INVITATION TO SYRIAC CHRISTIANITY

THE PUBLISHER AND THE UNIVERSITY OF CALIFORNIA PRESS
FOUNDATION GRATEFULLY ACKNOWLEDGE THE GENEROUS
SUPPORT OF THE JOAN PALEVSKY ENDOWMENT FUND IN
LITERATURE IN TRANSLATION.

INVITATION TO SYRIAC CHRISTIANITY

An Anthology

EDITED BY
Michael Philip Penn
Scott Fitzgerald Johnson
Christine Shepardson
Charles M. Stang

UNIVERSITY OF CALIFORNIA PRESS

University of California Press
Oakland, California

© 2022 by The Regents of the University of California

Library of Congress Cataloging-in-Publication Data

Names: Penn, Michael Philip, editor. | Johnson, Scott Fitzgerald, editor. | Shepardson, Christine C., editor. | Stang, Charles M., editor.
Title: Invitation to Syriac Christianity : an anthology / Michael Philip Penn, Scott Fitzgerald Johnson, Christine Shepardson, and Charles M. Stang, editors.
Description: [Oakland, California] : University of California Press, [2022] | Includes bibliographical references and index.
Identifiers: LCCN 2021023215 (print) | LCCN 2021023216 (ebook) | ISBN 9780520299191 (hardback) | ISBN 9780520299207 (paperback) | ISBN 9780520971035 (ebook)
Subjects: LCSH: Syriac Christians—History—To 1500—Sources. | Syriac Christians—History—Early works to 1800. | Syriac Christians—Translations into English. | Church history—Primitive and early church, ca. 30–600.
Classification: LCC DS59.S94 I58 2022 (print) | LCC DS59.S94 (ebook) | DDC 281/.63--dc23
LC record available at https://lccn.loc.gov/2021023215
LC ebook record available at https://lccn.loc.gov/2021023216

26 25 24 23 22
10 9 8 7 6 5 4 3 2 1

*To our teachers, especially Liz Clark, J. F. Coakley, and
Sebastian P. Brock, who have inspired and mentored so many*

CONTENTS

List of Illustrations · xiii
Acknowledgments · xv
Note on Translation, Transliteration, and Nomenclature · xix
Maps by David A. Michelson and Ian Mladjov · xxii

Introduction · 1

PART I. FOUNDATIONS

1. Origin Stories · 31
   Acts of Thomas · 32
   Ephrem, Hymns on Heresies 22 · 35
   Eusebius, Church History · 37
   Egeria, Pilgrimage Journal · 38
   Teaching of Addai · 40
   Chronicle of Edessa to 540 · 43
   Acts of Mar Mari · 44
   Alexander Romance · 46
   Michael the Great, Chronicle · 49

2. Poetry · 50
   Odes of Solomon 24, 19 · 52

>   *Hymn of the Pearl* · 54
>   *Ephrem, Hymns on Faith* 81 · 59
>   *Ephrem, Hymns on the Resurrection* 1 · 62
>   *Cyrillona, On the Huns* · 65
>   *Narsai, On Epiphany* · 67
>   *Jacob of Serug, On the Sinful Woman* · 69
>   *On Mary and the Gardener* · 74
>   *On the Cherub and the Thief* · 75
>   *Giwargis Warda, On Sin* · 81
>   *Khamis bar Qardaḥe, Wine Song* · 84
>   *'Abdisho' bar Brika, Metrical Catalogue of Syriac Authors* · 85

3. Doctrine and Disputation · 88
   Ephrem, Hymns on Faith 53 · 91
   Theodore of Mopsuestia, On the Incarnation · 92
   Severus of Antioch, To Nephalius · 96
   Babai the Great, Book of the Union · 99
   George of Resh'ayna, Life of Maximus the Confessor · 101
   A Syriac Fragment on the Sixth Council · 106
   Dionysius Bar Ṣalibi, Against the Melkites · 107

PART II. PRACTICES

4. Liturgy · 113
   Acts of Thomas · 115
   Didascalia · 117
   Chalcedonian Order for Emergency Baptism of a Child · 118
   Testament of Our Lord · 119
   Life of Rabban Hormizd · 124
   John of Mardin, Canons · 126
   Anaphora of Addai and Mari · 127
   Barhebraeus, Short Anaphora of Saint James · 131
   Service Book from Turfan · 137

5. Asceticism · 140
   Acts of Thomas · 142
   Aphrahat, Demonstrations 6 · 145
   Book of Steps · 147
   Rules of Rabbula of Edessa · 149
   Rules for Nuns · 151
   Philoxenus, First Letter of the Monks of Bet Gaugal; Letter Concerning Zeal · 153
   Jacob of Serug, On the Solitaries · 154
   Statutes of the School of Nisibis · 157

  Elias, Life of John of Tella · 160
  John of Ephesus, Life of Susan · 162
  Isaac of Nineveh, Treatises on the Behavior of Excellence 1; Whereby the Beauty of
    Solitary Life Is To Be Preserved · 165
  Barhebraeus, Book of the Dove · 167

6. Mysticism and Prayer · 170
  Timothy of Constantinople, On Those Who Come to the Church from
    the Heretics · 173
  Evagrius of Pontus, Praktikos, Skemmata, and Kephalaia Gnostika; Babai the Great,
    Commentary on the Skemmata and Commentary on the Kephalaia Gnostika · 175
  Evagrius of Pontus, Letter to Melania · 177
  Evagrius of Pontus, Kephalaia Gnostika; Babai the Great, Commentary on the
    Kephalaia Gnostika · 179
  Stephen bar Ṣudayli, Book of the Holy Hierotheus · 180
  Philoxenus of Mabbug, Letter to Abraham and Orestes · 183
  Isaac of Nineveh, On Gehenna · 185
  John of Apamea, On Prayer · 188
  Isaac of Nineveh, On Pure and Undistracted Prayer · 190
  Dadishoʻ Qaṭraya, Discourse on Stillness · 191
  John of Dalyata, Letters 12 · 193
  Joseph Ḥazzaya, On the Stirrings of the Mind during Prayer · 195

PART III. TEXTS AND TEXTUAL TRANSMISSION

7. Biblical Interpretation · 201
  Aphrahat, Demonstrations 12 · 203
  Ephrem, Commentary on the Diatessaron · 205
  Ephrem, The Repentance of Nineveh · 207
  Book of Steps · 209
  Narsai, On the Sacrifice of Isaac · 210
  Memra on Genesis 22 · 211
  Jacob of Serug, Memra on Tamar · 213
  Cave of Treasures · 215
  Daniel of Ṣalaḥ, Commentary on the Psalms, Psalm 1 · 219
  Syriac Apocalypse of Daniel · 221
  Solomon of Baṣra, Book of the Bee · 224

8. Hagiography · 229
  Jacob of Serug, On the Sleepers of Ephesus · 231
  John of Ephesus, Ecclesiastical History · 235
  Martyrdom of Abbot Barshebya · 237

    Martyrdom of Anahid · 238
    Stephen Mansūr, *Passion of Romanos the Neomartyr* · 242
    Theodoret, *History of the Monks of Syria* · 244
    Syriac Life of Mary · 250
    Thomas of Marga, *Book of Governors* · 253
    Life of Rabban Hormizd · 256

9. Books, Knowledge, and Translation · 259
    Book of the Laws of the Countries · 261
    Colophons from Syriac Manuscripts · 267
    Syro-Roman Law Book · 269
    Zacharias Rhetor, *Life of Severus of Antioch* · 273
    Philoxenus of Mabbug, *Commentary on the Prologue of John* · 275
    Sergius of Reshʿayna, *On the Aim of All of Aristotle's Writings* · 277
    Severus Sebokt, *Letter to the Periodeutes Basil of Cyprus* · 279
    Timothy I, *Letters 43, 48, and 47* · 280
    Thomas of Marga, *Book of Governors* · 286
    Moshe bar Kepha, *Introduction to the Psalter* · 287
    Hynayn ibn Isḥaq, *Risala* · 287

PART IV. INTERRELIGIOUS ENCOUNTERS

10. Judaism · 293
    Didascalia · 295
    Aphrahat, *Demonstrations* 11 · 298
    Ephrem, *Hymns on Unleavened Bread* 19; *Hymns on Faith* 87; *Hymns on Virginity* 28 · 299
    Teaching of Addai · 305
    Isaac of Antioch, *Homilies against the Jews* 2 · 307
    Simeon of Bet Arsham, *Letters* 1 · 309
    Book of the Himyarites · 311
    Letter of the Jews to the Emperor Marcian · 314
    History of the "Slave of Christ" · 315
    Disputation of Sergius the Stylite Against a Jew · 317
    Timothy I, *Letters* 40 · 319

11. Islam · 321
    Maronite Chronicle · 322
    Apocalypse of Pseudo-Methodius · 324
    Jacob of Edessa, *Letters* · 325
    Disputation of Bet Ḥale · 326
    Chronicle of Zuqnin · 331
    Timothy I, *Letters* 59 · 333

  Syriac Baḥira Legend · 335
  Dionysius Bar Ṣalibi, A Response to the Arabs · 339
  Michael the Great, Chronicle · 342
  Barhebraeus, Ecclesiastical Chronicle · 350

12. Religions of the Silk Road · 352
  Legend of Mar Qardagh · 354
  Theodore Abū Qurrah, On the Existence of God and the True Religion · 358
  Timothy I, Letters 41 and 47 · 359
  Jingjiao Stele · 360
  Discourse on the One God · 365
  History of the Life and Travels of Rabban Sauma · 368
  Mission of Friar William of Rubruck · 371

Appendix A. Translations and Editions · 375
Appendix B. Biographies of Named Authors · 389
Appendix C. Glossary · 407
Index · 413

ILLUSTRATIONS

MAPS

1. Near East before the Islamic Conquest · xxii
2. Near East after the Islamic Conquest · xxiv
3. East Asia · xxvi

FIGURES

1. Syriac slave contract · 4
2. Funerary couch mosaic · 6
3. Family portrait mosaic · 7
4. Syriac incantation bowl · 123
5. The Qalb Lawza basilica · 129
6. The basilica of Saint Sergius · 130
7. The *Rabbula Gospels* · 216
8. Mar Musa fresco of the Last Judgment · 223
9. An illustrated Syriac gospel lectionary · 226
10. Remains of Simeon the Stylite's pillar · 248
11. Plaque of Simeon the Stylite · 249

12. Earliest securely dated Syriac manuscript · 269
13. A scholarly gospel manuscript · 277
14. The *Kadamattom Cross* · 361
15. The *Kollam Plate* · 362
16. A rubbing from the *Jingjiao* stele · 366

ACKNOWLEDGMENTS

A project of this scale could never have come together without the help of numerous individuals and institutions. As a whole, the editors would like to thank: the group of almost ten external readers who each strengthened the book in numerous ways; a long list of colleagues whose advice on what to include in this anthology time and time again made it better; a truly incredible research assistant, Giovanni DiRusso, who is primarily responsible for appendices B and C, as well as images, image permissions, and captions; Adam Bremer-McCollum, whose expert translations can be found in almost every chapter; Dave Michelson and Ian Mladjov, whose maps begin the volume; our permissions editor Kenny Chumbley, our copy editor Gabriel Barlett, and our indexer Kate Mertes; and all the staff at the University of California Press, especially Eric Schmidt and Cindy Fulton, who made this book possible.

MICHAEL PENN

I would like to thank Stanford University's Department of Religious Studies, the Ptarmigan Fund, and the Abbasi Program in Islamic Studies at Stanford University for their financial support, which enabled the editors to have multiple in-person meetings and helped fund permission expenses. So, too, I want to acknowledge the kindness of the presses and individuals who granted us reprint permissions, particularly George Kiraz at Gorgias Press, who was especially generous in this regard. I would like to give special thanks to our editor Eric Schmidt, who first came up with the wonderfully crazy idea of this anthology. Eric put up with my adamant refusal to ever do something like this and then, a few days later, my reconsideration. For last-minute help in obtaining images, thanks go to Emma Loosley, Lucas Van Rompay, and David Taylor. Thanks also go to Zuyi Zhao for last-minute text entry. For their sustaining my enthusiasm for the project and all things Syriac, I want to acknowledge an amazing seminar involving the following Stanford graduate students: Philip Abbott, Anuj Amin, Meagan Khoury, Ana Nunez, and Sunny Persad. So, too, I am incredibly grateful for my partner Sarah Willburn and our daughters Sasha Willburn and Tabitha Penn, who now know more about Syriac Christianity than is healthy for any pair of seventh-graders. But most of all, lifelong thanks go to my Doktormutter Liz Clark, who many years ago took a huge risk on a molecular biology major interested in late antiquity.

SCOTT JOHNSON

I would like to acknowledge the generous financial support of the University of Oklahoma, its Department of Classics and Letters, and the John Simon Guggenheim Memorial Foundation. I also offer thanks to the following individuals for their invaluable assistance in preparing this book: Elizabeth Anderson, Giovanni DiRusso, Kyle Harper, Gillian Hasty, Fr. Columba Stewart, Jack Tannous, Matthew Wennerman, and Jeffrey Wickes. In addition, my wife Carol and our children Susanna, Daniel, and Thomas provide the deepest comfort and encouragement in all matters of life and work. The imprint of their love appears in every piece of my research and writing. Finally, I would like to express my most sincere gratitude to Sebastian P. Brock, my first teacher and mentor in Syriac; he remains an inspiration to all students and scholars of the language, its literature, and its people.

CHRISTINE SHEPARDSON

I would like to thank the Office of Research and Engagement at the University of Tennessee as well as the University of Tennessee Humanities Center for financial support of this project. I would also like to thank my colleagues Michael Penn, for the opportunity to participate in this project, and Dayna Kalleres, whose wonderful and patient company on a research trip to Turkey and Syria in 2010 made possible some of the images used in this volume. Most importantly, though, I want to thank my family and friends, and especially my partner Lyn, whose profound love, care, and compassion enrich my life and the lives of so many. In writing this volume, the editors have spoken often about the teachers and students who have inspired us, and the teachers and students that we in turn hope to inspire. In this regard, I am grateful to Amy-Jill Levine, whose energetic lectures first drew me into the study of early Christianity, and to Paula Fredriksen, whose electric intelligence inspired me and whose generous, mentoring friendship means the world to me. I also owe a great debt to Lucas Van Rompay and Susan Ashbrook Harvey for welcoming me into the field of Syriac Christianity. It is Liz Clark, though, who most indelibly shaped my own career and the study of late antiquity. Her decades of groundbreaking scholarship and the relationships she fostered have transformed the study of early Christianity, opening it to a richer diversity of scholars and scholarly questions from which we all benefit. Thank you, Liz, for everything.

CHARLES M. STANG

I would like to acknowledge the generous support of the Hugh Hackett Fund from the Center for the Study of World Religions at Harvard Divinity School, and the Loeb Faculty Research Grant from the Department of the Classics at Harvard University. I would also like to thank the following people for their invaluable assistance at crucial stages in the long process: Giovanni DiRusso, Michael Ennis, Julia Hintlian, Rong Huang, John Lamoureaux, Adam Bremer-McCollum, Corey O'Brien, Jeffrey Wickes, and John Zaleski. I would like to acknowledge and thank J. F. Coakley, who first taught me Syriac and who began my initiation into the vast world of Syriac Christianity. Finally, I would like to thank my wife Sarabinh, as well as my daughters Vivian and Saskia, for their support throughout, and especially for putting up with my travels.

As they start off the book proper, it is also appropriate to here note that the maps on pages xxii–xxvii were originally published in David A. Michelson and Ian Mladjov, "Diachronic Maps of Syriac Cultures and their Geographic Contexts," in *The Syriac World*, ed. Daniel King (New York: Routledge, 2019), xxvii–xxxiii, and maps 1–14, https://doi.org/10.4324/9781315708195. To further the growth of Syriac studies, the authors have made these maps available for reuse through the Vanderbilt University Institutional Repository at the following persistent link: http://hdl.handle.net/1803/16426. The maps are © 2017 by David A. Michelson and Ian Mladjov and are reused under the terms of the Creative Commons Attribution 4.0 International License: https://creativecommons.org/licenses/by/4.0.

A NOTE ON TRANSLATIONS, TRANS-LITERATION, AND NOMENCLATURE

TRANSLATIONS

For this volume, we have translated all previously untranslated texts, texts not previously translated into English, and those whose published versions we felt were outdated. In all other cases, we have utilized existing translations, although in the case of many older translations, we have done so with substantial modifications. Appendix A contains a complete list of these sources by chapter. Because of space considerations, we had to excerpt most works. We use the notation [. . .] to indicate where an excerpt skips over a section of the original text. We use the notation [___] to indicate where a word is missing or is illegible in the surviving manuscripts. Appendix A also serves as an important resource for helping locate unabridged versions of these texts.

TRANSLITERATION

In order to make the volume inviting and easy to read, we have adopted one of the simplest systems possible for transliterating Syriac script into roman characters. As the words we transliterate are usually common ones, this simplified system should not hinder scholars of Syriac. At the same time, it should provide enough information so that beginning students of Syriac can still identify basic Syriac words and see lexical relations between them. We transliterate the consonants and vowels of Syriac directly when they have an obvious roman equivalent. For example, the letter "mem" is represented by "m." There are, however, a few consonants that do not have an obvious roman equivalent. In these cases, we have used standard diacritical marks or combinations of consonants to identify them. These are: "ḥ" for "ḥeyt," ṭ for "ṭeyt," "sh" for "shin," "ṣ" for "ṣade," ' for "'ayn," and ' for "'alap."

We have not signaled the difference between long and short vowels. For example, to produce a particularly clean text we render both the long and short "a," two different characters in Syriac written vocalization, as "a." According to current scholarship, East Syrian pronunciation is the more ancient and it is what we have adopted in this book.

NOMENCLATURE

There has not yet emerged a consensus on how to best refer to the various branches of Syriac Christianity, and every proposed system of nomenclature has its disadvantages. To avoid potential anachronism, we have reserved terms such as the "Syrian Orthodox Church" and the "Church of the East" solely for modern communities. For the four pre-modern groups of Christians most prominent in our volume, we have chosen a particularly simple system of vocabulary to avoid the technical nature of terminology that can overwhelm beginning students of Syriac Christianity. In our case, we employ a single term for each set of Syriac Christians and use the same term to speak of their church. This results in a schema of four pairings:

1. The term "Melkite" (from the Syriac word for king) is often used for premodern supporters of the Council of Chalcedon who originally spoke Syriac and in later centuries spoke Arabic. Nevertheless, because this term so often has been used pejoratively to designate supporters of the Byzantine emperor, our own descriptions do not employ it. To avoid cumbersome constructions such as "Chalcedonian Christians who spoke Syriac or Arabic" or "the Chalcedonian Church outside the Byzantine Empire" we have simply referred to those Christians who supported the Council of Chalcedon as "Chalcedonian Christians" and their church as the "Chalcedonian Church." Context almost always clarifies whether we are referring to Greek or Syriac speakers.

2. The terms "Maronites" and the "Maronite Church" come from an early self-designation for a church that rapidly developed its own ecclesiastical structure. It continues as a self-designation up to the present. Maronites also support the Council of Chalcedon; so, to avoid confusion with Chalcedonian Christians who are not Maronites, we always specify Maronites when speaking of this subgroup of Chalcedonian Christians.

3. The Syriac Christians commonly called Nestorians were originally and predominately inhabitants of the Persian Empire. They adopted the dyophysite theology of Antiochene theologians such as Theodore of Mopsuestia and were forerunners of the modern Church of the East. Starting in the nineteenth century, they have often self-identified as "Assyrian Christians." Although

occasionally used as a self-designation, in most cases "Nestorian" is a polemical term and we do not use it in our own descriptions. When speaking of this ancient church, we simply employ "East Syrian Christian" and the "East Syrian Church."

4. Those Christians—regardless of geography—who opposed the Council of Chalcedon as well as the Christology of the East Syrian Church are often called "miaphysites" (or, especially in older scholarship, "monophysites"). For Syriac Christians of this confession, the word "Jacobite" is occasionally used. But, similarly to the term "Nestorian" for East Syrian Christians, "Jacobite" most often was a term of abuse and you will not find it in our own descriptions. In this case, "Syrian Miaphsyites" remains a possibility. But for simplicity and to preserve symmetry with our terminology of East Syrian Christians and the East Syrian Church, we here use the pairing "West Syrian Christians" and the "West Syrian Church" to speak of the forerunners of the modern Syrian Orthodox Church. We recognize that the term "West Syrian" has some potential ambiguity, as others occasionally use it also to include Maronite and Syriac-speaking Chalcedonian Christians. But, in this volume, we use West Syrian only when speaking of anti-Chalcedonian Christians.

The nomenclature of Chalcedonian, Maronite, East Syrian, and West Syrian has its problems. But we attempt consistency in our use of these terms in order to maintain clarity about the groups we are discussing.

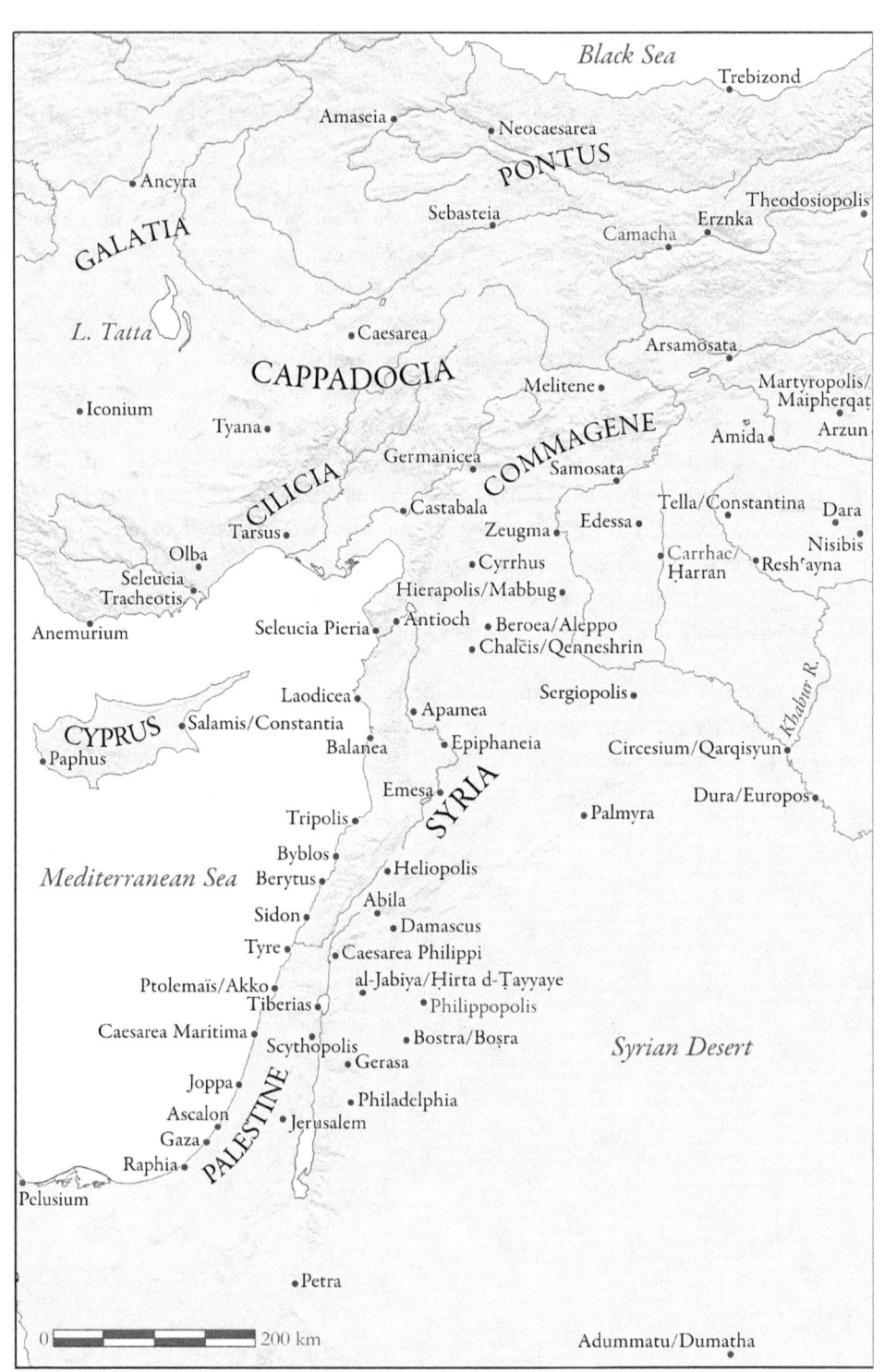

MAP 1.

Near East before the Islamic Conquest. By David A. Michelson and Ian Mladjov.

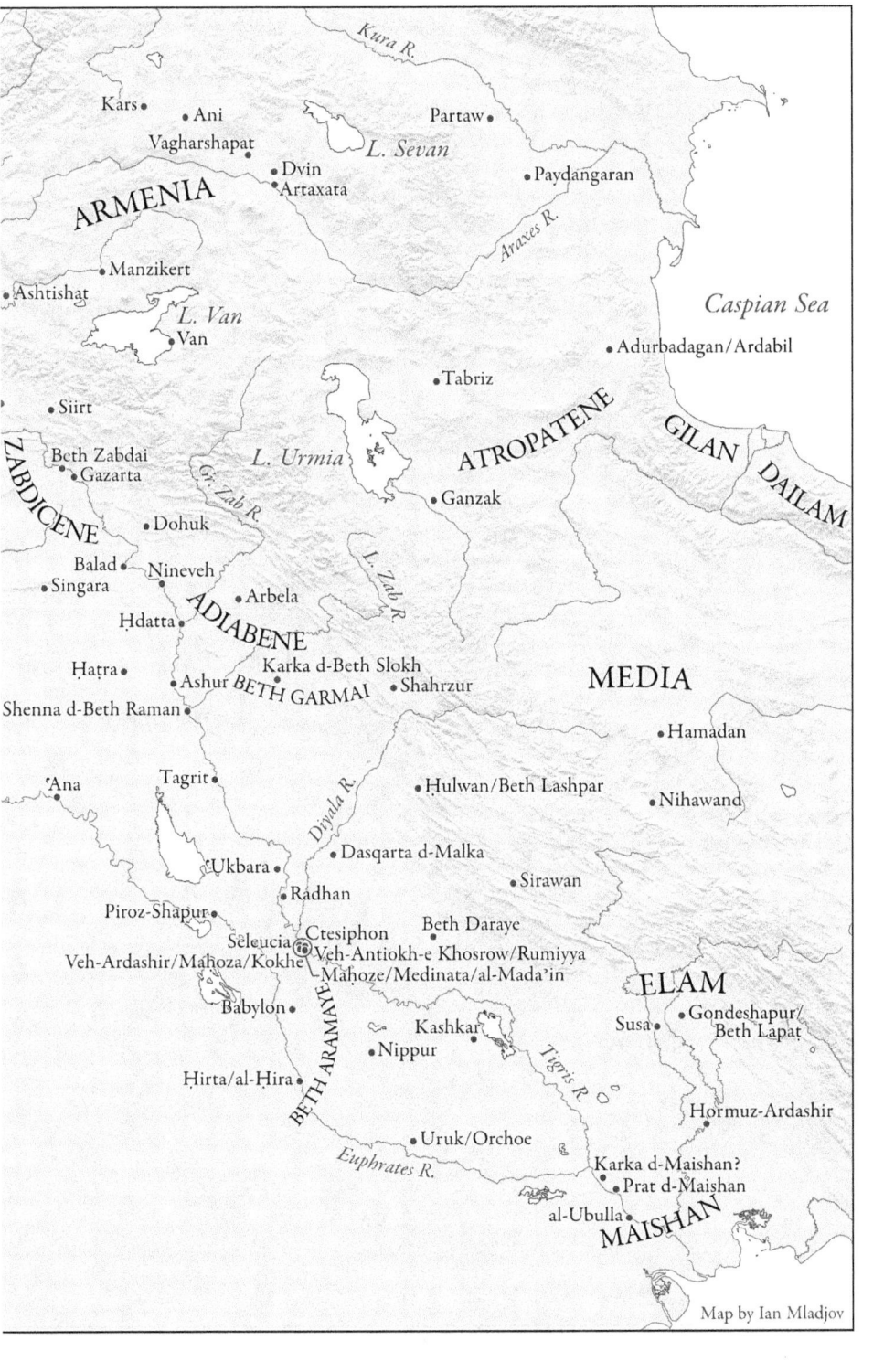

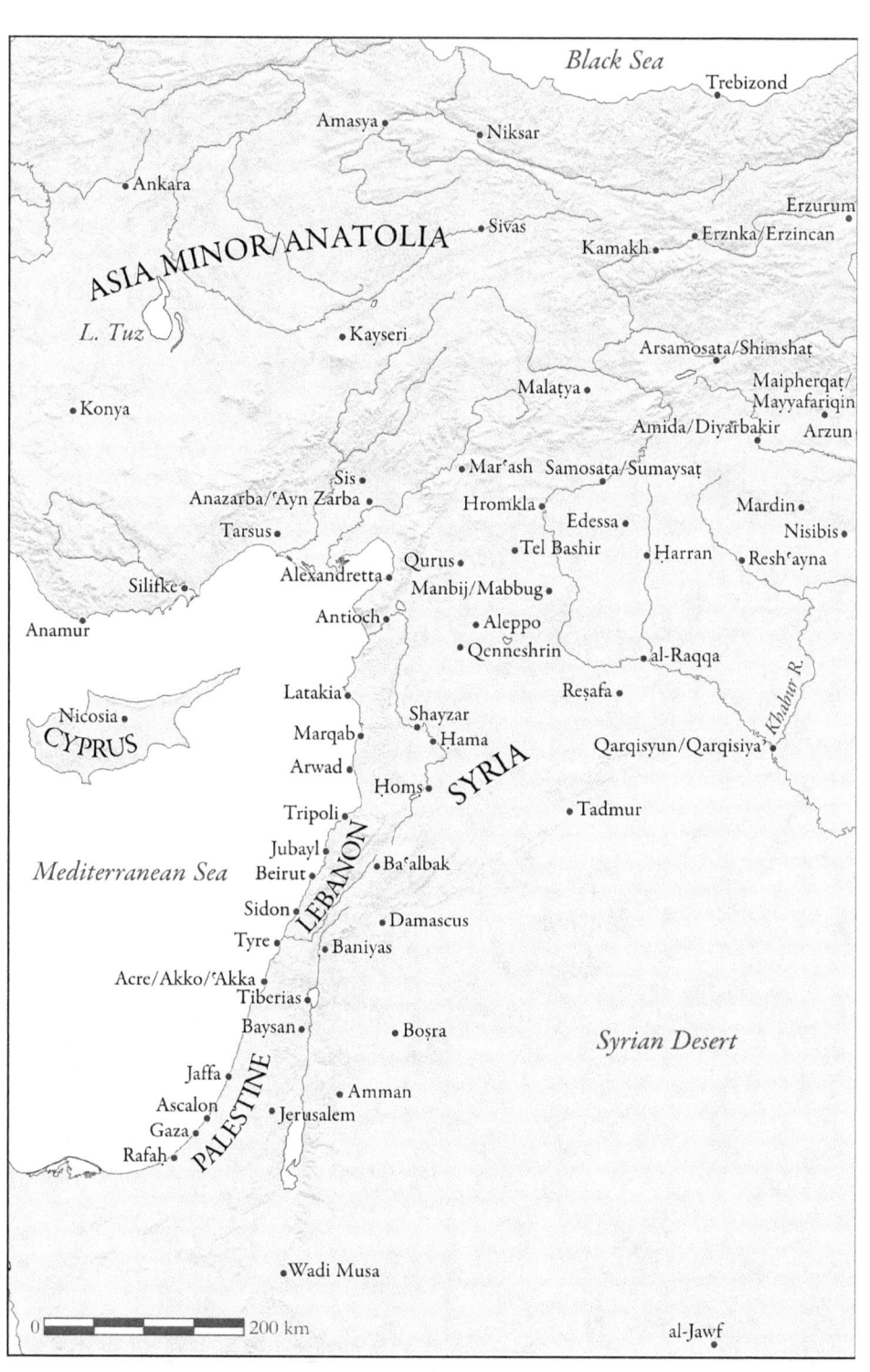

MAP 2.
Near East after the Islamic Conquest. By David A. Michelson and Ian Mladjov.

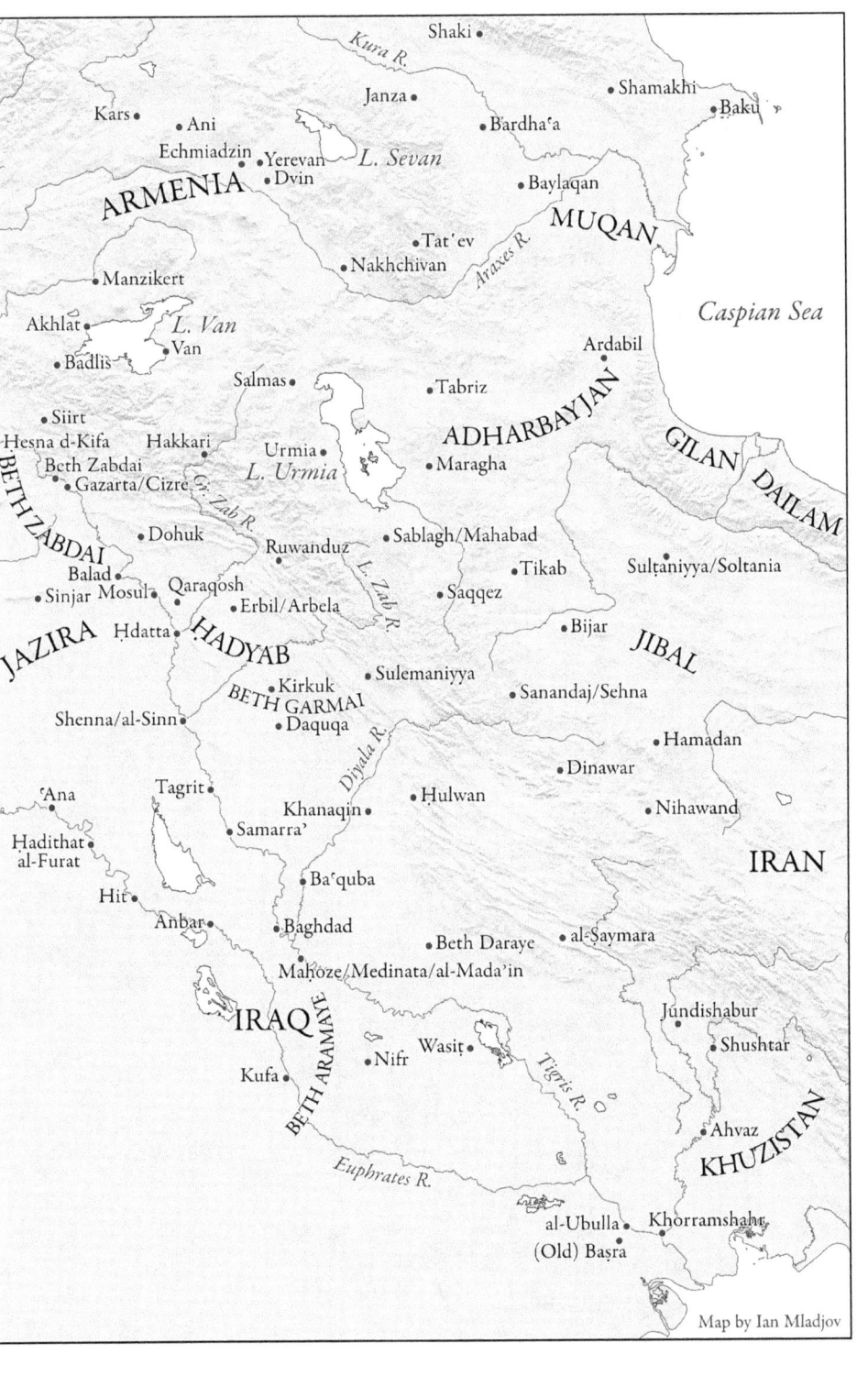

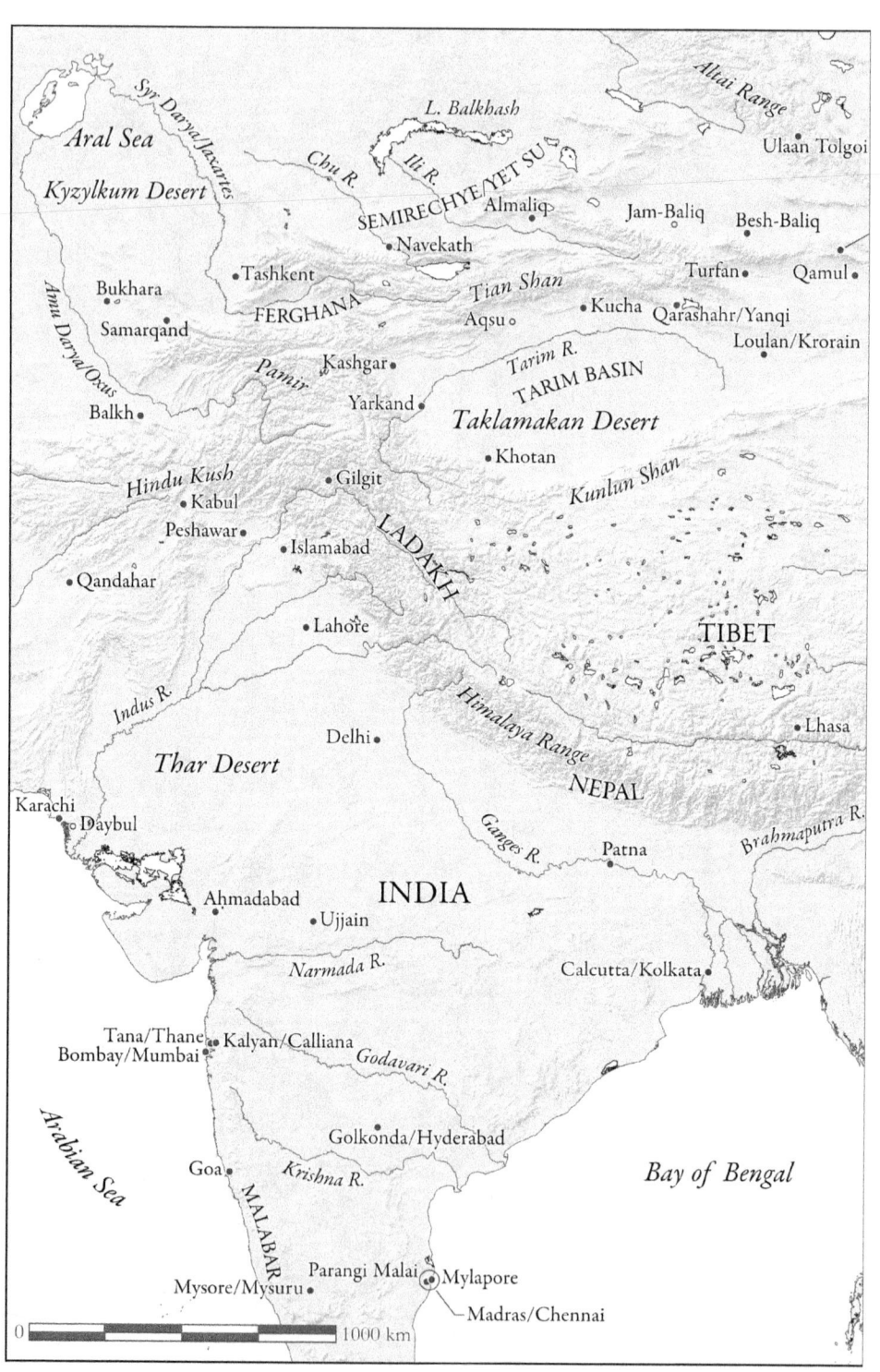

MAP 3.
East Asia. By David A. Michelson and Ian Mladjov.

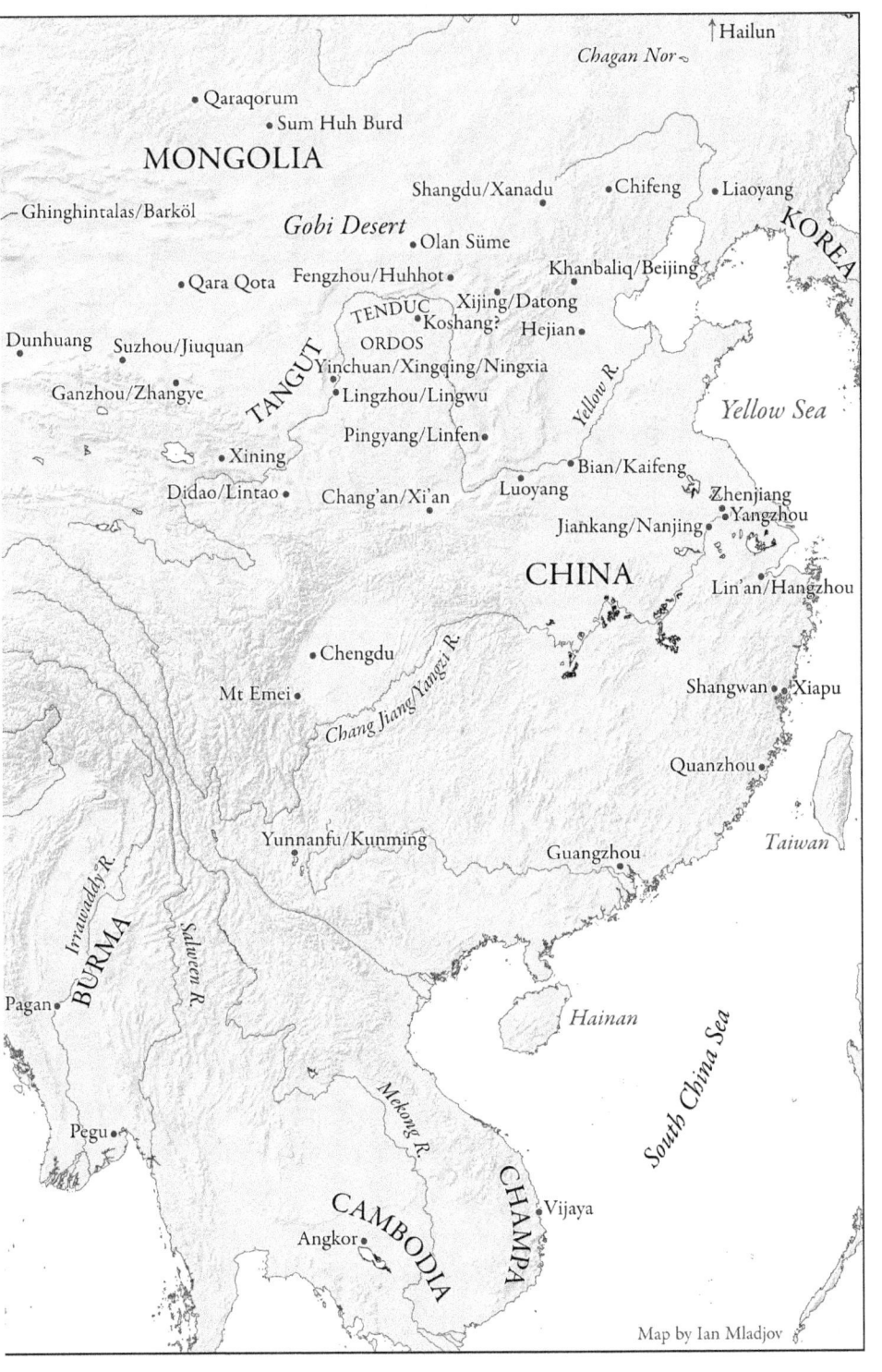

INTRODUCTION

When people think of premodern Christianity, they most often think of Christianity as a European religion or—at the very least—as a religion of the Mediterranean. That is, they picture Christianity's early spread corresponding roughly to that of the ancient Roman Empire. So, too, when people think of classics of Christian literature, they most often envisage works written by authors such as Athanasius, Augustine, or Aquinas. That is, they consider texts originally composed in Greek and Latin.

Although this represents fairly well modern impressions of premodern Christianity, it is actually a poor representation of early Christians themselves. Throughout much of premodernity, the most geographically expansive church was not the Roman Catholic Church or the Byzantine Orthodox Church, but rather churches that reached from modern-day Turkey, throughout the Middle East, across Afghanistan, down to India, up to Tibet, and into China. For these churches, the primary language of Christian scholarship and liturgy was the lingua franca of the late ancient Middle East, a dialect of Aramaic known as Syriac.

Syriac Christians developed their own theological, ecclesiastical, and monastic traditions. They produced the earliest surviving Christian translations of the Bible. They composed the most extensive collections of ancient Christian poetry. They were the first Christians to encounter Islam. They were a crucial link in the translation and preservation of Greek science and philosophy. They formed an essential cultural bridge between Asia, the Middle East, and Europe.

For historians living in the twenty-first century, Syriac texts are among the most valuable sources surviving from the late ancient and medieval Middle East. Syriac Christianity had complex interactions with early Jewish communities that challenged a clearly demarcated boundary between church and synagogue. Speaking a form of Aramaic, just as Jesus himself had, these Christians shared roots with the Jewish, Roman, and Persian worlds, as well as that of early Christianity. As a result, Syriac Christians had an incredibly rich historiographical tradition, and Syriac texts provide extensive and unique coverage of the Byzantine and Persian empires. So, too, Syriac works form the earliest and largest corpus of contemporary, textual evidence of the first Islamic dynasty, and they document events throughout the ancient silk road routes and Central Asia.

So, why have so few in the twenty-first century heard of these Syriac churches? Owing to a series of ancient theological controversies, Syriac Christians ended up being considered heretics by the forerunners of Roman Catholic, Greek Orthodox, and Protestant Christians. Because until recently the academic study of religion in Europe and the United States has been so closely tied to Catholic and Protestant theology, the combination of these Christians coming from the "wrong" place (that is, having relatively small American or European communities), having the "wrong" beliefs (that is, being considered heretics by Protestant and Roman Catholic theologians), and using the "wrong" language (consider how few even know the word "Syriac") has meant that Syriac Christians have essentially been written out of history.

At universities this has started to change. Whether as a unit in "Introduction to Christianity," a section of a survey course in church history, part of a class on the global Middle Ages, or as the focus of an upper-level seminar, select writings from Syriac Christians have begun to appear on undergraduate- and graduate-level syllabi. So, too, as a research field, Syriac studies has expanded exponentially; for example, more North American dissertations in Syriac Studies have been written in the last fifteen years than in the preceding 150 years combined.

But Syriac Christianity is not simply a subject of antiquarian interest. As a living tradition with over ten million modern practitioners, it is slowly coming to the attention of a wider public. Owing to ancient missionary movements, millions of modern Syriac Christians currently live in southern India. Until recently, millions of others remained in the lands of Syriac Christianity's birth: modern-day Iran, Iraq, Syria, Lebanon, and eastern Turkey. During the First World War, a genocide targeted Syriac Christians in the Ottoman Empire, killing between 250,000 and 500,000 of them, an event known among modern Syriac Christians as the *Sayfo* (sword). This was followed by periods of discrimination and persecution in Iran, Iraq, and Turkey. The twenty-first century is not looking much better. The chaos following the second Iraq war decimated the Syriac churches in Iraq and led to massive emigration and dislocation. The civil war in Syria has been even more destructive to these communities and their patrimony. Their congregations have been targeted by Islamists; their churches have been destroyed by the Islamic State movement; and their leaders have been kidnapped and killed.

As North America and Europe have become more aware of the plight of modern Syriac Christians, students, scholars, and the general public are increasingly interested in the history of Middle Eastern Christianity. As specialists in this branch of Christianity, the four of us have delivered dozens of public lectures about the Syriac tradition. Without fail, audience members ask us how they can learn more about the Syriac churches. In large part the impetus for this book arose from our inability to give a good answer. For, despite the ever-increasing interest in Syriac Christianity, most of the actual writings by Syriac Christians remain inaccessible to nonspecialists. No one has ever published a general, easily obtained, full-length anthology of Syriac texts in translation.

Invitation to Syriac Christianity is our attempt to help fill this gap. Until now, whenever professors wanted to include Syriac texts on their syllabi, modern Syriac Christians aspired to learn more about their heritage, graduate students wished to have Syriac Christianity as part of their studies, or the interested public desired to increase their knowledge of Middle Eastern Christianity, they needed to cobble together their own assortment of texts—a task for which few have the time or resources. The three years we spent selecting texts for this volume have not yielded a definitive compendium covering all the essentials of Syriac Christianity. But we have carefully curated this collection to serve as an entryway, an invitation into the Syriac tradition as well as a stimulus, we hope, for even further exploration.

We decided to organize the book thematically. This has the advantage of helping readers integrate Syriac sources into their existing frameworks of knowledge. For example, thematic organization allows one to choose more quickly texts for a new course syllabus or to explore more thoroughly how Syriac authors deal with a particular topic. But this schema has the disadvantage of giving little guidance concerning the chronological evolution of the Syriac tradition. So, especially for those who have a relatively light background in the history of Syriac Christianity, we wanted to provide as the center of the book's introduction a brief overview of some key events in the history of Syriac Christianity and its literature. Subsequent chapters, source descriptions, and texts will often allude to these developments.

THE FIRST THROUGH FOURTH CENTURIES

Syriac is a dialect of Aramaic, likely to have originated in Edessa (modern-day Urfa), in what is now southeastern Turkey. Edessa was an ancient Mesopotamia city called Adma' which was captured and re-founded by the successors of Alexander the Great, the Seleucids, in 303 BCE. It became the capital of the small province of Osrhoene, created by the Persian Parthians after their defeat of the Greek Seleucids in 130/129 BCE. Local kings ruled Osrhoene until the Romans made it a province in 195 CE and an official colony around 213. Edessa was a caravan city on a trade route hosting a diverse array of linguistic, cultural, and religious influences. How and when Christianity first arrived in Edessa is unknown, although legends from the fourth and fifth centuries claim that Jesus himself ordered his disciple Addai (or in Greek, Thaddeus) to evangelize the city at the invitation of its king, Abgar. Christians in and around Edessa spoke and wrote in Syriac. As these Christians moved further afield into Mesopotamia and eventually eastward as far as Persia, India, Central Asia, and China, Syriac spread with them. At the very least, we know that Syriac was one of the first languages, if not the first, into which the Christian Bible was translated.

Syriac is first attested in inscriptions in and around Edessa from 6 CE, and so predates Christianity's arrival. The presence of Syriac in a number of first through third-century pagan mosaics and a handful of legal documents also shows that non-Christians used Syriac. But apart from a few fragments, all surviving Syriac literature comes from Christian authors or has been transmitted by Christian scribes. Christian texts in Syriac appear in the second and third centuries, although it is impossible obtain a clear picture because many of these texts are anonymous, of uncertain date and origin, and were perhaps not originally composed in Syriac. Take, for example, the *Odes of Solomon*, a collection of forty-two short lyric poems that have survived almost entirely in Syriac. The authorship, the exact date, and the place of origin remain unknown, although most scholars place them in the early second century. If they were originally composed in Syriac, then they may be the earliest known non-inscriptional Syriac text. But they do not conform to any known Syriac verse form, and there are good reasons to believe that some, if not all, of the *Odes* were originally written in Greek. Although clearly Christian and strongly influenced by biblical language, the theology of the *Odes* is difficult to piece together, as is the community for whom they were presumably composed. One scholar has even claimed them as writings of the Essene Jews in the mid first century CE, perhaps among some converts from that community to Christianity.

We know considerably more about another Christian poet from the second century, Bardaisan (d. 222). He was active in the Edessene court of King Abgar VIII (d. 212), and he played the part of poet, philosopher, and—according to the chronicler Julius

---

FIGURE 1.

Syriac slave contract (*P. Euphrates* 6r). Owing to the relatively wet climate of Mesopotamia, very few Syriac papyri have survived. Nevertheless, three substantial Syriac parchments (sheets made from animal skin) dating from the third century were found around the cosmopolitan city Dura-Europos. They include one dated precisely to 243; this is a bill of sale for a slave written in Greek with a Syriac summary and signatures on the bottom and opposite side. In addition to its early date, there are several noteworthy features of this parchment. The date is given in multiple traditional systems, one of which starts with the colonization of Edessa by Rome in 212. Some of the signatures are in Greek, signifying the bilingual environment of Roman Mesopotamia. Finally, it mentions that a copy was placed in the archives of Edessa, signaling that both Syriac and Edessa were regionally significant and that Edessa's archives must have been extensive. Photo: Adam Bülow-Jacobsen.

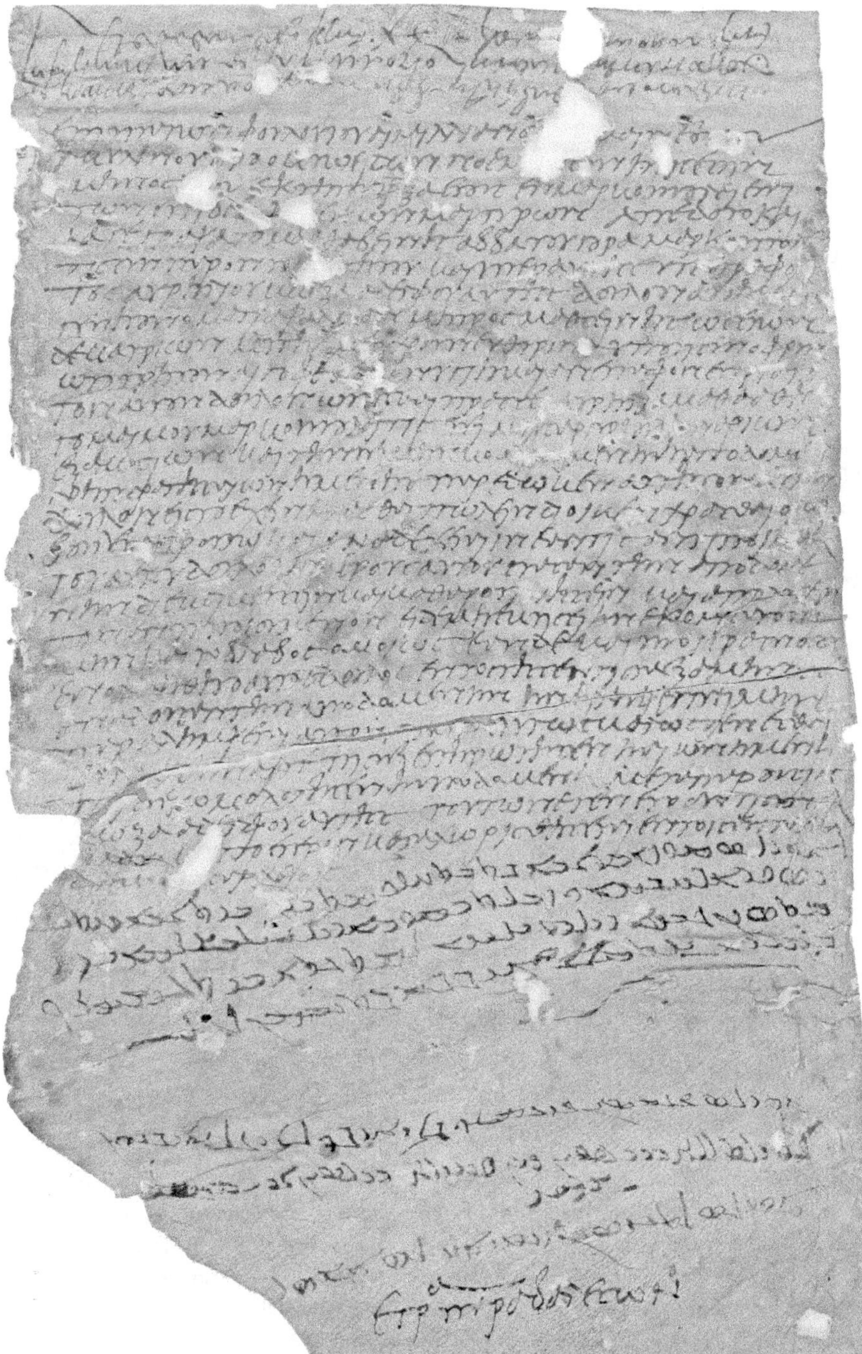

FIGURE 2.
Funerary couch mosaic. All surviving Syriac literature was either written or copied by Christians. But a number of early inscriptions, mosaics, and a handful of documentary sources (e.g., the slave contract in figure 1) attest to Syriac's use by non-Christians. Dated to ca. 278, this mosaic from southern Edessa was stolen in the late twentieth century. Our best record of it is a color drawing made in the mid-twentieth century. Note the names next to the figures written in Syriac. This mosaic depicts a recently deceased man surrounded by members of his family. Depictions of contemporary Edessans such as this are striking sources for understanding modes of dress and familial organization in pre-Christian Edessa. The survival of many such depictions of funerary couches from third-century Edessa suggests that the commemoration of the recently deceased through art was a fairly widespread practice. Photo by Mrs. Seton Lloyd from *The Dawn of Civilization: The First World Survey of Human Cultures in Early Times*, ed. Stuart Piggott (London: Thames & Hudson, 1961).

FIGURE 3.
Family portrait mosaic. As with the "Funerary couch mosaic," the "Family portrait mosaic" was stolen and our only remnant is a color drawing made in the mid-twentieth century. Originally found in Edessa and dated between 228 and 278, the "Family portrait mosaic" is a valuable source for understanding non-Christian Syriac culture in late antiquity. The figures' names and relations are written next to them in Syriac. The elaborate dress and hairstyles of the people suggest that this portrait depicts a noble family. The differing hats and hairstyles seem to mark different positions within the family and society more generally. Photo by Mrs. Seton Lloyd from *The Dawn of Civilization: The First World Survey of Human Cultures in Early Times*, ed. Stuart Piggott (London: Thames & Hudson, 1961).

Africanus, who met Bardaisan in 195—skilled archer. His own writings have unfortunately been lost, except for fragments quoted by later authors. But one of his students, Philip, has left us a philosophical dialogue on fate and freewill entitled *Book of the Laws of the Countries* (so named because of a long section on the "laws" or "customs" of different peoples), in which Bardaisan serves as the main character, much like Socrates in a Platonic dialogue. Bardaisan is reported to have articulated a speculative cosmology that was deemed heretical in retrospect and that almost certainly was influenced by Greek philosophy, and allegedly by Iranian and Gnostic cosmology as well. The *Book of the Laws of the Countries* was translated into Greek as *On Fate*, attributed to Bardaisan himself, and is quoted in other early Christian sources. The case of Bardaisan suggests that Syriac Christianity in Edessa was originally quite cosmopolitan.

Bardaisan is often paired with his slightly older contemporary, Tatian (d. ca. 185). A pagan born in "Assyria," and a self-described "barbarian philosopher," Tatian traveled west to Rome in search of true philosophy. He converted to Christianity and was a disciple of the Christian philosopher Justin Martyr until the latter's death, whereupon he is reported to have returned to the East in 170 to found his own school of philosophy somewhere in Mesopotamia. His single surviving philosophical work, *Oration to the Greeks*, is part savage indictment of everything Greek (written in Greek!), and part demonstration that Moses is more ancient than Homer. Later heresiologists associate Tatian with "encratism," an extreme form of asceticism based on the total renunciation of human sexuality, an asceticism some scholars believe was popular in Syria in the second and third centuries. While only faint traces of such asceticism are evident in Tatian's surviving works, the allegation has stayed with him over the centuries.

Tatian is most famous, however, as the author of the *Diatessaron*, a harmony that combines the four Gospels of Mark, Matthew, Luke, and John into a single text (hence its Greek name, *dia-tessaron*, "through [the] four [Gospels]"). This single-gospel narrative of Jesus's life was widely used among Syriac Christians until at least the fifth century. It is unclear what the original language of the *Diatessaron* was. If Tatian composed it during his time in Rome, then he likely would have composed it in Greek (or possibly even in Latin); if, after his return to the East, then it is likely that he composed it in Syriac. Regardless, the *Diatessaron* survives in part through quotations in a fragmentary Syriac commentary written by Ephrem the Syrian in the fourth century. In addition to this gospel harmony, by the third century more or less the entire Hebrew Bible was also translated into Syriac directly from Hebrew, perhaps by Syriac-speaking Jews in Edessa. The name "Peshitta" was given to this translation of the Old Testament in the ninth century, but the sense of this word is unclear: perhaps "Peshitta" meant it was a "simple" translation, although "widespread" or "common" are also possible meanings. These two biblical translations, Tatian's *Diatessaron* and the Peshitta, along with an early translation of the four separate gospels (the so-called Old Syriac Version), constitute the biblical matrix out of which Syriac Christianity emerged.

Apart from translations of the Old and New Testaments, like its Western counterparts, early Syriac Christianity was shaped by apocryphal literature, especially apocryphal acts of the apostles. Particularly beloved by Syriac Christians were the *Acts of Thomas*, originally composed in Syriac during the third century and translated into Greek soon afterward. The *Acts of Thomas* narrate the travels and travails of the apostle Judas Thomas, whose very name in Aramaic, "Thomas" (*T'oma*), is derived from the word "twin" (*ta'ma*) leading some Christians to describe Thomas as Jesus's twin brother. This theme of "twinning" was important for the early Christian tradition. In a number of Christian texts from the second and third centuries, the apostle Thomas, Jesus's "twin," becomes the model for every Christian, who is encouraged to discover that their innermost self is the "living Jesus," an inner divine light. This moment of self-knowledge transforms one into another twin of Jesus, a kind of divine double.

The *Acts* open with Jesus ordering Thomas to evangelize India, and most of the action takes place in India, where he is eventually martyred. Apart from the theme of twinning, one of the distinctive features of the *Acts* is that Thomas preaches complete sexual renunciation (once again invoking the specter of Tatian's "encratism"). Thomas runs afoul of local nobles and kings for persuading the wives of these powerful men to no longer sleep with their husbands. In two of the manuscripts of the *Acts*, Thomas sings a long hymn while he is imprisoned. Often called the *Hymn of the Pearl*, it is a story of a young prince from the East who travels to Egypt to recover a pearl from a dragon and is imprisoned there in a kind of stupor until his royal family sends emissaries to bring him home. The hymn has no obvious Christian content, and was probably an earlier, freestanding composition that at some point was incorporated into the *Acts*. This would be in keeping with the tendency of apocryphal acts to grow over time as successive editions and translations expand on or add new vignettes.

The *Acts of Thomas* narrate the apostle's journey to India from the Red Sea in such a way as to suggest that Thomas evangelized south India, where in fact there is a large community of Christians in Kerala that traces itself back to his first-century mission. It remains unknown, and perhaps unknowable, whether in fact the apostle Thomas himself evangelized India. But what remains certain is that Christian communities have flourished in India since at least the third century, and that at some point they became, in large part, members of the East Syrian Church, and so adopted Syriac as a liturgical language. With the arrival of Europeans (especially the Portuguese) in the sixteenth century, successive divisions have taken place, such that in contemporary Kerala there are now seven different churches associated with the Syriac tradition.

With the rise of imperial orthodoxy in the fourth- and fifth-century Roman Empire, there was a demand for stories about the origins of Syriac Christianity in and around Edessa that would highlight its own antiquity and its orthodoxy. The fifth century witnessed widespread controversies in the Christian East over matters of Christology—that is, debates about the constitution of the incarnate Christ. Especially in the wake of those controversies and the bitter divisions they engendered, some liked to look back on the first through fourth centuries as a time of an undivided church. The historical evidence, however, suggests a rather more diverse picture, as was the case throughout the Mediterranean world. Communities associated with heterodox Christian thinkers such as Marcion and Bardaisan seemed to flourish alongside proto-orthodox communities. A new religious group called "Manichaeans" emerged from Mesopotamia in the third century, claiming to be the true Christians with the true gospel and the caretakers of the true church. From Mesopotamia to China, Syriac Christians vied with Manichaean missionaries not only for converts but also for control over the name and legacy of Christianity. The emerging proto-orthodox community would itself eventually split along a fault line revealed by the Arian crisis. The fourth-century Egyptian presbyter Arius believed that God the Father was the only uncreated divine person; God the Son was created as a kind of secondary god, a mediator between God the Father and his creation. Some agreed with Arius's view, and others vigorously opposed it, arguing that God the Son was eternal, uncreated, and "consubstantial" (*homoousios*) with God the Father. The later view eventually prevailed at the Councils of Nicaea in 325 and Constantinople in 381, whose creeds established Trinitarian orthodoxy in the East and in the West.

We have access to a substantially larger quantity of Syriac texts from the fourth century on. From this period come the writings of Aphrahat (the first half of the fourth century), the anonymous *Book of Steps* (late fourth or early fifth century), and the extensive corpus of Ephrem (d. 373). Aphrahat lived in the Persian empire under the king Shapur II and was known as "the Persian Sage." He is the author of twenty-three so-called *Demonstrations*: roughly the first half concerns topics in Christian asceticism; and the second half is a polemic against Judaizing tendencies among his contemporary Christians. Aphrahat remains a crucial witness to forms of Syriac asceticism and protomonasticism, prior to the influence of Egyptian forms that would later predominate. He speaks of the *bnay* or *bnat qyama*, the "sons and daughters of the covenant." These were committed lay Christians who practiced a moderate form of asceticism in community with each other, with the expectation of celibacy. Their goal was the imitation of Christ, whose Greek title, "Only Begotten" (*monogenēs*), translates into Syriac as *iḥidaya*, the one who is "single" or "solitary." Christ's title is borrowed by these pious ascetics, such that the sons and daughters of the covenant become *iḥidaye* (plural), the solitary ones.

Further evidence for this protomonastic tradition is found in the *Book of Steps*, written sometime between the mid-fourth and early fifth centuries. The book categorizes two types of Christians: the so-called perfect, who are expected to be celibate, and the upright, who are not. The author evidently felt that standards were slipping, and the book is offered as an explanation of the two paths and an exhortation to practice with renewed faith and vigor. The *Book of Steps* was long thought to be representative of the Messalian movement. The name Messalian, Syriac for "one who prays" (Greek *Euchitēs*), was a slur given to monks who allegedly believed they could achieve a direct, sensible experience of the divine and thus had no need of the sacraments or the church that administered them. Although the *Book of Steps* is no longer thought to be a Messalian text, the charge of Messalianism haunts the Syriac mystical and ascetical tradition, especially its theology of prayer.

The fourth century also produced the most famous author of the Syriac Christian tradition, Ephrem the Syrian (d. 373). A deacon, poet, and theologian, Ephrem spent most of his life in the city of Nisibis, until that city was transferred from Roman to Persian hands in the year 363, at which time he relocated to Edessa for the last decade of his life. Ephrem's writings fall into four main categories: prose works, such as his commentary on the *Diatessaron* or his refutations of Bardaisan, Marcion, and Mani; so-called "artistic" prose; *madrashe* or hymns; and *memre* or verse sermons. Ephrem's fame derives primarily from the latter two. He stands at the head of a distinguished line of theologians in the Syriac tradition who chose to write in verse rather than prose, and whose theology is rich in imagery and symbolism while eschewing dialectics and disputation. His talent as a poet-theologian and his Nicene orthodoxy led Greek and Latin authors outside the Syriac world to embrace him. Early Greek biographical sketches of Ephrem sought to associate him with Basil the Great, one of the architects of Nicene orthodoxy and a founder of monasticism in Cappadocia. The fictional association with Basil appears also in the Syriac *Life of Ephrem*. Since Ephrem was a prestigious figure at the edges of the Roman Empire, the Greek church was eager to confer legitimacy on him, and then to claim him as its own.

In contrast to our earliest sources, Aphrahat, the *Book of Steps*, and Ephrem expressed little interest in the Greek influences coming from the West. This has led some to regard them and their age as somehow representing a purer Syriac Christian spirituality, free from the corrupting influences of Greek philosophy and science that would come with the fifth- and sixth-century translation movement. But sources from the second and third centuries suggest that the Syriac tradition was already negotiating the influence of Hellenism. Whatever their motivation for resisting Greek influence, then, it is unlikely that Aphrahat, the *Book of Steps*, and especially Ephrem did so out of some pure, uncorrupted ignorance. It is more accurate to think of them as deliberately turning away from Hellenism, in the hopes of developing a more idiomatic style of theology. So, rather than think of their spirituality as purer, or more pristine, it is better to think of them as investing in a religious and cultural retrenchment of sorts. Seen from the larger perspective of widespread cultural exchange in the region, they seem to have rather zealously guarded their own tradition in an increasingly multicultural world.

THE FIFTH AND SIXTH CENTURIES

The fifth and sixth centuries stand out as the formative period in which several Syriac-speaking Christian communities formally separated from imperial Roman orthodoxy, including the East Syrian community that became the modern Church of the East and the West Syrian community that became the modern Syrian Orthodox Church. Christological and ecclesiastical controversies coincided with flourishing ascetic traditions, both in individuals like the famous "stylites" (pillar-dwellers) and in the prominent monasteries of Syria and Mesopotamia. These monasteries played a critical role in the expression of distinctive mystical and exegetical traditions as the communities were restructuring their ecclesiastical identities in relation to empire. At this time, Rabbula, the bishop of Edessa (d. 435), and Philoxenus, the bishop of Mabbug (d. 523), circulated new Syriac translations of the New Testament, and the School of the Persians in Edessa was replaced by the famous School of Nisibis, which trained generations of exegetes, theologians, and church leaders for the East Syrian Church. The fifth and sixth centuries are renowned as a period with an extraordinary number of doctrinal conflicts. But this was also a period in which intellectual and ascetic creativity flourished.

It would be difficult to overstate the turbulence of Syriac-speaking Christians' relations with the empires with which they interacted. While in 325 the Council of Nicaea primarily addressed issues of the Trinity, it did not resolve questions of Christology—that is, the question of how best to express the belief that Christ was both fully human and fully divine. This was the issue that dominated fifth- and sixth-century controversies. In the early fifth century, church leaders adamantly disagreed about the nature and person of the incarnate Christ; this disagreement created a series of long-lasting rifts in the church. A conflict initially developed in the eastern Roman Empire between Cyril, the bishop of Alexandria (d. 444), and Nestorius, the bishop of Constantinople (d. 451). They agreed that Christ had both a human and a divine nature; they disagreed on how the two natures coexisted and what significance this had for Christ's role as savior. Cyril followed popular piety in acclaiming Mary *Theotokos* or "God bearer," because the child Mary bore was fully divine. Nestorius objected that this title confused Christ's two distinct natures, human and divine. In his view, Mary was the mother of the man Jesus, and so of his human nature. But she was not the mother of the Word, the Son eternally begotten from and "of one being" (*homoousios*) with God the Father. Nestorius preferred the title *Christotokos* or "Christ bearer" for Mary. These Christological debates became highly politicized as other powerful church leaders, as well as members of the imperial family, offered their support to one side or the other. In the end, Cyril gained the upper hand after a convoluted series of competing council meetings; in 431, the Council of Ephesus anathematized the teachings of Nestorius and set the standard for imperial orthodoxy.

East of the Roman Empire, however, Christians in the Sasanian Empire organized themselves around the bishop of the Persian capital Seleucia-Ctesiphon in 410. Reacting in part to regional pressures from their Zoroastrian rulers, whose ancient and dualist cosmology divided the world into opposing forces of good and evil and whose rituals centered on fire as a purifying element, these Eastern bishops reconvened in 424 and declared their independence from the Roman church. These two acts separated the East Syrian Church from the churches that still looked to Roman leaders to define Christian orthodoxy. Notably, these events preceded the Council of Ephesus in 431, and the East Syrian Church continued to accept as integral to its doctrine the teachings of Nestorius's mentor Theodore of Mopsuestia (d. 428), who argued that the two natures (and persons) of the incarnate Christ remained distinct. This was also a period of sporadic persecution for some Christians in the Sasanian Empire and the southern Arabian peninsula.

Back in the Roman Empire, however, the debates about the teachings of Cyril and the Council of Ephesus's condemnation of Nestorius were far from settled. In 449, Dioscorus (d. 454), who in 444 had succeeded Cyril as the bishop of Alexandria, persuaded Emperor Theodosius II to call the Second Council of Ephesus. This council was held in large part to address the teachings of Eutyches (d. 456), a presbyter in Constantinople who had taken to heart the condemnation of Nestorius's two-nature teachings, so much so that he taught there was one incarnate nature of Christ that was at once human and divine, a doctrine that his colleagues argued went too far in the opposite direction and compromised the Son's full humanity. The 449 council cleared Eutyches and condemned his most vocal opponent, Flavian of Constantinople (d. 449), who was severely beaten and died soon after he was sent into exile; it also condemned Hiba, the bishop of Edessa (d. 457) and Theodoret, the bishop of Cyrrhus (d. 457), for their close association with Nestorius and his teachings.

When Bishop Leo of Rome (d. 461) heard the results of this council, he rejected its legitimacy and wrote to the emperor Marcian (d. 457) and his wife Pulcheria, the sister of Theodosius II. In 451 the emperor called the Council of Chalcedon, which declared the 449 Council of Ephesus an illegitimate "robber council," condemned the teachings of Eutyches, deposed Dioscorus, and taught that the Son is one person (one *prosopon* or *hypostasis*) in two natures (two *physeis*). These events set the stage for another century of ecclesiastical and imperial conflicts around questions of correct doctrine and episcopal lineages. Immediately after the Council of Chalcedon there were violent struggles for the episcopacies in Jerusalem and Alexandria, and the use of imperial troops to enforce the emperor's wishes only aggravated the situation.

The decades that followed the Council of Chalcedon saw shifting imperial positions and numerous efforts to draft a successful compromise that could heal the growing rifts among these competing bishops and their loyal followers. For example, the emperor Zeno (d. 491) issued the *Henotikon* in 482 in an effort to present a definition of imperial orthodoxy that bypassed the most controversial language without explicitly condemning Chalcedon. In addition to failing to unite those who accepted or rejected Chalcedon, the *Henotikon* caused further schism by dividing those who signed it from those who refused to sign. When Zeno's successor Anastasius offered greater support to those who rejected the Council of Chalcedon than any later emperor would do, he added further to the upheaval and uncertainty over Roman definitions of orthodoxy. With Anastasius's death in 518, the fortunes of those who rejected Chalcedon declined dramatically, particularly under the rule of Anastasius's successor Justin I (d. 527), whose military and episcopal leaders imposed exile and sometimes physical violence on those who refused to accept Chalcedonian orthodoxy. Although Justin's successor Justinian (d. 565) and his wife Theodora once again sought reconciliation and compromise, those efforts did not survive for long after Theodora's death in 548. In 553 Justinian called the Second Council of Constantinople, which affirmed the Council of Chalcedon, condemned the teachings of Diodore of Tarsus (d. 390) and Theodore of Mopsuestia, and once and for all put an end to imperial debates over the legitimacy of the Council of Chalcedon. During this time, the miaphysite teachings of Chalcedon's opponents such as John Rufus (d. 518), Zacharias Rhetor (d. ca. 540), Philoxenus of Mabbug, and Severus of Antioch (d. 538) became foundational for the West Syrian Church.

In the decades that followed Justinian's Second Council of Constantinople, Syriac authors like John of Ephesus (d. 577/578) constructed heroic founding narratives for the West Syrian Church, including ascetics who preserved anti-Chalcedonian Christianity in the face of imperial rejection and the great evangelists Jacob Baradeus (d. 578) and John of Tella (d. 538), who helped their church to prosper through countless baptisms and ordinations. The fifth and sixth centuries thus saw the division of Syriac-speaking Christians among a number of newly distinct churches: some accepted the Chalcedonian orthodoxy of the Roman emperors Justin and Justinian; others in the East Syrian Church maintained Syriac traditions in the Persian Empire under the leadership of the patriarch or *katholikos* of Seleucia-Ctesiphon; and still others rejected the Council of Chalcedon and coalesced around the miaphysite teachings and episcopacies of the West Syrian Church. All these communities struggled with questions about their relation to the empire in which they found themselves and the processes of institutionalization that emerged from those definitions.

Side by side with the political and doctrinal schisms of the fifth and sixth centuries were the practices and teachings of the ascetics and monks who were often key players in those very controversies. Some of these ascetic leaders were deeply engaged in doctrinal and theological discussions of their day—sometimes directly related to their ascetic practice like the debates surrounding later "Origenism," the controversial fifth- and sixth-century teachings that many thought were based on the third-century teachings of Origen of Alexandria (d. 253). Others were active as interpreters and also as translators in monasteries as well as at educational centers like the School of the Persians in Edessa and its successor the School of Nisibis.

Many ascetic leaders were influential in Syriac Christian education and translation projects. While the origins of the Syriac translation of the Old Testament Peshiṭta and the Old Syriac Version of the New Testament are somewhat obscure, Rabbula, the powerful bishop of Edessa (d. 435/436), promoted a revised four-gospel translation of the twenty-two books known as the New Testament Peshiṭta. Although in the early sixth century Philoxenus of Mabbug commissioned a new Syriac translation (the Philoxenian Version) of all twenty-seven books of the Greek New Testament (and perhaps also some books of the Old Testament), his translation was not as widely used as the Peshiṭta, which to this day remains the standard Syriac biblical text. Apart from translations of scripture, the fifth and sixth centuries were also significant for a wave of translations of other Greek texts into Syriac that is sometimes collectively referred to as the first of two early Syriac Christian "translation movements." Paul, the early sixth-century West Syrian bishop of Kallinikos, for example, is renowned for having translated some of the Greek works of Severus of Antioch into Syriac soon after Severus produced them. Perhaps most prolific in the surviving manuscripts, however, are the translations of Sergius of Reshʿayna (d. 536). Educated in Alexandria, Sergius translated numerous Greek medical, philosophical, and theological writings into Syriac.

Close textual work was also at the heart of East Syrian intellectual and educational circles. The School of the Persians in Edessa was especially noteworthy since the influential School of Nisibis claimed it as its direct forerunner. Famous Syriac authors like Jacob of Serug (d. 521) and Narsai (d. ca. 500) studied at the School of Edessa. In Edessa and Nisibis these intellectual circles were well known by the middle of the fifth century for studying the controversial works of Diodore of Tarsus and Theodore of Mopsuestia that found favor in the East Syrian Church but were condemned as the root of Nestorius's heresy in other Christian traditions. As a result, the emperor Zeno ordered the closure of the School of the Persians in Edessa in 489. Later texts by Barḥadbshaba (d. early seventh century) from the School of Nisibis claim that the School of Edessa's most prominent teacher, Narsai, founded the School of Nisibis after he left Edessa in order to continue the Edessene school's deep intellectual traditions.

Ascetic practices played a significant role in the Syriac churches in the fifth and sixth centuries, as church leaders often relied on their own asceticism and the support of other famous ascetics to secure their legitimacy in lieu of imperial support. The fifth century saw the rise of the pillar-dwelling saints or "stylites" (most famously Simeon the Stylite), for example, as well as the wide variety of ascetic heroes praised in John of Ephesus's late sixth-century *Lives of the Eastern Saints* or Theodoret's fifth-century *History of the Monks of Syria*. Monasteries also became significant bases of support for church communities that were disenfranchised through the imperial politics of the late Roman or Sasanian Empires. In the East Syrian Church, the sixth century saw the famous monastic reform started in the "Great Monastery" of Abraham of Kashkar (d. 588), who issued his monastic rule in 570 after he had spent time with the ascetics at Scetis in the famous Egyptian desert. Abraham's Great Monastery came to be the center of East Syrian Christian monasticism, as did later monasteries founded by its alumni. Monasticism in the Church of the East had taken an unusual turn in 484 when the church accepted the values of their Zoroastrian rulers and neighbors, rejecting clerical celibacy, and encouraging monks to marry. Abraham's successors included some of the church's key figures, such as Babai the Great (d. 628) who studied at the School of Nisibis and went on to reform monasticism by requiring vows of celibacy for all monks and expelling any who had married.

Also relevant to the sixth-century doctrinal and ascetic conflicts were the challenges raised by the influential writings of the Greek mystical and ascetical writer Evagrius (d. 399) and the accusations of "Origenism" that swirled around the eastern Mediterranean in these decades. The fourth century had seen sharp controversies about the interpretations of the sophisticated theological and cosmological teachings of the Christian teacher Origen of Alexandria. Origen was greatly admired among many Christian leaders following his death, but later interpretations and extrapolations of his ideas became more controversial, particularly in the face of an increasingly circumscribed definition of Christian orthodoxy. Origen's ideas were perhaps most enthusiastically and creatively expanded in the writings of Evagrius. In fact, when the sixth-century controversies erupted and new concerns about "Origenism" were raised, they primarily focused on the writings and ideas of Evagrius rather than on Origen's own writings.

This renewed conflict over "Origenism" was in part a regional disagreement within Palestinian ascetic traditions, but the struggles escalated to such a degree that they were addressed at Justinian's Second Council of Constantinople in 553. This council anathematized both Origen and Evagrius, although the teachings deemed most objectionable derived from the latter. As a result of this condemnation, few of Evagrius's writings survive under his own name in the original Greek because the emperor ordered these controversial writings destroyed. Neither the East nor West Syrian traditions, however, accepted the validity of Justinian's council, nor did they associate Evagrius so clearly with Origen, whose works were not translated into Syriac. As a result, these Syriac churches continued to value, read, and comment on Evagrius's extensive writings. John of Apamea's teachings on prayer from the first half of the fifth century, for example, introduced Evagrian influence into Syriac ascetic traditions, and Sergius of Resh'ayna (d. 536) translated some of Evagrius's key works into Syriac. The East Syrian leader Babai the Great wrote a lengthy Syriac commentary on Evagrius's *Gnostic Chapters*, as did the much later West Syrian bishop Dionysius bar Ṣalibi (d. 1171).

The fifth and sixth centuries were a period of deeply divisive doctrinal discussions and imperial struggles that ultimately led to the creation of many of the Syriac churches that survive today. They were also a period of rich intellectual and ascetic exploration that set the stage for these communities to flourish in the challenging centuries that followed.

THE SEVENTH THROUGH NINTH CENTURIES

For those living in the late ancient world, the seventh century had a particularly dramatic opening: A series of rebellions in the Byzantine Empire put a new emperor named Heraclius (d. 641) on the throne, and they were used by the Persian king Khosrau II (d. 628) as a pretense for invading Byzantine territory, taking control of Jerusalem, and gaining possession of what was reputed to be the remains of Jesus's true cross. The Byzantine-Persian War ended only in 628, when a surprisingly successful counterattack by Heraclius prompted a Persian coup and subsequent capitulation. Two years later, Heraclius triumphally entered Jerusalem, returning the true cross. But, by that point, twenty-five years of warfare had already decimated many of the areas inhabited by Syriac Christians, and neither their respite nor Heraclius's was long lived.

About two years after Heraclius entered Jerusalem, 750 miles to the southeast, the prophet Muhammad died in the city of Mecca and his successors began a series of military expansions known as the Islamic Conquests. In response, Heraclius sent in substantial numbers of Byzantine troops. The Arabs defeated the majority of these and Heraclius withdrew. The Persians faced a similar phenomenon with a fairly continuous loss of territory throughout the late 630s and early 640s. Unlike the Byzantines, the Persians eventually lost their entire empire, with the last Persian king dying in 651.

The physical destruction from the Islamic Conquests was substantially less than that of the Byzantine-Persian Wars that preceded them. So, at first, many Syriac Christians may have viewed the change of rulers from Byzantine or Persian to Arab as either temporary or of little impact on their daily lives. At first, they may have been right. But the long-term effects are hard to overestimate. From the 630s onward most Syriac Christians lived under Islamic rule, putting them in direct contact with an emerging world religion.

Meanwhile, as part of an arguably foolhardy attempt to theologically unify the remnants of the Byzantine empire, Heraclius supported a new Christological compromise: Christ was to be viewed as having two natures but a single will. Heraclius began to forcefully impose this "monothelete" (one-will) doctrine even on fellow Chalcedonians. Among the initial supporters of Heraclius's one-will doctrine were the Chalcedonian monks of the monastery of Bet Maron. When, in 680, the Council of Constantinople declared monotheletism heretical, the monks of Maron and their followers broke off from other Chalcedonians forming the Maronite Church. Although in later centuries the Maronites would eventually reject monotheletism, by that point they had already established their own separate ecclesiastical organization. During the twelfth-century Crusades, the Maronites began establishing particularly close ties with the Roman Catholic Church and today they are in full communion with the Roman Catholic pope.

Because, starting in the seventh century, most Maronites, other Syriac speaking Chalcedonian Christians, West Syrian Christians, and East Syrian Christians lived under Arab rule, the fortunes of their four competing Syriac churches were directly tied to that of the newly formed Islamic Empire. After the first Arab civil war ended in 661, the Muslim governor of Syria named Muʿāwiya (d. 680) took control of the Islamic Empire and established the Umayyad dynasty. Toward the end of the seventh century, the caliph ʿAbd al-Malik (d. 705) further consolidated Umayyad power. Developments, such as ʿAbd al-Malik constructing the monumental Dome of the Rock in Jerusalem in 692 and his shift toward explicitly Islamic coinage, reflected his much more active role in championing Islam, promoting it as the supercessionary, state-sponsored religion of an increasingly Islamic empire. This led to a brief spate of late seventh-century Syriac apocalypses that interpreted these events as the harbingers of the world's imminent demise.

Contrary to such predictions, the world obviously did not end. But ʿAbd al-Malik's successors did increasingly intervene in church affairs, and they instigated specifically anti-Christian measures, including officially tying the tax rate to religious affiliation. An even more profound set of changes occurred in 750 when the ʿAbbasid family revolted against Umayyad rule, took control of the Islamic Empire, and began several long-term developments that shaped the fortunes of all Syriac communities.

The most important of these changes was increasingly greater contact between Syriac Christians and early Muslims. Such interactions took place in a number of different ways. For example, in 767 the ʿAbbasid caliph moved the capital from Damascus to the newly constructed city of Baghdad. This move was particularly advantageous for the East Syrian Church because Baghdad was located just a few kilometers from Seleucia-Ctesiphon, the traditional seat of its katholikos, and the East Syrian leader became a frequent attendee of the caliph's court. More broadly, as a result of the process of promoting Arabic that started a century earlier, many Syriac Christians were increasingly bilingual, allowing for more direct interactions with Muslims and a greater knowledge of Islam. But this also created a further distinction between Maronite and other Chalcedonian communities that more quickly adopted Arabic as their primary language when writing theology than did West Syrian and East Syrian Christians who underwent this linguistic shift more gradually. The move toward Arabic, both as a spoken language and later as a written language, further distinguished the Syriac churches, which were under Islam, from the Byzantine and Latin churches, which were not. Early 'Abbasid society also began a widespread project in which 'Abbasid authorities and private elites sought to translate all available texts of Greek science and philosophy into Arabic. During what modern scholars of Syriac often call the "first" translation movement, fifth- and sixth-century Syriac Christians had already translated numerous Greek texts into Syriac. As a result, Syriac scholars were active participants in the eighth-, ninth-, and tenth-century 'Abbasid translation movement of Greek works into Arabic (what modern scholars of Syriac sometimes refer to as the "second" translation movement). At the same time, cities and towns had increasingly mixed populations, which facilitated everyday contact between Christians and Muslims. This does not, however, mean that the eighth and ninth centuries were an age of universal tolerance and mutual respect. During the 'Abbasid period, conversion to Islam became increasingly prevalent and eventually led to a substantial decrease in the number of Syriac Christians. So, too, during the early 'Abbasid period, a set of discriminatory legal traditions designed to differentiate Muslims and non-Muslims began to reach its classic form.

The seventh through ninth centuries saw other types of cross-cultural interactions as well. Much to the dismay of the East Syrian Church, during this time period West Syrian Christians made further inroads eastward increasing the contact—and polemic—between West and East Syrians. But the East Syrian Church had, in turn, an even more dramatic geographic expansion. There is textual and archaeological evidence of Syriac Christianity in India and Central Asia prior the seventh century. But it was under East Syrian katholikoi such as the mid-seventh-century Isho'yahb III and the late eighth-century Timothy I that the East Syrian Church had its greatest missionary successes along the ancient silk road routes, with it establishing dioceses in India, Afghanistan, Tibet, Mongolia, and China. Three archaeological finds provide particularly important evidence for this expansion.

The first discovery took place in the Chinese city Xi'an (ancient Chang'an) which, in antiquity, was the capital of the Tang dynasty. In the 1620s, workers in Xi'an uncovered an almost three-meter-high limestone monument inscribed in Chinese and Syriac now known as the *Jingjiao Stele*. The inscription speaks of an East Syrian missionary named Aluoben who arrived in Xi'an in 635, and then it goes on to narrate Christian history in China up to the monument's dedication in the year 781.

The second find occurred in the early twentieth century, when a German expedition undertook a series of excavations within the central Asian oasis of Turfan (modern-day northwest China), a key staging post on the ancient silk routes. In the city of Bulayiq, archaeologists unearthed over one thousand textual fragments from an East Syrian monastic library. Primarily written between the ninth and thirteenth centuries, just under half of these fragments were in Syriac. The remainder were translations from Syriac into an array of other languages, especially Sogdian, the lingua franca of ancient Central Asia and the everyday language of the East Syrian Christians around Turfan. The recovered texts range from bibles to liturgical texts to hagiographies to an alleged cure for balding.

At the same time as the East Syrian community at Turfan was translating Syriac texts into central Asian languages, other East Syrian Christians were composing original Christian texts in Chinese. Key examples of these Chinese works were also uncovered in the early twentieth century, in this case at another oasis on the silk road. Among the almost fifty thousand Buddhist texts found in the "library cave" of the Chinese city Dunhuang were a handful of Christian works that were particularly striking in their use of Buddhist terminology to explain Christian theology. Together with the *Jingjiao Stele* and the Turfan fragments, the Dunhuang texts illustrate the vast geographic expanse of Syriac Christianity, as well as its constant interaction with other religious traditions.

In addition to being a period of substantial interreligious encounters and geographic expansion, the seventh through ninth centuries were also a time of key theological, scholastic, and liturgical development for all the Syriac churches. Competing Christological claims motivated the establishment of monastic schools that could provide new generations of clergy with sufficient theological acumen to defend their church's Christology and, ideally, to convert Christians from opposing communities. In the seventh through ninth centuries, several of the resulting monasteries grew to be especially prominent. Among West Syrian Christians, the bilingual Monastery of Qenneshre became a center of Greek and Syriac learning, and in just over a century five of its alumni were elected patriarch. Among Maronites, the Monastery of Maron was the starting point of their emergence as an independent church. For other Chalcedonian Christians, the Monastery of Mar Saba just outside Jerusalem became especially renowned and could count as one of its graduates the famous Chalcedonian theologian John of Damascus (d. 749). For East Syrian Christians, the late sixth-century monastic reforms of Abraham of Kashkar led to the founding of monasteries such as Mount Izla, Bet 'Abe, and Rabban Shapur. In addition to becoming future bishops and patriarchs, monks from these monasteries wrote many of their tradition's most important mystical texts.

Highly educated Christians from monasteries such as these engaged in other forms of scholarship as well. Partly in reaction to the rise of Islamic jurisprudence, Syriac authors—especially in the East Syrian Church—developed increasingly prolific and sophisticated codes of canon law. The seventh through ninth centuries also saw important developments in Syriac liturgy. Later writers credit this era's katholikoi, such as Katholikos Isho'yahb III (r. 649–659), with extensive liturgical reforms, and most of the earliest surviving Syriac liturgical manuscripts were composed in this time period.

This was also an age of important textual scholarship. Syriac Christians continued to translate Greek works into Syriac and, as part of the larger 'Abbasid translation movement, Greek and Syriac texts into Arabic. As a result, Syriac scholars were carefully searching out multiple manuscripts of earlier works, comparing them with each other, and adjudicating which readings they thought were most likely original. Because, in this period, Arabic was slowly replacing Syriac as the lingua franca, Christian scholars also became increasingly concerned with preserving the Syriac language. Like other Semitic languages, Syriac initially had no written vowels. But, as the number of native Syriac speakers who could accurately read unvocalized texts dwindled, scholars increasingly used various systems to mark how one pronounced a given word. So, too, they created fully vocalized copies of the Syriac Bible and many of the earliest surviving Syriac grammars.

In the seventh through ninth centuries the total number of Syriac Christians most likely began to wane as a result of conversions to Islam. But despite gradual demographic decline, in many other respects this was a time of substantial growth for Syriac Christianity. These centuries witnessed new interreligious interactions, the emergence of the Maronite Church, considerable geographic expansion, a rise in monasticism, and a blossoming of scholarship.

THE TENTH THROUGH FOURTEENTH CENTURIES

Recent scholarship has emphasized the vitality of seventh- through ninth-century Syriac literature, challenging any simplistic narrative of decline and revival. Nevertheless, many scholars still refer to the flowering of Syriac literature in the tenth through early fourteenth centuries as "the Syriac Renaissance." This high point in Syriac literature and learning was associated with changing fortunes for Syriac Christians in the Middle East and Iran, not least in response to the Crusades and the Mongol conquests. Two of the preeminent historians dominate later Syriac literature, Michael the Syrian (a.k.a. Michael the Great) and Barhebraeus, but many more lesser-known authors thrived during this period; and the genres and trends of earlier Syriac carried on, alongside grand and innovative new works.

Several East Syrian writers from the tenth and eleventh centuries speak to the efflorescence of Syriac during this period, even while Christian literature was increasingly written in Arabic. They compiled substantial technical works, including Bar Bahlul's highly significant tenth-century Syriac-Syriac lexicon, which represents the culmination of several centuries of Syriac lexicography and which continued to be added to after his death. Emmanuel bar Shahhare (d. 980) left a long verse commentary on the *Hexaemeron* (the six days of Creation). The tenth-century *Book of the Causes of Causes* is an anonymous theological work that is significant for its attempt to explain Christianity to Jews and Muslims. Elias of Nisibis (d. 1046) is best known for his *Chronography*, written in both Arabic and Syriac and containing sources that would otherwise have been lost. He was also a grammarian and lexicographer and wrote a Syriac-Arabic lexicon for the benefit of learners of Syriac, indicating perhaps that knowledge of Syriac had declined in his community. Most of the writers in the tenth and eleventh centuries also wrote liturgical treatises, canon law, theology, or apologetic works.

Above all, one must point to the manuscript collecting activities of Mushe of Nisibis, abbot of the Monastery of the Syrians in Egypt. Around 927 Mushe traveled to Baghdad to appeal new taxes levied by his governor. He returned with 250 high quality manuscripts. Manuscripts belonging to this monastery include one from 411, the oldest dated manuscript in the Western world, representing a collection of Syriac translations of Greek theological works, including Eusebius's *Theophania* and Titus of Bostra's *Against the Manichaeans*. Other texts uniquely preserved at the Monastery of the Syrians are the only complete manuscripts of Ephrem's *madrashe*, Aphrahat's *Demonstrations*, and the *Book of the Laws of the Countries*. The manuscripts are now for the most part divided between the Vatican and British libraries.

The Crusades of the twelfth century brought many changes to the experience of Christians in the Near East, even though Syriac Christians mostly stayed on the periphery of the conflicts. Relations between Muslim authorities and these "Suriani" deteriorated during Latin occupation. The low point was the destruction of Edessa in 1146, which resulted in the dislocation of its Christian inhabitants. Another result of the Crusades was the union of the Maronites with the Roman Catholic Church in the early thirteenth century. Close relations between the two led to the Latinization of the Maronite liturgy but, equally, to the flourishing of Syriac studies in Rome in the early modern period.

Syriac Christian literature in this period is known primarily through towering intellectual figures. Dionysius bar Ṣalibi (d. 1171) was the most significant Syriac writer of the early twelfth century. Like Michael the Great and Barhebraeus after him, he was born in Melitene in eastern Cappadocia. Under Michael he was appointed West Syrian metropolitan of Amid. Dionysius wrote commentaries on the Old and New Testaments, thus being the first Syriac author known to comment on the entire Bible. He drew on Greek commentators in Syriac translation and, even though he was West Syrian, incorporated exegetical works from the East Syrian Church. He also wrote commentaries on the logical works of Aristotle and Porphyry, a commentary on the Greek mystical and ascetical writer Evagrius, and polemical works against Muslims, Jews, and competing sects of Christians. We know of many works of his that have been lost, including a historical chronicle, a book of letters, and poems dealing with current events.

Michael the Great was patriarch of the West Syrian Church from 1166 until his death in 1199. He visited Latin-occupied Antioch and Jerusalem several times and, apart from a period in the 1180s, was recognized by the kingdoms of the Catholic crusaders. He was also in communication with the Seljuk sultan. He is best known for his massive and systematic world chronicle, which extends from the Creation up to his own day. In his role as patriarch he compiled liturgical works, theology, and canon law from the manuscripts he collected for his home monastery of Mar Barsawma (near Melitene). Among these manuscripts were histories that Michael used for his *Chronicle*, and some of them survive in large part through his excerpts, such as the ninth-century *Ecclesiastical History* of Dionysius of Tel Maḥre (also used in the important anonymous *Chronicle of 1234*). He arranged his narrative in separate columns, like historians before him, for the sake of chronological harmonization between sacred and secular events. In an appendix he applies his knowledge of world history to situating the Syriac Christians among the empires of the Near East. His *Chronicle* remains the apex of a long tradition of West Syrian historiography.

The renaissance of Syriac literature continued into the thirteenth and fourteenth centuries. Solomon, the East Syrian bishop of Baṣra, wrote the *Book of the Bee*, a collection of lore surrounding the Bible and the history of the Church. Like the Jewish *Book of Jubilees* (ca. 150 BCE) and the Syriac *Cave of Treasures* (ca. 600 CE), the *Book of the Bee* combines secular legends with imaginative stories inspired by the Bible. Here Solomon attempts to demonstrate, across the history of the ancient world, the work of God in the history of world events, while incorporating apocalyptic and other literature—for example, sections of the *Apocalypse of Pseudo-Methodius* (late seventh century) on the Muslim conquest and the tale of Gog and Magog from the popular *Alexander Romance* (mid-seventh century). Solomon's "bee" is a gatherer of nectar from flowers of all kinds.

Barhebraeus (d. 1286)—called, more properly, "Bar 'Ebroyo" or "Abū al Faraj"—was appointed bishop of Aleppo and ultimately became *maphrian* (subpatriarch) of the East for the West Syrian Church. He was a consummate polymath, read several languages, and composed over forty works on a diverse set of themes. His writings include the compendium of dogmatic theology titled the *Candelabra of the Sanctuary*, several books on philosophy and medicine, poems, grammatical treatises, and a two-part historical chronicle, split into the *Syriac Chronicle* (secular events) and *Ecclesiastical Chronicle* (church events). The latter deals with church history from its beginning to 1285 and covers both the West and East Syrian churches. His encyclopedia of Aristotelian philosophy, the *Cream of Wisdom*, relies on Avicenna, al-Ṭūsī, and a number of Greek writers. He wrote in Syriac and Arabic and frequently used the philosophical and scientific works of Arabic and Persian authors. In terms of his literary output, Barhebraeus is the chief representative of the Syriac Renaissance, but his crowning achievement may be his ability to synthesize Syriac thought and literature with a wide range of knowledge present in the Arabic and Iranian worlds.

The geographic expanse of Syriac Christianity during this time is perhaps best represented in a late thirteenth-century travelogue that recounts the journey of two East Syrian monks on pilgrimage from Beijing to Jerusalem. While en route, one of the monks, Markos, was elected katholikos in Baghdad in 1281, at which point he took the name Yahbalaha III. At the urging of the Ilkhanate khan, he commissioned his companion, Rabban Sauma, to continue to Europe as an ambassador. Rabban Sauma visited Constantinople, Rome, and Paris, among other cities, before returning to Baghdad. He kept a journal in Persian, which was translated into Syriac and incorporated into the travelogue by an anonymous compiler, who appears to have been an eyewitness to some of the events. This fascinating account is an important indicator of the spread of the East Syrian Church in China and Persia, particularly under the Mongol khans, and it uniquely relates the experiences of contemporary Western Christianity by a monk from the Mongol Empire. Rabban Sauma's journey to the West took place just prior to Marco Polo's to the East. Above all, the account demonstrates the wide geographical spread of the Syriac churches, their survival and inculturation under Chinese, Mongol, and Persian rule, and the increasing connections between West and East during the thirteenth century.

The greatest East Syrian verse of the medieval period appears in a collection attributed to George (Giwargis) Warda and comes down to us in manuscripts under the title *Book of the Rose* (*warda*). These 120 poems were incorporated into the East Syrian liturgies, primarily Eucharistic and they belong to the 'onita genre of Syriac strophic hymnography. Some of these poems were written during the Mongol invasions of the thirteenth century and address current events, but the collection was clearly added to as time went on. Most of the poems are liturgical, hagiographical, or penitential in nature and many are rhymed, unlike the bulk of Syriac poetry, thereby showing the influence of Arabic and Persian verse in this later period. The *Warda* became a foundation of liturgical poetry for the East Syrian Church.

Another thirteenth-century East Syrian poet, Khamis bar Qardaḥe also wrote strophic 'oniyata. These frequently deal with similar themes to the *Warda*, alongside which his poems appear in manuscripts. However, Khamis also wrote on secular themes: his satire, invective, and epigrams showcase his poetical skill.

The best-known Syriac writer of the fourteenth century is 'Abdisho' bar Brika (d. 1318), the East Syrian metropolitan of Soba (Nisibis). He wrote on a wide range of subjects in both Syriac and Arabic, and his corpus is usually seen as the culmination of the Syriac revival of learning in the high Middle Ages. He wrote an authoritative collection of canon law, the *Nomocanon*, a systematic theology for the East Syrian Church, the *Marganita* (The Pearl), and a collection of theological poetry called the *Paradise of Eden*. He is best known for his *Metrical Catalogue of Syriac Authors*, a long verse literary history of Syriac, particularly in the East, extending from the Bible to his own writings. The *Catalogue of Books* is a precious resource for the history of Syriac in that it names numerous works and authors we would not otherwise know. Even though his information is deficient for some authors, he attempts to be comprehensive, and the resulting work is a monumental poem testifying to the long and vibrant history of Syriac literature.

Syriac literature does not end; it continues to the present day. Furthermore, it is the liturgical language of millions of Christians across the world. However, the Mongol conquests of the thirteenth and fourteenth centuries—accompanied by tremendous anti-Christian violence and displacement—and the subsequent rise of the Ottomans drastically reduced the size and vitality of the Syriac churches in the late medieval period, and the so-called "Renaissance" of Syriac from the tenth to fourteenth centuries did not continue. This last efflorescence, both fueled and ultimately snuffed out by the vicissitudes of empire, brings to a close the history of classical Syriac. Nevertheless, it must be emphasized that the literature we have today would not have survived without subsequent readers and scribes who ensured that the Syriac literary heritage was preserved and passed on.

. . .

While writing this book, all four editors constantly struggled with the question of how to cull thousands of texts composed over this thousand-year period down to a hundred or so brief excerpts. Every discussion of what to include and what to exclude had a moment when we would fret about the inevitability of disappointed readers and reviewers. During such instances we kept reminding ourselves of the book's title. Our aim was not to codify a canon of Syriac literature and certainly not to present a comprehensive collection of texts. Rather, the goal was to create an *invitation*, a volume that balanced examples from what many consider the core of the Syriac traditions alongside other, lesser-known works. So, instead of striving toward the unreachable goal of complete coverage, the editorial team instead focused on the following question: what parts of what documents could entice the widest range of readers to further investigate the richness and diversity of this essential Christian tradition?

Even then, space constraints required us to make other difficult choices. Although Syriac Christianity continues to be vibrant and practiced by millions, we decided to focus on premodern Syriac Christianity, and thus limited ourselves to the time period of the earliest surviving sources through the Syriac Renaissance of the thirteenth and fourteenth centuries. During that millennium-long expanse, however, many Syriac Christians did not write in Syriac but rather in other languages such as Greek, Sogdian, and Arabic. So, too, the Syriac corpus contains a significant amount of translation literature, especially Syriac translations of Greek works. We included a few particularly influential documents written in other languages while maintaining a strong preference for texts originally composed and subsequently preserved in Syriac. This, in turn, affected confessional coverage and the majority of works in this volume come from the West Syrian and East Syrian churches. Their predominance partly reflects accidents of preservation; we simply have much more ancient literature from those two churches. But it also reflects the tendency of Chalcedonian authors to write in Greek or Arabic as opposed to Syriac. To maximize the amount of primary material, we also decided to provide only minimal framing for the sources themselves. Each chapter begins with a brief overview of its main theme, including a short list of additional suggested readings. Each excerpt has a short introduction. At the end of the book you will find a list of the translation and edition for each text as well as a concise, alphabetical biography of each named author and a short glossary of common terms. Fortunately, the *Gorgias Encyclopedic Dictionary of the Syriac Heritage: Electronic Edition* as well as *A Comprehensive Bibliography of Syriac Christianity* provide open-access online resources for further research and serve as effective supplements to this volume.

Each of these choices limited the book in one way in order to maximize its effectiveness in another. But even after we chose specific texts, a similar conundrum surrounded the question of how to cluster them. We quickly realized that every organizational structure was oversimplified, and often texts and topics that we first categorized one way could fit equally well another part of the book. Nevertheless, we eventually settled on a fairly simple system of four sections.

The first section, "Foundations," uses this term in two senses. Origin narratives, poetry, and doctrine are, of course, foundational to the various Syriac churches, and they continue to be lively topics among Syriac Christians. At the same time, they also have been foundational to the history of research on Syriac Christianity, and they were among the first issues to receive sustained attention from modern historians and scholars of religion. The second section, "Practices," responds in part to the danger involved in losing sight of lived religion. Scholars have noted that the tendency of reducing religious experience solely to texts has been particularly pronounced in work on traditions coded as "Eastern" and from subfields heavily indebted to philology. As a result, we wanted to foreground the interrelated phenomena of liturgy, asceticism, and mysticism. Although far from the only practices among premodern Syriac Christians, these are particularly illustrative of the creative, often contested, interplay between theology and performance. Section 3, "Texts and Textual Transmission," explores some of the most prominent genres of Syriac literature, including biblical exegesis, martyrology, and hagiography. It also includes Syriac writings about the acquisition, translation, and dissemination of books and the knowledge they contain. The section thus emphasizes both the richness of extant Syriac texts and also the effort premodern scholars put into the composition and preservation of the manuscripts containing them. The final section, "Interreligious Encounters," highlights Syriac Christianity's continual interaction with other religious traditions. Of all premodern Christian traditions, Syriac Christianity had the most direct and sustained encounters with Judaism, Zoroastrianism, Manichaeism, Islam, and Buddhism. This makes Syriac sources particularly valuable for the early history of each of these religions, and these sources provide some of the most in-depth historical examples of Christian interactions with non-Christians.

If you are a member of one of the modern Syriac churches or a member of an undergraduate classroom; if you consider yourself a specialist in Syriac studies, classics, late antiquity, medieval history, church history, or comparative religions, or if you consider yourself as someone simply curious about one of these subjects; if you are training in a seminary or if you are training for your PhD exams; if you have been assigned this book or if you are considering assigning it—you have been foremost in our discussion of how to best construct this volume. Along with the dozens of colleagues we have contacted for suggestions or who have anonymously reviewed our book manuscript, the editors have tried to keep you in mind as we have assembled these works. We hope the result of our deliberations will invite you to explore more deeply this vital and vibrant branch of Christianity.

ADDITIONAL RESOURCES

Many of the most important resources for the study of Syriac Christianity are now digital. An easily accessible starting point for many inquiries is the *Gorgias Encyclopedic Dictionary of the Syriac Heritage*, which is available in a print version through Gorgias Press or in a free electronic version. For the print version, see Sebastian P. Brock, Aaron Michael Butts, George Kiraz, and Lucas Van Rompay, eds., *Gorgias Encyclopedic Dictionary of the Syriac Heritage* (Piscataway, NJ: Gorgias Press, 2011). For the online version, see "Gorgias Encyclopedic Dictionary of the Syriac Heritage: Electronic Edition," e-GEDSH, https://gedsh.bethmardutho.org/index.html. The website devoted to the bibliography of Syriac Christianity provides searchable entries to over fourteen thousand publications dealing with Syriac Christianity. See "A Comprehensive Bibliography of Syriac Christianity," The Center for the Study of Christianity at the Hebrew University of Jerusalem, http://www.csc.org.il/db/db.aspx?db=SB. A principal journal dedicated to Syriac Studies, *Hugoye*, archives all issues and makes them freely accessible. See *Hugoye: Journal of Syriac Studies*, https://hugoye.bethmardutho.org/index.html.

There are also three particularly extensive collections of digital resources in Syriac Studies. Beth Mardutho: The Syriac Institute (http://bethmardutho.org/) has an ever-growing list of newly developed tools including online dictionaries, Syriac optical character recognition, and full-text searching of numerous Syriac texts. This institute also provides online courses for the Syriac language at the beginner and intermediate levels. Syri.ac (http://syri.ac/) seeks to be a comprehensive annotated bibliography for the Syriac world. This website includes links to open-access texts, a searchable bibliography, and a database of digitized Syriac manuscripts, as well as other research tools for the most significant topics in Syriac Christianity. Syriaca.org (https://syriaca.org/index.html) provides a portal to some of the most useful digital resources in Syriac studies, including extensive online guides to Syriac places, people, and texts. For a discussion of additional digital resources in Syriac studies, see Daniel King and David A. Michelson, "Online Resources for the Study of the Syriac World," in *The Syriac World*, ed. Daniel King (New York: Routledge, 2018), 814–23.

There are also a number of print publications that provide a general introduction to Syriac Christianity. The most recent is Daniel King, ed., *The Syriac World* (New York: Routledge, 2018), which contains thirty-nine chapters by top scholars in the field and, like the *Encyclopedic Dictionary of the Syriac Heritage*, can frequently provide a starting point for any given research topic. There are also several books that give a general overview of Syriac Christianity. These include the following: Sebastian P. Brock and David G. K. Taylor, eds., *The Hidden Pearl: The Syrian Orthodox Church and Its Ancient Aramaic Heritage*, 4. vols. (Rome: Trans World Film, 2001); Wilhelm Baum and Dietmar W. Winkler, *The Church of the East: A Concise History* (New York: Routledge, 2003); Sebastian P. Brock, *An Introduction to Syriac Studies* (Piscataway, NJ: Gorgias Press, 2006). See also Françoise Briquel Chattonet and Muriel Debié, *Le Monde Syriaque: Sur les routes d'un christianisme ignore* (Paris: Les Belles Lettres, 2017), which presents a particularly good overview of Syriac Christianity, along with plentiful color illustrations. Readers of French also should consult Muriel Debié, *L'écriture de l'histoire en Syriaque: Transmissions interculturelles et constructions identitaires entre hellénisme et islam* (Leuven: Peeters: 2015), which contains the most comprehensive discussion of Syriac historiography. There are also a number of shorter articles that provide quick summaries of Syriac Christianity and Syriac studies. These include the following: Susan Ashbrook Harvey, "Syria and Mesopotamia," in *Cambridge History of Christianity*, vol. 1, *Early Christianity: Origins to Constantine*, ed. Margaret Mitchell and Frances M. Young (Cambridge: Cambridge University Press, 2006), 351–65; Christine Shepardson, "Syria, Syriac, Syrian: Negotiating East and West in Late Antiquity," in *A Companion to Late Antiquity*, ed. Philip Rousseau (Malden, MA: Wiley-Blackwell, 2009), 455–66; and Muriel Debié and David Taylor, "Syriac and Syro-Arabic Historical Writing, c.500–c.1400," in *The Oxford History of Historical Writing*, vol. 2, *400–1400*, ed. Sarah Foot and Chase F. Robinson (Oxford: Oxford University Press, 2012), 155–79.

Suggestions for further resources on specific topics can be found at the end of each chapter introduction.

PART I

FOUNDATIONS

1

ORIGIN STORIES

The nature of our surviving sources obscures the historical origins of Syriac Christianity. But a rich variety of literary stories about those origins survives in the later traditions themselves. As Syriac traditions divided in the schisms of the fifth and sixth centuries, origin stories for Christianity in the different regions where Syriac Christianity thrived also multiplied. The early traditions of the apostle Thomas's travels to India and of Christianity arriving in Edessa were supplemented by more extended stories about the adventures of the apostle Addai, and later about the apostle Mari. By the twelfth century, texts like Michael the Great's *Chronicle* also included origin stories for the Syriac language itself, which Michael identified as the original human language before the Tower of Babel.

One of the earliest surviving Syriac narratives is the *Acts of Thomas*, which describe how Christianity arrived east of the Euphrates. In this tradition, after Jesus's resurrection, Jesus appoints his apostle Thomas to bring Christianity as far east as India. This tradition continues to be formative today, not least in the Syriac Christian communities of modern India in the region of Kerala. By the early fourth century, however, new origin stories focused on the city of Edessa, centered around a letter that King Abgar of Edessa ostensibly wrote to Jesus, and Jesus's alleged reply. Eusebius of Caesarea's early fourth-century *Church History* is our earliest source for this correspondence, a legend that expanded by the time the late fourth-century pilgrim Egeria wrote about her visit to Edessa, and that expanded further still in the early fifth-century *Teaching of Addai*. Edessa's long history with Christianity is also recorded in the sixth-century *Chronicle of Edessa to 540*, which mentions a flood in 201 that damaged an early church in the city. By the seventh century, East Syrian Christians celebrated their origins through the travels of Addai's disciple, the apostle Mari, whose evangelism in communities all over Mesopotamia is narrated in the *Acts of Mar Mari*. Other seventh-century Christians produced grander narratives that suggested a prehistory of Christianity in Mesopotamia with a Christianized narrative of Alexander the Great (d. 323 BCE) in the *Alexander Romance*.

A community's stories of origin are often closely tied to its efforts to distinguish itself clearly from other communities it sees as outside its boundaries. It is no surprise, therefore, that these origin stories are rife with polemic against religious "others"—Jews, pagans, and a wide variety of "heretical" Christians. The long-lived traditions of Christianity's arrival in Edessa thanks to the invitation of King Abgar are, for example, built on the anti-Jewish rhetoric of the king's letter; while other texts criticized Edessa's traditional worship of such gods as Bel, Nebo, and Atargatis; and the *Acts of Mar Mari* denigrate other pagan practices. Later traditions like the stories of Mari create a distinct origin story for the East Syrian Church in contrast to the West Syrian traditions. Perhaps most comprehensive in polemical self-definition among the excerpts collected here are the fourth-century writings of the theologian-poet Ephrem (d. 373), who denounces the falsehood of a vast number of other teachings while decrying the injustice of his own community's earlier followers being denied the name "Christians" in local competitions to claim that contested title.

Further Reading   While there are numerous places one could look for introductions to the origins of Syriac Christianity, the following are some of the most common. Two works from the 1970s represent older models of scholarship but nevertheless remain popular introductions. See Judah B. Segal, *Edessa: The Blessed City* (Oxford: Clarendon Press, 1970; repr., Piscataway, NJ: Gorgias Press, 2001) and Robert Murray, *Symbols of Church and Kingdom: A Study in Early Syriac Tradition*, rev. ed. (2004; repr., London: Bloomsbury T&T Clark, 2006). A brief overview with bibliography appears in Christine Shepardson, "Syria, Syriac, Syrian: Negotiating East and West in Late Antiquity," in *A Companion to Late Antiquity*, ed. Philip Rousseau (Malden, MA: Wiley-Blackwell, 2009), 455–66. On East Syrian traditions, see Wilhelm Baum and Dietmar Winkler, *The Church of the East: A Concise History* (New York: Routledge Press, 2010). For a French-language study, see Françoise Briquel Chatonnet and Muriel Debié, *Le Monde Syriaque: Sur les routes d'un christianisme ignoré* (Paris: Les Belles Lettres, 2017).

ACTS OF THOMAS

Third century. Originally Syriac. Taken here from the Greek translation of the Syriac.

The *Acts of Thomas* form one of many apocryphal *Acts* that each claims to narrate the life of one of Jesus's apostles beyond what is known from the New Testament texts. Although originally composed in Syriac, surviving Syriac manuscripts have a substantially edited version of the original text. As a result, the Greek translation of the Syriac often provides a version closer to the original narrative. The story advocates a strongly ascetic form of Christianity with a particular emphasis on celibacy, a theme prevalent in many early Syriac Christian texts. The *Acts of Thomas* are particularly significant as an origin story for Christianity in India. The excerpt here includes the call of the apostle Thomas to spread Jesus's teachings to India, Thomas's initial reluctance, and some of the dramatic conversions he performed on his travels, including that of a king's daughter and her new husband in their bridal chamber. For additional excerpts from the *Acts of Thomas*, see chapters 4 and 5.

At that time all of us, the apostles, were in Jerusalem: Simon, called Peter, and Andrew his brother, and James the son of Zebedee, and John his brother, Philip and Bartholomew, Thomas, and Matthew the toll collector, James the son of Alphaeus, Simon the Cananean, and Jude the son of James. We divided the regions of the world so that each of us would be in an allotted area and go to the nation to which the Lord had sent him. India fell to the lot of Judas Thomas, who is also called Didymus; but he did not want to go. [. . .]

While [Thomas] was speaking and pondering these things, there came along a certain merchant named Chaban, recently arrived from India. He had been sent by King Gundafar with a commission to buy and bring back a craftsperson. When the Lord saw him walking about at noon in the market he said to him, "Do you wish to buy a carpenter?" "Yes," he answered. Then the Lord told him, "I have a slave who's a carpenter, and I want to sell him." He showed him Thomas, some distance away, and settled with him on the price of three bars of unstamped silver. He drafted a bill of sale that read, "I, Jesus, son of Joseph the carpenter, agree to sell my slave, Judas by name, to you, Chaban, a merchant of Gundafar, king of India." When the paperwork was complete, the Savior took Judas, called Thomas, and brought him to Chaban the merchant. When Chaban saw him, he said to him, "Is this your master?" "Yes, he is, my lord," the apostle responded. Chaban said, "I've bought you from him." The apostle kept quiet. Early on the following day the apostle prayed and begged the Lord, "All right—I'll go where you want, Lord Jesus; enact your will." [. . .]

They then set sail with a favorable wind and proceeded rapidly until they reached Andrapolis, a royal city. They disembarked and entered the city to the sounds of flautists, organists, and trumpeters. The apostle asked, "What's the festival going on in this city?" The local people replied, "The gods have brought you to this city to be entertained. For the king has an only child, a daughter—at this very moment he's giving her away in marriage. What you see today is the joyful wedding celebration. The king has sent heralds to make a general proclamation: Everyone is to attend the wedding—rich and poor, slave and free, foreigners and citizens. If anyone refuses to attend, that person will be answerable to the king." When Chaban heard this, he said to the apostle, "We should go too, so we don't offend the king, especially since we are strangers"; to which the apostle said, "Certainly." [. . .]

While everyone else ate and drank, the apostle tasted nothing. So, the surrounding guests said, "Why did you come here if you're not going to eat or drink?" "I've come here," he answered, "for something more important than food or drink—to do the will of the king, of course." [. . .] Meanwhile, a flute girl, instrument in hand, mingled with the guests and played. When she came to the apostle's place, she stood at his head and played for a full hour. Now, that flute girl was a Hebrew.

The apostle was still as he was, staring at the ground, when one of the wine pourers raised his hand and slapped him. The apostle looked up, stared at his attacker, and said, "My God will forgive you this unrighteous act in the world to come, but in this world he will manifest his wonderful powers: I'll soon see this hand that struck me dragged along by dogs!" And having said that, he began to sing. [. . .]

When he had finished singing this poem, all the guests looked at him; but he kept quiet. They noticed his changed appearance but did not understand what he had said, since he was a Hebrew and had spoken in Hebrew. The flute player alone understood everything, since she, too, was a Hebrew. Standing apart from him, she played for the others, but frequently glanced back at him and kept watching him, for she loved him dearly as her fellow countryman. (He was also more handsome in appearance than anyone else present.) When the flute girl finished playing, she sat down opposite him and stared at him. For his part he did not look at or pay attention to anyone, but kept his eyes fixed on the ground, waiting for someone to release him from the spot.

Now, the same wine pourer who had slapped him went down to the well to draw water. A lion happened to be there—and it killed him, tore him apart, and left his limbs lying right there. Dogs immediately took his limbs away; and one, a black one, holding the right hand in its mouth, brought it into the banquet chamber. Seeing this, everyone was amazed and asked who among them was missing. When it became clear that the hand belonged to the wine pourer who had slapped the apostle, the flautist broke her flutes and threw them down. She went over to the apostle, sat at his feet, and said, "This man is either a god or an emissary of God; for I heard him say to the wine pourer in Hebrew, 'I shall soon see the hand that struck me dragged by dogs.' And that's precisely what you've now seen—it happened just as he said." Now some people believed her, but others did not.

When the king heard all this, he came in and addressed the apostle, "Get up, come with me, and pray for my daughter; she's my only child and today I shall give her away." The apostle did not want to go along with him, because the Lord had not yet appeared to him there, but the king led him off reluctantly to the bridal chamber, so he might pray for them. The apostle stood, then, and began to pray. [. . .]

Now the king asked the wedding attendants to come out of the bridal chamber. When everyone had come and the doors were locked, the groom lifted the veil of the bridal chamber to take the bride to himself. But he saw, speaking with the bride, the Lord Jesus, in the guise of Judas Thomas—the apostle who had just now blessed them and left them! So the groom said to him, "Didn't you leave before everyone else? How is it that you're still here?" The Lord said to him, "I'm not Judas who is also Thomas; I'm his brother."

The Lord sat down on the bed, ordered them to sit on the chairs, and began to speak to them: [. . .] When the young people heard this, they believed the Lord and pledged themselves as given to him: they refrained from filthy desire and spent the night in that place accordingly. [. . .] When the king heard this testimony from the groom and the bride, he tore his clothing and said to his guards nearby, "Go out, quickly, and make the rounds of the whole city. Arrest and bring me that sorcerer who by some ill chance has come to this city. To think that with my own hands I led him into my house!—and I myself told him to pray for my ill-fated daughter! To the man who finds and brings him to me I'll give whatever he asks."

So, they went out searching, but they did not find him, because he had sailed away. But when they went to the inn where he had lodged, they discovered the flute girl there, weeping and grieving because he had not taken her along with him. They related to her what had happened to the youths, and she heard this with great joy; so that, putting aside her grief, she said, "Now I, too, have found repose here." She got up to accompany them and was with them a long time, until they had informed the king as well. Many of the believers were still gathered there, until they heard a report that the apostle had been conveyed to the cities of India and was teaching there. At that they went off and joined him.

EPHREM, *HYMNS ON HERESIES* 22

Mid to late fourth century.

Ephrem (d. 373) lived in Nisibis until he moved to Edessa when the Roman emperor Jovian ceded Nisibis to the Persians in 363. He is one of the most revered and well-known writers of early Syriac Christianity and, having died well before the fifth-century schisms, he is honored in all Syriac traditions. While perhaps most famous for his poetry and his beautiful contributions to early Christian faith and theology, he also wrote artistic prose and covered a variety of topics—condemning heresies, praising virginity, encouraging the church, imagining paradise, and lauding his home city of Nisibis, to name a few. The excerpt below is noteworthy for the picture it paints of Ephrem's Nicene orthodoxy struggling to claim the name "Christian" in the midst of a rich variety of other communities who already identified themselves by that name. Thus, Ephrem condemns the followers of Marcion, Valentinus, Bardaisan, and Mani, along with Arians, Aetians (so-called "Neo-Arians"), and numerous others. He decries the fact that his community had earlier been called Palutians after their bishop Paluṭ, presumably because the name "Christians" was already claimed by one or more other communities. It is important to keep in mind that these hymns were sung liturgically, sometimes by Ephrem's famous women's choirs, with a response from the congregation after each verse. As such, it is easy to imagine the songs lingering in congregants' minds long after the service had ended, deepening the impact of their words on the community. For additional excerpts from Ephrem, see chapters 2, 3, 7, and 10.

> To the melody of "The Infants Have Been Killed"
>
> Like the form of the alphabet,
> Which is complete in its parts—
> It lacks no letter,
> Nor does it add another—
> So, too, is the truth written

In the holy gospel
With the letters of the alphabet,
A perfect measure that admits
Neither lack nor surplus.
Response: Blessed is your image that is in the alphabet!

Because Marcion added something fake,
The church has removed him and cast him out,
Valentinus, because he deceived,
The Quqite added and perverted,
Bardaisan ornamented his false copy,
Mani, who was wholly insane,
A bundle of thorns and thistles.
May the good one in his mercy turn them
From wandering into his pasture!
Response: Blessed is the one who is concerned about evil people!

Valentinus stole a flock
From the church and called it by his name;
The Quqite named one after his name;
The crafty Bardaisan stole one;
And they made the flock a common one.
Marcion kept his sheep separate,
Mani captured from him,
One rabid creature bit another,
They called a flock by their names.
Response: Blessed is the one who threw them out of his house!

The Arians, because they added and erred;
The Aetians, because they were subtle;
The Paulinians, because they acted perversely;
The Sabellians, because they acted with guile;
The Photinians, because they were cunning;
The Borborians, because they were defiled;
The Katharaites, because they kept themselves pure;
The Audians, because they were ensnared;
The Messalians, because they were unrestrained.
Response: May the good one turn them to his fold!

Look! Their hands have lost hold of everything,
And they have no handle to grasp.
They called us Palutians,
And we escaped that and rejected it.
Let there be an anathema on the one
Called by the name of Paluṭ,
If not by the name of Christ.
The furnace of the anathema has exposed them,

For they do not wish to be banned.
Response: Blessed is the one by whose anathema they have been exposed!

Paluṭ did not want
People to name themselves after him,
And were he alive, he would curse
With every anathema concerning this,
Because he was a disciple of the apostle
Who was clothed in suffering and brought to grief
Concerning the Corinthians, who had left
The name of Christ and called themselves
By the names of people.
Response: Blessed is the one who has truth!

A teacher who does not add
Anything shameful and hateful
To the teaching of Christ,
His disciples are Christians.
But if he adds a little deceit,
He leaves the name of Christ,
And his disciples call themselves
By the name of a weed,
Because what is false does not match the truth.
Response: Blessed is the one who has established us with his truth!

EUSEBIUS, *CHURCH HISTORY*

Early fourth century. Greek.

The city of Edessa had a unique claim to its Christian origins, in that it maintained that King Abgar of Edessa wrote a letter inviting Jesus to take refuge in his kingdom so that Jesus could heal the king of an illness. The tradition also claims that Jesus sent a response declining the invitation but promising to send one of his disciples instead. Although historians believe that these letters were created much later than the first-century reign of Abgar V, they nevertheless provided a powerful foundation story for Edessene Christianity that was expanded in the later *Teaching of Addai*. The letter's pointed reference to "Jews" as dangerous aggressors who are categorically distinct from Jesus and his followers is an anachronistic consequence of its origin centuries after Jesus's death.

> Copy of a letter written by Abgar the toparch to Jesus and sent to him in Jerusalem via the courier Ananias.
>
> Abgar Ukkama [V], toparch, to Jesus the good savior who has appeared in the region of Jerusalem, greetings. I have heard about you and your cures, that you effect them without drugs or herbs. For word has it that you make the blind see, the lame walk, cleanse lepers,

and cast out unclean spirits and demons, and that you cure those suffering from great illness and raise [people] from the dead. And having heard all of this about you, I can conceive one of two possibilities: either that you are God and, having come down from heaven you do all this, or that you who do this are Son of God. On account of this, therefore, I write, asking that you take the trouble to come to me and cure the ailment I have. I have heard, moreover, that the Jews murmur against you and plan to do you harm. My city is small, yet honorable, and enough for both of us. [. . .]

The reply of Jesus to the toparch Abgar, via the courier Ananias:

Blessed are you who have believed in me, without having seen me. For it is written about me that those who have seen me will not believe in me, even in order that those who have not seen me will believe and shall live. But about what you wrote me, that I come to you—it is necessary to fulfill everything for which I was sent here, and after fulfilling it thus to be taken up to the one who sent me. Yet, once I am taken up, I will send one of my disciples to you, in order to cure your ailment and to offer life to you and those with you.

EGERIA, *PILGRIMAGE JOURNAL*

Late fourth century. Latin.

The fourth-century travel journal of the female ascetic Egeria appears to be one of the rare texts from the period written by a woman. The adventurous Egeria left her monastery in modern Spain or southern France in 381 and spent three years traveling through the eastern Mediterranean world to see the places described in the Bible. Her depiction of her time in Edessa offers valuable descriptions about the city, including a tour of the palace said to have belonged to the king Abgar who wrote to Jesus. She also discusses the later history of Jesus's letter to Abgar, including its use to repel hostile armies from Edessa's gate, and copies of the famous letters that she received on her visit. Egeria also mentions the apostle Thomas's shrine in Edessa and his evangelism in Persia, but she does not seem familiar with the *Acts of Thomas* tradition, according to which he evangelized India. Anyone visiting Edessa (Urfa, Turkey) today will also be struck by her reference to the pools of fish of great size, similar to a landmark (the Pool of Abraham) that continues to draw pilgrims today, though now associated in the Muslim tradition with stories of the patriarch Abraham.

Then, setting out from there, we arrived in the name of Christ our God at Edessa. When we had arrived there, we immediately proceeded to the church and to the martyrium of holy Thomas. So, according to custom, having made prayers and the rest that was the custom to do in holy places, we also read there something from holy Thomas himself.

The church that is there is huge and very beautiful and of new construction, so that it is truly worthy to be a house of God; and as there were many things that I desired to see there, it was necessary for me to make a three-day stop there. Thus, I saw in that city very many martyria as well as holy monks, some living by the martyria, others having their cells farther from the city in more secluded places. And the holy bishop of that city, a truly pious man, both a monk and a confessor, receiving me willingly, said to me, "As I see, daughter, that you have taken on yourself such great labor for the sake of piety that you have come to these places from the farthest distant lands, therefore, if you are willing, we will show you whatever places here are pleasant for Christians to see." Then, giving thanks to God first, I asked him very much that he would be gracious enough to do as he said.

Thus, he led me first to the palace of King Abgar and there showed me a huge statue of him, very much like him, as they said, of marble, of such luster as if it were made of pearl. In Abgar's face from the front it appeared that this man had been very wise and honorable. Then the holy bishop said to me, "Behold King Abgar, who before he saw the Lord, believed in him, that he was truly the Son of God." For there was also nearby a statue similarly made of the same marble, which he said was of his son Manu, and similarly also having something of grace in the face. Then we went into the inner part of the palace; and there were springs full of fish, such as I never saw before, that is, of such size, and so bright and of such a good taste. For the city has no other water at all now except that which comes out of the palace, which is like a huge silver river.

And then the holy bishop told me about the water, saying, "At some time after King Abgar had written to the Lord and the Lord had replied to Abgar by the messenger Ananias, as is written in the letter itself, after some time had passed the Persians came against the city and surrounded it. But immediately Abgar, carrying the letter of the Lord to the gate with all his army, prayed publicly. And he said, 'Lord Jesus, you had promised us that no enemy should enter this city, and behold, now the Persians are attacking us.' When the king had said this, holding the letter open in his upraised hands, suddenly such darkness fell, but outside the city before the eyes of the Persians when they were already drawing so near to the city that they were about three miles from the city; but soon they were so confused by the darkness that they scarcely pitched their camp and surrounded the whole city three miles away. The Persians were so confused that they never saw afterward on which side to enter the city but they kept the city surrounded with troops three miles away, and [they] kept it for several months.

But afterward, when they saw that they could by no means enter the city, they wished to kill with thirst those who were in the city. For that little hill that you see above this city, daughter, at that time supplied water to this city. Then, seeing this, the Persians diverted that water from the city and made it run down the opposite way to that place where they had pitched their camp. On that day and at that hour when the Persians had diverted the water, immediately these springs, which you see in that place, at God's command at once burst forth; from that day until today these springs remain here by the grace of God. But the water that the Persians had diverted dried up at that hour, so that those who were besieging the city did not have anything to drink for even one day, as is also apparent down to this day; for afterward no moisture whatsoever has ever appeared there down to this day. So, by the will of God who had promised this would be, it was necessary for them immediately to return to their own land, that is, to Persia. For afterward also, whenever enemies have wanted to come and capture this city, this letter has been brought out and read at the gate, and immediately by the will of God all enemies have been driven back."

The holy bishop also related that [the place] where these springs burst forth had before been a level place within the city lying below Abgar's palace. "Abgar's palace had been located in a somewhat elevated place, as is also visible now, as you see. For the custom was such at that time that palaces, whenever they were built, were always in elevated places. But after these springs burst forth in that place, then Abgar himself built this palace in that place for his son Manu (that is, the one whose statue you see set up next to his father) so that these springs would be included within the palace."

After the holy bishop had related all this, he said to me, "Let us now go to the gate through which the messenger Ananias entered with that letter of which I had spoken." So, when we had come to that gate, the bishop, standing, made a prayer and read to us there those letters, and then blessing us, another prayer was made. The holy one also related this to us, saying, "From that day when the messenger Ananias entered through that gate with the Lord's letter down to the present day it has been maintained that no one unclean, no mourner should go through that gate, nor should the body of any dead person be carried out through that gate."

The holy bishop also showed us the grave of Abgar and of all his family, very beautiful but done in the ancient style. He also led us to that upper palace that King Abgar had had first and showed us whatever other places there were. It was also very gratifying to me that I should receive for myself from that holy one the letters themselves, whether of Abgar to the Lord or of the Lord to Abgar, which the holy bishop had read to us there. And although I had copies of them at home, yet it seemed more gratifying to me that I should also receive them there from him, lest perhaps something less had reached us at home; for what I received here is indeed fuller. If our God Jesus shall will it, and I shall come home from here, you will read them, ladies, my souls.

TEACHING OF ADDAI

Late fourth or early fifth century. West Syrian.

The *Teaching of Addai* is an early fifth-century expansion of the story begun in the letters between Jesus and King Abgar of Edessa, first cited by Eusebius in the early fourth century. The text provides the background to these letters, describing how the king's followers first encountered Jesus, and it describes the archivist Hanan painting a portrait of Jesus for the king, which is the earliest reference to the "mandylion" tradition that a physical representation of Jesus's face existed in Edessa. Primarily, however, the text focuses on the journey of Addai; it describes him as one of Jesus's seventy-two apostles whom, after Jesus's resurrection, the apostle Judas Thomas sent eastward. This excerpt focuses on Addai's conversion of the city of Edessa, and it reveals the conflicting ways in which Jews are portrayed in the text as both enemies of Jesus and locally as welcoming hosts of Jesus's apostle Addai. The end of the story also contains a noteworthy reference to the early bishop of Edessa, Paluṭ, who is mentioned in Ephrem's writings. For an additional excerpt from the *Teaching of Addai*, see chapter 10.

In the three hundred and forty-third year of the kingdom of the Greeks in the reign of our lord Tiberius, the Roman Caesar, in the reign of King Abgar, the son of King Manu, in the month of October on the twelfth day, Abgar Ukkama sent Maryahb and Shmeshgram, noble and honorable men of his kingdom, and Hanan the faithful archivist with them, to the city called Eleutheropolis (in Aramaic Betgubrin) to the honorable Sabinus, the son of Eustorgius, the procurator of our lord Caesar, who was governor over Syria, Phoenicia, Palestine, and all the country of Mesopotamia. They brought to him letters about the affairs of the kingdom. When they reached him, he received them happily and with honor; so they were there twenty-five days. Then he wrote for them a reply to the letters and sent them to King Abgar.

When they went out from his presence, they left and went on the road to Jerusalem. They saw many people coming from far away to see the messiah because a report of the wonders of his mighty deeds had gone out to distant places. When they saw them, Maryahb, Shmeshgram, and Hanan, the archivist, also went with them to Jerusalem. Upon entering Jerusalem, they saw the messiah and celebrated with the crowds who were following him. On the other hand, they saw the Jews standing in groups and plotting what they might do to him, for they were distressed at seeing that some of the multitude of the people were believing in him. Thus they were there in Jerusalem ten days. Hanan the archivist wrote down everything which he saw that the messiah was doing, along with the rest of the things done by him there before they had come there. Then they left and came to Edessa.

When they entered in before King Abgar, their lord who had sent them, they gave him the reply to the letters they had brought with them. After the letters had been read, they began to relate to the king everything that they had seen and everything that the messiah had done in Jerusalem. Hanan the archivist read to him everything that he had written and had brought with him. When King Abgar heard, he was speechless and astonished; so were his nobles who were standing before him. Abgar replied, "These powers are not of people but of God. For there is none who can restore life to the dead except God alone."

Abgar wished that he himself might cross over and go to Palestine and that he might see with his own eyes everything that the messiah was doing. But because he could not pass over a district of the Romans that was not his, lest this occasion should provoke bitter enmity, he wrote a letter and sent it to the messiah by Hanan the archivist. He went out from Edessa on the fourteenth of March, entered Jerusalem on the twelfth of April on the fourth day of the week, and found the messiah in the house of Gamaliel, a prince of the Jews. The letter was read to him, written as follows: [. . .]

When Jesus received the letter in the house of the chief priest of the Jews, he said to Hanan the archivist, "Go and say to your lord who sent you to me" [. . .]

When Hanan the archivist saw that Jesus had spoken thus to him, he took and painted the portrait of Jesus with choice pigments, since he was the king's artist, and he brought it with him to his lord King Abgar. When King Abgar saw the portrait, he received it with great joy and placed it with great honor in one of the buildings of his palaces. Hanan the archivist told him everything that he heard from Jesus, since his words had been placed by him in written documents.

After the messiah had ascended to heaven, Judas Thomas sent Addai, the apostle, one of the seventy-two apostles, to Abgar. When Addai came to the city of Edessa, he dwelt in the house of Tobias, the son of Tobias the Jew, who was from Palestine. When a report concerning him was heard throughout all the city, one of the nobles of Abgar (his name being Abdu the son of Abdu, one of the princes of Abgar's council) entered and told him [the following] about Addai: "Behold an ambassador has come and dwelt here. He is the one concerning whom Jesus sent to you [saying], 'I will send to you one of my disciples.'" When Abgar heard this, in addition to the great miracles that Addai was doing and the amazing cures that he was performing, he concluded, "Truly this is the one whom Jesus sent [saying], 'When I have ascended to heaven, I will send to you one of my disciples and he will heal your illness.'" Abgar sent and called Tobias and said to him, "I have heard that a mighty man has come and dwelt in your house. Bring him up to me. Perhaps by this one there will be found for me good hope for recovery."

So Tobias arose early the next day, took Addai the apostle, and brought him up to Abgar. Addai himself knew that it was by the power of God that he was being sent to him. When Addai went up and entered before Abgar, his nobles were standing with him. At his entrance before him a marvelous vision appeared to Abgar in the face of Addai. As soon as Abgar saw the vision he fell down and did obeisance to Addai. Great wonder seized all those who were standing before him for they did not see the vision that appeared to Abgar. Abgar said to Addai, "Truly you are the disciple of Jesus, that mighty man, the Son of God, who sent to me [saying], 'I will send to you one of my disciples for healing and for salvation.'" Addai replied, "Because at first you believed in the one who sent me to you, because of this I have been sent to you. Again because you believe in him, everything that you believe will come to you through him." Abgar returned, "I have so believed in him that against those Jews who crucified him I wish that I might lead an army myself and might go and destroy them. But because that kingdom belongs to the Romans, I have respect for the covenant of peace that was established by me as by my forefathers with our lord Caesar Tiberius." Addai responded, "Our Lord has completed the will of his Father. When he completed the will of his parent, he was raised to his Father, and sat down with him in glory, with whom he had been from eternity." Abgar replied, "Indeed I believe in him and in his Father." Addai returned, "Because thus you have believed, I lay my hand upon you in the name of the one in whom you believed." As soon as he laid his hand upon him, he was healed from the pain of his illness that he had had for a long time. Abgar marveled and was astonished for just as he had heard about Jesus that he worked and performed healings so also Addai himself without drugs of any kind performed healings in the name of Jesus. [. . .] Moreover, in all the city, he performed great healings and showed astonishing miracles.

Abgar said to him, "Now everyone knows that by the power of Jesus the messiah you are doing these wonders. Behold we are amazed at your deeds. Therefore I beseech you that you tell us concerning the coming of the messiah, how it came about, concerning his glorious power, and concerning the wonders that we have heard he was doing that you and the rest of your companions saw." Addai replied, "From proclaiming this I will not be silent. For because of this I was sent here in order that I might speak and teach everyone who, like you, is willing to believe. Tomorrow assemble all the city to me and I will sow in it the word of life by the preaching that I will proclaim to you." [. . .]

When Addai the apostle had spoken these things before the whole city of Edessa, and King Abgar had seen that all the city rejoiced in his teaching, men and women alike, and were saying to him, "True and faithful is the messiah who sent you to us," he also rejoiced much in this as he praised God; because, as he had heard from Hanan his archivist concerning the messiah, so he had seen amazing powers that Addai the apostle was doing in the name of the messiah. King Abgar said to Addai the apostle, "As I sent to the messiah in my letter, as he also sent to me, and I have received from you yourself today, so I will believe all the days of my life. In these very things I will remain and take glory because I know that there is no other power in whose name these signs and wonders are done than by the power of the messiah whom you proclaim in justice and truth. Now, therefore, I will worship him, I and Manu my son and Augustine and Shalmat the queen. Wherever you wish, therefore, build a church, a meeting-place, for those who have believed and continue to believe in your words. [. . .]

When King Abgar had gone down to his royal palace, he and his nobles with him rejoiced: Abdu, Garmai, Shmeshgram, Abubai, and Meherdat, with the rest of their companions, in everything that their eyes had seen and their ears had heard. In the rejoicing of their heart they also praised God who had turned their mind to himself, while they renounced the paganism in which they lived and acknowledged the gospel of the messiah. When Addai had built the church, they offered alms and oblations in it, they and the people of the city, and there they offered service all the days of their lives. [. . .]

Because [Addai's successor Aggai] died speedily and rapidly at the breaking of his legs he was unable to lay his hand upon Paluṭ. Paluṭ himself went to Antioch and received ordination to the priesthood from Serapion, the bishop of Antioch. Serapion himself, the bishop of Antioch, had also received ordination from Zephyrinus, the bishop of the city of Rome, from the succession of ordination to the priesthood of Simon Peter, who received it from our Lord, and who had been bishop there in Rome twenty-five years in the days of Caesar, who reigned there thirteen years.

CHRONICLE OF EDESSA TO 540

Sixth century. Chalcedonian.

The *Chronicle of Edessa to 540* is the earliest historical work in Syriac, preserving precious information about the history of Edessa. From the re-founding of the formerly Seleucid city by the Abgarid dynasty in 133/132 BCE to the year 540 CE, the *Chronicle* includes 106 independent events, which are dated precisely by year. It proceeds chronologically, except that the very first entry, presented here, describes a flood in Edessa in September of 201. This entry makes mention of damage done to the "sanctuary [or nave] of the church of the Christians." The appearance of a church in this text has led to debates over how early Christianity arrived in Edessa. One piece of evidence in favor of the *Chronicle*'s accuracy is that, at the end of this account, it notes the city archives at Edessa, to which scholars believe its author had direct access. In any event, the *Chronicle* serves as a testimony to the centrality of Edessa in the origins of Syriac Christianity.

In the year 513 [of the Greeks = 201 CE], in the reign of [Septimius] Severus [193–211] and the reign of King Abgar [VIII], son of King Manu, in the month of Second Teshrin [November], the spring of water that comes forth from the great palace of King Abgar the Great became abundant; and it rose abundantly as had been its wont previously, and it became full and overflowed on all sides. The royal courtyards and porticoes and rooms began to be filled with water. When our lord King Abgar saw this, he went up to a safe place on the hill, above his palace where the workers of the royal works reside and dwell. While the experts were considering what to do about the excess of waters that had been added, there took place a great and abundant downpour of rain during the night. The Daisan [River] came before the usual time and month and foreign waters came, and they found the sluices closed with large plated iron [bars] and with reinforced iron bolts. Since no ingress was found for the waters, a great lake formed outside the city walls and the waters began to descend between the battlements of the walls into the city. King Abgar, standing on the great tower called "[the tower] of the Persians," saw the waters by [the light of] burning torches and ordered that the gates and the eight sluices of the eastern wall of the city should be removed from [the place] where the river came out. But at that very moment, the waters broke down the western wall of the city and entered into the city. They destroyed the great and beautiful palace of our lord king and removed everything that was found in their path—the charming and beautiful buildings of the city, everything that was near the river to the south and north. They caused damage, moreover, to the nave of the church of the Christians. In this incident there died more than two thousand persons; while many of them were asleep at night, the waters entered upon them suddenly and they were drowned.

ACTS OF MAR MARI

Late sixth or seventh century. East Syrian.

The *Acts of Mar Mari* tell the story of Mari, whom it calls one of the original seventy of Jesus's apostles alluded to in the Gospel of Luke and a disciple of the apostle Addai. The text celebrates Mari for spreading Christianity throughout the Persian Empire. It relies on some of the details in the *Teaching of Addai*; it claims that Mari began teaching in Edessa before traveling to Nisibis and then around wide regions of Mesopotamia, including the south, where Mari claims to see the influence of the apostle Thomas from his travels to India. Notable about these conversion stories is not only the number of towns that it claims Mari turned to Christianity but also its specific references to Mari's building of churches and monasteries, as well as his establishing schools with teachers, all of which speak to the text's later context.

> Through the divine power, we are writing the story of Mar Mari the apostle, one of the seventy [disciples]: Our Lord, help me! Amen! [. . .]
> So far were [the stories] about the conversion of Mesopotamia. Let us now turn our attention to show how the fear of God moved from there to our own territories. Because this story is not told clearly, I am putting into writing the old tradition that is transmitted in the books, as follows.
> Before the blessed Addai died, he selected one of his disciples named Mari, who was living in the love of God and was adorned with virtuous manners. He placed his right hand

on Mari, as conferred to him by our Lord Jesus Christ, and sent him to the eastern region, to the land of Babylonia, ordering him to go and preach there the word of our Lord.

The blessed Mar Mari left Edessa to begin preaching until he reached the city of Nisibis. After the blessed one converted the city of Nisibis, planted in it the truth of the true faith, overthrew its idols, and shattered its statues, he built in it churches and monasteries and set up teachers and a school. [. . .]

When the blessed one reached the city of Arzen, he converted many people through the mighty acts that he was performing. Now the king of Arzen was stricken by the disease called gout. When he heard about the miracles and healings that took place at the hands of the blessed one, with great eagerness he ordered that they should bring the blessed one before him. When Mar Mari came and went into the presence of the king, the latter greatly rejoiced in him, because the blessed one bowed down happily before him. And when the king heard the word of the blessed one, he held him in increasing honor, because of his gentleness, humbleness, and joyful countenance—for Mar Mari was very meek and very kind toward everyone, and in him jealousy and anger had no place whatsoever. The king said to him, "Tell me! What is your religion? For I believe you are a god!" Then the blessed Mar Mari answered and said to the king, "God forbid! I am not God, O my lord the king, but I am a man, servant of the living God. My religion is Christianity, and I believe in Christ, the Son of God, who descended at the end of times from heaven, and turned the world away from the deception of the demons by which it was seized. I confess this One, O my lord the king, I perform these things in his name, bringing erring people [to God and] to the faith." The king answered and said to him, "According to your claim, can your Lord, therefore, heal this illness with which I have been stricken for a long time?" The blessed one said to him, "If you believe in him, your requests will be answered." Immediately, the king kneeled and bowed down before the blessed one, begging and saying, "My Lord, I believe! Help me!" At this point the blessed one came close and placed his hand on the spot, saying, "In the name of our Lord Jesus Christ, whom the Jews crucified in Jerusalem, get up on your feet!" Concomitant with the word of the blessed one, the king was healed, and was baptized along with the members of his house. When the entire city realized that the king was healed, they too came to the blessed one, and he healed their bruises. He thus converted the whole city, built in it a church, and appointed over it priests and deacons.

From there he left again and came to the land of Bet Zabdai. There he converted most of the local people, and from there the blessed one left for the land of Bet ʿArabaye, where he made many conversions. From there, he went down to the land of Erbil and Ator. [. . .] [He and his followers] came down to the city of Seleucia, which was located on the Tigris. Because Christianity did not exist in the region, nor could they find anyone who would receive them in his house for God's sake, the blessed one and those who were with him rented a house and settled in it. [. . .]

So he wrote a letter to the apostles, his colleagues, which he sent to the city of Edessa. He wrote to them as follows: "As I wrote to you in the past, the land to which you have sent me is full of thorns and thistles that I cannot tread under my feet, nor could I step upon the mountains and hills that are in it! And you wrote to me, 'You have no right to come here or to go elsewhere until you have subjected the mountains and the hills that are in it, have sown in it the living seed, and have sent from the fruits of its produce to heaven!'

When I realized that I had no other choice except to do so, I went to take my seat in the assembly of the elders and associated myself with them in eating, drinking, and singing like them. And through the help of God and through your prayers I converted among them the two presidents of the assembly. Now my turn to do the [food] service, as is the custom among them, has come. Send me now from the gold that you have, as well as skilled singers from there who can sing nicely, and the finest anointing oils, so that I will be able to do as they themselves do, because I have nothing here!" When the light-clad apostles heard these things, they rejoiced and sent him gold as he requested from them, along with fragrant herbs, tambourines, harps, cymbals, and all kinds of instruments that had no equal in Seleucia, and they reached the blessed Mar Mari in Babylonia.

When the day of service came, he did such a great service that no one in Seleucia had performed anything like it. And after the whole assembly had eaten and drunk, he ordered the singers to come in, and the singers went in and sang hymns in such a way that the three assemblies were deeply moved. They said, concerning the holy Mar Mari, "This man is a god, because he is different in every regard!" All of them came near the blessed Mar Mari and said to him, "We beg you that these singers remain here and that they should not return to their regions. And whenever your turn comes up to do the service, your service will be remitted against the wage of the singers." The holy man said to them, "I do not embezzle the wage of the singers, but if you want, I have one word to tell you and so listen to me!" They said to him, "Speak!" He said, "Become Christians, and these singers will be yours!" They too asked him, saying, "What is Christianity? We have never heard this name at all!" He said to them, "Have faith in God the omnipotent, who created heaven and earth—there is no God other than him—and in his Son Jesus Christ, who descended from heaven and assumed the body of the human beings whom he brought to himself. And believe in the Holy Spirit, she who placed in our hand the mighty things and the healing of the presidents of your assembly." [. . .]

After much discussion, the king ordered, and the temple was given to the blessed one. As for the idols, the king gave them to the blessed one as a gift. Mar Mari took them, ground them as fine as dust, and threw their powder into the Tigris. He demolished the temple of idols and instead he built a small church, establishing in it priests and deacons. In the same place he also founded schools and appointed one of his disciples in charge of the teachers. [. . .] Afterward, he descended to the lower territories, where he detected the traces of Saint Thomas the apostle and brought many people to our Lord. [. . .]

The blessed one circulated through the territories of the east for many years, consecrating churches and harmonizing them. [. . .] After these events, the blessed Mar Mari left this world, departing to the eternal life. His holy body was deposited and buried in the church that he himself built and completed in Dur-Qunni.

ALEXANDER ROMANCE

Seventh or eighth century. West Syrian.

Legends about the powerful leader Alexander the Great (d. 323 BCE) circulated widely in late antiquity. The *Chronicle of Zuqnin* (775/776), an important Syriac historiographical text, records a Christianized version of Alexander's exploits that scholars think originated soon after the Byzantine emperor Heraclius's victories in 629 and 630 over the Sasanians. Christian legends about Alexander multiplied over the centuries and took on particularly strident apocalyptic tones in the context of the Arab-Byzantine conflicts of the seventh century. The version of the story here begins by having Alexander proclaim his obedience to the messiah whenever he will come. The Son of God is then said to have appeared to Alexander and to have helped make him successful in his battles. The text contains several themes that appear also in the apocalyptic Christian literature of the late seventh and early eighth century after the dramatic military success of the followers of Muhammad, and it includes references to the opposing apocalyptic armies of Gog and Magog as well as passages describing the offering of Alexander's gold crown to God's Son.

When [Alexander] wanted to go out in expedition into the land, he stood up to make a vow, saying, "If the messiah Son of God comes in my days, I and all my troops would bow down and worship him, and if he does not come in my days, the crown that is on my head and my royal throne will be for his honor whenever he comes. And these eighty pounds of gold will be for his incense, light, and offerings when he comes." And he rose up to lead with him three hundred and twenty-four thousand soldiers and went to Egypt. [. . .] He marched up, going through that plain until the setting of the sun, as is written in [his] story. They saw the sun setting in the sky and the likeness of fiery balls falling from it at that moment, and all the people of that region and the animals and the birds fled into caves. Then Alexander and all his army rose up to return, marching to the east. He crossed many territories up to the territory that was between the Roman and Persian kingdoms and up to the land of Gog.

Alexander dispatched messengers to say, "The king of the Greeks is crossing over [your land] and he is not taking captives or destroying. [He says], 'Let everyone sit in peace, and let only the very old ones who are in this place come to me, for I need to ask them about a matter.'" When they came, he said to them, "Whose is this place?" They said to him, "Darius, king of Persia," He said to them, "And this great and mighty mountain, what do you call it?" They said to him, "This is a boundary that God placed between us and the nations on its other side, and it extends up to inner India where the people on the other side are sorcerers. When they wanted to march out to war, they would bring a pregnant woman near fire until her fetus came out and, on him they would practice sorcery: Wetting their weapons [in his blood], each one of them would look like two hundred cavalrymen, their shouts sounding like [those] of jackals." Alexander said to them, "Did they march out during your own time?" They said to him, "In this mountain there is an opening of about ten cubits, and they come out from it from time to time. And these Persian fortresses that you see, they destroyed them." He said to them, "What are the names of their kings?" They replied to him, "Gog, Magog, Gig, Tamerat, and Tamartan. Beyond them is Bet Amazerat, beyond it is Bet Kalbabarnosh, beyond the latter is Bet Mehanai, and beyond it are desolation, empty steppe, great mountains, dragons, and beasts. And beyond these is God's paradise, which seems to be situated far away, on a high place between earth and heaven, and day and night light is seen there from afar." He said to them, "And these rivers—Euphrates, Tigris, Pishon and Gihon—how does the Scripture say that they spring from there?" They said to him, "The Lord caused the rivers to spring up from paradise, and, lest people sail on them and enter paradise, God ordered these rivers to go down, running inside the earth many parasangs over. When people go to check, they realize that the rivers seen outside in the territories are far from each other." When Alexander heard many things from them, he dismissed them to go. And he ordered all the skilled people whom he brought from Egypt to make a great gate of iron for the opening that was in the mountain. And they blocked it with iron strengthened by bars.

The old men who left Alexander went to Darius to tell him [about the matter], and he ordered to gather eighty-two kings and their armies to attack him. As Ale[xan]der and all his army were sleeping and resting [during no]on time, the S[on] of God drew near him and awoke him, saying, "Why are you sleeping?" As for him, he grew very fearful, and replied to him, "What do you wish, my Lord." He said to him, "I am the Lord for whom you made a vow and you marched out under my name! Kings and their armies are now coming upon you now, but when they arrive, call upon me and I will come to your help." He got up and awoke his nobles, saying, "The Lord appeared to me at this moment and said to me, 'Behold, kings with their armies are coming upon you but call me and I will come to your help, for I am the Lord for whom you made a vow and you marched out under my name!' But let us go up to the summit of this mountain and see!" Some people among them went up and saw the whole land concealed by armies, and went down hurriedly, saying, "What shall we do? The whole land is concealed by armies that are coming upon us." Alexander rose up and ordered all his troops to offer incense to the Lord who appeared to him and to call upon him. And Alexander said, "Let the Lord come and find the whole camp whose smell is sweet!" And Alexander placed the crown and the royal apparel on the ground and said, "God: yours is the kingship and yours is the victory. Come to our aid!" And while they were standing, armies surrounded them from all sides. Now Alexander and his troops cried out, "To the Lord belong the battle and the victory!" and they then shouted and said, "Lord come to our aid!" And Alexander said, "Lord who appeared to me and said to me, 'Call me and I will come to your aid' come to our aid at this hour!" Then they saw the Lord coming in a chariot of cherubim and crowds of angels on his right and his left. And a great battle took place and the Lord came near Alexander and said to him, "Do not be afraid! Behold, I am with you." The voice of the Lord went away while thundering with the armies between the mountains. The troops of Alexander killed sixty-two kings and their armies, and the king of Persia who gathered them they seized alive. Alexander sought to kill him but he said to him, "What do you gain in killing me? Take away for yourself gold, silver, and all that is in my kingdom, and I subject Persia to you for fifteen years!" Alexander rose up, and marching down, he captured the Persian land, and descended toward India. Thereafter, Alexander, Darius, and Shapur agreed among themselves that each of them would establish six thousand guards at the gate that Alexander had made facing the land of Gog, and after fifteen years Assyria would be independent. And he returned, going to his land in great victory. He went to pray in Jerusalem to fulfill his vows, thanking the Lord on whose name he marched out and who gave him all this victory. He then left that place and went to reside in Alexandria to reign.

MICHAEL THE GREAT, *CHRONICLE*

Ca. 1190. West Syrian.

Michael the Great (d. 1199) is one of the principle historians and patriarchs of the West Syrian Church. His *Chronicle* is an impressive and sweeping history of the world from its creation until 1195. Michael lived at the intersections of various Muslim and Christian communities, including during his early life in Armenian territory, his visits as patriarch to the Latin Crusader States, and the conquest of his hometown by the Seljuk Turks in the 1170s. This brief excerpt from Michael's magisterial work demonstrates his pride in his Syriac heritage when he argues that his language, which he refers to as Aramaic, is the original human language. The text's special focus on the language and traditions of Edessa is characteristic of West Syrian Christianity. For an additional excerpt of Michael the Great's *Chronicle*, see chapter 11.

> At the start of the life of Reu, people began to build Babel and a tower in the land of Shinar. They were saying, "Let us build for ourselves a city and a tower. Let us make a name for ourselves, lest we be scattered and each goes to his own portion [of land]." The mighty Nimrud, son of Kush, fed the builders with his hunting. The building [project] took forty years. Disregarding the law, neglecting the commandment, and not keeping to the boundaries of the righteous Noah, they divided the land. And, so that they might find a way to save themselves from God's wrath at their transgressing the commandment, there was an agreement among them [to build the tower]. Scripture says that because of this, "The Lord descended and divided their speech and the one language was divided into seventy-two languages." This is why the land of Shinar was called Babel—because the confusion [of languages] occurred there. But that great elder Heber did not agree with their wish to divide [the land]. Rather, he said "Noah's commandment should be kept. Let us not incur a curse [from God]." Because he did not agree with them concerning the building of that tower, the first ancestral language was preserved by him. He named the land Babel. Our language of Aramaic fittingly interprets the name "Babel" as indicating confusion. The holy Mar Ephrem, Basil the Great, and other ancient ones among the wise, agree with this opinion. But, following certain ancient authors, Jacob, named "of Edessa," and John, bishop of Litharb, say, "The first language preserved by Heber is Hebrew, thus they are called Hebrews. Certain others say because Abraham crossed ['bar] the Euphrates River and entered the promised land, crossed ['bar] through troops in combat, and crossed ['bar] from the pagan customs of his ancestors to faith in God the creator of all—for all these reasons they say he was called a Hebrew ['barya]. But we say that all of this is true. The first language was Aramaic and, from it, Hebrew was born.

2

POETRY

Syriac authors used verse for every type of writing. Even in genres where prose was the dominant mode, such as with historiography, there are examples in verse. Above all, poetry was the distinctive medium of choice for theological exposition and exegesis. This mode of expression sets Syriac apart from other Christian languages in that Syriac writers adapted their theology to be expressed in verse form. So, too, poetic imagination affected how this theology was communicated and the settings in which it was received.

Most Syriac poems, whether metrical sermons or lyric poems, are devotional and hymnic in character: they include a refrain and are organized according to short stanzas or couplets. The hymns are simply poems, but these are poems that were often performed before audiences in church or monastic settings. Syriac poems were delivered by the poet, sometimes accompanied by choirs of women or men, and the congregation participated as well. Poetry in Syriac was a communal endeavor and was written with the hearts and voices of a congregation in mind.

Nevertheless, Syriac poetry is linguistically complex and adheres to specific melodies, patterns, and genres. The artistry of these hymns remains one of the most significant gifts from Syriac to the world of Christian literature. The aural melodies are lost to us, but the patterns of expression are clear and were shared between authors over centuries. The basic unit of organization is the syllable. Syriac verse was not quantitative, that is, they were not based the long/short quantity of vowels as in classical Greek and Latin. Instead, the number of syllables per line determines the distinctive style, tone, and effect of different genres.

The *memra* is a verse homily that is written in couplets with a standard number of syllables per line: for example, Ephrem used seven and Jacob of Serug used twelve. The *memra* was probably recited rather than sung. The *madrasha* is a lyric or stanzaic hymn that appears in numerous meters. The patterns could be simple or complex: Ephrem used around fifty different syllabic meters (*qale*) for his *madrashe*. The *qala* signified the melody, and the *madrasha* was usually sung. But the *qala* also denotes the meter and is associated with specific poems. A sub-category of the *madrasha* is the *sogita*. The most common *sogita* is the dialogue poem, in which two speakers debate, conjuring a dramatic scene. The Syriac dialogue poem is a legacy of dispute literature in the Ancient Near East. Finally, the *'onita* is a hymn that developed in later Syriac in concert with the Eucharistic liturgy, particularly in the East Syrian Church. A stanza in the *'onita* consists of four rhymed seven-syllable lines. Rhyme is largely absent in earlier poetry but comes into Syriac under the influence of Arabic verse from the ninth century on. Across these different genres word-play devices are common, such as the acrostic (beginning each verse with a different letter, to spell a word or a name, or proceeding through the alphabet). Many Syriac poems, even of very high quality, are anonymous.

The selections in this chapter represent Syriac poetry from its earliest appearance up to the fourteenth century. They have been chosen to appeal to a range of readers and students, highlighting preeminent authors and styles of Syriac verse over the centuries. The *Odes of Solomon* and the *Hymn of the Pearl*, which do not correspond to the standard genres, are examples of early Syriac poetry and represent some of the earliest Christian hymns anywhere. The *Hymn of the Pearl* initiates a motif, the pearl, that runs throughout Syriac literature. Ephrem's influential *madrasha* on the pearl imbues the image with Christian symbolism. Ephrem's rich theological expression appears here in his *madrasha* on the paradoxes of the incarnation. As a comparison, a Christological *memra* by Narsai on Epiphany shows how verse was used for dogmatic argumentation. Only six poems survive from Cyrillona, another early poet, who includes topical events such as the advances of the Huns. Jacob of Serug's *memra On the Sinful Woman* shows how the poet elaborates on scripture to create profound and meditative metrical sermons. Two anonymous *sogiyata* dialogue poems, on *Mary and the Gardener* and the *Cherub and the Thief* re-enact biblical motifs in vivid ways. The thirteenth-century Giwargis Warda offers a more personal and psychological *'onita* of repentance in an alphabetical acrostic poem. Khamis bar Qardaḥe is a preeminent example of later Syriac poets and one of the few who offered "secular" poems in the vein of medieval Arabic wine poetry (*khamriyya*). The important fourteenth-century catalogue of Syriac authors by 'Abdisho' bar Brika is a long *memra* on Syriac literary history that demonstrates how verse could be used for other literary modes. For additional examples of Syriac poetry, see chapters 1, 3, 7, 8, 9, and 10.

Further Reading   There are many studies to recommend on Ephrem. Sebastian P. Brock, *The Luminous Eye: The Spiritual World Vision of Saint Ephrem* (Kalamazoo, MI: Cistercian Publications, 1992) provides the most comprehensive overview of both the poetry and the recurrent motifs. For a modern literary analysis, see Jeffrey Wickes, *Bible and Poetry in Late Antique Mesopotamia: Ephrem's Hymns on Faith* (Berkeley: University of California Press, 2019). For a seminal and authoritative study of Ephrem's language and ideas, see Robert Murray, *Symbols of Church and Kingdom: A Study in Early Syriac Tradition*, rev. ed. (2004; repr., London: Bloomsbury T&T Clark, 2006). For poetry prior to Ephrem, see the survey in Scott Johnson, "Syriac Hymnography before Ephrem," in *Hymns, Homilies, and Hermeneutics in Byzantium*, ed. Sarah Gador-Whyte and Andrew Mellas (Leiden: Brill, 2021), 193–215. For later Syriac poetry, from the sixth century up to the present day, see Sebastian P. Brock, "Later Syriac Poetry," in *The Syriac World*, ed. Daniel King (New York: Routledge, 2018), 327–38.

ODES OF SOLOMON 24, 19

Early second to early third century.

The *Odes of Solomon* contain some of the most beautiful and enigmatic poems in the Syriac language. Possibly originally written in Greek, they survive for the most part through two Syriac manuscripts. Only one ode survives in Greek (Ode 11), known from a third-century papyrus. The odes, called *zmirata* ("psalms" or "songs"), may date from as early as the first quarter of the second century. They show significant Jewish influence, but many are clearly Christian. Specific scenes from Jesus's life are mentioned or alluded to: the virgin birth; the crucifixion; the walking on water; as well as the themes of baptism and eucharist. But here the savior is called Lord, messiah, and Son—never Jesus. The *Odes of Solomon* were used in some "gnosticizing" Coptic contexts but cannot be called Gnostic in any dogmatic sense. The two poems presented here are among the most famous. Ode 24 is a meditation on the descent of the dove, a probable allusion to Jesus's baptism. Ode 19 contains a very striking reference to the breasts of the Father as the inseminating agent for the virgin conception of the Son.

ODE 24

> The dove flew onto the head of our Lord messiah,
>   Because he was her head.
> And she cooed over him,
>   And her voice was heard.
> And the inhabitants were afraid,
>   And the sojourners were disturbed.
> The birds gave up their wing [beat],
>   And all creeping things died in their hole.
> And the primal depths were opened and covered.
>   And they sought the Lord like those who are about to give birth,
> But he was not given to them for food,

Because he was not their own.
But the primal depths were submerged in the submersion of the Lord
   And perished in that thought in which they had been from before.
For they were destructive from the beginning,
   And the goal of their destruction was life.
And all that was lacking was destroyed by them,
   Because they could not give the [pass]word, that they might abide.
And the Lord destroyed the thoughts
   Of all those with whom the truth was not.
For they lacked wisdom,
   Those who were arrogant in their hearts.
And they were rejected,
   Because the truth was not with them.
For the Lord showed his way
   And spread out his grace.
And those who understood it
   Understand his holiness.
Hallelujah.

ODE 19

A cup of milk was offered to me,
   And I drank it in the sweetness of the Lord's kindness.
The Son is the cup,
   And he who was milked, the Father,
And [the one] who milked him, the Spirit of holiness.
   Because his breasts were full
And it was not desirable that his milk should be poured out uselessly,
   The Spirit of holiness opened [the Father's] bosom
And mixed the milk of the two breasts of the Father.
   And she gave the mixture to the world, while they did not know,
And those who receive [it] are in the fullness of the right [hand].
   The womb of the virgin caught [it],
And she conceived and gave birth.
   And the virgin became a mother in great compassion
And she was in labor and bore a son.
   And she felt no pains,
Because it was not useless.
   And she did not require a midwife,
Because [God] kept her alive like a man.
   She brought forth by the will [of God]
And brought forth by [his] manifestation
   And acquired by [his] great power
And loved by [his] salvation

    And guarded by [his] kindness
And made known by [his] greatness.
    Hallelujah.

HYMN OF THE PEARL

Early third century.

The *Acts of Thomas*, one of the earliest literary prose texts in Syriac, contains two famous poems that are certainly earlier than the prose narrative. One of these, the *Hymn of the Pearl*, appears in two surviving manuscripts of the *Acts of Thomas*. In these manuscripts, it is sung by Thomas while he is in prison in India. In the poem, which is identified in the text as a *madrasha*, the author leaves his father's house to recover a pearl in Egypt that is guarded by a serpent. While in Egypt he eats Egyptian food and falls asleep. The father sends a letter, which awakens the son and, charming the serpent, the son takes the pearl home. He then receives the robe promised him on return. The *Hymn of the Pearl* is probably the single most famous poem in Syriac literature. It has been read in various ways, depending on how one identifies the potentially allegorical figures of the son, the father and mother, the pearl, the serpent, and the robe, as well as on how they should be interpreted as an ensemble. In one standard reading, the son is the soul, which is preexistent. It descends to the earth with a purpose, is corrupted, reawakens, gains the pearl, and then gets robed in heaven on its return. The author of the *Acts of Thomas*, a very pious Christian text, had no qualms about incorporating this very allusive, perhaps even Gnostic, poem into his text, even though the subject of the *Acts*—Thomas's mission to India—is very different in theme. As with the *Odes of Solomon*, how modern scholars interpret the *Hymn of the Pearl* often depends on how early they feel the poem was originally composed.

> And while he was praying, all those who were in the prison saw that he was praying and begged of him to pray for them too. And when he had prayed and sat down, Judas [Thomas] began to chant this hymn.
>
> When I was a little child
> And dwelling in my kingdom, in my father's house,
> And was content with the wealth and the luxuries
> Of my nourishers,
> From the East, our home,
> My parents equipped me [and] sent me forth;
> And of the wealth of our treasury
> They took abundantly [and] tied up for me a load
> Large and [yet] light,
> Which I myself could carry—
> Gold of Bet 'Ellaye

And silver of Gazak the Great,
And rubies of India,
And agates from Bet Kashan;
And they furnished me with adamant,
Which can crush iron.
And they took off from me the glittering robe,
Which in their affection they had made for me,
And the purple toga, which was measured [and] woven to my stature.
And they made a compact with me,
And wrote it in my heart, that it might not be forgotten:
"If you go down unto Egypt,
And bring the one pearl,
Which is in the midst of the sea
Around the loud-breathing serpent,
You shall put on your glittering robe
And your toga, with [which] you are contented,
And with your brother, who is next to us in authority,
You shall be heir in our kingdom."

I quit the East [and] went down,
There being with me two guardians.
For the way was dangerous and difficult,
And I was very young to travel it.
I passed through the borders of Maishan,
The meeting-place of the merchants of the East,
And I reached the land of Babel,
And I entered the walls of Sarbug.
I went down into Egypt,
And my companions parted from me.
I went straight to the serpent,
I dwelt around his abode,
[Waiting] till he should slumber and sleep,
And I could take my pearl from him.
And when I was single and was alone
[And] became strange to my family,
One of my race, a free-born man,
An Easterner, I saw there,
A youth fair and lovable,
The son of oil sellers;
And he came and attached himself to me,
And I made him my intimate friend,
An associate with whom I shared my merchandise.
I warned him against the Egyptians,
And against consorting with the unclean,

And dressed in their dress,
That they might not hold me in abhorrence,
Because I had come abroad in order to take the pearl,
And arouse the serpent against me.
But in some way or another
They found out that I was not their countryman,
And they dealt with me treacherously,
And gave me their food to eat.
I forgot that I was a son of kings,
And I served their king;
And I forgot the pearl,
For which my parents had sent me,
And because of the burden of their oppressions
I lay in a deep sleep.

But all these things that befell me
My parents perceived, and were grieved for me;
And a proclamation was made in our kingdom,
That everyone should come to our gate,
Kings and princes of Parthia,
And all the nobles of the East.
And they wove a plan on my behalf,
That I might not be left in Egypt;
And they wrote to me a letter,
And every noble signed his name to it:
"From your father, the king of kings,
And your mother, the mistress of the East,
And from your brother, our second [in authority],
To you, our son, who is in Egypt, greeting!
Up and arise from your sleep,
And listen to the words of our letter!
Call to mind that you are a son of kings!
See the slavery, whom you serve!
Remember the pearl
For which you were sent to Egypt!
Think of your robe,
And remember your splendid toga,
Which you shall wear and [with which] you shall be adorned,
When your name has been read out in the list of the valiant,
And with your brother, our viceroy,
You shall be in our kingdom!"

My letter is a letter,
Which the king sealed with his own right hand,
[To keep it] from the wicked ones, the children of Babel,

And from the savage demons of Sarbug.
It flew in the likeness of an eagle,
The king of all birds;
It flew and alighted beside me,
And became all speech.
At its voice and the sound of its rustling,
I started and arose from my sleep.
I took it up and kissed it,
And I began [and] read it;
And according to what was traced on my heart
Were the words of my letter written.
I remembered that I was a son of royal parents,
And my noble birth asserted its nature.
I remembered the pearl,
For which I had been sent to Egypt,
And I began to charm him,
The terrible loud-breathing serpent.
I hushed him to sleep and lulled him into slumber,
For my father's name I named over him,
And the name of our second [in power],
And of my mother, the queen of the East;
And I snatched away the pearl,
And turned to go back to my father's house.
And their filthy and unclean dress I stripped off,
And left it in their country;
And took my way straight to come
To the light of our home in the East.
And my letter, my awakener,
I found before me on the road;
And as with his voice it had awakened me,
[So], too, with its light it was leading me.
It, which dwelt in the palace,
Gave light before me with its form,
And with its voice and with its guidance
It also encouraged me to speed,
And with its love it drew me on.
I went forth [and] passed by Sarbug,
I left Babel on my left hand;
And I came to the great Maishan,
To the haven of the merchants,
Which sits on the shore of the sea,
And my bright robe, which I had stripped off,
And the toga that was wrapped with it,
From Ramta and Reken

My parents had sent thither,
By the hand of their treasurers,
Who in their truth could be trusted therewith.

And because I did not remember its fashion,
For in my childhood I had left it in my father's house,
On a sudden, when I received it,
The garment seemed to me to become like a mirror of myself.
I saw it all in all,
And I, too, received all in it,
For we were two in distinction,
And yet again one in one likeness.
And the treasurers too,
Who brought it to me, I saw in like manner
To be two [and yet] one likeness,
For one sign of the king was written on them [both],
Of the hands of him who restored to me through them
My trust and my wealth,
My decorated robe, which
Was adorned with glorious colors,
With gold and beryls,
And rubies and agates,
And sardonyxes, varied in color.
And was skillfully worked in its home on high,
And with diamond clasps were all its seams fastened;
And the image of the king of kings
Was embroidered and depicted in full all over it,
And like the stone of the sapphire too
Its hues were varied.

And I saw also that all over it
The instincts of knowledge were working,
And I saw, too, that it was preparing to speak.
I heard the sound of its tones
Which it uttered with its [___]:
"I am the active in deeds,
Whom they reared for him before my father;
And I perceived myself,
That my stature grew according to his labors."
And in its kingly movements
It poured itself entirely over me.
And on the hands of its givers
It hastened that I might take it.
And love urged me to run
To meet it and receive it;

And I stretched forth and took it.
With the beauty of its colors I adorned myself,
And I wrapped myself wholly in my toga
Of brilliant hues.
I clothed myself with it, and went up to the gate
Of salutation and prostration;
I bowed my head and worshipped the majesty
Of my father who sent me—
For I had done his commandments,
And he too had done what he promised—
And at the gate of his [___],
I mingled with his princes,
For he rejoiced in me and received me,
And I was with him in his kingdom,
And with the voice of [___] all his servants praise him.
And he promised that to the gate too
Of the king of kings with him I should go,
And with my offering and my pearl
With him should present myself to our king.

The hymn of Judas Thomas, the apostle, which he spoke in the prison, is ended.

EPHREM, *HYMNS ON FAITH* 81

Mid to late fourth century.

Ephrem the Syrian (d. 373), the most famous poet in the Syriac language, invoked the image of the pearl across a number of poems. At the end of his *Hymns on Faith*, Ephrem offers a famous cycle of five poems meditating on pearls. Exegetically, this motif depends on a parable of Jesus in Matthew 13:45–46, where a merchant, on discovering "a pearl of great price," sells all his possessions to buy the pearl for himself. Jesus applies this parable as an image of the kingdom of heaven. Ephrem, known for combining biblical metaphors with those derived from nature, finds in the pearl a number of symbols of Christian theology and biblical history. He sees the pearl as an image of the virgin birth, the church, the ark, and the manna in the desert. Ephrem extends the metaphor to the practice of pearl diving, a familiar image in ancient Mesopotamia but, among Christians, unique to Syriac theology. In Syriac, one word for "to baptize" is the same as "to dive" (*'mad*), a word that Ephrem uses elsewhere to play on the concepts. Here he emphasizes the depth of the sea as a metaphor for the depth of God's power. The admonition against "investigation" at the end is a commonplace in Ephrem: he considers the Arian questioning of the Son's created relationship to the Father in Trinitarian thought an offense against the received Nicene faith, and at odds with prayerful worship. For additional excerpts from Ephrem, see chapters 1, 3, 7, and 10.

One day, I took up
A pearl, my brothers. I saw in it symbols,
Things of the kingdom, images and types
Of that greatness. It became a fountain
And I drank from it symbols of the Son.

Refrain: Blessed is the one who compares the high kingdom to a pearl!

I placed it, my brothers, in the palm of my hand
To observe it. I began to look at it:
On one side, it had a face.
On every side, [it offered] examination of the Son,
Who is incomprehensible, because he is entirely light.

In its beauty, I saw the pure one,
Who is not moved. In its purity [I saw]
A great mystery: the body of our Lord,
Unsullied, without division.
I saw the truth that is undivided.

It was Mary that I saw there—
Her pure conception. It became the church,
And the Son was inside it. [It took on] the likeness of a cloud,
That one which carried him, and a heavenly mystery,
Which shone forth his fair splendor.

I saw in it his signs—of his triumphs
And of his crownings. I saw in it his aids,
Along with his profits. [I saw the signs of] his secrets
And his revelations. It became larger to me
Than an ark, so that I roamed around inside it.

I saw in it rooms without shadows,
Because it is born from light. [I saw] rational types
Without tongues; the speech of mysteries
Without lips. A silent lyre,
Voicelessly gave forth song.

[A trumpet] sounded, and thunder whispered:
"Do not be rash! Abandon hidden things,
Take up what is revealed!" I saw in a clear sky
Some rain—a fountain, from which my ears,
As from a cloud, were filled with interpretations.

Like that manna, which alone
Filled the people in place of meals,
It filled me with its tastes—
The pearl—in place of books
And their readings and interpretations.

But if I should ask whether there are
Other mysteries, it has no mouth
With which I could hear it, nor ears
That it might hear me. Nor [does it have] senses,
That [pearl] from which I have acquired new senses.

She responded and said to me—the child of the sea—
"I am infinite. As for that sea
From which I ascended, it is a great treasury
Of the symbols that are in my bosom. Inquire into the sea,
But do not examine the Lord of the sea.

"I saw divers descending after me.
[Terrified] of what was in the sea,
They returned to dry land. They could not wait
Even a brief moment: 'What is it we see?
Let us examine the depth of divinity!'

"The waves of the Son fill benefits
With harmful things. Do you not see
The sea's waves? If a ship resists,
[The waves] will break [it.] But if it [yields],
And does not resist, it is preserved.

"In the sea all the Egyptians were drowned,
Even without investigating. And without examination
The Hebrews were swallowed up on dry land.
How will you be saved? The Sodomites
Were licked with fire, so how will you be found innocent?

"[Seeing] these atrocities, the fish in the sea
Shake beside us. Do you then have
A heart of stone, that you read these things,
And [yet] are unmindful of them? Great fear!
Even righteousness was very silent.

"Examination is mingled with praise:
Which will win? Glory and
Investigation rise up from the tongue.
Which shall he heed? Examination and prayer
From one mouth, which shall he hear?

"For three days, Jonah was
Our neighbor in the sea. Creatures inside the sea
Shook, saying, 'Who is it that flees
From God?' Jonah fled
And [still] you dare to investigate [God]?"

EPHREM, *HYMNS ON THE RESURRECTION* 1

Mid to late fourth century.

This poem on the incarnation comes from Ephrem's *Hymns on the Resurrection*. As with Ephrem's hymn on the pearl, this poem blends biblical and natural metaphors. Each stanza is split thematically into two parts: first a wonder of the incarnation, then a wonder of the resurrection resulting from the incarnation. Christ is the rain that fell on the "thirsty earth," interpreted as Mary's womb, cultivating a seed of wheat; and then the seed springs up, after Christ's descent into hell, as a sheaf that provides the bread of life (also the "offering" of the Eucharist). Elsewhere, a similar metaphor describes the cross as a tree that bore fruit, that is Christ himself, who descended from the tree and ascended as the "first fruit" of the resurrection. The opening stanzas include an acrostic—in Syriac, each line begins with a letter of Ephrem's name. Each stanza throughout concludes with its own doxological refrain, such as "Blessed is his humiliation!" For additional excerpts from Ephrem, see chapters 1, 3, 7, and 10.

> The lamb has come for us from the house of David,
> The priest and pontiff from Abraham;
> He became for us both lamb and pontiff,
> Giving his body for sacrifice, his blood for sprinkling.
> Blessed is his perfecting!
> Refrain: Blessed is your rising up!

> The shepherd of all flew down
> In search of Adam, the sheep that had strayed;
> On his shoulders he carried him, taking him up:
> He was an offering for the Lord of the flock.
> Refrain: Blessed is his descent!

> He sprinkled dew and life-giving rain
> On Mary, the thirsty earth.
> Like a seed of wheat he fell again to Sheol
> To spring up as a sheaf, as the new bread.
> Refrain: Blessed is his offering!

> Knowledge of him chased error away
> From humanity that had become lost;
> The evil one was led astray by him and was confounded.
> [Knowledge of him] poured out all kinds of wisdom upon the peoples.
> Refrain: Blessed is his fountain!

> From on high did power descend to us,
> From within a womb did hope shine out for us,
> From the grave has salvation appeared for us,
> And on the right hand the king for us is seated.

Refrain: Blessed is his glory!

From on high he flowed like a river,
From Mary he [stemmed] as from a root,
From the cross he descended as fruit,
As the first fruit he ascended to heaven.
Refrain: Blessed is his will!

The Word came forth from the Father's womb,
He put on the body in another womb;
From one womb to another did he proceed,
And chaste wombs are filled with him.
Refrain: Blessed is he who has resided in us!

From on high he came down as Lord,
From within the womb he came forth as a servant;
Death knelt before him in Sheol,
And life worshipped him at his resurrection.
Refrain: Blessed is his victory!

Mary carried him as a child,
The priest [Simeon] carried him as an offering,
The cross carried him as one slain,
Heaven carried him as God.
Refrain: Praise to his Father!

From every side he stretched out and gave
Healing and promises:
Children ran to his healings,
The discerning ran to his promises.
Refrain: Blessed is his revelation!

From the fish's mouth he gave a coin
Whose imprint was temporal, whose currency passing;
From his own mouth he gave a new imprint,
Giving us the new covenant.
Refrain: Blessed is its giver!

From God is his divinity,
From mortals his humanity,
From Melkizedek his priesthood,
From David's line his kingship.
Refrain: Blessed is his combining them!

He was one of the guests at the wedding feast,
He was one of the fasters in the temptation,
He was one of the watchful in the agony,
He was a teacher in the temple.
Refrain: Blessed is his instruction!

He did not shrink from the unclean,
He did not turn away from sinners;
On the sincere he greatly delighted,
For the simple he greatly longed.
Refrain: Blessed is his teaching!

He did not hold back his footsteps from the sick
Or his words from the simple;
He extended his descent to the lowly,
And his ascension to the highest.
Refrain: Blessed is his sender!

His birth gives us purification,
His baptism gives us forgiveness,
His death is life to us,
His ascension is our exaltation.
Refrain: How we should thank him!

By the greedy he was considered a glutton,
But by those who know, the provider of all;
By drunkards he was considered a drinker,
But by the discerning, the one who gives everyone to drink.
Refrain: Blessed is his foresight!

To Caiaphas his conception was a scandal,
But to Gabriel his birth was glorious;
To the unbeliever his ascension is a source of difficulty,
But to his disciples his exaltation is a source of wonder.
Refrain: Blessed is his discernment!

With his begetter his birth is certain,
But to the investigator it is fraught with difficulty;
To supernal beings its truth is crystal clear,
But to those below, a subject of enquiry and hesitation
Refrain: Yet [a subject] that cannot be investigated!

By the evil one he was tempted,
By the [Jewish] people he was questioned,
By Herod he was interrogated:
He spurned him with silence when he wished to probe him.
Refrain: Blessed is his begetter!

They thought he was one of those baptized in the river [Jordan],
They accounted him among those that sleep while at sea,
They hung him like a slain man on the cross,
They laid him like a corpse in the grave.
Refrain: Blessed is his humiliation!

Who have we, Lord, like you—
The great one who became small, the wakeful who slept,

The pure one who was baptized, the living one who died,
The king who bore disgrace to ensure honor for all!
Refrain: Blessed is your honor!

CYRILLONA, *ON THE HUNS*

Late fourth century.

Only six poems survive from the poet Cyrillona, a younger contemporary of Ephrem. Nothing is known of his life and work beyond these poems. One of them, presented here, refers to the invasion by the Huns of northern Mesopotamia around 396. His other poems deal with various New Testament topics, such as foot washing, Holy Thursday, and the crucifixion. In this poem Cyrillona offers a vivid prayer of desperation to God during the incursions of the Huns. His pleas recall the Psalms in their personal appeal to God's protection and justice in the face of the decimation of his people.

And from the beginning
   To this day,
See how I am full
   Of every grief,
Of quotidian terrors,
   Of ill tidings every day,
Of torments every hour,
   Of all strife.
Your will has scourged
   The East with captivity,
And the towns that were laid waste
   Are uninhabited.
The West is stricken,
   And see how its cities
Are held by a people
   Who do not know you.
The merchants have died
   And oblations have been in vain.
The women are widowed
   And offerings have ceased.
The North is in distress
   And full of wars,
And if you turn away, O Lord,
   Again they shall lay waste to me.
If the Huns
   Conquer me, O Lord,
Then why take refuge

With the martyrs?
If their swords
   Lay waste to my offspring,
Then why hold fast
   To your great cross?
If you hand my cities
   Over to them,
Where is the glory
   Of your holy church?
Not yet a year
   Has passed
Since they came out to lay waste to me
   And take captive my children,
And see now,
   A second time
They have assaulted our country
   To vanquish it.
O Lord, do not deliver
   The lambs to leopards
And the sheep
   To filthy wolves!
May the hand of the wicked
   Not rule
Over a kingdom
   That honors you!
May kings who fear
   Your kingdom
Not be trodden down
   By infidels—
May those rather be trodden
   Under the feet
Of the kings who tread
   The gates of your church!
Stay your chastisement,
   For such is our communion with you
That if I am stricken,
   You have wounded yourself.
Your body is in me—
   May it not be dishonored.
Your mysteries are in me—
   May they not be mocked.
Grace is also
   Proper in the economy of things—
How much should it set a limit

    To your chastisement!
The South, which is full
    Of all your triumphs—
Your conception, your birth,
    And your crucifixion—
The fragrance of your footsteps
    Spreads from it,
Because you walked upon it
    And blessed it.

NARSAI, *ON EPIPHANY*

Mid to late fifth century. East Syrian.

Narsai (d. ca. 500) was one of the most prolific poets in early Syriac literature and was the first major East Syrian hymnographer. He was born in the Persian Empire but studied in Roman Edessa, where he was influenced by the exegesis of Theodore of Mopsuestia and where he eventually became head of the School of Edessa. Expelled after twenty years as director, he made his way to Nisibis where he founded a new school, which was to become the principal training ground for East Syrian scholars and monks. The statutes of the school (see chapter 5) are preserved under his name. Through his 81 surviving *memre* on various subjects, including biblical interpretation and individual theological and ethical topics, he propounded the East Syrian Church's dyophysite (two-nature) theology, emphasizing the unmixed relationship of Christ's humanity and divinity in the incarnation. In the poem presented here, Narsai dwells on the dual quality of Adam's humanity (body and soul), his corruption in the fall, and the second Adam's (i.e., Christ's) fully human nature, which was coupled with a heavenly lineage and authority. For additional excerpts from Narsai, see chapters 3 and 7.

    A rational image the creator willed to fashion for Adam;
        And he mixed a spirit with the colors of his lowly clay.
    Refrain: Blessed be the "spring" [i.e., Christ] that flowed into the Jordan
        And from which Adam drank and his thirst was quenched.
    He fashioned, first of all, an earthen vessel from dust
        And anointed it with a spirit; and the whole became a living soul.
    He depicted limbs on the colored visible clay
        And breathed an invisible spirit into [this] visible being.
    O painter, who has concealed his artistic power
        And set the beauty of his fair image within a tablet [of clay]!
    According to mortal art, exterior [qualities] charm
        And show viewers the beauty of their fashioning.
    According to divine art, interior [qualities] charm;

And the exterior is but a covering for the interior.
A twofold vessel the fashioner of the universe made for our nature:
  A visible body and a hidden soul—one person.
He made the exterior from dust that is lowly to look upon
  And fashioned the interior from the secret [recesses] of his majestic power.
He placed the precious [part], that contains life, in the mortal and lowly [clay],
  In order to give life to mortality by the power of its vitality.
The interior [part], containing intelligence, vibrated on the strings of [the human] body;
  And the clay became pleasing because of the melodious sound of the living spirit.
The living one chanted in the temple of clay a hymn of praise;
  And there assembled and came rational and dumb beings at the sound of its
    melodies.
The mortal one stood like a statue within a palace;
  And over his features marveled spiritual and corporeal [beings].
For a short time, there remained the beauty of the temporal image;
  But there arose a vile iniquity over its features [i.e., the fall].
The beautiful colors of his soul faded because of [his] desire for fruit:
  And he acquired the color of mortality by [his] eating of it.
Sin effaced the name of life [belonging to] the royal image
  And inscribed on his name corruption, and death upon his limbs.
[The image] became tarnished and wasted away for a long time in [his] mortal condition;
  And death trampled him and corrupted the beauty of his rational being.
His ill-wisher mocked and also laughed at his humiliation;
  And he lost hope that he would be renewed from his corruption.
The king who saw that the evil ones mocked the image of his image
  Took pity upon his image lest it be [further] outraged by the insolent.
The image proclaims the royal authority by his visible [aspect]
  And, by his features, shows the beauty of the one who constituted him.
In Adam's image was shown the authority of his Lord;
  And, in his features, was signified the power of his hiddenness [i.e., divine nature].
And because Adam fell and death corrupted the image [function] of his features,
  The king sent "pity" and "mercy" to raise him up.
Two messengers of peace he sent to honor his image,
  And he proclaimed on earth a message of renewal for mortality.
In his fashioning, he revealed to creatures the power of his hidden [divine nature],
  [While], in his renewal, he showed them the wealth of his love.
He exalted much more the name of his renewal than his fashioning,
  So that he might make the heavenly ones marvel over how much he loved him.
In his fashioning, [the angels] were bound [in kinship] from the beginning;
  And in his renewal, he gladdened those who were sad.
His [good] pleasure descended unto [one] whom he fashioned in fitting love;
  And he depicted on the tablet of Adam's body, a second Adam.
In the [same] order as Adam, he depicted a [second] Adam with the color of [his
    divine] will,

And renewed Adam and his offspring through [this] son of Adam.
The second Adam came forth from the womb as from the earth;
   And he is entirely like that first [Adam] whom the earth bore.
In body and soul, the second Adam is equal with the [first] Adam;
   But in authority, he is the lord of Adam and his offspring.
He is equal in nature, but greater in honor than all those who have come to be;
   And the witness is the vigilant one, who announced his conception and called him
      "Lord."
In many [ways], the second Adam is greater than Adam;
   And the rank that he attained [can] not be compared with that of creatures.
His conception is exalted because it has had no connection with human seed;
   And his birth is glorious because heavenly beings were its heralds.
He alone has received and inherited the name of lordship,
   So that heavenly and earthly beings might obey him.
His nature testifies that he is an Adamite from earthly beings;
   But the name of his authority cries out and proclaims that he is divine.
He is earthly because of [his] human body and soul,
   And he is heavenly because he has become the dwelling place for the God of the
      universe.

JACOB OF SERUG, *ON THE SINFUL WOMAN*

Late fifth to early sixth century. West Syrian.

Jacob of Serug (d. 521) is often lauded as the most accomplished Syriac poet after Ephrem. Like his older contemporary Narsai, Jacob studied at the School of Edessa and was acquainted with both dyophysite and miaphysite theology. Although he is today seen as firmly West Syrian dogmatically, he was equally claimed by the Chalcedonians in antiquity. He became bishop of Serug late in life, dying after only two years in office. His massive corpus, surviving in numerous manuscripts, contains 380 surviving *memre*, the majority of which are ruminations on biblical themes. Like Ephrem, he makes use of dialogue and the imaginative reconstruction of biblical scenes and characters. The poem presented here is a moving portrait of the sinful woman from the gospels who buys a costly perfume and anoints Jesus prior to his crucifixion. Jacob's poem, unlike some others on this theme, mixes accounts from all four gospels (Matthew 26, Mark 14, Luke 7, John 12), weaving together a masterful narrative that evokes the poignancy of the scene. Jacob was writing in a healthy tradition on this episode that included a poem by Ephrem, an anonymous *sogita*, and one by Jacob's younger contemporary, Romanos the Melode, who, though writing in Greek, was engaging the Syriac tradition. For additional excerpts from Jacob of Serug, see chapters 5, 7, and 8.

The prostitute wept because she saw that her wounds were many.
   Her soul understood, and terror seized her because of her corruption.

Jesus the sun rose and gave her light powerfully,
   And he showed her that her path was blocked by offences.
"Light had shined in the darkness" over the wretched girl,
   And she took hold of his feet and repented to him lovingly.
The radiance of the Father shined and gave light to the woman who was darkened,
   And in the beams of light she drew near to him so that she might be purified through him.
[Her] soul saw the glorious image of the great light,
   And it took from the light brightness so that it might flee from darkness.
She saw herself corrupted by odious iniquity,
   And she shed tears upon the physician so that he might heal her wounds.
She uncovered her many wounds to bring them near to him,
   And she shed tears with passion to show that it was bitter to her.
She sprinkled the physician with excellent perfume when he was healing her,
   So that everyone might see a token of her love in the fragrance of the oil.
She poured this oil on both his head and his feet,
   Because on every side he was full of mercy to the one who approaches him.
He offered himself to the one full of blemishes to approach him,
   And, just as she had sought to do, she caressed him discerningly.
She took hold of his head, and he did not forbid this defiled woman from doing so.
   She grasped his feet, and he let her do as she wished.
She sprinkled him with tears, and he did not draw back from the wretched girl.
   She kissed him with passion, and, although she was a prostitute, he did not drive her away.
Wherever she wanted she drew near and grabbed [him] shamelessly.
   And because she trembled from [her] love, she was allowed to approach.
The whole treasury of divinity was let open in front of her,
   In order that she might be a model in her proximity [to the Lord] for those who repent.
She descended there to the baptismal font so that she might be purified.
   If she had been ashamed, she would have left without forgiveness.
Oil and tears she poured out there upon the holy one,
   With the result that the entire ritual of baptism was completed.
The excellent oil and the little water were mixed.
   The great high priest made atonement for the defiled girl by performing his own part.
The wise woman knelt before the forgiver,
   In order to come to spiritual birth, which she lacked.
She bent her head over to wipe his feet with her hair.
   And just as in baptism she received holiness from the holy one.
She entered into the second womb, the place of atonement,
   So that in new birth she might become beautiful in a spiritual sense.
She grasped his feet to find a sea of mercy at the banquet.
   She was baptized in him, and he cleaned and polished her, and she arose pure.

She exposed her soul before the great flood of holiness.
    He poured forth on her waves of his mercy so that she might be atoned.
She presented herself to the living fire clothed in the body.
    It burned the thicket of her soul and [the evil] vanished completely.
Her love brought [her soul] into the crucible of mercy and smelted it there.
    Its [refined] gold showed its beauty so that it might be a cast ornament to the Lord
        of kings.
Our Lord was reclining to eat the supper of the Pharisee.
    His love moved the sinful woman so that she might draw near to him.
He was hungry to forgive because of his mercy, which is woven into him.
    And at the banquet of Simon he found what he hungered for.
They invited him as a prophet to eat supper.
    But he made use of forgiveness like God.
The weeping that he heard from the prostitute was more pleasing to him.
    Than the preparations that Simon brought to present to him.
The teardrops that he received there were more lovely to him
    Than all the drinking that came with the meal.
The sound of the groans that were being poured out was more beautiful to him
    Than what Simon had prepared for the supper.
The dinner party asks questions about the food that was set out.
    But our Lord gives heed to the prayers that are murmured.
Everyone was expecting to get the beverage that will delight him.
    But Jesus drinks in the melodies of suffering that are sung unto him.
They were engrossed in the delicacies that Simon brought in.
    [Jesus] was delighted in the repentance that he loves.
He eats with them, but his attention is directed at the prostitute,
    For he was very hungry for [her] supplication, that it might be presented to him.
At that time Simon was divided about the true one.
    He considered him ignorant of the things [she] had done.
The ignorance of Simon assailed the omniscient one,
    And he was considered to be ignorant of the hidden things.
The ignorant one was doubting the knower,
    Because if he were a prophet, he would know [so it says] who approached him.
Simon understood that the woman who had entered was sinful.
    And he did not allow the polluted woman to draw near to himself.
If [Jesus] had been close to divine revelations, [so Simon thought]
    He would have rebuked the polluted woman, and she would have fled from him.
If he had a secret eye that could see mysteries,
    He would have recognized her blemishes for she is so foul.
If he had an intellect that controlled the hidden things,
    He would not give permission to the polluted woman to grasp his feet.
It is obvious indeed that he is not at all a prophet;
    He did not restrict the sinful woman from himself since he did not recognize her.
Simon seethed with these thoughts for he did not understand.

And he was divided concerning the omniscient one, whom he himself had invited.
The good physician was eager to heal the polluted woman.
And he was rejected by the onlookers when he healed [as if] he did not know her.
If he is a prophet, he would know [so they say] who this woman is.
And [Simon] would have called him a prophet only on the strength of [recognizing the woman].
Before his doubts, the Pharisee, who had invited [Jesus], called him a prophet.
But after he had doubted, [Jesus] was considered [by Simon] to be not even a prophet.
[Simon's] integrity was divided even when he set out from the start.
Therefore, he was susceptible to the doubt that assailed him.
When [Simon] honored the lord of the prophets [by inviting him], he reckoned [Jesus] a prophet.
[Simon] was divided because the emotion of his love was wanting.
If he had acknowledged from the beginning that the Son is the Son,
[Certainly] not at the end would he have not even regarded him as a prophet.
The foundation of his faith was empty.
Therefore it was powerless against doubt when doubt struck it.
"If he is a prophet, he would have known," as one may say,
"For he is not even a prophet, though I supposed that he was a prophet."
But the knower turned to Simon calmly:
"I have something to tell you: judge rightly."
The good shepherd holds his sheep lovingly,
So that when he seeks to find one, he will not lose another.
He had visited to drive out the offense from [Simon] with various tricks,
So that [Simon] might also repent, together with her, that is, the woman he [already] found.
"I have something to tell you," he said.
And Simon answered to our savior, "Speak, Rabbi."
He caught [Simon] humbly so that he might be judged because he doubted.
But it was lovingly that he himself said to him, "Speak, Rabbi."
The wise of mind made Simon into a judge,
So that he might accuse himself because he was divided concerning the true one.
"There were two debtors to one creditor.
One owed five hundred and the other owed fifty.
And because they did not have anything to give back to him, he remitted both.
Which of these do you say should love him more?"
Simon said, "The former should love him more;
His debt is greater than that of his companion.
His love for the remitter should be as great as the remission.
It is appropriate that he love the creditor more."
Simon became a judge for his own soul concerning the hidden things.
He did not understand the hidden speech from his own mind.
He accused himself and was proud that he was appointed to make a judgment.

He was not good enough, yet he considered himself a judge.
He entered his verdict and was eager to settle [the case] uprightly.
   But because the truth surrounded him justly, he emerged guilty.
The judge was judged—he was found guilty by himself—
   While thinking that the verdict he entered referred to another.
He entered his verdict and he was found guilty and he emerged not knowing [what had happened].
   He became a judge and he accused himself, but he did not understand.
He judged rightly, but did not know he would be found guilty,
   Lest he exalt himself over the one who knows the hidden things.
Both he and the sinful woman were considered the two guilty ones.
   He entered an opinion, but by it he was exposed as guilty.
The wise of mind trapped him in his words just like David
   He was found guilty by his own words, just like the son of Jesse, when he was asked.
The prophet Nathan condemned David through his responses.
   And the Lord of Nathan similarly condemned the Pharisee.
The prophet and his Lord judged the king and the Pharisee.
   And they condemned them through their own words when they were interrogated.
The judges were judged by their actions.
   And they pronounced condemnation for themselves.
The woman full of sins grabbed by his feet the one who is full of compassion.
   But when Simon had found fault with her, he was judged wisely.
Our Lord began to explain to him how things really are;
   And he showed him that the verdict he entered is not another's [but is for Simon himself].
[Jesus] turned his face to the prostitute in great love.
   And he began to explain to Simon about her.
He sought to display her great love in the presence of those who were reclining;
   [And] how much had her love exceeded the discrimination of the one who had invited him.
"I entered your house," he had said to the Pharisee.
   "But you did not even bring water for my feet, to offer it to me.
But she drenched them discerningly with her tears.
   She in truth offered me the very hair of her head instead of a cloth.
You did not kiss me so that everyone might see the sign of your love,
   But she did not cease from kissing my feet.
You did not anoint me although it was demanded from your [absent] decorum,
   But she sprinkled me lovingly with excellent oil.
Your decorum was far below what is acceptable,
   But she showed her love to me in many ways.
You brought before me a feast of bread and wine,
   But she offered her prayer, her tears, her perfume, and her hair.
You mix the kind of thing [i.e., wine] that comes to nothing,

> But she kissed my feet all over.
> You showed your love in perishable tastes,
> > But she repeated her petition with penitent cries.
> Her love is greater than your meal and your delicacies,
> > And because she loved so much, her sins, which were many, are forgiven."

ON MARY AND THE GARDENER

Sixth to seventh century. West Syrian.

The *sogita* was a genre of poetry, modeled on a simple form of the *madrasha*, that reimagined biblical scenes or theological themes through dramatic dialogue. This genre derives, ultimately, from ancient Mesopotamian dispute texts in which the participants vie for precedence. The *sogiyata* are usually written in either two- or four-line stanzas of 7+7 syllables and often include an acrostic, with the disputants speaking in alternating verses. Surviving *sogiyata* are almost always anonymous or attributed pseudonymously to famous poets such as Ephrem and Jacob of Serug. Examples include disputes between death and Satan, Cain and Abel, and Abraham and Isaac. The short poem presented here is a dialogue between Mary and the post-resurrection Jesus. As in John 20, Mary thinks he is the gardener but recognizes him as her risen Lord when he speaks her name. The poem is typical of the genre in that it embellishes a short scriptural scene with imaginary dialogue.

> On Sunday, in the morning early
> > Along came Mary to the tomb.
> Mary: "Who will show me," she was saying,
> > "My son and my Lord for whom I am seeking"?
> As a gardener did our Lord appear
> > To her, answering and speaking to her:
> Gardener: "Disclose to me, O Lady, what it is
> > You are seeking today in this garden."
> Mary: "O Gardener, please do not refuse me,
> > Do not drive me from your garden.
> In it is a single fruit that is mine;
> > Apart from it there is nothing else that I seek."
> Gardener: "At this season you should realize
> > That no fruits are to be found in any garden;
> So how is it that you are telling me
> > That you are looking for fruit today?"
> Mary: "You should know, O gardener,
> > That the fruit for which I am searching
> Will give me life—such is my hope—
> > If I should but happen to see it."

Gardener: "What is this fruit, young lady,
   About which you speak such astonishing words?"
Mary: "I know very well and am quite certain
   That the sight of it is too exalted for the eye."
Gardener: "How you weary me with your talk,
   How you vex me with what you say."
Mary: "Where have you removed him? Disclose this to me,
   For I am going after him, after him."
Gardener: "Why, Lady, do you seek
   The living in Sheol the devourer?
He concerning whom you are asking
   Left the tomb this very night,
[While] the guards [were] wielding swords,
   Resembling raving dogs."
Mary: "Concerning his resurrection, disclose and explain to me
   So that I may be believing in him.
[For] he flew down from highest heaven
   And dwelt in a virgin womb."
Gardener: "Incline your ear, O lady, and listen,
   So that I may be the one to show you concerning him.
His resurrection gives witness to her who bore him,
   His mother gives witness to his resurrection;
Height and depth are my witnesses
   That, transcending nature, he was both born and [now] has risen."
She heard his voice and recognized him,
   For he repeated the words "Mary, Mary."
Mary: "Come to me, my Lord and my master,
   For I now forget my anguish."
Come in your compassion, O son of Mary,
   Just as you came to Mary;
And with you, at your resurrection, let your light shine forth
   On me and on him who composed this.

ON THE CHERUB AND THE THIEF

Sixth to seventh century. West Syrian.

The anonymous *sogita*, *On the Cherub and the Thief*, imagines the dialogue between the angel guarding the gate of paradise and the thief on the cross to whom Jesus said, "today you will be with me in paradise" (Luke 23:43). In ancient Christian thought the thief was the first Christian since he was the first to die after Christ's sacrifice. The poem, following early Syriac tradition, equates heaven with a renewed Garden of Eden, and the angel is the same one that God set to guard the Garden with a flaming sword in Genesis after the fall. The thief offers the sign of the cross as a key to open the gate of paradise. While told in the mode of dramatic dialogue, the poem meditates on the doctrine of the crucifixion and in that way is typical of Syriac biblical exegesis through typology and narrative. This dialogue is still performed in some Syriac liturgies today.

At the crucifixion I beheld a marvel
When the thief cried out to our Lord,
"Remember me, my Lord, on the day when you come
To that kingdom which does not pass away."

Refrain: Praise to you, Lord, for at your coming
Sinners turned back from their wickedness,
They entered and found shelter
In the Garden of Eden—which is the holy church.

He made a petition, stretched out and gave it
To the crucified king, asking for mercy,
And he who is full of mercy heard his cry
And opened the door to his request.

"Remember me, Lord," did he call out on the cross,
"In that kingdom which does not pass away,
And in that glory in which you will be revealed
May I behold your rest, seeing that I have acknowledged you."

Our Lord replied, "Because you have acknowledged me
This very day you shall be in the Garden of Eden;
In very truth, man, you will not be kept back
From that kingdom toward which you look.

"Take with you the cross as a sign, and be off:
It is the great key whereby the great gate
Of that garden shall be opened,
And Adam, who has been expelled, shall enter again."

The word of our Lord was sealed
Like a royal missive from the palace;
It was handed over to the thief
Who took it and made off for the Garden of Eden.

The cherub heard and rushed up;
He grabbed the thief at the gate,
Stopping him with the sharp blade he held.
All astonished, he said as follows:

Cherub: "Tell me, my man, who has sent you?
What is it you want, and how did you come?
What reason summoned you here?
Reveal and explain to me who has sent you."

Thief: "I will tell you who sent me;
Just hold back your blade and listen to my words.
I am a thief, but I supplicated for mercy,
And it was your Lord who sent me on my way here."

Cherub: "By what power did your coming take place?
Who brought you to this dread spot?
Who transported you across the sea of fire
So that you could enter Eden? Who is it who has sent you?"

Thief: "It was through the power of the Son, who sent me,
That I crossed over and came here without hindrance.
Through him I subdued all powers
And I have come to enter here, seeing that he has given me confidence."

Cherub: "You are indeed a thief, just as you have said,
But our region cannot be stolen into:
It is fenced in with the sword that guards it.
Turn back, man, you have lost your way."

Thief: "I was indeed a thief, but I have changed:
It was not to steal that I came here.
Look, I have upon me the key to Eden,
To open it up and enter, and I will not be prevented."

Cherub: "Our region is awe-inspiring and cannot be trodden,
For fire is its indomitable wall;
The blade flashes out all around it.
How is it you have made bold to come here?"

Thief: "Your region is awe-inspiring, just as you have told me
—But only until our Lord mounted the cross
When he transfixed the sword of all suffering
So that your blade no longer kills."

Cherub: "Ever since the time that Adam left
I have never seen anyone turn up here:
Your race has been banished from the garden.
You will not enter it, so do not argue anymore."

Thief: "Ever since the time that Adam left
Your Lord was angered at our race,
But now he is reconciled and has opened up the gate.
You are standing here to no purpose at all."

Cherub: "You should realize that it is not possible
For an unclean man to enter in here
—And you are a murderer, and one who sheds blood.
Whoever has brought you to this pure place?"

Thief: "You should realize that such is the wish

Of him who makes the unclean clean, who was crucified with me;
With the blood of his side did he thoroughly cleanse and wash me.
It was he who has sent me to paradise."

Cherub: "Be off with you, man, and do not argue any more,
For thus have I been commanded
To guard from your race by means of the sword
The tree of life that is to be found in here."

Thief: "Be off with you, angel; learn and see
That I have left behind hanging on Golgotha
The fruit of salvation that is in your garden,
So that our race may enter without any hindrance."

Cherub: "Eve and Adam fell into debt and wrote out
A document that will not be erased:
Under sentence did they go out from here
To live in humble estate in the land of thorns."

Thief: "The debt is repaid; just listen, O cherub:
The document has now been transfixed on the cross.
With both blood and water has your Lord wiped it out,
He has pinned it with nails and it will not be exacted."

Cherub: "Adam was driven out from this garden
And there is no means whereby he can reenter here,
For the blade of the sword revolves
And it will meet him if he should come near."

Thief: "He who was driven out has returned to his father's house,
For the great shepherd has gone out and found
That sheep that had left the garden,
And, carrying him on his shoulders, he has escorted him back."

Cherub: "Today it is something novel that I have seen:
A track entering inside the garden.
But here are Adam's footprints, take a look;
He left here and has not returned again."

Thief: "Jesus your Lord has performed a novel deed,
For he has now released Adam, who had been confined;
He has raised up whole crowds from inside Sheol,
And they sent me in advance so that I might open up for them."

Cherub: "I am a cherub, and how is it you have transgressed
Against my office of guarding, with which I have been entrusted?
A fiery being cannot be vanquished,
But as for you, son of Adam, how bold you are!"

Thief: "I am your companion and we have but one Lord
Who is in common for both me and for you:

His authority is higher than either yours or mine,
And, so, I have no fear, for it was he who sent me."

Cherub: "You simply cannot enter here,
For it is a resplendent place that no one can tread:
The Shechina [i.e., divine glory] is escorted around inside it,
And the sword of fire guards it."

Thief: "You cannot hold anyone back,
For the sword is now blunted and dulled.
The cross has opened up the Garden of Eden;
There is no means by which it can still be closed."

Cherub: "Have you not heard from scripture
How the cherub and the sword go round,
Guarding the way to the Garden of Eden,
So that none from Adam's house may enter?"

Thief: "Have you not heard from the revelation
That your Lord came down and became man,
Thus reconciling Adam, who was in a state of anger,
Bringing back to Eden the one who had been driven out?"

Cherub: "The sign of the revolving sword
That guards the tree of life
Frightened off Adam when he was driven out,
So how is it that you are not afraid?"

Thief: "The sign of your Lord is with me,
And by it the sharp sword is blunted;
By it, too, is the sentence remitted,
And by it Adam, once driven out, shall return."

Cherub: "The ranks of fire are standing here,
Thousands of them, in bands innumerable;
The multitudes are awe-inspiring, and you simply are unable
To travel on and enter among them."

Thief: "The multitudinous ranks of which you have told me
Are themselves in awe as they look upon the cross:
The sign of the Son inspires the awe
And they worship before it, while me they hold in honor."

Cherub: "The sign of my Lord is upon the chariot,
Resplendent upon the throne, but from us it is hidden,
So how is it that you—as you are claiming—
Carry this sign of his and escort it?"

Thief: "His sign is upon the chariot above,
But look, his cross is on Golgotha below.
And with his own blood he has written, a new missive

Allowing Adam to return inside the garden."

Cherub: "O agent in blood, who has brought you here?
Who has sent you, a murderer?
The sword is drawn and if you make too bold
The blade will flash out against you."

Thief: "O agent for the king, do not be upset;
Your authority is repealed, for your Lord has so willed it.
It is the cross that I have brought to you as a sign:
Look and see if it is genuine, and do not be so angry."

Cherub: "This cross of the Son that you have brought to me
I dare not look upon at all.
It is both genuine and awe-inspiring; no longer will you be debarred
From entering Eden, seeing that he has so willed."

Thief: "The cross of your Lord has breached the fence
That had been built up between us and you.
Anger has passed away and peace has come,
And the path to Eden is no longer cut off."

Cherub: "He who has slain has sent to me and testified with his own blood
That I should let go of the blade that I have been wielding.
Fearful is this sign that you have brought me;
Enter in, O heir, I will not turn you back."

Thief: "Resurrection has occurred for the human race
Who had been thrust forth from their home.
You cherubim and angels, rejoice with us,
For we have returned to your city."

Cherub: "Great is the compassion that has been shown to you,
The descendants of Adam who sinned and thus died.
Enter, thief, you will not be kept back,
For the gate is now open for those who repent."

Thief: "Great and most glorious is the compassion of my Lord,
For his mercy has affected it and his love has compelled him.
Rejoice with us, O spiritual beings,
For we have been mingled into your race."

Cherub: "The gentle one has held back from your race
The blade and the sword that I was wielding.
Outcasts who have returned, have no fear,
Enter inside the garden with exultation."

Thief: "Praise be in Eden, which has been pacified,
Peace on earth, which has been liberated.
Blessed is the crucified one who has reconciled us
So that we shall no longer be deprived of your race."

Thanks be to you, O Lord of all,
Who have brought back Adam who had been driven out,
While to the thief who asked for mercy
You opened up the gate that had been closed.

Thanks be to you, at whose word
The thief entered into the Garden of Eden,
And there was good hope for Adam again,
And he returned to the place from which he had gone out.

GIWARGIS WARDA, *ON SIN*

Thirteenth century. East Syrian.

An important medieval collection of poems in the East Syrian tradition has come down to us under the name of Giwargis Warda (George Warda; also called the *Ktaba Warda*, "The Book of the Rose"). It is a collection of around 150 poems for festivals of the Christian year, added to over time. Some poems reference the Mongol invasions of the thirteenth century, which marks the date of its compilation. The poems are written in the *'onita* genre associated with the Eucharistic liturgy. A typical stanza consists of four rhymed, seven-syllable lines (rhyme only enters Syriac verse through the influence of Arabic). The poem presented here on the theme of sin and repentance is very self-reflective and contains little of the biblical reimagining from earlier Syriac poetry. An alphabetical acrostic structures most of the stanzas, followed by the poet's name (here shortened to Giwarga). Alongside its high literary quality, the poem powerfully evokes a communal practice of contrition prior to receiving the communion of grace.

I have sinned and instigated to sin and am sinning again.
I am sinning and instigating to sin.
I teach but do not know.
And I do not know yet I teach.

I convert yet I do not convert myself.
And I do not convert myself yet convert.
I enlighten yet do not give light.
I adorn yet I am not fair.
Refrain: I sinned unto you only.

O you, who are filled with all sorts of goodness,
Have mercy on the one filled with all sorts of vices.
For your goodness remains,
While my vices are transitory.

My vices, however great they are,
Are covered with the stream of your love.

And my outrages, however foul they are,
Are smoothed over with the fairness of your fairness.

Your treasury is boundless;
Your wealth is immeasurable;
Your nature is indefinable;
And your love is inextinguishable.

For to do good is eternally intrinsic of you.
And to do evil is never intrinsic of you.
To do whatever you like is intrinsic of you.
To change your qualities is not intrinsic of you.

That good one, when the lawlessness
Of our stock had increased, overcame it.
The beloved Son he had, who was like himself,
He gave on behalf of us.

And also the Son, who was like his parent,
Fulfilled his work with love.
And subjected his flesh to the Law.
And baptized it notwithstanding our filth.

Sin became in every way righteous,
And the curse became in every way blessed.
And the eternally alive one became dead.
And who is capable of such grace!

His mind is terrified here,
And reason shut the door on him.
The ear of the listener is helpless
From listening to such news.

Very complicated and very easy.
Very easy and very complicated.
It is quite clear for God,
But very complicated for humans.

The presenter of righteousness,
Who heard what was sin,
Granted life and blessings
By dying with a humiliating death.

When our Lord met with sin,
Sin came to an end.
And, after he was buried because of the curse,
The curse came to an end.

There was no sin in his person,
Nor any curse on his face.
He brought glory to the disgraced,

And brought glorification with his feats.

Righteousness is impossible
To become sin by its nature.
But sin is possible to turn
Into righteousness through grace.

But it is possible that grass
And brushwood and dry litter would become fire.
But it is impossible that fire should be called
Brushwood or grass.

Fire sputters and dies out,
But [God's grace] does not die out from anything.
And with this design our Lord took [away]
The curse and lawlessness on our behalf.

The fire of righteousness became inflamed,
And sin burned down before it:
As brushwood disappears and perishes
From the strength of the flame.

The roots of sin are dug up;
Shoots of curses are cut off.
And blessings and righteousness
Covered mountains and heights.

Humankind is already saved
From these three evils:
The curse, death, and sin—
Which were the origins of its ruin.

He was inflamed with righteousness
Like the shining sun.
And the sin ceased in him, fleeing
Like darkness at light.

Death is killed, sin is dead,
And curses are destroyed.
Humankind has been saved, has become righteous,
And has received blessings forever.

This matter is very great,
But though great it is not too great
That justice be done for us,
For our Lord was called "sin [offering]."

All numbers and measurements are abolished.
Measures and scales became inefficient,
And small for this quantity
And qualities.

Life established itself, blessings triumphed
With the divinization of humankind.
And there is no end to grace
And no end to righteousness.

The mighty one, if we measure him,
The sea waters will be in his cupped hand.
If our lawlessness is measured with his measure,
There will not be a drop in it.

O you, the one who measured out heaven with his span,
What, to the grandeur of his glory,
Is the dirt and filth of our stock?
Naught, just naught.

And he who has gripped Earth in his palm,
How will he deem the lawlessness of the generation,
Our stock, with its reluctance?
It is as imperceptible as a particle in his mountain.

More, if it could be weighed,
Than any mountain or eminence, on the scales
Would weigh the goodness to us.
It is innumerable like onion skins.

Men and women of humankind,
Who were and are among the creation,
Are innumerable like drops in the kettle
And the number of grains in sand.

O forgiving
And merciful one,
Who gave his soul for sinners
To save them from sins,
Forgive our meanness captured by the wicked one
For you are our victory and honor!

KHAMIS BAR QARDAḤE, *WINE SONG*

Thirteenth century. East Syrian.

This short excerpt from Khamis bar Qardaḥe's *Wine Song* represents a rare example of "secular" poetry in Syriac. Clearly influenced by Arabic poetry on the same theme, Khamis directs his praise to the preeminent elixir of clear thought, though it is couched even still in theological typology of the wine of the Eucharist and the blood from Christ's side on the cross. Like the poem attributed to Warda above, Khamis's poems are *'oniyata* and cover many different themes. Some are penitential and liturgical, while others, such as this one, deal with profane matters. In addition to the *'oniyata*, Khamis wrote numerous epigrams on various themes as well as verse commentaries on the Bible. His writings stand as the apex of poetic experimentation in the long history of Syriac verse.

> The truly undivided soul longs and desires
> For a cup mixed with love, from the hand of a sleek gazelle
> Who captivates lions with his glances.
>
> O guest, why do you hold back? Unstop the flask,
> Choose the lasting draft and the moon-faced cup bearer,
> And pour away your riches and treasures.
>
> With a full cup overflowing with an ancient living wine,
> Relieve your anguished heart, for bereft of money and coin,
> Tomorrow you must depart.
>
> And when you are ready to drink, choose a true friend
> Who can tell right from wrong, and occupy a private court
> Where the fool cannot see you.
>
> When the fumes go to your head, and you are freed of dross,
> Loose every knot from your heart, and taste the wine of his side,
> Pressed with the sacramental lance.
>
> So, go in past the boundaries, draw aside all secrets and veils,
> Transcend spheres and wheels, renounce mind and matter,
> That to you the invisible one might appear.
>
> This wine is not of grapes, nor did he choose a place on the stock,
> But it is from a wild vine shoot, possessing hidden clusters,
> Which the Father of truth tended.

'ABDISHO' BAR BRIKA, *METRICAL CATALOGUE OF SYRIAC AUTHORS*

Late thirteenth to early fourteenth century. East Syrian.

The prolific scholar, poet, and theologian 'Abdisho' bar Brika left to posterity a large corpus of writings in several different genres. In many ways he represents the culmination of the ancient and medieval East Syrian literary tradition. His *Metrical Catalogue of Syriac Authors* is a chief Syriac source for East Syrian literary history, presenting a history of texts known to 'Abdisho' from the beginning of Syriac literature up to his own day, including those early writers shared by both East and West Syrian Christians alike. Many of the authors and texts he mentions no longer survive. The *Catalogue* is a prime example of how Syriac authors could use poetry for a wide variety of purposes. The selections presented here include fulsome descriptions of Ephrem's and Narsai's writings (though by no means complete) as well as very short notices that show 'Abdisho' knew little more than the name of the author (without which, however, we would not know these authors even existed). Finally, 'Abdisho' places himself in this long history of literature, demonstrating the impressive scope of what he was able to achieve in this late period of classical Syriac.

> Ephrem the Great, called the prophet of the Syrians, published commentaries on Genesis, Exodus, Leviticus, Joshua son of Nun, Judges, Samuel, the Book of Kings, David [i.e., the Psalms], Isaiah, the Twelve [Prophets], Jeremiah, Ezekiel, and blessed Daniel. He wrote also books and epistles on the faith of the church. In addition, metrical sermons, hymns with songs, and all the songs for the departed [i.e., services for the dead] survive. He wrote also treatises on the alphabet, a disputation with the Jews, as well as against Simon and Bardaisan, and also against Marcion and the Ophites, and an answer to the blasphemy of Julian. [. . .]

> Narsai, the harp of the spirit, wrote commentaries on Genesis, Exodus, Leviticus, Numbers, [Joshua] son of Nun, the books of Judges, Ecclesiastes, Isaiah, the Twelve [Prophets], Jeremiah, Ezekiel, and the prophecy of Daniel. Further, twelve other books of *memre*, which are in number three hundred and sixty. He wrote a liturgy, an exposition of the sacraments and baptism, sermons of consolation, hymns of praise, litanies, exhortations, and a treatise concerning the disgraceful manner of life. [. . .]

> John of Dalyata. He composed two books, along with epistles on penitence that concern the monastic life.

> Isaac of Nineveh wrote seven volumes concerning the spiritual manner of life, concerning the divine sacraments, and [concerning] judgments and stewardship.

> Abraham of Natpar wrote various compositions.

> Jacob of Edessa wrote annals and chronicles. [. . .]

> Abraham Katina wrote opinions and questions.

> Simeon of Kurdlah wrote metrical *memre* along with interpretations.

> Father Yazidad wrote a book which is called *A Gleaning*.

> Bar Jacob wrote a book.

> Damniyas wrote metrical *memre*.

> Susai of Shus composed a book of thanksgivings.

> Abraham Saba wrote a book of various questions. [. . .]

> Bod Peryadeuta wrote *memre* on the faith, and against the Manichaeans, and against the followers of Marcion. [He wrote] also questions in Greek, entitled *Aleph-Migin*. And he translated from Indian [Sanskrit?] the book of *Kalilag and Damnag* [i.e., *Kalila and Dimnah*] [. . .]

The books that I myself, the humble 'Abdisho' from Sauba, composed: A book of exposition on scripture, both Old and New [Testaments]; a catholic book on the amazing dispensation; a book of psalms, which is entitled *Paradise of Eden*; a short collection of the canons of synods; a book *Shah Marourid*, which I composed in Arabic; a book *Marganita* [i.e., the *Pearl*], which concerns the true faith; a book of obscure mysteries from the philosophy of the Greeks; a scholastic book on the repudiation of all heresies; a book of the organization of judgments and church laws; and a book containing twelve *memre* comprising all disciplines of knowledge; interpretations with consolations and *memre* concerning diverse subjects; a commentary on the great letter of the admirable Aristotle that he wrote to Alexander on the great art; various letters that concern demonstrations of multiple arguments; a resolution for difficult questions; and riddles, titles, and parables.

3

DOCTRINE AND DISPUTATION

Syriac Christianity was riven by doctrinal controversies in the fifth through seventh centuries, which resulted in the separation of three Syriac-speaking communities from imperial Chalcedonian orthodoxy—namely, the East Syrian community that would become the Church of the East, the West Syrian community that would become the Syrian Orthodox Church, and the originally monothelete Maronites. Long before the fifth century, however, Syriac Christians were involved in disputes over doctrine.

In the year 313, the emperor Constantine issued the Edict of Milan, which ended the persecution of Christians in the Roman Empire. Although he was baptized only on his deathbed in 337, Constantine was deeply involved with the affairs of the church long before that. Above all else, he wished to unify Christianity for the sake of the integrity of the empire. The most significant challenge to Christian unity in his reign was the so-called "Arian" controversy. The fourth-century Egyptian presbyter Arius believed that God the Father was the only uncreated divine person; God the Son, he maintained, was created as a kind of secondary god, a mediator between God the Father and his creation. Some agreed with Arius's view, and others vigorously opposed it, arguing that God the Son was eternal, uncreated, and "consubstantial" (*homoousios*) with God the Father. The later view eventually prevailed at the Council of Nicaea in 325 and the Council of Constantinople in 381, whose creeds established "Nicene" Trinitarian orthodoxy in the East and in the West. The controversy engulfed Christians everywhere, including Syriac-speaking Christians, who found themselves on different sides of this debate. For example, as seen in the first selection below, Ephrem the Syrian (d. 373) was an ardent defender of Nicene orthodoxy.

As soon as the Arian controversy was resolved in the late fourth century, a new confessional division reared its head. If, as Nicene orthodoxy maintained, God the Son was fully divine, "consubstantial" with the Father, then the question arose: how did the two natures, human and divine, coexist in the incarnate Christ? Questions such as these are the domain of "Christology," which means at its most basic something like "an account of who Christ is," but in this context refers to something more specific—namely, whether and how the incarnate Christ contains and even unites these distinct natures. What is ultimately at stake in both the Trinitarian and Christological controversies is salvation: it was thought that Christ can save humans only by being both fully human and divine, and so Christians felt the need to agree on a confession of *how* the incarnate Christ is both human and divine.

Theodore of Mopsuestia (d. 428) and the Antiochene tradition for which he stands had a distinctive answer to this question. His Christology emphasizes a clear distinction between the human and divine natures in the incarnate Christ. He insisted that Christ's two natures, human and divine, each had its own "face" or *prosōpon* (which can also be translated "person"). The human face of Christ lent itself to the pair, and thus in Christ the two natures were not united but "conjoined." The second selection below showcases Theodore's distinctive Christology. Although he died a defender of Nicene orthodoxy, he posthumously ran afoul of Christological orthodoxy, and was posthumously condemned at the Second Council of Constantinople in 553. His writings were translated into Syriac early, perhaps even during his own life, and his teachings served as the basis of the curriculum for the Schools of Edessa and Nisibis.

Nestorius (d. 450), bishop of Constantinople, was deeply influenced by Theodore's Christology. Theodore's insistence on the clear distinction between Christ's human and divine natures led Nestorius to object to Christians calling Mary "God bearer" (*Theotokos*) for, strictly speaking, Mary gave birth to the human nature, not the divine. It would be better, Nestorius said, if we acclaimed Mary *Christotokos*, the "Christ bearer." Cyril of Alexandria (d. 444) disagreed sharply with Nestorius, and their dispute inaugurated the Christological controversies. Cyril's Christology was defined by his insistence that, despite the distinction of two natures, there was only ever one, single person in the incarnate Christ, who mysteriously united the two natures in a single "hypostasis." This sounds very much like what would eventually be established as Chalcedonian orthodoxy. But in less guarded moments Cyril also spoke more strongly of the union of the two natures, and even of Christ having one nature (*mia physis*) out of the two. Some of Cyril's followers took up this stronger formulation and formed a miaphysite tradition that became the West Syrian Church and eventually the modern Syrian Orthodox Church.

As this book's introduction showed, a series of councils and schisms arose from the events set in motion by this dispute between Nestorius and Cyril. As a result, the fifth and sixth centuries saw the division of Syriac-speaking Christians into a number of newly distinct churches that this volume calls the Chalcedonian Church, the Maronite Church, the East Syrian Church, and the West Syrian Church. Chalcedonian Christians who accepted the orthodoxy of the Roman emperors Justin and Justinian were perceived as

Byzantine sympathizers and, from the eighth century, were often called by their opponents "Melkites" (from the Syriac term *malka* for emperor). In the course of the seventh and eighth centuries, a subset of Chalcedonian Christians split off from others to form the Maronite Church. East Syrian Christians maintained their traditions in the Persian Empire under the leadership of the patriarch or *katholikos* of the city Seleucia-Ctesiphon. Still other Syriac Christians rejected the Council of Chalcedon and coalesced around the miaphysite teachings and episcopacies that became the West Syrian Church.

Selections below include some of the premier representatives of these different confessions and communities. Severus of Antioch (d. 538) is generally recognized as one of the most important Greek theologians of the sixth century and, together with Philoxenus of Mabbug (d. 523), the main proponent of the miaphysite tradition, which became the West Syrian Church and eventually the modern Syrian Orthodox Church. Babai the Great (d. 628) authored the *Book of the Union*, which remains a fundamental statement of the Christology of the modern Church of the East.

Repeated efforts to heal the breach between imperial Chalcedonian orthodoxy and the various miaphysite churches led to a series of Christological compromises in the sixth and seventh centuries. It was hoped that these compromises, which emphasized Christ's unity, would bring the miaphysite West Syrian churches into the fold of imperial Chalcedonian orthodoxy. One such compromise was the emperor Heraclius's (d. 641) promotion of "monotheletism," the teaching that Christ has two natures but only one will (*thelēma*). Included below is a monothelete "antihagiography" of Maximus the Confessor (d. 662), who was a defender of Chalcedonian orthodoxy and who suffered greatly for vocally resisting the emperor's efforts. Maximus was vindicated at the Third Council of Constantinople in 680/681, which rejected monotheletism. The penultimate selection is a fragment from a monothelete, and more specifically a Maronite, complaint about this council (also known as the Sixth Ecumenical Council). The final excerpt is from Dionysius bar Ṣalibi (d. 1171), a West Syrian author who, in his polemical work *Against the Melkites*, resists any efforts to soften the distinction between what is in his mind (miaphysite) orthodoxy and (dyophysite, Chalcedonian) heresy.

Further Reading   The best place to start for the Trinitarian and Christological controversies is Frances M. Young, and Andrew Teal, *From Nicaea to Chalcedon: A Guide to the Literature and Its Background*, 2nd ed. (Grand Rapids, MI: Baker Academic, 2010). Those who wish to go deeper into the Christological controversies will benefit from John A. McGuckin, *Saint Cyril of Alexandria and the Christological Controversy* (Leiden: E. J. Brill, 1994). Aloys Grillmeier's two-volume *Christ in Christian Tradition* is a magisterial study, but it is for advanced students. See Aloys Grillmeier, ed., *Christ in Christian Tradition*, vol. 1, *From the Apostolic Age to Chalcedon*, trans. John Bowden(Atlanta: John Knox Press, 1975); Aloys Grillmeier and Theresia Hainthaler, eds., *Christ in Christian Tradition*, vol. 2, part 1, *From Chalcedon to Justinian I*, trans. Pauline Allen and John Cawte (Atlanta: John Knox Press, 1987); vol. 2, part 2, *The Church of Constantinople in the Sixth Century*, trans. Pauline Allen and John Cawte (Atlanta: John Knox Press, 1995); vol. 2, part 4, *The Church of Alexandria with Nubia and Ethiopia*, trans. O. C. Dean (Atlanta: John Knox Press, 1996); vol. 2, part 3, *The Churches of Jerusalem and Antioch*, trans. Marianne Ehrhardt (Oxford: Oxford University Press, 2013). On various forms of miaphysitism in the sixth century, together with more primary sources, see Iain Torrance, *Christology after Chalcedon: Severus of Antioch & Sergius the Monophysite* (Norwich: Canterbury Press, 1988). For the same, but in the seventh century, see Pauline Allen and Bronwen Neil, eds. and trans., *Maximus the Confessor and his Companions: Documents from Exile* (Oxford: Oxford University Press, 2002). For more recent synthetic studies of the Christological controversies, see Volker Menze, *Justinian and the Making of the Syrian Orthodox Church* (Oxford: Oxford University Press, 2008); David Michelson, *The Practical Christology of Philoxenos of Mabbug* (New York: Oxford University Press, 2014); and Yonatan Moss, *Incorruptible Bodies: Christology, Society, and Authority in Late Antiquity* (Berkeley: University of California Press, 2016).

EPHREM, *HYMNS ON FAITH* 53

Mid to Late Fourth century.

The fourth century was witness to the so-called "Arian" controversy: Arius, eager to defend the monotheism of God the Father, believed that the Son must be somehow subordinate to the Father, created as a subordinate deity—in other words, a "creature." The opposing view, which eventually won the day at the Councils of Nicaea and Constantinople, insisted that the Son was "of one being" (*homoousios*) with the Father—not created but eternally begotten. The deacon-poet Ephrem (d. 373) was an ardent defender of Nicene orthodoxy. In this hymn, he targets those who look to Proverbs 8:22, where wisdom (which is understood to be equivalent to the Son) speaks of herself as a "creature," as evidence for a subordinate Son. For additional excerpts from Ephrem, see chapters 1, 2, 7, and 10.

> Who would not marvel at the just one [Moses], who did not neglect
> To write of exalted things, or inscribe lowly things?
> He writes of created things, and includes everything,
> Even the staff and the story of the mandrakes
> About which simple women spoke. He dictated through the Holy Spirit,
> And it was placed in the ark.
>
> Refrain: Praise to your teaching!
>
> Who would not fear? There is scandal throughout the land,
> Bickering in the inhabited earth, and debate in the marketplace.
> There are schisms among congregations, and in the churches,
> Destruction and dagger. Women fall upon women,
> Men upon their friends, and priests upon kings.
> The whole world clamors!
>
> Who would not weep at how often the earth
> Has quaked, and then settled again, while the quakes and the controversies

Of the churches have not grown silent? Waves and storms
Quiet down over the sea, but fools and debaters
Are stirred up on dry land. It is a blessing for sailors,
But woe to the scribes! [. . .]

They can say to us, like most excellent scribes,
Conversant with the law, and practiced in the things of the prophets:
"See how Solomon encourages controversy? [Proverbs 8:22]
For he perceives and calls him 'creature' and 'thing-made.'"
Thus Solomon becomes a great refuge
For all their sophisms.

From my simplicity, hear succinctly:
All of this smallness that is in the books
Is fulfilled in the humanity of our savior.
But if you are able, pass beyond his humanity
And come to his divinity, and you will find that above all
These things he is exalted.

Come and fly to his side on the feathers of the mind,
And the wings of thought. Polish and cleanse
The eyes of your mind. Ascend and look upon the Son.
Look upon him and look upon his Father, and see [the Son] entirely
Like his begetter. For the Father is hidden from all
And the Son is concealed from all.

Count, therefore, how many times he is called "Son" and "Begotten,"
And then add up how often he is called "creature."
And once the words have been compiled, the names that predominate,
Persuade those who are discerning of the accurate name.
The [true] name is repeated every time instead of the title—
Two, three, and more [times].

We have counted and found that in one parable alone,
Solomon calls out "creature." We have made a calculation and have not [even] finished.
For the Father is in all marvels, the prophets in all mouths,
The apostles in all words, and the demons in all scourging.
As one, they have proclaimed him "Son." Who would not believe
And rebuke the quarrelsome?

THEODORE OF MOPSUESTIA, *ON THE INCARNATION*

Ca. 380. Originally Greek. Survives to various degrees in Greek, Latin, and Syriac.

In addition to his biblical commentaries, Theodore is famous for his distinctive Christology, which deeply influenced Nestorius and others in the East Syrian Church where, along with Diodore of Tarsus (d. ca. 390) and Nestorius (d. 451), he is remembered as one of the three "doctors" of the church. The following selection is a collection of passages that have been preserved (in the original Greek [book 7] and in Latin translation [books 2 and 5]) from Theodore's major work, *On the Incarnation*. Theodore was eventually condemned at the Second Council of Constantinople in 553. These passages from *On the Incarnation* were preserved by his adversaries, because they were thought to represent what they regarded as Theodore's heretical teaching about the union of Christ's human and divine nature. Notice some of Theodore's distinctive Christological teachings: Jesus's human nature was the same as ours and, although his humanity was graced by God, his human nature is not changed; God "assumes" the human Jesus in an act of gracious indwelling; Jesus is therefore the "assumed one," whose human nature is united to the divine nature in a "prosopic union"; God dwells in Christ neither in substance (because he is present to all equally in substance) nor in operation or activity, but according to his "good pleasure" and "as in [his] son."

[Book 2] Jesus the man. For "What is a human being that You are mindful of him?" [Psalms 8:5]. The apostle affirms that this has been said of Jesus. For he says that "The one whom we see who has been made a little less than the angels [is] Jesus" [Hebrews 2:9]. How is this so? For Jesus is a human being like all human beings, differing in no way from those sharing his nature, other than that [God] has graced him. But the grace given to him does not change his nature. Then, after incurring death, "God gave him a name above every name" [Philippians 2:9]. God is the one giving, and the one given [this grace] is Jesus Christ, the first fruits of those who will rise. For he is "the firstborn of the dead" [Colossians 1:18]. He has ascended, sits at the right hand of God, and is over all. What an all-surpassing grace has been given to Jesus—a grace that transcends every nature! Although he has the same nature as my own, he has been shown to be above the heavens, sitting at the right hand of the Father. [. . .]

[Book 5] When anyone considers the natures, he necessarily discovers [that they are different from] one another. Nor do I think that there is any controversy here, since God the Word is one by nature and the other is admitted to have been assumed (whatever this may mean). Yet this latter is said to be simultaneously the same person (Latin *persona* = Greek *prosōpon*) whose [two] natures are in no way confused, but [are one] because of the assumed one's union with the assuming one. For, if one willingly grants that the latter is other than the former by nature, it is evident that the one assumed is not equal to the one assuming. However, each will be clearly found to be the same one in a prosopic union. Therefore, one has to make distinctions in regard to Christ without there being any contradiction here. For these [distinctions] closely conform to what the divine scriptures [state]. So the natures are not to be confused, nor the person to be perversely divided. Both the way the natures relate to one another must stay unconfused and the person must be acknowledged as undivided. On one hand, the natures exist by what is proper to [each], with the assumed one being distinguished from [his] assumer. Yet, on the other hand, [they are undivided] in their prosopic union. For they are said to be as one because the natures of the assumer and the assumed are [each] considered as belonging to their [natures'] whole [union]. And, if I may say so, we call God the Word by the name of Son and at the same time also affirm [the same] of the assumed nature on account of his union to the [Word]. [. . .]

[Book 7] For, if we learn how the indwelling takes place, we will know both its mode and its modal difference. Some declare that the indwelling has occurred in a substantial way and others [that it has occurred] in an operational way. Let there be, therefore, a careful examination [to learn] if there is any truth to these [statements]. First of all, let us agree: does [the Word] dwell in all or not? But it is evident: not in all. For God has promised that his [indwelling] comes as a special relationship to the saints or, generally speaking, to those whom he wants set apart for himself. But, if this is so, what was [God] promising when he said, "I will dwell and walk among these [faithful ones] and be their God, and they will be my people" [Leviticus 26:12], showing them thereby some special favor? But [how] do those human beings who disobey [God] publicly share this [favor]? For if he does not dwell in all—and clearly I am speaking here not only of things but also of human beings—there needs to be some special reason for his indwelling, whereby he is present only to those in whom he said he would dwell.

To say, therefore, that God dwells [in Christ's humanity] in a substantial way is wrong. For then one would have to restrict his substance to only those in whom he said he would dwell, thereby being distant from all others—which is absurd to say about an infinite nature that is present everywhere and limited by nothing. So, if someone states that God is present everywhere, by reason of his substance, he [must] also attribute his indwelling to all, not merely to humans but also to irrational and inanimate beings, [that is,] if we maintain that he dwells by means of his substance. Both of these [statements] are clearly false. For to say that God dwells in all is to state an outright absurdity, and to equate this [universal] substance with him is unbecoming. Therefore, to say that the indwelling occurs by reason of substance should be [considered] utmost folly.

Someone can also say the same about [God being present] by means of his activity. For his operational presence ought again to be limited to those [who experience his power] alone. How, then, will we account for the fact that God foresees all things and governs all things and acts upon everything in an appropriate and correct way that accords in a consistent way with [each nature] by means of those serving as his agents in the universe? For, since he endows all things with the power for each to be itself and to work according to its own nature, we [can] say that he does dwell in all things. Thus, [we can] clearly state that it is in neither a substantial nor operational way that God has effected these kinds of indwelling. What, then, is left? What reason can we offer that seems to preserve what is special about these [indwellings]? Clearly, it is fair to state that [God's] indwelling has taken place by good pleasure. Good pleasure is said to be God's most excellent and noblest desire to benefit those who are pleasing to him because of their effort to be devoted to him. For those deeds that are [done] well in a noble way are seen to be pleasing to him, [a view] usually taken for granted by the scriptures and found in them, as the blessed David says, "His will does not [rely] on the strength of a horse, nor is he well pleased about a one's speed. The Lord takes pleasure in those who fear him and hope in his mercy" [Psalms 147:10–11]. Although [God] affirms his refusal to cooperate with some and his unwillingness to work with others, yet [God] says to those [reverentially] fearing him that he esteems them greatly and is pleased to work with them and aid them. In this way, then, it is fitting to speak of an indwelling. For, being infinite and unlimited in his nature, [God] is present to all. But by his good pleasure he is thus distant from some and near to others. [The scripture] agrees with this viewpoint: "The Lord is near to the brokenhearted and will save the humble in spirit" [Psalms 34:18]; and elsewhere: "Do not cast me away from your presence and do not take away your Holy Spirit from me" [Psalms 51:11]. Thus, he is near because he is [fondly] disposed toward those worthy of his nearness, and again far from sinners, although he is neither separated [from them] nor found to be closer by reason of his nature. He responds to both in light of how his will is disposed [toward them]. So he is near and distant by his good pleasure, as is evident from what we have said when we spoke about [God's] good pleasure.

Therefore, we have discussed in precise ways what is meant by the assertion that [God] effects [his] indwelling by good pleasure. He is not limiting his substance or operation in these instances, because he exists apart from all others. Rather, he is present to all in a substantial way, but separated from the unworthy by how he is now disposed [toward them]. For in this way his unlimited [existence] is better preserved, since his unlimited nature appears here not to be essentially restrained. If he were indeed present everywhere by [his] good pleasure, then he would once again be found to be necessarily constrained to be there. He would then not be present in a voluntary way but by means of his infinite nature, with his will being [by necessity] in agreement with this. Since he is both present to all by [his] nature and separated from those from whom he voluntarily wants to be, then in no way do the unworthy profit from the presence of God. In this way, his infinite nature is preserved, and is true and complete. [. . .]

So, therefore, [God] is present to some and separated from others by [his] good pleasure, to the extent that, even though separated from all the rest, he is [nevertheless] with all these by [his] substance. In the same way that the indwelling occurs according to [God's] good pleasure, so too does [his] good pleasure vary its mode of indwelling. For what prompts God to dwell in some, and to reveal to them that he is present everywhere by reason of [his] substance, and dwells in even the most unlikely beings—I am speaking here about [his] good pleasure—[this is what] conditions the mode of [God's] indwelling in all cases. For just as he is said to be dwelling not in all when he is present to all by his substance, but only to those in whom he is present by his good pleasure, so [in this sense] he can be said to dwell. But this [mode] of indwelling is not found to be equally everywhere but is dependent upon the extent to which God dwells by his good pleasure. Therefore, when he is said to dwell either in the apostles or generally in the just, then he dwells there insofar as he is pleased with these upright individuals, just as [he does] when pleased with the virtuous. However, we do not maintain that the indwelling took place in [Christ] in this way—for we would never be so mad, but as in [his] Son. For, since [God] was well pleased [with him], he dwelt [within him] in this way. What, then, is [meant by] "as in [his] Son"? [It should be understood] in the sense that, when [the Word] dwells [within his humanity], he has united himself wholly to the assumed one and made him share in every honor that [the Son] shares, because he is the one in whom [God's] Son dwells by nature, to such an extent that he is accounted to be one person (*prosōpon*) because of his union with him. [God], therefore, shares all his power with [his humanity], so that all things will be accomplished by means of him and [the Father] will pass judgment on all, by examining through him when [Christ] will come [at the end of time], but with the clear understanding that [the Father and Jesus] differ [from each other] in accordance with what correctly pertains to their natures.

SEVERUS OF ANTIOCH, *TO NEPHALIUS*

Early sixth century. Originally in Greek, preserved in Syriac.

Severus of Antioch (d. 538) is one of the most important Greek theologians of the sixth century; along with Philoxenus of Mabbug (d. 523), he had the most theological authority in the miaphysite West Syrian tradition, a tradition that became the modern Syrian Orthodox Church. He was the patriarch of Antioch, but spent much of his life between Beirut, Gaza, Constantinople, and Egypt, where he died in exile. He was a fierce opponent of imperial Chalcedonian orthodoxy. In 536 the emperor Justinian had Severus's writings condemned, with the result that most of them survive only in Syriac translation. In this selection, addressed to a Chalcedonian named Nephalius, Severus aligns himself with Athanasius of Alexandria (d. 373) and Cyril of Alexandria (d. 444) against the Antiochene tradition represented by Nestorius (d. 451), Theodoret of Cyrrhus (d. 466), and a certain Andrew, the bishop of Samosata and a supporter of Nestorius. Severus here argues that the Chalcedonian confession of Christ—"in two natures" and yet also "united and not divided" and moreover united in "one hypostasis"—introduced an absurdity into the faith.

> Of the same man again, a second discourse to Nephalius. To the same people who assert that Christ is to be recognized in two natures after the union, and add the phrase, "which are united and not divided."
>
> Now we ourselves, according to the saving and truly divine statement of the three hundred and eighteen [fathers at the Council of Nicaea], believe and confess that the only begotten Son of God, who is equal in essence to the Father through whose power all things existed, came down at the end of days and became incarnate and was made human—that is, he was united to flesh that had a soul possessed of reason and intelligence by means of a free and hypostatic union from the Holy Spirit and from the ever-virgin Mary, Mother of God; and that his nature was one, even when the Word had become incarnate, just as the God-inspired men and mystagogues of the church have instructed us; and we know him as simple, and not compound, in that which he is understood to be God, and composite in that which he is understood to be human. For since we believe him to be Emmanuel, even the same God the Word incarnate out of two natures that possess integrity (I mean out of divinity and out of humanity), we know one Son, one Christ, one Lord. We do not affirm that he is known in two natures, as the Synod of Chalcedon declared as dogma, putting the expression "indivisibly" onto its declaration as a kind of apology.

For that very synod bears witness that it is not the same thing to say that after the union he is "out of two natures" as it is to say that he is "in two natures," even if the word "united" be added. [. . .]

See how [Athanasius] has affirmed him as being one Christ, one person (*prosōpon*) and one nature and one hypostasis. Furthermore, with the same words that holy Cyril comes forward. For [Cyril] says, in the second treatise against the blasphemies of Nestorius, "Leave off from dividing the natures after the union." But immediately a malicious hearer disputes this and says, "Look, he forbids us to divide the natures after the union, and I declare that they are united!" But that person shall hear from us: "We do not pay attention to your disputations; but we shall enquire of the source of the statement what he defines as the meaning of [the instruction] that we should 'not divide the natures.'" Now, in the same discourse he had stated earlier: "Thus everything shall be spoken of as if referring to one person: for one nature is perceived as existing after the union, that of the Word himself incarnate." Now, according to you [Nephalius], he ought to have said, "For the two natures are perceived as united after the union." But he himself knows that the union demonstrated to me one nature incarnate, that of the Word himself; and the fact that he also calls that same Christ "hypostasis" we can observe without any trouble. For [Cyril] wrote as follows in the third chapter of his anathemas: "If anyone divides the hypostases in Christ after the union, joining them together merely by a conjunction in dignity or authority or might and not rather by a conjunction of a union according to nature, let him be anathema."

But yet again those who attack these things that have been stated are calumniators and assert that that union according to hypostasis allows us to speak of two hypostases, that is, two natures, after the union. But I do not need many words to deal with this, since I shall give testimony from the enemies themselves to the effect that this conjunction of hypostases, which is effected through a natural union, brings about one incarnate hypostasis in the composition of the Son himself. For Andrew says, in his complaint against this anathema, "Again, let us remind him of these words of his, since they show him speaking of two hypostases (in those matters which he discusses in the first volume): 'So then, that word which is from the Father was not sanctified with us according to his own nature, even if one were to suppose that he alone was also born of the holy virgin, was anointed, and sanctified; and because of this also assumed the title Christ.' How, then, as if disregarding these words of his, does he gather [the natures] into one hypostasis by confusing the natures, when he calls the divine union 'natural'"?

Look: he evidently complains of the anathema as something that introduces one hypostasis. How, then, do you presume to call the gathering together of the hypostases according to a natural union "two natures," that is, two hypostases united, when you do not perceive as a result of the union one entity in composition? Now that this is indeed the case, hear along with the testimony of the enemies the voice of Cyril himself as well. For [Cyril] states in that letter to Nestorius, in which he also cites the anathema: "Therefore let us ascribe to one person all the gospel expressions, to one hypostasis of the Word incarnate. For the Lord Jesus Christ is one according to the scriptures."

Thus it is clear that those who were at Chalcedon, when they promoted the dogma that Christ is in two natures, threw in for us the term "one hypostasis" to lead to deception. For if there is one hypostasis, there is, in short, also one nature, as has been demonstrated before. For the God-inspired voice of the fathers clearly affirmed neither two natures nor two hypostases for the one Son, regardless of whether anyone should say that the natures were either united or separated. For the lack of definition of both terms is understandable and challenging because it is generic, according to external authorities as well as general opinions. Furthermore, on account of irreverent mouths especially is added also that phrase "but one nature of God the Word incarnate." Nor may they assert that by saying "incarnate" he established that other nature separately: for that God-inspired man who had Christ speaking within him did not utter an expression so base and perverse but had stated clearly that there were not two natures divided but two united.

Why, then, do you frighten those who are more simple when you say, "See! the holy Cyril in sending letters to Nestorius states that the natures that were gathered together into the true union were different from one another"; and thence you bring forth those matters that come out of your own heart when you assert, "So, then, if the natures are gathered together into a union, is it necessary for us to speak of them as two natures united"? For that man deserves to be believed rather than your opinion or your soothsaying, as though he were explaining himself and saying, "Now one Christ and Son and Lord is understood from the two [natures], not as if the difference, but rather the separation of the natures were taken away on account of the union." With understanding indeed let us add this: for the natures from which comes the one Christ are in fact different, inasmuch as divinity and humanity are not the same. But we do not make their difference a cause of duality, in that they are gathered together into the union; for from them Emmanuel is composed. For the teacher cries aloud: "Cease from dividing the natures after the union!" However, this command that we should not divide the natures does not mean that we should affirm (as you yourselves affirm) that the two natures are united; but it means this—that we should affirm one incarnate nature, as [Cyril] himself says. For he declares as follows (just as he also asserts above when he says): "So, just as everything is spoken of the one person—for one nature is recognized as existing after the union, namely that of the Word incarnate." Thus, these words "after the union" were said not with reference to distinction. It is not the case, as certain people supposed as a result of this, that before the union there were two natures of Christ; for these words are the words of a drunken mind, and mere twaddle.

For indeed before the union and the incarnation, the Word was simple and incorporeal; but when, according to the scripture, it pleased him to become flesh, that is, to be united to flesh that possessed a rational soul; then, from that conception, God the Word was incarnate and yielded himself for our sake to our composition in a manner inconceivable and inexpressible and as he himself alone knew. For we do not set up the human nature separately, in the manner of the foolish Nestorians, and then make God the Word dwell in it afterward. For this would constitute an indwelling and not incarnation; with the consequence that God would not be incarnate and made man, but rather there would be found a man inspired by God, a Christ. For indeed when we examine things altogether, we know that the divinity is one thing and the humanity another, and that they are greatly distant from one another. But when we consider the divine union, that is to say, the incarnation as conceivable for us, we see that out of two, divinity and humanity that are perfect, is composed Emmanuel in a union that is indivisible. And this is what was meant by the holy Cyril: "Leave off from dividing the natures after the union," that is, after we have affirmed the union.

BABAI THE GREAT, *BOOK OF THE UNION*

Early seventh century. East Syrian.

Babai the Great (d. 628) was a theologian and a monastic author of the East Syrian Church. He studied at the School of Nisibis and became a monk of the "Great Monastery" founded in 571 by Abraham of Kashkar (d. 588). His *Book of the Union* remains a fundamental statement of the Christology of the Church of the East to this day. In it, Babai defends the Christological position that Christ is two natures and two hypostases—that is, concrete instantiations of a nature—united in a single person. This position grew out of debates at the School of Nisibis and was directed against miaphysite views, as well as against intermediary positions (e.g., those who maintained Christ had two natures but one hypostasis). Largely through Babai's efforts, the two-hypostasis Christology came to define the orthodoxy of the East Syrian Church. Babai clarifies the meaning of the key terms "nature" (*kyana*), "hypostasis" (*qnoma*), and "person" (*parṣopa*). Through definitions, arguments, and analogies, he argues that affirming two natures in Christ necessitates affirming two hypostases. He also explains how two hypostases can coexist in the one person of Christ. For additional excerpts from Babai, see chapter 6.

> On the distinction between hypostasis and person, and how person is assumed, but hypostasis is not.
>
> A unique essence is termed hypostasis, subsisting in its sole being, in number just one, and separate from the many, but not in that it is something combined together: rather, in the case of those who are made, rational, and free, the hypostasis is receptive to various accidents, such as of virtue or vice, of knowledge or ignorance, while in the case of the irrational, here, too, hypostasis is receptive to various accidents, whether in the combining of opposite characteristics or in some other way. As I have said, these accidents are not created and made alone, for hypostasis is firmly fixed in the disposition of its nature, and a hypostasis is contained under its own species and nature together with any number of its co-hypostases, but it is distinct from these co-hypostases by the unique property it possesses in its person—for example, of Gabriel and not Michael, of Paul and not Peter. Yet the whole common nature is recognizable in each and every hypostasis, and what the one nature that contains the hypostases in common is can be recognized conceptually, whether of human beings or something else, but hypostasis does not contain what is common.
>
> Person is also a property of any hypostasis that distinguishes it from others, as Paul's hypostasis is not Peter's, even though they are equal in terms of nature and hypostasis, since both of them possess bodies and a soul, are living, rational, and corporeal, but in person each is distinct from the other in the unique individuality that each one possesses, whether in age, appearance, temperament, wisdom, position of authority, being a father, a son, male, female, or in some other way that distinguishes and demonstrates the unique, individual property of this one as opposed to that one, and that one as opposed to this one, even if they are equal in terms of nature, since the category "person" makes a distinction by virtue of the unique property that this hypostasis, which is not that one, possesses. [. . .]

Just as the natures have been combined in one person, their names, too, are combined in what a single person is called. In this unity of the single person of Christ, which is in the single connection of divinity and humanity, they are not far removed from each other in nature, power, authority, honor, lordship, or reverence due, but the natures are kept separate, with no mix-up, forever. But this one person is common to two combined hypostases—that is, that of God the Word and of his temple—but not of the whole trinity, even if they are one in nature, will, power, authority, and lordship. For God the Word, it is said, became flesh, and God sent his Son in the image of flesh and the image of God: that is, God the Word, one of the hypostases of the Trinity, assumed the image of a slave, one of the hypostases of human beings, the human Jesus Christ. [. . .]

Those who say there are two natures in Christ without at the same time connecting the two hypostases in one person belittle this right confession of God's plan, since the person is common to God the Word and his temple, which is the second human being, and is one of the hypostases of human beings. What is combined is God the Word, one of the hypostases of the Trinity, by the single combined connection of the two natures in their hypostases in a single kind of being, a Son. For not all human hypostases are with God the Word, the single, unique Son. Nor are the Father or the Holy Spirit called human being, in terms of person, along with our humanity, but rather God the Word with his temple, in the single unity in one common person, and they give and take names mutually, which is why the fathers called this unity of person natural and hypostatic, so we can say that the natures in their hypostases—and not the natures apart from their hypostases—are recognized in this single person of Christ, the Son of God, and actually, using the names Christ and Son, from their unity and beyond, makes known two natures and two hypostases in one person, since natures are recognizable in the hypostases that are under them, as we have said in the previous sections. [. . .]

We have learned and believed and continue to hold that there is a unity of the two natures, that is, of the two hypostases, the image of God and the image of the slave, of the temple and its resident, in a single connection, in a single name, in a single power, in single reverence, with the two properties of the hypostases kept without mixture, that of the divinity of Christ and that of his humanity, in the person of being a Son. (Those who have kept the Lord's commands together with the right confession are truly alive.)

How this can be is unsearchable and impossible to reason out: how the limitless is in the limited, the forever with the temporal, and one whom no one has ever seen nor is able to see, and dwells in blissful light that no one can approach, has come to this wonderful descent, that he might be a single Son in a single connection and unity distinct in kind, together with his humanity, which is a nature that feels, is created, and made, which he exalted and applied to his person, so that we might be honored, worshipped, and praised along with him, and possess everything of divinity except his nature! Who knows all this as it really is? How can this miracle that cannot be reasoned out be described as it is, this wonder that is unsearchable, that a human being should be with God the Word, the single, unique Son of God, in one person? For this mystery is ungraspable and impossible to reason out. [. . .]

God the Word does not, in terms of nature, have two natural persons, so that there are two sons, so that a human is not said to be two animals. It is impossible for a hypostasis to have two natural persons in terms of nature, as nasty people nonsensically say. Look, it has been demonstrated that one person can belong to two hypostases, but that two natural and hypostatic persons can belong to one natural hypostasis? This is impossible, that the hypostasis of God the Word together with its person should be one hypostasis with the human hypostasis and its person.

Divinity is in this: three hypostases in one nature. Many human beings, too, are one nature. Further, Christ is of two natures and two hypostases in one person: this is God's plan and true, as has been demonstrated. For it is not that the one who took up and the one taken up have sonship separately, otherwise there would be two sons. Rather, sonship belongs to the humanity of the Son together with God the Word, who is the forever Son, who exalted and applied the human Son to his person: they have a connection and partnership together, in a single unity, in a single name of being a Son, in single praise and authority, never combined with the Father and never combined with the Holy Spirit. And there are not two sons, as the human Son, too, is not two, with two persons: one who is named in terms of unity and, in his natural limitlessness, is in heaven, and one who is a descendant of David and Abraham, who was handed over to the nations, who treated him derisively, crucified him, and he died in weakness, and rose with God's power that was in him, as it is said, "to hand over the human Son" and "destroy this temple, and I will raise it back up in three days."

The person of Christ, Son of God, is one in his divinity and his humanity, and he is one person, the Son of the most high, the Lord, Jesus, the unique, firstborn human Son, Christ. The two natures are recognizable in this one person, which is the one Christ, Son of God, and the names, while distinguished by the properties of their hypostases are combined with no mix-up, and while combined with no mix-up, are distinguished in their properties, in the single unity of the one person of Christ, Son of God forever.

GEORGE OF RESH'AYNA, *LIFE OF MAXIMUS THE CONFESSOR*

Mid-seventh century. Maronite.

Maximus the Confessor (d. 662) was a prolific Greek author, a brilliant theologian, and an ardent defender of the dyophysite (two-nature) Christology of the Council of Chalcedon. He rejected monotheletism, insisting instead that Christ had both a human and a divine will (i.e., dyotheletism). Monotheletism was in favor with both the emperor (first Heraclius and then Constans II) and the patriarch of Constantinople. For his resistance, Maximus was imprisoned, tried, and tortured: he had his tongue cut out and his right hand cut off, and he died shortly thereafter. He was vindicated at the Third Council of Constantinople in 681, which condemned monotheletism and defined Christ as having two wills, human and divine. This biography of Maximus, written by the monothelete George Resh'ayna sometime between 662 and 680, is an "antihagiography" meant to discredit him, as is clear from the text's title, "The Narrative Concerning the Wicked Maximus of Palestine, Who Blasphemed against His Creator and His Tongue Was Cut

Out." Notice how the author says that Maximus was essentially a "Nestorian," and that God punished the lands that accepted Maximus's error (dyotheletism) by means of the Arabs. The Arabs' conquest of Roman North Africa and the islands of the Mediterranean is thereby interpreted as God's retribution for Maximus's heresy. The one surviving copy of this text breaks off before the story's end so we do not know how the work originally concluded.

This Maximus was from the village of Ḥeṣfin, for it was there that this bitter tare was born, his father being a Samaritan from Sychar, while his mother was a Persian, the slave girl of a certain Jew named Zadok from the town of Tiberias. Now, the father of this Maximus used to go and sell his work in Tiberias—he was a maker of linen and he sold luxurious goods—and when he was in Tiberias, next door to the house of Zadok, he committed adultery with the Persian slave girl, for she was very pretty. And when she became pregnant, she told him on the next occasion that he came to sell his work: "Either ransom me from my master before he notices my state and disgraces me or I will inform on you at once, and they will seize you and you will become an object of ridicule and scorn; for I am certainly pregnant." He, being placed in an awkward position, took two hundred darics and ransomed her from Zadok her master.

When his relatives and fellow Samaritans saw what he had done, they were in great consternation, and they all met together and told him, "Either allow us to burn this pregnant woman in order to remove the disgrace from us and our people, or we will expel you from our community." But he was unwilling to consent to them in this, saying, "Although I agree to do what you want, I shall not carry it out today." They, however, were plotting to kill him and the girl with him, secretly; but when he learnt of their plot against him, he made his escape by night, taking her with him. He arrived at the above-mentioned village of Ḥeṣfin and entered it, going to the house of a priest called Martyrius. He stayed with him for two years, and he and his wife were secretly baptized by him, Maximus's father receiving the name Theonas instead of Abna, and his mother the name Mary instead of Šndh—for that was her name in Persian. Now this Martyrius who baptized them was the son of the maternal uncle of Gennadius, the governor who was at that time in charge of Tiberias and all the surrounding area, and it was through his authority that [Martyrius] escaped any punishment from the Samaritan people.

When this fruit of wickedness [i.e., Maximus] was born, this priest Martyrius gave him the name of Moschion at baptism. The priest Martyrius also gave his parents a place in Ḥeṣfin, settling them near himself, on church property. Nine years later his father died of dropsy, leaving his children to the priest Martyrius to act as guardian to them. His mother also died a year after her husband, as a result of a fall from a pomegranate bush, leaving behind three children in all, two boys and one girl. His sister fell into the grate of a hearth and was badly burned, as the result of which she died.

The priest Martyrius took Moschion to the monastery of Palaia Lavra, where the abbot Pantoleon received him. His younger brother died in this monastery, three years after Moschion's novitiate, as the result of a bite he received from a vicious camel belonging to some Easterners who were staying there; this occurred on the day of the adoration of the holy cross. Moschion's teacher Pantoleon changed his name to Maximus, after the son of

[Pantoleon's] nephew, of whom he was very fond but who had died while still a child: it was in memory of him that he gave the name to this rascal.

Now this priest Martyrius of Ḥeṣfin wrote a record about this Maximus and his father. All this was related to me by the priest Eulogius, who was closely acquainted with the affairs of the persons mentioned and who turned his back on their wicked teaching. And all this I have diligently set down—I, George from Reshʿayna, a disciple of Sophronius the bishop of Jerusalem; I have set down these records for [the benefit of] the faithful: they represent what I have seen, heard, and taken over from persons who are worthy of credence.

Now this Pantoleon poured out and filled this disciple of his Maximus with the entire bitterness of his evil teaching, finding in him a vessel capable of receiving all the foul dregs of his blasphemy. For I frequently encountered this man full of hateful things, both in disputes and in sophistic discourses, for he was full of a murderous pride, and his tongue was swift in deceitful replies; for Sophronius used to praise Maximus as someone endowed with a lofty understanding.

After his teacher the wicked Origenist Pantoleon had died, this wretch made manifest his fraud, relying henceforth on the leaders and authorities who had accepted the foul teaching of his master. Furthermore, he had the opportunity for Sophronius, who had previously been captivated by his error, to show forth his own wickedness openly: Maximus reminded Sophronius, who was in the same error, of the letter in which "Arcadius the archbishop of Cyprus showed you contempt."

Now Sophronius, in that he held a grudge against Arcadius, readily accepted all that the rascal had to say, and Maximus [then] told Sophronius: "Send and gather for me those who are in doubt about this, and I will unite them with a defense." This Sophronius at once sent a letter to Arcadius, inviting him to send to the holy Cyrus of Alexandria and to Honorius Patriarch of Rome and to Sergius Patriarch of Constantinople, [saying] that there should be a synod and gathering of bishops wherever they liked, and they should make trial of these things, saying, "It is not pleasing to the Lord that we should consume the revenues of the sheep and of the church, while there is an upheaval of dissension in our midst; why should we come to destruction on behalf of the flock that the head shepherd has entrusted to us?"

For there was disagreement and dispute between the patriarchs over this foul doctrine, and Maximus did not cease from causing trouble and disturbance until he had completely corrupted the place where he was and its whole neighborhood with his foul teaching, saying that "we should not say 'who was crucified for us' in the Trisagion." And he wrote four books, acknowledging in them two wills and two energies and two minds, acknowledging everything to do with Christ to be double, apart from the matter of the persons only.

When the holy Arcadius received the letter from Sophronius's notary and from the deacon John, who was going round the churches of Mount Sinai, and when he had read it, he did not delay from carrying this out, and he wrote off sending [letters] to the above-mentioned patriarchs. The holy Cyrus of Alexandria did not shrink from the labor of the journey but came at once without any delay to Arcadius in Cyprus, together with five bishops from his jurisdiction. Honorius sent his deacon Gaios, a virtuous man, wise in understanding and illustrious in the divine scriptures; Sergius, the chaste patriarch of Constantinople, sent to them his archdeacon Petrus. And when they [all] arrived in Cyprus, Arcadius sent to Sophronius, saying, "Come to us now, and we will make inquiry into the matters over which the church is disturbed."

When Maximus learned which bishops were there in Cyprus, he was afraid to go [himself], saying, "I cannot undertake this today, but let Anastasius, my pupil, go with you, and I will give him a book on this subject." So we set off and arrived on the island of Cyprus—I, George, and two of my pupils, together with eight other bishops from Sophronius's jurisdiction.

When we arrived, they received us with great joy and fitting honor, and on the following morning we sat down to make inquiry into this matter. After much had been said, some of the bishops were saying that "we should accept Maximus's doctrine," while others said, "No, it is pernicious"; and they decided to put this doctrine down in writing and send it to the victorious emperor Heraclius. When they had done this, they sent it by the hands of Georgius, the archdeacon of the holy Arcadius, Bishop of Cyprus, and of Leon, the deacon of the holy Cyrus of Alexandria, and of Elias, the notary of Sophronius. Now Sophronius was also afraid of the disturbance that had taken place there because of him shortly before.

Those who gathered were forty-six persons. When the letter in which Maximus's doctrine was outlined had been written, the holy Arcadius, remembering what had happened to Sophronius's letter, which had previously been sent to him, said, "Everyone who accepts this doctrine and believes it from his heart shall be anathema."

Sophronius says to him, "What then do you want—that this should reach the emperor?" Arcadius replies to him, "It is because of your lack of belief, and because of the false doctrine you and your companions hold, in that you resist the truth." The holy Cyrus of Alexandria, however, gave orders and silenced the dispute by means of a veto, saying, "We did not assemble so as to make strife, but to inquire into and uncover the truth, and to lay bare and refute error." And thus everyone left for his own city and country, awaiting the outcome of the [letter] that had been sent.

When the above-mentioned men reached the imperial city, they entered before the victorious emperor Heraclius, and the letter containing the doctrine of Sophronius and the rascal Maximus was read out in their presence, whereupon they perceived that it was alien to the entire Christian teaching. The emperor at once made a document called an "edict," and sent it to the four [patriarchal] sees. In it he rejected this despicable doctrine and ordered it to be brought to naught as being pernicious, and he laid down in the definition he made that everyone who confessed [this doctrine], or believed on such lines, should be ejected from his position.

When this order from the emperor arrived and was received by the four sees and all the bishops, they added the signatures of their agreement and anathematized everyone who added or subtracted anything. Thereupon, all who held this doctrine were in fear, and in this way there was peace until the death of the victorious emperor Heraclius, and [the doctrine] came to nothing and faded out.

Now Maximus confined himself in a small cell out of fear of the emperor and the patriarchs who had anathematized his teaching. Serving him was Anastasius his pupil, as well as his own disciple Sergius. He stayed in this cell until the Arabs appeared and took control of Syria and many other areas.

And because heresy is accustomed to join forces with paganism, and to take strength to establish itself as a result of some punishment sent, this wretch [i.e., Maximus], seeing that the land was in the control of the Arabs and there was no longer anyone to restrain and nullify his doctrine, manifested his fraudulence once again openly, and began to sow his teaching among certain individuals in the regions of Syria. And because the victorious emperor Heraclius had died, together with Constantinus his son and Heracleon and his mother, and Constans son of Constantinus, [still] a young child, had received the Roman Empire, and because Africa was in rebellion against the emperor at this time, Maximus was encouraged, and at once took Anastasius and the other brethren with him, and they went up and came to Africa.

Now Anastasius was well known in these regions, having been born there, as we mentioned before. They set off and arrived at a monastery at the upper tip of Africa, called in Latin *Hippo Diarrhytus*, where some students from Nisibis were living. The abbot of the monastery was Esha'ya, and there was his son, called Isho'. There were about eighty-seven monks there, and they were Nestorians; and when they found that Maximus and Anastasius agreed in their teaching with Nestorius their master, they received them and agreed with their doctrine. [Thus,] they led astray the whole of Africa, and there was no one who disputed with them in Africa, apart from one God-loving recluse whose name was Luke; through him they were refuted by God's might, and he immediately sent [message] about them to Constantinople. It was to this recluse that the holy Macarius, the patriarch of Antioch, addressed three books against the doctrine of Maximus.

After they had sown their tares and led astray as many as they could in Africa, even deceiving the eparch there, whose name was George, they then removed from there and came to Sicily, fear of the Arabs having disturbed them—for by their agency the wrath of God had reached the whole of Africa. And when they had made the rounds of all the islands of the sea, they then went up to Rome itself and by means of their deceitfulness even Martinus the patriarch there was ensnared, and he fully accepted his doctrine, with the result that he gathered a synod of 190 bishops to confirm the doctrine of Maximus.

And he anathematized the patriarchs of Constantinople because they had refused to agree with him. For this reason the emperor Constans was angry with him and sent for him and brought him to the imperial city, urging him to change from his pernicious doctrine. When he remained unpersuaded, [the emperor] sent him into exile to Lazika, in the time of the holy Pyrrhos, patriarch of that city, and of Macedonius of Antioch; and there he died an evil death. For it was not at Constans's orders that he became patriarch but through the fraudulence of some documents he had forged; and through the wiles of a clever man who was a *patrikios*, called Theodorus, he came down to Constantinople.

And [all] this "*rmg[]bwlqr*" [unknown name], who succeeded Theodorus the emperor's brother, told me when he came down to pray in the holy city Jerusalem, when there was peace between Mu'āwiya, the Arab amir, and the emperor Constans. And all the other things that I am about to write down concern Maximus and Anastasius and those monks who fled from Africa in the face of the Arabs and went up to Rome to the aforementioned Martinus; for I have taken great care to write down this history truthfully.

After Maximus went up to Rome, the Arabs seized control of the islands of the sea, and entered Cyprus and Arvad, ravaging them and taking [their inhabitants] captive; and they gained control over Africa and subdued virtually all the islands of the [Mediterranean]. For, following the wicked Maximus, the wrath of God punished every place that had accepted his error.

The students who had been in the monastery of Hippo Diarrhytus, which we mentioned above, fled in front of the Arabs and came up to Rome, where they were received by Martinus as having the same faith as he, and he gave them a monastery, called in the Latin tongue *Cellae novae*, which means "nine cells." And they remained in their error, leading astray all they could.

And when Maximus saw that Rome had accepted the foul mire of his blasphemies, he also went down to Constantinople at the time when Muʿāwiya made peace with the emperor Constans, having started a war with Abū Turāb, the amir of Ḥirta, at Ṣiffin, and defeated him. The emperor Constans was in Azorbaijan, and at that point Maximus entered Constantinople, hoping to corrupt it too with his deception, just as everywhere else.

Maximus immediately went and stayed at a convent of nuns called Plakidias, which was in the city; and through his wickedness he was able to lead them astray away from the truth, and he [taught] them his pernicious belief, and he [ ] in the throw[ing] of the offering of . . . [manuscript breaks off at this point].

A SYRIAC FRAGMENT ON THE SIXTH COUNCIL

Late seventh century. Maronite.

In the year 680, the emperor Constantine IV convened the Third Council of Constantinople (also known as the Sixth Ecumenical Council), which condemned monotheletism and defined Christ as having two wills, human and divine. This selection is a Syriac fragment of a report critical of that council, probably written shortly after its end in September, 681. The report is critical for reasons procedural (laymen sitting in front of bishops), political (murderous imperial intrigue), and theological. Among other things, the monotheletes argued that if Christ has a distinct will with respect to each of his two natures, then he has two moral wills, which could imply moral confusion on Christ's part.

Of it [i.e., the Synod], the laymen being inscribed before the bishops, and they were sitting in front of the bishops.

And again we find fault with it, because it named the emperor who gathered it "the new David," while, until halfway through the synod, his two brothers were sitting with him—that is to say, Heraclius and Tiberius.

These, his own brothers who were reigning with him when his synod gathered, he rose against and mutilated; and because his mother spoke to him on their behalf, he removed her from his kingdom and sent her into exile. And again, because the commanders of the forces rose up and besought him in tears, saying that he should not mutilate them and crying out, "May the years of the Christian king be many," and that "we have three kings, and a Trinity rules over us in heaven, and a Trinity rules over us on earth," [as a result of this] he seized the Patricius Leon by craft, together with eleven [army] commanders, and crucified and killed them.

Again we find fault with it, because it spoke of a will proper to each nature, which implies more than one moral will.

It is also censured because it confessed a [separate] will in the flesh of Christ, which is a sin, as all the scriptures testify.

It is also censured because it confessed that there is one [faculty] that subjects and another that is subjected, one that is master and another that is servant; one that rules by force, another that is ruled by force; one that wills and is effective, another that does not will and is not effective.

It is censured because it laid down two [faculties] that will and are active, and that strive equally for the salvation of humankind. For these and similar reasons we reject it, and do not accept it.

DIONYSIUS BAR ṢALIBI, *AGAINST THE MELKITES*

Late twelfth century. West Syrian.

Dionysius bar Ṣalibi (d. 1171) was a prolific West Syrian author and the metropolitan of Amid. Most of his surviving works are commentaries, including on the New Testament, the liturgy, Evagrius's writings, and Aristotle's logical works. *Against the Melkites* is one of his polemical works; other targets of his ire include Armenians, Jews, and Muslims. "Melkite" (from Syriac *malka*, meaning "king" or "emperor") is a pejorative name for Chalcedonians who lived outside the domain of the Roman Empire but remained loyal to imperial orthodoxy. Dionysius refers to them here as "Greeks" and "Chalcedonians." The treatise is addressed to a certain Rabban Ishoʻ, who was considering leaving or had already left the miaphysite West Syrian Church to join the Chalcedonian Church. Dionysius is replying to ʻIshoʻ's letter explaining his decision and he tries to refute it point by point. In this chapter, Dionysius refuses any attempt to blur the distinctions between the two communities and their confessions. He lays claim to the Councils of Nicaea, Constantinople, and Ephesus, but refuses "that unholy Council of Chalcedon." For an additional excerpt from Dionysius, see chapter 10.

On his hidden falsehood that has been exposed and on how he is a protagonist of the believers in two natures.

You write: "Why should we have greater truth than all? We do not agree with them in the matter of two natures, but we should not reject them and consider them as heretics."

See how this discloses your intention to favor those who differ from us in their faith. I will now ask you a question: Are the Syrians right or are they wrong? If they are wrong, why do you not reject them completely? And if they are right, why do you not reject the Chalcedonians? If you refuse to believe in two natures, you should reject also the truth of the orthodox Syrians. As light is opposed to darkness, and good health to illness, so that they are mutually repellent and cannot remain concomitantly in one place, so also the one who believes in two natures in Christ after the union is opposed to the one who believes in one nature in the Word who became flesh. You will not contradict that the two are opposed to each other, how then do you pretend that you do not believe in two natures like them and at the same time not reject them? You are like the one who holds the two ends of a rope and is unable to climb up with either of them.

You write, "Why should we not accept them? The apostle said, 'Who art thou that judgest the servant of another? To his own lord he stands or falls" [Romans 14:4]. He also said, 'Pray for one another,' and he did not say, 'anathematize.'"

Your words would have been very true, if only the Chalcedonians would listen to you. For your sake we shall compromise and accept them: but come now to Melitene, which is not under their power, and see how they tear at our people like wolves. Anyone who, through his instability and weakness, falls [and joins them], they baptize again, and they openly call us heretics and untruthful, and out of their own free will they do not allow anyone to enter their churches. I remonstrated several times with them, but because of their arrogance they did not desist. Were it not for a reason that I will not disclose and for the fact that they would have been sneered at by outsiders, I would have revealed their falsehood, and they would have been despised by all; but mendacity often succeeds.

Now repair in your imagination to the city of their pride. You will see that it contains a mosque for the Mohammedans, but it has no church for the Syrians and the Armenians. Do they do this out of their good nature or out of their wickedness? By their actions they show that the faith of the Mohammedans is better than the orthodox faith of ours.

About a hundred years ago, in the time of Ignatius of Melitene, we had a church in Constantinople but, impelled by Satan, they took possession of it and their patriarch of that time ordered our books that were in it, and the church vestry, and the holy chrism, to be burned in the middle of the bazaars. On that very night that patriarch was struck by a sudden illness and lost his life. What do you say about these? Glory be to the one who deprived them of their power! If they had the power they would not have left a single Christian alive, as their fathers did in the times of yore.

As to the quotation that you brought forth to the effect, "Who are you who judges another's servant," it has not the significance that you attribute to it, and it has not been said of the heretics. If it were, we should not be allowed to bring an accusation against the Jews and the pagans, or to reprove the immoral people and the adulterers, or to punish the criminals, the sedition mongers, the robbers, and the murderers. Will the apostle come in these cases and tell us, "Who are you that judges these who are the servants of another?" But for the tranquility of your conscience I am going to disclose for you the mind of the apostle.

The Jews who had believed in Christ used to keep also the law of Moses, and not to eat the food that that law considered to be unclean; but the Gentiles who had believed in Christ used to eat everything. A disturbance arose on this account between Jewish Christians and Christians. Paul then rose, strong in truth, against the Jews who had believed, and he maintained that food does not bring someone nearer to God or farther from him; why do you force, therefore, the Gentiles to observe the old law? And he further added, "The one that is weak eats herbs." He meant by these words that as you Jews are weak in faith you distinguish between this and that food (as a weak stomach does) with regard to herbs, but one who is strong in faith eats everything and despises distinctions between foods; "let not the one who eats not judge the Christian that eats, for God has received that one"; that is to say, he has made them to be related to him and not to the law; you, therefore, O Jew, why do you judge them? They are the servant of God, how dare you then judge them? If they stand—that is to say, by faith—they are to their Lord and not to you; and if they fall, as you believe, because they do not observe the legal distinction between the foods, they are also to their own Lord. This is in short terms the meaning of the sentence of the apostle.

As to your other point, that we are commanded to pray for one another, it does not mean that we are commanded to pray for one to go astray from the truth of the faith and walk in error; nor are we commanded to pray for this particular person in relation to that particular person, but only to pray in such general terms as: O God, call all and bring them to yourself. As to your saying "Paul did not say: anathematize;" but Paul did say, "If somebody should preach to you other than that which we preached to you, let them be anathema" [Galatians 1:8]. What answer do you want us now to give to Paul? He said, "Let them be anathema," and you say that we should not anathematize.

Three hundred and eighteen bishops assembled once [at Nicaea] and defined the catholic faith in the Father and the Son and reached in the creed as far as the passage, "And in the Holy Spirit," and they anathematized Arius and Sabellius. Then one hundred and fifty others gathered together in Constantinople, completed the creed, and said, "And in one Holy Spirit the Lord and vivifier of all, who proceeds from the Father," and so on, till the end of the creed; and they anathematized the Macedonians. Then again, two hundred and fifty bishops assembled at Ephesus in the time of the emperor Theodosius and of the patriarch Cyril, but they did not write a new profession of faith nor did they add anything to the creed in one God, but they said that the faith of the two previous councils was sufficient; and they enacted in the synod a canon of anathemas and curses against anyone who would introduce a new faith, or would add anything to it, or diminish anything from it; and after anathematizing Nestorius and his teachers, they went back.

Then, after a time, the emperor Marcian assembled that unholy Council of Chalcedon. The fathers of it, however, did not follow in the steps of the fathers who had preceded them, but through the pressure brought upon them by the wicked emperor and by his accursed wife, Pulcheria, and by other heretics who were present there, such as Theodoret, they trespassed against the anathema of the Council of Ephesus, and wrote a new creed, which begins: "We believe in the Father, in the Son, and in the Holy Spirit, and in the incarnation of the Son." They thus made the Trinity a quaternity; and then they defined the two natures.

Now, if the Greeks are anathematized, it is the fathers of the first council who anathematize them; what blame then attaches to us from it? Where did you hear in the faith of the ancients the mention of the two natures, which the Greeks have added? And so on.

PART II

PRACTICES

4

LITURGY

More Syriac manuscript copies of liturgical works survive than that of any other genre. This should not be surprising. In their everyday lives, Syriac Christians needed liturgical texts more often than other documents. Whether for regularly scheduled rituals, such as prayers, Sunday services, and feast days, or for occasional rituals, such as baptisms, funerals, and even exorcisms, liturgical manuscripts were in constant use. As a result, these works provide a window into the day-to-day practices of what it meant to be a Syriac Christian.

Discussions of liturgy took place in a variety of formats: manuals listing how to conduct a given ceremony, canon laws specifying what is ritually permissible, narratives describing a ritual performance, liturgical commentaries deliberating symbolic meaning, lectionaries excerpting biblical passages to be read during a service, as well as calendars, prayers, hymnals, and homilies. These sources show how Syriac worship had strong connections with that of other churches, especially the Byzantine church. Ancient Syriac texts, such as the *Acts of Thomas* (found in this chapter) or the *Odes of Solomon* (found in chapter 2), even provide some of our earliest witnesses to Christian rituals in any language making them especially valuable for the history of Christian liturgy more generally.

But the various Syriac churches also developed ritual forms that varied from non-Syriac churches and from each other. Such differences reified confessional boundaries and became important identity markers. In other words, at the same time the liturgy helped unify a given community, it also was a frequent subject of intra-Christian contention. So, too, liturgical development held in creative tension innovation and conservatism. On the one hand, each church had moments of profound change: seventh-century liturgical reforms in the East Syrian Church, West Syrian Christians adopting and modifying the Byzantine eight-tone system for their music, the adoption of Arabic in Chalcedonian worship, the Roman Church's effect on the Maronites. On the other hand, the Syriac churches are remarkable in their preservation of ancient traditions. One can walk into a modern Syriac church and still hear the chanting of hymns originally written in the fourth century or attend a Eucharist that still follows a fifth-century service order.

The sheer number and complexity of Syriac liturgical texts prevents a few excepts from providing anything close to a representative sampling. Instead, these selections try to illustrate various ways liturgy matters—how it mattered for early Syriac Christians and how it matters for modern historians trying to better understand the everyday dynamics of Syriac Christianity. The first six texts focus on the Christian initiation ritual of baptism. They range in genre from service orders to canon laws to one of the earliest surviving exorcism manuals. Together they show how baptismal practice could both reflect and affect topics such as women's role in the clergy, intra-Christian polemic, and interactions with Islam. The next two texts consist of complete Eucharistic service orders (anaphoras), one the oldest surviving example, the other from the thirteenth century. This section also contains images of the archaeological remains from late ancient basilica, helping one visualize where Syriac liturgy often took place. The final excerpt focuses on one of the less studied Christian rituals, in this case coming from a recently published Syriac funerary manual found in western China reminding one of the distance Syriac liturgical texts traveled and the breadth of their influence.

Further Reading Few published works on Syriac liturgy are in English. For those who can read French, German, or Latin, consult the bibliography by Sebastian Brock. See "Syriac Liturgy," syri.ac, http://syri.ac/brock/liturgy. This should be supplemented by more recent items in Baby Varghese "The Liturgies of the Syriac Churches" in Daniel King, ed., *The Syriac World* (New York: Routledge, 2018), 402–4. In terms of primary source material translated into English, a large collection of ancient anaphoras currently used by the Syrian Orthodox Church can be easily accessed at "Anaphoras: The Book of the Divine Liturgies," trans. Archdeacon Murad Saliba Barsom, ed. Metropolitan Mar Athanasius Yeshue Samuel, Syriac Orthodox Resources, http://syriacorthodoxresources.org/Liturgy/Anaphora/. For a particularly intriguing example of East Syrian liturgy, see Erica Hunter and J. F. Coakley, *A Syriac Service-Book from Turfan* (Turnhout: Brepols, 2017). This introduces and translates an entire liturgical manuscript used by East Syrian Christians in ninth-century China. For English language publications that are especially attentive to the theology embodied in Syriac liturgies, see Sebastian P. Brock, *Fire from Heaven* (London: Variorum Reprints, 2006); Sebastian P. Brock, *The Holy Spirit in the Syrian Baptismal Tradition* (Piscataway, NJ: Gorgias Press, 2008); R. H. Connolly, *The Liturgical Homilies of* Narsai (Cambridge: Cambridge University Press, 1909); Baby Varghese, *West Syrian Liturgical Theology* (London: Ashgate, 2004).

ACTS OF THOMAS

Third century. Originally in Syriac; translation from the Greek version.

In the second and third centuries, Christians wrote a number of accounts about Jesus's earliest apostles that modern scholars often call the "apocryphal acts of the apostles." Particularly popular were the *Acts of Thomas* in which Jesus's apostle Thomas evangelizes India. Although this text was originally written in Syriac, the Greek manuscript tradition often better preserves the original story. This text includes some of the earliest surviving literary depictions of Christian liturgy that, though set in the first century, likely reflect (however imperfectly) third-century practices. The following descriptions of prayer, baptism, and the Eucharist come from a scene where Thomas baptizes the Indian prince Vizan, his wife Manashar, and the king's wife Tertia. The ritual participation of the woman Mygdonia is similar to how the next excerpt appearing in this chapter (*Didascalia*) describes the role of a deaconess. For additional excerpts from the *Acts of Thomas*, see chapters 1 and 4.

> While they were conversing, Judas [Thomas], along with Sifor, his wife and daughter, Tertia, Mygdonia, and Narkia, came to Vizan's house. When Vizan's wife, Manashar, saw him, she did obeisance and said, "Have you come to be our savior from the troublesome disease? You're the one I saw in the night giving this youth to lead me to the prison; your gentleness didn't let me grow weary, and you yourself came to me."
>
> After speaking, she turned around and saw the youth no longer. When she did not find him, she said to the apostle: "I'm unable to walk by myself; the youth you gave me isn't here." Judas said, "Hereafter Jesus will lead you by the hand." Then she came to him at a run. When they entered the house of Vizan, the son of Mizdai the king, though it was still night, abundant light surrounded and shone on them. Then Judas began to pray, saying:

"Friend and ally, hope of the sick, confidence of the humble,
  Refuge and lodging of those who have fallen asleep,
Voice come from on high,
  Consoler who dwells in the midst,
Lodging and harbor of those
  Who go through the rulers' realms,
  Physician who accepts no pay;
You who were crucified by men on behalf of many,
  You are he who descended into Hades with great power;
You, whose sight the powers of death could not bear,
  You ascended with great glory,
  Leading all who have taken refuge in you.
You prepared for them a way,
  And all those you liberated followed in your footsteps.
Bringing them into your own flock,
  You mingled them with your sheep.

Son of mercies, you who were sent to us
>   From the perfect fatherland above;
> Lord of all possessions, who enslave your servants
>   So that they might live;
> You who fill creation with your own wealth,
>   You who became needy and fasted for forty days,
>   You who satisfy souls thirsty for your goods:
> Be with Vizan, the son of Mizdai, and Tertia and Manashar,
>   Gather them to your fold
>   And include them in your number.
> Be their guide in a place of error,
>   Be their physician in a place of illness.
> Be their rest in a place of weary people.
>   Sanctify them in an unclean place.
> Be the physician of their bodies and souls.
>   Make them your holy temples,
>   And let your holy spirit dwell in them."

After he prayed in this way, the apostle said to Mygdonia, "Undress your sisters." She undressed them, tied loincloths around them, and led them in. Vizan had entered first and they came after him. Judas took oil in a silver vessel and made this invocation over it:

"O fruit more beautiful than the other fruits,
>   To which no other fruit can be compared;
> Altogether merciful one,
>   Heated by the force of the word;
> Power of the wood,
>   Clothed with which people overcome their adversaries;
> You who crown the victors,
>   Symbol and joy of those who are weary;
> You who proclaimed to people their salvation,
>   You who showed forth light in darkness;
> You whose leaves are bitter,
>   But who are well formed with fruit most sweet;
> You who are rough to the sight, but smooth to the taste,
>   You who seem to be weak, but in an abundance of power
>   Bear the power that contemplates all things!"

After saying this, he added, "Jesus, let your victorious power come and let it be established in this oil, as your power was established in the wood akin to you, the power whose word those who crucified you could not endure. Therefore, let the gift come, through which you breathed on your enemies and made them retreat and fall prone, and may it dwell in this oil on which we invoke your holy name."

When he had said all this, he poured [oil] first on the head of Vizan, then on the heads of the women, saying, "In your name, Jesus Christ, may it become for these people remission of sins, defense from the hostile one, and salvation for their souls." He ordered Mygdonia to anoint the women, but he himself anointed Vizan. When he finished the anointing he led them down to the water in the name of the Father, Son, and Holy Spirit. When they emerged, he took bread and a cup, blessed them, and said,

"We eat your holy body that was crucified for us,
   And we drink for our salvation your blood
   That was shed for us.
Therefore, let your body become our salvation
   And your blood produce remission of sins.
In return for the gall that you drank on our account,
   Let the gall of the devil be removed from us.
In return for the vinegar that you drank for us,
   Let our weakness be empowered.
In return for the spittle that you received on our account,
   May we receive the dew of your beneficence.
By the reed with which they beat you on our account,
   May we receive the perfect dwelling.
Because you received a crown of thorns on our account,
   May we who love you put on an unfading crown.
In return for the shroud in which you were wrapped,
   Let us gird ourselves with your unconquerable power.
In return for the new tomb and the burial,
   May we receive renewal of soul and body.
Because you arose and came back to life,
   May we arise to life
   And stand before you in just judgment."

He broke the eucharistic bread and gave it to Vizan, Tertia, Manashar, and Sifor's wife and daughter and said, "May this Eucharist bring you salvation, joy, and health of soul." And they said, "Amen." Then a voice was heard saying, "Amen. Fear not, but only believe."

DIDASCALIA

Third century. Originally in Greek; translation from the Syriac version.

The *Didascalia* is one of many surviving early Christian documents that appropriate apostolic authority to forward their author's vision for how the church should be structured and run. The *Didascalia* claims to have been written by Jesus's twelve apostles (and Paul). But, in reality, its true author was almost certainly an anonymous third-century Christian. Although originally composed in Greek, only a few Greek fragments have been preserved. By contrast, it was immensely popular among Syriac Christians, and dozens of Syriac manuscripts contain a complete copy of this lengthy text. Amid topics ranging from heresy to sexual ethics to the relationship with Judaism appear several discussions of early Christian rituals. The following excerpt focuses on the role of a deaconess in the baptism of women. But it also discusses other duties performed by this female member of the clergy. For an additional excerpt from the *Didascalia*, see chapter 10.

> Therefore, bishop, you should appoint yourself righteous workers and helpers to help bring your people to [eternal] life. You may choose and appoint as deacons whomever you like from all the people: a man to take care of numerous necessities, and a woman for the service of the women. For there are houses where you cannot send a deacon to the women, because of pagans, but do send deaconesses. The office of a woman deaconess is also necessary for many other reasons. First, when women have gone down into the water, those who have gone down into the water must be anointed with anointing oil by deaconesses. Where no woman is present, particularly a deaconess, the one who baptizes must anoint the woman being baptized. But where there is a woman, particularly a deaconess, it is not right for women to be seen by men. Rather, at the laying-on of hands, anoint only the head. Just as previously the priests and kings of Israel were anointed through the laying-on of hands, in the very same way you should also anoint the head of whoever receives baptism, whether men or women. And afterward, whether you yourself are baptizing or whether you command deacons or priests to baptize, as we just said, let a woman deaconess anoint the women. But a man should mention the names of the divine invocation over them, over the water. And when the woman being baptized has come up from the water, the deaconess will receive, teach, and educate her so that the seal of baptism will be unbroken in chastity and holiness. Therefore, we say that the ministry of a woman deaconess is urgent and necessary. For our Lord and savior was also served by women deaconesses—that is, Mary Magdalene, Mary the daughter of Jacob, the mother of Jose, and the mother of the Sons of Zebedee, along with other women. You also need the deaconess' ministry for many things. In the houses of pagans where there are Christian women, the deaconess is needed to enter and visit those who are sick, to serve them however they need, and to wash those who have begun to recover from their sickness.

CHALCEDONIAN ORDER FOR EMERGENCY BAPTISM OF A CHILD

Before the thirteenth century. Chalcedonian.

Most surviving Chalcedonian liturgical texts are in Greek. An important exception is a Syriac manuscript now found in the British Library, most likely from the twelfth or thirteenth century. It preserves a particularly old form of the Chalcedonian baptismal liturgy and is especially notable for including a shortened version of the baptismal rite designed for an infant who might otherwise die unbaptized. As, for expediency's sake, a purposefully condensed version, it illustrates those parts of the ritual Chalcedonian Christians found most essential.

> The order for the short baptismal [service], in cases of need, when a child is in danger after seven days from birth.

They bring [the child] to the priest and he seals the child with the cross, saying, "_____ is signed to the glory of God the Father, and to the knowledge of the only begotten Son, and to the worship of the Spirit of holiness, amen."

Then the priest prays the prayer of incense: this is written in the long baptismal service.

Then he prays as follows: "Blessed is your holy, glorious, and exalted name, O Lord God, merciful and pitying—you who sent, in your grace and great mercy, the Lord your Christ, for the life and salvation of all humankind. He came and chose for himself twelve men, valiant and just, and showed them the mystery of holy baptism. Everyone who believes in it and is baptized lives, while everyone who does not believe is judged. I, too, have received [the tradition] and I beseech you, O Lord God, Lord of all, and our Lord Jesus Christ, your Son and your beloved one."

Here the priest bends over the water and blows on it, saying gently, "May your Spirit, living and holy, be sent, and may it come and dwell and rest and reside on this water, and sanctify it, and make it like the water that flowed from your side on your cross."

He raises his voice, "And may this water be a sprinkling and purification, and a beneficial healing and forgiveness of sins for this your servant standing [here] now and being baptized in it. And sanctify them in their soul and in their body and in their spirit, and may they become a new child, and a holy one, unto eternal life; and cause them to share in your holy body and blood, so that they may receive from them propitiation of faults and forgiveness of sins, unto eternal life."

Then the priest casts the holy oil on the water, signing it with the cross and saying "Halleluiah" three times, saying, "This water is sanctified in the name of the Father and the Son [and the Holy Spirit]."

Here the priest anoints and baptizes [the child]. And then he gives [the child] the holy mysteries [of the Eucharist], and prays this prayer over [the child]: "The God who has been pleased to choose you for adoption, and who puts on you his living sign and has mingled you among the sheep of his flock, and put on your head the helmet of salvation, and who puts the sword of salvation in your right hand—may he make you worthy of his heavenly reward, that the conduct of your life may be in peace, and may he, who has shown us the holy mystery of baptism by his baptism in the Jordan, give you a portion, a lot, and an inheritance, and life in the kingdom of heaven, now and always."

End of the short service.

TESTAMENT OF OUR LORD

Fourth or fifth century. Originally in Greek; translation from the Syriac version.

Although originally written in Greek, the *Testament of Our Lord* appears in multiple Syriac manuscripts. It claims to come from Jesus himself. The text was actually written in the fourth or fifth century. Nevertheless, much of its content comes from a third-century ritual manual known as the *Apostolic Tradition*. The *Testament of Our Lord* eventually became part of a large West Syrian collection of ritual instructions, council decisions, letters, and canon law known as the *Synodicon*. The following excerpt begins with a discussion of catechumens, those who wish to join the Christian community but have not yet been baptized. It continues to specify their preparation for baptism, provides one of the longest early Christian discussions of exorcism, and concludes with the candidates' baptism.

Should any catechumens be apprehended because of my name and be sentenced to torture, they should hasten and press on to be baptized. The shepherd is not to hesitate in this matter but is to confer baptism. But if any are violently killed before receiving baptism, be not anxious about them because they were justified by being baptized in their own blood.

May all those selected to be baptized be examined beforehand as to their way of life while still under instruction, whether they have respected widows, visited the sick, walked in all humility and love; whether they have shown themselves to be steadfast in doing good works. Also to be presented is the testimony of those who brought them.

Each day, after hearing the gospel, they are to receive the laying-on of hands.

From the day on which they were selected for baptism, they are to be exorcised. Let them be baptized on the day of the Pasch [i.e., Easter]. When these days approach, the bishop is to exorcise each individually so that he might be persuaded that each is clean. Should it happen that someone is not clean or is possessed by an unclean spirit, that person is to be convicted by that impure spirit.

Those discovered to be restrained by such an impediment are to be removed from among the candidates, and since the evil and foreign spirit still dwells within, they should be reproached and censured for not having faithfully heard what was commanded and advised.

Those to be baptized are to be instructed to wash themselves and to cleanse their heads only on Thursday of the last week.

Should a woman be menstruous, she may also choose another day on which to bathe herself and wash beforehand.

They are to fast on Friday and on Saturday.

On Saturday the bishop is to gather together those who will be baptized and, as the deacon proclaims, he tells them to kneel. After a short period of silence he lays his hand on them and gives the exorcism.

"O God of heaven, God of the stars, God of the archangels who are subject to you, O God of the angels who are under your power, O king of glories and dominions, O God of the holy ones, the Father of our Lord Jesus Christ, you have freed the souls that were confined by death. Through the nailing on the cross of your suffering and only begotten Son you have enlightened those who were enclosed and pinned down by the darkness. You have broken our bonds and removed our burdens [and] you [have] warded off from us Satan's hostile attack. O Son and Word of God, by your death you made us immortal, by your glory you glorified us, by your passion you dissolved all the bonds of our sins, by your cross you bore the curse of our sins, and by your resurrection you taught that we pass from being human to being divine. You have taken upon yourself our misfortune. For us you have laid out the path to heaven, and from corruptibility to incorruptibility you changed us. Lord, hear me. To you I cry out with pain and fear. Lord God and Father of our Lord Jesus Christ—before whom stand the holy power of the archangels, the cherubim, the innumerable armies of princes and of seraphim—your veil is the light, and before your face the fire burns; the throne of your glory is ineffable, and ineffable are the dwellings of your delights that you have prepared for your holy ones, whose covering and riches are visible only to your holy angels. All things tremble before you. Together they praise you. Your glance measures out the mountains, and your name, when spoken, divides the depths. The heavens, contained in our hand, hide you. Before you the heavens and the earth tremble together; the sea and the animals within it are moved. The untamed beast, trembling, turns to you. Through you the mountains and the earth's firmament melt out of fear; due to your power the wind of winter trembles and quakes. Because of you the angry winds keep within their defined limits. [. . .] Lord, hear me and breathe the spirit of peace upon these your servants so that protected by you they may produce through you the gifts of faith, strength, wisdom, purity, self-discipline, patience, hope, unity, modesty, and praise because in the name of Jesus Christ you have called them to be your servants when they are baptized in the Trinity, in the name of the Father and the Son and the Holy Spirit, with as witnesses the angels, the glories, the dominions, and the whole heavenly army. Lord, as the foundation of our life and of theirs, guard their hearts, O God, because you are strong and wonderful forever."

All the people and priests are to say, "Amen. So be it. So be it. So be it."

If, while the bishop is performing the exorcism, someone becomes excited, suddenly jumps up, and cries out, or shouts violently, or foams at the mouth, or gnashes the teeth, or shamelessly stares, or is lifted up or simply runs away, being quickly carried off, the deacons are to isolate such a person so that there be no commotion while the bishop is speaking. Those acting in this way are to be exorcised by the priests till they are made clean; then they are baptized.

After the priest has exorcised those who were brought near or who were found to be unclean, he is to breathe upon them, sign them on the forehead, on the nose, on the chest, on the ears, and so may he raise them up.

During the forty days of the Pasch [i.e., during Lent] the people are to remain in the church, keeping vigil, praying, listening to the scriptures, to hymns, and to doctrinal instruction.

On the last Saturday the faithful are to rise early in the night when the catechumens are being exorcised, till the middle of the night on the same Saturday.

The baptismal candidates are to bring nothing with them other than one loaf of bread for the Eucharist.

This is how they are to be baptized when they approach the water, which should be pure and flowing; first the children, then the men, and then the women.

If anyone wishes to make a vow of virginity to God, this person is the first to be baptized by the bishop.

Women are to loosen their hair for baptism.

All the children who can respond while being baptized do so, repeating the words after the priest; but if they are unable to do this, then their parents or some family member reply on their behalf.

When, after their response, those to be baptized go down into the water, the bishop is to see to it that no man is wearing a ring, that no woman has a gold ornament on her, for no one is to have any foreign object on him or her while in the water; such is to be handed over to those standing close-by.

When the candidates are about to be signed with the oil for the anointing, the bishop is to pray over the oil and give thanks. He is also to exorcise another oil for the catechumens. A deacon carries the exorcised oil, with a presbyter standing near him. Whoever stands near the oil over which praise has been given is to be on the right; whoever stands near the oil that has been exorcised is to be on the left.

When the bishop takes hold of each of those to be baptized—they are facing the west—the bishop says, "You are to say, 'I renounce you, Satan, all your service, all your pretext, all your desires, all your works,'" and, after the candidate has said and professed this, he or she is to be anointed with the oil of exorcism while the bishop who does the anointing says, "I anoint you with this oil so that you be free from every evil and impure spirit, that you be free from all evil."

The bishop turns the candidate toward the east and says, "You are to say, 'I submit to you, Father, Son, and Holy Spirit, before whom all nature trembles and quakes; grant that I might without sin do all that you desire.'"

The bishop is then to hand over this person to the presbyter who baptizes.

Those to be baptized stand naked in the water. A deacon is to descend in like manner with these candidates.

And when those to be baptized have gone down in the water, the one baptizing places his hand upon each of them and says, "Do you believe in God, the almighty Father?" and the person to be baptized says, "I do believe." Immediately, each is baptized a first time. Then the priest says, "Do you believe in Jesus Christ, the Son of God, who came from the Father, who from the beginning is with the Father, who through the Holy Spirit was born of Virgin Mary, who was crucified under Pontius Pilate, who died, who rose from the dead with new life on the third day, who ascended into heaven, who sits at the right hand of the Father, and who will come to judge the living and the dead?" The candidate, having responded, "I do believe," is then baptized a second time. Then the one baptizing is to say, "Do you believe in the Holy Spirit, in the holy church?" and the candidate, having responded, "I do believe," is baptized a third time.

When the newly baptized come up out of the water, they are anointed by the presbyter with the oil over which the thanksgiving was given. He says, "I anoint you with oil in the name of Jesus Christ."

Women are to be anointed by the widows who sit in the front during the gathering, doing so while the presbyter recites over them the formula. These widows, during the baptism, under a veil, are to receive them with a veil while the bishop says the profession and also the things that are renounced.

When they have gathered again in the church, the bishop places his hand upon each of them and says the following:

"Lord God, through your beloved Son Jesus Christ you filled your holy apostles with your Holy Spirit. Through this same Spirit you allowed your holy prophets to speak. You made these your servants worthy to merit through Christ the forgiveness of sins through the washing of regeneration, and you washed away from them all mist of error and the darkness of infidelity. Through your goodness make them worthy to be filled with your

FIGURE 4.
Syriac incantation bowl. Magical bowls from late antiquity have been found in several dialects and scripts of Aramaic, including Jewish Babylonian Aramaic using the square script, Mandaic using the Mandaic script, and Syriac using the Estrangela script or another script that has been called "proto-Manichaean." This bowl was unearthed in the Diyala region in 1976. Here the bowl's inscription is in Syriac and uses Estrangela script, the oldest script that Christians used to write Syriac. Despite the prominent and relatively uncommon cross imagery in this bowl, scholars continue to debate which, if any, of the Syriac incantation bowls were actually made by Christians. Magical bowls such as this feature incantations that sought to protect the possessor and their household from demonic influences. They thus provide an important witness to popular religious and magical practices in the late antique Near East, as well as important data about the development of the Aramaic language. The writing in this bowl moves outwards in a clockwise direction. Markku Haverinen, National Museum of Finland.

Holy Spirit. Grant them your grace so that, O God, they might truly serve you according to your will. In holiness may they fulfill your commands so that at all times, doing the things that please you, they might enter your eternal tabernacles through you and through your beloved Son Jesus Christ, through whom glory and might forever be to you with the Holy Spirit."

Likewise the bishop, pouring the oil and placing his hand upon the head of the recently baptized, says, "Anointing, I anoint you in the all-powerful God, in Christ Jesus, and in the Holy Spirit, so that you be a worker having perfect faith and a vessel pleasing to him." Signing the person on the forehead, the bishop gives him or her the peace, saying, "May the God of the humble be with you." The person who is signed responds, "And with your spirit." This the bishop does for each individual.

Henceforth, the recently baptized are to pray with the whole assembly.

LIFE OF RABBAN HORMIZD

Eighth century or later. East Syrian.

This long hagiographic text often focuses on conflicts between the East Syrian ascetic Rabban Hormizd and neighboring West Syrian Christians, especially those from the West Syrian Monastery of Bezkin. In the following episode, a Muslim governor visits Hormizd hoping the holy man might cure his son. The son's death in transit forces Rabban Hormizd to up his ante, and the ascetic's eventual resurrection of the youth prompts both father and son to seek baptism. An argument over which Syriac church has the true baptism is then resolved by the seventh-century equivalent of a science fair experiment premised on the widespread Christian belief that one should never be baptized a second time. This excerpt presents a particularly vivid example of how Syriac discussions of ritual often played a prominent role in intra-Christian polemics. For an additional excerpt from the *Life of Rabban Hormizd,* see chapter 8.

> The Arab Shaiben, the son of 'Uqbe, the governor of Mosul, became sick. [. . .] His father became quite distraught over him as the doctors despaired, saying, "Our knowledge has failed [to cure] this boy's sickness. Our amir 'Uqbe, we counsel you to carry your son gently in a chariot and take him to the holy Rabban Hormizd. For when he places his right hand upon him, [your son] will be completely healed of whatever sickness he has." When the amir 'Uqbe heard these things, he ordered that they prepare a chariot for his son. He sat him in it, led out his forces with him, and left to go to holy Rabban Hormizd on Mount 'Edrai. But when they approached the village of Alqosh, [. . .] [the son] was overpowered with pain, convulsed with his sickness, and died. [. . .] The inhabitants of the town of Alqosh gathered alongside Rabban's servant Gabriel and they approached 'Uqbe, saying to him: [. . .] "Our good amir, do not be disturbed, for we all counsel you to bring your dead son up to Rabban. By the God whom the righteous one serves, we believe he will revive your son from the dead." [. . .] Because he was a good as well as a faithful man, the amir 'Uqbe gladly listened to those believers. He immediately issued a command and they placed the dead

boy on a pack animal. ['Uqbe,] along with ten of his companions, brought him up to the blessed one. [. . .] When they reached the holy one, the governor greeted the holy one and sat by him. [. . .] And the holy one answered and commanded his servant Gabriel to bring the dead [boy] and place him before him. Gabriel did this and [Rabban Hormizd] turned toward the east and prayed to our Lord, saying, [. . .] "Shaiben, in the name of Jesus of Nazareth rise up from your state of death." At this word, his life came [back] into him. [. . .] Immediately, his eyes opened, they set him upright, and he sat up. The holy one approached him and gave him a washing [i.e., holy water] to drink and he drank. He also broke off a piece of eucharistic bread and gave it to him to eat. And as he ate and drank, everyone standing there was amazed in awe and joy. They cried out, saying, "Truly the Christians profess the truth and in purity they blamelessly worship their Lord Christ. For by the name of Jesus of Nazareth this dead [boy] was resurrected."

At this moment of joy for the Arabs and the residents of Alqosh, suddenly there fell upon them the arrival of the cursed tonsured sons of [the West Syrian monastery of] Bezkin [who came] to greet the amir and to console him at the death of his son. And behold, they saw that the governor's son had been resurrected. [. . .] They greeted the governor and blessed him. [. . .] The amir said to Rabban, [. . .] "[let me] be baptized in the name of him in whose name my son was resurrected from the dead." [. . .] The holy one said to him, "you know that I do not have here the supplies and holy elements for baptism." [. . .] Instead of the amir, John the cursed, the anathematized, tonsured abbot of Bezkin responded, saying, "My Lord amir, consider our monastery, which is prepared with all the things for baptism. You can be baptized by us just as by Rabban because our baptism and his baptism are the same." When they heard these things from John, Rabban and the crowd that had gathered there were shocked at his audacity. Rabban answered and said to the wretched John, "Wicked one it is not so. Our baptism and your baptism are not the same just as God is not [the same] as Satan and light is not [the same] as darkness. Audacious one, if you want, I will show you this with this deed."

John said to Rabban, "If, as you said, through a deed you can show me [this], then you would be true and I a liar." Rabban made the governor and all those gathered there witnesses to this. Then Rabban approached his servant Gabriel and said to him, "Quickly bring a large, bronze basin and two children who have been baptized, one the son of Nestorian [parents] and the other the son of Jacobite [parents]." Gabriel rapidly did this. Rabban poured water into the basin and sanctified it through the Holy Spirit. He placed in it the son of [Nestorian] Christians who had been baptized, and he baptized him in the font of water. But, as if in wineskins, the water—[being of] fluid nature—wonderfully and miraculously stayed on the sides of the basin. When they saw [this], they praised God. And while the water was still staying on the sides of the basin, [Rabban] took the son of the Jacobites and placed him in "the Jordan" [i.e., the baptismal font]. The water immediately surrounded the son of the Jacobites and he was baptized in the water. The crowd there was amazed and said to Rabban, "What is this amazing change in the water that we saw? Now, explain [it] to us." Rabban said to them, "That child who first descended into the water is the son of Nestorians. Because he had [already] been baptized one time, when he descended into the water of baptism the holy water fled from him, just as you saw, and did not [re]baptize him. The second child who descended for baptism was the son of Jacobites; he needed baptism.

When he descended into the water of baptism, the water surrounded and baptized him because he did not [yet] possess holy baptism, rather profane and false [baptism]. When that crowd saw this great and glorious marvel, they all glorified God, saying, "There is no true faith except the faith Rabban Hormizd, the servant of the living God, preaches." The [previously] dead and [now] resurrected Shabein first descended into the font and was baptized. After him, were baptized his father the amir 'Uqbe and, in succession, the ten Arabs, the companions of the governor, who had also believed in Rabban. And in great shame those heretics, who had previously come to tempt the governor, returned to their defiled, accursed, and barren monastery.

JOHN OF MARDIN, *CANONS*

1153. West Syrian.

In 1153, a West Syrian bishop in southeast Turkey named John of Mardin oversaw a church council that produced forty canons. Several of these discuss the proper performance of baptism and provide important evidence for Syriac ritual practice during the crusader period. But what particularly stands out is the last canon on baptism, which refers to the baptism of Muslim children. This is not a conversion ritual per se. The council carefully delineates two different rituals. For the children of Christian parents, they participate in a ritual that makes them Christian. For the children of Muslim parents, they participate in a different sort of baptism, after which they still remain Muslim. Nevertheless, at least some Muslim parents felt that such a ritual would provide a sort of spiritual protection for their children. John and his compatriots did not seem to discourage this practice but rather chose to regulate and institutionalize it.

CANON 24

On holy baptism. The holy apostles and fathers have ordered that people coming to be baptized should, on the day before, approach the bishop or the priests in charge of the admonitory service for the people to be baptized, and an admonition fitting for them to hear should be read over them, their presenter, and sponsors, from the teaching of John Chrysostom about the mysteries of baptism and being baptized, so that all the hearers know and learn the great mystery of holy baptism and what a great grace, as an adoption, they have been made worthy of in debt-propitiating baptism, and so that, even though they were children when baptized, they understand the great mystery now, and adorn their faith with acts in line with the reading they have been read.

After that, the names of all the people to be baptized should be recorded one by one in order of their lifetimes and ages, whether children of priests, leaders, or the underprivileged, without partiality, so that there is no disturbance or quarrel at the time of the baptism.

On the next day, they should come to holy baptism, the older ones standing first at the entryway to the baptismal font, with the first baptismal service being for them, and the evil one should be thrown out beyond the entryway. Then, while repeating the creed, they should enter and come to the Jordan, that is, the holy baptismal font, and mix the waters, and the baptism will be sanctified, and each one should be baptized in order, as we said above.

Anyone who attacks someone else should be excluded and banished from baptism as a nonbeliever, since the power and the gift of those first and last is one and the same.

The basin itself should be wide, and there should be plenty of water, sufficient for a person's head to be baptized, according to the rite, and it should be midway at the north side of the church, but not right at the wall.

Whoever keeps this carefully will be kept, but whoever disregards it will be liable.

CANON 25

As for the children of Muslims, we command carefully and tell you with an apostolic command that there is no divine authority for priests to baptize them together with the children of believers in our sanctified basin. Rather, they should have a different baptism, separately on another day, either before or after, with regular water, with only the service of repentance taking place, which is a hymn cycle, a chant, a repentance melody, and so on. The priest should baptize them while saying the following: "So-and-so is baptized in the name of the Lord, in the baptism of John, for the absolution of debts and the forgiveness of sins, amen." And they should anoint the person to be baptized with regular oil.

ANAPHORA OF ADDAI AND MARI

Third, fourth, or fifth century.

Dozens of Syriac Eucharist services known as anaphoras survive. The liturgical reforms attributed to the East Syrian katholikos Isho'yahb III (d. 659) reduced the official number in the East Syrian Church to three, and these three continue to be used up to the present day. The oldest Syriac anaphora is attributed to the alleged first-century missionaries, Addai and Mari. In actuality, it likely was composed between the third and fifth centuries. This short Eucharist service can be found in full below. At least in the form preserved by the oldest surviving manuscripts, the *Anaphora of Addai and Mari* differs from most other anaphoras in that it does not include any narrative explicitly connecting the Eucharist with Jesus's last supper.

> PRIEST: "Peace be with you."
> ANSWER: "And with you and your spirit."
> PRIEST: "The grace of our Lord Jesus Christ and the love of God the Father, and the fellowship of the Holy Spirit be with us all now and for ever world without end."
> ANSWER: "Amen."
> PRIEST: "Up with your minds."
> ANSWER: "They are with you, O God."

PRIEST:	"The oblation is offered to God, the Lord of all."
ANSWER:	"It is fitting and right."
THE PRIEST SAYS QUIETLY:	"Worthy of glory from every mouth and thanksgiving from every tongue is the adorable and glorious name of the Father and of the Son and of the Holy Spirit. He created the world through his grace and its inhabitants in his compassion, he saved all people through his mercy, and gave great grace to mortals. Your majesty, O Lord, a thousand heavenly beings adore; myriad myriads of angels, and ranks of spiritual beings, ministers of fire and of spirit together with the holy cherubim and seraphim glorify your name, crying out and glorifying unceasingly calling to one another and saying:"
PEOPLE:	"Holy, holy, holy, Lord God almighty, heaven and earth are full of his praises."
THE PRIEST SAYS QUIETLY:	"And with these heavenly armies we, yes we your lowly, weak, and miserable servants, Lord, give you thanks because you have brought about us a great grace that cannot be repaid. You took upon yourself our human nature in order to give us life through your divine nature; you raise us from our lowly state; you restored our fall; you restored our immortality; you forgave our debts; you justified our sinfulness; you enlightened our understanding. You, our Lord and our God, conquered our enemies and made the lowliness of our weak nature to triumph through the abundant mercy of your grace."
ALOUD:	"And for all your help and grace toward us, let us raise to you praise and honor and thanksgiving and worship, now and ever and world without end."
PEOPLE:	"Amen."
THE PRIEST SAYS QUIETLY:	"You, Lord, through your many mercies that cannot be told, be graciously mindful of all the pious and righteous fathers who were pleasing in your sight, in the commemoration of the body and blood of your Christ, which we offer to you on the pure and holy altar, as you taught us. And grant us your tranquility and your peace for all the days of this age."
PEOPLE:	"Amen."
[PRIEST:]	"That all the inhabitants of the earth may know you, that you alone are the true God and Father, and you sent our Lord Jesus Christ, your beloved Son, and he, our Lord and our God, taught us through his life-giving gospel all the purity and holiness of the prophets, apostles, martyrs, confessors, bishops, priests, deacons, and all children of the holy catholic

FIGURE 5.
The Qalb Lawza basilica. This fifth-century basilica sits in the "Dead Cities" region of Syria, a region northwest of Aleppo that contains the ruins of many Roman and Byzantine cities and churches. The basilica is notable for exemplifying several trends of late antique Byzantine and Syriac architecture on a massive scale. It is one of the earliest large examples of the broad-isled layout, which used broad arches to separate the nave and side aisles instead of rows of columns, such that the nave and side aisles were integrated into one continuous space. In addition to this distinct layout, several examples of architectural sculpture are extant in the basilica. These sculptures include various plant motifs as well as the common Christian symbols of the cross and chalice. Yasser Tabbaa Archive, courtesy of Aga Khan Documentation Center, Massachusetts Institute of Technology Libraries (AKDC@MIT).

church who have been sealed with the living seal of holy baptism. And we also, Lord, your lowly, weak, and miserable servants, who have gathered and stand before you, [and] have received through tradition the form that is from you, rejoicing, glorifying, exalting, commemorating, and celebrating this great mystery of the passion, death, and resurrection of our Lord Jesus Christ. May your Holy Spirit, Lord, come and rest on this offering of your servants, and bless and sanctify it that it may be to us, Lord, for remission of debts, forgiveness of sins, and the great hope of resurrection from the dead, and new life in the kingdom of heaven, with all who have been pleasing in your sight. And because of all your wonderful dispensations toward us, with open mouths and uncovered

FIGURE 6.
The basilica of Saint Sergius. This church found in Sergiopolis (modern Resafa), Syria was dedicated to Saint Sergius. Resafa has had a rich history beginning since at least the ninth century BCE. In late antiquity and the early medieval period, it became an important Byzantine city in part owing to its proximity to the border with Persia. In the fourth century, Resafa became a popular pilgrimage site because of its association with Saint Sergius, who was said to have been martyred there. For this reason, the city was renamed Sergiopolis, and this basilica was built with imperial sponsorship. The Byzantine emperor Justinian supported additional building projects in the city. In the sixth century, it also became a center for Arab Christianity. The city fell to Muslim forces in the seventh century, but it remained occupied at least until the Mongol period. The surviving ruins of the city and especially the remains of this large basilica demonstrate the importance of the city, like others in modern-day Syria, for the Byzantine Empire, and they provide valuable information for archaeologists. The basilica's size and storied history point to the popularity of the cult of Saint Sergius in late antiquity, the importance of pilgrimage practices, and the multiethnic appeal of Christianity in late antique Syria. Photo: Christine Shepardson.

faces we give you thanks and glorify you without ceasing in your church, which has been redeemed by the precious blood of your Christ, offering up praise, honor, thanksgiving, and adoration to your living and life-giving name, now and at all times for ever and ever."

PEOPLE: "Amen."

BARHEBRAEUS, *SHORT ANAPHORA OF SAINT JAMES*

Thirteenth century. West Syrian.

In contrast to the East Syrian Church, which eventually limited its Eucharist service orders to three, West Syrian Christians continued to expand their anaphoras to over seventy (almost a dozen of which are still used in the modern Syrian Orthodox Church). Perhaps the most popular of these is the *Anaphora of Saint James*. Although attributed to Jesus's brother James, this is a Syriac translation of what was most likely a fourth-century Greek liturgy. In the thirteenth century, the West Syrian theologian Barhebraeus created an abridged version of this anaphora found in full below. Like many anaphoras, this one includes key words and ellipses to indicate longer prayers that were well known by the priest and the congregation. This shorter version of the *Anaphora of Saint James* continues to be used among modern Syrian Orthodox churches, especially those in India. For additional excerpts from Barhebraeus, see chapters 5 and 11.

Anaphora of Saint James, brother of our Lord, and the first archbishop of Jerusalem, apostle and martyr. Learned from the mouth of the Lord.

PRAYER BEFORE THE PEACE: "God of all and Lord, hold us, we who are unworthy, to be worthy of this salvation, so that without guile and united by the bond of love, we may greet one another with a holy kiss, and we may offer up glory and thanksgiving to you and to your only begotten Son and to your Holy Spirit."

PEOPLE: "Amen."

PRIEST: "Peace."

DEACON: "Let us give . . ."

PRIEST: "O you, who alone are merciful Lord, who dwell on high and behold the humblest things, send [your] blessings to those who have bowed down their necks before you, and bless them by the grace of your only begotten Son and of your Holy Spirit. Now and always."

PEOPLE: "Amen."

PRIEST: "God the Father, who by your great love for humankind sent your Son to the world to bring back the sheep that had gone astray. Do not reject, O Lord, this service of this bloodless sacrifice, for we rely not on our righteousness but on your mercies. Let not this mystery, which was instituted for our salvation, be for our condemnation, but for the blotting out of our sins and for the rendering of thanks to you and to your only begotten Son and to your Holy Spirit."

DEACON: "Let us stand . . ."

PEOPLE:	"Mercies . . ."
PRIEST:	"Love . . ."
PEOPLE:	"And to your spirit."
PRIEST:	"On high . . ."
PEOPLE:	"They are . . ."
PRIEST:	"Let us give thanks to the Lord."
PEOPLE:	"It is meet and right."
[PRIEST] INCLINED:	"Truly it is meet and right to thank, to worship, and to glorify the maker of the whole creation."
AND HE RAISES HIS VOICE:	"He whom the heavenly hosts glorify, the corporeal and incorporeal, the sun, the moon and all the stars, the earth, the seas and the first born inscribed in the heavenly Jerusalem, angels, princedoms, authorities, thrones, dominions, powers, the many-eyed cherubim and the six-winged seraphim who cover their faces and feet, fly to one another, sanctifying, crying out and saying:"
PEOPLE:	"Holy . . ."
[PRIEST] INCLINED:	"In truth you are holy, and the one who makes holy, O king of the worlds; holy is your Son, our Lord Jesus Christ; holy is also your Holy Spirit, who searches your mysteries. You created humans out of earth and placed them in paradise, and when they transgressed the commandment, you did not leave them straying, but did guide them through the prophets, and finally you sent also your only begotten Son to the world, who, when he had taken body of the Holy Spirit and from the Virgin Mary, renewed your image, which was worn out."
HE RAISES HIS VOICE:	"When the sinless one was prepared to receive voluntary death for us sinners, he took bread in his holy hands, and when he had given thanks, he blessed, [priest makes sign of the cross] sanctified [makes sign of the cross], and broke and gave to his holy apostles, saying, 'Take, eat of it. This is my body, which for you and for many is broken, and given for the remission of sins and for the life that is forever.'"
PEOPLE:	"Amen."
PRIEST:	"Similarly, [he took] the cup and, when he had given thanks, he blessed [makes sign of the cross], sanctified [makes sign of the cross], and gave to his holy apostles, saying, 'Take, drink of it all of you. This is my blood, which is for you and

	for many is shed and given for the remission of sins and for the life that is for ever.'"
PEOPLE:	"Amen."
PRIEST:	"'Do this in my memory: when you partake of this mystery, you are commemorating my death and resurrection until I come.'"
PEOPLE:	"Your death . . ."
PRIEST:	"Remembering[, therefore], O Lord, your death and resurrection on the third day, and your ascension to heaven and your session at the right hand of God the Father and your second coming in which you judge the world with justice and reward every one according to their deeds; on account of this we offer you this bloodless sacrifice, so that you may not deal with us according to our debts, nor reward us according to our sins. But according to your abundant mercies, blot out the sins of your servants, for your people and your inheritance beseech you and, through you, your Father, saying:"
PEOPLE:	"Have mercy . . ."
PRIEST:	"And we also . . ."
DEACON:	"How awful . . ."
PRIEST INCLINED:	"Have mercy upon us God the Father, and send upon these offerings your Holy Spirit, the Lord who is equal to you and to [your] Son in throne, kingship, and eternal substance, who spoke through your Old and New Testament and descended like a dove on our Lord Jesus Christ in the River Jordan, and like the tongues of fire on the apostles in the upper room."
PRIEST:	"Answer me, O Lord . . ."
PRIEST:	"So that, by tabernacling, he may make this bread the life-giving body [makes sign of the cross], the redeeming body [makes sign of the cross], [and] the body of Christ our God [makes sign of the cross]."
PEOPLE:	"Amen."
PRIEST:	"And he may perfect this cup, the blood of the new covenant [makes sign of the cross], the redeeming blood [makes sign of the cross], and the same blood of Christ our God [makes sign of the cross]."
PEOPLE:	"Amen."
PRIEST:	"So that the souls and bodies of those who partake of them may be sanctified, for the bearing of the fruits of good deeds, for the confirmation of the holy church, which is founded on the strong rock of faith, and the gates of Sheol

                                cannot overpower it. Deliver her from the offenses of heresies even unto the end, that she may offer up glory and thanksgiving to you and to your only begotten Son . . ."

INCLINED: "We offer you this bloodless sacrifice on behalf of holy Zion, the mother of all churches, and on behalf of the holy church throughout the world, so that you may grant her the grace [and] gifts of your Holy Spirit. Remember, O Lord, our fathers, the just and the upright: our patriarch, our bishop Mar _____, the presbyters, the deacons, and all the orders of the church along with my wretchedness. Do not remember the sins of my youth; but make me live, according to your mercy. And remember our brethren: the prisoners, the sick, the infirm, the afflicted, and those who are tormented by evil spirits. 'Bless the air and the crown of the year,' filling all the living with good will."

HE RAISES HIS VOICE: "Deliver us, O Lord, from every insurrection of evil ones, the assault and oppression of demons, and from every scourge brought upon us by reason of our sins. Preserve us in the observance of your holy commandments, for you are a merciful Lord and we offer up glory to you and to your only begotten [Son]."

INCLINED: "Remember, O Lord, [our] parents and siblings who are [now] standing with us and praying, and those who have departed from us, and those who wished to make offering, but could not, and to each one grant their good petition."

HE RAISES HIS VOICE: "Remember, O Lord, all those whom we have mentioned and have not mentioned and receive their sacrifices on the breadths of your heaven. Reward them with the joy of salvation and hold them worthy of the succor that is from you. Strengthen them by your power; arm them with your might, for you are merciful, and we offer up glory to you and to your only begotten Son."

INCLINED: "Remember, O Lord, the pious kings and queens, and aid them with the spiritual armor; and subdue all their enemies to them, that we may lead a peaceful life."

HE RAISES HIS VOICE: "For you are the savior, the helper, and the giver of victory to all who hope in you. We offer up glory to you."

INCLINED: "Because you have authority over life and death, O Lord, remember the holy fathers, the prophets, the apostles, virgin mother of God, John the Baptist, Saint Stephen the martyr, together with all the righteous."

HE RAISES HIS VOICE: "We beseech you, O mighty one, strengthen our impossibilities; unite us with the assembly of the firstborn inscribed in

	heaven. We remember them, that they also may remember us before you and partake with us in this spiritual sacrifice for the admonition of the living and for the encouragement of us, the miserable, and for the repose of the faithful departed, our parents, siblings, and masters, by the grace and mercies and the love for humanity of the only begotten Son."
INCLINED:	"Remember, O Lord, the true shepherds, who from James the archbishop until this day have confirmed the orthodox [faith] in your church."
HE LIFTS UP HIS VOICE:	"Confirm in our souls the doctrines of the enlightened and the doctors who carried your holy name before the Gentiles and kings and the children of Israel. Remove the heresies that trouble us. Hold us worthy of the blameless standing before [your] terrible throne, for you are holy, the sanctified of the saints. We offer up glory to you and to your only begotten."
INCLINED:	"Remember, O Lord, all the orders of the church that, in orthodox faith, have departed before and are at rest, and all those for whom they offered and those who are now mentioned."
HE RAISES HIS VOICE:	"O Lord, God of the spirits and all flesh, remember those who have departed from us in orthodox faith. Give rest to their bodies, souls, and spirits. Deliver them from endless condemnation. Make them rejoice in the place where the light of your countenance visits, and do not enter into judgment with them, for there is none innocent before you except your only begotten Son, through whom we also hope to find mercies, for his sake both for us and for them."
PEOPLE:	"Remove . . ."
INCLINED:	"Remove [and] pardon our offenses [committed] in thought, word, and deed—those that are manifest and those that are hidden, yet evident to you."
HE RAISES HIS VOICE:	"Keep us, O Lord, without sin until our end and gather us at the feet of your elect ones, when, where, and as you will, only without shame by reason of our offenses, so that in this also as in all things, your all-honored and blessed name may be glorified and praised with that of our Jesus Christ and of your [Holy] Spirit."
PEOPLE:	"As it was . . ."
	(Priest breaks and signs the bread [with the sign of the cross]).
PRAYER:	"Our Father who are in heaven: O God, Father of our Lord Jesus Christ, who are blessed by the cherubim and sanctified

by the seraphim, and exalted by thousands of thousands, and myriads of myriads of the rational hosts, you who sanctify and make perfect the offerings and ripe fruits, which have been offered for a sweet-smelling fragrance, sanctify also our bodies, souls, and spirits, so that with a pure heart and a face unashamed we may call upon you, O God the heavenly Father, and pray, saying, Our Father who are in heaven."

PEOPLE: "Our Father who are in heaven."

PRIEST: "Yea, Lord, our God, do not let us enter us into intolerable temptation; but deliver us from the evil one, making a way of escaping from temptation, and to you we will offer up glory and thanksgiving and to the only begotten."

DEACON: "[Let us bow down] our heads."

PRIEST: "Peace . . ."

PEOPLE: "And with [your] spirit."

PRIEST: "Unto you [your] servants who are waiting for your rich mercies, have bowed down their heads. Send forth, O Lord, [your] blessings and sanctify the bodies, souls, and spirits of all of us, and hold us worthy to partake of the life-giving mysteries of Christ, our savior, and to you we will offer up glory and thanksgiving and to your only begotten."

PRIEST: "May the grace . . ."

DEACON: "With fear . . ."

PRIEST: "Holy things to the holy."

PEOPLE: "And with [your spirit]."

PRIEST: "We give thanks to you, O Lord, for the abundance of your mercies, by which we have been made worthy to partake of your heavenly table. May we not be condemned for receiving your holy mysteries, but, being worthy, may we be in fellowship with your Holy Spirit, and find a portion and an inheritance with all the righteous who have been from the beginning and we will offer up glory and thanksgiving to you and to your only begotten."

PRIEST: "Peace . . ."

PEOPLE: "And to your spirit."

PRIEST: "O great and wonderful God, who lowered the heaven and came down for the salvation of the human race, have compassion and mercy upon us, so that we may always glorify you and God the Father, your begetter, and your Holy Spirit, now and at all times and forever."

Here ends this anaphora of Maphrian Gregory [Barhebraeus]. May his prayer be with us always.

SERVICE BOOK FROM TURFAN

Late eighth or ninth centuries. East Syrian.

In the early twentieth century, archaeologists uncovered the library of an East Syrian monastery near the oasis of Turfan, located in what is now southwest China. Among fragments from almost five hundred Syriac manuscripts appears a nearly complete service book. Radiocarbon dating suggests that this book was most likely written between the years 771 and 884. Alongside many other rituals found in this 120-page manuscript is the earliest known Syriac funerary service. The service includes extensive directions for how to conduct funerary rites for Syriac Christians with variations depending on whether the deceased was a clergy member, an ascetic, a layperson, or even an unknown stranger; this suggests that this Chinese monastery served a wide range of Christians in the surrounding community. The following excerpts contain a series of responsive hymns that could be included in the service. They begin with a chorus and then include a series of verses, each ending with an asterisk showing where participants should repeat the initial response. Although this part of the manuscript is in a fairly good state of preservation, there are several places where a word or short series of words is no longer legible; those places are marked as [____].

A MEMRA FOR ALL RANKS

RESPONSE: O race of mortals, consider the changes yesterday in this world; today in the one to come.

VERSES: Like a traveler, pass the night in the world of the departed, and rise early and set out from it to the Eden of delight.* In the eye of the mind I saw paradise and wondered at its glory, so beautiful and desirable.* The garden of joys in which is the Eden of paradise: let it be your dwelling and the place of your rest.* Our savior made it a habitation for the just and a haven of joys for Adam and for his children.* See, there are the just of Noah's house and Elijah, people who will not ever taste death:* Abel the innocent, Job the righteous, Abraham the faithful, and Melchizedek the blessed.* The company of all the saints are invited to the great feast in the bridechamber of paradise.* They rejoice and are glad, everyone, at his supper; and at the [____] of light they rejoice continually.* He sprinkles the dew of joys on their [faces]. And light without compare shines on them all.* All the assembly of spiritual beings longs and desires to see the crown of their glory.* Everyone according to their labor receives their reward from that judge who examines hidden things.* Do not, Lord, bring me into the judgment of your justice, for no one living will be acquitted before you by works.* How bitter is death and sweet [is] revival, and bright [is] paradise. And its dwellers are full of blessings.*

RESPONSE ([IN] CHANT, [TITLED] "FOR CHILDREN"): In paradise children find pasture without danger. Our Lord, gather them into the treasury of the kingdom.*

VERSES: At evening in the west I saw a spiritual being standing above my head and wishing to carry me away.* I saw him and was shaken and my face was terrified. And I began to beseech him,* "Leave me a little while." He did not heed what I said to him and did not accept my plea. And he began to separate one bone from another.* I turned and asked him, "Where do you dwell?" And he answered and said to me, "In Eden of paradise."* I saw a dwelling-place there, and a tabernacle of light, and a voice that was saying, "Blessed is the robber."* Who is worthy to see the [____] of the [holy ones] where angels stand and dwell?* [____] On that day of the preparation of their crowns, make me worthy to join the companies of their ranks.* Fasting had taken away the color of their faces—they are beautiful and joyful in the tabernacles of paradise.* At the head of them all, the heavenly bridegroom sits. And he writes their names in the book of his kingdom.* Woe to the one who has borne children. For cruel and fearsome is the day when death separates her beloved one.* If you have siblings and friends and loved ones, they are accompanying you as far as the mouth of the tomb, O our brethren.* Our Lord alone goes [from there] by your side, and he will protect your body and soothe your soul.* Please, gracious one, save me by your grace and forgive me my sins and make me worthy of your bridechamber.*

RESPONSE: Your body has reached your end, that you should go [to be] among your people.

([IN] CHANT): And your day has come that you should become a traveler within the tomb.*

VERSES: Let the one who has carried you from among us, from the company of your brethren, bring you by his grace to the bosom of Abraham.* Do not be sad, O our brethren, that you have departed from this world. For you will go and enjoy the bridechamber of the kingdom.* May our Lord in his grace raise you up to his right hand when he comes in the great glory of his kingdom.* May our Lord by his cross raise you up to his right hand and number you with the just who have been pleasing to his lordship.* O my brethren and my friends, may our Lord pay you the wage of your tears that you have shed for me.* In your prayer, my brethren, remember the love that was with me, at the time of the holy [Eucharist], that he may make me worthy of his kingdom.* A traveler has come upon me and snatched me from your company. Now pray for me that I shall go and be received.* May the one who formed you from dust and brought you into being give you delight by his mercies with the just who have loved him.

A MEMRA FOR BISHOPS AND FOR AN EMINENT PERSON

RESPONSE: I come and do not fear, for my Lord calls me and sets on me a crown of glory and gladdens me.

VERSES: Our father, the day of your departure has saddened us, and the day of your separation has pained us exceedingly.* In what meeting-place shall we seek you, O treasure of our pride with whose beauty our whole congregation was adorned?* Your clear and pure spring has dried up for us, that flowed sweetly and gave us all to drink.* Your teaching dawned on us and gladdened us like the sun, which lights up the creation by its light.* Your love itself watered us abundantly, in which you set us in order and taught us good rules.* And who should again instruct our childish state like you? With bridles of love and fear you set us in order.* You invited us to the feast of life. Indeed you made us ready that we might prepare seemly garments for that banquet.* You showed us a good example in yourself. You clothed us in [____] from your modesty.* Blessing to you henceforth, [O our father]—and dread to us: who will give us someone like you, O our example?* [Today] your labor has rested and your danger is over. You prepared provisions and have crossed the troubled sea.* Your crown is prepared on high, for all your victorious deeds. And praise has multiplied in our land, [but] to us it is sorrow.* We are sad not that you have fallen asleep and your danger is over, but that you have gone away from us and left us and left us lonely.* Who may endure away from your company, O our example? And who can give quietness, or console?* Your voice was soothing and the sound of your words gladdened us. By your sweetness you brought calmness to our anxiety.* Our congregation is greatly sad, O our father, that it has not your society. For you were the crown on our head, of which we are not worthy.* Upon us has been fulfilled what the prophet too said: "There is none to repair our breach." They have stripped bare our beauty.* Whose mouth shall be able to speak of your victories? For in diligence and love you were most perfected.* Your prayer daily was that we should be victorious. For [our] confidence was exceedingly dear to you.* Your Lord will call you, O our father, on the day of revival, and you will enter with him the bridechamber, with your head high.* The high one who saw you that you served him from your childhood until your old age in perfection*—praise to him who by his cross preserved your ship that it should not sink among the waves of [earthly] pleasures.* Thanks [be] to you from our congregation, O one who takes pleasure in our life, that in the haven of the tomb you cause us to rest until the revival.

5

ASCETICISM

Vows of celibacy and other acts of renouncing the physical pleasures of this world are visible in Christianity from its beginnings. But many early Syriac traditions seem to have had a particularly strong affinity for ascetic teachings. Asceticism, from the Greek term *askēsis*, traditionally referred to the careful control that athletes demonstrated over their bodies in their rigorous daily trainings and diet. Early Christians began to apply the terms "athlete" and "*askēsis*" to the bodily disciplines associated with exceptional daily devotion to God, including vows of lifelong celibacy, a meager diet, frequent prayer, and other practices of piety. Christian women and men practiced asceticism in varying degrees and locations, whether in a house, a structured community of other ascetics called a monastery, or in more extreme forms as individuals or loosely networked communities in deserts, forests, mountains, and caves. The most remarkable ascetics, both female and male, came to be famous saints. They were visited by pilgrims and recognized for their miraculous abilities and astonishing feats of endurance like those shown by the stylites who spent decades atop a tall pillar or the dendrites who lived in trees.

Early Syriac Christian texts like the third-century *Acts of Thomas* and the fourth-century writings of Aphrahat (d. after 345) and Ephrem (d. 373) reflect a strong emphasis on the value of celibacy. When the apostle Thomas converts the royal newlyweds to Christianity in the *Acts of Thomas*, for example, their conversion is concurrently a commitment to a life of celibacy. Syriac Christians like Jacob of Serug (d. 521) praised those they called solitaries, people who had vowed to live a single life in devotion to God. Such a person was called a single one, *iḥidaya*, a term also used in Syriac to refer to Christ as the only begotten Son of God. Aphrahat and Ephrem, along with later authors like Rabbula of Edessa (d. 435), also referred to the "sons and daughters of the covenant," or the celibate male *bnay qyama* and female *bnat qyama*, who committed themselves to Christian piety and prayer. On the other hand, the *Book of Steps* prefers to distinguish instead between the "perfect" celibate ascetic Christians, and noncelibate Christians it calls the "upright."

Some Syriac ascetics gathered into intentional communities, often governed through sets of rules that provided order and guidance for their discipline. The earliest monastic movements in Syriac were unlike the early traditions coming out of Egypt: the "single ones" and "sons and daughters of the covenant" are unique offices or identities in Syriac Christianity. Documents illustrating governance of communal (coenobitic) communities in Syriac offer crucial evidence for the rise of institutional monastic movements that appeared among Syriac Christians from the late fourth century. Such documents show a close attention to the life of the monks and the lay Christians surrounding them. Instructions for education, communal living, and worship are combined with meditations on the role of the church and monks. In many ways, as with earlier admonitions to the "children of the covenant," monastic rules were paradigmatic for Syriac Christians of all stripes and remain important meditations on early Christian spirituality and practice.

The arrival of monasticism in its communal Egyptian form is associated in Syriac with various figures: Mar Mari, himself a disciple of Addai (or in Greek Thaddeus), one of Jesus's seventy disciples and the legendary founder of churches and monasteries across the Persian Empire; Mar Awgen (Eugenius), a fabled monastic founder from Roman Syria; and Julian Saba (d. 367), who settled in the region around Edessa. Whether or not these particular origin stories have any basis in fact, Syriac monasticism flourished, often in concert with more solitary forms of asceticism. Not unlike in Palestine, where clusters of ascetics often gathered, each in their own cell, Syriac monasteries frequently had holy women and men associated with a monastery yet living separately from other monks; one such example is Simeon the Stylite (the Elder) at Qal'at Sim'ān. Women monastics were separated from the men and seem to have been self-governed.

In the centuries that followed the fifth- and sixth-century doctrinal divisions among Syriac-speaking Christians, ascetic, mystical, and spiritual practices flourished in a variety of ways. The West Syrian ascetics remembered in the *Lives of the Eastern Saints* by John of Ephesus (d. 586/587), for example, often either lived in exile from their monasteries for refusing to accept the Council of Chalcedon or found a place among the more extreme solitaries living alone in caves and trees. Many seventh- and eighth-century East Syrian texts, such as writings by Isaac of Nineveh, are by mystical ascetic authors themselves, and they express the teachings and theological understandings behind their ascetic behavior.

From the sixth century on, communal monasticism came to dominate the Syriac religious landscape. In the East Syrian world, Abraham of Kashkar reformed Syriac monasticism and established patterns of monastic founding and regulation that persisted for centuries. Such foundations included standard structures, such as libraries, refectories, and guest quarters. Remains of Syriac monasteries have been found as far afield as Kharg Island in the Persian Gulf, where over sixty cells accompanied the central buildings. In the West Syrian tradition, John of Ephesus highlights Amida as having one thousand monks already in the sixth century, and the monasteries of Tur 'Abdin in southeastern Turkey flourished throughout the medieval period. A common thread that cuts across chronological, geographical, and doctrinal lines is the powerful insistence on the spiritual benefits of renouncing material possessions and bodily pleasures. From the poetry of Jacob of Serug, to Elias's hagiographic praise of John of Tella (d. 538), to the warnings of Philoxenus (d. 523) and Barhebraeus (d. 1286) about the vigilance lifelong asceticism required, Christians stressed the spiritual reward that awaited those who voluntarily renounced material comforts in order to devote their lives fully to God.

Further Reading Asceticism has been a popular focus in the study of Syriac Christianity, so there are numerous excellent books for further study. As in so many areas of Syriac studies, the work of Sebastian P. Brock is central. A particularly rich study of hagiography is Sebastian P. Brock and Susan Ashbrook Harvey, *Holy Women of the Syrian Orient* (Berkeley: University of California, 1987). For earlier ascetic traditions, see Naomi Koltun-Fromm, *Hermeneutics of Holiness: Ancient Jewish and Christian Notions of Sexuality and Religious Community* (New York: Oxford University Press, 2010). Susan Ashbrook Harvey's work has also been central to the study of Syrian asceticism and women's roles in those traditions. For one of her most substantive works, see Susan Ashbrook Harvey, *Asceticism and Society in Crisis: John of Ephesus and the Lives of the Eastern Saints* (Berkeley: University of California Press, 1990). Two other foundational early works are Arthur Vööbus, *History of Asceticism in the Syrian Orient: A Contribution to the History of Culture in the Near East*, 3 vols. CSCO 184/14, 197/17, 500/81 (Louvain: CSCO, 1958); and Sidney H. Griffith, "Asceticism in the Church of Syria: The Hermeneutics of Early Syrian Monasticism," in *Asceticism*, ed. V. Wimbush and R. Valantasis (Oxford: Oxford University Press, 1998), 220–45. More recently, see Cornelia Horn, *Asceticism and Christological Controversy in Fifth-Century Palestine: The Career of Peter the Iberian* (New York: Oxford University Press, 2006).

ACTS OF THOMAS

Third century. Greek translation of Syriac.

The third-century *Acts of Thomas* is both a story of the introduction of Christianity east of the Euphrates and a narrative that privileges Christian celibacy and asceticism. It reveals some of the ways in which ascetic teachings have been deeply ingrained in Syriac Christianity since its early history. The *Acts of Thomas* claims to tell the story of the travels undertaken by Jesus's apostle after the resurrection and Thomas's successful spreading of Christianity as far as India. In this excerpt, Thomas has arrived at the court of a king whose only daughter is about to be married. The king insists that Thomas pray for the bride and groom in the bridal chamber, but the king is unhappily surprised to learn that Thomas (and then Jesus in the form of Thomas) persuaded the young newlyweds to lead celibate Christian lives. For additional excerpts from the *Acts of Thomas*, see chapters 1 and 4.

When the king heard all this, he came in and addressed the apostle: "Get up, come with me, and pray for my daughter; she's my only child and today I will give her away." The apostle did not want to go along with him, because the Lord had not yet appeared to him there, but the king led him off reluctantly to the bridal chamber, so he might pray for them. The apostle stood, then, and began to pray.

"My Lord and my God, who accompanies his servants,
    Who leads and guides those who believe in him;
Refuge and rest of the afflicted,
    The hope of the poor and redeemer of the imprisoned;
The healer of souls laid low by disease
    And savior of all creation,
    Who gives life to the world and strength to human souls:
You understand what things are to be,
    And bring them to completion through us;
You, Lord, reveal hidden mysteries,
    And disclose secret words;
You, Lord, tend the good tree,
    And through your hands
    All good works are generated;
You, Lord, are in all things, pervade all things,
    Are present in all your works,
    And become manifest
    Through the activity of all things,
Jesus Christ, compassionate Son and perfect savior,
    Christ, Son of the living God,
    Undaunted power that has overthrown the enemy;
Voice that has been heard by the rulers,
    That has shaken all of their powers,
    Ambassador sent from on high
    Who has descended as far as Hades;
You who have opened the doors,
    And led up from there those who for long ages
    Have been locked in the storehouse of darkness,
    And have shown them the way that ascends on high:
I ask you, Lord Jesus, I bring my petition to you on behalf of these young people:
That you do what is helpful, suitable, and beneficial for them."

   He then laid his hands on them and said, "The Lord be with you." Then he left them in that place and went on his way.

Now the king asked the wedding attendants to come out of the bridal chamber. When everyone had come and the doors were locked, the groom lifted the veil of the bridal chamber to take the bride to himself. But he saw, speaking with the bride, the Lord Jesus in the guise of Judas Thomas—the apostle who had just now blessed them and left them! So the groom said to him, "Didn't you leave before everyone else? How is it that you're still here?" The Lord said to him, "I'm not Judas who is also Thomas; I'm his brother." The Lord sat down on the bed, ordered them to sit on the chairs, and began to speak to them:

"Remember, my children, what my brother told you and to whom he commended you. Know this, that if you abandon this sordid intercourse, you'll become holy temples, pure, freed from afflictions and pains, both visible and hidden, and you'll not take on the troubles of livelihood or children, the final result of which is destruction. It's so, isn't it? If you have many children, because of them you become thieves and cheats, beating orphans and defrauding widows, and when you do such things, you subject yourselves to dreadful punishments. Not only that, but most children turn out to be useless, afflicted by demons—some openly, some in secret: they're either epileptic, half-withered, lame, deaf, mute, paralytic, or foolish. And if they do happen to be healthy, they'll be unproductive anyway, doing useless or dreadful things. Perhaps they'll be involved in adultery, murder, theft, or fornication; you, too, will be tormented by all these things. But if you obey and keep your souls pure for God, you'll have living children—no harm can touch them. You'll also be carefree, living an undisturbed life, without grief or anxiety, waiting to welcome the imperishable, the true marriage. You'll be members of the wedding party who go into that bridal chamber that is full of immortality and light."

When the young people heard this, they believed the Lord and pledged themselves as given to him: they refrained from filthy desire and spent the night in that place accordingly. The Lord left their company, saying, "The grace of the Lord be with you."

At dawn, the king entered, laid out a breakfast table, and set it before the groom and bride. He found them sitting opposite one another, the face of the bride uncovered and the groom obviously happy. But when her mother approached, she said to the bride, "Why do you sit so, child, and show no shame but act as if you've lived with your husband for a long time?" Her father added, "Is it because of your great love for your husband that you don't cover yourself?" The bride responded, "Truly, father, I'm deeply in love. I pray to my Lord that the love I've felt tonight may remain with me, and I'll ask for the husband I recognized today. So I'll no longer remain covered, since the garment of shame has been taken away from me. I'm no longer ashamed or embarrassed, since the shameful and embarrassing deed has departed far from me; nor am I terrified, since there's no terror left in me. Instead I'm joyful and glad, since the joyful day hasn't been disturbed. I've come to despise this man, and this wedding celebration that fades before my very eyes, now that I've been united in another marriage. I've not had intercourse with a husband who passes away—something that ends up in lewdness and bitterness of soul—because now I've been joined to a real husband." The bride went on in this vein. Then the groom joined in:

"I give thanks to you, Lord,
  Who were proclaimed through the stranger,
  And found among us;

Who distanced me from corruption,
   And sowed life in me;
Who released me from this eternally lingering disease
   That is so difficult to treat or cure,
   And provided me with chaste health;
Who showed yourself to me,
   And revealed to me everything about my condition;
Who rescued me from disaster,
   And led me to what is better;
Who have released me from what is temporary,
   And instead have made me worthy
   Of things that are immortal and exist forever;
Who humbled yourself to me and my smallness,
   So that, by introducing me to majesty,
   You might unite me with yourself;
Who did not withhold your mercy from me
   When I was perishing,
   But showed me how to seek after myself
   And to know who I was,
Who I am, and how I exist in the present,
   So that I might again become what I was.
You whom I didn't know
   Have sought me out;
You whom I haven't grasped—
You have taken hold of me.

   The one I've come to perceive—I can't forget him now. His love throbs inside me, and I cannot speak as I should: all that I'm able to say is brief, altogether paltry, and inadequate to his glory. But I can't be blamed for speaking to him—shamelessly, it must seem—about things I don't really understand, because it's his love that makes me speak as I do."

   When the king heard this testimony from the groom and the bride, he tore his clothing and said to his guards nearby, "Go out, quickly, and make the rounds of the whole city. Arrest and bring me that sorcerer who by some ill chance has come to this city. To think that with my own hands I led him into my house!—and I myself told him to pray for my ill-fated daughter! To the one who finds and brings him to me I'll give whatever they ask." So they went out searching, but they did not find him, because he had sailed away.

APHRAHAT, *DEMONSTRATIONS* 6

336 or 337.

The early fourth-century Christian author Aphrahat (d. after 345) is best known for a series of Syriac *Demonstrations* that he wrote from his home in the Persian Empire. These texts offer his audience instruction on a wide range of topics, many of which try to create a clearer distinction between Christian and Jewish communities whose scripture and traditions overlapped. Aphrahat produced *Demonstration 6* in 336 or 337 and writes to encourage his audience (male and female) to persevere in an ascetic form of Christianity as they await the imminent return of Christ their bridegroom. Aphrahat advocates for rigorous prayer, fasting, and the renunciation of material possessions, but he especially advocates for lifelong celibacy for single men and women alike. This text uses the distinctive Syriac Christian language of "the covenanters," or the male and female "children of the covenant" (*bnay qyama; bnat qyama*), and "single ones" (*iḥidaye*) to describe members of his audience. The sons and daughters of the covenant were encouraged in sexual abstinence—to return to sex in marriage is likened to adultery. The "single ones" are the ultimate paradigm of ascetic virtue, being called to live alone and remain virgins. For additional excerpts from Aphrahat's *Demonstrations*, see chapters 7 and 10.

> For this reason, my brothers, [if there is] anyone who is a covenanter or a holy one who loves singleness yet wants a female covenanter ([who is] like him) to live with him, it would be better for him to take a wife openly and not become wild with lust. Likewise for the woman: if she does not wish to be separated from a [male] single one, she should be [united] to the man openly. It is good for a woman to live with a woman, and a man ought to live with a man. Furthermore, if a man wishes to remain in holiness, his wife should not live with him, so that he will not return to his former state and be considered an adulterer. This counsel that I give myself is good and proper and beautiful, as it is also for you, my friends, [who are] single ones (who do not take wives) and female virgins (who do not belong to husbands) and those who love holiness: even if a person encounters difficulty, it is proper and right and good that they should remain alone. In this way, it is appropriate for them to live as it is written in the prophet Jeremiah: "Blessed is the one who takes up your yoke in their youth and dwells alone and is quiet, for that one carries their yoke upon themself." For this reason, my friend, it is good for whoever carries the yoke of Christ to carry their yoke in purity. [. . .]
>
> You [female] virgins who have betrothed yourselves to Christ: if a [male] covenanter says to one of you, "I will live with you and you will serve me," you should say to him, "I am betrothed to a man of royalty, and I am serving him. If I leave his service and serve you, my betrothed will be angry with me and will write me a letter of divorce and send me away from his house. May you seek to be honored by me and I by you, so that harm will not come upon [either] you or me. Do not become inflamed with desire, or you will burn your garments. Rather, remain in honor on your own, and I [will remain] alone in my honor. These are the ones whom the Bridegroom is preparing for his eternal wedding feast. Make yourself a wedding gift and prepare yourself to meet him, and I will prepare oil so that I might enter in with the wise and not be left outside the door with the foolish virgins."
>
> Pay attention to what I am writing to you concerning what is appropriate for single ones, the covenanters ([who are] virgins), and holy ones. In the first place, the one upon whom the yoke is laid ought to have a firm faith, as I wrote to you in the first letter. They should be diligent in fasting and prayer, intense in their love for Christ, and humble and moderate and reasonable. Let their speech be peaceful and pleasant, and let their mind be clear toward

everyone. Let them weigh their words carefully and set a fence against harmful words around their mouth, and may foolish laughter be far from them. They should not love the adornment of clothing, nor let their hair grow long in order to decorate it, nor should they anoint it with aromatic oils. They should not recline at banquets, nor is it appropriate for them to wear fancy clothing. They should not boldly drink too much wine, and a proud mind should be far from them. It is not appropriate for them to look at fancy clothing, or to wear stylish cloaks. They should get rid of a deceitful tongue, put away envy and strife, and cast away lying lips. When words are spoken about a person who is not present, let [the covenanter] not listen or receive [such words], so as to not sin, until they investigate [the matter]. Mockery is a repulsive blemish, and it is wrong for it to arise in the heart. They should not demand interest when lending, nor should they love greed. They should suffer wrong but not do wrong [to others]. Let them stay away from commotion, and not speak frivolous words. They should not scoff at the person who repents of their sins, nor mock their brother who is fasting, nor shame the one who is not able to fast. Where they are received, let them rebuke, but where they are not received, let them keep their honor. At an appropriate time, let them speak their word, but [if there is no opportunity] let them be silent. They should not despise themselves on account of the demands of their stomach but should reveal their secret to one who fears God and keep themselves from the evil one. They should not respond to an evil person, nor to their enemy. Let them fight in such a way as to have no enemies at all. When they are envied because of what is good, let them add to their goodness and not be plagued by jealousy. When they are able to give to the poor, let them rejoice, but when they are not able, they should not be sad. Let them not be acquainted with an evil person, nor let them speak with a disgraceful person, so that they will not give themselves over to disgrace. They should not dispute with a blasphemous person, or their Lord will be reviled because of them. They should stay away from the slanderer and should not try to make one person pleasing to another with flattering words. These things are fitting for single ones, those who have received the heavenly yoke and have become disciples of Christ. It is fitting for disciples of Christ to be like their Lord.

BOOK OF STEPS

Mid-fourth to early fifth century.

The Syriac *Book of Steps* focuses on encouraging a spiritual life of Christian asceticism. This collection of thirty discourses (*memre*) most likely originates from a community in northern Iraq and offers guidance for two statuses of Christian practice: "uprightness," describing those who follow some commandments like treating others well, and "perfection," describing those who are expected to live a strongly regulated and celibate ascetic life. The *Book of Steps* combines practical advice for liturgical practice with a more mystical approach to achieving spiritual maturity. It pairs acts of contemplating the divine with ascetical vows to poverty and fasting, among other disciplines. This selection addresses questions about Adam and Eve, and God's original plan for human desire, marriage, and reproduction. The *Book of Steps* argues that human lust and the desire for sexual intercourse were the result of Satan corrupting Adam's initial angelic state; marriage, thus, is presented as a compromise and a consequence of sin. The text hopes that its audience will renounce marriage, sexual intercourse, and lust in order to return to being like angels. For an additional excerpt from the *Book of Steps,* see chapter 7.

So now let us explain this marital desire that came into being through Adam, how it came to be in him, and how it might be removed from his children. After he had sinned and was censured, a law was established for him, inferior to that first [law]. By this same law [God] permitted him to marry. Because he had desired to become physical and not spiritual, that is, earthly and not heavenly; it was then that carnal desire came to exist in him, for Adam desired intercourse as a result of the teaching of the evil one who had plotted to make him fall from the sanctity of the angels and imitate wild beasts.

Now Adam had turned his thoughts to these [things] before [God] had permitted him to marry, seeing that the evil one had taught him while he was [still] without lust, and Adam and Eve supposed that everything that the evil one had taught them would come to be. But if God had not had compassion upon Adam, the evil one would have cast him into the pit; Satan desired that [Adam] become like him and be subservient to him. Blessed is the good [God] who opens the door to everyone who repents.

At first Adam and Eve accepted the evil idea and coveted the beauty of the earth. The woman saw the tree—how it was desirable to eat from—and it became an object of lust to the eyes, just as today we know that gold and silver, property and clothing, and the delicacies of the earth are desirable. They initially desired these things in the hope that they could become like their Creator, through the deadly appetite that the evil one had put into their ears and after which their mind speedily followed. There did not exist in them any lust to desire intercourse, but they greatly desired it because the evil one had directed their gaze [to it] through cattle. That is why David said, "A person who has not taken notice of his honor," because he was holy like the angels and peaceful like the heavenly ones. But he saw an animal and wished to imitate it in sexual intercourse.

They had not had any desire of the instinct for [sexual] union until they had been persuaded by the evil one to become earthly people and to acquire earthly toil and wealth. So God permitted them to marry and to labor after he had cursed them. Lust and the procreative instinct were in them because they had sinned and had violated his commandment. They hated holiness and loved intercourse. They did not really desire it, but [they did so] in that hope that they could become great like God. Now let us show from this that Adam and Eve had no lust while they had not yet sinned. [. . .]

Before Adam and Eve had sinned, they were naked like infants, but since the lust in their heart was not aroused, they were not ashamed, just as infants are not ashamed. Once they had sinned, and sin existed in their heart, directing them to desire intercourse, [then] "They saw that they were naked"; that is, they knew the shame they had not known. Just as from the [moment] sin existed in the heart of Adam and Eve, and they desired intercourse. God allowed them to marry—the instinct and lust of intercourse being in them; so today, when the descendants of Adam, who love holiness, have striven against and killed the sin from the heart with lowliness and love, then they will abandon physical lust and turn away from it, ascending to the desire for God. Then God will command that lust be removed from the heart and the instinct from the body completely. Then they will become "holy" like children, as our Lord said, "If you do not turn around and become like these children, you shall not become as you were before you had sinned, in this purity in which I created your father, while he had not yet transgressed against my commandment. And if you do not become like this, you are not worthy of me to be perfected and glorified with me."

Now infants neither lust nor judge, nor are they anxious, but they may cry at any time. We who are purified, however, judge and are anxious, but cannot cry at any time since we fall short of our Lord. Our Lord said, "Those who are worthy of the resurrection are like the angels of God and are not able to die." That is, those who know my words and keep them are like the angels." [. . .]

Therefore, if there is a person who is in the conjugal state while he is in the uprightness of the upright, a pledge of the Holy Spirit exists in him. If he elevates himself above marriage while he is in the uprightness of the upright, he will grow even more above marriage. If he has elevated himself above marriage, he will elevate himself above intercourse to the way of life of the apostles, [then] quickly he will be perfected and receive the Paraclete [i.e., the Holy Spirit] and hear the voice of God.

If virginity comes up to the [level of the] way of life of the apostles, it will be much superior and will receive the Paraclete and become perfect and hear the voice of God. If marriage sanctifies and lowers itself more than physical virginity, it will be superior to it, but if it is only a little ahead of [virginity] in lowliness, it will [only] be equal to it.

If, however, physical virginity becomes spiritual and empties and lowers itself more than everything, there is nothing surpassing it among people. Yet marriage, which, like it, has lowered and sanctified itself spiritually, can reach it while still being inferior to it.

RULES OF RABBULA OF EDESSA

Early fifth century. West Syrian.

The rules attributed to Rabbula of Edessa (d. 435) cover the gamut of monastic experience in the early fifth century. These rules concern, not least, the relationship of monks to secular activities, particularly the ownership of property. Even more, Rabbula's rules seek to confine monks to the monastery and, in the case of novices, to prohibit them from roles above their station. The rules read very much like a list of activities that require ongoing vigilance. The titles of "sons and daughters of the covenant" continue into the communal phase, but they are not separated from other monastic offices: in particular, the priests and deacons carefully manage the covenanters' roles at the monasteries. Rabbula's rules cover many different intramonastic problems encountered on a daily basis, such as interaction between the sexes, the serving of the Eucharist, and psalm recitation. More extreme cases, such as self-castration, are also addressed.

Admonitions for the Monks of My Lord Rabbula, Bishop of Edessa.
1. First of all, let the monks be diligent so that no woman might enter their monasteries.

2. The brothers of a monastery may not go out into the villages, except for the administrator of the monastery, all the while maintaining the order of chastity.

3. An administrator who enters a village or a city may not lodge at an inn and may not spend the night in a house of worldly [persons] but [may lodge only] in a church or a monastery if one is nearby.

4. Monks may not drink wine, lest they blaspheme, and they must be especially careful not to purchase [wine to] drink.

5. Monks may not grow their hair or wear or carry around iron [weights], except those who are solitary hermits and do not go anywhere.

6. Neither the administrators who go out for the work of the monastery nor any of the brothers may wear a coat of hair outside the monastery, so that they not sully the dignity of the [monastic] habit.

7. None of the monks may give oil [for anointing], especially not to women. If someone manifestly possesses the charism [of healing], he may give the oil to men, but if there are women in need [of it], let it be sent to them by their husbands.

8. Monasteries may not have memorials [i.e., services for the dead] with a public assembly but only [with] the monastery's own brothers.

9. Monks may not possess sheep, goats, horses, mules, or calves of cattle as property, except for one donkey for what is necessary, or a yoke of oxen for those who do the plowing.

10. Books outside the faith of the church may not be in the monasteries.

11. Commercial transactions of buying and selling may not take place in the monasteries, except [to procure] whatever is necessary for their supply, [and so long as it is done] without avarice.

12. No one of the brothers who are in the monasteries may possess anything solely for himself other than whatever is common to the brotherhood and under the authority of the head of the monastery.

13. The heads of the monasteries may not allow the brothers to meet their family or to leave and go to them, lest they become weak.

14. The brothers may not desert their monasteries and go about in the cities or in the villages on the pretext of illness. They must bear their infirmities within their monasteries for the sake of the love of God.

15. Monks may not forsake their dwelling and take on lawsuits on behalf of others and go to the cities or before judges.

16. The monks may not skip the times that are fixed for the service, by day or by night, on account of duty or work.

17. They must receive strangers lovingly, and they may not shut the door on any of the brothers.

18. One of the brothers may not dwell alone unless he gives proof of his works for a duration of time.

19. A monk may not deliver a sermon from the [Bible] to anyone.
20. No brother who is neither a presbyter nor a deacon may dare to distribute holy [communion].
21. Those who are presbyters or deacons in the monasteries and to whom have been entrusted churches in the countryside: the heads of the monasteries must appoint those in their monasteries who have demonstrated proof and are able to manage the brotherhood, and they must remain with their churches.
22. The bones of martyrs are not permitted in the monasteries, but all [monasteries] that have any [bones] must bring them before us: if they are real, they will be placed among the martyrs, and if not, they will be placed in the charnel house.
23. [Regarding] the urns of the dead, which some monks desire to make for them[selves], they must hide them in the ground so that they are not at all visible.
24. If a head of a monastery or a brother of one of the monasteries goes out from the world, only those brothers of the same monastery will bury him quietly. If they cannot, they will call over to them brothers from a monastery that is near them. Neither the people from the countryside nor secular people may be [present] for the procession.
25. If someone buys grain for the use of the monastery, he may not keep any profit. He must buy it at the price at which they are selling [it] at the time of threshing, while not coveting [anything] in the name of the monastery.
25a. Diviners and charmers, those who write out amulets, and those who anoint men and women while acting under the guise of medicine: drive them out of every place and take from them a guarantee that they will not enter into our territory [again].
25b. The children of the church will not have fellowship with heretics, neither in word nor in deed.
26. No one may accept a brother who moves from monastery to monastery, unless on the order of the head of the monastery to which he belongs.

The end of the admonitions for the monks.

RULES FOR NUNS

Early fifth century. West Syrian.

These fragmentary canons provide evidence of the flourishing of women's monastic communities and how such communities were strictly circumscribed by the abbess—that is, the head of the monastery (*rishat dayra*). This text survives only in a single manuscript that is not well preserved, so there are numerous gaps in the text. These gaps will be marked as "[____]". Female ascetics were kept separate from men and were not allowed, presumably in part for their protection, to travel alone outside the community. Even though the rules are largely prohibitions, the rules for nuns do not differ significantly from those for new male monks. These rules indicate a bustling life of monastics of different stripes, and they include a reference to an East Syrian monastery that the West Syrian nuns are prohibited from visiting.

1. It is not lawful for any of the sisters to go out from [the monastery] [____] alone, without one of the sisters, these who [have received] the garment, [____] without [telling?] the head of the monastery expressly as to where she wishes to go nor to go [anywhere] except to where she has asked [to go] [____]

2. It is not lawful for any of the sisters of the monastery to go out to an eating house to eat and drink [____], nor to go to the vigils in the assembly [in honor] of the martyrs, not in the town nor outside the town and also not to go to the vigils [____] or wakes or funerals, and also not to banquets; but whoever wants to go to pray in the church of the holy ones on the days [____] she shall go if she has with her a female companion according to the authority of the first canon.

3. It is not lawful for any of the sisters [____] something from outside the monastery and because of this to go and to roam. And also no stranger shall place something with her [____] except only a book, unless he is her father or fleshly brother or her mother or her sister [____] through the permission of the head of the monastery.

4. It is not lawful for any of the sisters to eat anything in the whole town [____] to drink except only water.

5. It is not lawful for any of the sisters to eat with a man, not in the monastery nor outside the monastery, unless he is her father or her fleshly brother or her [paternal] uncle or her mother's brother; and this through the permission of the head of the monastery. And she also shall not eat bread outside the refectory destined for this purpose, or in the gate porch, unless she goes on a necessary journey [____] and if she sits at the table of the refectory of the entire house, she [shall not] let [a man] sleep nor let a man enter into the inner monastery, entirely not [____]

6. It is not lawful for any of the sisters to enter alone a house with a man, not inside the monastery nor outside the monastery; she shall also not speak with a man on the street without her female companion [____] who goes out with her, except [____] greeting [____], if he is her father or fleshly brother; it also shall not be lawful for them to engage [in conversation] with the monks on the [____] in order that they do not betray [____]

7. It is not lawful for any of the sisters to enter inside the vestibule or the court of the monastery of the [male] monks [nor shall they let in] the monks inside the gate of their monasteries, except if the monk is an old priest [____] on Sunday in order to consecrate for them the Eucharist; and they shall not enter the monastery of the eastern ones nor the monastery [____] except in case [of a funeral] they enter with the departed one and go out with the entire community of them who accompany the departed one. And they shall not [visit the solitaries] on the mount or recluses or the stylites with the pretext to make alms to them, or to bring them an offering;

[except] an old itinerant priest who has been appointed by each monastery for the purpose that through his hands the alms shall be sent.

8. It is not lawful for any of the sisters to receive [a responsibility in the case of?] baptism, except if the one to be baptized is a pagan or a little girl [to be baptized] in exigency of [____] only [so] it is permitted [____] and through the permission of the administrator or the head of the monastery.

9. It is not lawful for any of the sisters to borrow from somebody nor to lend; nor to write a letter nor to receive from anybody, without the knowledge of the head of the monastery, except [her father] or her mother or her fleshly brother or her [paternal] uncle or her mother's brother or her sister.

10. It is not lawful for any [of the sisters] [to neglect] [____] or the evening or the morning prayer or the eucharistic liturgy on the day of Sunday, or to go on the day of Sunday from her monastery at all [____] Eucharist, except in suffering [____] necessity; except those who are being sent or [who remain] in the outskirts [____] or because of other pressing business that exists in the community; but who neglects one of these [____] except in the case of sickness, she shall fast from the meal and from wine for two days. [____]

11. It is not lawful for any of the sisters to go on a journey that is more than one mile without [the permission] of the administrator.

12. It is not lawful for any of the sisters to raise a hand against her companion or to abuse [her] and to [____] [but whoever dares and] beats her companion shall be excluded from the Eucharist and from the meal and from wine for one month [____] and abuses [her] boldly, and calls her companion with foul names, and [____] her, she shall fast from [the meal]. [____]

13. It is not lawful for any of the sisters that she engage herself [in worldly business?] [____] except [it be] because of necessary business, except she has an evident [cause], she shall not go out of her monastery.

14. It is not lawful for any of the sisters to go to the monastery of the [male] monks on any pretext [____]

PHILOXENUS, *FIRST LETTER TO THE MONKS OF BET GAUGAL; LETTER CONCERNING ZEAL*

Late fifth century. West Syrian.

Philoxenus (d. 523) was the West Syrian bishop of Mabbug (Manbij, Syria) in the early sixth century, although he spent his last years in exile. He was a very influential leader during his lifetime and his works were important in the development of the West Syrian Church. The first excerpt below is from one of two surviving letters that Philoxenus wrote to the monks of Bet Gaugal, a monastery in the region of Nisibis. Philoxenus wrote this text between 482 and 484, when he had been exiled from the city of Antioch but before he was bishop of Mabbug. In this excerpt he praises monks who have not accepted bribes or other pressures to accept Chalcedonian Christianity. The second excerpt from another letter condemns monks who have been bribed in order to support the controversial Council of Chalcedon, whose followers the second text polemically calls the "new Jews." As seen in these texts, monasteries were important allies for West Syrian bishops during the protracted conflicts over the status of Chalcedonian doctrine. For additional excerpts from Philoxenus, see chapters 6 and 9.

FIRST LETTER TO THE MONKS OF BET GAUGAL

Where has the fame of your holy monastery not spread? Who has not admired, who has not wondered at the cruel persecutions [that] you [have suffered]? The mention of your rule causes the lax to fear, for the weak are wont to be afraid when they hear of your courageous works. But as these tremble at the mention of your fervor, so also the strong take heart, and try to imitate the zeal [of] your works. [. . .] Today you form an illustrious remnant among all the disciples. [. . .] Neither the fear of [others] nor the flattery of the great has ruled over you. You have not bartered the truth for earthly presents, and you have not ceased from your zeal for the faith for the sake of temporal gifts, and your monastery is not addicted to begging like those that subsist in that way. You have not sold Christ for sheaves of barley and loaves of bread like those who sell him for such prices. It is written that Judas sold him for thirty [pieces] of silver; but those disciples in name [only] sell him every day for things more contemptible and abominable than that. Those who act thus serve their belly and not God. [. . .] They were born for the earth and not for heaven; their eyes are fixed completely on the things of the earth.

LETTER CONCERNING ZEAL

A monk, indeed, who because of [receiving] a present relaxes from the zeal, is a partaker of the traitor Judas. That one sold the messiah for money and he is selling him for handfuls of barley and loaves of bread; that one sold him for one time, but this one sells him every day. [. . .] A monk who is frightened before the powerful, and ceases from zeal, is not conscious of the messiah. [. . .] A monk who puts on sackcloth but becomes silent about the truth, has the leprosy of Gehazi for his garment. A monk who is being visited by grace but becomes silent regarding the faith, on the last day his mouth shall be shut like that of Legion. A monk who is a companion to the new Jews [i.e., the Chalcedonian Christians], crucifies God together with the old Jews. A monk who at a time when he is expected for war, on the pretext of the peace of the ministry remains silent, is a servant of Satan.

JACOB OF SERUG, *ON THE SOLITARIES*

Late fifth or early sixth century. West Syrian.

Jacob of Serug (d. 521), the famed "flute of the spirit and harp of the church," was a Syriac Christian ascetic and prolific poet. Jacob was doctrinally miaphysite, but he has been revered for his beautiful poetry by Syrian Orthodox and Chalcedonian Christians alike. This excerpt is taken from a series of homilies Jacob wrote on the "solitary" Christians (*iḥidaye*) who withdrew from society to practice Christian asceticism in a celibate life devoted to God. It emphasizes the spiritual value of renunciation, including of worldly possessions and bodily concerns. As Jacob reminds his audience, material poverty in this world produces spiritual wealth in the next realm. So, those who would devote themselves to the life of a Christian solitary should flee from the world and focus on the development of their soul and the accumulation of spiritual treasure in heaven. Although many women practiced asceticism in the Syrian traditions, here Jacob imagines a male practitioner. For additional excerpts from Jacob of Serug, see chapters 2, 7, and 8.

> Poverty is the solitary's entire beauty,
>   But if he is well-supplied, he suffers loss and lacks his beauty.
> Nakedness is his proper clothing if he is discerning;
>   Abundant food has robbed him also of keeping vigil with hope.
> If he has a money bag, he has renounced trust;
>   [If] he has deposited a denarius, [then] Christ has left his abode;
> [If] he has worried about tomorrow, [then] he has taken up a load too big for him;
>   [If] he has considered what to wear, [then] he has trodden on the commandment that would have sustained him.
> [If] he has bought or sold, [then] with a whip of cords our Lord
>   Will drive him away from the monastic community.
> [If] he has desired possessions, [then] he has become a stranger to the promises;
>   And if he should call his brother a fool, [then] he is guilty before the tribunal.
> The solitary never hates the one who hates him,
>   For regarding that, he has stripped off the world to put on the love of the Son.
> Because of what he has, he does not stoop down to acquire the world;
>   The hidden wealth of regal treasuries is not equal to [what he has].
> He is to seek what is above, and unless he is nourished from above,
>   He receives these things here superfluously.
> Inasmuch as he has another world for which to long,
>   [This] world is worthless to him, for his soul looks at his [other] world.
> Wealth is there, but poverty is here,
>   For these present matters here are not ideal.
> This world is grass, a flower, and even a blooming flower;
>   [It is] a leaf that falls off, a blossom that withers, and its beauty vanishes.
> Because of this, solitaries are to flee from it,
>   Lest they be deceived by its superficial, fleeting beauty.
> It resembles a dream and flees like a vision of the night,
>   For, as with sleep, deception is cast upon [the world's] beloved.
> If the solitary is a discerning man, he does not belong to the night
>   To be deceived by dreams and by things that are not real.
> His light is in him and he is not enslaved to the darkness,

And he remains vigilant in God and the dream of the night cannot deceive him.
As for the world's friend, his way is beset with stumbling blocks
    And he journeys in the darkness and stillness does not befall him.
Look, our Lord is a great daylight for whoever he encounters,
    For whoever is smoothing out the rugged place and leveling the road before [his] steps.
By it the soul is illumined to journey without stumbling blocks,
    Along a road full of great peace to the place of the Father.
The blind man is incapable of knowing how to distinguish colors;
    Since he lacks light, he is deprived of seeing beautiful things.
Love of the world blinds humanity and they cannot see
    These hidden beauties in the new world.
Blindness hinders the light of the eye, and there is no way
    To see properly because of the disease disturbing it.
And if the soul has been drawn away by anxiety, its understanding dims,
    So that it becomes blind and cannot see the light above.
[But] the soul has looked up, open to receive
    The great wealth from the unshakable essence.
Its gaze withdrew from the world slightly, and the waves
    Of the Father's splendor carried it away to graze upon his choicest spiritual portions.
To the degree that the mind does not gaze at the earth or its adornments,
    It finds comfort above where the Trinity resides.
If it flees from the love of the world, it draws near
    To become a companion of that army of heavenly beings.
If it has been freed from the slavery of the vexing world,
    It has ascended to him who reigns in a glorious place without suffering.
But if it has begun to arrange [its] affairs like a worrier,
    The heights have cast it down, and it descends to graze with the animals.
Because of this, the cultivators of the spirit were commanded to seek what is above,
    [And] not to be caught up in earthly things.
He taught them not to lay up treasure on earth,
    Lest the heart be buried with [that] treasure in the dust of the earth.
"Lay up your treasure in heaven above," he commanded them,
    So that, because of [that] treasure, the heart might ascend to his high place.
For the heart does not abandon [its] treasure and depart from it,
    For it stands there to guard the treasure wherever it is.
If on earth, the heart dwells with it on earth,
    And if in heaven, moreover, it remains near it without abandoning it.
Whoever has spiritual treasure above, in heaven,
    Though his heart should descend to wander on earth, it is not enslaved.
But if the heart withdraws from [the treasure], it also is removed,
    For no treasure remains without guards.
Whoever has sent his treasure to God on high,
    Let him leave his heart there in that place and [God] will guard it.

Inasmuch as the heart is above with God on high,
   His treasury is guarded, not to be despoiled by raiders.
Inasmuch as the soul gazes at God, it is filled with light,
   And if the soul turns back to look at the world, darkness envelopes it.

STATUTES OF THE SCHOOL OF NISIBIS

Late fifth or early sixth century. East Syrian.

The most elaborate Syriac text regarding monastic governance is the *Statutes of the School of Nisibis*. Nisibis became the home of East Syrian scholarship and education from the late fifth century, after the School of Edessa was closed by the emperor Zeno in 489. Subsequently, the School of Nisibis provided a blueprint for monastic establishments throughout Persia and further east. These *Statutes* concern a wide range of topics, from the election of the head of the monastery (*rish dayra*) or abbot (*rabban*) and the subabbot (*rabbaita*), to personal wills and inheritance, to caring for sick monks, to study and teaching duties, to sheltering enslaved persons who have run away. There are prohibitions against traveling across the border into the Roman Empire. Many different offices are cited, including the teachers (*malpane*), who must have been numerous. Above all, the *Statutes* demonstrate the complicated business of ordering a vibrant monastery and how discipline and self-governance became critical issues as Syriac ascetic practices became institutionalized and spread throughout the Christian Near East.

> The first canon. At the time when it is proper, that the subabbot should be [set apart] and made known according to the order and custom year by year, with the counsel of our abbot, the head teacher of the school and with that of the whole community with one consent they shall elect a reliable person who is fitting for the guidance of the community. No one is permitted to stand up and to make a party, quarrel, and confusion about something that was right. And whosoever is found that he does one of these [things], and stands up against the truth and disputes, shall receive punishment. He shall become foreign to the community and the residence in the town.
>
> The second canon. The subabbot, however, that one who has been elected and entrusted with the guidance of the community, shall not judge by taking favor, and shall not be directed by his own conscience, and shall not proceed with income and expense of the school without two or three witnesses. And without the counsel of our abbot and that of the outstanding brothers he shall not bring punishment on the offenders, but every act, appointing punishment or remission or something else, he shall do with the counsel of the brothers.
>
> The third canon. Some of the brothers who come to the school to learn instruction and abandon their promises and slip away to take wives or are detected in adultery or in fornication or in stealing or in witchcraft or in a mind perverted from the true faith or are deceived to be distracted in vanities—which are slander, plotting, confusion, lie, intrigue

in the houses on the occasion of the banquets or contention of rebellion—the whole community determines that these shall not be received in the school, and also shall not be in the town.

The fourth canon. Those brothers who are in the school are not allowed to go over to the region of the Romans without precept and order of the brothers and that of the subabbot of the school, neither for the cause of instruction nor because of a pretense of prayer, also not in order to buy or to sell. Whoever, however, enters on the occasion of instruction or prayer without permission, shall not be received in the community. For the purpose of trade it is not lawful to get permission because it is outside the will of the canons and it is entirely foreign to the occupation of the community. But who, then, dares and enters the region of the Romans to do business, he shall not be received in the community. But if it seems [good] to the subabbot and to the brothers of the community to grant grace to them while they are not deserving it, because only once they were caught treading outside the custom of the community—those who entered because of teaching and prayer shall agree under strict stipulation that they shall not enter again without permission. And after they receive censure and rebuke that they deserve, they shall be received. From those who entered because of trade, what they brought from the region of the Romans shall be taken and it shall enter the treasury of the school, and then they shall be received. If, however, those brothers who have a good name, nothing being heard against them either in the community or in another place, have done business, a half of that which they have brought shall be taken from them for the treasury of the school. [Through these proceedings] they shall be received in the community. [As to] the second journey—if they are captured, they shall be driven away entirely from the community.

The fifth canon. No one of the brothers shall practice business or craft. But if it is necessary to buy and sell [then] from the month of Ab [i.e., August] until [the month of] the former Teshri [i.e., December] outside Nisibis in other countries. In Nisibis, however, except the workers, they are not allowed to practice business. A craft, however, that is not shameful, they may work for three months.

The sixth canon. No one of the brothers who has earned dinars beyond his need and seeks to lend them shall lend on usury. On interest, however, as this is in the church, that is one hundredth of a dinar per year, he may lend in order that the community may not be reviled because of his affair if he takes more.

The seventh [canon]. The brothers, however, who enter the community newly, shall not be received until they have appeared before the subabbot and the brothers, and have received instruction as to how they ought to be.

The eighth [canon]. The brothers, however, who [already] are in the rank of the scribe are not allowed to cease from writing, reading, and interpretation of the school and the recitation of the choirs without an urgent affair.

The ninth [canon]. In the time, however, of the great *mautba* [i.e., part of the service sung seated], when they have recited the psalm of the evening, everyone shall go into his cell. And when the cock crows, everybody shall come and take [his] place. The one that was taken from the evening is not valid. Those, however, who come at the cock's crow shall leave one row before the bench to be for the brothers and presbyters and shall take places in the other row.

The tenth [canon]. The brothers, however, who come to the school shall not dwell singly and by twos in the cell but shall be with others without confusion.

The eleventh [canon]. The brothers who reside in one cell, if it happens that one of them become sick, shall be with him and serve him as is becoming.

The twelfth [canon]. A brother who has a contention with his companion or against someone else, shall not go to the court of the outsiders out of his will without permission of the brothers and the subabbot. And a brother who dares and transgresses one of these canons and does not repent, shall become foreign to the community and the town.

The thirteenth [canon]. Those brothers, however, who are in the school—if, before they appear to be trained and know the order of the word, they are found that they speak in the school about an affair of the community, and cause confusion in the school—shall be driven away from the community and from the town.

The fourteenth [canon]. A brother who finds something lost and does not come and notify the subabbot about this in order that the affair may be announced in the community and the one who lost it may hear and take his own; or he requests a book from the subabbot in order to read in it or to copy from it, and it happens that the subabbot forgets [about it], the one who does not come to notify him shall receive punishment and shall go from the town.

The fifteenth [canon]. A brother from among the brothers who notices that his companion is troubled by some offense and offers him correction, and he does not regret—and he neglects and does not come to inform the subabbot, and the matter becomes known after a certain time through another one, he shall share in the punishment of that one who offended.

The sixteenth [canon]. A brother who accuses his companion regarding some offense and does not prove it, and it is found that he falsely told about him, shall receive punishment that that offense deserves regarding which he has accused his companion.

The seventeenth [canon]. When someone of the brothers becomes ill and approaches death—if he shall make a will in the presence of the subabbot and the brothers, something he has made shall be valid; if, however, he shall make it when the subabbot is far off, the will he has made shall be void, and all he has shall enter [the funds of] the school.

The eighteenth [canon]. If someone of the brothers stretches out [his] hand because of one of the reasons that he may have and beats his companion or reviles him and is proved by those who have seen it, he is to be scourged before the entire community.

The nineteenth [canon]. If someone of the brothers is scourged in the community because of a matter of offense for three times, and does not reform, and if, after this he shall commit another offense like one of the previous ones, he shall receive punishment, and shall go from the community and from the town.

The twentieth [canon]. But the teacher of reading and the vocalizer, those in the school, if they despise and neglect the order of reading by syllables and reading that is laid upon them without a reason of sickness and permission of our abbot, they shall receive a rebuke; sustenance that they are entitled to receive is withheld from them; and they cannot be present to hear the judgment of the school.

The twenty-first [canon]. Whoever is detected because of some offense, and the brothers and the subabbot of the community have determined the punishment upon him that he is to receive according to his offense, but he does not obey the decision that they have determined over him, and he goes and takes refuge with some cleric or one of the seculars and seeks for himself patrons and a defender—he shall not be worthy of mercy even if his offense is small. And he shall be driven away from the fellowship of the community and from the dwelling place that is in the town [because] he persisted obstinately and did not accept the decision that was [made] against him.

The twenty-second [canon]. Everyone who has become a subabbot is not allowed to act contrary to these [rules] that are written in this book. And if he shows himself that he acts otherwise, he shall give to the school as a recompense ten dinars of gold and shall leave the community and the town in shame.

ELIAS, *LIFE OF JOHN OF TELLA*

Early sixth century. West Syrian.

John of Tella (d. 538) joined a monastery at Kallinikos in the early sixth century and was ordained bishop of Tella by Jacob of Serug and his colleagues in 519. Because the new emperor Justin I oversaw the ousting of anti-Chalcedonian bishops from the sees of the Eastern Roman Empire, John spent the years from the early 520s until his death in exile in the eastern borderlands. There he is said to have ordained thousands of deacons and priests for the West Syrian church, helping it to survive despite imperial opposition. This hagiographical text identifies itself as the work of one of John's close followers named Elias, who focuses on John's devout ascetic practice since the time of his youth. It describes John's efforts to extract himself from the marriage to which his mother had promised him, and his mother's initial chagrin at his rejection of a traditional family life in order to devote himself to Christian asceticism.

> [John's mother] betrothed him to a woman, and in gladness of heart prepared to make for him a great and expensive wedding feast. But while these preparations were being made, divine providence watched them all in secret and let them be done so that, finally, it would become apparent to many people that love for Christ had, since his youth, taken a stronger hold on him than love for this world. He put before his eyes, as on a pair of scales, the two loves, comparing one with the other. Thereupon he entered a period of trial and struggle with his thoughts as to which one of the two beauties and pleasures would remain unchanged and uncorrupted, the transitory or the permanent one, the divine or the human, the heavenly possessions and wealth, or those that are here on earth that in time and like time will vanish, although sometimes they last for a little while. But there will come a moment when they will be carried away—like a shadow and like a dream they shall disappear. Because his mind was inflamed by the spirit, and the fire that our savior has lit in the world was burning in his soul, the strength of his spirit did not falter, nor did the care for a wife, for children, and for the possessions of this world excite him. Hope in them and their remembrance [of him] did not prevail in his mind over the thought of God, of the

promises to come, of the real life in him, or over the recognition of his fearful judgments and the punishment of the wicked and the vengeance that should be taken on evildoers in the fire's flame.

So, while his mother was concerned with the details, he was silent and quiet, wrestling with his thoughts, which were now springing up, now vanishing away, to see which of them would have the victory for which he was fighting. He called God to help him and he said, "Show me, O Lord, your way so that I may walk in it. How can a young man keep his way pure to observe your commandments? By the mouth of your prophet you proclaimed happy whoever has borne your yoke in his youth." And he put in his mind this thought, saying, "Unless I completely escape from the world I shall not be delivered from sin." At once he fled to a holy man who had shut himself in a cell a short distance from [the city of] Sura of the Romans and whose name was Abgar—a saint, just, and of great and divine labors. John's purpose was to receive his blessing, to be in his company, and to reveal secretly to him his determination. When his mother—very upset because her son had gone from her sight—knew where he had gone, she arose quickly with her male and female servants and went after him. And when she brought him back to her home, the saint obeyed his mother, respectfully and prudently, yet he was determined to leave her and, without causing her sorrow, return to the monastery. Thus it was for five years. And when his mother said to him, "You can please God and still stay in the world, as these or those people, who still were well off and possessors of wealth in the world, did please him." He said to her, "It belongs to the strong ones, mother, to do perfect justice to the two things when they render to Caesar the things that are Caesar's and to God the things that are God's, and to live in this world like the upright fathers and the just men whose names you mentioned to me. But I, myself, cannot please God and yet be entangled with the world's affairs."

On a certain day he picked up the book of the *Life of the Blessed Thecla*, the one who was Saint Paul's disciple, and read in it. Since he was a chosen vessel, unlike the other young men of his age who did not accept the discipline, he was not struck by the burning arrows of evil, nor was he involved in the passions of the world. Because he was preserved by God's grace and by his parents' vigilance, the love of Christ started with vigor in his soul. Immediately, he took the book of the blessed apostle and started to read it diligently, and, like the blessed Thecla, he became the disciple of the holy apostle.

He built for himself in his house a little upper chamber in which he stayed constantly alone except for his tutor. And they made a pact with each other not to let his mother learn his thoughts and what he was doing. He refrained from eating meat and from drinking wine, and his tutor used to eat the food that was brought to him. And from one evening until the next was well advanced he would eat only a parched piece of bread. Later, he ate but one meal every other day. Still no one had detected so far the secret that was between them. When the tutor sat to enjoy the food that they had brought up to the saint in the evening, as the tutor himself narrated it to us, then the saint, bent like a hook, with his hands bound together on his back and the hair of his head resting on the floor, would proceed to perform his prostrations. He would remain in this state until late in the evening, and afterward he would throw himself on the floor and sleep for a little while. He also learned the Psalms in Syriac and both of them would recite together—for his tutor had learned them along with him. And when his mother, of blessed memory, saw that the color of her son's face and the brightness of his youth had changed, she asked his tutor, "What sort of sign is this that I see in my son, that he looks sad so much?" To calm her, at least with a word, he said to her, "Because he remains up until late at night reading." And she was happy that he was drilling in the reading of foreign languages and the arts, but he really cared only for what was really useful to him.

JOHN OF EPHESUS, *LIFE OF SUSAN*

Sixth century. West Syrian.

John of Ephesus (d. 588/589) was one of the great sixth-century advocates for the West Syrian Christian communities. His three-part *Church History* and his moving *Lives of the Eastern Saints* preserved stories of anti-Chalcedonian saints for the generations that followed. While most of the ascetic heroes of these stories are men, John also recorded some stories of heroic women as well, including this story of Susan. As with most of John's saints, the story of Susan's ascetic valor is explicitly intertwined with her uncompromising defense of West Syrian orthodoxy and the stalwart rejection of the Council of Chalcedon. Susan's story begins when she devotes herself to asceticism at the young age of eight, and it ends in a desert cave where she fights demons, cures the sick, and receives visits from men and women who seek her comfort and counsel. For an additional excerpt from John of Ephesus, see chapter 8.

> And now the twenty-seventh story, about the blessed virgin of Christ whose name was Susan.
>
> The mighty strength of Christ God is wont to be celebrated and manifested in human weakness so that no flesh may glorify itself before him, the strengthener of the weak. However, it is apt to show its activity not only in men who are powerful in appearance and mighty and forceful but also in weak, feeble, frail women. Thus it fortifies and gives them courage until they, too, bear the struggle with undaunted strength—not simply with flesh and blood, enticing passions, the yearnings of fleshly lusts, and so on; but even against principalities, powers, and those ruling the world of this darkness, and against evil spirits under heaven. Against these are they mightily given courage, and they mock them as a powerful man mocks a band of children or infants preparing to come and fight against him. This was also revealed to us through Paul, wise in all things, when he said, "In Christ Jesus there is neither male nor female, nor slave nor free." This woman, then, holy and manly in Christ, so astonished me by her appearance, words, and strength in God that she seemed to me not at all out of place in this series of stories of holy men, with whom she strains to enter the same narrow gate, as indeed she already has done.
>
> Now this blessed woman (as we discovered when we managed to learn the details from her) belonged to a family from Persian Arzanene. It was a noble family; but from the beginning, since the age of eight, the light of her life shone out in her mind until people marveled

at her sensibility, modesty, and devotion. For, as if through prophecy, her parents had named her "Blessing," she who truly received a heavenly blessing.

This virtuous girl decided that she should go and worship in the holy places, where the salvation of our lives took place, and she implored her parents. But they laughed at her, a mere child, and said, "You haven't even learned to understand the scriptures, and yet you want to go to Jerusalem!" So she was silent, keeping watch in her heart; and during that time she prayed and said, "Lord if you wish for the salvation of my miserable soul, 'Make straight your way for me,' and present me with an escort. Save my soul from the defilement of this world's filthy mire!" Then the child (as she related to us when I pressed her greatly) placed her soul in the hands of God and ran away. [. . .]

She searched around to find a female monastery where she could live, and, learning that there was a large community of women between Ascalon and Gaza, she set her course there. She revealed her desire to the woman at the gate, but because of that monastery's strictness, the old woman said to her: "My daughter, you can't live here because you are a child. You couldn't bear the hardship and labor. Besides, your genteel upbringing doesn't make you suited for a monastery."

The devout girl, because she was a stranger and in a foreign country, was very upset, and sat at the gate weeping for seven days. The women tried to drive her away, but she would not leave. Then, learning that she was a foreigner, they took her in; and she entered, though they looked down on her because she was so young. But when they learned where she had come from and where she had gone, they said to her as if concerned, "What good is it, child, for you to go out and ruin your soul this way in the mire of sin? For seeing you so young and, what's more, alone, who—even if he were unwilling—would Satan not bring against you in order to destroy you prematurely?" Then (as the blessed women with her used to relate to me, and as they themselves had learned at the outset from her), she said, "For our Lord's sake pray for me, since I trust in him to whom I have committed my soul, that he did not desert me to be destroyed, and he does not desert me now." And so they praised God.

From that time forward she took up great ascetic practices and virtuous feats of labor, abstinence, and devotion, while they hindered her and would slap her because she was a child, so that she would not apply herself to these things more than the other sisters. But she would strive even more and would keep vigil all night, standing in a corner. Not a single word would leave her mouth for anyone all day unless begged for; nor, from her arrival at the monastery, did any of her companions ever see her face uncovered or all of her eye exposed; and no laughter came from her mouth. [. . .]

After she had been laboring ten years in these practices, persecution fell upon their monastery, forcing them either to submit to the Chalcedonian faith or to leave. Since theirs was a great and well-known community of women, the majority of them were seized and these then submitted to their persecutors; but some scattered here and there. Thus, two choices were facing the blessed woman: either to leave the monastery or to risk falling into evil faith; so she decided to go out, and, entering the desert beyond Alexandria, live there. Immediately she left. But there was great division even among those sisters who had surrendered themselves, and some women were saying, "Since Susan has gone, we won't stay."

Then five of the more prominent women from those who had not surrendered joined themselves to her, although she had intended to go alone, saying, "There is no way that we will be parted from you."

So Susan revealed her intentions to them, since they compelled her, and said, "Do not come with me. For to be brief, if the Lord profits me as is his wont, I am going to the desert." They also declared their decision: "We, too, will come with you to the desert." Then, as they would not be dissuaded, they boarded a ship together and crossed over to Alexandria.

There the blessed woman heard rumor of a place in the desert outside the monastery of Mar Menas, and she directed her course there—about two miles from a village called Mendis. This place eventually belonged to the blessed Syrians, but its beginning lay with Susan's arrival. Now, there was a tower there that had been built as a watchtower against barbarians; and, entering it enthusiastically, she and the five others dwelt there. Then one of them went and brought them work from the village. Thus they labored with their hands for their needs, and they sustained themselves. And God took care of them, seeing their zeal and trust in him. [. . .]

Now the blessed woman gained valiance against demons through the strength that comes from grace, as night and day they arrayed themselves in successive ranks for battle against her in the form of men and attacked her with every kind of weapon. But she mocked them, as a mighty man would despise sickly men who were threatening him. Report of her strength was heard everywhere; and after she had been in that desert for fifteen years, the news of her perfection incited us, as well, to desire the sight of her and of the holy men who were also there. Still, when we were deemed worthy of seeing her whom I can hardly call a woman, I was astonished at the words of suffering and wisdom of God that issued from her mouth [. . .]

She also received the gift of healing, so that she could cure every sickness or disease she stretched her hand against. Now, while we were there, a certain blessed man, great and God-loving, dwelt in a place in the desert not far away. Against him the demons would openly prepare for combat, and he would see their battle with the blessed woman, and she his. But because she was stronger than he, she both conquered the demons and had no fear at all of them. She became firm like stone and unmovable—so much so that the demons would cry out at her: "This is a woman, but she is stone, and instead of flesh she is iron!" Such were the things the demons said to her. [. . .]

[M]arveling at her spiritual strength and courage, I said to [another monk], "Why can one not see the face of this woman?" He told me, "One day while we were speaking, I said to her, 'Why do you conceal your face from us?' And she swore an oath to me, saying, 'He who placed his yoke upon me by his grace knows, our brother, that ever since I accepted his yoke twenty-five years ago, I have not seen a man's face. And do you want me to look at yours now?' So I said to her: 'For our Lord's sake, tell me the truth. Are you afraid that you will suffer harm at the sight of a man, or that he would at the sight of you?' She answered, 'Because of both these things.'"

So, marveling at the practice of the holy woman and the constancy of Susan, Christ's virgin, we departed from there praising God. The story of the blessed virgin of Christ whose name was Susan is ended.

ISAAC OF NINEVEH, *TREATISES ON THE BEHAVIOR OF EXCELLENCE* 1; WHEREBY THE BEAUTY OF SOLITARY LIFE IS TO BE PRESERVED

Late seventh century. East Syrian.

Isaac of Nineveh, a respected monk, was briefly the bishop of Nineveh (Mosul, Iraq) and an influential spiritual teacher for the East Syrian Church in the late seventh century. Starting his ascetic life on the east coast of the Arabian Peninsula, he temporarily moved north to Nineveh to be that city's bishop but returned to be a solitary ascetic farther south again, east of the Tigris and not far north of the Persian Gulf. Isaac's spiritual teachings were influenced by the earlier teachings of Evagrius (d. 399) that came to be rejected in Greek churches after their condemnation at the Second Council of Constantinople under the emperor Justinian in 553. West and East Syrian traditions did not accept that council, however, and often saw Evagrius's teachings as beneficial to the practice of Christian asceticism. The excerpts below come from two of Isaac's teachings. The first is the opening of his six *Treatises on the Behavior of Excellence*, and it introduces readers to the practice of asceticism, along with the fear of God and the renunciation of the world that it requires. The second is all but the final sentences of his short treatise on the beauty of the solitary life and the role model that Christian solitaries should be for others. As with so many early texts, the imagined subject is male, although women also practiced asceticism as the story of Susan above shows. For an additional excerpt from Isaac of Nineveh, see chapter 6.

TREATISES ON THE BEHAVIOR OF EXCELLENCE 1

The fear of God is the foundation of excellence; for excellence is said to be the offspring of faith. It is sown in a man's heart, when he allows his mind to confine the wandering impulses to continual meditation on the order of things to come, away from the distractions of the world. As to the foundation of excellence, the first among its peculiar elements is the concentration of the self, by freeing it from practical things, upon the enlightened word of the straight and holy ways, the word that by the inspired psalmist is called the teacher.

There is scarcely to be found a man who is able to bear honors, or possibly such a one does not exist; because man is very prone to err, even if he be an angel in his way.

The foundation of the way of life consists in accustoming the mind to the words of God and the practice of patience. For the draft provided by the former is helpful toward acquiring perfection in the latter; and, further, increased development toward accomplishment in the latter will cause a heightened desire of the former. And the help provided by both of them will quickly bring about the rise of the whole building.

No one is able to come near to God except only the one who is far from the world. For I do not call separation the departure from the body but from bodily things.

Excellence consists therein that a man in his mind be a void as regards the world. As long as the senses are occupied with [outward] things, it is not possible for the heart to rest from imagining them. Nor do the affections cease, nor evil thoughts end except in the desert and the wilderness.

While the soul has not yet become drunk by the faith in God in that it has received an impression of its powers, the weakness of the senses cannot be healed and it is not able to tread down with force visible matter that is a screen before what is within and not perceived [by the senses].

Reason is the cause of freedom and the fruit of both [is the] liability to err. Without the first, the second cannot be. And where the second fails, there is the third bound as it were with halters.

When grace is abundant in a person, then the fear of death is despised on account of the love of righteousness. He finds many arguments in his soul [proving] that it is becoming to bear troubles for the sake of the fear of God. And those things that are supposed to injure the body and to repel nature unfairly, which consequently are of a nature to cause suffering, are reckoned in his eye as nothing in comparison with what is expected to be. And his mind convinces him firmly of the fact that it is not possible to recognize truth without gaining experience of the affections, and that God bestows great care upon people, and that they are not abandoned to chance. Especially those who are trained in praying to him and who bear suffering for his sake, see [these truths] clearly [as if painted] in colors. But when little faith takes root in our heart, then all these things are felt as contrary, not as serving for testing us.

WHEREBY THE BEAUTY OF SOLITARY LIFE IS TO BE PRESERVED AND HOW IT CAN BE A CAUSE OF GOD'S BEING GLORIFIED

It is becoming for the solitary to be in every way a vision of stimulation to those who look at him, so that because of the beauties that radiate from him on all sides as the rays of the sun, even the enemies of truth unwillingly acknowledge that the Christians have a well-founded hope; and from every side they will flow to their place of refuge, and thus the head of the church will be elevated above its enemies. Thus the glory of the solitary's deeds will be a stimulus for many to withdraw from the world. And [it is becoming] that he be revered by everyone on account of his excellence, so that the mouth of the members of the church will be opened on his account and their head exalted above all creeds.

The pride of Christ's church consists in the behavior of the solitaries. Therefore it is becoming to the solitary that the beauties of his habits shine on all sides; in the humble attitude of his limbs, in the simplicity of his habit, in his elevation above visible things, in the veracity of his renunciation, in his rigorous fasting, in his being continuous silent, in the subduing of his senses, in the continence of his aspect, in his not being quarrelsome with other people for any reason, in the sparingness of his speech, in his being pure from rancor, in his discriminate conscious simplicity. And [it is becoming for him] that it be known that he is alien to this harmful and fleeting life and near to true and spiritual life, from his constantly being by himself, from his being unknown among people, from his not being tied to any one by the bonds of comradeship and intimacy, from his quiet dwelling place, from the small space of his habitation, from his few and mean utensils, from his avoiding people, from his constant prayer, from his hating and avoiding honor, from his not being bound by temporal life, from his great patience, from his endurance in temptations, from his keeping aloof from rumors and from inquiries into worldly affairs, from his constant care for and meditation upon his true country, known by his sad countenance and his shriveled face, from his constantly weeping night and day, and above all from his cautious chastity and his freedom from covetousness in small and great things.

These are, in short, the manifest beauties of the solitary that testify to his being wholly dead to the world and near to God. It is becoming for him to think of these things constantly in order to acquire them.

BARHEBRAEUS, *BOOK OF THE DOVE*

Thirteenth century. West Syrian.

Barhebraeus (d. 1286) was a West Syrian scholar and church leader who played a powerful role in the renaissance of the Syriac language, which had been replaced by Arabic as the lingua franca in the Christian communities under Muslim rule. Barhebraeus was from the region of Melitene in late Roman Armenia and modern Turkey, was educated in centers of learning in the Latin Crusader States, and in 1260 witnessed the Mongol conquest of Aleppo where he was bishop. He moved to Mosul in 1264 when he was appointed to the position of *maphrian,* second only to the patriarch. In charge of the West Syrian churches of the eastern territories, he was regularly in conversation with leaders from Muslim and East Syrian communities in the region and knew work, for example, by the famous Muslim scholar al-Ghazali (d. 1111). Barhebraeus was a prolific author and the mystical *Book of the Dove* represents only one of the wide variety of topics his writings covered. This excerpt describes its teachings as spiritual medicine and instructs its readers on living a life of Christian asceticism. The excerpt ends with Barhebraeus's reminder that even accomplished ascetics must continue to be vigilant against the temptations of the world that could lead them astray. For additional excerpts from Barhebraeus, see chapters 4 and 11.

In the same way as we find, O my brother, in bodily medicine books describing the behavior of patients not attended by a physician, it is becoming, in psychic medicine, to give instructions concerning the behavior of those patients who are without or far from a leader; especially in this our age, in which the Syriac world is bereft of an initiated who has personally experienced the narrowness of the way leading to the kingdom and the narrowness of the gate giving entrance to it. It is, therefore, our aim to give this sort of clear and simple instruction.

This book, which is small in extent but great in power, is divided into four chapters. The first [contains] instruction concerning the bodily labor accomplished in the monastery. The second [describes] the quality of psychic labor performed in the cell. The third explains the spiritual rest that the consoling dove imparts to the perfect, elevating them to royal rank and introducing them into the divine cloud where the Lord is said to abide. The fourth is a tale of the author's gradual progress in teachings and some sentences communicated to him in revelation.

These four kinds [of states] are represented by the four periods of Noah's life: the first, that of the works of his righteousness, which made him pleasant to God. The second, that of his entering the ark, which saved him from the destruction of the deluge. The third, that of his leaving the ark, when the dove had announced to him that the waters had disappeared from the surface of the earth. The fourth, that of the revelations he received and the covenant established with him; the planting of the vineyard, his drinking wine, and his getting drunk.

However, Noah's dove was irrational and mortal; but this dove is rational and immortal. She even gives reason to the rational and life to the living. She flies without leaving her nest above, the church of the firstborn in heaven. She reaches all quarters without stirring from her place. All images are represented in her without her possessing color herself. She abides in the East, yet the West is full of her. Her food is fire, and whoever is crowned by her with wings will breathe forth flames from his mouth. All those who are burning from love and sick from affection reveal their secrets to her and she slakes their thirst. Her speech touches every ear, but few hear her voice. She calls everyone by their name, but one of a thousand answers her. Her cooing is much sweeter than the sound of the organ. As the poet describes her:

She's very pure and full of shame,
No mouth can put on her a blame.
She bears no sign of things material,
Being spiritual, incorporeal. [. . .]

The habitation of the cell has to take place with distinction, not falling into it casually, as is the case with many persons who become recluses without having fixed an aim, toward which the labor of their behavior shall be directed. This aim consists in expecting from the Lord the gift of the illumination of the mind and the aptitude to behold the spiritual things in their nature and to have communion with them; together with many other things that are effectuated to [the recluse].

When he has fulfilled this, the duties of the cell are given him. They are: solitude, true asceticism, which is accomplished by prayer, invocation, reciting, and meditation; definite ritual prayers at fixed times; vigils; weeping; fasting; manual labor; abiding abroad; guarding the heart against evil passions, which are: dejectedness, wantonness, lasciviousness, anger, rancor, envy, desires, covetousness, vain glory, [assuming] a false appearance, haughtiness, boasting, reprehension.

When the heart is purified from such evil passions, it has necessarily to be adorned with good qualities, as patients, beside shunning things that cause harm, have also to make use of remedies. They are: love of teachings, faith, thanksgiving, hope, fear of God, poverty, confidence, purity of deliberations, remembrance of death. This is the behavior of the pure in heart, which shall see God. We shall describe each of these [qualities] peculiarly. [. . .]

Prayer, forgiving the faults of the one who has sinned against him, turning eastward, elevating his hands, and looking to the earth as if being ashamed before his Lord, the solitary shall begin his prayer by saying several times, "O God, be merciful to me, a sinner. My Lord, have mercy upon me. My Lord, endow me with those things that you know to be profitable to me." Then God will give him that of which he has no idea to ask. [. . .]

When the mind becomes united with the good one, it ascends from glory to glory by the Lord the spirit, forgetting not only the things of the world but also itself, and in the light with which it is clad in that apartment it sees itself in the likeness of God. [. . .]

Though the body is sanctified, the heart purified, and the mind made bright in the rank of perfection, still, if the perfect is not cautious against the snares laid by the evil one, he will quickly fall from that height of elevation, as also Beliar has fallen. He is, however, drawn away from evil deliberations, as soon as he, beatified by wonderful revelations, rejoices at himself and desires to reveal those gifts that no eye has seen, that no ear has heard, and of which he has been deemed worthy. So he is zealous to go to towns and villages as a teacher and a redeemer of souls, as an edification and an example to be imitated by many. And he imagines demons that howl and complain of him, saying, "What have we to do with you, servant of God, that you are come here to torment us?" And further his imagination sees people being healed and a crowd pressing near to touch his garments. And he places at his door those who seek him and, if he is not willing to go with them, drag him along with ropes.

If he is allured thus, he is on the way to return to the world. Then, if he sees one of his colleagues, whose speeches are in better favor than his and whose teaching is more beloved, he envies him and begins to hate him, as for instance Heron of Alexandria, the punctual in behavior, who used to take food once every three days. When he was captivated by self-exaltation, his intellect was blinded and he began to disdain Aba Evagrius, saying, "Those who follow your teaching, err; for they want no teacher beside Christ. For he has said, 'Call no person your master on the earth.'"

And when Satan incited him to go to Alexandria and he had come there, he immersed himself in the mud of fornication so that his genitals became rotten and had to be cut off. And when he was healed, being without those members, he returned anew to steadiness of mind. Therefore, even if a man reaches perfection, he has constantly to beseech his Lord: "Do not cast me away from your presence; and do not take your Holy Spirit from me."

6

MYSTICISM AND PRAYER

For our purposes, "mysticism" refers to those practices that aim for a direct and unmediated encounter with the mystery of God. Such encounters could take the form of a vision, an intellectual contemplation, or an experience of union or "commingling"—just to name a few. The Syriac tradition has a long and rich tradition of mystical theology, with several distinct influences and features. This chapter views that long tradition through three lenses: (1) the specter of "Messalianism," an ascetic movement whose members allegedly claimed a sensible perception of the very essence of the Trinity, as well as the ability to achieve perfection in this life, such that they were freed from conventional laws and norms; (2) managing the influence of Evagrius of Pontus (d. 399), whose ascetical and mystical theology was both an inspiration and at times a source of anxiety for Syriac mystical theologians; (3) the flowering of mystical theologies of prayer, especially in the East Syrian Church of the seventh and eighth centuries.

The first two selections below give a taste of how "Messalianism" shaped the imagination of the Syriac mystical tradition. "Messalianism" was an ascetic movement whose name derives from the Syriac *msallyana*, "one who prays." What we know of the Messalians we know from their opponents, and scholars debate whether they were in fact a real group with distinctive beliefs and practices or whether they were merely a rhetorical construct, an imagined heresy with which ecclesiastical authorities could better police the mystical excesses of monks. We first hear of them in the fourth century, but the specter of Messalianism continued to haunt the Syriac mystical tradition until the eighth century. Although different views were attributed to Messalians over the centuries, the most relevant are as follows: that they spurn the church's sacraments and authorities because they believe that fervent prayer is the only way to have a sensible perception of the essence of the Trinity; such sensible perceptions render the monk perfect so that the perfected monk is thereafter freed from conventional laws and norms. The Messalians came to serve as a sort of "specter" for the Syriac mystical tradition, almost like a photographic negative. Their alleged belief in a sensible perception of the essence of the Trinity, for example, led Syriac mystical theologians to develop accounts of the vision and contemplation of God that was neither sensible, nor claimed to comprehend the incomprehensible divine essence. Their alleged belief in their ability to achieve perfect freedom from passion (*apatheia*) was a source of particular concern, leading other writers to chasten confidence in ever achieving such perfection in this world. Their alleged disdain for the church and its sacraments, as well as for conventional laws and norms—what one might call their mystical "antinomianism"—echoes down through the centuries and prompted some writers to insist on guard rails for mystical practice. Their emphasis on prayer as the means of directly encountering God is reflected in the subsequent tradition, even as that tradition articulates very different understandings of mystical prayer. Nevertheless, throughout these centuries, Syriac mystical theologians were often suspected of being influenced by Messalians or by Messalian ideas.

Evagrius of Pontus was a Greek theologian whose writings exerted an enormous influence on the Syriac ascetical and mystical tradition. He spent the last stage of his life as a monk in Lower Egypt among the famous desert monks of Nitria and Kellia. He in turn was shaped by another Egyptian theologian, Origen of Alexandria (d. ca. 253), whose writings inspired a movement we call "Origenism," popular especially among Eastern monks as early as the fourth century. Both Origen and Evagrius were condemned by the imperial church at the Second Council of Constantinople in 553. Evagrius's writings were translated into Syriac, where his reputation flourished among both the West and East Syrian communities, neither of whom felt bound by the condemnation of the imperial church. Evagrius divided the monastic life into two stages, practice (*praktikē*) and contemplation (*theōria*), with the threshold between the two being freedom from passion (*apatheia*). At times, his views on *apatheia* veered close to the Messalians', and so Syriac authors, such as Babai the Great (d. 628), had to work to interpret him safely for his own monastic charges. Babai's commentary on Evagrius's *Gnostic Chapters* (*Kephalaia Gnostika*) facilitated the acceptance of a revised Evagrian mysticism in the East Syrian Church. Like Origen, Evagrius believed in universal salvation, the rehabilitation and restoration of all rational minds (angels, humans, and demons)—often referred to as the *apokatastasis* (Acts 3:21). Evagrius imagined the minds returning to and mingling with God in a kind of mystical (re)union. Some Syriac authors, such as Babai and Philoxenus of Mabbug (d. 523), sought to hem in such speculation, while others, such as Stephen bar Ṣudayli (sixth century) in his *Book of the Holy Hierotheus*, took it much further. Almost all Syriac theologians esteemed Evagrius, but they had to manage how his esoteric mystical theology, centered on the mind's contemplation of and eventual return to the divine source, could be translated for their own lives and communities.

The Syriac mystical tradition is also characterized by an intense interest in the theory and practice of prayer (and what lies beyond prayer) as the means for having a direct and unmediated encounter with God. The roots of this go back to such foundational figures as Ephrem and Aphrahat in the fourth century. The first selection of this section, however, is from John of Apamea (first half of the fifth century) who recommended silent, spiritual prayer as the means of encountering God, who "is silence." In the wake of Abraham of Kashkar's monastic reforms in the late sixth century, a distinctive monastic culture emerged in the East Syrian Church that was conducive to the rise of mystical literature. The most significant monastic center in the southern dioceses of the East Syrian Church was the monastery of Rabban Shapur in Khuzestan, where two late seventh-century authors resided for a time: Isaac of Nineveh and Dadisho' Qaṭraya. Specifically, discussions of prayer—and, crucially, what lies beyond prayer—picked up in the seventh century among these two, as well as in the eighth century among two other East Syrian monastic and mystical theologians, John of Dalyata and Joseph Ḥazzaya. All four authors state, or at least suggest, that there is a state *beyond* prayer, although perhaps only reached *through* prayer, in which the mind no longer needs words or thoughts but is rapt in silent wonder, where (at least in Joseph Ḥazzaya) the light of the monk's mind is enveloped in, and indistinguishable from, the light of the holy Trinity.

These theories of a state beyond prayer could well be seen as a critique of the Messalians, who believed prayer and only prayer offered the means for a direct and sensible perception of the essence of the Trinity. Nevertheless, in the late 780s, three of these four authors—John of Apamea, John of Dalyata, and Joseph Ḥazzaya—were condemned by the katholikos Timothy I (d. 823) for alleged Messalian tendencies. Forty years later, the three authors were rehabilitated by the katholikos Isho' bar Nun (d. 828). Nevertheless, this condemnation halted the momentum of the Syriac mystical tradition in the eighth century and instead initiated a process of retrospective canonization of the great mystical theologians of the past. The ninth-century monastic histories of Isho'dnah of Baṣra and Thomas of Marga seem aware that the golden age had passed.

Further Reading   The best place to begin is Sebastian Brock's anthology, which includes a wealth of sources from the fourth to the eighth centuries: Sebastian P. Brock, *The Syriac Fathers on Prayer and the Spiritual Life*. (Kalamazoo, MI: Cistercian Publications, 1987). For a recent and high-altitude survey of the East Syrian mystical tradition, see Adrian C. Pirtea, "The Mysticism of the Church of the East," in *The Syriac World*, ed. Daniel King (London: Routledge, 2018), 355–76. For the early period of Messalianism, see Columba Stewart, *"Working the Earth of the Heart": The Messalian Controversy in History, Texts, and Language to AD 431* (Oxford: Clarendon Press, 1991). For its continued relevance to the Syriac tradition, see Brouria Bitton-Ashkelony, "'Neither Beginning nor End': The Messalian Imaginaire and Syriac Asceticism," *Adamantius* 19 (2013): 222–39. To appreciate

Evagrius's complicated influence on the Syriac mystical tradition, see Joel Kalvesmaki and Robin A. Darling Young, eds., *Evagrius and His Legacy* (South Bend, IN: University of Notre Dame Press, 2016). The long Syriac tradition of mystical prayer has been masterfully handled by Brouria Bitton-Ashkelony, *The Ladder of Prayer and the Ship of Stirrings: The Praying Self in Late Antique East Syrian Christianity* (Leuven: Peeters, 2019). For further reading and bibliography, see Grigory Kessel and Karl Pinggéra, *A Bibliography of Syriac Ascetic and Mystical Literature* (Leuven: Peeters, 2011); Grigory Kessel, "Syriac Ascetic and Mystical Literature: An Update (2011–2017)," *Hugoye: Journal of Syriac Studies* 20, no. 2 (2017): 435–88.

MESSALIANISM

TIMOTHY OF CONSTANTINOPLE, *ON THOSE WHO COME TO THE CHURCH FROM THE HERETICS*

Ca. 600. Greek (alternative dating puts him in the early eighth century)

Timothy was a priest in Constantinople. His work *On Those Who Come to the Church from the Heretics* includes a list of doctrines associated with the Messalians. Timothy's is just one of five such lists we have, which all may go back to a single original. In this text, the Messalians are said to believe that a demon dwells in each and every human soul, which baptism cannot expel; only prayer can. They are said to believe that once Christians have achieved freedom from passion (*apatheia*), they have no need for any discipline or teaching of the body or soul; furthermore, they can passionlessly pursue whatever they wish, however (im)moral. Messalians are also said to believe that one can have a sensible perception of the Trinity; and that one should shun work in favor of sleep and spurn the sacraments of the church, including the Eucharist.

> [The Messalians or "Those who pray"] say that intense prayer alone can drive out this demon.
>
> They say that a demon is substantially joined immediately to each person who is born, this having befallen [humanity] from the condemnation of Adam, and that this demon incites the person to unseemly deeds, remaining with him substantially. [. . .]
>
> Yet they say that holy baptism contributes nothing to the driving out of this demon: nor is holy baptism enough to cut out the roots of sin, [the roots that] have coexisted with people from the beginning. [. . .]
>
> This demon is made to flee through the coughing and spitting of the one praying, [and] is visible as smoke or as a serpent in its coming out. [. . .]
>
> They say that the expulsion of the demon that has coexisted with people has occurred through coughing and spitting [. . .]
>
> And that when this happens, then the coming of the Holy Spirit occurs to the one praying, the Holy Spirit visiting and appearing perceptibly. [. . .]

He says that after what is called *apatheia* by them, the soul feels such communion occur to it with the heavenly Bridegroom as a woman feels in being with a man. [. . .]

As the body is freed from the bitterness of the passions and the soul is no longer prone to the inclination toward worse things, as both soul and body then come into *apatheia*. [. . .]

No longer is one needful of fasting or other discipline of soul or body for the instruction of the body, nor of teaching for the training of the soul.

They say that giving oneself to wantonness and licentiousness after the so-called *apatheia* is guiltless and not dangerous: for one is no longer oppressed by any passion but is free to pursue licentiously the passions that had been forbidden.

They say that after what they call *apatheia*, then people can foresee the things to come and behold invisible powers perceptibly.

They say that the all-holy and life-giving and blessed Trinity, which is by nature invisible to every creature, can be seen with the eyes of the flesh by those who have come into what they call *apatheia*: and to such people alone occurs the vision seen by them bodily.

Suddenly leaping up, they imagine demons to be jumping about, and with their fingers they fancy that they shoot the demons.

They say that they see in what condition are the souls of the perfected, and they fancy themselves knowers of hearts, as if they could see accurately the dispositions of people through intentions and manners.

They say that the work of the hands is to be shunned as loathsome. And so they call themselves "spiritual ones," not considering it possible or right for such people as these to touch perceptible work: they are repudiating in this way the tradition of the apostles.

They say not to give alms to those who ask, or to widows or orphans, to those in various circumstances, either to those who have maimed bodies, or to those who have encountered incursions of robbers or barbarians, or to those fallen into situations such as these; but rather they hold on to everything themselves, for they are truly "the ones who are poor in spirit."

They say that after what is called by them *apatheia*, they give themselves over to much sleep, and the dreams that occur by the inspiration of the evil demon energizing them they herald as prophecies; and they teach that these things are to be believed as inspired by the Holy Spirit. These possessions they regard and name as holy: they are deceiving and deceived.

They say that the holy reception of the holy body and blood of Christ our true God neither benefits nor harms those who receive them worthily or unworthily. And that on account of this alone it is not necessary to separate from ecclesiastical communion, regarding this as indifferent. And they do not receive these things as life-giving, with fear and faith, as being and believed to be of God incarnate.

These, when asked about their own teachings, become deniers; and immediately and willingly anathematize all the ones who think or thought this way. They swear without fear that they hate and reject such beliefs, for after *apatheia* neither perjury nor cursing can harm those who have become, as they say, "spiritual ones." They have from the tradition of their teachers that they can perjure and anathematize themselves freely.

EVAGRIUS OF PONTUS, *PRAKTIKOS*, *SKEMMATA*, AND *KEPHALAIA GNOSTIKA*; BABAI THE GREAT, *COMMENTARY ON THE* SKEMMATA *AND COMMENTARY ON THE* KEPHALAIA GNOSTIKA

Fourth century. Greek.
Early seventh century. East Syrian.

Evagrius of Pontus (d. 399) was a Greek ascetical and mystical theologian whose writings exerted an enormous influence on the Syriac tradition. He argued that monastic practice delivered the monk into a state of freedom from passion or *apatheia*, which was a threshold the monk had to cross on his way from being a monastic practitioner (*praktikos*) to becoming a monastic "knower" (*gnostikos*), given over to contemplation (*theoria*), first of the created world and then of its creator, the Triune God. Evagrius's views on perfect *apatheia* and contemplation of the Trinity were felt to be dangerously close to Messalian teachings, and so Syriac commentators had to guard against any heretical implications of his teachings. His strongest articulation of perfect *apatheia* in *Praktikos* 68 (quoted below) was simply omitted from the Syriac translation of that work. Babai the Great (d. 628) was a theologian and monastic author of the East Syrian Church. He wrote commentaries on Syriac translations of Evagrius's works, the *Skemmata* and the baffling *Gnostic Chapters* (*Kephalaia Gnostika* [*KG*]). The Syriac translation of the *Gnostic Chapters* (the so-called S1 version) had already gone some distance in domesticating Evagrius's thinking. In the selection below, Babai is at pains to show that Evagrius is opposed not only to the Eunomians (i.e., Neo-Arians) but, more importantly, to the Messalians. Babai insists that perfect *apatheia* is on offer only in the afterlife, and that in this life we need the sacrament of baptism and ongoing disciplines of body and spirit to make us ever more holy. For additional excerpts from Babai the Great, see chapter 3.

> *Praktikos* 68 [omitted from the Syriac translation]: The perfect person does not practice self-control, and the one who has attained freedom from passion [*apatheia*] does not practice patient endurance, since endurance is for the one subject to the passions, and self-control for the one who is troubled.
>
> *Skemmata* 3: Freedom from passion [*apatheia*] is the quiet state of the rational soul, which is established through humility and chastity.
>
> Babai, *Commentary on the* Skemmata 3: Evagrius indicates what freedom from passion [*apatheia*] is, and that it is not like the impiety of the filthy Messalians, who perform all vile deeds and say that they do them without passion, on the grounds that they are free of passion as if in the New World—or as if there were no judgment.
>
> Evagrius rejects their impiety when he says: "Freedom from passion [*apatheia*] is the quiet state of the rational soul, which is established through humility and chastity." It is not thus [i.e., in the manner that the Messalians claim], you wicked troublemakers! You

sons of demons! Wanderers in the city streets and performers of all types of vile deeds—in their satanic pride, they preach about themselves, "We are perfect."

Now, listen: in every moment of the "quiet state of the rational soul," which is obtained by tranquility and by abstinence from all visible things, without the humility that considers itself dust and ashes and without the chastity, which is resplendent, holy, and pure—not only [freedom] from intercourse with or looking at lewd women but also freedom from all whispers of the movements of all sorts of vile deeds, above which the intellect is exalted—[without such humility and chastity] one cannot obtain this freedom from passion [*apatheia*], as in a pledge in this life.

KG 3.9 (S1): In the world to come the ignorance of rational beings will come to an end, and in them the knowledge of distinctions will abound, those distinctions from which joy and sadness flow: joy for the diligent, sadness for the negligent.

Babai, *Commentary on the* KG 3.9 (S1): [Evagrius] lays low two impious heresies, that of the followers of Eunomius, who foolishly claim to be perfect in divine knowledge, and that of the filthy Messalians, who preach *apatheia* and that they can become perfect in this life, since they imagine [that they perform] spiritual prayer. Not so, you wicked men! [. . .] In the house of judgment, all rational creatures will receive perfect knowledge: Demons and wicked men [will receive perfect knowledge] of their suffering, and they will testify to the righteousness of God. The holy angels and blessed men [will receive perfect knowledge] of their delight, and they will rejoice in the kingdom that the ages never make to pass, on account of their diligence here, which is in the love of toil and love toward their Lord."

KG 3.85 (S1): All those who in water are baptized share in the fragrance of the Holy Spirit, but he who baptizes is he who has the perfumed oil.

Babai, *Commentary on the* KG 3.85 (S1): Here [Evagrius] rejects and uncovers the wicked heresy of the Messalians, whose very name is deceitful, who deny and reject holy baptism and who [claim that] spiritual prayer gives us the grace of the Holy Spirit, and that they are perfect in this world and baptism would profit us nothing. Blessed Mark [the Monk] uncovered this wicked heresy in his *memra* on baptism. Concerning this, also, blessed Evagrius says that all those who are baptized in the water of baptism receive the pledge of the grace of the Holy Spirit.

KG 4.39 (S1): If in the world to come God shows his wealth to rational beings, it is certain that in this world they grasp [only] a part of it.

Babai, *Commentary on the* KG 4.39 (S1): This chapter is against the Eunomians, who wickedly assert that they are perfect in the knowledge of God in this life; and against the Messalians—whose very name is deceitful—who foolishly claim perfection in this passible world . . . through holy baptism, we receive as in the beginnings and as in a pledge all the things that you [i.e., Eunomians and Messalians] claim.

KG 6.60 (S1): Sterile is the mind deprived of spiritual teaching, or lacking the seeds sown by the Holy Spirit.

Babai, *Commentary on the* KG 6.60 (S1): [Messalians] reject reading the scriptures and virtuous conduct; they live in idleness and pleasure; they preach prayer without works; and they claim to have *apatheia*.

EVAGRIAN INFLUENCES

EVAGRIUS OF PONTUS, *LETTER TO MELANIA*

Late fourth century. Greek.

While the *Gnostic Chapters* (*Kephalaia Gnostika*) are the most elaborate and esoteric articulation of Evagrius's mystical theology, his *Letter to Melania* (also called the *Great Letter*) is a much clearer expression of the same. Evagrius was a follower of Origen of Alexandria (d. 253), who taught that all rational beings (angels, humans, and demons) will be restored to their original condition as minds (*noes*, sing. *nous*) in a final "restoration of all things" or *apokatastasis pantōn* (Acts 3:21). In this selection Evagrius anticipates what will happen in the final restoration. Notice that Evagrius imagines that the distinguishing names and qualities of the rational minds will disappear as they are united to God, whose three persons—Father, Son, and Spirit—will remain for all eternity. Also notice his daring image of how the restored minds will mingle with God: land (i.e., sin) will disappear, and rivers (i.e., minds) will merge with the ocean (i.e., God), "one with him and undifferentiated."

Just as there will be a time when the names and numbers associated with "body," "soul," and "mind" will be taken away, by virtue of the fact that they will be raised to the order of mind (as in, "Grant them that they be one in us, as you and I are one" [John 17.22]), so too there will be a time when the names and numbers of "Father," "his Son," "his Spirit," "his rational creation"—that is, his body—will be taken away (as in "God will be all in all" [1 Corinthians 15:28]).

But do not think, because I said that the names and numbers of rational creation and its creator will be taken away, that the persons and names of the Father, Son, and Spirit will be erased. Rather, just as the nature of the mind is united to the nature of the Father—in that the mind is the Father's body; so too the names "soul" and "body" will be absorbed into the persons of the Son and Spirit, and the one nature, three persons of God and of his image will abide without end, as it was before the minds' descent into bodies and will be again after [their] descent into bodies, because of the agreement among wills.

For it is on this account that there is number in body and soul and mind, namely because of the differences among wills. But the names and numbers that came upon the mind because of movement will be taken away; so too will the many names by which God is named. Because of the differences among rational beings, God is necessarily called—causally, providentially, and figuratively—"judge" because of evildoers, "avenger" because of sins, "doctor" because of the sick, "resurrector" because of the dead, "executioner" and "penitent" because of enmity and sin, and so on and so forth.

It is not as if all these distinctions do not exist but rather that those who need them do not exist. But the names and persons of the Son and the Spirit do not pass away, because they have no beginning or end; since they have not been named from some transient cause, they do not pass away. But when, and as long as, their cause exists, they exist. But the Son and Spirit are not like rational creation, whose cause is also the Father: he caused rational creation by grace, but the Son and the Spirit by the nature of his essence.

But this mind, as we said, is one in its nature and person and order. At some time, because of its own sovereign free will, it fell from its original order, and was named soul. And when again it descended it was called body. At one and the same time, there is body, soul, and mind, because of the differences among wills. And because there will be a time when their different wills and movements will pass away, it will rise again to its original creation. Its nature and person and name will be one, which God knows. That which rises in its nature is surely alone among all beings in that neither its place nor its name is known. And as for the mind, surely when again it is naked it will say what its nature is.

Do not be amazed when I said that in the union of the rational beings with God the Father they will be one nature in three persons, without addition or difference. For if the perceptible sea that is one in its nature and color and taste when many rivers of different tastes mingle with it not only is not changed to their distinctive qualities but rather, completely and effortlessly, changes them to its own nature, color, and taste, how much more so the intelligible sea, infinite and unchanging (which is God the Father), when like torrents to the sea the minds return to it, it completely changes all of them to its own nature, color, and taste. Thereafter they are not many but one, in their unity without end or distinction, because of their union and mixture with it.

Just as in the mingling of the rivers with the sea, there is found no addition in its nature or change in its color or taste, so too in the mingling of the minds with the Father, there is no addition of a second nature or a fourth person. But just as the sea is one in its nature and color and taste before the rivers mingle with it and even after they do so, so too the nature of God is one in the three persons of Father, Son, and Spirit, even after the minds mingle with him, just as before they do.

For we see that, before the waters of the sea manifested in one place and the dry land became visible, the rivers in it were one. But afterward they were separated from the sea, becoming many and different because each and every one of them was differentiated by the taste of the land in which it happened to be. Thus, by analogy, before sin separated minds from God—like the land separated the sea from the rivers—they were one with him without difference. But when their sin became known, they were separated from him and were estranged from him and from his taste and color, because each and every one of them took the taste of that body to which it was joined. But when the land is taken away from their midst, the sea and the rivers will again be one without difference. Thus, when the sin between minds and God is erased, they will be one and not many.

But although I said that as the rivers were originally in the sea, so the rational beings were in God, do not infer from this that they were with him eternally, in their nature. Even if they were with him eternally in his wisdom and in his creative power, their creation had a beginning. But there is no end to them because of their union with him who has neither beginning nor end.

EVAGRIUS OF PONTUS, *KEPHALAIA GNOSTIKA*; BABAI THE GREAT, *COMMENTARY ON THE* KEPHALAIA GNOSTIKA

Fourth century. Originally in Greek, preserved in Syriac.
Early seventh century. East Syrian.

Apart from a number of fragments, the original Greek text of Evagrius's *Kephalaia Gnostika* is lost. Two Syriac translations, however, do survive: judging from the surviving Greek fragments, one of them (S2) seems to be more or less faithful to the original, and the other (S1) seems to take a fair bit of license, sometimes shoehorning Evagrius into later orthodoxies, sometimes softening the edge of his ascetical and mystical speculations. Here are two "chapters" in both translations, along with Babai's commentary (he was working with the S1 version). Evagrius borrowed Origen's account of creation, according to which God created all rational minds equal; when they turned away, they fell into souls and bodies, and became, according to the degree of their sin, angels, humans, or demons—what Evagrius calls "the rank of practice." But Origen was very unpopular in the Syriac tradition, and so the S1 translation attempts to obscure the Origenist frame for Evagrius's speculations about the descent of the mind. Babai very much continues in the vein of the S1 translation. Notice, however, that the S1 translation still holds out the promise that in the *apokatastasis* the restored mind will be made equal to the image of the holy Trinity, and will be made equal to its original teacher, none other than the Holy Spirit. The restoration of the fallen mind amounts to its deification. For additional excerpts from Babai the Great, see chapter 3.

> KG 3:28 (S2): The soul is the mind that through its carelessness fell from unity; and from its heedlessness has descended to the rank of practice.
>
> KG 3:28 (S1): The sinful soul is the pure mind that through its carelessness fell from contemplation of the Holy Unity; it needs by means of great labor to be made equal to the perfect image of the holy Trinity, from which [image] it fell.
>
> KG 3.55 (S2): In the beginning the mind had the incorruptible God as a teacher of immaterial intellections, but now it has received corruptible sensation as a teacher of material intellections.
>
> KG 3.55 (S1): In the beginning the rational mind had as teacher the revelation of the spirit, but it turned away and became a student of the senses. But in the perfection of Christ it will again be made equal to the original teacher.
>
> Babai, *Commentary on the* KG 3.28 (S1): Showing what the image is from which we fell, and how we may return to our inheritance, he says: "The sinful soul is the pure mind that through its carelessness fell from the contemplation of the Holy Unity; it needs by means of great labor to be made equal to the perfect image of the holy Trinity, from which [image] it fell" [KG 3.28 (S1)]. He calls the soul *nous* and the *nous* soul, that [soul] which, as he says many times about it, has three distinct faculties. Sometimes he calls the rational part of the

soul *nous*, or [sometimes he calls] the entirety of the soul *nous*, in order to distinguish it from the soul of animals, which consists of their blood in place of a soul, just as he says in another place: "In the beginning, the rational mind [nous] had as teacher the revelation of the spirit, but it turned away and became a student of the senses. But in the perfection of Christ it will again be made equal to the first teacher" [*KG* 3.55 (S1)].

STEPHEN BAR ṢUDAYLI, *THE BOOK OF THE HOLY HIEROTHEUS*

Sixth century. East Syrian.

In the early sixth century, a collection of Greek texts appeared under the pseudonym Pseudo-Dionysius the Areopagite, the Athenian judge whom the apostle Paul is said to have converted to Christianity (Acts 17). The pseudonymous author identifies a certain "Hierotheus" as his teacher in mystical theology. Already in the early sixth century, the Pseudo-Dionysian corpus was translated into Syriac, and another pseudonymous work soon appeared in its wake, this one claiming to be authored by that very Hierotheus. The author is thought to be Stephen bar Ṣudayli. *The Book of the Holy Hierotheus* narrates the mind's ascent to God, and it owes much to the theology of Origen of Alexandria and Evagrius of Pontus but it also goes beyond both. Origen taught that in the *apokatastasis pantōn* or "restoration of all things" to God (Acts 3:21) all rational minds will be restored to their proper status, equal to Christ. This text, however, imagines the restored minds surpassing Christ, and even the Godhead, as they vault beyond "unification" into an undifferentiated "commingling" with God. Notice that the text also uses the metaphor of waters flowing together to illustrate this, an image that echoes Evagrius's *Letter to Melania*. But whereas Evagrius insisted that the three persons of the Trinity would remain for eternity, this text claims that in the *apokatastasis* all names—even God, Christ, and Spirit—will pass away, and only the divine "Essence" will remain. It stands as one of the most radical articulations of universal salvation and mystical union in the history of Christianity.

> Fourth Discourse, Chapter 18: Of the Infinity of the Mind.
> For, when the Mind is accounted worthy of these things, it will not see by vision, nor by "form"; and it will no longer ascend and descend and will no more see above and below; for, then, the shape of the world passes away, and [the mind] is no longer limited but limits all. For it is expanded and not compact; it is hidden and not perceived; and so it becomes the object not of knowledge but of faith, which those who saw will see no more; it is henceforth exalted, in glorious and divine mystery, to become above "sight" and "form."
>
> Fourth Discourse, Chapter 19: That the Mind Abandons the Great Name of Christ
> And henceforth it abandons even the name of Christ; and thenceforth, when it passes beyond speech and language, it is neither called nor named; since, now, in mystery, it attains to those things that are not [to be] reduced to speech: for it puts away [every] distinctive

designation, and is no longer called "Son" or "heir" [Hebrews 1:2], and they will no longer say, "This is my Son, my beloved, in whom I am well-pleased" [Matthew 3:17, 17:5]; and neither, perchance, will it now say, "Father, glorify your Son, that your Son may glorify you"[John 17:1]; since, now, the order of distinction in which [some] are glorifiers and [some] glorified passes away, and so [the mind] neither loves nor desires to be brought near.

Fourth Discourse, Chapter 21: That the Mind Abandons the Name of Godhead

And now the mind does not receive the name of "Godhead"; that [name] also is the title of "that which is exalted and holy"; "I have made you God to Pharaoh," says [the scripture], and, "I said, 'You are gods'" [Exodus 7:1; Psalms 82:6; John 10:34]. This name, therefore, is not that which indicates "that which is exalted above speech and above language." But, with regard to the perfect mind, I know that it has now become "above speech and above language." It is evident, therefore, my son, that the perfect mind does not long remain or continue in the title of "Godhead."

But, for my own part, my son, I do not know [how] to put into words what things belong to the mind at that time of commingling, since all the glorious and holy secrets of which the mind is accounted worthy at the time when it becomes "without vision" are, perhaps, beyond the power of speech. Remember, then, my son, the Word that says, "The vision of the prophets will come to an end, and the Holy of Holies will belong to Christ" [Daniel 9:24]; and understand what is the significance of "the Holy of Holies" and [what is] the meaning of "the vision of the prophets."

But the mind will not regard "similitude" nor give heed to "vision" when it is accounted worthy of this contemplation; and now it will begin by a new and holy brooding to create a new world; and will create a new human in its own image without image, and in its own likeness without likeness; and will mete out the heavens with its span, and will measure the dust of the earth in its measure, and will number the drops of the sea, and will weigh the hills in a balance; and who now will say that which cannot be said, and who will name that which cannot be named? Perhaps, then, with the apostle, we will marvel at the mystery and say, "O the depth and the riches and the wisdom and the intellect—[far] above the designation of 'Godhead'—of the perfect mind that has been fulfilled! For no one searches out its judgments, and its ways cannot be traced; for who knows its thought, or who has become counselor to it?"

Such, then, my friend, shortly and inadequately [stated], are the glorious praises of the glorified mind when it fulfills and completes all and is commingled with the all-creating goodness. [...]

Let us, then, for our part, my son, put away unification and speak of commingling, of which divine minds also are accounted worthy at that time when they become "above unification"; and let us say what commingling is, and what unification [is], and whether [he who is] "Christ" and "Son" and "beloved" is united or commingled. Now, for my own part, I know that unification is very close and near to that which is called "commingling"; that is to say, that something distinct appears in it, [though] not [as] a very distinct thing, for those who have been united [only] cannot remove all distinction, there remains in them something distinct; but in those who have been commingled, we may say, nothing distinct and different is known or seen. Therefore, we glorify "Christ" and "Son" and "offspring," the designation of our unification, but the name of commingling is far more sublime and exceeding than all the designations of unification. Now those who have been united may possibly be separated, but those who have been commingled are no more torn asunder; and I myself know many minds that, after unification, have been cast away: therefore, the designation of "commingling" is proper for minds that have become "above unification."

For even they who make investigations concerning nature know that the name of "commingling" is more akin and nearer to "simplicity" than [is the name of] "unification." Perhaps, then, it [will] not be [considered] contemptible or unworthy, my son, if we introduce into our discussion an analogy from inanimate nature.

For if you divide the simple species water into diversity, into five portions or ten or however many, you can see the self-same essence of water in all the distinct portions but you observe a matter of one or of two or of many portions distinct from each other, for their number is just as great as the number of the vessels that receive them. If, then, you desire to gather together that which is scattered and to unite that which is divided, you cannot do this unless you first do away with the instruments of separation. But if you incorporate the measures into each other, and empty the many vessels into one vessel, then separation has passed away and diversity is removed, and it is impossible in [the] one measure to see the number of the measures that were poured into it. And, in the same way, we cannot see the distinctions of minds when they have "commingled" with the good and they are no longer in subjection to numbers, for thenceforth they are not numbered or accounted one or two or many.

Fifth Discourse, Chapter 1

Now, my son, I have handed on to you, without stint and in simplicity, all [the] words of our divine discussion. But as for this secret of which I will now speak, it may be that not even to the angels of God are the mysteries that it discloses revealed, "but to us God has revealed [it] by his Spirit"; so now, my son, we are not receivers of revelations but givers of revelations. But speech, perhaps, has not power to utter the glorified mysteries of this secret; I fear greatly and quake because of the demons and minds that are not pure, lest I become to them a cause of slackness. Conceal, then, my son, this secret not only from the minds that are not pure but also from all "unified" minds.

Fifth Discourse, Chapter 2: Cautions Concerning the Third Secret

The sin that is after knowledge, which is without expiation, will be upon you, my son, if you expose this mystery. As for me, my son, henceforth I am prepared for suffering, and the time has arrived that I should be rejected on account of these things that I have handed on; but this is the friendship of the friend, that he lay down his life for the sake of his friend; [this is the proof] of my love toward you, that for your sake I should be rejected by everyone.

Know, then, my son, that all things are destined to be commingled in the Father; nothing perishes and nothing is destroyed, nothing is annihilated; all returns, all is sanctified, all is made one, all is commingled, and the word is fulfilled that was said, "God shall be all and in all" [1 Corinthians 15:28]. Hells shall pass, and torments shall be done away; prisoners shall be released; for even reprobates are absolved, and outcasts return, and those that are far off are brought near; and chastisement ceases, my son, and the scourger scourges not, and the judge shall judge no more, and the officer shall not condemn, and the last farthing is given, and the prisoner who was bound is loosed (but he who has repented before the imprisonment has given the last farthing); for demons receive grace, and people receive mercy; and angels minister not, and seraphs consecrate no more, and thrones keep not their primacy; for the orders that are above pass away, and the distinctions that are below are abolished, and everything becomes one thing: for even God shall pass, and Christ shall be done away, and the Spirit shall no more be called the Spirit—for names pass away and not essence; for if distinction pass, who will call whom? And who, on the other hand, will answer whom? For one neither names nor is named. This is the limit of all and the end of everything; and take heed.

PHILOXENUS OF MABBUG, *LETTER TO ABRAHAM AND ORESTES*

Early sixth century. West Syrian.

Philoxenus (d. 523) was a prominent West Syrian theologian and the bishop of Mabbug in northern Syria. In this letter, he warns Abraham and Orestes, two presbyters from Edessa, of Stephen bar Ṣudayli, the presumed author of the pseudonymous *Book of the Holy Hierotheus*. His two principal complaints against Stephen are: first, that he is a pantheist (i.e., he confesses that "everything is of one nature with God"); and second, that he is a universalist (i.e., he believes that all rational minds will be saved). Both views are attested in *The Book of the Holy Hierotheus*. In a section of the letter not included below, Philoxenus acknowledges Stephen's debt to Evagrius. We know from Philoxenus's other writings that he was also an admirer of Evagrius, and so the proper interpretation of Evagrius emerges as a fault line in the Syriac mystical tradition. For additional excerpts from Philoxenus, see chapters 5 and 9.

> I have learned that Stephen the scribe, who departed from among us some time since and now resides in the country of Jerusalem, sent to you, some time ago, followers of his with letters and books composed by him; taking care at the same time that the arrival of those whom he had sent, as well as what he was astutely desirous of accomplishing, should be concealed from us. For he thought that, were I to learn that he had sent to you men and also writings, his hopes might be disappointed. He has insanely imagined—whence I know not, but certainly from Satan, for he is the father and cause of every heresy—to put forth in a book an impious and foolish doctrine, which is worthy of being reputed not only a heresy but worse than paganism and Judaism, because it openly assimilates the creation to God, and teaches that it is necessary for everything to become like him. It also falsifies the holy scriptures, and even destroys faith in Christianity, teaching that everyone may sin as they please, and dissuading pagans, Jews, and heretics from Christian instruction and from being converted to God. It makes of no effect holy baptism, and the giving of the divine mysteries, and labors and struggles for righteousness. For if, according to his impious words, not only will there be no judgment but all will receive the same measure of retribution, then the same honor will be accorded to the apostle Peter and to Simon Magus, to the preacher Paul and to the traitor Judas, to the apostles and evangelists. And what is

especially full of an impiety akin to insanity is that he says that everything is of one nature with God. What has just been detailed is most important and most completely reprehensible; for then the apostles have in vain worked, and converted all nations from heathenism to Christianity, if even without instruction in the faith and baptism they are to be equals of the apostles, and are to become consubstantial with God, the Lord of the universe. Hence there is no difference between those who died for Christ and those who killed them, for they who were confessors of the faith will receive nothing more, and they who killed them nothing less, because all together, as he says, will arrive at one perfection; and as the members of the body are of the same nature as each other and as the body itself, so, as he means and even says, are we in God and with him in unity the one with the other. These things may be known, he says, by the mystery of the first day of the week, when, as he says, God will be all in all: one nature, one substance, one divinity. If, then, it is possible that men should become consubstantial with the divinity, then the dispensation of the flesh and the incarnation were superfluous. From misunderstanding, therefore, this saying of the apostle, "that God may be all in all" [1 Corinthians 15:28], he has foolishly imagined and produced this impious and foolish doctrine, which perhaps would not even be accepted among demons; for I think they would tremble simply to hear that they were to become consubstantial with God; for also concerning them, as well as all the angelic host that did not fall, does he assert, that they will become consubstantial with the divinity and godhead. And as he did not know how to understand this saying or to perceive what preceded it, neither was he able to consider all the things that are said in the holy scriptures on the reward of the righteous and the punishment of the wicked. Neither did he know how to distinguish between the divinity and the creation, and that it is not possible for the divinity through change to become the creation, or creation the divinity. Furthermore, he does not accord with the doctors who have interpreted this saying in an orthodox manner. He desired, being puffed up like a vain and proud man, to originate heresies himself also, like John the Egyptian, whom for a short time he even followed. [. . .]

But [Stephen] not being able to see these things himself, nor willing to learn them from those who were able, wrote this book in which he consulted his own vain thoughts and not the holy scriptures, and constructed a new doctrine full of wickedness and impiety, in an insipid and foolish language. For although he is not even able to command a language worthy of writing, still, being desirous of making a display, he came forward as an inventor of heresies. I will not, furthermore, omit the following fact, although it is apparent from his writings. There came unto me trustworthy men who said that on entering his cell they found written by him on the wall: "All nature is consubstantial with the divine essence"; and on account of their strongly accusing him of blasphemy, and it becoming known to many monks who murmured at it, he was afraid and removed it from the wall; but secretly put it into his writings. [. . .]

If therefore he has either written to you, as I have learned, or has sent to you his blasphemous books, be careful lest they fall into any person's hands and especially into those of nuns dwelling within church precincts, lest they be led astray through the simplicity and weakness natural to women. For the wise must all, as is written, "take up the stumbling-block out of the way" [Isaiah 57:14], lest he receive many wounds and become the companion of many others who stumble and fall.

Write also to him, if it seem proper to you, that he cease from his blasphemies on an ineffable, pure, incomprehensible, and holy doctrine. Concerning which I do not know that he has yet a single disciple, for, of the many arguments that he has collected from the scriptures, when he applies them, he does not discover the [real] force, but he imagines that they support his view.

I remember that I once wrote to him a letter by means of one of his disciples, Abraham by name; a copy of which also I now send unto you. At that time I did not well know that he had dared to imagine such blasphemies, for I had only met with his commentaries on a few of the Psalms, in which he also glorifies himself and ascribes to himself revelations and visions, and [says] that to him alone is it given to understand the scriptures correctly. In them he also calls the scriptures dreams, and his commentaries the interpretation of dreams.

Afterward he craftily devised to send his books to you and to write to you, in order to deceive the simple people there [at Jerusalem]; for I have heard that he says to them, that even in Edessa is his heresy received, and is furthermore much praised by us—until some of the monks there happened upon the letter that I had written, of which I now send you a copy, and found that [on the contrary] he was strongly censured by me. When therefore you shall have received these letters of mine, that which you know to be just write to him, and reprove him, and that not feebly but forcibly. I myself would write to the bishop of Jerusalem respecting him, were it not for differences concerning the faith, and that the fact of our not being of the same communion is a middle wall [of partition] between us. For [Stephen] has sinned not a little, and the offenses that he has committed are not small; for he says that dogs, pigs, serpents, scorpions, mice, and other reptiles of the earth, are consubstantial with God: that is, [they] will become so. He also strives to persuade others to believe likewise, and says thus: "As the Father and the Son and the Spirit are of one nature, and as the body of the Word is consubstantial with his divinity," through ignorance he also blasphemes concerning this part [of Church doctrine], adding, "all creation also will become consubstantial with the divine nature": and magicians and murderers, crucifiers and apostles, persecutors and martyrs, adulterers and virgins, the chaste and those who satisfy their lusts, all, he says, will be changed and become consubstantial with God, and there will be no one who shall excel, neither anyone who shall be lacking.

ISAAC OF NINEVEH, *ON GEHENNA*

Late seventh century. East Syrian.

Isaac was an East Syrian ascetic theologian from Bet Qaṭraye in northeast Arabia. After a brief tenure as the bishop of Nineveh, he became a hermit attached to the monastery of Rabban Shapur. His writings survive in several "parts," of which three are known. This selection, from the second "part," concerns "Gehenna," the biblical name for the pit where the condemned are thrown to burn in unquenchable fire. Isaac takes up the question of whether God punishes sinners for eternity and confesses instead that all suffering has a providential end: God will lead all rational minds, including demons, to salvation, even if the path is painful. This is the mystery of God's providence. Throughout his writings, Isaac quotes Theodore of Mopsuestia and Diodore of Tarsus, prominent authorities in the East Syrian Church, in support of his universalism. For an additional excerpt from Isaac of Niveveh, see chapter 5.

> Contemplation on the topic of Gehenna, in so far as grace can be granted to human nature to hold opinions on these mysteries.[. . .]
>
> A right way of thinking about God would be the following: the kind Lord, who in everything he does looks to ways of assisting rational beings, directs thought concerning judgment to the advantage of those who accept this difficult matter. For it would be most odious and utterly blasphemous to think that hate or resentment exists with God, even against demonic beings; or to imagine any other weakness, or passibility, or whatever else might be involved in the course of retribution of good or bad as applying, in a retributive way, to that glorious [divine] nature. Rather, he acts toward us in ways he knows will be advantageous to us, whether by way of things that cause suffering, or by way of things that cause relief, whether they cause joy or grief, whether they are insignificant or glorious: all are directed toward the single eternal good, whether each receives judgment or something of glory from him—not by way of retribution, far from it!—but with a view to the advantage that is going to come from all these things. [. . .]
>
> I am of the opinion that he is going to manifest some wonderful outcome, a matter of immense and ineffable compassion on the part of the glorious creator, with respect to the ordering of this difficult matter of [Gehenna's] torment: out of it the wealth of his love and power and wisdom will become known all the more—and so will the insistent might of the waves of his goodness.
>
> It is not [the way of] the compassionate maker to create rational beings in order to deliver them over mercilessly to unending affliction [in punishment] for things of which he knew even before they were fashioned, [aware] how they would turn out when he created them—and whom [nonetheless] he created. All the more since the foreplanning of evil and the taking of vengeance are characteristics of the passions of created beings, and do not belong to the creator. For all this [characterizes] people who do not know or who are unaware of what they are doing or thinking when something has happened with us [human beings], for as a result of some matter that has occurred unexpectedly to them, they are incited by the vehemence of anger to take vengeance. Such action does not belong to the creator who, even before the cycle of the depiction of creation had been portrayed, knew of all that was before and all that was after in connection with the actions and intentions of rational beings. [. . .]
>
> If we consider that there is in truth some kind of providence hidden within the course that creation takes, and [if] we examine the divine judgments that convey a certain mystery—for these terms and their usage are inappropriate when we approach the nature of the creator in contemplation, seeing that they do not correspond to the knowledge and properties of that [divine] nature when compared with [ordinary] actions—[then] come, let us cry out to God with the blessed David, saying, "Your judgments are like the great deep" [Psalms 36:6]. Truly, this is an understanding that has become aware, through the gift of spiritual knowledge, of what is above the body, and what is more interior than [outward] phrases and corporeal images.

Just because [the terms] wrath, anger, hatred, and the rest are used of the creator, we should not imagine that he [actually] does anything in anger or hatred or zeal. Many figurative terms are employed in the scriptures of God, terms that are far removed from his [true] nature. And just as [our] rational nature has [already] become gradually more illumined and wise in a holy understanding of the mysteries that are hidden in [scripture's] discourse about God—that we should not understand everything [literally] as it is written, but rather that we should see, [concealed] inside the bodily exterior of the narratives, the hidden providence and eternal knowledge that guides all—so, too, we shall in the future come to know and be aware of many things for which our present understanding will be seen as contrary to what it will be then; and the whole ordering of things yonder will undo any precise opinion we possess now in [our] supposition about truth. For there are many, indeed endless, things that do not even enter our minds here, not even as promises of any kind.

Accordingly, we say that, even in the matter of the afflictions and sentence of Gehenna, there is some [hidden] mystery, whereby the wise maker has taken as a starting point for its future outcome the wickedness of our actions and willfulness, using it as a way of bringing to perfection his dispensation wherein lies the teaching that makes wise and the advantage beyond description, hidden from both angels and human beings, [hidden] too from those who are being chastised, whether they be demons or human beings, [hidden] for as long as the ordained period of time holds sway.

If the world to come is entirely [the domain] of grace, love, mercy, and goodness, and because the resurrection from the dead is also a demonstration of the mercifulness of God and of the overflowing abundance of his love that cannot be repaid, how [can one think of] a dispensation in which are included requitals for our own good or evil [actions]? For one speaks of requital when one who is the requiter is gradually instructed about the requital [needed] as a result of, and corresponding to, the good and bad actions that take place: along with actions that differ from day to day, he acquires a different knowledge, and his [consequent] thoughts are subject to [outside] causes and take their origin from temporal circumstances.

If the kingdom and Gehenna had not been foreseen in the purpose of our good God, as a result of the coming into being of good and evil actions, [then God's] thoughts concerning these would not be eternal; but righteousness and sin were known by him before they revealed themselves. Accordingly, the kingdom and Gehenna are matters belonging to mercy, which were conceived of in their essence by God as a result of his eternal goodness. It was not a matter of requiting, even though he gave them the name of requital.

That we should further say or think that the matter is not full of love and mingled with compassion would be an opinion full of blasphemy and insult to our Lord God. [By saying] that he will even hand us over to burning for the sake of sufferings, torment, and all sorts of ills, we are attributing to the divine nature an enmity toward the very rational beings that he created through grace; [the same is true if we say] that he acts or thinks with spite and with a vengeful purpose, as though he was avenging himself.

Among all his actions there is none that is not entirely a matter of mercy, love, and compassion: this constitutes the beginning and the end of his dealings with us.

As far as he is concerned, there is no beginning to the setting in motion of the actions that he foresees with regard to us; but, as far as we are concerned, the initiative is understood as being within time and as having a beginning.

How much to be worshipped is our Lord God's gentle compassion and his immeasurable munificence: he makes many threats but he makes the punishment small out of grace, all in order to increase love for him in ourselves. May his name be blessed! Amen.

MYSTICAL PRAYER

JOHN OF APAMEA, *ON PRAYER*

First half of the fifth century.

We know almost nothing of the life John of Apamea, also known as John the Solitary (*iḥidaya*). A number of his works have survived in both the West and East Syrian Churches, and he seems to have exerted a considerable influence on the Syriac mystical tradition. In this short treatise, John recommends silent prayer as the most appropriate and spiritual form of address to God, who "is silence, and in silence is he sung." One who prays aloud is "just," but one who prays in silence is a "spiritual being." He names five different kinds of silence, the highest of which is "the silence of the spirit" in which "the mind ceases even from stirrings caused by spiritual beings and all movements are stirred solely by being."

Do not imagine, brother, that prayer consists solely of words, or that it can be learned by means of words. No, the truth of the matter, you should understand, is that spiritual prayer does not reach fullness as a result of either learning or the repetition of words. For it is not to a human that you are praying, before whom you can repeat a well-composed speech: it is to him who is spirit that you are directing the movements of your prayer. You should pray therefore in spirit, seeing that he is spirit.

No special place is required for someone who prays in fullness to God. Our Lord said, "The hour is coming when you will not be worshipping the Father in this mountain or in Jerusalem" [John 4:21]; and again, to show that no special place was required, he also taught that those who worship the Father should "worship him in spirit and in truth" [John 4:23]; and in the course of his instructing us why we should pray thus he said, "For God is a spirit" [John 4:24], and he should be praised spiritually, in the spirit. Paul, too, tells us about this spiritual prayer and psalmody that we should employ: "What then shall I do?", he says, "I will pray in spirit and pray in my mind; I will sing in the spirit and I will sing in my mind" [1 Corinthians 14:15]. It is in spirit and in mind, then, that he says one should pray and sing to God; he does not say anything at all about the tongue. The reason is that this spiritual prayer is more interior than the tongue, more deeply interiorized than anything on the lips, more interiorized than any words or vocal song. When someone prays this kind of prayer, one has sunk deeper than all speech, and one stands where spiritual beings and angels are to be found; like them, one utters "holy" without any words. But if one ceases from this kind of prayer and recommences the prayer of vocal song, then one is outside the region of the angels and becomes an ordinary person again.

Whoever sings, using tongue and body, and perseveres in this worship both night and day, such a person is one of the "just." But the person who has been held worthy to enter deeper than this, singing in mind and spirit, such a person is a "spiritual being." A "spiritual being" is more exalted than the "just," but one becomes a "spiritual being" after being "just." For until one has worshipped for a considerable time in this exterior manner, employing fasting, using the voice for psalmody, with long periods on the knees, constant vigils, recitation of the psalms, arduous labors, supplication, abstinence, paucity of food, and all such things, one's soul continuously being filled with the remembrance of God, full of due fear and trembling at his name, humble before all, considering everyone better than oneself even when one sees someone's actions: should one see a debauched person, or an adulterer, or someone grasping, or a drunkard, one still acts humbly before them and in one's hidden innermost thoughts really considers them better than oneself, not just making an outward pretense, but, seeing someone amid all these evil things, one goes up to him and acts in a humble way before him, begging him, "pray for me, for I am a sinner before God, I am guilty of many things, for not one of which have I paid the price." Only when someone achieves all this—and greater things than those I have mentioned—will one arrive at singing to God in the psalmody that spiritual beings use to praise him.

For God is silence, and in silence is he sung by means of that psalmody that is worthy of him. I am not speaking of the silence of the tongue, for if someone merely keeps their tongue silent, without knowing how to sing in mind and spirit, then one is simply unoccupied and becomes filled with evil thoughts: one is just keeping an exterior silence and one does not know how to sing in an interior way, seeing that the tongue of one's "hidden person" has not yet learned to stretch itself out even to babble. You should look on the spiritual infant that is within you in the same way as you do on an ordinary child or infant: just as the tongue placed in an infant's mouth is still because it does not yet know speech or the right movements for speaking, so it is with that interior tongue of the mind; it will be still from all speech and from all thought: it will simply be placed there, ready to learn the first babblings of spiritual utterance.

Thus there is a silence of the tongue; there is a silence of the whole body; there is the silence of the soul; there is the silence of the mind; and there is the silence of the spirit. The silence of the tongue is merely when it is not incited to evil speech; the silence of the entire body is when all its senses are unoccupied; the silence of the soul is when there are no ugly thoughts bursting forth within it; the silence of the mind is when it is not reflecting on any harmful knowledge or wisdom; the silence of the spirit is when the mind ceases even from stirrings caused by created spiritual beings and all its movements are stirred solely by being, at the wondrous awe of the silence that surrounds being.

These are the degrees and measures to be found in speech and silence. But if you have not reached these and find yourself still far away from them, remain where you are and sing to God using the voice and the tongue in love and awe. Sing with application, toil in your service until you arrive at love. Stand in awe of God, as is only right, and thus you will be held worthy to love him with a natural love—him who was given to us at our renewal.

And when you recite the words of the prayer that I have written for you, be careful not just to repeat them, but let your very self become these words. For there is no advantage in the reciting unless the word actually becomes embodied in you and becomes a deed, with the result that you are seen in the world to be a person of God—to whom glory, honor, and exaltation are fitting, for eternal ages, amen.

ISAAC OF NINEVEH, *ON PURE AND UNDISTRACTYED PRAYER*

Late seventh century. East Syrian.

Like the selection above, this comes from the second of Isaac's three surviving "parts." In this short chapter, Isaac discusses "pure prayer," wherein the mind does not maintain stillness but in fact wanders in contemplation of God's glory and majesty. This is the height of prayer, but beyond even this pure prayer lies the "silence of the mind," a state in which "the mind is entirely without any kind of reflection." Isaac's criticism of the Messalians was in part motivated by their presumption that they could, by their own efforts, pray their way to this highest state. Isaac insists rather that is a gift, "not within the reach of pure prayer, or a matter of the will." The "fools" mentioned may very well be Messalians, real or imagined.

> By the same Mar Isaac, a section that nicely indicates and clearly explains what is pure and undistracted prayer.
>
> [. . .]
>
> Purity of prayer, O disciple of truth, and the recollection of mind that exists in it, consist in the exact reflection on virtue in which we carefully engage at the time of prayer. Just as purity of heart, concerning which the fathers diligently exhort, is not a matter of someone being totally without thought or reflection or stirring, but rather it consists in the heart being purified of all evil, and in gazing favorably on everything, and considering it from God's point of view, so it is the same with pure and undistracted prayer. This does not mean that the mind is entirely devoid of any thought or wandering of any kind but that it does not wander about on empty subjects during the time of prayer. It is not the case that the mind is outside purity of prayer unless it wanders about on something specifically good; but it may also ponder things that are appropriate and think thoughts pleasing to God during the time of prayer. Nor is it required of someone that empty recollections should not come at all when they pray but that they should not occupy themselves with them and be distracted by them.
>
> For there is a good kind of wandering and a bad kind of wandering. When you are in prayer, do not seek to be entirely free from mental wandering, which is impossible, but seek to wander following something that is good. For even pure prayer consists in a wandering that follows something—but this wandering is excellent, seeing that the search for something good is excellent.
>
> Wandering is bad when someone is distracted by empty thoughts or by reflecting on something bad, and so thinks evil thoughts when one is praying before God.
>
> Wandering is good when the mind wanders to God during the entire extent of its prayer, to his glory and majesty, stemming from a recollection of the scriptures, and at insights into the divine utterances and holy words of the spirit. In the case of someone who struggles to tie down their thought from wandering on such things, or their mind from wandering of its own accord on them during prayer, one is of unparalleled stupidity if one thinks that this kind of wandering is alien to, and outside the limits of, pure prayer. For we do not consider as alien to purity of prayer and as detrimental to collectedness of thoughts in prayer any profitable recollections that may spring up in the mind from the writings of the spirit, resulting in insights and spiritual understanding of the divine world during the time of prayer. For

someone to examine and think in a recollected manner about the object of their supplication and the request of their prayer is an excellent kind of prayer, provided it is consonant with the intention of our Lord's commandments. This kind of collectedness of mind is very good.

If the mind is released from this prayer and becomes diffused in things divine, or if some excellent reflection occurs to it, arising out of scripture's insights on God, insights that are either individual to the person or belong to the [whole] community, insights into God's dispensations and acts of providence, whether they be those belonging to each successive day or universal ones—all things by which the depth of the heart is stirred toward the praise of God or to thanksgiving and joy at the immensity and exalted nature of his compassion and love toward us; [if this happens], this kind of wandering is even better than prayer! However exalted and pure someone's supplication may be, this is the culmination of every kind of collectedness of mind and of excellence of prayer.

When the mind is entirely without any kind of reflection, this is silence of the mind and not purity of prayer. It is one thing to pray purely, and quite another for the mind to be silent from any wandering at all or insight into the words of prayer, and to remain without any stirrings. No one is so stupid as to want to find this by means of struggle and the strength of his own will; for this is the gift of the revelation of the intellect, and it is not within the reach of pure prayer, or a matter of the will.

Apart from this, the mind is able to wander in prayer in the two ways we spoke of, either in reflection on its requests or in contemplation on the scriptures and a sage reflection on God, the Lord of all, carried out in a sensible way.

If anyone thinks otherwise with respect to purity of thoughts and collectedness of mind, supposing that there is some other means of finding them, then he is infirm in his ignorance and he is impeded by a boorish mind.

You are wise enough not to require of the mind motionlessness—as do the fools; for this cannot be asked of [human] nature. Rather, strive to discover stirrings that are good during the time of prayer, as the wise do. These consist in reflection on the spirit's insights, and a sagacious purpose that considers during the time of prayer how to please the will of the maker of all: this is the final end of all virtue and of all prayer.

When in these matters you receive the power that stems from grace to be bound firmly to their continual stirrings, you will become a person of God and will be close to spiritual things; close, too, to finding that for which you yearn without your being aware of it, namely, the apperception of God, the wonderment of mind that is free from all images, and the spiritual silence of which the Fathers speak. Blessed will you be and held worthy of the great joy and gladness that exist in our Lord—to whom be praise and honor. And may he perfect us with knowledge of his mysteries, for ever and ever, amen.

DADISHOʻ QAṬRAYA, *DISCOURSE ON STILLNESS*

Late seventh century. East Syrian.

Dadishoʻ was an East Syrian monk, a contemporary of Isaac of Nineveh, also from Bet Qaṭraye, and also associated with the monastery of Rabban Shapur. Nothing more is known of his life. In this excerpt from his *Discourse on Stillness*, Dadisho' discusses "pure prayer" and the virtues and commandments that sustain it. There are four virtues—two of the body (fasting and vigil), and two of the soul (peaceableness and humility)—and four corresponding vices. He attributes this teaching to Evagrius of Pontus and Mark the Hermit, a theologian and ascetic writer of the fifth century. It is unclear whether "the spiritual way of life" discussed near the end of this excerpt is another name for "pure prayer," or whether, like Isaac in the excerpt above, Dadisho' is describing something beyond prayer.

> Pure prayer that is without any distraction and without any disturbance is accomplished, brought to perfection, established, and preserved by means of four virtues; and by four passions it is diminished, tarnished, rendered ineffective, and obstructed. The four virtues are these: fasting, vigil, peaceableness, and humility. Two of these concern the soul and two the body. The passions that render it ineffective are greediness for food, and too much sleep, anger, and vainglory, as I indicated above [in a previous section]. Those illuminated instructors of solitaries, the blessed Mark [the Hermit] and the blessed Evagrius, give us clear teaching on the subject of these four virtues that constitute the pure prayer whereby the solitary can vanquish all the passions and demons. The blessed Mark teaches us concerning them in one of his *Kephalaia* [i.e., *Chapters*] as follows: "One who wishes to cross with discernment the spiritual sea of the passions and demons, just as Moses and the Israelites discerningly crossed the Red Sea, should show patience, humble himself, keep vigil, persevere in asceticism. Without these four virtues, even if someone forces himself to enter [this sea], he will be forcing his heart to do so, but he will not be able to proceed with discernment."
>
> He goes on: "Stillness is advantageous, provided it has ceased from anything evil. But if one receives assistance in prayer with these four virtues, no one will more speedily reach perfect well-being." Again, he says: "The intellect cannot be stilled apart from the body. Nor can it dismantle the barrier to these four virtues without stillness and prayer." He calls peaceableness "patience," for in another passage he shows that these two are the same, saying: "A patient person is exceedingly wise," and again, "One who is gentle in our Lord is wiser than the wise." He attributes wisdom to both patience and peaceableness, as having the same meaning.
>
> These two virtues of the soul by which pure prayer is constituted—I mean peaceableness and humility—are the ones taught by our Lord: "Learn from me, for I am peaceable and humble in my heart, and you shall find peace for your souls" [Matthew 11:29].
>
> Rest of soul and pure prayer are in truth established by these two virtues, according to our Lord's word. When the two other virtues of the body, fasting and keeping vigil, are joined with them, according to the sure verdict of our Lord, "The species of passions and demons does not depart except by means of fasting and prayer" [Matthew 17:21]—the power and beauty of which are constituted particularly in vigils.
>
> As for the fourth virtue, which Abba Mark calls perseverance of asceticism, he is accustomed to name it "fasting." In other words, when someone fasts, he will need to put up with less. This sense can be found in other *Kephalaia*, as when he says that "the ascetic who perseveres is far removed from gluttony." From all this it is apparent that Abba Mark

is everywhere calling the virtue of fasting and small amounts of food "perseverance" and "asceticism."

These are the four virtues, two of the soul and two of the body, by which pure prayer is perfected into the first haven of peace. The solitary should meditate on these every day and take care to pray that they may acquire them, until they actually find them.

This, too, one should realize: that the entire way of life of stillness is interwoven with the following three virtues: with faith that comes from listening, and with hope and with love, out of which real faith is made known. Once someone enters his cell and commences on the way of life of faith, that is to say, employing bodily labors, until he reaches the way of life of hope, which is the way of life of the mind, consisting in meditation on God, he labors and struggles by means of these four virtues indicated above against the four passions that sully pure prayer, hindering and preventing him from arriving at meditation on God—which is the way of life of hope. The virtues, as I have said, correspond to the "comprehensive commandments" of every commandment, out of which spiritual prayer is constituted and established: fasting, vigil, humility, peaceableness. The opposite passions are love of the belly, sleep, anger, vain glory.

When someone commences on the way of life of hope, which consists of meditation on God, and until he reaches the way of life of love that is the way of life of the spirit, in which is revealed real faith, which is the vision of our Lord in the spirit, this person labors and conducts himself with three great commandments, the most comprehensive of all commandments: they are these—prayer without ceasing and without distraction; instantaneous destruction of evil thoughts the moment they begin to stir in the heart; endurance of all afflictions and every temptation that comes upon one in stillness, originating from the passions or from demons or from people.

When the solitary is fully perfected in this way of life of hope, which is the way of life of the mind, namely meditation on our Lord, he is raised up and enters upon the way of life of the spirit, which is the spiritual way of life, in which all the fruits of the spirit are manifested and produced, the ones that the apostle laid out [c.f. Galatians 5:22], those first fruits, among which are these three: the delight in the pledge of the love of our Lord Jesus Christ and of the love of his Father; complete humility; real faith, which is the spiritual vision of our Lord and of the heavenly good things through the revelation of the Holy Spirit.

"I bend my knees" [Ephesians 3:14] and I pray for you, says the apostle Paul, that you may be empowered with the Holy Spirit, so that Christ may dwell in your inner person in faith and in your hearts in love, in all humility of mind. These are the four virtues out of which the prayer of the mind is constituted, and these are the three great and binding commandments, by which spiritual prayer is constituted.

JOHN OF DALYATA, *LETTERS* 12

Eighth century. East Syrian.

John of Dalyata, also known as John the Elder, was an East Syrian monk, who, after seven years in a monastery, took up a solitary life in the mountains of Bet Dalyata. In this letter,

John, much like Isaac of Nineveh, insists that there is a state beyond prayer, which he calls "wonder." Like Isaac before him, he bases this on a mistranslation of a saying by Evagrius. In Syriac, Evagrius's saying reads, "Prayer is *cut off* by means of wonder at the light," whereas the original Greek read "happens." This gives John (and Isaac) license to insist that the consummation of prayer is a state beyond prayer, "wonder at the mysteries," where "there is no place for words, no place the pen's torrent could travel along the paths of ink." John's writings, along with John of Apamea's and Joseph Ḥazzaya's (below), were condemned by the katholikos Timothy I (d. 823) at a synod in the late 780s, for alleged Messalian tendencies. John of Dalyata was exonerated and rehabilitated soon thereafter, but his reputation in the East Syrian Church suffered as a result.

> The monk who continually prays to God accompanied by stirrings of one sort or another still stands below the consummate grade. You will object, saying, "Do not blaspheme, brother; our fathers exalt this form of prayer more than all other labors." Indeed, I too am one of those who extol it, and I ask of my God that I may complete the rest of my life in such prayer; I acknowledge that it is something magnificent and much more exalted than all other labors. Though it is fatiguing, yet it gives rest to the weary, ensuring that, once they are rested, they never weary again.
>
> Understand this well, my brother: Christ said to Simon, the head of the apostles, "To you do I give the keys of the kingdom of heaven, so that you may close and open to whomever you wish" [Matthew 16:19]. It is not to one alone that he gave this authority, but to all lovers of truth. Now prayer is just the one knocking on the door of one who gives. So how can the person who has entered the kingdom and received authority over its treasuries knock at the door? One enjoys the blessings within and is utterly astounded at the beauty of the good one. It is ridiculous to say that such a person is actually praying: rather, he is completely intoxicated with the beauty of the most wondrous bridegroom.
>
> Evagrius says, "Prayer is purity of the mind, the movements of whose prayer are not interrupted except once the holy light of the Trinity has shone out in the mind." For, he says, "Prayer is cut off by means of wonder at the light." Thus, the consummation consists in wonder at God, as we have said, and not in the continual stirrings of prayer. The person who has entered the place of the mysteries remains in wonder at them, and this is the true prayer that opens the door to the treasures of God, allowing those who seek to have their fill of all they need. "Freely have you received, do yourselves give freely" [Matthew 10:8] to everyone you wish. How could anyone dare to say of those who have been given authority over wealth, to give it as if it were their own to everyone they wished, that they are knocking at the door like beggars asking for alms to meet their needs? No; rather, they distribute life, raise the dead, convey hope, give light to the blind; "you are the light of the world, he said: I will give you the keys" [Matthew 5:14, 16:19]. You are no longer someone who asks, for you have acquired authority—as though over what belonged to yourself—to bind and to loose, in this world and in the age of ages. How can such a person prostrate himself at the door and beg like a vagabond, seeing that the keys to the treasury are already placed in his hands, enabling him to take and give, have life and provide life? [. . .]

This prayer is the greatest of all labors: it opens the door to the place of wonderment, it gives rest to weariness, it stills all movements. Maybe you will say, "You are speaking about wonderment, and I do not know the meaning of wonderment." Let me adduce as testimony the words of a certain brother, who is worthy to be believed; he used to say, "When the grace of my God so wills it within me, it draws my intellect to wonder at the sight of him, so that it remains the entire day motionless, in the place of wonderment. Then, once it has left there, it again prays and supplicates that the light of hidden being that is hidden within him may shine forth in the world full of wonder." From that point onward there is no place for words, no place where the pen's torrent could travel along the paths of ink. Here the boundary is set, namely, silence. Only the mind is permitted to cross over and have a sight of that place where all symbols find their rest. For the mind is authorized to enter and wonder at the wondrous beauty that is beyond all, yet hidden within all.

Thus any prayer that is not from time to time transformed in wonder at the mysteries has not yet reached consummation, as we explained above. Nor can prayer consisting of stirrings last continuously if it has not tasted at all of the wonder that comes with the joy of God. Continuous prayer is wonder at God: that is the sum of our message. You may go on to say, "Do not speak about things with which you are not acquainted; do not talk about matters that you have not explained." I too hang my head in shame, and will keep silent, taking refuge in divine mercy. Assist me in prayer.

JOSEPH ḤAZZAYA, *ON THE STIRRINGS OF THE MIND DURING PRAYER*

Eighth century. East Syrian.

Joseph Ḥazzaya, or the "Visionary," was an East Syrian monk, about whose life we know rather more than his contemporaries. Born to Zoroastrian parents around 710, he was captured and enslaved as a child; when he exhibited interest in the monks he saw in the region of Mount Qardu, he was baptized, and he was eventually freed in order to pursue his own monastic vocation. He was both an abbot and a hermit at different times of his life. A number of his writings have survived, although some of them circulated under the name of his brother ʿAbdishoʿ, including the text from which the following excerpt is taken, *On the Stirrings of the Mind during Prayer*. Joseph's analysis owes much to Evagrius's division of the monastic enterprise into two stages, practice (*praktikē*) and contemplation (*theōria*), corresponding roughly to the material and immaterial stirrings during prayer. Notice that among the immaterial stirrings are some that are "uncircumscribed": these are stirrings from God, "the [only] one who is uncircumscribed," and they usher the monk into a contemplation of the holy Trinity, in which the light of his mind is indistinguishable from the divine light, a state of wonder beyond all thought. This state is a pledge of what is to come for all rational minds, recalling Evagrius's (and Origen's) universalism. Like John of Apamea and John of Dalyata, Joseph was condemned by the katholikos Timothy I at a synod in the 780s for alleged Messalian tendencies, a decision that was later reversed by Timothy's successor.

By the same, concerning the operation of the impulses that arise in the mind during the time of prayer: which are material, and which are immaterial, and which are uncircumscribed and without form.

During the time of prayer the soul resembles a ship positioned in the middle of the sea. The mind is like the steersman in charge of the boat. The impulses convey the boat like the winds.

Just as it is the case that not all the winds that blow are suitable for the course of the ship, similarly, with the impulses that are aroused in the soul during the time of prayer, not all are suitable for the ship's course, enabling it without any cause for fear to reach harbor, safe from the waves. Rather, some of them are suitable, whereas others are not. The latter imprint in the soul some material form, and these hinder the course of the boat of the mind, the steersman preventing it from reaching the harbor they are aiming for. The former impulses stirred up in the soul during prayer are immaterial: these are the gentle breezes that convey the ship of the soul over the waves to a harbor that is totally restful.

There are yet other impulses that arise during prayer, accompanied by light: these are called "uncircumscribed": they are neither material nor immaterial but uncircumscribed, as I have just said; for not all immaterial impulses are also uncircumscribed. For the holy angels and the nature of our souls are immaterial, but they are by no means also uncircumscribed; for they are immaterial things subject to circumscription, whereas out of all things there is [only] one who is uncircumscribed. Now the impulses that concern that Being are uncircumscribed—just as the prophet said: "there is no limit to his understanding" [Psalms 147:5].

Material impulses consist in all the understandings that are stirred up in the soul through the medium of the body's senses. These are material, and they are harmful to the soul's course during the time of prayer. Even though at other times they may be advantageous, nevertheless during the time of prayer they cause the soul harm. This is because, during the time of prayer only the immaterial impulses direct the soul toward those that are without limit.

The immaterial impulses consist in the hidden spiritual knowledge concealed in the natural created world, wonderful insights concerning incorporeal contemplation, and insights arising from the contemplation of providence's judgment. All these impulses may occur during the time of prayer, and these are immaterial. Therefore, every time they are revealed to the mind during prayer, they give a sweet taste to the mind's palate, like a honeycomb, and they kindle all the faculties of both soul and body with their warmth, so that tears without measure pour down from a person's eyes whenever these impulses are set in motion in his mind. These are not tears stemming from the passions or from sorrow because of wrongdoings, but rather they arise from joy and delight, and from a sense of wonder at God's creation, compassion, and care for everything—at how his compassion is poured out abundantly over us human beings, at the extent of our ingratitude toward him; at how, whereas we did not exist before, nor are we able to come into being of our own volition, yet in his compassion he brought us into existence and well-being, even though he was aware of our future ingratitude and wickedness even before he created us; at how, once we had sinned and incited his anger through our choice of evil deeds, out of his fatherly love he still does not hold back from us the gifts of his divine care for us and his providence;

at how, when our nature had reached despair, he sent his beloved Son, our Lord Jesus, and handed him over to suffering and death on our behalf in order to save us who are befouled by sin; at how he tasted vinegar and bitter herbs for us, in order to render harmless the bitter venom of the serpent that slew us in Eden; and at how, after all the wickedness and blasphemies that we perpetrated against him, in his ineffable grace he prepared for us another world full of every imaginable good thing, decreeing for us the gift of resurrection by means of which we shall be raised up from the passions of mortality, and will become incorruptible, immortal, unchangeable, impassible, and without needs, being continuously raised up with him in an understanding of his mysteries and in the glorious vision of him.

Thus, as a result of recollecting all these things the impulses of the mind are extended from the sphere of material things toward those impulses that are without limit, that is to say, wonder at the new world, and the faculty of vision that belongs to contemplation of the holy Trinity. For when the vision of the mind is mingled with the light of the glorious Trinity, all its impulses become infinite. For none of the visionaries or "gnostics" is able to distinguish the identity of the mind as a result of the vision of that glorious light that is seen of the holy Trinity, for all the innermost chambers of the heart are filled by that blessed light and there are no shapes or forms or anything material, or number or color; rather that light who cannot be separated out into shapes and forms is single owing to the simpleness of the faculty of sight.

This, too, I have to tell you: at such a time there is no longer any kind of movement there, or any kind of thought, or any kind of mental process, only a state of wonder that is beyond all mental processes, impulses, or thoughts. This is the pledge of the good things that are to come, which have been prepared through the mediation of our Lord Jesus Christ for the human race; that is to say, for all rational beings, as a result of the abundance of the compassion of the revered Father, who created us when we did not exist and allowed us to share in a knowledge of his glory, so that we might become like him, having no end forever, and that we might enjoy his glory. May he in his mercy make us all worthy of his glorious vision—here in pledge, but there in reality. Amen.

PART III

TEXTS AND TEXTUAL TRANSMISSION

7

BIBLICAL INTERPRETATION

Reading the Bible in any context is already an act of interpretation, as readers choose which translation and edition to read, which passages to stress, and how to understand what they read. Among early Syriac Christians, a number of different biblical translations both facilitated and complicated this task of scriptural interpretation. In terms of the Old Testament, early Christians generally used a Greek translation of the Hebrew Bible known as the Septuagint. Alternatively, they sometimes translated this Greek version of the Hebrew into their native language. In contrast, by the third century many Syriac Christians used what scholars today call the Old Testament Peshiṭta, a Syriac translation made directly from the Hebrew. Centuries later, Philoxenus of Mabbug commissioned a new translation that was produced by Polycarp in 507/8, portions of which might survive in the Syro-Lucianic fragments. Later, Paul of Tella produced an early seventh-century translation based on Origen's text of the Septuagint, a translation known as the Syro-Hexapla. Jacob of Edessa (d. 708) produced yet another edition of the Old Testament, which was a hybrid version based on the Syriac Peshiṭta, the Hebrew text, and the Greek Septuagint. Jacob's version, though, never rivaled the Old Testament Peshiṭta in popularity.

In terms of the New Testament, Syriac Christians had many choices. The first was the harmonized text of Tatian's *Diatessaron* that combined the Gospels of Mark, Matthew, Luke, and John into a single narrative. Two other translations kept these four gospels separate: the Old Syriac translation (which may have relied on the *Diatessaron*) and a revision of the Old Syriac that came to be known as the New Testament Peshiṭta. In the fifth century, Rabbula, the bishop of Edessa, strongly supported his own revision of the

New Testament to replace the *Diatessaron*. But it had some competition in the form of two later New Testament translations, one produced in 507/508 and commissioned by the early sixth-century West Syrian bishop Philoxenus, and the other produced in 616 and known as the Harqlean Version, some parts of which might have relied on Philoxenus's earlier translation. In reaction to the Christological debates of their time, these newer versions were more word-for-word translations of the Greek in an attempt at theological precision. Although the Harqlean Version appears in many early manuscripts, eventually both the Old Testament and New Testament Peshiṭta became the standard biblical translation in all later Syriac churches. The New Testament Peshiṭta differed from Western translations not only because it was in Syriac but also because of its canon, as it initially contained only twenty-two of the twenty-seven books in the Greek New Testament.

But even readers of the same translation can come to vastly different conclusions about what a given text means. Like their contemporaries writing in other languages, Syriac church leaders often litigated the controversies of their day by citing and interpreting scripture to support their claims. This was true, for example, in arguments such as those by Aphrahat and Ephrem that aimed to prove the superiority of Christianity over Judaism. Syriac Christians, like their non-Syriac Christian colleagues, interpreted their Old Testament as full of symbols and signs that they believed pointed to later Christian events and teachings. For example, the authors here excerpted—Aphrahat, Ephrem, the author of the *Book of Steps*, Narsai, Jacob of Serug, and Daniel of Ṣalaḥ—all understand their Old Testament through a distinctly Christian lens.

Early Syriac authors also used biblical interpretation to support their claims in the complex Christological controversies of the fifth and sixth centuries that came to form the Chalcedonian, East Syrian, and West Syrian churches as distinctive interpretive communities. These exegetical arguments revolved not only around theological and Christological concerns; they also concerned the spiritual and ascetic practices of the leaders involved in the arguments. These leaders were enmeshed in lineages linked to lines of education, ordination, and monastic training, all of which shaped what readings of scripture they found most persuasive. While the teachings of Theodore of Mopsuestia, for example, were posthumously condemned as heretical by Roman imperial orthodoxy, his interpretations of scripture were foundational for East Syrian traditions.

Syriac-speaking Christians also produced a number of beautifully creative textual interpretations, such as the anonymous *Homily on Genesis 22*, as well as distinctive histories of the world that were grounded in biblical narratives, such as the *Cave of Treasures* and the *Book of the Bee*. Illustrations such as those found in the sixth-century *Rabbula Gospel* or in the thirteen-century lectionary now labeled *British Library Additional* 7170 show how Syriac manuscript art also played a role in biblical interpretation. So, too, paintings such as the thirteenth-century frescos at the monastery of Mar Musa, demonstrate another, highly visual venue for biblical exegesis. Whether in words or in images, these works include windows into each author's and artist's views of the world.

Further Reading   There are many studies of Syriac biblical interpretation. In English, on the Bible itself, see Michael Weitzman, *The Syriac Version of the Old Testament: An Introduction* (New York: Cambridge University Press, 1999); and Sebastian Brock, *The Bible in the Syriac Tradition* (Kottayam: St. Ephrem Ecumenical Research Institute, 1989; repr., Piscataway, NJ: Gorgias Press, 2006). For the poetic metaphors ingrained in the symbolic interpretations of Ephrem and Aphrahat, see Sebastian P. Brock, *The Luminous Eye: The Spiritual World Vision of Saint Ephrem the Syrian* (Kalamazoo, MI: Cistercian Publications, 1992); Kees den Biesen, *Simple and Bold: Ephrem's Art of Symbolic Thought* (Piscataway, NJ: Gorgias Press, 2006); and Stephanie Skoyles, *Aphrahat the Persian Sage and the Temple of God: A Study of Early Syriac Theological Anthropology* (Piscataway, NJ: Gorgias Press, 2008). For an overview of early exegetical traditions, see J. F. Coakley, "Syriac Exegesis," in *The New Cambridge History of the Bible: From the Beginnings to 600*, ed. James Carleton Paget and Joachim Schaper (Cambridge: Cambridge University Press 2013), 697–713.

APHRAHAT, *DEMONSTRATIONS* 12

344.

Aphrahat, the "Persian Sage," is the author of twenty-three *Demonstrations* written between 336 and 345. Many of these teachings address the value of ascetic practices and the importance of differentiating the biblical interpretations—and thus the beliefs and practices—of those in Aphrahat's audience from those of the region's Jews. In the Zoroastrian Persian Empire where Aphrahat lived, Christians sometimes faced hostility from Shapur II's government, and Judaism seems to have appealed to some as a similar but safer alternative. This excerpt from *On Passover* is part of Aphrahat's concerted effort to distinguish the Christian "peoples" (whom he designated with the plural) from the Jewish "people" (whom he designated with the singular). He also stresses the superiority of the new covenant (of Jesus) over the old covenant (of Moses). In this section, Aphrahat emphasizes that not only is the crucifixion of God's Son greater than the sacrifice of the Passover lamb, and so Easter is greater than Passover, but also that even by contemporary Jews' own scriptural requirements, their celebrations of Passover that Aphrahat's congregants might be tempted to join are invalid by the Bible's own standards, as they are held outside Jerusalem and without the requisite Temple sacrifice. For additional excerpts from Aphrahat's *Demonstrations*, see chapters 5 and 10.

> See these mysteries, my friend, that [were expressed] when the holy one commanded the offering of the Passover sacrifice. He warned them concerning all its laws and said to them: "You must eat it in one house and must not take any of it outside the house." Moses commanded them as follows: "When you enter the land that the Lord has given you and offer the Passover sacrifice in its time, it is forbidden to slaughter the Passover sacrifice in [any]

one of your towns, except in the place that the Lord your God will choose. You and your household will rejoice in your festival." He also commanded them as follows: "No stranger or hired hand should eat of the Passover sacrifice, but a servant who has become yours [by being] bought with money may eat of the Passover sacrifice when you have circumcised the flesh of his foreskin."

Great and wonderful are these mysteries, my friend! When the Israelites were in their own land, it was forbidden to offer the Passover sacrifice, unless [it was] in Jerusalem. In our day, [the Israelites] are scattered throughout all peoples and languages, among the unclean and the uncircumcised, and they eat their bread in uncleanness among the peoples. Ezekiel spoke about them, when [God] showed him a sign that he would eat his bread in uncleanness, and he petitioned by saying, "O Lord of lords! My soul has not been defiled, nor has defiled flesh entered my mouth!" And [God] said to Ezekiel, "This will be the sign: the Israelites will eat their bread in defilement among the peoples where I will scatter them." Now if, as I said above, it was forbidden, while the Israelites were in their land, to slaughter the Passover sacrifice at any place except before a single altar in Jerusalem, how is it possible [for them] to perform the mystery of the Passover sacrifice in our [own] day, when they are scattered among foreign peoples? They now have no authority [to do so]! [God] testifies about them as follows in the prophet: "The Israelites will live for many days without sacrifices and without an altar, without [anyone] to wear the ephod or to offer incense." Again, he said to Jerusalem, "I will bring an end to her celebrations and her festivals, her new moon [rituals] and her sabbaths." About the ark of the covenant he said, "They will not again say 'the ark of the covenant of the Lord'; they will not remember it, and it will not be made again." Now that [God] has said that they will not remember it, [that] it will not be made again, and [that] it will not come to mind, why are they determined to do it? Earlier, Moses had said about them: "I will make them jealous by a people that is not a people, and I will anger them with a foolish people." I ask you, O wise debater of the people who does not examine the words of the law: show me when this word that God would make his people jealous by a people that is not a people was fulfilled? And when did he anger them with a foolish people? If you are made jealous by the people that is from the peoples, you fulfill the word that is written, which Moses earlier inscribed in the book. And if you offer the Passover sacrifice in any of the places where you live, you offer it in transgression of the commandment. Because [of this], a letter of divorce has been written for you. [. . .]

The Passover of the Jews is on the day of the fourteenth [of the month of Nisan], its night-time and day-time. Our day of great suffering, however, is Friday, the fifteenth day [of Nisan], its nighttime and daytime. After the Passover, Israel eats unleavened bread for seven days until the twenty-first day of the month, but we observe the [days of] unleavened bread as the festival of our savior. They eat unleavened bread with bitter herbs, but our savior rejected that cup of bitterness and removed all the bitterness of the peoples when he tasted but did not wish to drink. The Jews bring their sins to mind from season to season, but we remember the crucifixion and humiliation of our savior. They departed from the slavery of Pharoah by means of the Passover sacrifice, but we were saved from the slavery of Satan on the day of [Christ's] crucifixion. They sacrificed a lamb from the flock and by its blood were delivered from the destroyer, but we have been saved from the destructive actions that we were doing by the blood of the Son [who is] approved. Moses was a leader for them, but for us Jesus has become a guide and savior. Moses divided the sea for them and enabled them to pass through, but our savior divided Sheol and broke down its gates when he went inside it and opened them and prepared a way for all those who believed in him. Manna was given to [the Israelites] to eat, but our Lord gave us his body to eat. [Moses] brought forth water from a rock, but for us our savior let living water flow from within himself. [God] promised them the land of the Canaanites as an inheritance, but through a declaration he promised us the land of life. Moses lifted up the bronze serpent for them, so that whoever looked at it would survive the bite of the serpent, but Jesus lifted up himself for us so that when we look to him, we might be saved from the bite of the serpent who is Satan. Moses made the temporary tabernacle for them, so that they might bring sacrifices and offerings into it and be purged of their sins, but Jesus raised up the tent of David, which had fallen, and it [continues] to stand. He said to the Jews, "After you destroy this temple that you see, I will raise it up in three days," and his disciples understood that he was speaking about his body when he said that after they destroyed it, he would raise it up in three days. In that tent he has promised us life, and in it our sins have been purged. [Moses] called their [tent] the "temporary" tabernacle because it would function for [only] a short time, but ours [is called] the temple of the Holy Spirit, which is forever.

EPHREM, *COMMENTARY ON THE* DIATESSARON

Mid to late fourth century.

It is difficult to overstate the influence on Syriac Christian traditions of Ephrem (d. 373), the prolific deacon and poet from Nisibis who spent the last ten years of his life in Edessa. In addition to Ephrem's famous *memre*, or metrical verse homilies, and hundreds of liturgical hymns known as *madrashe*, his commentaries on Genesis, parts of Exodus, Acts, and some of the Pauline letters survive alongside his commentary on the late second-century *Diatessaron*, a text attributed to Tatian that harmonized the four canonical Greek gospels. While the Old Syriac Version of the New Testament also existed in Ephrem's time, the *Diatessaron* seems to have been Ephrem's primary Syriac version of the gospel stories and it remained very popular until the fifth century. This excerpt exemplifies Ephrem's characteristic reading of biblical "symbols" or "signs," whether Old Testament stories that he read as symbols of later Christian events or, in this case, a story about Jesus that Ephrem reads as a symbolic rejection of Judaism. The challenges posed by the story of Jesus cursing a fig tree for not producing fruit out of season presented a chance to foreground Ephrem's interpretive skills. For additional excerpts from Ephrem, see chapters 1, 2, 3, and 10.

> [Jesus] cursed the fig tree. [He did this] because it is written, "Whenever you reap your harvest, leave the gleaning for the poor, and whenever you beat your olives, do likewise;

thus shall you do in every instance." The owner of the fig tree did not obey the law but spurned it. Our Lord came and found that there was [nothing] left on it so he cursed it, lest its owner eat from it again, since he had left [nothing] for the orphan and widows. It is also said that in a similar fashion the Gadarenes had made a decision not to go out to him. Therefore, [the Lord] drowned their swine so that he might attract their hearts to go out [to him], even though they were unwilling. The owner of the fig tree likewise had made up his mind not to go out to him. [The Lord] dried up his fig tree so that he might go out, even though unwilling. On all [possible] occasions, therefore, [the Lord] was solicitous for the salvation of humanity.

Or [it was] because he had said, "Destroy the temple and in three days I will raise it up." They said to him, "It took forty-six years to build, and you would build it up in three days?" So it was evident that they did not believe. Moreover, when they showed him its ornamentation, he said, "The days will come when it will be destroyed, and Jerusalem will be devastated."

He cursed the fig tree and it shriveled up to show them the power of his divinity, so that by means of [this] action near at hand that they could see, they might believe that which was to come. Because [Jerusalem] had not accepted the law he cursed [the fig tree], so that there might no longer be fruit on it, according to its law. He sought fruit from the fig tree at an inopportune time, that it might be a symbol of one who had deceitfully withheld the fruits of the law at the opportune time. For, if he had sought fruit from it at the opportune time, no one would have known that there was a parable [in question] here. Instead of the fig tree, therefore, he showed that it was Jerusalem that he was reproaching, for he had sought love in her but she had despised the fruit of repentance. He was hungry and came to the fig tree, and, since he did not find [anything] on it, he cursed it. The fact that he was hungry can be attributed to the body, that is, whenever the [divine] power wished it. But how could he, who was informed concerning the hidden things of the heart, have looked for fruit at an inopportune time? Understand therefore, that it was not because of hunger that he cursed the fig tree. For, even if it had been the opportune time, and they had not reserved [the fruit] for him beforehand, that he might find some on it, it would not have been fitting that it should have been shriveled up and uprooted. [. . .]

Let us examine [further] concerning this question of the fig tree, since it is not Jerusalem, as other people say. It is likely that the apostles were thinking in their simplicity, as they were wont, and then doubted. So, in order to frighten them by a miracle, he dried up this fig tree before them. When they returned, they said to him, "See this fig tree that you cursed! How quickly it has dried up!" He said to them, "As for you too, if you had faith and did not doubt, you would speak to this mountain, and it would be transported." If this [fig tree] had [only] been a parable, he would not have been obliged to say, "If you had faith," but rather, "If you had insight." This [fig tree] is a sign, therefore, and not a parable. [. . .]

Why, therefore, did this person who was good and gentle, who everywhere revealed great things out of little things, and completion out of imperfection, why did he command the fig tree to dry up? For he healed the sufferings of everyone, changed water to wine, made an abundance from a little bread, opened the eyes of the blind, cleansed lepers, and raised the dead to life. But this fig tree alone did he cause to wither. It was because the time of his suffering was near, and, lest it be thought that he was captured because he was unable to free himself, he cursed the fig tree, that it might be a sign for his friends and a miracle for his enemies. Thus, the disciples would be strengthened by his word, and foreigners would be amazed at his power. Because he did all things well, and [the time] for him to suffer was near, it might be thought, as indeed it was, that he was captured because he possessed no power. He showed in advance, therefore, by means of an inanimate plant that he caused to wither, that he would have been able to destroy his crucifiers with a word. Just as he did this here, so too, lest his divine power be derided through an inferior member of the body, he likewise said to Simon, "Put back your sword in its place." [. . .]

It was also said that when Adam sinned and was deprived of that glory with which he was clothed, he hid his nakedness with the leaves of the fig tree. Our Lord came and endured sufferings for him, to heal the wounds of Adam, and to provide a garment of glory for his nakedness. Therefore, he caused the fig tree to wither, to make it known that the leaves of the fig tree were no longer required for the clothing of Adam, because he had restored him to his former glory, which, when in possession of it, he had no need of fig leaves, nor of clothing made from skins. Henceforth, there is no longer any use for the withered fig tree, whose leaves, when moist, were a garment of shame, and a clothing of mockery.

EPHREM, *THE REPENTANCE OF NINEVEH*

Mid to late fourth century.

Ephrem (d. 373), the beloved deacon from Nisibis who spent his final years in Edessa, was a master of poetic artistry. Even his lengthy homilies, or *memre*, were written in his trademark couplets of seven syllables each. This particular *memra* on the biblical story of Jonah exemplifies Ephrem's interest in emphasizing the superiority of Christians' worship of God over that of Jews, often polarized as the gentile "peoples" versus the Jewish "people." In the biblical story, the prophet Jonah warns the gentile Ninevites that God will overthrow their city if they do not repent of their ungodly ways and turn to the God of Israel. Ephrem's interpretation emphasized and expanded on the sincerity and depth of the Ninevites' repentance. For the Christian Ephrem, this was an ideal opportunity to offer his audience exemplary role models of repentance while concurrently reaffirming the superiority of the Gentiles' worship of God over that of the Jews, as Ephrem reads the Ninevites as symbols of later Christians. For additional excerpts from Ephrem, see chapters 1, 2, 3, and 10.

> The king [of Nineveh] stood up and stripped off his cloak,
>   and they all stripped off their cloaks.
> The king rushed to put on sackcloth,
>   and his troops [put on] black like him.
> The Assyrians who were living luxuriously
>   were suddenly 'Ethiopians'.
> The hair that was on their sackcloth

   assumed the symbol of Jacob,
So that they deceived Jonah and stole
   victory through repentance. [. . .]
The king called his army leader
   and he went out and inspected his camp.
Criers went through the camp
   so that everyone would repent,
"Let the unclean shed their uncleanness,
   so that it not conquer him in the battle." [. . .]
The king remained in mourning
   and nobly inspected the troops;
He proclaimed a fast for his camp
   and gave them a breastplate of glory;
He called them and drew them to prayer,
   the shield that was the salvation of all of them;
He proclaimed to them humility,
   the bow whose arrows are victorious;
He drew them to living love,
   the sword that causes those who grasp it to rejoice. [. . .]
Jonah saw, and wonder seized him;
   he was ashamed of his people.
With the Ninevites he saw victory,
   and he wept for the seed of Abraham.
He saw that the seed of Canaan was restored,
   and the seed of Jacob was acting wickedly.
He saw that the uncircumcised people circumcised their heart,
   and that the circumcised people hardened their heart.
He saw that without the Sabbaths being observed,
   the commandments were being kept;
Without the Sabbath there was salvation,
   and without circumcision there was victory.
Jonah despised his people
   who had boasted about the Sabbaths;
He despised them also because circumcision
   they placed between life and death.
The king of Nineveh knew
   that the cause of the anger was [their] foolish behavior;
He cut off the cause of the evils
   and quickly cut off the storms.
He was a physician who inspected his province,
   and he knew the medicine appropriate for it.
Through the fast, the victorious medicine,
   he healed the sickness of the city;
And with sackcloth and ash he banished

the sin from within the walls.
Because they left behind their debts,
   the good one increased his forgiveness.
Through the principal and interest that they paid,
   the province and the city were delivered.
Jonah had required the debts;
   the fast had forgiven the sins.
They came together and took counsel,
   the Ninevites, about how they might live;
The whole people established a contract
   so that through it they might appease God.

BOOK OF STEPS

Mid-fourth to early fifth century.

The *Book of Steps* is a collection of Syriac teachings that focuses on asceticism and the spiritual life. It distinguishes two types of Christians, which the text calls the perfect, who live celibate ascetic lives, and the upright, whose practices are not so strict. This excerpt comes from a section that uses a study of Adam and Eve from Genesis as a way of expanding the reader's understanding of Paul's teachings in 1 Corinthians. The text argues that God intended men's genitals only for urination, and that Adam erred by lustfully engaging in sexual intercourse with Eve. Marriage and sexual intercourse are thus subordinated to the ideal of a celibate ascetic life without lust. For an additional excerpt from the *Book of Steps*, see chapter 5.

> "Food," Paul said, "does not commend us before God," because those who have walked this way have not been helped but have forgotten God after they had eaten and reveled, and the anger of God rose up against them. Do you see how food and pleasures do not allow us to stand before God? Therefore, on account of that hope, the evil one had taught Adam and Eve: "In this way you shall become as great as God"; and then, "There is a way for you to be fruitful and multiply, and to do everything you desire, as does the creator."
>
> Adam wanted to rebel and consented to imitate the intercourse of animals. Adam did not know, however, that if they had kept the commandment, they would have been fruitful and multiplied, as he had made Eve fruitful by the Word of our Lord without lust. Although they would not have been able to do a thing without the Word of the Lord, still they believed that without our Lord what the evil one had said would come to be. Adam sinned and erred in this because he obeyed the advice of the evil one. He was not able to perform a deed without the creator but was overthrown and departed from the paradise of the kingdom.
>
> Perhaps you will say, "Since he was not able to do a single thing without the creator, why did [God] drive him out and close the door of paradise so that he may not reenter?" Was his error small, seeing he desired to become an opponent to his creator, to sit opposite him and resist him, since he thought he could become like [God] and challenge him with

power? For had he not thought, "I take no account of him," he would have been afraid of his commandment and would have listened to him. But he was also defiled without lust by what the evil one had placed in their ears. Immediately after they had obeyed and had given their attention, the evil thought made the taste of death enter and it was impressed on their heart.

If you say, "Look, the [genital] members were meant for intercourse," but you [really] do not desire intercourse, [you should say] that the creator made them in order for you to urinate.

Therefore, keep the commandments today as [God] has spoken to you and come to that perfection that Adam had wasted. When you have come to that thing from which Adam fell, see, it has removed the lust from you. When you became a celibate without lust you will see that these members are for urinating and not for intercourse. Because, when you become a celibate, lust will never ascend again upon your heart, and you will no longer desire intercourse just as a dead person whose soul is removed does not desire it. [. . .]

Therefore, when Adam and Eve left heaven and loved the earth and these visible things, they transgressed against the law of the creator. God came to find fault with them but had compassion upon them, establishing for them another law after they had transgressed against the first [law], and God allowed them to marry. Then the lustful instinct of marriage came to exist in Adam and Eve, and, because of all their transgressions, they were married.

NARSAI, *ON THE SACRIFICE OF ISAAC*

Fifth century. East Syrian.

The fifth-century Mesopotamian scholar and poet Narsai played an important role in intellectual conversations of his time, and he was an influential figure in the development of the East Syrian Church. Perhaps most famously, Narsai was the director of the School of Edessa until the emperor Zeno closed it in 489, whereafter Narsai was welcomed in Nisibis and founded the celebrated School of Nisibis. Narsai's exegetical traditions were strongly influenced by the Greek theologian Theodore of Mopsuestia, whose teachings were condemned in the Roman Empire under the emperor Justinian for their association with Nestorius. In this excerpt Narsai explores the struggle that Abraham faced when God asked him to sacrifice his son Isaac (Genesis 22), and he finds in it a symbol of Christ's sacrifice in the Crucifixion. For an additional excerpt from Narsai, see chapter 2.

The sweetness of passionate love for his Lord enabled the just man to constrain and neutralize the poison that was mingled in his natural feelings.

O Abraham, true friend of faith, who forgot all the lovely things that nature had acquired. Well did God choose you when he chose you from all the peoples, making you an example for anyone wanting to imitate your passionate love. Through love for his master did the fervent man carry out his master's will, taking his son to go to the place that had been shown him. The voice bade him make his sacrifice in a distant place, so that he might be observed by the inhabitants of both earth and heaven: to the sight of all creation was God demonstrating his fortitude of soul, how resolute he was, showing no weakness in the labor of his journey.

Three days did he travel, silent, without doubt in his mind. He did not reveal the secret of his master's will to his household; from everyone did he hide the secret between him and his Lord, not even revealing to Sarah the preparations he had in mind. He kept the secret between his Lord and himself hidden, so that the genuineness of his love might be assured for the Lord who had chosen him. His Lord's command was weighty upon him above all else, but he made ready his own will in accordance with his Lord's: by that will his soul's emotions were held fast, while he was looking to the outcome at the end of his journey.

The three days' course of his journey came to an end, and, raising up his eyes, he beheld the place, at which he rejoiced: for with bodily eyes God showed him the place of his son's sacrifice, while in his mind God revealed the type of what was to come, for on that symbolic site Christ was to become a sacrifice, and God foretold him, before these things took place, by means of the symbol of the sacrifice, since Isaac's sacrifice was a symbol of that of Christ. Most appropriate it was that the one sacrifice should resemble the other. The creator's power made similar love's intent, so that those who hear these words may not show doubt at what was carried out.

Such was Abraham's mind on this three-day journey, so that the one sacrifice might prove a witness to the other, the symbol to the reality. Abraham directed his mind to this intention and his soul found rest at the site of the sacrifice that his Lord had shown him. On this sacrificial site he brought to perfection his own will and that of his Lord. He built the altar, laid out the wood, bound his son, drew out the knife—and, with the knife, he drew out his will. But a voice held him back, checking his hand from his beloved one: "Abram, Abram!" did the spiritual being call out to the mortal: "Hold back your hand; stop from your son's sacrificial death; stop from the sacrifice of mortal blood that I requested of you. Take and offer to me the blood of a mute animal instead of a rational being; I do not ask for the blood of a human being at this time, for he is insufficient to wipe out with his blood the document of debt: humanity's debts cannot be repaid with human blood until the time that, from humanity, there shall come the perfect man. [. . .]

I have revealed to you, Abram, by means of this sacrifice, the delivery of humankind, so that all may know to watch for the time of humanity's salvation. By what has occurred with you I have trodden the path that leads to what is to come, so that humanity may travel to meet hope of death's annulment."

MEMRA ON GENESIS 22

Likely fifth century.

We know little about the origins of this anonymous Syriac *memra* on Genesis 22. This reading of the story of Abraham's near sacrifice of his son Isaac is particularly notable for how it expands his wife Sarah's role. In ways that were common in Syriac dialogue hymns (*sogiyata*), this expansion of the biblical text constructs a remarkable conversation between

Sarah and Abraham after he returned and Sarah believed that he had sacrificed their son to God.

> Once they had arrived and reached home, Abraham said to his son,
> "My son, please stay back for a little, while I go in and return to your mother.
> I will see how she receives me; I will spy out her mind and her thought."
> The old man returned and entered in peace. Sarah rose up to receive him;
> She brought in a bowl to wash his feet, and she began to speak as follows,
> "Welcome, blessed old man, husband who has loved God;
> Welcome, happy man, who has sacrificed my only child on the pyre;
> Welcome, O slaughterer, who did not spare the body of my only child.
> Did he weep when he was bound, or groan as he died?
> He was eagerly looking out for me, but I was not there to come to his side;
> His eyes were wandering over the mountains, but I was not there to deliver him.
> By the God whom you worship, relate to me the whole affair."
> Abraham answered and said to Sarah, in reply to her words,
> "Your son did not weep when he was bound, he gave no groan as he died.
> You have put me under oath by God, saying, 'Did he ask to see you on the pyre?'
> When the pyre was built and set up, and the bonds were on his hands,
> And the knife above his head, then did he remember you there,
> And he asked to see you on the pyre."
> "May the soul of my only child be accepted, for he
> Hearkened to the words of his mother.
> If only I were an eagle, or had the speed of a turtledove,
> So that I might go and behold that place where my only
> Child, my beloved, was sacrificed,
> So that I might see the place of his ashes, the site where he
> Was bound, and bring back a little of his blood to be comforted by its smell.
> I had some of his hair to put in a place inside my clothes,
> And when grief overcame me, I placed it over my eyes. I had
> Some of his garments, so that I might imagine him, as I placed
> Them in front of my eyes, and when suffering sorrow overcame me,
> I gained relief through gazing upon them. I had wished I
> Could see his pyre and the place where his bones were burned, and
> Could bring a little of his ashes, to gaze on them always and be comforted."
> As she stood there, her heart mourning, her mind and
> Thought intent, greatly upset with emotion, her mind dazed as
> She grieved, the child came in, returning safe and sound. Sarah
> Arose to receive him, she embraced him and kissed him amid
> Tears, and she began to address him as follows: "Welcome, my
> Son, my beloved; welcome, child of my vows; welcome, a dead
> One who has come back to life."
> The child began to speak, saying as follows, "A son does
> Not last forever, nor do wealth and possessions, but God endures

Forever for whoever performs his will. But for the voice that
Called out, 'Abraham, hold off from the child' I would yesterday
Have died and my bones would have been consumed by fire."
Then Sarah began to repay, with utterances of thanksgiving,
The good God who had brought back her only child: "I give
Thanks to God who has given you to me a second time; I do
Obeisance to that voice that delivered you, my son, from the
Knife. I praise him who saved you from burning on the pyre.
Henceforth, my son, it will not be 'Sarah's son' that people will
Call you, but 'child of the pyre,' an 'offering that died and was resurrected.'
And to you be glory, O God, for all passes away, but you endure."

JACOB OF SERUG, *MEMRA ON TAMAR*

Late fifth or early sixth century. West Syrian.

Jacob of Serug (d. 521) was born in a village on the east shore of the Euphrates River, southwest of Edessa. His preeminence as a Syriac poet is second only to Ephrem, and Jacob's hundreds of twelve-syllable *memr*e, or verse homilies, are a testament to his talent, devotion, and the time he spent learning at the School of Edessa. This particular *memra* examines the complex story of Genesis 38 in which Tamar dressed as a prostitute to seduce her father-in-law Judah, who has refused to give his third son to Tamar in marriage after his first and second sons consecutively married her and soon died, leaving the family without heirs. Jacob's homily offers a creative reading of the gender and sexuality dynamics in the story, while also Christianizing the story to focus on the priceless seed of Abraham that ran through Judah to Jesus. For additional excerpts from Jacob of Serug, see chapters 2, 5, and 8.

> To Abraham the Father spoke in revelation,
>   [Saying] that all the peoples would be blessed in his elect seed.
> And because of this the Son of God was expected,
>   For the world had become aware that he would come in a mysterious way.
> All the upright were desirous to see his day,
>   And were expecting he would shine forth on earth in their own days.
> In various places women were yearning for the choice seed—
>   That from them he who was expected to come to earth might shine forth:
> Leah and Rachel, straightforward women of integrity,
>   Were contending over him in the land of Aram.
> They had heard that in the seed of the House of Abraham
>   All the peoples were going to be blessed—and fire fell upon their minds!
> For this reason there befell a dispute between the two of them,
>   And, as if over some treasure, they fought over a righteous man.

They performed an action that was most hateful to chaste women:
    One desired, and one asked, impudently;
They acted without restraint, showing no shame, because they were aware
    Of what wealth was concealed in the godly man.
Rachel, importunate and like a prostitute, demanded of him,
    Saying, "Give me children, otherwise I will die."
Leah, like someone infatuated and loving adultery, hired him,
    And she was not ashamed to plunder the wealth that she so desired.
It was not with the lust of adulterous women that they were fired,
    But it was for the seed of their weighty man that they longed.
Ruth, too, acted in like fashion over Boaz,
    Going out in the night like a thief to despoil,
So that she might steal from him the great wealth that was hidden within him.
    She was not ashamed, chaste woman that she was, to seize hold of his legs.
She went out to the threshing floor to steal away the seed of the House of Abraham.
    In her vigilance she stole it, just as she had wanted, in an impudent way.
When and how have women so run after men,
    As these women who contended over the medicine of life?
The divine plan, mistress of mysteries, incited these women
    With love of the only begotten before he had ever come.
It was because of him that they acted without restraint and schemed,
    Putting on the outward guise of wanton women,
Despising female modesty and nobility,
    Not being ashamed as they panted for men.
Someone who wants to get hold of a treasure, if they could,
    Would perform a murder in order to gain the gold they so desired.
These women, while running after men,
    Were yearning for the Son of God's great epiphany,
And they struggled for the seed of the House of Abraham,
    Since they had learned that in it the peoples of the earth would be blessed.
It was not harlotry in the case of these sincere women,
    But love for the blessed seed that incited them. [. . .]
But what should I say concerning Tamar, who is filled with mysteries?
    For the wonder that fills her case surpasses that of her companions:
This woman openly became a wanton-hearted prostitute,
    She went out and sat by the crossroads to ensnare a man!
It was for you, O Son of God, that she was gazing out, [waiting for] you to come to her,
    And it was because of you that she despised women's nobility.
She went out after you like an infatuated woman in the streets,
    For she was wanting you to sprinkle sanctity on her limbs.
Now Tamar saw that if she sat like an honorable woman,
    She would not ensnare the wealth after which she had gone out.
Therefore she dressed like a prostitute, went out and sat there,
    To fall in with a merchant on the road, like some impudent woman.

In the case of all the mystery-filled narratives of the Only Begotten
  It is right to listen with great love, O discerning [reader],
For if love does not open the gate of your ear,
  Then there is no passage to your hearing for the words.
In the case of the story of Tamar, unless a mind that has faith
  Listens to it, the discerning woman will seem worthy of reproach,
Whereas if an intellect that loves to listen to the mysteries
  Should hear the tale, it will render back in return for it praise.
All the words that the spirit of God has placed in scripture
  Are filled with riches, like treasures, hidden in the books.
Moses the scribe set the story of Tamar
  Like a jewel in his book so that its beauty might shine out among its readings.
Why would he have written of a woman who sat like a prostitute
  By the crossroads had she not been filled with some mystery?
Why did Moses, who drove away all prostitutes from his people,
  Extol this one who had adorned herself like a prostitute?
Her action would have been wrong had there not been some mystery there,
  And it would not have been successful had it been something hateful to God.
Her action was [indeed] ugly, but her faith made it beautiful,
  And it was resplendent and dear because of the mystery that was performed
    in her. [. . .]
O soul who, like a prostitute, loves the world,
  Supplicate Christ by the wayside, and once you have found him,
Take refuge in faith that is filled with light.
  Clothe yourself in baptism, as the armor of righteousness,
And hang the cross of light around your neck, as a necklace;
  Then you will have confidence that the flame will not touch you.
Let Tamar serve as a mirror for the entire world:
  Let everyone preserve their faith and their baptism,
And when the fire of judgment is revealed in this life,
  Blessed is [Christ] who rescues from the flame the person who loves him.

CAVE OF TREASURES

Fifth or sixth century. Attested in East and West Syrian manuscripts.

The anonymous *Cave of Treasures* is a fascinating example of Syriac exegesis. Cited in the sixth century and likely not produced before the fifth century, this work presents biblical history from creation to Pentecost with numerous distinctive traditions woven into its summary of the biblical narratives. One recurring thread is its location of numerous biblical events at the same earthly place, which it calls the center of the world or Golgotha. Golgotha, it claims, was where Adam, whose body was taken on the ark by Noah, was reburied after the flood, as well as where Abraham prepared to offer Isaac as a sacrifice

FIGURE 7.

The Rabbula Gospels (*Biblioteca Medicea Laurenziana, Ms. Plut.* 1.56, fol. 13a). In addition to preserving text, Syriac manuscripts often include artwork ranging from doodling, to small geometric drawings, to lavish illustrations. The *Rabbula Gospels* are a manuscript containing the Peshiṭta version of the canonical gospels, completed by the scribe Rabbula in 586. The manuscript is famed for its illuminations, which feature bold colors, dynamic figures, detailed backgrounds, and geometric patterns. The codex constitutes one of the earliest surviving gospel manuscripts with large illustrations and some of the only surviving Christian painting from the sixth century. The illustrations show both Hellenistic and Persian stylistic influences, indicative of the diverse influences on late antique Syriac Christian art and scribal culture. Florence, *Biblioteca Medicea Laurenziana, Ms. Plut.* 1.56, fol. 13a, courtesy of MiBACT. Any further reproduction by any means is prohibited.

to God. It was also the site of the Crucifixion where the blood of Christ, the new Adam, soaked into the ancient burial ground and baptized the first Adam. This text differs in its Eastern and Western recensions and its origins are uncertain; these excerpts are just small portions of the much longer text and include some sections from each recension.

[On Creation]

On the third day God commanded the waters under the firmament to gather into one place and for the dry land to appear. When the veil of waters had been rolled back from the earth's surface, it was seen to be uninhabited and unprepared, that is, loose, lax in its nature. And the waters gathered together in the seas under the earth, in it and above it. And God made a ford below for the earth, and a channel and streams for the water-ford and for the wind, so it could come up from within the earth, and through those channels and fords there might be heat and cold in service of the earth. The earth on the bottom side is like a thickly formed sponge, since it is set on water. And on that day God commanded the earth and it pushed grass up from below. And within it conceived all kinds of trees, seeds, plants, and roots. [. . .]

And God formed Adam with his holy hands, with his image, and with his shape. And when the angels had seen Adam's image and glorious appearance, they were moved by his beautiful form. For they had seen his face burning with a light bright like the solar orb, the light of his eyes like the sun's rays, and his body's shape like ice's bright light. And when he had stretched and stood in the middle of the earth, and he had set both his feet in the place where our savior's cross was stuck, there he donned royal clothing and a gleaming crown was placed on his head; there he was made king, priest, and prophet; there God set him on the royal throne, and there all the animals, birds, and livestock gathered, passing before Adam, and Adam designated names for them and they bowed their heads, worshipping him. The angels and heavenly powers heard God's voice, saying to Adam, "Look! I have made you king, priest, prophet, master, chief, handler of all things made and created, and to you alone have I given them, and I have put you in charge over everything I have created." And when the angels, archangels, thrones, masters, cherubs, seraphs, and all the heavenly powers heard this, they blessed and worshipped him.

[. . .]

[On Noah and the Ark]

The entrance into the ark was on a Wednesday, in the month of Iyyar [i.e., May], in which Noah entered the ark. On the fourteenth, a Friday, beginning in the morning, animals and livestock entered the lower level; at midday, the birds and reptiles entered the middle level; and at sunset Noah entered the ark, he and his sons on the eastern side of the ark, while his wife and the wives of his sons entered the western side. And the body of Adam was placed inside the ark. Because all the mysteries of the church are depicted in the ark, that men should be on the east in the church, women on the west, with the men not seeing the women's faces, and the women not seeing the men's faces, this way, too, within the ark the men lived on the east, the women on the west, and like a pedestal, Adam's body had been placed in the middle. And as peace reigns within the church between men and women and children, so peace reigned within the ark among animals, birds, livestock, and reptiles. [. . .]

After a bit, once the water had dried from the earth, [Noah] sent out a dove, but it found no resting place and went back to Noah in the ark. And after seven days, he sent the dove out again, and it came back to him with an olive leaf in its mouth. This dove depicts the two covenants for us: with the first, the spirit that spoke through the prophets found no resting place among that difficult, quarrelsome people, but with the second, it rested on the peoples in the waters of baptism, and they were saved through the anointing. [. . .]

[On Babel and the Syriac Language]

From Adam to the tower [of Babel] they would speak Syriac, which is more expansive and far-reaching than all other languages and is called Aramaic: it is the king of all languages. The early writers made a mistake when they recorded Hebrew as the first language, and here is a nasty error in their writing, for all the languages in the world are derived from Syriac, and all languages have mixed with it, but it has overcome them all. [. . .]

[On Mary's Ancestors]

Since none of the early teachers found out the succession of their fathers, they seriously pressed the people of the church to show them the parents of the blessed Mary, the succession of their families, for them to really want to carefully research the succession of their fathers and to show them the truth. Because of this, they called Mary an adulterer, but here the mouth of the Jews can shut up, and they believed that Mary is the seed of David and of Abraham. [. . .]

And since Joseph was Mary's cousin—God in his foreknowledge knew that Mary was going to be persecuted by the Jews—she was given to Joseph, who was her cousin, so that, with her guarding him, he might guard her. See, brother Namosaya, that Mary's ancestors are from the genealogical succession of Abraham, son of David. [. . .]

[On Jesus's Birth]

[The magi] thought they would find a royal palace in Israel, with golden beds spread with carpets and covers, a royal child wrapped in purple, armies and ranks of the king's swift servants, the kingdom's nobles offering him tables and gifts, readied and arranged, regal fare and the food that kings want, royal tableware of gold and silver, and enslaved men and women serving fearfully. They were expecting to see things this way, but they saw things even greater. When they entered the cave, they saw Joseph, the old man, sitting in wonder, and Mary was in amazement—no extravagant bed, no prepared table, and not one of the marks of earthly royalty. But when they saw all this loathsome poverty, they had no doubts, but fearfully approached, worshipped him honorably, and offered their gifts: gold, myrrh, and incense. Mary and Joseph were deeply sad that they had nothing to offer them, but they nourished themselves from their provisions. Christ was eight days old when they brought him the offerings, and it was right that on the eighth day, the day of circumcision, offerings should be brought to him, for at the time that Joseph circumcised him, in the evening, Mary received the offerings. In truth, Joseph circumcised him in accordance with the law, but he performed the circumcision without anything having been cut away: like iron that has crossed and cuts the rays of the sun or fire, with nothing cutting it, thus, too, Christ was circumcised, with nothing being taken from him. [. . .]

[On the Crucifixion]

In everything, Christ made himself like Adam, as it is written, and in the spot Melchizedek served as priest, where Abraham offered up a lamb as a sacrifice, there the wood of the cross was stuck. This place is the middle of the earth, and there the four corners embrace together. Because, when God made the earth, his great power would run ahead of him, and the earth would run after him from the four corners; there, at Golgotha, God's power arose and stopped; and there the four corners of the world embraced each other: this place is the door of the universe, and the place was opened. When Shem and Melchizedek put Adam's body in the middle of the earth, the four corners ran and embraced Adam, and the door was shut immediately, and none of Adam's children could open it. But when the cross of Christ—the savior of Adam and his children—was placed over it, the door of the place opened on Adam's face. And when the cross was fixed over him, Christ was wounded by the spear, and blood and water flowed from his side, they flowed into Adam's mouth and became his baptism, and he was baptized with them.

DANIEL OF ṢALAḤ, *COMMENTARY ON THE PSALMS*, PSALM 1

542. West Syrian.

Daniel of Ṣalaḥ was an influential scholar, monastic leader, and author who seems to have mainly written during the reign of the emperor Justinian in the middle of the sixth century. A staunch opponent of the Council of Chalcedon as well as of the controversial teachings of the strongly anti-Chalcedonian teacher Julian of Halicarnassus, Daniel became a hero of the West Syrian Church. Although not many of Daniel's writings survive, his *Commentary on the Psalms* alone fills over a thousand manuscript pages. The excerpt here demonstrates the flexibility of his exegetical style, ranging from comments on his understanding of the historical context of the Psalms' composition (traditionally ascribed to King David) to the "spiritual understanding" that is key for the Christian spirituality Daniel hopes to foster in his audience.

Those who are desirous of the blessings granted by the Holy Spirit should proffer the ear of their soul to listen to what has been granted through the divine psalmist David. Keeping away from the things in which the Holy Spirit takes no pleasure, let them approach the spiritual occupation that draws God's will to them. For any approach to the divine blessings involves complete separation from the works of wickedness: just as participation in the divine light effects in us a distancing from the darkness of sin, so too, by means of desire for the heavenly blessings we distance ourselves from any association with the woes that apply to the wicked. Now, it is impossible for anyone to enjoy the blessings unless they escape from any occupation to which woes are attached—this occupation to which woe is attached being the wicked way of life of evildoers. This is why the blessed David—who knew of the divine blessings through the revelation of the Holy Spirit that he received in his soul, and who was aware, too, of the punishments that had come upon evildoers by means of just judgments—made a beginning of his psalmody with the blessed state of the upright.

Now we should inquire into the reason why he sang this first psalm, so that in this way it may prove easy for us to look fully at the aim of its interpretation.

It is said by those who are acquainted with the Hebrew language that David uttered it with reference to Saul when he went to raise Samuel by witchcraft [1 Samuel 28], that is, when the king of Israel abandoned the path of uprightness and walked in the path of the wicked, in other words, in the path that leads to the darkness of the error of demons: this was when he descended from the throne of righteousness and sat upon the seat of the woman who worked witchcraft in ʿAdoʿir.

For this reason, the blessed David was stirred, uttering this song of praise in flight, in response to the change that had come over Saul. Without any hesitation he openly cried out to the king who had been called by him "anointed of the Lord," singing, "Blessed is the one who has not walked in the path of the wicked, and has not stood with the mind of sinners, and has not sat upon the seat of scorners" [Psalms 1:1]—in contrast to Saul, who had abandoned the path of uprightness, having previously spurned, nullified, and abandoned the company of the prophets who speak in the spirit; a man who believed in the demons who rose up from the ground and prophesied to him what was going to happen to him.

Maybe you will object and say, "It was not the demons, but Samuel that the woman said that she had seen." Listen, O wise and discerning reader, look carefully at what the woman said when Saul asked her, "What have you seen?" [1 Samuel 28:13]: she said, "I have seen gods ascending from the earth"—that is, demons who were considered by her to be gods, and whom she worshipped; these were in the habit of appearing to her when she used incantations. and thus they deceived those who erred after her. Then, subsequently, she said, "An old man has come up, wrapped in a cloak" [1 Samuel 28:14], to which Saul said, "It is Samuel," for the demon that had come up and deceived Saul had changed appearances and taken on that of the prophet in order to deceive the sinful king.

It was on seeing and hearing this hateful deed that the blessed David accorded blessing to the man who had not walked in the path of the wicked.

Now, when we ascend toward the height of the spiritual understanding of this first "blessed," we find the divine David looking in prophecy to the first-formed human being: Adam existed in a realm exalted above woes when he was in paradise, but once he had turned his footsteps away from that luminous path that travels amid the luminous plants of paradise, he left for the outer fence of paradise on a pathless course of wandering, having become a disciple of the serpent, through Eve's counsel—just as Saul became a disciple to witchcraft that leads astray by means of the woman's teaching. So that first human being left the garden of life and incorruptibility. Now Saul, who was also called "Adam" by David, fell from kingship over that holy people after he had been initiated into witchcraft.

These two spiritual meanings, therefore, we have taken from the beginning of this psalm. But let us expend a little sweat on these first three phrases.

Every human being is divided up separately into body, soul, and mind, and his occupation is likewise separated out as having three goals: when we attribute the "walking" to the soul, the "standing" to the mind, and the "seat" to the body, then we discover that the blessed David has uttered these verses in a sage way. The words, "Blessed is the one who has not walked in the path of the wicked," are fulfilled and completed when the feet of the soul are restrained from walking in the dark path of the workers of evil. The wise Qohelet, too, realizing that "walking" applies to the soul, used to say, "The sight of the eyes is preferable to the walking about of the soul" [Ecclesiastes 6:9].

Now, a person who "stands in the mind of sinners" is someone who has stopped from "walking" and who has reached the point of action. And the person who "sits on the seat of scorners" is someone who ends up in an occupation of despair, having alighted upon the occupation of evil-doers that is filled with scorn.

SYRIAC APOCALYPSE OF DANIEL

Early seventh century. Likely Chalcedonian.

The seventh-century military successes of Muhammad's followers in the Christian-majority regions around Jerusalem and Damascus prompted a series of Christian apocalyptic writings; the *Syriac Apocalypse of Daniel* seems to emerge from this period, possibly in a Greek original, although it does not clearly refer to these events. While most of these seventh-century apocalypses rely on earlier apocalyptic writings like the scriptural book of Daniel, the *Syriac Apocalypse of Daniel* also echoes some earlier noncanonical Jewish apocalyptic literature, and scholars debate whether it also references the book of Revelation. Although Revelation was considered canonical in Western New Testament traditions from the fourth century onward, the text's canonical status was much more controversial in the eastern Mediterranean and it never attained the same level of canonicity in the Syriac New Testament. This excerpt reveals this apocalypse's rich interpretive traditions as it weaves together earlier traditions to predict a violent apocalyptic upheaval, a time of peace, the arrival of an Antichrist, and the final welcoming of God's true followers into the heavenly city of God. Its early seventh-century context makes its apocalyptic fervor particularly interesting to anyone tracing Christians' first encounters with the followers of Muhammad and the development of the new religion of Islam.

> Then will be gathered the four winds of heaven,
> One to the other,
> And there will be a great and vicious battle.
> Also, the corpses of the slain will be gathered like mounds.
> The western horn will rise and break the winds of heaven
> And it will hold fast until the end of days.
>
> Signs will appear on earth:
> A commotion on the islands,
> And fire will be burning on them day and night.

And there will be these signs in those times:
The sun will be blotted out like sackcloth,
And the moon clothed as with blood.
The earth will quiver and the sea,
And many people will fall.
In those times there will also be fallacy on earth:
A son will renounce his father, a brother his brother,
And even a friend will deceive his friend.

God will reject the earth.
In those days there will be a great famine and pestilence,
Much rebellion and heat and blight,
The sword and locust and crawling locust,
Which will devour the grass of the land.

There will be in those days a great darkness covering the earth,
A gloom for generations.
The earth will conceive deceit,
And will travail and bear iniquity.
Dew will be withheld from heaven,
Rain from the clouds.
And fire from the sun
Will devour the stones of the earth and inflame the northern regions;
It will be burning day and night,
While devouring dust and roots and stones and trees.

In those days the earth will be in uproar and the sea.
People will rise against people, kingdom against kingdom,
And cities against cities.
The strongholds of the earth,
One against the other will rebel.

In those days angels will go out to the four winds of heaven
To make the requital of anger from the midst of the earth.
They will begin to strike and to destroy with the sword and with pestilence,
Also with all kinds of trials.
After this there will be silence on earth,
And peace will abound.
Those who dwell in the world will be healed. [. . .]

It will be in those days, a woman will bear a son from the tribe of Levi. And there will appear on him these signs: something will be represented on his skin like weapons of war, the details of a breastplate, a bow, and a sword, a spear, an iron dagger, and chariots of war. His countenance will be like the countenance of a burning furnace, and his eyes like burning coals. Between his eyes he has a horn whose tip is broken off, and something that has the appearance of a serpent is coming out of it.

FIGURE 8.

Mar Musa fresco of the Last Judgment. In addition to textual interpretations, Syriac Christians also created elaborate artistic depictions of biblical scenes. Particularly stunning examples can be found in frescos from Deir Mar Musa al-Habashi (Monastery of Saint Moses the Abyssinian), al-Nabek, Syria that were painted in 1207/1208. A collection of scenes of the last judgment is the best-preserved fresco from Deir Mar Musa and one of the only surviving examples of medieval painting from the Syriac tradition. This fresco presents a distinct West Syrian perspective on the final judgment. The left half of the fresco depicts the elect in ascending order from West Syrian monks and nuns (bottom) to church fathers and the Virgin Mary (top, not visible). On the right are the damned: these include murderers, non-Christian priests, Muslims, and, near the top, Chalcedonian Christians. Therefore, in addition to its art historical significance, this fresco articulates specific perspectives on religious and theological differences. © Emma Loosley / *Architecture and Asceticism;* licensed under the CreativeCommons Attribution-NonCommercial-ShareAlike 4.0 license; available online at http://architectureandasceticism.exeter.ac.uk/items/show/665.

When these signs are about to occur, then the advent of the senseless, the crooked serpent, Antichrist, will be about to appear. He will come from the ends of the land of the East to seduce the inhabitants of the world. He will say about himself, "I am Christ!" [. . .]

Then the mighty Lord will gather all the elect of Israel,
All the scattered of Judah,
And the entire offspring of Abraham,
And will celebrate a banquet for Zion
And a feast for Jerusalem,
Also, the paschal feast and joy and glory,
A banquet of peace,
In the days of Christ, at the salvation of Zion,
Also, at the assembling of the exiles of Israel,
And all of the just and righteous.

SOLOMON OF BAṢRA, *BOOK OF THE BEE*

Thirteenth century. East Syrian.

Like the *Cave of Treasures*, the *Book of the Bee* is an overview of the history of the world, from creation to Christ's resurrection. The *Book of the Bee* was produced by Solomon, a bishop of Baṣra in the East Syrian Church, about whom we know little else beyond his attendance at a consecration in 1222. This excerpt includes an observation about the order of creation in Genesis, which Solomon says intentionally disallowed later philosophers from claiming that the sun and not God created the earth's plants. Like many Syriac texts, it also recognizes Syriac as the primordial human language, and makes an argument for the priority of its own (East Syrian) tradition over other forms of Christianity. It also teaches that the crossbar of Jesus's cross had earlier been the rod of Moses and had begun as a branch of the tree of the knowledge of good and evil that Adam took with him when he left paradise.

It is well for us to take the materials for our discourse from the divine scriptures, that we may not stray from the straight paths of the way of truth. The blessed David says, "Lord, you have been our dwelling-place in all generations, before the mountains were conceived." David, the harpist of the spirit, thereby makes known that although there was a beginning of the framing of Adam and the other creatures when they were made, yet in the mind of God it had no beginning; that it might not be thought that God has a new thought in respect of anything that is renewed day by day, or that the construction of creation was newly planned in the mind of God: but everything that he has created and is about to create, even the marvelous construction of the world to come, has been planned from everlasting in the immutable mind of God. As the natural child in the womb of his mother does not know her who bears him, nor is conscious of his father, who, after God, is the cause of his formation; so also Adam, being in the mind of the creator, knew him not. And when he was created, and recognized himself as being created, he remained with this knowledge six hours only, and there came over him a change, from knowledge to ignorance and from good to evil. Hence, when divine providence wished to create the world, the framing of Adam was first designed and conceived in the mind of God, and then that of the [other] creatures; as David says, "Before the mountains were conceived." Consequently, Adam is older than the [other] creatures with respect to his conception, and the [other] creatures are older than Adam with respect to their birth and their being made. And whereas God created all creatures in silence and by a word, he brought forth Adam out of his thoughts, and formed him with his holy hands, and breathed the breath of life into him from his spirit, and Adam became a living soul, and God gave him the knowledge of the difference between good and evil. When he perceived his creator, then was God formed and conceived within the mind of the man; and the man became a temple to God his maker, as it is written, "Do you not know that you are the temple of God, and that the spirit of God dwells in you?" And again, "I will dwell in them, and walk in them."

When God in his mercy wished to make known all his power and his wisdom, in the beginning, on the evening of the first day, which is Sunday, he created seven natures in silence, without voice. And because there was as yet none to hear a sound, he did well to create them in silence, that he might not make anything uselessly; but he willed, and heaven, earth, water, air, fire, and the angels and darkness, came into being from nothing. [...]

On the third day God commanded that the waters should be gathered together into the pits and depths of the earth, and that the dry land should appear. When the waters were gathered together into the depths of the earth, and the mountains and hills had appeared, God placed the sand as a limit for the waters of the seas, that they might not pass over and cover the earth. And God commanded the earth to put forth herbs and grass and every green thing; and the earth brought forth trees and herbs and plants of all kinds, complete and perfect with respect to flowers and fruit and seed, each according to its kind. Some say that before the transgression of the command, the earth brought forth neither thorns nor briars, and that even the rose had no thorns as it has now; but that after the transgression of the command, the earth put forth thorns and briars on account of the curse that it had received. The reason why God created the trees and plants before the creation of the luminaries was that the philosophers, who discourse on natural phenomena, might not imagine that the earth brought forth herbs and trees through the power of the heat of the sun. Concerning the making of paradise, it is not mentioned in the Pentateuch on what day it was created; but according to the opinion of those who may be relied upon, it was made on the same day in which the trees were made: and if the Lord will, we will speak about it in its proper place. [...]

From Adam to the building of the tower, there was only one language, and that was Syriac. Some have said that it was Hebrew; but the Hebrews were not called by this name until after Abraham had crossed the river Euphrates and dwelled in Ḥarran; and from his crossing they were called Hebrews. [...]

When Adam and Eve went forth from paradise, Adam, as if knowing that he was never to return to his place, cut off a branch from the tree of good and evil—which is the fig tree—and took it with him and went forth; and it served him as a staff all the days of his life. After the death of Adam, his son Seth took it, for there were no weapons as yet at that time. This rod was passed on from hand to hand to Noah, and from Noah to Shem; and it was handed down from Shem to Abraham as a blessed thing from the paradise of God. With this rod Abraham broke the images and graven idols that his father made, and therefore God said to him, "Get out of your father's house," and so on. It was in his hand in every region as far as Egypt, and from Egypt to Palestine. [. . .]

And Moses took the rod, and it was with him until God spoke with him on Mount Sinai. When God said to him, "Cast the rod upon the ground," he did so, and it became a great serpent; and the Lord said, "Take it," and he did so, and it became a rod as at first. This is the rod that God gave him for a help and a deliverance, that it might be a wonder, and that with it he might deliver Israel from the oppression of the Egyptians. [. . .]

And Phineas hid the rod in the desert, in the dust at the gate of Jerusalem, where it remained until our Lord Christ was born. And he, by the will of his divinity, showed the rod to Joseph the husband of Mary, and it was in his hand when he fled to Egypt with our Lord and Mary, until he returned to Nazareth. From Joseph his son [James], who was surnamed the brother of our Lord, took it; and from [James] Judas Iscariot, who was a thief, stole it. When the Jews crucified our Lord, they lacked wood for the arms of our Lord; and Judas in his wickedness gave them the rod, which became a judgment and a fall to them, but an uprising to many. [. . .]

It is moreover right to know that Eliezer fathered two sons, Mattan and Jotham. Mattan fathered Jacob, and Jacob fathered Joseph; Jotham fathered Zadok, and Zadok fathered Mary. From this it is clear that Joseph's father and Mary's father were cousins. [. . .]

FIGURE 9.
An illustrated Syriac gospel lectionary (*British Library Additional* 7170, fol. 6a). There are many Syriac manuscripts containing an entire biblical text or a collection of entire biblical texts. But the most common Syriac biblical manuscript was a lectionary. Lectionaries contain short biblical passages meant to be read aloud during a church service. This page of a Syriac lectionary dated to between 1216 and 1240 depicts the evangelists John and Luke writing their gospels. Syriac text near each evangelist identifies them. For each evangelist, a hand comes from a partially visible orb to aid them, symbolizing God's inspiration and assistance in writing the gospels. The platforms on which the evangelists are working are architecturally simple but feature highly elaborate geometric decoration, as does the border of the illustration. It is worthwhile to compare the style of this illustration to the depiction of the crucifixion and resurrection in the "Rabbula Gospels" (Figure 7). Both illustrations incorporate vibrant colors, geometric motifs, and plants in the background. This image features more elaborate brushwork and more crisp facial details. The plant life is also given a more fantastic appearance. As a lectionary, this manuscript played a prominent role in liturgical practice, and this image served to emphasize one of the central events of the Christian narrative and liturgical calendar. © Trustees of the British Library.

Some people have a tradition that when our Lord broke his body for his disciples in the upper chamber, John the son of Zebedee hid a part of his portion until our Lord rose from the dead. And when our Lord appeared to his disciples and to Thomas with them, he said to Thomas, "Take with your finger and lay it on my side, and do not be unbelieving, but believing." Thomas put his finger near to our Lord's side, and it rested upon the mark of the spear, and the disciples saw the blood from the marks of the spear and nails. And John took that piece of consecrated bread and wiped up that blood with it; and the Eastern [apostles], Mar Addai and Mar Mari, took that piece, and with it they sanctified this unleavened bread that has been handed down among us. The other disciples did not take any of it, because they said, "We will consecrate for ourselves whenever we wish." As for the oil for baptism, some say that it was part of the oil with which they anointed the kings; others say that it was part of the unguent with which they embalmed our Lord; and many agree with this [statement]. Others again say that when John took that piece of consecrated bread of the Passover in his hand, it burst into flame and burned in the palm of his hand, and the palm of his hand sweated, and he took that sweat and hid it for the sign of the cross of baptism. This account we have heard by ear from the mouth of a recluse and visitor, and we have not received it from scripture. [. . .]

It is said that each one of the twelve and of the seventy wrote a gospel; but in order that there might be no contention and that the number of [written] acts might not be multiplied, the apostles adopted a plan and chose two of the seventy, Luke and Mark, and two of the twelve, Matthew and John [to write gospels].

8

HAGIOGRAPHY

Syriac Christianity is particularly well-known for its hagiographic works. This is partly owing to the large number of surviving saint stories; the most recent estimate suggests that over 1,200 Syriac hagiographic texts survive. Many of these have strong connections to more Western stories of sanctity. Syriac writers often translated hagiographic narratives from Greek into Syriac, and such translated texts had considerable influence on subsequent Syriac writers. So, too, some hagiographic works originally written in Syriac were later translated into Greek or Latin. But even in cases when an entire work did not cross a linguistic border, characters, plots, and hagiographic conventions were still constantly circulating among all the late ancient and medieval churches. As a result, the Syriac tradition of hagiography bears a strong familial resemblance to how other premodern Christians wrote about holy women and holy men.

But the renown of Syriac hagiography also lies in the tradition's diversity. Even in the earliest martyrological texts such as those commemorating fourth-century martyrs from Edessa, Syriac discussions of sanctity often stemmed from political, theological, or social contexts that varied substantially from those of other Christians. As a result, Syriac hagiographic texts provide an entryway into understanding some of the factors that distinguish Syriac Christians from their contemporaries. It is in Syriac hagiography, for example, that one finds some of the most explicit discussions of what it meant to be a Christian under non-Christian rule or under the rule of a Christian empire that considered one's church to be heretical. Hagiographic works also point to specific ascetic practices most closely associated with Syriac Christianity, such as stylitism (living on top of a pillar), dendritism (living in a tree), or membership in a form of non-monastic community known as the *bnay/bnat qyama* or "sons and daughters of the covenant."

Nevertheless, like with all hagiographic literature, one must always keep in mind the literary aspect of Syriac works. Many of the figures discussed in Syriac narratives may have truly existed. Nevertheless, the texts themselves were usually written long afterward and clearly reflect a specific agenda. Modern readers should not mistake them for unbiased accounts of what actually happened but should read them as heavily stylized works aiming to provide models for Christian sanctity that their authors considered worthy of emulation.

Syriac discussions of holy people occurred in a variety of formats including prose narratives, homilies, hymns, and liturgical calendars. The vastness of Syriac hagiographic material makes it particularly challenging to cull down to just a few examples. Nevertheless, even this small collection provides a taste of the richness of the Syriac hagiographic tradition.

The chapter's first half focuses on martyrological texts, works that celebrate Christians who died (or almost died) for their faith. The organizational schema is by setting—hagiographic works set in the Roman, Byzantine, Persian, and Islamic Empires. These narratives illustrate how various Syriac communities positioned themselves vis-à-vis dominant political powers and competing religious traditions. The chapter's second half focusses on ascetic superstars. In this case the organization is both chronological (earliest to latest) and geographic (west to east). For additional excerpts from hagiographic texts, see chapters 1, 4, 5, 9, 10, and 12.

Further Reading The amount of martyrological and hagiographic works that survives in Syriac is truly immense. Fortunately, many of these texts are now available in translation. Sebastian P. Brock and Susan Ashbrook Harvey, *Holy Women of the Syrian Orient* (Berkeley: University of California Press, 1987) presents one of the most accessible readers in Syriac hagiography. Also of note, the Persian Martyr Acts in Syriac series at Gorgias Press provides an ever-expanding set of editions and English translations of Syriac martyrologies set in the Sasanian Empire. In terms of secondary scholarship, a starting point for research on Syriac hagiography is the digital database at Syriaca.org. See Jeanne-Nicole Mellon Saint-Laurent, "Gateway to Syriac Saints: A Database Project," Syriaca.org, https://www.syriaca.org/saints/index.html. It provides extensive information on over 1800 hagiographic texts. Also see Jeanne-Nicole Mellon Saint-Laurent, "Syriac Hagiographic Literature," in *The Syriac World*, ed. Daniel King (New York: Routledge, 2019), 339–54 and Sebastian P. Brock, "Saints in Syriac: A Little-Tapped Resource," *Journal of Early Christian Studies* 16 (2008), 181–96. Elizabeth Key Fowden, *The Barbarian Plain: Saint Sergius Between Rome and Iran* (Berkeley: University of California Press, 1999) contains an especially rich examination of a particular martyr cult. For a recent set of scholarly essays that reflects a variety of approaches to Syriac hagiographic material, see Sergey Minov and Flavia Ruani, eds. *Syriac Hagiography: Texts and Beyond* (Leiden: Brill, 2021).

JACOB OF SERUG, *ON THE SLEEPERS OF EPHESUS*

Early sixth century. West Syrian.

As with other branches of Christianity, the Syriac churches composed numerous accounts of pagan-led persecutions. Although almost all these works are set in the Roman Empire before the fourth-century emperor Constantine converted to Christianity, the majority were actually written long afterward. One of the most popular of such martyrdom accounts was the *Sleepers of Ephesus*, initially set in the mid-third century. Although most likely the original account of this martyrology was composed in Greek, the story quickly spread eastward and variations of the story can be found in Arabic, Coptic, Ethiopic, Sogdian, and Syriac manuscripts. A version of the story also appears in the Qur'an. This account by Jacob of Serug (d. 521) is the earliest securely datable narrative of the *Sleepers of Ephesus* composed in Syriac. For additional excerpts from Jacob of Serug, see chapters 2, 5, and 7.

O Son of God, whose door is open to whoever calls on him,
   Open your door to me, so that I may sing of the beauty of the children of light.
O good shepherd who chose lambs from the midst of his flock,
   And gathered them into the sheepfold on high to be with him.
Blessed is the farmer who selected the wheat from the tares,
   And sowed them in the field of life, in the kingdom.
It is concerning the offspring of the leading men of Ephesus
   That I am to utter a discourse before [my] listeners.
Give ear to me, laborers, and sing praise, O children of the bridal chamber.
The emperor Decius set out from his place to another one.
   To visit the towns and cities in his realm;
He entered Ephesus and threw it into great commotion,
   Making a festival to Zeus, Apollo, and to Artemis too.
He wrote a missive to the lords of his realm
   That everyone should come and place incense before the gods.
He assembled the leaders, old men, and infants, along with the children,
   And they placed incense for the deaf images, the work of [human] hands.
Now there were there some dear boys, sons of leading men,
   Who despised the order and did not subject themselves to it, like their companions.
They went in and hid themselves in the sheepfold of Jesus,
   So that the unclean smell of impure incense should not ascend for them.
Their companions saw, and denounced them in the emperor's presence:
   "There are some boys here who have rebelled against your order."
The emperor listened and was clothed in anger against the innocent.
   The emperor gave orders that the boys be brought for him to see them.
The wolves rushed off and grabbed the lambs from the midst of the sheep,
   Bringing them in haste to the emperor's presence.

The emperor saw how admirable were their persons,
    And he spoke to them with blandishments, saying,
"Tell me, boys, why have you transgressed my orders?
    Come along and sacrifice, and I will make you leaders."
The son of a cavalry officer opened his mouth, along with his seven companions:
    "We will not worship deaf images, the work of [human] hands:
We have the Lord of heaven, and he will assist us.
    It is him whom we worship, and to him do we offer the purity of our hearts.
You have as king Zeus and Apollo, along with Artemis,
    But we have as king Father, Son, and Holy Spirit."
The emperor gave orders and they beat them with rods.
    He gave orders again: "Leave them until I come;"
For he was in a hurry to visit the towns and the cities
    And [then] to return back to Ephesus with this intention.
[So] the emperor departed from Ephesus on his business.
    The dear boys deliberated among themselves,
"Let us leave and escape from this town of Ephesus
    Before the accursed emperor comes to judge us."
There was there a rock cave on the top of the mountain,
    And the dear boys decided to hide there.
They took with them some of their parents' money
    So that it might serve them [both] as an accusation and as a source of pride.
They did not take with them choice clothing or fineries.
    It was some of the coinage of the pagan emperors that they took with them.
    For whoever carries any of that coinage meets with accusation.
They ascended the mountain and went into the cave to spend the night there,
    And they called upon the Lord with a plaintive voice, saying,
"We beg you, good shepherd who has chosen his sheep,
    Preserve your flock from that wolf who is thirsting for our blood."
The Lord saw the faith of the dear lambs
    And came to give a good reward as their recompense.
He took their spirits and raised them up above, to heaven,
    And left a watcher to be guarding their limbs.
The emperor returned, entered Ephesus, and was asking,
    "Where are the boys who rebelled against the commandment?"
In answer they told him, "They are hidden in a cave at the top of the mountain."
    The tyrant emperor thought he would make them die there.
He gave orders once more, and along came craftsmen with their skills.
    They cut stones with skill and placed them against the entrance.
There were there two sophists, sons of the leading men,
    And they reckoned that the Lord would resurrect them,
So they made tablets of lead and placed them beside them;
    On them they wrote down the names of the children of light,
And why the young men had gone to hide in the cave,

And at what time they had fled from the presence of the emperor Decius.
The time of the pagan emperors and their rule passed away,
   And the Lord wished to arouse these children of light.
There was there in Ephesus a wealthy man
   Who wanted to build a fold for his sheep at the top of the mountain.
He gathered stones and built the fold for his sheep there,
   And he saw the cut stones and tore them down:
   The light entered in and awoke the children of light.
They shook off sleep and sat up on the ground—a wonder to tell.
   The dear boys deliberated among themselves,
"Who will go down and see if the emperor has come,
   And [so] we will learn and see what he has ordered concerning us.
   Let him go down and show us whether he has required us or not."
There was there one of them whose name was Iamlikha;
   He said, "I will go down and I will find out;
I will go into the palace as a poor person,
   And learn and see what he has commanded concerning us."
They answered him and said, "Take some small change and bring back some bread:
   Ever since evening we have been short of bread, and we have not had a meal."
The boy dashed down from the top of the mountain and reached the city.
   He called on the Lord with a plaintive voice, saying,
"I beg of you, good shepherd who has chosen his sheep,
   Guard your flock from that wolf who thirsts after our blood."
He lifted up his gaze and saw a cross above the gate;
   He bowed his head in veneration before it, feelingly.
He began to look round, in case any of the pagans had seen him;
   He began to say in his mind, "What is this?
In the evening the cross was hidden from pagan eyes,
   But here it is today, openly placed above the gate!"
The boy turned back to go and enter by another gate;
   He lifted up his gaze and saw a cross above the gate.
He began to say, "I have gone completely mad, and I am crazy:
   Is this not Ephesus, the city where I was brought up?"
He saw a man sitting in the street; he approached him and asked,
   "Tell me, sir, this city—what is it?"
The man said, "This city is named Ephesus."
   And he was wondering in his mind what had happened to him.
The boy ran among the streets, unperturbed;
   He arrived at the palace, and saw its door closed in front of him.
He went out to the street to buy some bread to take it [back] with him;
   He took out and produced some of the small change he had in his purse.
The man who was selling took it and examined it;
   He gave it to his companion, so that his [companion] too might examine it.
The small change passed through the hands of five people as they examined it,

[and they began] whispering amongst themselves over it.
The boy saw that they were whispering and he answered and said,
  "Give me some bread if you are going to give me any; otherwise I am off."
The man who was selling came up and grabbed the boy:
  "Tell me, boy, where are you from, and what is your country?
As for the treasure you have found, let us be sharers with you in it;
  If you do not reveal it to me, I will hand you over to the law court."
The boy said, "This is not at all the case, it is not true:
  I have never seen any treasure or been aware of any."
Gossip fell on all the streets of the Ephesians
  That a boy has found some treasure; and they immediately grabbed hold of him.
Word entered the holy church, reaching the bishop;
  He sent and snatched him from their hands; he asks him,
"Tell me, boy, where are you from, and what is your country?
  What is your family, and where is the treasure they are saying you have found?"
The boy said, "I am from Ephesus;
  I am the son of Rufus, the elect, one of the leading men."
Iamlikha began looking around all the crowd
  In case he might see one of his family or relations,
Or one of his friends and neighbors and acquaintances,
  So that he might summon his father to come and snatch him from their hands.
But he did not see any of his family or relations:
  Tears welled up in his eyes, and he began to cry.
There was there a sophist in the holy church
  Who took hold of the boy and questioned him discerningly:
"Tell me the truth, boy; why should you die?
  Disclose and explain to me where you are from, and do not hide it from me."
The boy said, "I will show you the truth,
  [But] do reveal and show me what I truly should say to you."
He went on and said, "Where is the emperor Decius?
  Then I will reveal to you concerning the affair."
The sophist heard; a gasp seized him as he wondered greatly
  At that youth who was showing forth deep matters.
He bent his fingers and stretched them as he spoke with him:
  "Crazy idiot, you deserve to die for mocking me;
I can see that you are about twelve years old,
  And the person you are talking about was a great long time ago.
By the reckoning and accounting among the Greeks
  The emperor [would be] 372 years [old]!"
The boy said, "It was from him that I and my companions ran away;
  We went to sleep at the top of the mountain, I and my seven companions."
The head men and elders, the nobles and youths, gathered
  To go up and see the living treasure that had been revealed to them.
Talk went out in all the district of the Ephesians:

"Come and see this treasure that has been revealed to us."
The youths in the cave heard, and trembled in fright,
   Supposing that the emperor had sent to take them off.
The son of a calvary officer encouraged them, saying as follows:
   "Stand up and take courage; put on the armor of faith,
And we will rely on God, for it is he who assists us,
   Giving us strength and guiding us according to his will."
While he was encouraging them, the boy entered and stood beside them,
   And the bishop, and the leaders too, entered with him.
They saw the boys sitting on the ground;
   They greeted them, saying, "Peace be with you."
And straightway they wrote a missive to the emperor Theodosius:
   "Come, my lord, and see a living treasure that has been revealed to us."
The emperor made haste and came down and saw them;
   He greeted them, saying, '"Peace be with you."
He took the lead tablet and began to read
   [The reason] why the youths had gone into the cave to hide.
Theodosius the emperor urged them to come down with him
   In the midst of Ephesus, and he would build a shrine over their bodies.
They say in reply, "Here we shall be, for here we love;
   The shepherd who chose us is the one who bade us be here.
For your sake has Christ our Lord awoken us
   So that you might see and hold firm that the resurrection truly exists."
He took a mantle [with which] he was covered, and covered them up;
   And he left them, and they slept the sleep of repose.
Blessed is the shepherd who chose the lambs from his sheep
   And caused them to inherit the bridal chamber, the garden, and the kingdom on high.

JOHN OF EPHESUS, *ECCLESIASTICAL HISTORY*

Late sixth century. West Syrian.

A distinguishing factor of Syriac martyrological literature is that much of it depicts intra-Christian persecution. That is, Byzantine governmental and ecclesiastical authorities often pressured Syriac Christians to conform with the Christology put forth in church councils such as the Council of Chalcedon. For West and East Syrian Christians, opposition to this theology became a key factor in their confessional identity. Accounts of Byzantine Christian persecution of Syriac Christians were especially important in drawing boundaries between the various churches. John of Ephesus's (d. 586) *Ecclesiastical History* is a prime example of this phenomenon. Although the entire work no longer survives, substantial sections of it were incorporated into the late eighth-century *Chronicle of Zuqnin*, which preserves the following account featuring the Chalcedonian bishop of

Amida, Abraham Bar Kayli, and a West Syrian priest named Cyrus. For an additional excerpt from John of Ephesus, see chapter 5.

Concerning the martyr priest Cyrus. [A martyrdom] that was again more terrible, harsh, and bitter than all of them.

One priest whose name was Cyrus, of the Ligin village, was arrested and compelled to receive the Eucharist. When he did not consent, they brought him into the city to the bishop. The latter shouted at him harshly and in indignation, saying, "Why do you not take the Eucharist?" He answered, "You are teaching me to suspect your Eucharist and not to take it, for the Eucharist given by such force is not the Eucharist!" Then the bishop swore, "You will not go far from here before you take the Eucharist!" But he swore, "I will absolutely not take from you the Eucharist of compulsion!" When the bishop gave orders and the Eucharist was brought, he commanded that they seize that priest and that they fill a spoon and put it into his mouth. Since the priest shut his mouth, they were not able to put in the spoon. He then ordered that a whip be brought and its handle be placed into his mouth, and in this way they would get the spoon into his mouth. They pulled his teeth apart to such an extent that they almost came out. When they had placed the handle into his mouth, he stammered to them, since he could not move his tongue and speak correctly. He asserted and said, "By truth of Christ, if you put the Eucharist in my mouth, I will spit it in your faces!" And thus, in bitter anger and under the threat of death, they inserted the spoon by one side of the whip and shoved it into his mouth. But he spluttered and spat the Eucharist out of his mouth, and was thus appropriately nicknamed "the Spitter" in accordance with what he did.

When Bar Kayli saw what that priest had done, he took the matter as a pretext for his death. But this was exactly what he intended to do: to kill him like the others who perished at his hands. And while intoxicated by the cruelty and violence of Satan, who from the beginning was a murderer, he quickly ordered that wood and fire be brought to the Tetrapylon [i.e., a four-arched monument] of the city and that the priest be burned. The day was Wednesday of the Holy Week of Lent. And in this way he caused that priest to stand in the Tetrapylon: wood was piled up all around him, fire was set, and he was burned while the city watched, wailed, and lamented at this atrocious and heart-breaking sight. They watched a human being burned and his dense smoke going up like that of dumb and irrational animals! This was shameful and alien to humankind, that they used all this cruelty, stubbornness, and hardness of heart, found in dumb animals.

While the whole city was confused and perturbed on account of this evil act of setting someone—a priest—on fire unjustly and wickedly, people planned to act in the same way Bar Kayli acted, and burn him as he burned that priest. There were people among the notables of the city who, for fear of the emperor, prevented them from doing so. But many split away from him, considered him a killer and a Jew, and separated themselves from his communion. As Bar Kayli feared that this matter might become known to the emperor, and that he would sanction him to be burned as he had burned others, he made the first move and wrote a lie, informing [the emperor] that a certain priest had trodden the Eucharist under his feet and because of this he had been burned. And thus he was able to mislead others and dismiss the murder.

In writing about these matters, we did not deviate from the truth nor did we slander: the Lord is our witness, and so are all the contemporaries of this wicked and cruel deed. This evil also became known throughout East and West, everyone being moved by what had been done by those who were clad with the priestly apparel but were far from its virtue. If we were to undertake to write about the rest of the evil deeds of this [Bar Kayli], which we have seen with our eyes and touched with our hands and also heard with our ears, we would require numerous books: how he was fabricating strange designs and devising plans, as it is written, issuing various evil sentences every day against those who did not submit to the heresy of the two natures, while he himself did not adhere to it willingly but hypocritically. Sometimes he used to send shaven monks, called them "troops," to stay in the houses of the believers who did not agree with him, and they did what the barbarians themselves would never recognize at all [as legitimate]; sometimes [he would send] the barbarian forces themselves, who belonged to a [military] detachment stationed in the same city; and sometimes he would even order total destruction against whoever resisted him.

MARTYRDOM OF ABBOT BARSHEBYA

Likely sixth century. East Syrian.

A distinctive feature of the East Syrian hagiographic corpus is the presence of approximately sixty works describing Christians martyred by Persian authorities. The accounts themselves were usually composed centuries after the events they depict and, like most martyrological texts, their historical accuracy often remains suspect. Scholars continue to debate how often Syriac Christians faced persecution under Zoroastrian rulers, especially because the mere fact of being Christian was never illegal in the Persian Empire. But conversion from Zoroastrianism to another religion could be a capital offense, as could desecration of Zoroastrian sacred places such as a fire temple. Like many Persian martyr accounts, the *Martyrdom of Abbot Barshebya* is set during the rule of Shapur II (d. 379), even if the text itself was most likely composed in the sixth century. It tells the story of a Zoroastrian priest (a mobed) persecuting Christians and how the Christians' bravery so impressed a Zoroastrian (here: magus, plural: magi) passing by that he also becomes a martyr. The entire work appears below. Although extremely succinct, it nevertheless includes a large number of plot and literary motifs common to most Persian martyr acts.

At the time when blessed Miles was crowned, there was an abbot in the land of the Persians whose name was Barshebya ["son of the captivity"]. He dwelt in a monastery, and with him were ten disciples.

Impious and evil men accused them before the mobed of the city of Istakhr, saying, "He corrupts many people, and he teaches sorcery in our land, destroying the teachings of the magi with his instruction." [The mobed] ordered that [Barshebya] be arrested, he and the brothers with him, and they brought them to [the mobed] in shackles. He imposed cruel tortures and intense suffering upon them until even their knees were hacked down with a hammer. He destroyed their shins, arms, and sides with a spiked staff, and he mutilated their faces, ears, and eyes.

When the iniquitous judge saw—during all this destruction of their limbs and all the suffering they endured—that the true ones were not defeated and that the upright ones were not shaken or turned from their God or lapsed in their faith, he ordered that they be taken to the outskirts of the city to be executed. While they were being led away, they sang psalms and glorified God, and a great crowd surrounded them.

When they had begun to be executed, a certain magus came out from the city and passed by along the road. With him was his wife, who was sitting on a mule, and two of his sons and some of his servants. He raised up his eyes and saw the gathered multitude of people, and he said to those who were with him, "Come this way for a moment so I can find out the reason for this assembly." And he went ahead on his horse with one of his servants with him.

He went over and stood beside the martyrs while they were being killed, and he saw the courageous abbot holding the hands of each of the disciples whom he chose, one after the next, and whom he then gave over to be killed. [The abbot] comforted them with *madrashe* sung in sweet and dulcet tones. Then the Lord opened the eyes of this magus, and he saw tongues of fire standing up in the form of the cross, and the fire blazed and flared and stood upon the corpses of those who had been killed. [The magus] was terrified, and, trembling, he got down from his horse. He exchanged his clothes for those of his servant, and he drew near to the glorious one and whispered to him, "I have seen a strange vision, and your god has truly chosen me to die with you because he is God, he alone, and in him I put my faith with all my heart. So now let no one know that I have not come from among you and hold me as [you held] each of your disciples and give me over to be killed. For I have a great longing to be killed with you, the holy and true and believing people."

And the blessed one believed him all the more because a wondrous vision was shown to him. After the nine others, [Barshebya] took [the magus] by the hands and gave him to be killed, and the killers did not know. And after him the eleventh was killed as well, with the abbot killed last of all as the seal of the twelve. In this the magus was perfected.

Then they brought their heads into the city and hung them upon the temple of Anahid, the goddess of the Persians, to display them for the masses in order to deter them. Wild animals and birds of the heavens devoured their bodies.

Afterward, this thing became known about this magus himself, and there was great amazement throughout the land. Many converted to the truth because of him, and even his wife and sons and servants became true believers because of him, and they lived all the days of their lives in the fear of God.

These holy ones were crowned on the seventeenth day of the lunar month Ḥaziran [i.e., June].

MARTYRDOM OF ANAHID

Likely sixth century. East Syrian.

In contrast to the very short *Martyrdom of Abbot Barshebya* reprinted in full above, the following passages come from the longest surviving Persian martyrdom act known as the

Petion Cycle, which was most likely composed in the sixth century. Set during the rule of Yazdgard II (d. 457), this portion of the *Petion Cycle* focuses on Anahid, the daughter of a Zoroastrian priest. According to the narrative, when she was a child, Anahid suffered from demonic possession. Having exhausted other options, Anahid's father sought out the Christian holy man Petion who promptly healed his daughter. Both father and daughter soon converted to Christianity. Their conversion from Zoroastrianism to Christianity later prompted their arrest. The following excerpts concerning Anahid's torture and martyrdom are particularly striking in their depiction of gender, religious authority, and violence.

The Magian [i.e., Zoroastrian] [Adurfrazgard] ordered that she be brought before him. Both [Adurfrazgard] and his attendants gazed at the girl in their amazement at her beauty and fair appearance. Everyone's anger disappeared and they ceased from their menacing threats. The chief Magian [Adurfrazgard] then addressed her pleasantly and gently, supposing that she would be the more easily ensnared by his coaxing her. But when she paid no attention to his cajolements, he looked hard at her and said, "[. . .] [Y]our family is held in great honor by the king of kings and by everyone in the realm. What, then, has happened to you that such utter folly and ridiculous stupidity has overtaken you? Even though your father Adurhormizd, having spent night and day unceasingly in the performance of Avesta [i.e., Zoroastrian scripture], Yasht [i.e., Zoroastrian hymns], and Drōn [i.e., Zoroastrian ritual], has gone out of his mind, his brain having dried up and been filled with nonsense with the result that he has gone off after the magic practices of the Christians so that he needed to be healed of his sickness and to recover—what, my pretty girl, has happened to you? I hear that you too are wanting to go off after the magic practices of the utterly despicable Christians. Is not whosoever you should want to marry from among all the Magians and nobles held in great favor and honor? No, my daughter, do not pay any attention to the misguided opinions of your distracted father; do not lose the position of great honor and reputation that your noble birth holds. If you are willing to accept me, I will raise you above all the noble women in the realm; if, however, you refuse me, here is my son, Adursroshay, who is the king's own official; he has 170 special soldiers. Marry him and do not destroy your life, led astray by Ahriman [i.e., the Zoroastrian god of evil]. I too will honor you above all my sons and daughters, making you mistress in charge of everything in my household." [. . .]

Then the holy woman opened her mouth and addressed him: "I am telling you, greatest and most famed of the Magians, that I have once and for all been betrothed to Christ, and so I cannot belong to anyone else; I have already received from him the pledge of the spirit, and I cannot leave him. Nor indeed will my Lord and my king who has betrothed me allow me to be taken off by anyone else to marry, for he is extremely powerful and strong, and no one can take anything from him. So, if you have something else to say, or if there is some other action to take, carry it out; it is no use wasting time with empty words."

At this the Magian [Adurfrazgard] became very angry and said, "You wicked and impertinent woman, I can see that in your folly you are traveling along the same road to perdition as your father. I am telling you not to destroy your own life by this madness of yours. Hold on to the religion of your parents, do not be led astray. Find refuge in the worship of the luminaries and fire, following after Hormizd [i.e., the Zoroastrian god of good]: if you do so, you will be saved from all the terrible things you will otherwise have to endure. For I can see that your folly may bring you great harm."

"Alas for old age," said Anahid, "when it grows foolish and is given to senseless speech, thus becoming the object of laughter—and here you are in your venerable old age yourself talking nonsense by introducing the subject of fire and the luminaries. O chief among Magians, do you say that these children of Hormizd were conceived and given birth to by Hormizd or by someone else? On the basis of observation we can see that those who father children or give birth to them do so as a result of cohabitation of two persons, a male and a female; a person cannot achieve this on his or her own accord. If Hormizd on his own conceived in his own belly and gave birth to children, like his father Zurvan, then he is androgynous—as the Manichaeans say. But if he fathered them from his mother, daughter, and sister, as your crazy and senseless teaching maintains, how is it he does not resemble us in everything? For God has no mother, daughter, or sister, since he is one and he alone is God, having control over all his treasure stores. But Zurvan and Khwashizag his mother testify that Hormizd is like us, subject to a beginning, an end, and corruption: for just as they ceased from life, so too will their children and grandchildren. There is something written in our scriptures concerning such as these: 'Do not put your confidence in humans, for they are no source of confidence; rather, put your confidence in the living God.'"

At this point Adurfrazgard lost his temper and he ordered those standing in his presence to hit her hard on the mouth until all her teeth fell out onto the ground. Those ordered came up at once and hit her on the cheeks, mouth, and head, until her face was so swollen that her eyes were covered up and she had lost all her teeth. Her body was drenched with blood, which ran from her mouth and cheeks—it was as though she was swimming in it.

He gave orders that she be trussed up like a dog and thrown into prison under close guard. No one was to give her any food or anything to drink until the God of the dispersed Christians, in whom she trusted, should come and rescue her. They carried out his orders on the spot. [. . .]

When morning came, the nobles assembled in the presence of Adurfrazgard and sent for the holy woman. [. . .] A close relative of hers went up to her and said, [. . .] "Even if you do not revert to Magianism, at least say, 'I am not a Christian,' and then I can save you and carry you off to somewhere where there are Christians, and you can live there in Christianity all the rest of your life."

The wise woman replied, "You silly and senseless man, how can I deny him in whom we live and move and have our being—we and all created things? [. . .] I have already renounced your gods—which are not gods—and I continue to do so; and I have confessed him and will continue to confess him right up to death."

When the Magian heard this, he ordered that her clothes be ripped off and that she should be stripped naked. "Bring a caning frame," he said, "and four pairs of men, and I will show you what to do." They brought this as instructed, and he gave orders for her to be stripped naked. She was still trussed up like a dog, with her head between her knees. He gave orders that she be scourged on the caning frame by two men, one on either side, until the flesh on her back and thighs was cut into from every direction, reaching the bones.

The men came up to scourge her, and when they had struck the virgin only twice with the rods, her flesh was at once deeply cut into, and streams of blood began to flow, so that the place where she was lying trussed up was running like streams of water with blood. The men did not stop beating her but rather lashed out at her even more assiduously than farmers hack at uncultivated ground to soften it.

When the first pair of men grew tired, a second pair took their place to scourge her. In this manner they continued the scourging until she became silent and her tongue ceased from praising God. When her voice could no longer be heard, they imagined that she must have expired, and the Magians gave orders that she be taken off and thrown to one side. Guards were appointed to watch over her, lest some Christians might snatch away her corpse. [. . .]

He then ordered two thin threads of cobblers' string to be brought in. This was done. He then told them to tie them into a hangman's noose round her breasts, one thread on each. Two men were to hold on to and pull at each thread until her breasts were severed and fell to the ground. [. . .]

Her two breasts were quickly cut through and hung each by a mere sinew. The holy woman stretched out her hands, grabbed her breasts, and placed them in front of the Magian, with the words, "Seeing that you very much wanted them, O Magian, here they are, do with them whatever takes your fancy. If I have any other limbs you would like, give the order and I will cut them off and put them in front of you. I will not hold back anything I have from your banquet."

The Magian was furious and said, "Am I a dog, that I should want to eat human flesh?"

The wise woman replied, "A dog is better than you—and you know it: a dog guards the palace door, but you guard the door to Gehenna; just as the dog belongs to the palace, so you belong to Gehenna."

At this he grew even more angry and gave orders that she be carried off to prison in fetters. He had a piece of wood placed under her two armpits, and her hands were tied, doglike. They were to place her upside down on the wood all night in the prison. They then took her off as instructed.

The next morning he had her brought [. . .] When she was brought in, they saw that all the bones in her arms had been broken so that she could not move any of her limbs. He gave orders that she be conveyed at once to the hillside where she had been living. They were to smear her body with honey and stretch her out on the mountainside attached to four stakes. This was to frighten her and deter all who saw her from her superstition. [. . .]

A considerable crowd accompanied the holy woman to see what would be done to her. When they reached the hillside, [the provincial governor] Nehormizd ordered that the girdle be taken from her; then they stretched her out on a flat spot on the hillside, beneath the crag there, attaching her to four huge iron stakes. They smeared her with honey and left her, stationing over her some guards from among the horsemen and the local landlords, four hundred men in all, while Nehormizd went to see if there were any further instructions concerning her.

Before they had reached the lower slopes of the hill in their descent, an enormous swarm of wasps collected, such that the entire mountain in every direction was covered up by their presence. They were heaped up on one another in clusters more than an arm's span wide. So threatening were they with their stings at the ready that they prevented anyone approaching anywhere near the mountain—not just human beings and cattle, but even birds. They did not touch the pure woman's body but were heaped up on each other in swarms, some five arms' lengths thick, around the martyr's body, as though it were some festival, and their mass acted as it were as a canopy above her body. This lasted seven days, preventing anyone from approaching the mountain.

On the seventh day the clergy of the deported community who lived a little further up from there took the gospel along with candles and incense and processed with a large crowd of the faithful, carrying scented water and clean burial garments. When the group of clergy arrived in procession, the wasps separated themselves from their swarm and settled, piling onto one another to the right and to the left, like huge heaps of rocks; they did not hurt anyone and did not make a move to fly off either to the right or to the left.

Before they reached her, the holy girl was addressing God in her prayers [. . .] All the clergy at once answered "amen" with a loud voice. As the "amen" was pronounced, she yielded up her spirit and fell asleep. When the clergy reached her, she was already resting in the sleep of death.

STEPHEN MANSŪR, *PASSION OF ROMANOS THE NEOMARTYR*

Late eighth century. Chalcedonian. Originally Greek now surviving only in Georgian.

In the Islamic Empire, Christianity was a legally protected religion. As a result, very few Christians were martyred under early Islam. Among East Syrian sources, there are no surviving accounts of such martyrdoms. Among West Syrian sources, there is a single, poorly preserved martyrological account set in the Islamic Empire that appears at the end of the late eight-century *Chronicle of Zuqnin*. Only among Chalcedonian texts can one find a handful of accounts depicting Christians martyred by Muslim authorities. A particularly intriguing example, the *Passion of Romanos the Neomartyr*, was written by a monk from the Chalcedonian monastery of Mar Saba named Stephen Mansūr (d. 780). Although Stephen most likely originally wrote his text in Greek, it survives solely in Georgian. It tells of a Christian monk who was abducted by Muslim bandits, who was falsely accused of being a foreign spy, and whom the caliph al-Mahdi eventually killed because Romanos convinced some recent converts to Islam to return to Christianity. The following excerpts begin with a Muslim official named Rabi learning of Romanos's reconversion efforts and Romanos's subsequent martyrdom by Caliph al-Mahdi (here called Amir al-Mu'minin, that is "commander of the faithful"). Of particularly interest is how radically different this depiction of al-Mahdi is from that found in chapter 11. There, the very same caliph appears as the kind, supportive, and polite interlocutor to the East Syrian katholikos Timothy I.

The martyrdom of Saint Romanos the neomartyr, who was martyred in the reign of King Mahdi, the servant of the devil, which the blessed Stephen of Damascus wrote, who was one of the fathers of the lavra [i.e., monastic community] of our holy father Sabas. [. . .]

And at that time some people were led away as captives from the land of the Greeks [i.e., Byzantines], and when they were brought in before Amir al-Mu'minin, through fear of torture and death the wretches denied true salvation, abandoned the Christian faith, and joined themselves to the faith of the Saracens [i.e., Muslims]. And when these wretched apostates saw Saint Romanos praying to Christ God, they were saddened and captured by remorse. Then Sunday night came, and Saint Romanos was awake standing and alert in prayer with praise to God. The Greek apostates were standing near him, and they saw him and were longing for it and lamenting for themselves, because they had driven away from themselves a blessed eternity and had exchanged eternal life for this short, fleeting span of time. And when it was dawn, they went to him with tears and confessed their sins and asked him if there was something that they ought to do and they would do it. Then the saint rebuked them for the cowardice of their treachery and falling away from the true faith. But after that he promised them and encouraged them and taught them what they ought to do for the betterment of their souls. And he said, "If then you have sinned and thrown yourselves into the depths of godlessness and have chosen this fleeting, corruptible life instead of the eternal one, but you have turned back to the life of God and repented of what you have done, truly your souls will be saved, for he is good and loves humankind. He will have mercy on you if you confess him boldly, for he does not wish the death of the sinner but turning back and repentance." This and other such things the beloved one taught these men who had gone astray.

Then the guards saw them weeping at the feet of Saint Romanos. They then made this known to the amir, and he called upon the saint and said, "O enemy of God and enemy of his officials, was not the treachery and betrayal that you committed against Amir al-Mu'minin sufficient for you? But now you have persuaded these faithful Saracen men to become Christian!" [. . .]

[Amir al-Mu'minin] said to him: "I can no longer endure you, Romanos. Nevertheless, one possibility remains for you to save yourself—if you will yield to my command. If you will die a good death, now you will obey me, for I urge you to do what is best for you. Abandon your error and follow my faith, and you will receive countless gifts and unimaginable honors. And if you will not heed my good advice, I will hand you over to painful tortures and merciless beatings, and in the end you will meet with a bitter death, as one who resists the authority of the ruler and foolishly does not obey what is for his own good. Now if you will obey me, I will change your offenses, which you have unknowingly endured with us, and the ignorant tortures. And I will also order my physicians to care for you properly for the sake of your healing. And they will quickly heal your wounds, and in an instant you will be set free from their pains." [. . .]

The holy martyr answered and said: "Why are you striving in vain, O Amir al-Mu'minin, and amusing yourself, speaking to me as if I were a small child. Even if I endure myriad torments and death for Christ, I will regard them joyfully and gladly on account of the desire that I have for him, since there is this one death, which human nature undoubtedly owes, and it is not at all possible for anyone to save themselves from it with an abundance of possessions and fear of power. Nevertheless the honor and gifts that you promise me and all the glory of your kingdom are like dry grass to me, and like a passing dream and a vanished shadow. And you cannot persuade me with them to deny my creator and God, Jesus Christ, and his ineffable Father and the unattainable Holy Spirit, the holy Trinity, alike in essence and held in awe by the demons, whom you worship. Now then do what you wish, and do not make any trouble for yourself in vain about this." [. . .]

Then, when he saw that he was like a hard and solid rock, his heart was filled even more with rage because of this, for he did not give any response to what he said. Then he ordered that they bring a sewn pelt and spread it out on him, and he ordered the executioner to frighten him with the sword until he would give a response. Nevertheless the saint placed his hands behind himself and turned himself to the east, and he offered his neck to the sword, but in his mind he was praying to God. Nevertheless the tyrant did not want to add one word more. And Amir al-Mu'minin and all his companions were amazed at the saint's boldness before death. Then he ordered that his head should be cut off. And the executioner struck and cut off his holy head. Then the infidel ordered that they throw his body with his head into the river that was near them—that is, the great Euphrates.

THEODORET, *HISTORY OF THE MONKS OF SYRIA*

Ca. 440. Greek.

Perhaps the most famous of Syriac saints is Simeon the Stylite (d. 459), also known as Simeon the Elder. There are multiple accounts of his life, numerous artistic depictions of Simeon, and a huge pilgrimage complex at Qal'at Sim'ān in Syria whose impressive ruins still survive (see figure 10). Sources claim that Simeon was the first to practice stylitism, the ascetic practice of living on top of a pillar. This practice became fairly widespread among Syriac ascetics and even spurred a related ascetic discipline, dendritism, in which one lived not on a pillar but in a tall tree. There are two early Greek and one Syriac account of Simeon's life. The earliest comes from the bishop Theodoret (d. 466) who met Simeon and wrote about him while the stylite was still alive. Theodoret's text also provides an example of how an ancient author might present Syriac Christianity to a more Western audience.

> The famous Simeon, the great wonder of the world, is known of by all the subjects of the Roman Empire and has also been heard of by the Persians, the Medes, the Ethiopians; and the rapid spread of his fame as far as the nomadic Scythians has taught his love of labor and his philosophy. I myself, though having everyone, so to speak, as witnesses of his contests that beggar description, am afraid that the narrative may seem to posterity to be a myth totally devoid of truth. For the facts surpass human nature, and people are wont to use nature to measure what is said; if anything is said that lies beyond the limits of nature, the account is judged to be false by those uninitiated into divine things. But since earth and sea are full of pious souls educated in divine things and instructed in the grace of the all-Holy Spirit, who will not disbelieve what is said but have complete faith in it, I shall make my narration with eagerness and confidence. I shall begin from the point at which he received his call from on high.
>
> There is a village lying on the border between our region and Cilicia; they call it Sisa. Originating from this village, [Simeon] was taught by his parents first to shepherd animals. Once, when there was much snow and the sheep were compelled to stay indoors, he took

advantage of the respite to go with his parents to the house of God. I heard his sacred tongue recount the following: he told how he heard the gospel utterance, which declares blessed those who weep and mourn, calls wretched those who laugh, terms enviable those who possess a pure soul, and all the other blessings conjoined with them. He then asked one of those present what one should do to obtain each of these. He suggested the solitary life and pointed to that consummate philosophy.

Therefore, having received the seeds of the divine word and stored them well in the deep furrows of his soul, he hastened—he said—to a nearby shrine of the holy martyrs. [. . .]

Getting up from there, he repaired to the dwelling of some neighboring ascetics. After spending two years with them and falling in love with more perfect virtue, he repaired to that village of Teleda. [. . .] The wonderful Heliodorus succeeded to the office of superior over the community. He lived for sixty-five years and spent sixty-two years immured within; for it was after three years of rearing by his parents that he entered this flock, without ever beholding the occurrences of life. He claimed not even to know the shape of pigs or cocks or the other animals of this kind. I too had often the benefit of seeing him; I admired his simplicity of character and was especially amazed at his purity of soul.

After coming to [Heliodorus], this all-round contestant in piety spent ten years contending. [. . .] On one occasion Simeon took a cord made from palms—it was extremely rough even to touch with the hands—and girded it round his waist, not wearing it on the outside but making it touch the skin itself. He tied it so tightly as to lacerate in a circle the whole part it went round. When he had continued in this manner for more than ten days and the now severe wound was letting fall drops of blood, someone who saw him asked what was the cause of the blood. When he replied that he had nothing wrong with him, his fellow contestant forcibly inserted his hand, discovered the cause, and disclosed it to the superior. Immediately reproaching and exhorting, and inveighing against the cruelty of the thing, he undid the belt, with difficulty, but not even so could he persuade him to give the wound any treatment. Seeing him do other things of the kind as well, they ordered him to depart from this wrestling school [i.e., Heliodorus's monastery], lest he should be a cause of harm to those with a weaker bodily constitution who might try to emulate what was beyond their powers. [. . .]

From that time till today—twenty-eight years have passed—he spends the forty days [of Lent] without food. Time and practice have allayed most of the effort. For it was his custom during the first days to chant hymns to God standing; then, when because of the fasting his body no longer had the strength to bear the standing, thereafter to perform the divine liturgy seated; and during the final days actually to lie down—for as his strength was gradually exhausted and extinguished he was compelled to lie half dead. But when he took his stand on the pillar, he was not willing to come down, but contrived his standing posture differently: it was by attaching a beam to the pillar and then tying himself to the beam with cords that he lasted the forty days. Subsequently, enjoying henceforward still more grace from above, he has not needed even this support, but stands throughout the forty days, not taking food but strengthened by zeal and divine grace.

After spending three years, as I said, in this cottage, he repaired to that celebrated hilltop, where he ordered a circular enclosure to be made. [. . .] As his fame circulated everywhere, everyone hastened to him, not only the people of the neighborhood but also people many days' journey distant, some bringing the paralyzed in body, others requesting health for the sick, others asking to become fathers; and they begged to receive from him what they could not receive from nature. On receiving it and obtaining their requests, they returned with joy; and by proclaiming the benefits they had gained, they sent out many times more, asking for the same things. So, with everyone arriving from every side and every road resembling a river, one can behold a sea of people standing together in that place, receiving rivers from every side. Not only do the inhabitants of our part of the world flock together, but also Ishmaelites, Persians, Armenians subject to them, Iberians, Homerites, and people even more distant than these; and there came many inhabitants of the extreme West, Spaniards, Britons, and the Gauls who live between them. Of Italy it is superfluous to speak. It is said that the man became so celebrated in the great city of Rome that at the entrance of all the workshops people have set up small representations of him, to provide thereby some protection and safety for themselves.

Since the visitors were beyond counting and they all tried to touch him and reap some blessing from his garments of skins, while he at first thought the excess of honor absurd and later could not abide the wearisomeness of it, he devised the standing on a pillar, ordering the cutting of a pillar first of six cubits, then of twelve, afterward of twenty-two and now of thirty-six—for he yearns to fly up to heaven and to be separated from this life on earth. I myself do not think that this standing has occurred without the dispensation of God, and because of this I ask faultfinders to curb their tongue and not to let it be carried away at random, but to consider how often the master [i.e., God] has contrived such things for the benefit of the more easygoing.

[So], too, he has ordained this new and singular sight in order by its strangeness to draw all to look, and to make the proffered exhortation persuasive to those who come—for the novelty of the sight is a trustworthy pledge of the teaching, and the one who comes to look departs instructed in divine things. Just as those who have obtained kingship alter periodically the images on their coins, at one time striking representations of lions, at another of stars and angels, and at another trying to make the gold piece more valuable by the strangeness of the type; so the universal sovereign of all things, by attaching to piety like coin types these new and various modes of life, stirs to eulogy the tongues not only of those nurtured in the faith but also of those afflicted by lack of faith.

Words do not testify that these things have this character, but the facts themselves proclaim it; for the Ishmaelites, who were enslaved in their many tens of thousands to the darkness of impiety, have been illuminated by his standing on the pillar. For this dazzling lamp, as if placed on a lampstand, has sent out rays in all directions, like the sun. [. . .]

I myself was an eyewitness of this, and I have heard them disowning their ancestral impiety and assenting to the teaching of the gospel. And I once underwent great danger: [Simeon] told them to come up and receive from me the priestly blessing, saying they would reap the greatest profit therefrom. But they rushed up in a somewhat barbarous manner, and some pulled at me from in front, some from behind, others from the sides, while those further back trod on the others and stretched out their hands, and some pulled at my beard and others grabbed at my clothing. I would have been suffocated by their too ardent approach, if [Simeon] had not used a shout to disperse them. Such is the benefit that the pillar mocked by lovers of mockery has poured forth; such is the ray of divine knowledge that it has made descend into the minds of barbarians. [. . .]

I have been, not only an eyewitness of his miracles, but also a hearer of his predictions of the future. The drought that occurred, the great crop failure of that year, and the simultaneous famine and plague that followed, he foretold two years beforehand, saying that he had seen a rod threatening humankind and indicating the scourging it would cause.

His reputation is also great with the king of the Persians. As the envoys who came to see Simeon related, he wished to inquire carefully about the man's way of life and the nature of his miracles; and his spouse is said to have asked for oil honored by his blessing and to have received it as a very great gift. [. . .]

More than all this, I myself admire his endurance. Night and day he is standing within view of all; for, having removed the doors and demolished a sizeable part of the enclosing wall, he is exposed to all as a new and extraordinary spectacle—now standing for a long time, and now bending down repeatedly and offering worship to God. Many of those standing by count the number of these acts of worship. Once one of those with me counted one thousand two hundred and forty-four of them, before slackening and giving up count. In bending down he always makes his forehead touch his toes—for his stomach's receiving food once a week, and little of it, enables his back to bend easily. [. . .]

Despite such labors and the mass of his achievements and the quantity of his miracles, he is as modest in spirit as if he were the last of all people in worth. In addition to his modest spirit, he is extremely approachable, sweet, and charming, and makes answer to everyone who addresses him, whether they be artisan, beggar, or peasant. And he has received from the munificent master the gift also of teaching. Making exhortation two times each day, he floods the ears of his hearers, as he speaks most gracefully and offers the lessons of the divine spirit, bidding them look up to heaven and take flight, depart from the earth, imagine the expected kingdom, fear the threat of hell, despise earthly things, and await what is to come.

He can be seen judging and delivering verdicts that are right and just. These and similar activities he performs after the ninth hour—for the whole night and the day till the ninth hour he spends praying. But after the ninth hour he first offers divine instruction to those present, and then, after receiving everyone's request and working some cures, he resolves the strife of those in dispute. At sunset he begins to converse from then on with God.

Although engaged in these activities and performing them all, he does not neglect care of the holy churches—now fighting pagan impiety; now defeating the insolence of the Jews; at other times scattering the bands of the heretics; sometimes sending instructions on these matters to the emperor; sometimes rousing the governors to divine zeal; at other times charging the very shepherds of the churches to take still greater care of their flocks.

I have proceeded through all this trying from a drop to indicate the rain, and, using my forefinger, to give readers of the account a taste of the sweetness of the honey. The facts celebrated by all are many times more numerous than these, but I did not promise to record everything, but to show by a few instances the character of the life of each [holy person].

FIGURE 10.
Remains of Simeon the Stylite's pillar. In addition to three early hagiographic texts written about Simeon, there are extensive archaeological remains that attest to Simeon's popularity in late antiquity. In the fifth century, a large complex of churches was built around the pillar on which Simeon stood. The complex included four basilicas, a monastery, and a baptistry, making it one of the earliest Christian church complexes. Because of Simeon's fame, the complex became a popular site for pilgrimages. Although it was captured by Arab forces in the seventh century and converted into a fortress in the tenth century (Qalʻat Simʻān), Christian pilgrims continued to visit the complex for religious purposes. Today, it is considered part of the "Dead Cities" region in Syria. Simeon's pillar has been worn down in part because of pilgrims repeatedly breaking off small chunks of it to keep as relics. Ultimately, the elaborate architecture and lengthy history of the pilgrimage site reflect the enormous popularity of Simeon's cult across the Christian East, even after the rise of Islam. Photo: Christine Shepardson.

FIGURE 11.

Plaque of Simeon the Stylite. Simeon's emergence as an "ascetic superstar" is also attested by artistic images of the stylite. This late sixth-century silver plaque depicting Simeon the Stylite comes from a church in Ma'arrat an-Nu'man, Syria. A dedicatory inscription is written in Greek at the bottom of the plaque, suggesting this was offered as thanks for a fulfilled request. A calm look is visible on Simeon's face, and he is crouched and reading a book. The snake slithering up the pillar may refer to an episode in the anonymous Syriac *Life of Simeon* in which a snake climbs Simeon's pillar in an attempt to disturb him but fails. This icon is a striking testimony to the popularity of Simeon the Stylite in the eastern Mediterranean and, more generally, to the development of the cult of saints in the region. It suggests that individuals made both prayers and votive offerings to deceased holy men and shows awareness of some details of Simeon's story, indicating its widespread dissemination. © RMN, Musée du Louvre / Hervé Lewandowski.

SYRIAC LIFE OF MARY

Pre-779. West Syrian.

There are a number of hagiographic texts whose protagonists modern scholars sometimes call "transvestite saints." In these accounts of female ascetics, male authors explored what for them were both the possibilities and the limitations of female holiness. For modern readers, these texts are particularly important sources for analyzing ancient conceptions of gender, bodies, and sexuality. One of the most beloved of such hagiographic works was the story of a woman named Mary who joined a monastery while pretending to be a man. There are multiple Syriac versions of this narrative as well as examples in other languages. Mary's popularity crossed confessional divides in the Syriac church, though she became especially prominent in later Maronite traditions.

Next, the story of the blessed Mary who was called Marinus.

As we said, the door of God's house is open. For whoever wants to, works in the vineyard of righteousness—not only men, but also women for whom the weakness attached to them is fitting for them to enter the kingdom. Women have been celebrated in all generations and have even surpassed men. We'll mention a few of these women in this account: Moses's sister Miriam was called a prophetess. Back then she led Israel and, through her, God redeemed Israel. So, too, through Judith God redeemed them. Hanna was named a prophetess because she sat in the Lord's temple in holiness for many years until she became worthy to carry our Lord in her arms. By holiness one approaches God. As the apostle says, "Pursue holiness. For without it, no one will see God." Through holiness many women have prospered. One of them was the blessed Mary concerning whom we composed this account we are now beginning. We begin reciting the splendid conduct and powerful endurance of this admirable, praiseworthy, blessed woman.

There was a man in Bithynia and he had a wife who bore him a single daughter. He named her Mary. After her mother's departure from this world, her father raised her with careful teaching and in proper conduct. When she reached maturity he said to her, "See my daughter. Everything that I have is given to you. For I am leaving in order to take care of my soul." But when the girl heard this from her father, she answered and said to her father, "My father, do you want to save your life but destroy mine? Don't you know what was said by our Lord, 'I lay down my life for my sheep.' And he also said, 'Whoever redeems a soul is like he who created it.'" When her father heard these things from her, he was moved by her words, especially when he saw her weeping and mourning. He said to her, "My daughter, what can I do for you as you are a woman and I plan to enter a monastery and to be taken away from this world's burdens. How could you be with us?" [. . .] When the girl heard [this], she answered, "No my lord. I will not enter the monastery as you said. Rather, I will shave the hair off my head and will clothe myself in a man's attire. Then I will enter a monastery with you." When he agreed to consent to his daughter's words, he divvied up everything he owned and gave it to the poor. He shaved the hair off his daughter's head and, just as she had said to him, he clothed her in manly attire. And he changed her name and named her Marinus. [. . .] He led her and entered the coenobium [i.e., the monastery]. [. . .]

The brethren supposed that she was a eunuch because she did not have a beard and also on account of the fineness of her voice. But others thought [this came] from the many labors of asceticism with which she afflicted herself. And it happened that her father departed from the world. She [then] further increased her ascetic conduct and self-control so that she received from God gifts of grace against demons and various sufferings. When she put her hand on someone who was sick, by God's help she received healing for them without delay. Now there were in that coenobium forty brothers, that is, holy men. Every month four of the brothers were sent out for the monastery's business, because there were other monasteries beside just their own. So, they were constantly visiting and overseeing [the other monasteries]. Midway down the road that they usually traveled there was an inn where those who had been sent out for the monastery's business entered and spent the night in order to rest since it was not easy to travel the entire road in a single day. And with great care the innkeeper would bring them in. To provide them with the most rest, he would give them shelter apart from [the other rooms].

One day the abbot summoned Marinus and said to him, "My brother, I am convinced of the sincerity of your conduct and I know that you are perfect in all of it, that is, in humility and in your careful obedience. Thus, depart, leave, and go out to visit [the other] monastery. For even the brothers are distressed that you have not gone out to visit [the other] monastery. When you obey, do this, and depart, you will obtain greater reward from God." And when the humble one heard these things from the abbot, immediately he fell prostrate at the abbot's feet saying to him, "My father, pray for me and I will go wherever you have commanded." Now, when this happened and Marinus departed with three brothers to visit the [other] monastery, they spent the night in the inn we mentioned.

And while they were spending the night there, it happened that a certain soldier defiled the innkeeper's daughter such that she conceived by him. With the devil's counsel the soldier who did this defilement said to the innkeeper's daughter, "If this becomes known to your father, say to him, 'That young monk slept with me.'" Day by day her belly grew so that the shameful thing perpetrated on his daughter became known even to her father. And when he found out, he spoke, demanding from her, "From where did this evil come upon you?" Then she cast the blame on Marinus saying, "The monk whom you boast of as being holy, he did this to me and by him I conceived." Then her father came to the monastery and, tearing at himself, he said, "Where is the false Christian whom you say is holy?"

When the abbot questioned the innkeeper to learn from him why such commotion arose from his visit, the abbot said to him, "My brother, tell me the reason for your accusation so that I, too, may apologize to you." Then that innkeeper answered, "What you ask, I will tell you. I had only one daughter whom I hoped to remain with in my old age. But see what Marinus, whom you say is blessed, has done to me. See, he defiled her and she conceived." When the abbot heard these things from him, he was stunned. [. . .]

When Marinus heard these things, he threw himself prostrate on the ground, crying out with bitter weeping and with choking tears. He said to the abbot, "My father, on account of our Lord forgive me because. like a human, I stumbled." But, being angry with him, the abbot expelled him from the monastery, saying, "Never again enter our monastery." Then

Marinus went out of the monastery and sat outside enduring the cold and the heat. Those who were entering and leaving the monastery kept asking him, "Why are you sitting outside the monastery's door?" He would answer them, "On account of my sin. For I fornicated and was driven out of the monastery." But when the time was completed and the day arrived that the innkeeper's daughter should give birth, she bore a male child. Then the girl's father took him and brought him to the monastery. When he discovered Marinus sitting outside the monastery's door, the innkeeper cast the infant before him saying, "Take your son whom you wickedly spawned." He left the infant with him and went away. Marinus lifted up the infant. Crying out, he said, "Lord my God, if I am being repaid for my sins, why should this poor infant die here with me?" And troubled so, Marinus began to bring the baby milk from shepherds so that, as a father, he might raise the boy. The accusation he already had was not enough for Marinus, the infant with his frequent tears also made Marinus's clothes stink. For three years the blessed Marinus endured this pain and grief. At the end of three years, the brothers felt pity for Marinus and they said to the abbot, "All this disgrace is enough. For he has made his transgression known before everyone." [. . .] When he heard all of this, he said to them, "Thanks to your affection, I'll take him back." [. . .]

And when the boy before Marinus grew to maturity, he carefully behaved in the monastery with a proper order of virtue. For no one remains in the simplicity of thought into which they are born. Rather, just as one is taught, so one grows up. And the boy became worthy of the monastic garb. A little while later, the abbot one day questioned the brethren, saying, "Where is Marinus? For three days I have not seen him at the Eucharist; he has always been the first one to be at the service. So, in case he has some sort of sickness, enter his cell and look in." When the brothers entered the cell, they found him dead and they informed the abbot, saying, "Poor Marinus has passed away." The abbot said, "How did his poor soul depart? Indeed, what excuse might he have before God." While saying these things, the abbot commanded that they dress him. And, when—in accord with the abbot's command—the brothers had gone out to dress him, they discovered that she was a woman. Seeing her, their limbs became weak and their eyesight blurred. Once they had recovered a little, they began to cry out "*Kyrie Eleison*" [i.e., "Lord have mercy"]. When the abbot heard the sound of the cry, he inquired what was the cause of their cry. They said to him, "Brother Marinus is a woman." After the abbot came and saw her, great amazement seized him because of the endurance she had possessed. He fell prostrate upon the ground, cried out with mournful tears, and said, "Forgive me for I have sinned against God and against you. Thus, I will die here before your holy feet that I might receive forgiveness for my sins—those that I committed against you and other such sins that are even greater." With his face prostrate at the holy woman's feet, he uttered groans and lamentation for three days. At the end of three days a voice came to him saying, "If you had knowingly done these things against me, this sin would not have been forgiven you. But the sin is forgiven you because you acted unknowingly." Then, when the abbot had gotten up from before the holy woman's feet, he summoned the innkeeper and had him brought [to him]. When he arrived, the abbot said to him, "See, poor Marinus has died." Upon hearing this, the innkeeper answered and said to him, "May God forgive him for he shamed my house." Then the abbot said to him, "May God forgive you because you troubled me as well as my monastery. Do not remain in sin but repent. For you have sinned against God and you even caused me to sin. You seized me with your words, and because of you, I sinned. For although Marinus's knowledge and attire were those of a man, by nature she was a woman." But when the innkeeper heard that she was a woman, he was amazed and astonished at these things [. . .]

While this commotion was going on, they dressed her holy body and, with an appropriate service, placed her in an honored place. Inside the monastery they praised God who had imparted such endurance to her. And at the conclusion of all these things, the innkeeper's daughter entered. While being dashed about by a demon, she confessed the entire truth, saying, "It was a soldier who defiled me, impregnated me, and counseled me to wrong the servant of God and the monastery." And when she said these things, without delay the girl was healed by the grave of holy Mary. For this action and miracle that took place they all praised the Lord, who gives such endurance to those who love him. For she never revealed herself as a woman to anyone and persisted in this way until death.

My beloved ones, may we also seek to emulate her manly perseverance and endurance so that, along with her, our Lord might give us grace, mercy, and the holy ones' portion on the fearful day of judgment. By our Lord Jesus Christ to whom—along with his Father and his living Holy Spirit—be glory, honor, and worship for ever and ever.

The story of the blessed Mary/Marinus is finished.

THOMAS OF MARGA, *BOOK OF GOVERNORS*

840s. East Syrian.

The East Syrian bishop Thomas of Marga composed a mammoth hagiographic work—almost six hundred pages in translation. Most commonly known as the *Book of Governors*, this sprawling account relates the miraculous deeds of hundreds of East Syrian ascetics, especially those who were alumni of Bet 'Abe, Thomas's monastery. For modern readers, the *Book of Governors* is a surprising mix of well-known historical figures alongside teleporting trees, petrified dragons, and a temporarily resurrected dog. This combination makes it a particularly rich, albeit challenging, source for reconstructing ninth-century Syriac Christianity under Islamic rule. The following excerpts center around an abbot of Bet 'Abe named Rabban Cyriacus and his dealings with the Muslim official, 'Amran bar Muhammad, who wishes to confiscate the monastery. For an additional excerpt from Thomas of Marga's *Book of Governors*, see chapter 9.

> There was a disturbing Ishmaelite whose name was 'Amran Bar Muhammad, about whom I also wrote in the *History of Rabban Gabriel*—a harsh, violent, cold man, and a murderer. Now, when he began to enter this country from Bet Bozai, he killed people and took control of the provinces of Birta, Helaphta, Hetra, Bashosh, Herpa, the villages of Saphsapha, and little by little, many other places. He planned to take possession of the estates of this holy monastery, but this holy father stood up for us and fenced in our paths against his wickedness, just as the blessed Moses, Joshua, and David did in their times.

When he entered this monastery and pressured all the brothers to sign over to him the deed of sale, the blessed old man, Rabban Cyriacus, stood heroically before him, shamed him, and despised him with the rebukes of his words and with the flow of his proofs, saying, "'Amran bar Muhammad, I affirm and swear by the hope of the Christians that this monastery will never be yours, nor your sons, nor your grandsons! See all the land before you, leave from this holy house, and, as the Lord lives, if you leave, it will be much the better for you, and you will do very well for yourself. But, if you dare to seek to enter the monastery through the power of your threats, you will soon eat the bitter reward of your evil deeds. See, I have warned you and I have advised you for good! Leave us and it will be well for you, lest you quickly go to the house of the dead. Know this as well: because of all the blood of the believers that you have shed and the poor people whom you have killed and whose houses you have taken, it is written with an iron reed on adamantine stone in the archives of God's justice. This will be a sign to you: when you die, the earth from which you were taken and to which you will return will not receive you. No, rather, your body will be rejected, and the earth will not accept your evil body."

Now, when, by all this strength of trust in divine providence, the passion of his temperament, and the sharpness of his tongue, he had put 'Amran to shame, 'Amran rose up angrily and went to Helaphta having evil in his heart to secretly send and kill the holy one. When 'Amran left, the blessed one saw that the monks were terrified and afraid of 'Amran's threats. And he said to them, "Blessed brothers, do not be afraid, neither of his words, nor of any stumbling block that 'Amran can put in our way. For this monastery will forever be preserved from this man and from all his descendants. Let no one fear that 'Amran will send people here to kill someone. For now, he has decided to flatter you. Behold, he will shortly send for some of you. Just go and do not be afraid. For I will go with you, and you will hear me pour things greater than these into his ears."

When a few days had gone by, 'Amran sent ten horsemen for some of the elders from the assembly. When they sounded the gong and were all gathered together, all the brothers were oppressed with fear, because the horsemen would not allow the holy old man to go with his companions, for they said, "We were ordered not to bring Rabban Cyriacus with us."

Now, when the holy old man saw that they were desperate and afraid, he drew them to one side and said to them, "Do not be afraid to go. For when you enter 'Amran's presence, you will find me sitting before Amran on his seat." With this reassurance, they set out and made their way to depart. The horsemen left that blessed man on the portico in front of the church and, until the horsemen passed Risha, the blessed elder and the brothers remained in the evening prayer chapel.

But, when everyone had returned to his cell, that divine force—the one that snatched the prophet Habakkuk to Babylon, the one by which the disciples' ship came suddenly to the land where they were going, and the one that raised up the blessed Paul to heaven and to paradise—visited this poor monastery when there was no king and when this Arab wanted to force those blessed ones to hand over the monastery and its estates to him. By the power of the Holy Spirit, that divine force took the blessed old man like it had his companion [i.e., the apostle Paul], and brought him before 'Amran prior to those elders and the horsemen who were with them arriving. The divine force hid the blessed old man from 'Amran's sight while he stood above 'Amran's head until the moment when the horsemen knocked at the door. Immediately, the blessed old man appeared among them. When 'Amran saw him, he was amazed. And he looked with bitter anger upon those whom he had sent and upon the elders, saying, "Why did you bring Cyriacus with you when I commanded that he shouldn't come?"

They all swore, "We did not see him from the time we left him in the monastery until now." The blessed old man said to 'Amran, "I came here before you could look in the mirror and comb your head and beard. Do not be angry with these innocent men. You will never inherit our monastery. Let go of this desire. Let your hard heart be softened. Let your greed be done with. Look, you have inherited a lot. And thus you have made yourself such that none of your contemporaries will proceed you to hell."

While 'Amran was astonished and amazed at the words of the blessed older man, he knew that the boldness of all his flowing words was not ordinary. The blessed old man's swift coming and his entrance before him—for which he did not need a door—and his being hidden from his sight until the entrance of his companions also testified to this. So, he was afraid, trembled before him, and answered, "Get up and go in peace to your monastery. I have no dispute with you." So, the blessed ones left and returned to their cells.

But the accuser, the evil enemy of Christians and especially of holy ones, counseled 'Amran and hardened his heart. 'Amran considered everything that had been done to be magic and judged that Cyriacus did that which had been done in front of 'Amran through his witchcraft. 'Amran secretly called five bold men who were used to shedding blood and doing all kinds of evil. And he commanded them, saying, "Go to Bet 'Abe. When it is night, secretly go down to the cell of Cyriacus, take his head, and bring it to me." When those men came without anyone's knowledge, and late in the evening went down by the descent that is called "Path to Shikon," and little by little drew close to the small hill north of his cell, they saw him walking back and forth in the enclosure in his cell. They were waiting until he fell asleep in order to seize him.

Now because the holy old man turned his nights into days and, like the blessed Arsenius, spent the entire night in vigil, he went up to the enclosure in the center of his cell and began the Psalms of David from the beginning. That divine power which the blessed Elisha had, when spiritual hosts appeared to the young boy his servant with their horsemen and horses of fire, encircling the entire space where Elisha was, according to the custom of the greatness of God's power, which strengthens all things, it surrounded the entire enclosure where this holy old man was with fire. They saw the fire and were astonished. And it appeared to them that not only was an unapproachable fire surrounding him with smoke; they also saw that his body was like light. And whenever he fell prostrate, stood up, and spread out his fingers to heaven, ten bright lights came out from his fingers and rose to the sky.

After these things, they saw another man like him standing to his right. They were dazed and fearful, and they thought that the fire would suddenly come from him and consume them. But when they wanted to leave, their bellies stuck to the ground where they were lying until dawn. When they were seen by some of the brothers, they went toward them. The brothers asked them why they were there. And the men showed them exactly why they were there. Now, the elder, Henanisho', the neighbor of Cyriacus, swore [an oath] and said, "I was one of those brothers who went to those men." When the men had gone to 'Amran, who sent them, and recounted all these things to him, ['Amran] refrained from all the evil that he had prepared to do to us. At the end of his life, he commanded his sons, saying, "The monastery of Bet 'Abe will never be yours." And when 'Amran died, the earth would not receive him. Three times he was buried, and three times he was cast out of it, according to the word previously spoken by the blessed Cyriacus about 'Amran.

LIFE OF RABBAN HORMIZD

Eighth century or later. East Syrian.

Although likely written centuries later, this lengthy account of the holy man Rabban Hormizd is set in the mid-seventh century and runs to over 150 pages in translation. Of particular focus are the ongoing conflicts between the East Syrian Hormizd and local West Syrian Christians, especially West Syrian monks from the monastery of Bezkin. In the course of these monastic battles, Rabban Hormizd also had multiple run-ins with various Muslim governors, each of whom eventually served as a witness to the veracity of East Syrian Christianity and the fallacies of West Syrian Christians. The *Life of Rabban Hormizd* thus provides particularly illustrative examples of the frequent Syriac motif of Muslim characters adjudicating intra-Christian struggles (another instance from a different confessional perspective appears in the *Maronite Chronicle* found in chapter 11). The following excerpts come from a single narrative episode in which the West Syrian monks of Bezkin try to frame Rabban Hormizd but are foiled by divine intervention. For an additional excerpt from the *Life of Rabban Hormizd*, see chapter 4.

> Concerning the prostitute at Bezkin and her postmortem resurrection by Rabban Hormizd.
>
> There was a prostitute [living] with an inhabitant of the filthy "tavern" of Bezkin, which in pretense was called the monastery of Bezkin. Publicly, [the monks] were tonsured, but secretly they were evil doers. They even wanted to associate our Rabban with the defiled business of their defiled fornication, in that a group of five or so of those unclean people would gather together to satisfy their fornication, shamefully like a dog, indifferent to either appearance or nature, intemperate like Sodom, like raving dogs. They were consumed with passion for this woman and her ilk.
>   Then, after the woman stayed with them for a while, conceived, and gave birth to a male child in this monastery, those with whom the woman had been expanded their business to another kind [even] worse than before. The five who impregnated this woman and made her have a child feared that the area's ruler would notice and sentence them in accord with their crime. So, they plotted against the prostitute and said to her, "Get up and we will take you to the town of Arsham. Because of the child's crying it is impossible for you to stay with us in the monastery. For if it should happen that the ruler noticed, in the worst way he would destroy us and you." When the prostitute heard these things from those tonsured ones, she became quite afraid and said to them, "Do everything that you wish."

That evening the five of them got up, took the woman and her son, went out together, and reached the outskirts of Rabban Hormizd's cave. They took the woman, mercilessly dashed her to the ground, took out a knife, slew her, threw her by the entrance to the holy one's cave along with her son, and left. The defiled ones immediately ran off, went to the city, informed the ruler, and said, "That one whom all of you consider to be righteous among the Nestorians, behold a woman from the town of Arsham came to him requesting that the deceiver Hormizd pray for her. Because there was no other person with the woman, he fornicated with her, corrupted her, and then killed her and her young son." When the ruler heard these things, he was troubled and, along with a crowd, he left the city. When the ruler and the crowd with him approached the entrance to [Hormizd's] cave, they saw the slain woman and her baby lying upon her alive. [. . .] Rabban's servant, Gabriel of Alqosh, restrained the ruler saying to him, "Concerning rebellious actions such as these, a ruler should not rush [to judgment] unless he has first investigated and examined both sides." [. . .] [Gabriel] turned to Rabban and said to him, "Now go and ask your Lord that he might bring your truth to light and that every falsehood might be revealed." And Rabban compassionately and humbly prayed to this effect. When he finished his prayer and said "amen," he turned to this corpse and said aloud to it, "Dead corpse, in the name of Jesus of Nazareth, rise up from being slain and convict your murderer." And at [the moment] of Rabban's utterance to the murdered woman, the spirit entered her limbs and amazingly she began to speak. Rabban approached her and said to her, "Tell me truthfully, who sinned against you and killed you?" She answered Rabban, saying to him before the ruler and this crowd, that in the monastery of Bezkin five of them fornicated with her for a long time in this monastery. And after they had fornicated with her, she said, "Then they brought me to this place at night and killed me. I don't know anything else except that it is you who called and awoke me from the abyss of Sheol." Suddenly she was silent and spoke no more.

Then Rabban spoke up and said to the ruler, "Take the murdered woman's baby and place him on your knees." He did this and Rabban spoke to the baby and commanded him, "I am speaking to you, speechless baby. By God's command I tell you that you will say before all of us who your father is, for your mother did not mention him." The Lord opened the baby's mouth and he began to say, "From the semen of two of them I was formed in the womb of my mother." For he said at Bezkin five men were having sex with his mother, three of whom were sterile. And he said that his birth into the world came from [the other] two of them. [Then] the child was mute and no longer spoke. And when the crowd saw this wonder, all fell prostrate before the blessed one's feet and kissed them. [. . .] They took the dust from the blessed one's cave as though a heavenly gift, the Alqoshites went back to their town, brought [back] a bed, took away the woman's corpse, and descended from Rabban's mountain just as the holy one had commanded them. They buried her at the base of that mountain, and Rabban's faithful [companion] Gabriel took her son, a child nine months old, and gave him to a wet nurse and she raised him. (When he grew up and reached the age of twenty, he became a monk in the Rabban's monastery. He succeeded in the glorious way of life and went out of this world with inexpressible victory.) And the ruler, along with all the crowd that saw the miracle Christ had performed through the mediation of Rabban Hormizd, was filled with divine zeal. They beat those tonsured ones with harsh blows, damaged [their] monastery, and plundered everything in it. The ruler harshly bound the inhabitants of Satan's tavern [i.e., the monks of the monastery of Bezkin] with chains, took them with him, and locked them in the prison of the city of Balad.

He wrote to the governor of Mosul about their crimes. But the governor of Mosul accepted a large bribe from the heretics of Balad and Mosul. He commanded them to return to their monastery and, without injury, to rebuild it as they wished. And these tonsured ones returned to their monastery rejoicing and exultant because they had obtained much money from their fellow heretics in the cities of Mosul and Balad, and they began to excavate the ruins [of their monastery] and to rebuild [it].

9

BOOKS, KNOWLEDGE, AND TRANSLATION

Many Syriac authors expressed a keen interest in philosophy, science, law, and other traditional Greco-Roman intellectual pursuits. In specific Syriac contexts, these were combined with textual practices stemming from the manuscript culture of the early medieval Near East. Owing to the spread of Hellenistic culture following the eastern conquests of Alexander the Great in the fourth century BCE, the earliest Syriac authors engaged with Greek ideas and the legacy of ancient philosophy. Among surviving texts this close relationship between Syriac and Greek is evident both on the linguistic level and in themes and forms of argumentation. The translation of Greek literature was a constituent part of Syriac textual engagement throughout its history and—along with scribal techniques of translation, copying, and cross-linguistic engagement—supplies the context for philosophical and scientific works.

Translations from Greek illustrate a close but often complicated relationship between languages and cultures. Syriac translation technique is usually seen as moving over the centuries from an early fluidity toward more precision, with the end result being—from the sixth century on—an extremely close attention to the original Greek, to the detriment of the Syriac style. This trajectory has been labeled "from antagonism to assimilation," emphasizing both the intentional and culturally determined aspects of what is often called the "first" translation movement. This pattern is especially true for biblical translations that began in the early centuries with an idiomatic style but, by the seventh century, followed the Greek to the degree of becoming "mirror translations." The passages presented here attempt to illustrate such concerns across the range of translation practice.

Colophons—that is, short notes by scribes usually at the end of manuscripts—also provide rich information about the history of knowledge transmission in Syriac. The earliest securely dated Syriac colophon comes from 411 and is reproduced here, as is a later one that discusses the manuscript collecting activities at a single tenth-century monastery. They point to the larger phenomenon of philosophical and scientific translations often made in bilingual monasteries. For Syriac translators, Aristotle was a major focus. Many of the philosophical texts available in the medieval West to philosophers such as Thomas Aquinas were originally translated from Greek to Syriac, later translated during a "second" translation movement into Arabic in medieval Baghdad, and finally carried across North Africa to Muslim Spain, where they eventually appeared in Latin.

We know of the practices of scholars both through scribal colophons and also through contemporary writers who discuss the composition, translation, and transmission of ancient books. In the absence of the library catalogues we are familiar with today, such evidence is particularly important for understanding the crucial role that Syriac played in the transmission of ancient culture. This was true even for more practical forms of knowledge, such as law. Some Syriac Christians, including the famous bishop, Severus of Antioch, achieved careers in Roman legal service and studied at famous secular centers such as Beirut and Alexandria. As the biography of Severus makes clear—further substantiated by the *Syro-Roman Lawbook*—translation of texts (and concepts) went hand in hand with the shared education system, and early Syriac Christianity never strayed far from the Greco-Roman intellectual milieu.

The selections presented here attempt to capture not only different types of scholarly endeavor in Syriac but also the ethos of their work. From ethnography to hagiography to translation, Syriac literature reveals not only an awareness of what was available in Greek; it also foregrounds the new directions that Syriac authors took in developing their own approaches to education and scholarship.

Further Reading   This broad section can be approached from various angles. The knowledge and transmission of Greek thought is an underlying theme, profitably explored, with reference to Ephrem and early Syriac, by Ute Possekel, *Evidence of Greek Philosophical Concepts in the Writings of Ephrem the Syrian* (Leuven: Peeters, 1999). The scholastic world of the West Syrian churches became one of the primary venues for translation from Greek to Syriac as described by Sebastian P. Brock, "From Antagonism to Assimilation: Syriac Attitudes to Greek Learning," in *East of Byzantium: Syria and Armenia in the Formative Period,* ed. Nina G. Garsoïan, Thomas F. Mathews, and Robert W. Thomson (Washington, DC: Dumbarton Oaks, 1982), 17–34. See also, Jack Tannous, "You Are What You Read: Qenneshre and the Miaphysite Church in the Seventh Century," in *History and Identity in the Late Antique Near East,* ed. Philip J. Wood (Oxford: Oxford University Press, 2013), 83–102. Manuscript colophons as evidence of textual, social, and intellectual history are the subject of this foundational article: Marlia Mundell Mango, "Patrons and Scribes Indicated in Syriac Manuscripts, 411 to 800 AD," *Jahrbuch der Österreichischen Byzantinis-*

tik, 32 (1983): 3–12. The Syriac background of the 'Abbasid translation movement has been investigated by Sebastian P. Brock, "The Syriac Background to Hunayn's Translation Techniques," *ARAM* 3 (1991): 139–62. Historiography and textual scholarship were prime movers in the Syriac renaissance of the eleventh to fourteenth centuries: see Herman G. B. Teule and Carmen Fotescu Tauwinkl, eds., *The Syriac Renaissance* (Leuven: Peeters, 2010).

BOOK OF THE LAWS OF THE COUNTRIES

Early third century.

The *Book of the Laws of the Countries* or *On Fate* is a philosophical prose dialogue in a Platonic mode on the subject of fate and free will. It was written down by Philip, a student of Bardaisan of Edessa who is the principal figure in the dialogue. The work has two halves: the first is a refutation of the concept of the "Chaldean [Persian] astronomers" that human lives are determined by the stars; the second is an ethnography of foreign customs proving that human lives are in fact not fully determined. In the second half, a portion of which is reproduced here, Bardaisan describes the customs of around twenty cultures, giving evidence for his earlier argument that people often behave contrary to astrological or climatological expectations. In the last section, he offers what he claims is the strongest argument against determinism, that Jews "keep to the law laid upon them by their fathers" regardless of where they live or when they were born. Bardaisan is the earliest Syriac author known by name. At the end of the work he identifies himself as a Christian, though his views on cosmology, in particular, were deemed heretical by later Christian authors. The *Book of the Laws of the Countries* was translated into Greek and was known to several later writers in a variety of languages. It also may have influenced Mani, the founder of the religion Manicheism, in third-century Persia. Bardaisan is also credited with 150 hymns, a treatise against the Marcionites, and a history of Armenia, among other writings. Beyond this work, only fragments of his hymns survive; Ephrem quotes them in his *Hymns Against Heresies*. Ephrem claims that Bardaisan was the first to add music and chanting to the Syriac lyric poem or *madrasha*, which was also one of Ephrem's chosen genres (see chapter 2). From Ephrem's testimony it seems that followers of Bardaisan, the Bardaisanites, were still active in fourth-century Edessa. Nevertheless, it remains unclear how this and later "Bardaisanism"—including that mentioned by medieval Muslim writers—relate to Bardaisan's own thought and writings.

> To this Bardaisan said, "Because of the fact that people do not lead their lives in the same manner, you are convinced that they do not sin through their natural constitution. Now you will also feel convinced that they do not by any means sin because of their personal fate, if we can show you that the decision of fate, that is, of the rulers, does not cause all people to act in the same manner, but that we have liberty to dispose over ourselves, so that we are not slaves of physical nature, or determined by the guidance of the rulers."

Then Awida said, "Demonstrate this to me and I will believe you and do everything you charge me to."

Bardaisan said then, "Have you read the books of the Babylonian Chaldaeans, in which it is described what influence the stars in their constellations exercise upon people's horoscopes? And the books of the Egyptians, in which all the different things that may befall people are described?"

Awida replied, "I have read books on the Chaldean doctrine, but I do not know which are Babylonian, and which are Egyptian."

Bardaisan said, "The doctrine of both countries is the same."

To this Awida said, "It is known that it is so."

Then Bardaisan said, "Now listen, and try to understand that not all people over the whole world do that which the stars determine by their fate and in their sectors, in the same way. For people have established laws in each country by that liberty given them from God, for this gift counteracts the fate of the rulers, who have appropriated something not given to them. I shall now begin to relate these, insofar as I remember them, beginning in the extreme east of the whole world.

Laws of the Seres [the "people of silk"—i.e., the Chinese]: The Seres have laws that they shall not kill, shall not commit fornication, and shall not worship idols. And in the whole country of the Seres there is no idol, no prostitute, no murderer, and no one murdered, although they too are born at all hours and on all days. And not even mighty Mars, standing in midheaven, so forces the liberty of the Seres as to make a people shed the blood of their fellow with an iron sword. Nor does Venus, when in conjunction with Mars, force any of the Serian men to have intercourse with the wife of his neighbor or with any other woman. Yet there are rich and poor there, sick and healthy, rulers and subjects, because these things are given unto the power of the guiding signs.

Laws of the Brahmans in India: Furthermore, there is a law among the Indians for the Brahmans, which [says that the] many thousands and tens of thousands of them are not to kill, to worship no idols, to commit no fornication, to eat no meat, and to drink no wine. And among them not one of these things takes place and behold, these people have been living for thousands of years already according to that law which they have established for themselves.

Another law in India: There is another law in India and in the same territory, which obtains for people who do not belong to the caste of the Brahmans and are not followers of their doctrine. According to this law they may worship idols, commit fornication, kill, and do other evil things that the Brahmans do not approve. And in the same part of India there are people who are accustomed to eat human flesh, as other peoples eat the flesh of animals. And the malign stars have not forced the Brahmans to do evil and impure things, neither have the benign stars induced the other Indians not to do evil things. Also, those stars that have a favorable position in their fitting place and in the human signs of the zodiac have not brought the eaters of human flesh to cease partaking of the impure and disgusting meats.

Law of the Persians: Then the Persians have made themselves laws to take their sisters, daughters, and granddaughters to wife; some go even farther and take their own mother to wife. Some of these Persians have left their country and live in Media, in Atrapatene, in

Parthia, in Egypt, and in Phrygia. They are called Magians. And in all places and climates where they live, they live according to this law enjoined upon their fathers. Yet we cannot say that all Magians and other Persians have Venus in the house of Saturn with the moon and Saturn in her sectors, and in the presence of Mars. There are many parts of the empire of the Parthians where the men kill their wives, brothers, and sons and incur no punishment. Yet among the Romans and Greeks everyone who kills one of these is punished with death, because they have made themselves deeply guilty.

Laws of the Geli: Among the Geli the women sow and reap, build houses, and do all kinds of manual work. They do not wear colorful clothes or shoes, and they do not use fragrant oils. No one reproaches them if they commit adultery with strangers or if they have intercourse with their domestic slaves. But the husbands of the Gelian women wear colorful clothing, adorn themselves with gold and jewels, and use fragrant oils. They do not behave like this from effeminacy, however, but because of the law they have. And all men are fond of hunting and wage war. Yet we cannot say that all the women of the Geli have Venus in Capricorn or in Aquarius, in the ill-fated position. Nor can we say that all the Gelian men have Mars in Aries with Venus, a place of which, it is written, that brave but effeminate men are born then.

Laws of the Bactrians: Among the Bactrians who are called Kushanians the women are fond of wearing fine male attire, a lot of gold, and beautiful ornaments. And the slaves and slave women do more service to them than to their husbands, and they ride on horses caparisoned with gold and jewels. Now these women do not remain chaste but have intercourse with their slaves and with the foreigners who come to that country. Their husbands do not reproach them with this and they are not afraid, because the Kushanians have their wives to mistress. Yet we cannot aver that all Bactrian women have Venus with Mars and Jupiter in the house of Mars, in midheaven, a situation whereby rich and adulterous women are born, who lord it over their husbands in every way.

Laws of the Rakamaeans, Edessenes, and Arabs: Among the Rakamaeans not only is the adulterous wife killed but even she who is suspected of adultery is punished.

Laws in Hatra: In Hatra there is the law that everyone who steals a trifle, if only water, is punished with stoning. The Kushanians spit in the face of anyone who has committed a theft of this kind. Among the Romans everyone who has stolen some trifle is scourged and then set free. On the further side of the Euphrates, toward the east, no one called a thief or a murderer will become very angry. But if a man is accused of having had sexual intercourse with boys, he avenges himself and does not even shrink from murder. [text breaks here] Further, all over the East those who are openly reviled [for this] and are known to be such are killed by their fathers and brothers, and usually these do not even let their graves be known. These were the laws of the Easterners.

In the North, however, in the territory of the Germans and their neighbors, the boys who are handsome serve the men as wives, and a wedding feast, too, is held then. This is not considered shameful or a matter of contempt by them, because of the law obtaining among them. Yet it is impossible that all those in Gaul who are guilty of this infamy should have Mercury in their nativity together with Venus in the house of Saturn, in the field of Mars and in the western signs of the zodiac. For, regarding the men who are born under this constellation, it is written that they shall be shamefully used, as if they were women.

Laws of the Britons: Among the Britons many men together take one wife.

Laws of the Parthians: Among the Parthians one man takes many wives and they all submit themselves in chastity to his command, because of the law obtaining in that country.

Laws of the Amazons: All Amazons, the entire people, have no husbands, but, like the animals, they leave their territory once a year, in the spring, and cross a river. And when they have crossed it, they hold a great feast on a mountain. Then the men of those parts come and spend a fortnight with them, having intercourse with them, and the women conceive from them and then return to their country. And when they have born children, they expose the male children and bring up the female ones. Now, it is obvious that, as they all conceived in the same month, they will by the rules of nature all bring forth in the same month also, a little earlier or a little later. And, as we have heard, they are all strong and warlike. Yet none of the stars can save all the little boys who are born from being exposed.

The *Book of the Chaldeans:* It is written in the *Book of the Chaldeans* that when Mercury stands with Venus in the house of Mercury, this gives rise to sculptors, painters, and money changers, but that when they stand in the house of Venus they produce perfumers, dancers, singers, and poets. But in the whole region of the Tayites, of the Saracens, in Upper Libya, among the Mauretanians, in the country of the Numidians, which lies at the mouth of the Oceanus, in Outer Germany, in Upper Sarmatia, in Spain, in all the countries to the north of Pontus, in the whole region of the Alanians, among the Albanians, and among the Sasaye and in Brusa, which lies across the Duru, no one sees sculptors, or painters, or perfumers, or money changers, or poets. The influence of Mercury and Venus is powerless along the outskirts of the whole world.

All over Media, when people die, they are thrown to the dogs, even while there is still life in them, and the dogs eat the dead of all Media. Yet we cannot say that all Medes are born when the moon stands together with Mars in Cancer for them, by day beneath the earth. For so it is written that those are born whom the dogs eat.

All Hindus, when they have died, are burned with fire and their wives are burned alive with them in great numbers. But we cannot maintain that all the wives of the Hindus who are burned have a nativity in which Mars with the sun stands in Leo, by night beneath the earth, circumstances in which people are born who are burned with fire.

The Germans all die by strangulation, except those who fall in war. Yet it is impossible that all Germans have the moon and Hora between Mars and Saturn in their nativity.

In all places, every day and each hour, people are born with different nativities, but the laws of people are stronger than fate, and they lead their lives according to their own customs. Fate does not force the Seres to commit murder if they do not want to, nor the Brahmans to eat meat; it does not prevent the Persians from marrying their daughters and sisters, the Hindus from being cremated, the Medes from being eaten by dogs, the Parthians from marrying many wives, the Britons from a plurality of men taking one wife together, the inhabitants of Edessa from living chastely, the Greeks from practicing gymnastics, the Romans from always conquering new territories, the Gallic men from having sexual intercourse with one another, or the Amazons from not bringing up their little boys. Their nativity forces no one on the outskirts of the world to exercise the art of the Muses. But, as I have already said, in each country and each nation people use the liberty belonging to their nature as they please. Yet they are subject to fate and to nature because of the body they are endowed with, sometimes according to their desire and sometimes against it. For in every country and in every nation there are rich and poor, masters and servants, healthy and sick, as fate and their nativity happen to fall out for each person."

Then I [i.e., Philip] said to him, "O father Bardaisan, of this you have convinced us and we know that it is true. Yet you are also aware, that the Chaldeans maintain that the earth is divided into seven parts named climates, and that one of the seven rules over each of these parts, and that in each of these regions the will of his government rules and is called law?"

He replied to me, "In the first place you must know, my son Philip, that the Chaldeans have invented this doctrine to bolster up their fallacy. Even if the earth is divided into seven parts, yet in each of these parts many laws are found that differ from one another. For we do not see seven laws in the world according to the number of the seven stars, nor twelve according to the number of the signs of the zodiac, nor thirty-six according to the number of the decanal stars, but there are numerous laws in every reign, in every region, in every district, and in every inhabited place that differ one from the other. You surely remember I told you that in the one climate of the Hindus there are people who do not eat the flesh of animals and others who eat human flesh. Then I have told you of the Persians and the Magians, who not only marry their daughters and sisters in the climate of Persia, but in every place they came to, they have kept to the law of their fathers and observed the secret practices they transmitted to them.

Remember also the many peoples I have named to you living all over the world, not in one climate but in all quarters of the winds and in all the climates, who are not acquainted with the arts that Mars and Venus give when they are in conjunction. If the laws depended on the climates, this could not happen, but it is obvious that their way of living is quite different, because they see very little of other people. Consider how many wise people have abrogated the laws of their country that did not seem good to them, and how many laws have been done away with because necessity demanded it. Consider how many kings, having conquered foreign countries, abrogated the laws in vigor there and established the laws they wished. And when this happened, none of the stars could maintain the law, as you can observe in your own surroundings. Recently, the Romans have conquered Arabia and done away with all the laws there used to be, particularly circumcision, which was a custom they used. For someone of their sovereign free will submits himself to the law laid upon them by another, who also possesses sovereign free will.

But I shall tell you another thing too, more convincing than all the rest to fools and unbelievers: All the Jews that have received the law of Moses circumcise their male children on the eighth day, without waiting for the coming of stars and without regard for the local law. And the star that rules the climate they are in has no compulsive power over them. But whether they live in Edom or in Arabia, in Greece or in Persia, in the North or in the South, they keep to the law laid upon them by their parents. And clearly, they do not do this because of their horoscope, for it is impossible that on the eighth day, when they are circumcised, Mars should be in such a position with regard to all Jews, that iron comes over them and their blood is spilled. Everywhere they are, they do not worship the idols and on one day in the week they and their children let all work rest; they do not build and do not travel; they do not buy and do not sell. Neither do they kill any animal on the

Sabbath, light any fire, or give judgment. And among them there is found no one who is charged by fate to go to law and gain his suit on the Sabbath or to do the same and have it given against him, or to pull down his house or build it up again, or to do a single one of those things that all people do who have not received this law. They have other precepts also, through which they lead a life different from that of other people, although on this day, too, they beget children, are born, fall ill, and die, for over these things no one has power.

In Syria and Edessa there was the custom of self-emasculation in honor of Tar'ata, but when King Abgar had come to the faith, he ordered that every man who emasculated himself should have his hand chopped off. And from that day to this no one emasculates himself in the territory of Edessa.

What shall we say of the new people of us Christians, that the Messiah has caused to arise in every place and in all climates by his coming? For behold, we all, wherever we may be, are called Christians after the one name of the Messiah. And upon one day, the first of the week, we gather together and on the appointed days we abstain from food. And our brothers who live in Gaul do not marry men, and they who live in Parthia do not marry two women, and in Judea they are not circumcised. Our sisters among the Geli and the Kushanians do not have intercourse with foreigners, and they who live in Persia do not marry their daughters. Those who live in Media do not flee away from their dead or bury them alive or throw them for food to the dogs. Those who live in Edessa do not kill their wives or sisters who have committed adultery but have nothing more to do with them and leave them to the judgment of God. And those who live in Hatra do not stone thieves. But in whatever place they are and wherever they may find themselves, the local laws cannot force them to give up the law of their Messiah; nor does the fate of the guiding signs force them to do things that are unclean for them. But sickness and health, wealth and poverty, that which does not depend on their free will, comes over them wherever they are.

As the liberty of humankind is not subject to the guidance of the fate of these seven and, when it is subjected to it, can oppose its influence, so neither can one, as one offers himself to our view, immediately free himself from the power of his guiding signs, for one is a slave, and in subjection. For if we could do everything, we should be everything, but if nothing lay in our power to do, we should be instruments of others. Yet if God wills, all things can take place without hindrance, for there is nothing that can withstand this great and holy will. Even they who think they can resist him do not do so of their own strength but from wickedness and error. Now this may last for a short time, because he is mild and allows all natures to exist in their own fashion and to live according to their own free will. But they are bound by the works that have been done and the ordinations that have been instituted for their sake. For this order and rule that is given, and the mingling of one with the other, restrict the force of the natural elements, that they might not become completely harmful nor completely harmed, as they caused and suffered harm before the creation of the world. But a time will come when even the possibility of causing harm still existing with them will disappear through the doctrine that is founded on a different intermixture. In the condition of this new world all evil damaging influences will have ceased and all revolts will have ended, the foolish will be convinced and every lack supplied, and peace and perfect quiet will reign through the gift of the Lord of all natures."

COLOPHONS FROM SYRIAC MANUSCRIPTS

Colophons are an important part of Syriac manuscript culture. They are short notes, usually placed at the end of the manuscript, which describe when and by whom the text was copied, and they sometimes offer other information, such as when the library acquired it. The earliest dated Syriac colophon is from 411 and comes from a manuscript of theological texts translated from Greek. Because of its colophon—which gives not only its date but also the name of the scribe, Jacob, and its location of copying, Edessa—we know that this represents the earliest dated manuscript in any language from the Western world. In addition to the colophon dated to 411 found below, this same manuscript also contains a marginal note from an eleventh-century reader that also documents the manuscript's composition date (see figure 12 and its caption).

To show the continuity of colophon practice in Syriac, we also include below a much later colophon from the Monastery of the Syrians in Egypt, dated to 932. This colophon explains that the book was part of the collecting activities of the abbot Mushe of Nisibis, who brought back 250 fine books from his trip to Baghdad and Syria: many of these are among the earliest extant in Syriac, including the 411 manuscript. Often, as in the 932 colophon, the scribe declares a curse against anyone who would deface the manuscript in the future.

COLOPHON DATED 411 (*BRITISH LIBRARY ADDITIONAL* 12150). WEST SYRIAN

This volume was completed in Edessa, a city in Mesopotamia in the Second Tishri [i.e., November] of the year 723 [of the Greeks = 411 CE].

COLOPHON DATED 932 (*BRITISH LIBRARY ADDITIONAL* 14445). WEST SYRIAN

To the honor and glory and magnificence of this Syrian Orthodox monastery of the Mother of God in the desert of Sketis, Mushe, known as "of Nisibis," an insignificant sinner and abbot, strove to acquire this book, together with 250 others (many of which he himself bought, while others were given to him as a present), when he went to Baghdad on behalf of this holy desert and the monks dwelling in it. May God, for whose glory, and for the benefit of those who read these books, grant forgiveness to them and to their departed, and to everyone who has shared with them. By the living word of God, no one is permitted to cause harm to any of them in any way; nor to appropriate them to themselves. Nor should anyone delete this commemorative note, nor make any erasure or cut anything out—nor order anyone else to do so; nor may they be given away from the monastery. If anyone dares to do so, let them realize that they are under an anathema. These books arrived with the above-mentioned abbot Mushe in the year 1243 of the Greeks [= 932 CE].

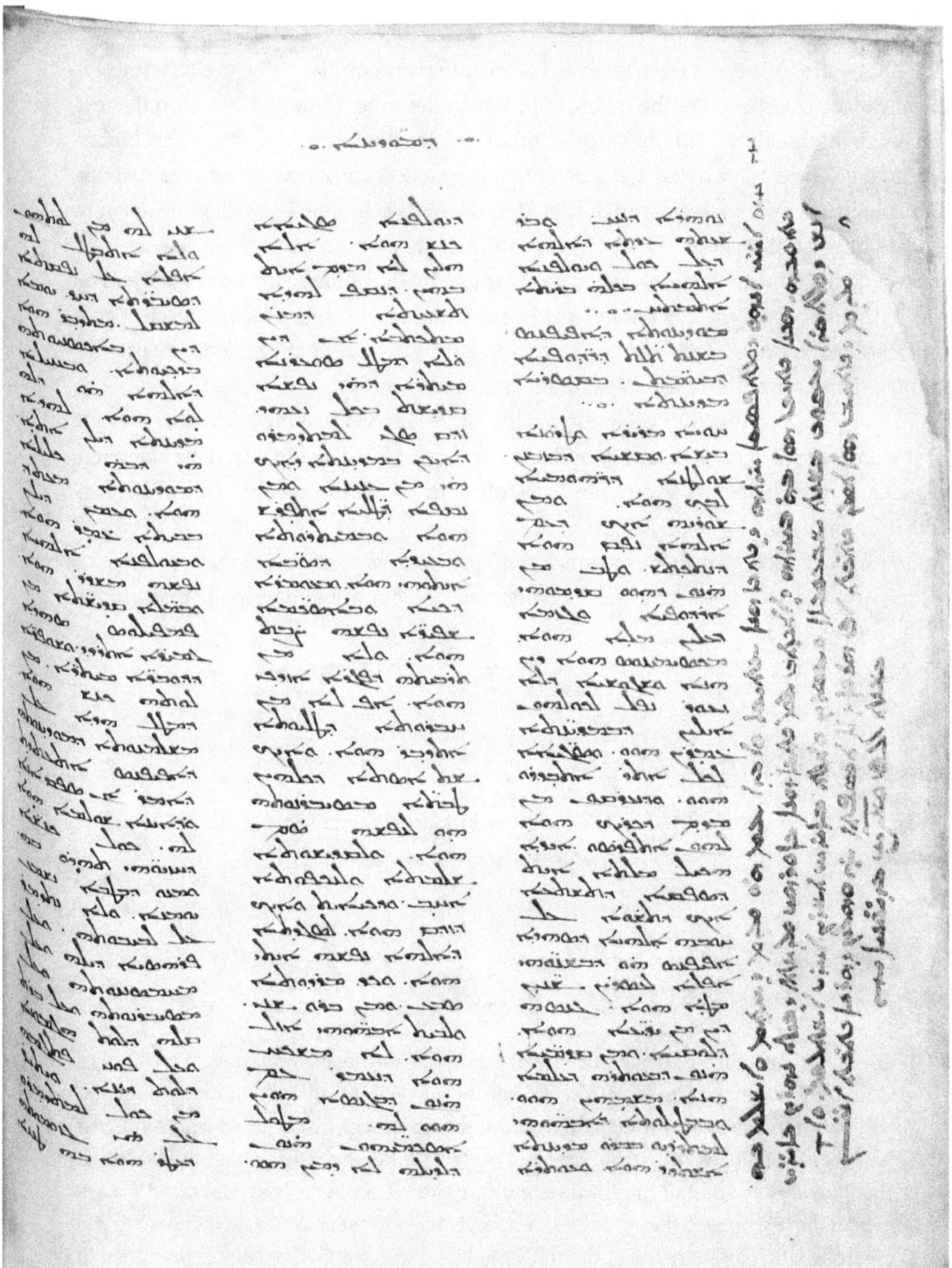

SYRO-ROMAN LAW BOOK

Fifth century. Originally Greek, earliest surviving version in Syriac.

The text called the *Syro-Roman Lawbook* is a unique piece of literature that offers important evidence for the perspective of Syriac Christians on Roman law and social norms. It represents a collection of various interpretations of specific laws dealing with property, marriage, private life, and slaves. Its relationship to the law school of Beirut (see the *Life of Severus* below) is unknown but certainly represents traditions present in Syria at the time of the law school's influence. It thus offers a documentary complement to the story of Severus's career and conversion, though with a monastic background. The *Lawbook* was incorporated into both West and East Syrian juridical collections and from there it was translated into Arabic and Armenian. The selections presented here deal with laws concerning slaves and divorce. They show how Roman law was mediated through ecclesiastical hierarchies but, equally, how Syriac churches did not see themselves as above the Roman authorities, even in cases of capital punishment. The close study of Roman law, its translation into Syriac, and its application in ecclesiastical matters all speak to the transmission of knowledge across linguistic and cultural lines in early Syriac Christianity.

> Is it legitimate that a slave whom his master frees before witnesses is freed? [Yes, if it is before] the bishops and presbyters. Or, if he is in the country, before the chorepiscopus, called *periodeutes* or the presbyters, according to the order of the praiseworthy and blessed king Constantinus.

FIGURE 12.
Earliest securely dated Syriac manuscript (*British Library Additional* 12,150, fol. 239b). The final colophon in this manuscript locates its production in Edessa in 411, making it the oldest book in any Western language securely dated by a colophon. The contents of the text include the pseudo-Clementine *Recognitions*, an anti-Manichean discourse, translations of works by Eusebius of Caesarea, and an anonymous martyrology. This codex's antiquity impressed not only modern scholars. As can be seen on the right side of this page, in the eleventh century a reader wrote in the book's margin: "If the end of this ancient book should be cut off and perish along with what its scribe finished and sealed it with, see my brethren, here is what was written at its end: 'This book was written in Edessa a city of Mesopotamia by the hands of a man called Jacob. It was finished in November 723 [of the Greeks = 411 CE].' Just as it was written there, I have also written here without addition. I wrote these things here in the year 1398 of the Greeks [=1086/1087 CE]." What makes this manuscript's story particularly compelling is that the last pages of *British Library Additional* 12,150 did indeed become separated from the rest of the book, just as this medieval reader had feared. But their marginal note set the mid-nineteenth-century assistant keeper of the British Museum manuscripts, William Cureton, on a quest to find the missing colophon. In 1847 Cureton discovered the corresponding colophon among recent fragments obtained from the Monastery Deir al-Surian reconfirming the 411 date for this manuscript's composition. © Trustees of the British Library.

If a man decrees in writing that he frees his slave and, together with the slave, his private property, he is free. If, however, he does not write it out explicitly, after the death of the one who freed them, his inheritors take the private property that the slave owns.

Can one who frees a slave get him back to enslave him? He can, if, during his lifetime, he accuses him that he was dishonored and despised by him. And if he accuses him that he treated him shamefully—then the slave is subjugated to his former master.

Can he who frees a slave leave a legacy to his slave and to the sons of the slave who are from a slave woman? The law orders that that can take place.

If a man buys an [allegedly] good slave who is not a runaway, the transaction allows him to test the slave during the period of six months. If, before the completion of this time of six months, he does not like him, the buyer is entitled by the orders of the laws to return the slave and to deliver the slave to his former master who sold him and to receive from him the money that he gave as his price. If, before the time of six months is completed, the slave escapes the one who bought a good slave, he who bought him must search for him and demand back the money he gave for the slave.

If a man sells a slave to another, whether he is good or bad, under the stipulation that neither of them has any recourse against the companion, that which is called in Greek *hapleone*, and [yet] he who bought wishes to return him to the one who sold, the law does not allow him to send him away and [so] he cannot return him, unless he finds that a demon lives in the slave. If it can be proved it is in him and he so desires, he may return him to that one who sold him.

If a man orders his slave to have a legal process for him, the law does not allow him. It is not authorized because a slave and a free man cannot go to law, for they are not equal in honor.

If someone receives a slave that is not his while knowing that he is a slave and that he will be accused, the law orders that the one who received him shall be consigned to slavery.

If a man receives a laborer who is not his, which is written *apographa*, while knowing that he whom he received is a laborer of another one, he will be consigned as a laborer to his accuser.

If a man buys an object and gives an earnest in money, and the seller withdraws, the law orders that he [be paid] double the earnest that he received on the basis of the [entire] sum of money. But if the buyer who gave the earnest does not want to buy, he loses his earnest that he had previously given.

If a slave buys an object, he is entitled to, for what he buys belongs to his master and he is entitled to buy.

The laws do not give a man authority to kill his slave by his own hands. If, however, a deed that deserves death has been done to him by the slave, he must give him over to the authorities, and they shall punish him according to his deeds. If, however, a man, one who does not have authority from the state, dares and kills a robber or a murderer or kills a servant who deserves death, he shall be killed according to the laws—the one who dares and who kills and has no authority for this.

If a man wants to free his slave under the stipulation that, after the emancipation, he shall stay with his son or his inheritors for a certain number of years and that he, although a free man, should work for the inheritors, the law orders that he is so entitled.

Can a man free a slave under stipulation? He can free [him] before the church or before the judge or through the testament if he writes the stipulation into the document of emancipation.

[What to do] if a free man when questioned says about himself that he is a slave and agrees with him who buys him? If a man who says about himself that he is a slave is twenty years of age, he loses his freedom and cannot appeal to the help of the laws. Particularly, if he has received the half of the price of himself or has eaten it with the deceiver who sold him, he remains a slave of him who bought him.

[What to do] if a woman, a free person, says about herself that she is a slave woman, and she will be taken so that she will be sold or given as a dowry of a woman? If she is younger than twenty years, the laws help her and she can rise against slavery and can return to freedom. But if she is twenty years old or above, she injures her freedom and remains a slave woman of the one who bought her or to the one who took her as a dowry of a woman.

In regard to those men and women who receive stolen objects from slaves. The laws order that they have to return them to the owners fourfold.

If a man buys a slave by a good-faith contract and, before the completion of six months, that which is the term limit set up by the laws and reckoned since the day of the selling of the slave, finds in him something, a hidden sickness or a demon, the law orders the return of the slave to the man who sold him, and he will receive the money he paid [originally]. But if the six months since he received him are completed, and [he has not noticed] a hidden sickness in the slave, the one who bought [him] is not entitled to return him to the one who sold him.

Thus is the regulation about the slaves and slave women in the [legal] judgment: If a man buys a slave or slave woman in a bad-faith contract, by simple purchase with no retreat, and the one who bought wants to give back the slave or slave girl to the seller, he cannot because he has bought by a bad contract. But if he finds a demon in the slave or slave woman, he is entitled to return him to the seller and receive his money. If it happens that the slave or slave woman flees back to the house of their former master or turns out to be a thief, the buyer can return the slave or the slave woman and not only this but the buyer can demand the price of what was stolen.

When a slave is freed by his masters and becomes a free man and the slave inclines to take a slave woman for his wife after he is freed and he has children by her, the law orders that the children from the slave woman shall not inherit but those masters who freed him shall inherit him.

The one who wishes to free a slave shall free him in the following way: If the freeing of the slaves takes place in a town, then [it shall take place] before a bishop and six presbyters from his clergy. If the freeing of the slaves takes place in a village, then before the *periodeutes* and the presbyters of the village so that with them five other priests are present, and before the inhabitants of his village so that as witnesses they give their signature to the act of the emancipation of the slaves. If a slave is freed in this way, his emancipation [procedures] are valid and he shall be a free man. If, however, his emancipation does not take place before the clergy, the emancipation of the slave is not valid, and he shall be under the hand of his former masters, serving in slavery as the precept of the laws orders. [. . .]

If it happens that there is a separation between the husband and his wife, whether this be through death or through another cause that gives the wife the claim to take the dowry, it is right to take the following [into account]: If the garments of the dowry still exist and are not yet mutilated and worn out, she shall take the garments of her dowry with her. If, however, they are mutilated and worn out, the price shall be fixed as it was when the garments were new—the kinds of garments and their prices are known to the merchants of every town. Thus, the wife shall take this price of the garments of her dowry with her. If she has gold in her dowry or darics [i.e., Persian gold coins] or land, she shall take with her that which she had brought from the house of her parents. If she, in the dowry, has brought to the husband oxen or camels or sheep, and if something has been sold from the species of animals, she shall take the price instead of the sold animals. If all of them are still existing, she shall take the [full] number she has brought [plus] a half of the increase of all kinds [of animals] and of the sheep, but the other half she shall separate for her husband for the sustenance of the animals because they were supported by his [means]. With respect to the marriage settlement, however, which her husband brought her according to the dowry—as the computation of the marriage settlement indicates, so shall she receive gold according to the property written [in the record]. If one of the animals is dead, he does not owe her a recompensation. In like manner, if she has brought in her dowry, a slave or a slave woman; if the slave or slave woman is still alive, she shall take these slaves. But if they have been sold, her husband shall return to her [their price]. If the slave woman has children, she shall take half of her children. If one of the slaves is dead, he owes her nothing.

Can a husband dismiss his wife, depriving her of her dowry, if he cannot accuse her in matters that, according to the law, involve the loss of it? The husband cannot, except he can prove the matter as punishable by the law. These are: If she has committed adultery with another. If she has spent the night in another house that is not hers, [namely, other than] the chamber of her husband. If she has gone to a theater to see improper things and all that is related to these things. If he can prove one of these things, he can dismiss her so that she does not take her dowry. If, however, he wants to dismiss her for [other] reasons, though he cannot prove one of these things, he cannot dismiss her without [her taking] the dowry; nor may he deduct anything from her dowry.

Can a wife give a bill of divorce to her father-in-law or to her husband and take her dowry when she cannot prove an offense against her? A wife cannot carry out a divorce and take the dowry without the agreement of her husband and her father-in-law except in the following cases: The testimony of two or three witnesses who testify and swear that her husband has beaten her in an illegal way. Or he has done to her such things as deserve divorce—such as, namely: witchcraft, brigandage, or adultery. Or that he brought a harlot into the house over against his wife. Or that, instead of his wife, he has taken a concubine. And not only this—but also if he has beaten her with a rod or a kick or a whip like a slave or has lifted an iron instrument against her. Under such circumstances she can. With such an argument, the laws command to give her the bill when she reclaims her dowry without any impediment. However, she cannot enter into a legal procedure against her father-in-law unless he has given his agreement to her dowry. If her dowry was made with his approval, his having given his signature to it, this [opens the] way for legal procedures also against her father-in-law to reclaim her dowry.

ZACHARIAS RHETOR, *LIFE OF SEVERUS OF ANTIOCH*

Sixth century. West Syrian.

Severus of Antioch was arguably the most important theologian of the sixth century. This was particularly true for the West Syrian Church, even though Severus wrote exclusively in Greek. He studied in Alexandria and at the famous Roman law school of Beirut. While in Beirut, Severus converted to Christianity. Later, he became a monk in Gaza, advocated for the anti-Chalcedonian cause in Constantinople, and was ultimately elected bishop of Antioch. The *Life of Severus* offers an important testimony to higher education and, particularly, to the law school of Beirut during late antiquity. It was still clearly thriving in Severus's time and it attracted both pagan and Christian students. Severus and his biographer and colleague Zacharias Rhetor sought to integrate their study of law with their study of the Bible and the theologians of the Church. This mode of life required abstinence from the entertainments of the world and intense focus on study, worship, and prayer.

> When the most illustrious Severus was ready to move from Alexandria to Phoenicia [i.e., Beirut] to study law, intending to become a lawyer, he urged me to accompany him. But when I said that I still needed to study further the speeches of the rhetoricians and philosophers—because of the pagans, who are so excessively proud of these studies, so that we would easily manage to dispute with them—he went ahead, just one year before me.
>
> After this [year] had ended, I, too, went to Beirut to study civil law, and I was expecting to suffer everything that newcomers in the city, who had come for the purpose of law, had to go through—and what they were going through was downright foolish and nothing, just to make those who saw it laugh, and to show the power of those who were mocking them and making fun of them—from those called *ediktalioi*, and particularly from Severus, the now holy, for I thought that since he was still young he would adopt the habits of the others.
>
> So, when, on the first day, I went to the school of Leontius, Eudoxius's son, who at that time was teaching law and whose glory is well-known to everyone who takes an interest in law, I found the worthy Severus among those who were sitting with him, listening to a lecture on law. Then, taking for granted that he would be my enemy, I noted that he was actually kindly disposed to me, for he greeted me first, cordially and cheerfully, and I thanked God for this glorious miracle. [. . .]
>
> I said to Severus, "Thus, what is needed, dear friend, is that all those who [have the ability to] think well take refuge in him, the creator of life, through baptism."
>
> "You have spoken well," he said, "but now we must decide how to carry this out, since I am busy studying law."
>
> And I said to him, "If you want to obey me—or, rather, the divine words and the universal doctors of the church—flee, first of all, from shameful shows, from horse racing and the theater, and from games with animals against wretched people. Furthermore, keep your body clean, and offer evening prayers to God every day after having worked devotedly with the law. For we, having the knowledge, must do the evening services in the holy churches while others spend a lot of time occupied with playing chess, rolling in drunkenness, drinking with whores, and making a complete disgrace of themselves."

He, then, promised to stick to this. "Just don't make me a monk," he said, "for I am a lawyer and devoted to law! Now, tell me if there is something else you require."

And I, rejoicing, said, "I came to this city for the sake of civil law, for I am devoted to the art of pleading [cases]. Now that you are concerned with your redemption, I suggest something that neither interferes with the love of work with law, nor requires a lot of spare time, but provides practice in rhetoric and philosophy and, at the same time, understanding of the divine words and the doctrines."

"What would that be?" he said, "For the promise is great and powerful, if it is possible, without neglecting the study of law, that we could obtain such benefits, too, particularly that which is the best of all!"

"We study law, as I understand it, all week except Sunday and the evening from which it dawns. We read the lessons of law that we finish during the other days with our teachers, and afterward we work with them again, at home by ourselves. We rest half the day before Sunday, which civil law, too, commands us to consecrate to God. If you agree, I said to him, we could appoint this time to the doctors of the church, to the companions of the great Athanasius, I say, and Basil, Gregory, John, Cyril, and the others. Letting the other friends occupy themselves with whatever they please, we will delight our souls with theology, and with the meanings, and with learning as much as possible the writings of the church."

He said, "This is why, dear friend, I started by asking if you had brought this material with you. Now that things, through God, have turned out this way for us, we will do as you said, and I will stay with you during the said moments." Thus he agreed with me, and this is what we did.

Starting with the antipagan writings of various authors of the church, we went on to read the *Six Days* [i.e., the *Hexaemeron*] by Basil, the all-knowing, and after that his separate homilies, his letters, the homily against Amphilochius, the refutation of Eunomius, and the allocution directed to the youth in which he teaches them how to profit from pagan speeches. Later, as we proceeded, we read the homilies of the three divine Gregories, and those of the illustrious John and Cyril.

This he and I acquired on our own, during the said moments. Every day, we also attended the evening service together, in the company of the worthy Evagrius, whom God had brought to Beirut to persuade young people to exchange the nothingness of forensic oratory for divine philosophy.

Being from Samosata, [Evagrius] had been instructed at the school in the great [city of] Antioch. It happened, however, that he became affected by youth, when he was young, and went to see a show in the city and was beaten in a sedition that took place there. Afterward, when he had been restored from the injury, he hated excessive spectacles, and took to spending all his time in the holy churches, joining those who, at that time, sang all night in the church of the all-illustrious Stephen, the first martyr, men who are devoted to practical philosophy and in many ways [are] not inferior to the secluded ones. After diligently studying the preparatory teaching, [Evagrius] wanted to rise to this [true philosophy] and choose the monastic life for good. His father had, however, forced him to go to Phoenicia to study law at the time when I, too, came there.

Now, for this very reason and at the same time, the worthy Elisa, who was from Lycia, arrived [in Beirut]; a man who was very calm, humble, and simple, and lavishly filled with love for those who lacked food and clothes. Since they [Evagrius and Elisa] had become as parents to me, and I saw that they were ready for the love of God, I suggested that we should offer evening prayers to God together in the holy churches, and we agreed to do so.

Having completed the exercises of reading law, and having fulfilled the tasks connected therewith, we gathered every evening at the church called Resurrection, and many others joined us—first of all, according to our agreement, the illustrious Severus, and, after him, Anastasius from Edessa and Philippus from Patara in Lycia, and also Anatolius the Alexandrian. [They were] God-loving men, and prominent in civil law, which they had been studying for four years, and they wanted to be ranged among us. Zenodorus, of Christ-loving memory, who came to Beirut after us, joined us too—like me he was from the coast of Gaza. and he, who was a celebrity among the lawyers here, in the imperial stoa, has now departed from mortal life—took part in our fellowship, as did Stephen the Palestinian, who also arrived later.

The leader of this holy group was Evagrius, a philosopher, in practice, of our Lord Jesus Christ, who fasted every day, as it is said, and who destroyed the splendid blossom of youth by divine philosophy, tormenting his body by vigils and never washing himself except on one single day: the day before the Easter festival [in celebration] of the great resurrection of the savior of us all, Christ.

Gradually, though, the great Severus rivaled him, both in practice and theory. He was studying with me in the way that I mentioned and, having become skilled in the words of the doctors of the church, from which he acquired some of the theory of divine philosophy, as well as what was said about practical philosophy, he now looked at the practice of the worthy Evagrius as a living example, a model and an icon, recognizing a Christian philosopher not only in words—such as myself and many others—but in practice, too. And so he took after him and his virtues, tormenting his body by fasting, and he imitated his chastity and his other virtues by abstaining from eating meat—not because it was sinful, as the Manichaeans say, but because abstention from it made it easier to attain philosophy—and not washing himself during most of the year, until the very day when he, like him [Evagrius], did so.

PHILOXENUS OF MABBUG, *COMMENTARY ON THE PROLOGUE OF JOHN*

Early sixth century. West Syrian.

Philoxenus (d. 523) was a leading Syriac opponent of the Council of Chalcedon. He was appointed the bishop of Mabbug (modern Manbij, Syria) in 485 and spent the last years of his episcopacy under the emperor Justin I in exile. Philoxenus was a prolific author and theologian with a deep commitment to the text and interpretation of the New Testament, so much so that he commissioned a new translation of the Greek New Testament into Syriac, known as the Philoxenian New Testament. This excerpt is taken from Philoxenus's *Commentary on the Prologue of John*, a text from the gospels that was seen as key to the fifth- and sixth-century controversies over the human and divine aspects of God's Son for their description of the incarnation of the preexisting Word of God. This selection includes Philoxenus's close study of Greek and Syriac translations, and his argument that current and less accurate Syriac translations obscure the nuances of the Greek that support his Christological views. For addition excerpts from Philoxenus, see chapters 5 and 6.

> The apostle Paul too spoke well, saying, "He became [flesh]," and not, "He was born" in the flesh [Romans 1:3]—which was how it pleased those first translators [of the Peshiṭta] who translated from the Greek to interpret, thus giving strength to the heretics to understand that one being was born in another. The apostle also concurs here as well with the evangelists and the angel, each of whom spoke first of a "becoming" and then of birth.
> If those who translated supposed that it was not elegant in the Syriac language to speak of the "becoming" of Christ, or of God, or of the Son, they should have realized that someone who is concerned to translate the truth ought not to select those words that are appropriate for each particular language, but to seek out what are the utterances and terms that come from God or from his Spirit and were spoken through the prophets and apostles. For things placed in the holy scriptures are not the offspring of human thoughts, so that they should receive correction or adjustment by means of human knowledge.
> Among the Greeks, each one of these words and terms, which we have mentioned as having been spoken by the evangelists and the apostle, is put exactly as we have said, namely, "He came into being from the seed of David in the flesh" [Romans 1:3], and not "he was born in the flesh"; and again, "The book of the coming into being of Jesus Christ" [Matthew 1:1], and "Of Jesus Christ the coming into being is as follows" [Matthew 1:18]. And because the books of the New Testament were uttered in their own tongue [of Greek], it is all the more fitting to incline toward what is set down in Greek with them, and not to those things that were interpreted by just anyone—things that merely belong to that person's supposition and are not part of the teaching that comes from the spirit.
> Consequently, whoever who alters, or interprets differently, the words and terms spoken by the Spirit, is not only reprehensible and to be rebuked, but is also an impious blasphemer and a companion of the Marcionites and Manichaeans—people who themselves removed from the scriptures things that had been spoken by God, and changed certain things, replacing them by others considered by them to be an improvement. Having fallen into this impiety, Theodore and Nestorius, the leaders of the heresy of human-worshippers, also audaciously altered certain words of scripture, and gave a contrary interpretation to others. [. . .]
> Likewise, with the passage in the Letter to the Hebrews that reads, "Jesus the Son, by grace of God"—that is, of the Father—"on behalf of everyone tasted death" [Hebrews 2:9]: they altered this and wrote "apart from God," and their concern was to transmit that this Jesus, who received death on our behalf, is not God.
> Also, instead of what the Evangelist wrote, namely, "The Word became flesh and tabernacled in us" [John 1:14], Nestorius understood and read it as follows: "Flesh came into being, and the Word tabernacled in it."
> By inclining toward views such as these, those who originally translated the scriptures into Syriac erred in many things—whether intentionally or through ignorance. This was not just in matters that teach about the economy in the flesh, but various other things that are written about other topics. It was for this reason that we have now taken the trouble to have the holy books of the New Testament interpreted anew from Greek into Syriac.

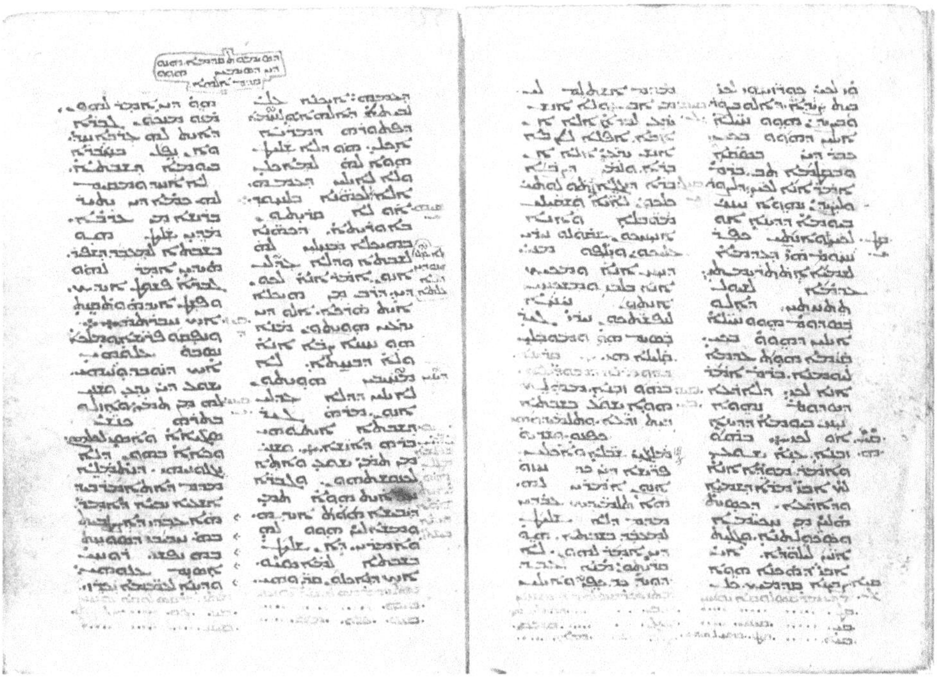

FIGURE 13.

A scholarly gospel manuscript (*British Library Additional* 14,456, fols. 14b–15a). These pages come from an eighth-century scholarly manuscript of the gospels in Syriac, written on parchment. In addition to the text of the gospels themselves, this manuscript includes limited vocalizations, variant readings in the margin from the Ḥarqlean Version of the New Testament, and additional marginal emendations. The gospels are divided according to the Eusebian canons or Ammonian chapters, a method of dividing the gospels that was widespread in late antiquity. With its detailed paratextual apparatuses, this manuscript embodies the meticulous scholarship and scribal culture that developed around late antique and medieval Syriac monasteries. © Trustees of the British Library.

SERGIUS OF RESHʿAYNA, *ON THE AIM OF ALL OF ARISTOTLE'S WRITINGS*

Early sixth century. West Syrian.

After having studied medicine in Alexandria, Sergius of Reshʿayna (d. 536) translated a large number of Greek works in both science and theology: for instance, he translated the famous second-century doctor Galen, as well as the important Greek theologian Pseudo-Dionysius the Areopagite. In this passage, Sergius briefly describes his oral translation practice before explaining how Aristotle is the chief philosopher and how training in logic is the basis of all knowledge. The continuity of interest in Greek philosophy and medicine among Syriac authors is striking and it extends from Sergius through the whole medieval period. Later translators relied on Sergius's translations, and he is often seen as an inaugurator of the first translation movement. Passages from Ḥunayn ibn Isḥaq reproduced later in this chapter discuss the reception of Sergius's translations in ninth-century Baghdad.

> There is a saying uttered by the ancients, my brother Theodore, that the bird called the stork rejoices and becomes strong when it separates itself from cultivated ground and moves off to the wilderness to live in its former lair until the time when its life comes to an end. In the same way, it seems to me, no one can understand the opinions of the ancients or enter into the mysteries of the knowledge contained in their writings unless he has separated himself from the entire world and its dealings and distanced himself from the body as well—not in space, but in mind—leaving behind him all its delights. Only then will the mind be emptied in order to turn toward its own being, and gaze at itself, seeing clearly the things that have been written by the ancients, and judging well which have been said correctly and which have not been set down in this way. That is, once there is nothing present from the things that oppose a person's swift progress as a result of the body's inclinations that hinder him in the course of such a journey.
>
> When we were translating certain works of the doctor Galen from Greek into Syriac, I used to translate, while you would write it down after me, correcting the Syriac wording, in accordance with the requirements of the idiom of this language. And when you saw the fine divisions of speech that are to be found in the writings of this man, along with the definitions and demonstrations that occur so frequently and excellently in it, you asked me, "From where did this man receive the source and beginning of his education? Did he acquire such a fullness of knowledge from himself, or from some other writer before his time?"
>
> I replied to the question that you, in your love of learning, had put: "The ultimate source and beginning of all education was Aristotle. This does not just apply to Galen and his fellow doctors, but to all the writers and renowned philosophers who came after him. For up to the time when nature had brought this man into the world inhabited by humans, all the parts of philosophy and education were extended like roots, scattered and dispersed chaotically and ignorantly among all sorts of authors. But this man alone, like a wise doctor, assembled all the scattered writings and put them together in a craftsmanlike and intelligent way, seasoning them with the unique and complete assistance of his teaching. For in the case of those who approach his writings diligently, he uproots and removes from their souls the sicknesses of ignorance, whether these be serious or less so. It is like the case of people who make statues: they cast each part of the image separately, and only then do they put them together, each piece in turn, as their skill demands, thus completing the statue. So, too, did Aristotle fit and put together each of the parts of philosophy in the place required by its nature, forging out of them in all his writings a complete and wondrous portrait of the knowledge of all things that come into being."
>
> When you heard this from me, my brother Theodore, you immediately wanted to know what was the purpose of this man's teaching, and what was the order of his writings, and

the sequence of his ideas. I attempted to tell you a little of what you had mentioned, and now you have asked me to commit to writing something of what I related to you orally. In view of the exalted nature of the subject I excused myself from this, saying that I had already composed a brief treatise on the purpose of Aristotle's writings, and that this would suffice for anyone who encountered it to make them aware, as far as is possible, of the man's views. But you were not persuaded by this; instead, you lovingly urged me to make—not a general work concerning the sage's entire teaching on the cause of the universe, such as I have already done—but individual brief introductions to each of his writings in turn. Therefore, since I am unable to escape from your request, before I commence on this, I urge you and all who may come across this work, not to turn at once, after just a single reading, to unpleasant charges and complaints, but to persevere reading and taking it in, once, twice, three times, and even four times over, should the subject matter require it. If even so something appears obscure, then one should not neglect to go to someone who can instruct and show them what they do not know. In this way one will save themselves from the confusion that exists in the mind of those who do not understand what they are reading; and one will, furthermore, restrain themselves from laying accusations and complaints—which are of no help at all to the author of the words.

Without all this [i.e., Aristotle's works on logic] neither can the meaning of writings on medicine be grasped, nor can the opinions of the philosophers be known, nor indeed the true sense of the divine scriptures in which the hope of our salvation is revealed—unless a person receive divine power as a result of the exalted nature of their way of life, with the result that one has no need of human training. As far as human power is concerned, however, there can be no other course or path to all the areas of knowledge except by way of training in logic.

SEVERUS SEBOKT, *LETTER TO THE PERIODEUTES BASIL OF CYPRUS*

Mid-seventh century. West Syrian.

Severus Sebokt (d. 666/667) was associated with the school of Qenneshre, a West Syrian monastery on the Euphrates northeast of Aleppo that became a major center of study for scholars who knew both Syriac and Greek. Severus was an astronomer, philosopher, and mathematician, and he is said to have held debates in front of the Muslim caliph at Damascus. His philosophical works, like most Syriac philosophy of the period, concerned Aristotle, especially the subject of logic. He may also have translated Middle Persian works of Paul the Persian on Aristotle into Syriac—a signal of Severus's multilingual scholarly environment. The following selected passage appears in a short chapter from an unnamed work by Severus found in the manuscript *Paris Syriac* 346. Here Severus quotes Plato's dialogue the *Timaeus* as proof that the Greeks were not the first philosophers or scientists, and he suggests they looked to the Indians, who surpassed both the Greeks and Babylonians in astronomy.

On the subject of the tardiness in knowledge, and the lack of learning of the Greeks, let them listen to what the Greeks themselves have to say. I am referring to Plato the first philosopher of such renown among them, and what he writes in the *Timaeus*: "On returning from Egypt, Solon, the wisest of the wise, told Arkitanis [i.e., Critias] what he had heard from an Egyptian priest who was of great age. He said to him, 'O Solon, you Greeks are children all the time. There is not a Greek who has grown to old age.' Later, he further said, 'You Greeks are all babes in your souls: you do not have a single ancient opinion in them, or any doctrine aged by time. Writing passed you by for many generations, and you have died without a voice.'" This quotation shows that the Greeks did not even know writing for many generations, but "they all died without a voice," that is, in a dumb way, and unintelligent. How then do some of them boast that they were the first discoverers of the science of mathematics and astronomy? Neither is the case!

At this point I shall refrain from speaking about the science of the Indians, who were not even Syrians, or about their exact discoveries in the science of astronomy—discoveries that are far more skilled than those of the Greeks or Babylonians—and the logical method of their calculations and the way of counting that surpasses description: I am speaking of the method that uses nine signs. Had they been aware of these, the people who imagine of themselves that they alone have reached the summit of wisdom just because they speak Greek would perhaps have been persuaded, even though rather late in the day, that there are other people who have some knowledge: it is not just the Greeks, but also some of the peoples who speak different languages as well.

TIMOTHY I, *LETTERS* 43, 48, AND 47

Late eighth century. East Syrian

Elected katholikos of the East Syriac Church following the poisoning of his predecessor, Timothy I (d. 823) stayed in office for forty-three years. As katholikos, Timothy interceded on behalf of the church under the 'Abbasid caliphate and reorganized the church structure to the east of Persia—namely, in China, Tibet, India, Yemen, and Central Asia. He held a debate with the caliph al-Mahdi (d. 785), a later description of which survives to today (see chapter 11). As a scholar he was an inveterate supporter of translating Greek philosophy into Syriac and Arabic. As exemplified by the selections here from his *Letters*, he was eager to make sure his translations from Greek were as accurate as possible. In *Letter* 43 he seeks to know whether the West Syrian monastery of Mar Mattai in northern Iraq has commentaries (*scholia*) on the works of Aristotle and he reveals he has been discussing Greek translation with a Chalcedonian colleague. In *Letter* 48 he has a long discussion with a fellow Greek scholar about a specific Greek word and he reveals that he translated Aristotle's *Topics* into Arabic. In *Letter* 47 Timothy describes a manuscript of the Syro-Hexapla he received and had recopied with great care—this was a translation of the Old Testament made by Paul of Tella in the seventh century from the third-century theologian Origen's famous multicolumned edition. Timothy's copy includes many scholarly annotations. Timothy also describes the discovery of Hebrew manuscripts in a cave near Jericho—under remarkably similar circumstances to the Dead Sea Scrolls. Here he also mentions appointments for bishoprics in Tibet and Iran, showing that the scholarly interests of this important figure always shared time with ecclesiastical matters. For additional excerpts from Timothy I's *Letters*, see chapters 10, 11, and 12.

LETTERS 43

To the God-loving priest and teacher, Rabban Mar Pethion. Timothy the sinner greets you and hopes to see you.

The royal command required of us to translate the *Topika* [i.e., the *Topics*] of the philosopher Aristotle from Syriac into the Arabic tongue. This was achieved, with God's help, through the agency of the teacher Abū Nuḥ. A small part was done by us as far as the Syriac was concerned, whereas he did it in its entirety, both in Syriac and Arabic; the work has already reached a conclusion and has been completed. And although there were some others who were translating this from Greek into Arabic (we have written to inform you how and in what way it happened that all this took place) nevertheless [the king] did not consider it worth even looking at the labors of those other people on the grounds that they were barbaric, not only in phraseology but also in sense, whether because of the natural difficulty of the subject (for you are aware of the style of the philosopher in matters of logic, and how and to what extent he infuses obscurity into the beauty of [his] meaning and sense) or as a result of the lack of training of those who approached such things. For you know the extent and magnitude of the toils and labors such a task requires. But [the king] entirely approved of our labors, all the more so when from time to time he compared the versions with each other.

Let your eminence sagely ask and inquire whether there is some commentary or scholia by anyone, whether in Syriac or not, to this book, the *Topika*, or to the *Refutation of the Sophists*, or to the *Rhetorika* [i.e., the *Rhetoric*], or to the *Poetika* [i.e., the *Poetics*]; and if there is, find out by whom and for whom [it was made], and where it is. Inquiries about this should be directed to the [West Syrian] Monastery of Mar Mattai—but the inquiries should not be made too eagerly, lest the information, [the purpose of the inquiry] being perceived, be kept hidden, rather than disclosed.

Job the Chalcedonian told me that he has seen a small [number] of scholia on the *Topika*, but only, he said, on certain chapters. But let your chastity doubly enquire about scholia or a commentary on these books.

Send us the other volume of Athanasius, so that we can copy it out. We have the first. I think the translation is by Paula, for on the title of the book the following is inscribed: "First volume of the holy God-clothed Gregory the Theologian, which the abbas Mar Paula translated from Greek into Syriac on the island of Cyprus." The revision, so it says, is by Athanasius. So much for this.

Search out, too, for the treatises on the natural principles of bodies, written by someone of the Platonic school; it begins, "Concerning the natural principle of bodies some have said . . . ." The first treatise gives the opinion of all the earlier philosophers and sets out the ideas and Platonic forms. The second treatise begins by speaking of matter, species, and negation, following Aristotelian teaching. [The author] deals with it in five sections, but the treatise is incomplete. Search out to see if these treatises can be found—both what remains from the second treatise, and the rest of what follows from these.

Search out for a work by a certain philosopher called Nemesius, on the structure of human beings, which begins: "Human beings are excellently constructed as a rational soul and body . . . ." He brings the subject to an end in roughly five sections; at the end he promises to deal with the soul, but this second part is missing.

Please search out and copy for us [Pseudo-]Dionysius [the Areopagite] in the translation of Athanasius [of Balad] or that of Phokas [of Edessa].

Peace to you and to all the brethren.

LETTER 48

To the reverend and elect of God, Mar Sergius, the metropolitan of Elam. Timothy the insignificant servant of Jesus our Lord and our God does obeisance to your chastity and hopes to see you.

I do not wish to conduct the present discussion with your eminence in a hasty fashion or anything of that sort; I wanted rather to do it leisurely, at a gentle pace, and in a more detailed manner. Nevertheless, because the order from the victorious king came upon us all of a sudden to set off to Roman [i.e., Byzantine] territory to join him, we temporarily put a stop to what we were planning, and we have simply acted in an extemporizing fashion.

Your eminence is aware that after seven days of the month Ḥziran [i.e., June] in the present year of 183 [in the year of the Hegira—that is, 799 CE] had passed, we started out on the journey to the victorious king, seeing that he had commanded us to go to him, [according us] honors, expenses, and regal presents: if we wanted [we were to use] the public transport, or if we liked [we could use] animals that belonged to us. The matter ended in our traveling by public transport, owing to haste. May your eminence pray that our Lord's will be brought to perfection in us, and that our going prove to be for the common good, and not result in any harm.

[The Greek word] a*ulētrides* does not mean "playing" or "drunkenness," or even "wine presses." [No,] they are "[flute-]playing women." We learned this first of all from the translation that Athanasius [of Balad] made of the *Epideictics*, from Greek into Syriac; there he wrote "[flute-]playing women," corresponding to a*ulētrides*. Later, we also [learned it] from the book of the *Topika*, for there he everywhere puts "[flute-]playing" for a*ulētridion*, and "[flute-]playing women" for a*ulētrides*. It will be clear to your eminence how much difference [in meaning] there is between "[flute-]playing" and "[flute-]playing women," and between *aulētridion* and *aulētrides*; for the term "[flute-]playing women" indicates both the persons and the actions, while "[flute-]playing" indicates the action rather than the person.

I think that [here] the "[flute-]playing women" have nothing to do with the art of music that has reference to philosophy, which is one of the *mathēmatika*. Rather, it concerns the female sort [of music], which has to do with women. For when the *mathēmatika* are under discussion, [*aulētrides*] is never [given] as a technical term for music, [but instead] "musician" is used as the technical term. They speak of *musiqara* and *musiqos* as the terms combining both the person and the action.

We have described this following what we have learnt from the books of the commentator. I think the word [here means] something different: it is not because there is no vineyard, as being the distant cause, that there are no [flute-]playing women in Scythia; for neither the vineyard nor the wine is the cause of the *aulētrides*, since even when there is no wine and no vineyard it is possible for *aulētrides* to be found. I think that [Aristotle] is speaking of rites and libations accompanying sacrifices and pagan mysteries; for everywhere they used to make libations to demons together with the sacrifices. Among the Scythians, however, because they had no wine, they [only] offered up sacrifices, and did not make libations in the rites of their mysteries. Thus, he gives the reason why there are no *aulētrides* among the Scythians; and when he should have mentioned the proximate and direct cause—because there was no wine at all—he removed altogether the proximate cause [and put] the distant cause, namely, "because there was not even a vineyard."

This is just [my] conjecture, and I have not spoken out of precise [knowledge]. If it is true, or near the truth, let it be accepted; otherwise, let the wind take it.

Nevertheless, your eminence should be aware that the word is a strange one and unusual, even in Greek, as I believe. For when we were translating the book of the *Topika* into Arabic from Syriac, we had with us some Greeks, and one of them was the patriarch of the Melkites; only with difficulty could they understand the word, and the fact that they accepted [the translation] "[flute-]playing women" was either the result of our happening upon it in the translation of Athanasius, or as a result of their own achievement.

I have written this in great haste. If our Lord grant to us life, we shall make a reply to your book.

We send greetings to all the church of God with you, and to our brother Babai, head of the monastery; tell him that he is under the ban of the word of God until he accepts the yoke of priesthood, either at Hormizd-Ardashir, or somewhere else. Pray for me.

LETTERS 47

To the revered bishop Mar Sergius, the metropolitan of Elam. The sinner Timothy does obeisance to your reverence and asks for your prayer.

We have read the letters which your reverence sent to us on the subject of the [Syro-]Hexapla, and we have learned from all that you wrote in them. We give thanks to God for your good health and the fair course of your episcopal governance, and we, who are sinners, ask God's mercy that your affairs may have a successful and glorious outcome.

On the subject of the book of the Hexapla about which your reverence wrote, we have already written and informed you last year that a copy of the Hexapla, written on sheets using the Nisibene format, was sent to us through the diligence of our brother Gabriel, *synkellos* [i.e., advisor] of the resplendent king. We hired six scribes and two people to dictate, who dictated to the scribes from the text of the exemplar. We wrote out the entire Old Testament, with Chronicles, Ezra, Susanna, Esther, and Judith, producing three manuscripts, one for us and two for the resplendent Gabriel; of those two, one was for Gabriel himself, and the other for Bet Lapat, for this is what Gabriel had instructed in writing. The manuscripts have now been written out with much diligence and care, at the expense of great trouble and much labor, over six months more or less; for no text is so difficult to copy out or to read as this, seeing that there are so many things in the margin, I mean readings of Aquila, Theodotion, Symmachus, and others, taking up almost as much space as the text of the Septuagint in the body of the manuscript. There is also a large number of different signs above them—how many, it is not possible for anyone to say. But we had bad and greedy scribes, eight men for just under six months. The copying was done as far as possible using correction, seeing that it had been made from dictation; the copies were gone over a second time and read out. As a result of the excessive labor and work of correction, my eyes were harmed and I nearly lost my sight—you can get an idea of the weakness of our vision from these shapeless letters that we are writing now.

Even the exemplar from which we were copying, however, contained errors, and most of the Greek names were written in reverse: the person who wrote them must have had a knowledge of Greek as weak as our own, apart only from the fact that he was not aware of the reversal of the characters he was writing, whereas we were at least aware of that! For he had not noticed the replacement and interchange of the characters, sometimes writing the letter *chi* in place of *kappa*, and *zeta* in place of *chi* as well as putting all sorts of other things. We, however, recognized the situation.

At the end of every biblical book the following was written: "This was written, collated, and compared with the exemplar of Eusebius, Pamphilus, and Origen".

This, then, is the way the Hexapla had been copied. It has endless differences from the text which we employ [i.e., the Peshiṭta]. I am of the opinion that the person who translated this exemplar in our possession was working from the versions of Theodotion, Aquila, and Symmachus, since for the most part there is a greater resemblance to them than to the Septuagint. I had imagined that a copy of the Hexapla had already been sent to your reverence, so when you wrote we immediately wrote off to the noble Gabriel, telling him to fulfill his promise to you; but if he does not want to send it to you, let him write to us, for we will copy it out again and send it to you. So much for that topic.

We have learned from certain Jews who are worthy of credence, who have recently been converted to Christianity, that ten years ago some books were discovered in the vicinity of Jericho, in a cave dwelling in the mountain. They say that the dog of an Arab who was hunting game went into a cleft after an animal and did not come out; his owner then went in after him and found a chamber inside the mountain containing many books. The huntsman went to Jerusalem and reported this to some Jews. A lot of people set off and arrived there; they found books of the Old Testament, and, apart from that, other books in the Hebrew script. Because the person who told me this knows the script and is skilled in reading it, I asked him about certain verses adduced in our New Testament as being from the Old Testament, but of which there is no mention at all in the Old Testament, neither among us Christians, nor among the Jews. He told me that they were to be found in the books that had been discovered there.

When I heard this from that catechumen, I asked other people as well, beside him, and I discovered the same story without any difference. I wrote about the matter to the resplendent Gabriel, and also to Shubhalmaran, metropolitan of Damascus, in order that they might make investigation into these books and see if there is to be found in the prophets [passages] that testify to, "He will be called Nazarene" [Matthew 2:23], or "That which eye has not seen and ear has not heard" [1 Corinthians 2:9], or "Cursed is everyone who is hung on the wood" [Galatians 3:13], or "He turned back the boundary to Israel, in accordance with the word of the Lord that he spoke through Jonah the prophet from Gad Hfar," and other passages like them that were adduced by the New Testament and the Old Testament but are not to be found at all in the Bible we possess. I further asked him, if they found these phrases in those books, by all means to translate them. For it is written in the Psalm, beginning "Have mercy, O God, according to your grace" [Psalm 51:1], "Sprinkle upon me with the hyssop of the blood of your cross and cleanse me." This phrase is not in the Septuagint, nor in the other versions, nor in the Hebrew. Now that Hebrew man told me, "We found a David [i.e., a psalter] among those books, containing more than two hundred psalms." I wrote concerning all this to them.

I suppose that these books may have been deposited either by Jeremiah the prophet, or by [Jeremiah's scribe] Baruch, or by someone else from those who heard the word and trembled at it. For when the prophets learned through divine revelations of the captivity, plunder, and burning that was going to come upon the people as a result of their sins, they, being men who were firmly assured that not one of God's words would fall to the earth, hid the books in the mountains and caves to prevent their being burned by fire or taken as plunder by captors. Then those who had hidden them died after a period of seventy or fewer years, and when the people returned from Babylon there was no one surviving of those who had deposited the books. This was why Ezra and others had to make investigations, thus discovering what books the Hebrews possessed. The Bible among the Hebrews consists of three volumes, one [i.e., the Pentateuch] being the volume that the seventy interpreters subsequently translated for King Ptolemy [in Alexandria]—who is worthy of a wreath of accolades; another was the volume from which others translated at a later time; while the third is preserved among them.

If any of these phrases are to be found in the aforementioned books it will be evident that they are more reliable than the texts in currency among the Hebrews and among us. Although I wrote, I have received no answer from them on this matter. I have not got anyone sufficiently capable with me whom I can send. The matter has been like a burning fire in my heart and it has set my bones alight.

Pray for me: my frame is very weak; my hands are not very good at writing; and my eyes are feeble. Such things are indications and messengers of death. Pray for me that I may not be condemned at our Lord's judgment.

The Holy Spirit recently anointed a metropolitan for Turkestan and we are making preparations to anoint another for Bet Tuptaye [i.e., Tibet]. We have sent another to Shiarzur and another for Radan, since Nestorius the metropolitan of Radan has died. We are also making preparations for another at Ray [i.e., Tehran region], since Theodorus has died; another for Gurgan, another for Balad—Cyriacus of Bet 'Abe; another for Dasen since Jacob has sunk into the pit from which there is no resurrection; another for Bet Nuhadra, which has no bishop. So, pray with us to the Lord of the harvest that he may send out laborers for his harvest.

Shubhalisho' of Bet Daylamaye has plaited a crown of martyrdom. We have sent in his place ten monks from Bet 'Abe. Pray for me, reverend father, in God my Lord.

Send me the *Apologia for Origen* by Eusebius of Caesarea, so that I may read it and then send it back. Make a search for the *Discourses on the Soul* by the great patriarch Mar 'Aba: there are three of them, but only one is available here. And copy out and send the *Homilies* of Mar Narsai, since we have not got them; for Mar Ephrem, of holy memory, wrote to us to say that there is a great deal there with you that is not available here. Write to "the Tyrant of Fars" and inform him that every metropolitan who is appointed by a bishop with his coordainers is subject to the canon of the church of God, the Synod of the 318 Fathers [i.e., the Council of Nicaea], and the canons of Mar 'Aba.

THOMAS OF MARGA, *BOOK OF GOVERNORS*

840s. East Syrian.

Thomas of Marga was a monk at the monastery of Bet 'Abe, the "Forest Monastery" northeast of Mosul, Iraq. Thomas was the author of a major work of monastic history, the *Book of the Governors*, more properly called the "Book of the Abbots of Bet 'Abe" since it tells the history of his monastery and especially its relations to the many East Syrian monasteries founded from the sixth to the ninth centuries. Vignettes regarding specific East Syrian monks are among the most compelling stories in the book. This particular story about the life of Mar 'Anan'isho highlights Mar 'Anan'isho's superior learning, even within a highly academic monastery. He uses, for instance, the walls of his monastic cell to write out philosophy in an Aristotelian mode. The story also shows the value that books had in the monastery, suggesting that Bet 'Abe had a substantial library. For an additional excerpt from Thomas, see chapter 8.

> Now when they came to this monastery and dwelled in silence according to the rule of ascetics, Rabban 'Anan'isho, the wise of understanding, labored so hard in the study of books, that he surpassed in his knowledge all who came before and after him. When Mar Isho'yabh was metropolitan of Arbela and he wished to draw up in order a book of the canons—so that he might send copies of it to all the countries of his patriarchate—he made the wise abba 'Ananisho', the love of whom is very dear and sweet to me, to sit with him during the drawing up of the canons. [This was] because of the institutes and rules that 'Ananisho' had composed, and because Isho'yahb found that he alone possessed in a sufficient measure a clear mind, a natural talent for the art of chanting, and a sense [for the meaning of words]. Now the excellent man, and elect of God, Isho'yabh, the brother of 'Ananisho', was appointed bishop of Kardilabad, that is Shenna, a city of Bet Ramman. And the noble 'Ananisho' composed definitions and divisions of various things, which were written upon the walls of his cell. And when his brother Mar Isho'yabh came to pray in this monastery and saw the divisions of the science of philosophy of his brother 'Ananisho', he begged him to write a commentary on them for him, and to send it to him, which 'Ananisho' did. He wrote to him a clear exposition in many lines, and everyone who reads them will perceive the greatness of his wisdom. Now the title of this work is "A letter that a brother wrote to his brother; to the excellent and holy Mar Isho'yabh the Bishop, 'Ananisho', greetings in our Lord." He also wrote a work on the correct pronunciation of the words and of the difficult [or obscure] words that are used with different significations in the writings of the fathers. This exists among the books in the library of this monastery, and it surpasses

all other collations in its accuracy. According to what I have learned concerning these [books] of his from the aged elders, they were completed and given to us by him.

MUSHE BAR KEPHA, *INTRODUCTION TO THE PSALTER*

Late ninth century. West Syrian.

Mushe bar Kepha (d. 903) was bishop of Bet Ramman, north of Tikrit, Iraq. He produced a massive collection of biblical exegesis and theology and is recognized as one of the preeminent writers in the West Syrian tradition. His scholarship depended on compiling sections of previous works, showing him to have been well versed in tradition and having had access to many books. As a result, he was very well aware of the differing perspectives on translation technique that preceded him. He relies on the comments of Jacob of Edessa (d. 708) regarding the versions of the Syriac Old Testament—namely, the Peshiṭta (translated from the Hebrew by the third century) and the Syro-Hexapla (translated from the Greek Septuagint in the early seventh century). Although one might assume that the older Peshiṭta was more exact because it was translated from Hebrew, Jacob notes that Philoxenus—in line with the other selections offered in this chapter—privileges the Greek version of the Old Testament. Jacob argues that most of the Old Testament quotations in the New Testament are from the Septuagint, which is quite true. He includes here the legend perpetuated by Jacob that Addai and the converted king Abgar sent a translator to Palestine to produce a Syriac version of the Old Testament from Hebrew.

> In our own Syriac tongue there are two translations of the Old Testament. One is the Peshiṭta, which we read; this was translated from Hebrew into Syriac. The Peshiṭta was translated from Hebrew into Syriac in the time of King Abgar of Edessa, as Mar Jacob has said. Mar Jacob says that Addai the apostle and the believing king Abgar sent a man to Jerusalem and the region of Palestine, and they translated the Old Testament from Hebrew into Syriac. The version of the seventy-two [i.e., the Septuagint] was translated from Greek into Syriac by Paul, bishop of Tella d-Mauzelat, in the time of the emperor Heraclius [r. 610–41], according to some people. Of all these translations the Peshiṭta, which was translated from Hebrew into Syriac, is the most exact, in that they say that the Hebrew tongue is closely related to Syriac. But Philoxenus of Mabbug says that of all the versions that of the seventy-two is the most exact: this is clear from the fact that our Lord and his disciples adduced testimonies from it in the gospel and Acts, and so too did Paul [the apostle].

ḤUNAYN IBN ISḤAQ, *RISALA*

Mid-ninth century. East Syrian. Arabic.

In ninth-century ʿAbbasid Baghdad Ḥunayn ibn Isḥaq (d. 973) became famous as a translator of Greek philosophical and medical works into Syriac and Arabic. Ḥunayn cultivated a school of translators that produced Syriac and Arabic versions of almost all the writings of the ancient physician Galen. They also translated Plato and Aristotle, among other Greek philosophers. The selections here are taken from a letter Ḥunayn wrote in which he describes his travels across the East in search of ancient Greek manuscripts. The original version of this was in Syriac, but what has come down to us is a revised and expanded edition in Arabic, translated from Syriac. He also discusses previous translations into Syriac, such as those by the sixth-century Sergius of Resh'ayna (see earlier in this chapter). Ḥunayn often felt the need either to revise the earlier translations or to retranslate completely. His Arabic translations were usually made via the Syriac, which were made, in turn, from the Greek. From his own records, we can see that he translated Galen into Syriac much more than into Arabic. Ḥunayn also became the royal physician to the caliph al-Mutawakkil (d. 861) and he wrote numerous medical treatises of his own, as well as grammatical and theological texts. Ḥunayn's writings illustrate how a Syriac-Greek-Arabic matrix was definitive for the intellectual climate of Baghdad in the 'Abbasid period and beyond.

PREFACE TO THE ARABIC TREATISE

Ḥunayn ibn Isḥaq said: You mentioned—may God give you honor—the need for a book containing a list of what is needed and known of the books of the ancients on medicine, an exposition of the purpose of each of them, and an enumeration of the volumes of each book, as well as what subjects are treated in each volume. Through it, there would be a lightening of the burden of the person looking for any particular one of these subjects, should the need arise to examine it; and one might know in which book it is found, and in which of its volumes and where in the volume, and in which chapter. [This you mentioned, intending] that I undertake [to write] it for you. I informed you—may God give you support—that my memory was incapable of encompassing all those books, since I had lost all of them that I had collected, and that a certain man, a speaker of Syriac, had asked me, after I lost my books, for something similar to this with regard to the books of Galen in particular, wanting me to exposit for him which of those books I myself and others had translated into Syriac and Arabic. I thus wrote for him a book in Syriac along the lines of what he had in mind when he asked me to write it. You thus bade—may God give you honor—that I translate that book for you, for now, until such time as God might deign to do that of which he is worthy, returning those books through your aid, and further that I add to the books of Galen that I mentioned in that book anything that is necessary, as well as an account of the rest of the books of the ancients on medicine that we have found. It is my intention to do what you have bade, God willing.

PREFACE TO THE EARLIER SYRIAC TREATISE

You asked me to describe for you the number of Galen's books, by what [titles] they are known, and what was his purpose in each of them, as well as how many volumes each has, and what he describes in each of those volumes. I informed you that Galen has written a book along these lines, in it outlining his books—he entitles it the *Pinax*, which, translated, means "the Catalogue"—and that he has written another volume in which he described the order in which his books should be read. Surely it is better to seek to understand the books of Galen from Galen rather than from me. You answered as follows: "Even if the matter is as you describe, we and all our contemporaries who read the books [of Galen] in Syriac and Arabic need to know: which have been translated into Arabic and Syriac and which have not been translated; which translated works you alone undertook to translate and which others alone have translated; which were translated by someone else before you that you then either translated again or corrected; who those other people were that translated each of these books and the skill of each of them as translators; for whom you translated each of those books that you translated and how old you were when you translated it (it is necessary to know these two things in that [the value of] a translation accords solely with the skill of the book's translator and the person for whom it was translated); for which of those books hitherto not translated has a Greek copy been discovered and for which of them has one not been discovered or discovered only in part (this must [be known] both that care might be taken to translate what we have discovered and that the undiscovered ones might be sought)."

When you responded to me in this fashion, I realized that you had hit on the truth in what you said and that you had summoned me to a task of benefit both to me and to you, and to many others. Regardless, I delayed for a time, first opposing your request and then seeking to put you off by reason of my having lost all my books. These books I gathered one by one, during the whole of my life, since the time I came of age, from the various lands in which I traveled. These books, all of them, I completely lost. I do not even have any longer that book I just mentioned, the one in which Galen listed his works. When you persisted in your request, you compelled me to accede to what you asked, despite the loss of what I needed to prepare such a work, when I saw that you would be satisfied and content with what I could remember on this subject. I shall now begin that task, in it relying on the heavenly aid for which I hope through your prayers, keeping it as short as possible, as you requested, while at the same time recounting everything I remember about those books. I begin with a description of what one should know about the two books I just mentioned. [. . .]

Causes of Breathing: He composed this book in two volumes, during his first visit to Rome, for Boethus. His purpose in it is to show which organs give rise to breathing, both that which is unforced and that which is forced. Job has produced an unintelligible translation. Isṭifan also translated it into Arabic. Abū Jaʿfar made the same request regarding it that he made regarding the preceding book. He bade Isṭifan to collate it with me, and I corrected the Syriac and Arabic together until the Syriac became stylistically intelligible, with nothing to fault (as I desired to have a copy for my son) and the same regarding the Arabic, except that it was far more accurate than the Syriac.

Difficult Respiration: He composed this book in three volumes. His purpose in it is to describe the different kinds of difficult respiration, what causes them, and what they indicate. He mentions in its first volume the different kinds of respiration and their causes and in the second volume poor respiration and what each of its kinds indicates, while in the third volume he cites Hippocratic proof texts for the validity of his statements. Job has translated it into Syriac. I collated it with the Greek and corrected it for my son. I have translated it into Arabic for Abū Jaʿfar. [. . .]

Properties of Foodstuffs: He composed this book in three volumes. In it [he treated] all the foods and drinks by which one in nourished, describing the properties in each one of them. Sergius al-Raʾsī has translated it; and later, Job. Initially, I myself translated it for Salmawayh, from a copy that was corrupt. Later, I wanted a copy for my son: I accordingly collated a number of copies that I had collected and thus produced a correct copy. I also made an epitome of it in Syriac and in Arabic, adding to them whatever else the ancients said on this subject, in three volumes. [. . .]

The Best Doctor Must Be a Philosopher: This book consists of a single, small volume. Job translated it into Syriac. Later, I translated it into Syriac for my son and into Arabic for Isḥāq ibn Sulaymān. I translated it a second time into Arabic for ʿAbd Allāh ibn Isḥāq. [. . .]

Authentic and Spurious Works of Hippocrates: This book also consists of a single volume. It is a nice book, and beneficial. There is a copy in Greek among my books, but I have not had time to translate it, nor do I know whether anyone else translated it. Later, I translated it into Syriac for ʿĪsā. I also made an epitome of it.

PART IV

INTERRELIGIOUS ENCOUNTERS

10

JUDAISM

Early Syriac Christianity had a rich but complicated relationship with Judaism. Those who understood Jesus to be the messiah foretold in the Jewish Bible and who believed his followers would inherit God's covenant with Abraham struggled to draw distinctions between their communities and those who followed the laws of Moses but did not believe that Jesus was the Son of God. While we today often label these communities simply "Christians" and "Jews," early intersections among them were varied and complex—perhaps nowhere more so or for longer than in Palestine, Syria, and Mesopotamia, where many Aramaic- (including Syriac-) speaking followers of Jesus lived. After Roman soldiers destroyed the Jerusalem Temple in 70 CE, all these communities struggled to reinterpret scripture to determine how God wanted them to live. Each of the interpretive communities that developed in the region's churches and synagogues understood themselves to be the true covenanted people of the God of Abraham.

Modern scholars have long noted evidence in texts like the *Didascalia* for some shared biblical translations, interpretations, and practices that did not fit neatly into later expectations of a sharp distinction between Christianity and rabbinic Judaism. The Syriac writings of Aphrahat (d. after 345) and Ephrem (d. 373), as well as John Chrysostom's Greek homilies from Syrian Antioch, suggest that some churchgoers celebrated Passover with "Jews." Jews continued to live in these regions throughout this early period, leading to shared scriptural traditions and regular interactions with their Christian neighbors. Textual and social proximity, as well as so-called "Judaizing" practices, were not, however, welcomed by the majority of later church leaders, and Christians concurrently developed sharp and violent anti-Jewish rhetoric. Syriac texts repeatedly contrast the singular noun "people" ('*amma*) of the Jews with the plural noun they used for gentile Christian "peoples" or "nations" ('*amme*, a translation of the Greek *ethnē*), such that Syriac authors often refer simple to "the people" or "the peoples" without further clarification. Texts like those by Ephrem and the *Teaching of Addai* insult the Jews, calling them blind and foolish and referring to them as "crucifiers" in reference to the role that Matthew 27:25 gives the crowd and their descendants at Jesus's crucifixion. Texts like the *Didascalia* and those by Aphrahat, Ephrem, and Isaac of Antioch offer a supersessionist Christian narrative and interpret scripture to argue that God's earlier expectations, such as those connected to circumcision and food laws, have been replaced by a new covenant of baptism and Christian faith. In later texts, such as the *Martyrdom of Habsa, Hayya, and Hayya*, the *Letter* of Simeon of Bet Arsham, and the *History of the "Slave of Christ,"* violent anti-Jewish caricatures appear in Christian martyrdom stories. So, too, supersessionist arguments are expanded in disputation texts, such as the work by Sergius the Stylite, which represent a Jewish interlocutor as a foil for Christian instruction.

Anti-Jewish language, however, was not limited to Christian conflicts with Jews themselves; early Christian authors frequently used anti-Jewish arguments to try to delegitimize other opponents who, in their mind, shared something in common with Jews. Ephrem, for example, deployed anti-Jewish rhetoric not only against anyone who joined a local Passover celebration but also against so-called "Arian" Christian heretics. He reasoned that Arius's denial of the Son's full divinity was equivalent to the Jews' denial that Jesus was the messiah or the Son of God. Subsequent decades brought new Christian "heresies" and a further use of anti-Jewish polemic, including against the dyophysite teachings associated with Nestorius. For their opponents, these so-called "Jewish" heretics included not only Nestorius himself but also the East Syrian Christians who followed the dyophysite teachings of Theodore of Mopsuestia, as well as (for miaphysite Christians) Christians whose acceptance of the Council of Chalcedon seemed to their opponents to be a revival of Nestorius's teachings. Leaders like Timothy I would later also use this rhetoric to denigrate Muslims as the latest in this long line of "new Jews." Syriac Christianity thus has a history of sharing more in common with its contemporary Jewish communities than did many other Christians while concurrently mirroring other forms of Christianity in its development of sharp anti-Jewish narrative traditions. Modern readers should be attuned to the dangerous and harmful potential of these violent representations for later communities.

Further Reading   For one of the foundational studies on this topic, see Jacob Neusner, *Aphrahat and Judaism: The Christian-Jewish Argument in Fourth-Century Iran* (Leiden: Brill, 1971). Two essays are particularly noteworthy for their contributions to this area of study: Giles Rouwhorst, "Jewish Liturgical Traditions in Early Syriac Christianity," *Vigiliae Christianae* 51 (1997): 74–82; and Charlotte Fonrobert, "The Didascalia Apostolorum: A Mishnah for the Disciples of Jesus," *Journal of Early Christian Studies* 9 (2001): 483–511.

More recently, see Christine Shepardson, *Anti-Judaism and Christian Orthodoxy: Ephrem's Hymns in Fourth-Century Syria* (Washington, DC: Catholic University of America Press, 2003) and *Jews and Syriac Christians: Intersections across the First Millenium,* Aaron Michael Butts and Simcha Gross, eds. (Tübingen: Mohr Siebeck, 2020).

DIDASCALIA

Third century. Syriac translation of Greek original.

The *Didascalia Apostolorum*, or "teachings of the apostles," is one of many early Christian texts whose origins remain difficult to pinpoint. While the text itself claims to be teachings agreed upon and narrated by the twelve apostles along with Paul and Jesus's brother James, most scholars agree that third-century Syria is a likely provenance for this text, which originated in Greek but has had a particularly long manuscript history in Syriac. The *Didascalia* addresses followers of Christ whose practices it considered too "Jewish" to be appropriately "Christian." The text instructs them to stop following what it calls the "reiterated law" (which modern scholars often translate as the "second legislation"), the expectations of Jewish law laid out in the Hebrew Bible that most Christians believed were no longer necessary after Jesus's resurrection. Rather, Christians should follow only the "first law," or what many Christians today call the ten commandments. In addition to arguing that the time of the reiterated law has passed, this excerpt tries to draw a sharp distinction between "the people" of the Jews and the followers of Christ in order to encourage a clearer separation between the practices of these communities, particularly around the Passover holiday. For an additional excerpt from the *Didascalia*, see chapter 4.

> Because of the blindness of the people [i.e., the Jews] a great darkness was surrounding them. For they had seen Jesus, but they did not realize or understand that he is Christ, neither from the books of the prophets, nor even from the things he did and the healings he performed. And to those of you from the people [i.e., the Jews] who believe in Jesus we say, "Learn how scripture attests concerning us and says, 'they have seen a great light.'" Thus, you who have believed in him, you have seen a great light, Jesus Christ our Lord, and furthermore, may those who will believe in him see!
>
> But those "who sit in the shadows of death," you are those from among the peoples [i.e., the Gentiles] because you were in the shadows of death, for you were trusting in idolatry and did not know God. But when Jesus Christ our Lord and teacher appeared to us, a light dawned over you, since you looked for and trusted in the promise of the eternal kingdom. You separated yourselves from the custom and lifestyle of your previous error, and you no longer worship idols as you previously had been doing. Rather, a long time ago you believed and were baptized in him, and a great light has dawned over you. So, then, because the people did not obey, it got dark, but the obedience of you who are from among the peoples has become light. Because of this, pray, then, and petition for them, and especially during

the days of Passover, so that by your prayers they might become worthy of forgiveness and turn toward our Lord Jesus Christ. [. . .]

You who have turned away from the people [i.e., the Jews] to believe in God our savior, Jesus Christ, do not continue any further in your former lifestyle, friends [lit., brothers], by keeping useless restrictions: purifications, sprinklings, ritual bathings, and distinction of foods. For our Lord said to you, "Do not remember former things: look, I am making everything new! I am telling you the good news of these present matters, so that you might recognize them. And I will make a road in the desert." Thus the churches used to be deserts, places where there is now an immense road, with knowledge of the unerring, new, and clear religion [lit., fear of God]—that is, Jesus Christ and all his guidance from the beginning.

For you knew that he gave a simple, pure, and holy law of life, in which our savior has put his name: he made ten statements, and thus indicated "Jesus," since "ten" indicates the letter *yod* [the tenth letter of Syriac script], and *yod* is the beginning of Jesus's name [in Syriac].

Thus, through David the Lord testifies about the law and says, "The Lord's law is faultless and restores souls." And, so too, everywhere many other similar things have been mentioned. For in another place at the end of the books of the prophets, the Lord spoke through the messenger Malachi and said, "Remember the law of Moses, the Lord's slave, according to the commandments and judgments he has given you." In addition, our savior, to show that he would not destroy the law, when he had cleansed the leper, he pointed him to the law and said to him, "Go, show yourself to the chief priests and make an offering for your cleansing, just like Moses commanded, as a witness to them." But our savior teaches a reiterated law, and why a reiterated law? Because he said, "I have not come to destroy either the law or the prophets, but to fulfill them." The law, then, cannot be undone, but the reiterated law is temporary and can be. [. . .]

Thus, then the law is easy and light, without being quiet. But when the people denied God [. . .] and said, "We have no God to go before us," and they cast a molten calf for themselves, bowed down to it, and sacrificed to what they had shaped. So, the Lord was angry, and in the heat of his anger, along with the mercy of his grace, he bound them with the reiterated law. He put heavy burdens on them and a harsh yoke on their necks. And he no longer says, as before, "if you should do . . .," but rather—as if he had need of them—he says, "Make an altar, and be sacrificing continually."

Therefore he required continual burnt sacrifices of them and he separated them from certain foods using food distinctions. For from that point animals were recognized as clean and unclean meat. From that point there were distinctions, purifications, ritual bathings, and sprinklings. From that point sacrifices, offerings, and ritual meals. From that point burnt sacrifices, offerings, showbread, sending up sacrifices, first-borns, redemptions, young goats for sins, vows, and many other shocking things that had been prescribed to them as unspeakable customs thanks to a large amount of sins. But they did not persevere in any of them, but rather, they angered God again, so, with the reiterated law he further increased over them the blindness worthy of their deeds. [. . .]

If, woman, as you say, during your time of menstruation you are empty [of the holy spirit], unclean spirits will fill you. For when an unclean spirit turns to you and finds an opportunity in you, it can enter and dwell in you forever, and then there will be the entrance of an unclean spirit, with the exit of the holy spirit, and an on-going battle. Because of this, you foolish women, thanks to your views and thanks to these observances you keep, these things will happen to you, and thanks to your set opinion you will be emptied of the holy spirit, filled with unclean spirits, and be cast out of eternal life into unending, fiery burning.

Woman, again I say to you: as it is in the reiterated law, you should consider yourself unclean during your seven days of menstruation, so how can you be cleansed after seven days without ritual bathing? And if you should bathe in that way through which you believe you would be purified, you would annul God's perfect baptism, which has completely forgiven your sins, and you would be found in the evils of your previous sins and would be delivered to eternal fire. But if, in accord with your set opinion, you do not bathe, you will continue to be unclean and the vain seven-day observance will not have helped you at all, but rather will actually be extremely harmful to you, since in your opinion you are unclean, and you will incur guilt as an unclean person.

This is how to think about everyone who observes restrictions having to do with seminal emissions and having sex. For all these observances are stupid and harmful, for if, when someone has sex or a seminal emission, he has to bathe and wash his mattress, it is going to become a chore and an incessant annoyance to him: he would just be bathing and washing his clothes and mattress and unable to do anything else. For if you bathe after a seminal emission or having sex, as in the reiterated law, you are even obligated for a mouse. If you should step on one, you have to bathe, but you will never become pure, since even the shoes on your feet come from the skin of dead animals and you wear shoes from hide that was sacrificed to idols. In addition, you are wearing clothes made of wool that comes from similar animals. If you step on a bone or go into a cemetery, you are obligated to bathe, but you would never become pure and you would annul God's baptism. You will renew your offenses; you will be found in your previous sins; you will affirm the reiterated law; and you will accept the idolatry of the calf as your own. For if you accept the reiterated law as your own, accept idolatry, too, since the reiterated law was established because of idolatry. You are pulling and piling your previous sins onto yourself like pulling a long rope or a wagon strap, and also piling woe onto yourself. For when you affirm the reiterated law, you are happy with the curse against our savior and you denounce the blessed Christ, he who distributes a blessing to those who are worthy. So you will inherit a curse, for all who curse someone will be cursed, and all who bless will be blessed. May those who affirm the curse against our savior, Lord, and God be handed over to whatever curses, whatever judgment, or whatever condemnation!

So you have to run away and distance yourselves from observances like these, for you have been liberated: don't tie yourselves up again, and don't reburden yourself with what our Lord and savior has unburdened you of. Don't be observing these things and thinking they have to do with uncleanness. Don't be abstaining because of them. Don't be looking for sprinklings, bathings, or purifications like this. For in the reiterated law, if someone comes close to a corpse or a grave, they bathe. But you, just as in the gospel and according to the power of the Holy Spirit, may gather and read scripture even in cemeteries, you may complete your worship and petitions to God without observances, and may offer an acceptable Eucharist.

APHRAHAT, *DEMONSTRATIONS* 11

344.

Aphrahat is a rare early witness to Syriac Christianity in the Sasanian Empire. He seems to have written from among the Persians during a period when the region's Jews were sometimes more welcomed by the Sasanian government than were the Christians, whose loyalties may have been considered to be increasingly suspect with the rise of other Christians' imperial power in the neighboring Roman Empire. A number of Aphrahat's twenty-three *Demonstrations* address a concern that his audience is participating in Jewish traditions such as the celebration of Passover. In this excerpt Aphrahat discusses a succession of covenants with God in order to argue that Jesus's covenant supersedes the earlier covenant that required male circumcision, and that Christian faith rather than Jewish circumcision is the new mark of God's true people. For additional excerpts from Aphrahat's *Demonstrations*, see chapters 5 and 7.

> When God blessed Abraham and made him the leader of all the faithful, the righteous, and the upright, God was not making him the father of one people, but of many peoples, since he said to him, "Your name will not be 'Abram,' but rather your name will be 'Abraham,' for I have made you the father of a multitude of peoples." Now, dear friend, listen [as I discuss] the significance of [this] saying, and the basis of the dispute that we are justified in having with that people who preceded us, who believe that they are the seed of Abraham. They do not understand that they have been called "rulers of Sodom" and "people of Gomorrah," that their father was an Amorite and their mother a Hittite, and that they are rejected silver and rebellious children. [. . .]
>
> This is known to all who consider [the matter]: circumcision is of no use without faith, [nor is there] any profit [in it], since faith is before circumcision, and circumcision [was only] a mark. A covenant was given to Abraham when God said to him, "This is my covenant, that you will keep by circumcising every male." During the time that it pleased the one who gave it, [circumcision] was kept along with the commandments of the law, [and] it benefited and gave [them] life. But during the time when the law was not kept, circumcision did not benefit [them] at all. Jereboam, son of Nabat, from the descendants of Joseph, from the tribe of Ephraim, was circumcised as the holy one commanded Abraham, and as Moses admonished in the law. All the kings of Israel who walked in the law of Jereboam were circumcised and set apart, but because of their sins, a good memory of them was not preserved. How did Jereboam benefit from his circumcision, [he] and all the kings of Israel who walked in his footsteps? And what use or benefit was [circumcision] to Manessah son of Hezekiah, on account of whose sins[, which multiplied,] God was unable to forgive Jerusalem again?
>
> In each generation, as it pleased him, God gave his covenants to all generations and tribes, and they were kept in their [various] times but [then] replaced. He commanded Adam not to eat from the tree of the knowledge of good and evil, but because he did not keep the commandment and the covenant, he was condemned. As for Enoch, who was pleasing to

God, it was not [because] the commandment about the tree was kept by him that [God] took him to [the land of] life, but because he was faithful. [Being] pleasing [to God] did not resemble [keeping] the commandment not to eat from the tree. [God] saved Noah, who kept [his] integrity and righteousness, from the wrath of the flood. He made a covenant with him and with the generations after him, so that they might increase and multiply: the covenant of the rainbow, between God, the earth, and all flesh. Circumcision was not given with one of these covenants. When [God] chose Abraham, it was not because of circumcision that he called him and chose him and named him to become a father for all peoples, but because of faith. [. . .]

In each case the law and the covenant were changed. First, God changed the covenant of Adam and gave another [one] to Noah. He also gave [one] to Abraham, but he changed that [one] and gave another [one] to Moses. When [the covenant] of Moses was not kept, he gave another [one] in the final generation, a covenant that will not be changed. [. . .] The circumcision that pleases the one who gave the covenants is that concerning which Jeremiah spoke: "Circumcise the foreskin of your hearts." [. . .] Our God is true, and his covenants are very trustworthy, and each covenant in its time was true and [able to] be trusted. Those who are circumcised in heart live, and they are circumcised a second time at the true Jordan, the baptism of the forgiveness of sins.

EPHREM, *HYMNS ON UNLEAVENED BREAD* 19; *HYMNS ON FAITH* 87; *HYMNS ON VIRGINITY* 28

Mid to late fourth century.

The poet-deacon Ephrem (d. 373) is celebrated in Syriac traditions as the "Harp of the Spirit" for his beautiful poetry, some of which was performed liturgically by women's choirs. In addition to playing a foundational role in Syriac theology and biblical interpretation, however, Ephrem was also a sharp polemicist against those whose teachings he believed were harmful, such as Mani, Marcion, Bardaisan, and "Arian" Christians who did not accept the Council of Nicaea. Much of his criticism, though, was reserved for Jews and those among his own audience who, in his view, shared too much in common with Jews' beliefs or practices. The first excerpt below comes from a series of hymns directed against the unleavened bread of the Passover. Reproduced in full, this hymn includes virulent anti-Jewish language that associates fourth-century Jews in Ephrem's region with the crowd that called for Jesus's death in Matthew 27:25. The second excerpt addresses the doctrinal concerns that followed the Council of Nicaea in 325, using anti-Jewish rhetoric to condemn other Christians with whom Ephrem disagreed. In particular, Ephrem criticizes Christians who, like the Eunomians and Anomeans (so-called "Neo-Arians"), claimed to be able to use human logic to understand God rather than relying simply on faith. In this hymn, Ephrem claims that Satan exchanged "the people" of the Jews, who earlier abused Jesus, for these new Christian heretics, through whom Satan abuses Christ anew. The third excerpt illustrates yet another way in which Ephrem relied on anti-Judaism to define Christianity. In this hymn, Ephrem speaks of the "symbols" of the Christian Old Testament that he understands to have been fulfilled in the life, death, and resurrection of Jesus as the messiah. Ephrem argues that the Jews misunderstand their own scripture and that only Christians read and understand correctly the ways in which Jesus's story was prophetically foretold. In the process of claiming authority over these shared texts, Ephrem further denigrates Jews by referring to them simply as "the crucifiers." In its early context, such language served the purpose of trying to draw sharper boundaries around Christianity and grant Christians authority over Jewish scripture. The same language of course became increasingly harmful as Christians gained more power. For additional excerpts from Ephrem, see chapters 1, 2, 3, and 7.

HYMNS ON UNLEAVENED BREAD 19

The lamb of truth arose and broke his body
    For the innocent ones who ate the lamb of Passover.
Refrain: Glory be to Christ through whose body the unleavened bread of the [Jewish]
    people became obsolete, together with the people itself.
The paschal lamb he slaughtered and ate, and he broke his body.
    He caused the shadow to pass over and he provided the truth.
He had eaten the unleavened bread. Within the unleavened bread
    His body became for us the unleavened bread of truth.
Ended there was the symbol that ran
    From the days of Moses until there.
But the evil people that wants our death,
    Enticing, gives us death in food.
Desirable was the tree that Eve saw,
    And equally desirable is the unleavened bread.
From that desirable [tree], a manifest death;
    In the beautiful unleavened bread, a concealed death.
Although the dead lion was impure,
    Its bitterness gave sweetness [Judges 14:8–9].
In the bitter lion, beautiful honey;
    In the sweet unleavened bread, the bitterness of death.
On account of its symbol, the angels yearned
    For that unleavened bread that Sarah had baked [Genesis 18:1–15].
Loathe the unleavened bread, you, my friends [lit., brothers],
    In which the symbol of [Judas] Iscariot dwells!
Moreover, flee, my friends, from the unleavened bread
    Because stench dwells within its purity.
For that putrid reputation that Moses described
    Indeed dwells in the purity of that unleavened bread.
Garlic and onions the people had desired [Numbers 11:5].

Their unleavened bread itself stank, together with the eating of it.
From the impure ravens Elijah took
   Loaves because he knew that they were pure [1 Kings 17:6].
Do not take, my friends, that unleavened bread
   From the people whose hands are covered with blood,
Lest it cling to that unleavened bread
   From that filth that fills their hands.
Although flesh is pure, no one eats
   From that which was sacrificed [to idols] because it is unclean.
How impure therefore is that unleavened bread
   That the hands that killed the Son kneaded!
The hand that is defiled with the blood of animals,
   One is loathe to take food from that [hand].
Who would therefore take from that hand
   That is completely defiled with the blood of the prophets?
Let us not eat, my friends, along with the drug of life [i.e., the Eucharist]
   The unleavened bread of the people as a deadly drug.
For the blood of Christ mixed in and dwells
   In the unleavened bread of the people and in our [Eucharist] offering.
The one who received it in our offering received the drug of life.
   The one who ate it with the people received a deadly drug.
For that blood for which they cried out that it might be upon them [Matthew 27.25]
   Is mixed in their festivals and in their Sabbaths.
And whoever is joined together in their festivals,
   To that one the sprinkling of the blood also comes.
The people that does not eat from a pig
   Is a pig that wallows in much blood.
Flee and distance yourself from [the Jewish people]! Look, it shakes itself off!
   Do not let the sprinkling of the blood contaminate you!

HYMNS ON FAITH 87

As in a contest, I saw debaters,
Prideful. They were worn down
From [trying to] taste fire, see the wind,
Touch the light. On the basis of [just] a beam,
They strained to make distinctions.

Refrain: Glory to the Father, and to his Son Jesus, and to his Holy Spirit.

The Son, who is more subtle than the mind,
They wanted to explore. The Holy Spirit,
Who cannot be touched, they thought they could touch
With their questions. And the Father, who is eternally
Inexplicable, his debaters [tried to] explain.

A good example of our faith
[Is that] of Abraham, of our repentance,
The Ninevites, and the house of Rahab,
Of our hope. For us there are the prophets,
For us there are the apostles. The evil one grows envious. [. . .]

That bitter one saw good order
And upturned it. He saw hateful things
And sowed them. He saw hope
And suppressed and severed it. The debating that he planted,
Look: it has yielded the fruit of the poison of [the serpent's] teeth.

Satan saw that the truth had strangled him
And his weeds, and he went off
To devise [new] plots and lay snares
For the faith. He shot at priests
The arrows that those in authority love. [. . .]

Satan stripped off the first scribes
And put on others. The people, worn out,
The worm and the locust had gnawed and consumed them,
Then abandoned and left them. The worm has come
To the new garment of the new people.

He saw the crucifiers, that they were rejected and cast away
As strangers. From among those of the same family,
He made investigators. From worshippers
There came debaters. From that garment
He brought forth the worm and placed it all around.

He brought forth the locust in a wheat granary,
And sat and watched. A pure storehouse,
Look: it was desolated. Look: the garments of glory
Have been eaten. He mocks us,
And we [mock] ourselves, for we are drunk.

He sowed weeds and planted brambles
In a pure vineyard. He defiled the flock
And leprosy spread. Lambs upon lambs
Became his possessions. He began among the people,
But came to the peoples to finish.

Instead of that reed that the first people
Held out to the Son, the last [peoples], presuming
In their treatises, have written with a reed
That he is [only] human. The evil one has exchanged
A reed for a reed against our redeemer.

Instead of the garments of many colors
In which [the people] clothed him, they have dyed a title

Falsely. Many names
He has put on, whether creature
Or thing-made, though he is the maker.

While [the people] [braided] a crown for him from mute,
Quiet thorns, wordy thorns
Of the mind he has woven together out loud
As hymns. And he has hidden unnoticed
Briars inside songs.

Satan saw that he had been exposed
In the former things, when he manifested the spitting,
The vinegar, the thorns, the nails, the cross,
The garments, the reed, and the lance that smote him.
They were despised and obvious, so he changed his plans.

He introduced error, instead of the slap
That our Lord received. Instead of spitting,
Disputing arose, and instead of garments,
Hidden schisms. Instead of the reed,
Controversy arose to afflict all.

Pride called out to anger, her sister.
Envy and wrath, arrogance and guile
Replied and came along. They have taken counsel
Against our savior, just as on that day
They took counsel, when [our savior] suffered.

Instead of the cross, controversy is
A hidden cross. Instead of nails,
Questions have entered. Instead of Sheol,
Denial. A second passion
Satan wished to renew.

Instead of the sponge moistened with vinegar,
He has given arrows—investigation, utterly
Soaked with death. The gall that he gave,
Our Lord spit out. The fraudulent investigation
That the bitter one gave has pleased fools.

Though in that time there was a judge
Against them, look: judges
[Stand] as if against us. And instead of an inscription,
Their ordinances. The crown is absolved,
For priests have placed stumbling blocks before kings.

Instead of the priesthood praying
On behalf of the kingdom that wars would cease
From humanity, they have urged them

Toward a perverse war, so that kings begin
To fight against their cities.

O our Lord, reconcile priests and kings.
In one church, let priests pray
For their kings, and kings show mercy
To their cities. And the quiet within,
Through you, may it be for us a wall without.

HYMNS ON VIRGINITY 28

Refrain: Glory to your highness

The scattered symbols you [God] have gathered
From the Torah toward your beauty,
And you set forth the prototypes in your gospel
And powers and signs from nature.
You mixed pigments for your portrait.
You were observed by yourself and you portray yourself,
O painter who also portrayed his Father in himself!
The two portray one another.

Prophets, kings, and priests, all of them created,
Have portrayed you, though they were unlike you.
Created servants are not at all sufficient,
For you alone are sufficient to portray yourself.
Your portrait has been fully drawn.
You perfected it by your advent.
The drawings were swallowed up by the strength of the pigments,
Resplendent in all colors.

Faded is the drawing of the temporal lamb.
Resplendent is the glory of the true lamb.
Very weak too is the drawing of the staff
[___] the cross of light
[___] and the fixed serpent:
In the wilderness it portrayed the crucified body.
The transitory symbols have been completed and swallowed up
By the truth that does not pass away.

The daybreak that is from you, the dawn that is from you
Confined and swallowed [___]
By the shining forth of your advent the shadows have been illuminated.
The types have come to an end, but the allusions persist.
The flash of the symbols has been swallowed up by your rays.
Your symbols have passed away, but your prophets have not passed away.
The [Jewish] people have erred in their reading of the prophets,
And they maintained that you were not you. [. . .]

He is the glorious, immutable nature,
But because of his love, he acquired changes.
Colors were put on: the symbols and types,
And also all the prototypes and all the life stages.
The crucifiers saw him and dishonored him.
The tares saw him and made him alien.
The church has seen him and, while knowing his nature,
Worships his changes.

TEACHING OF ADDAI

Late fourth or early fifth century. West Syrian.

The *Teaching of Addai* includes a number of noteworthy stories, including an early tradition of letters that were exchanged between Jesus and Abgar, the king of Edessa, along with the arrival of a painted portrait of Jesus. This excerpt is one of numerous places in the text that are sharply negative toward Jews. In this part of the story, the wife of the first-century Roman emperor Claudius, who was allegedly an ancestor of Constantine, renounces her pagan traditions after seeing miracles performed by one of Jesus's apostles; she then travels to Jerusalem to see the place of his crucifixion, where she ostensibly discovers the true cross on which Jesus was crucified. This story is a successor to an earlier fourth-century tradition that Constantine's mother Helena discovered the true cross. The so-called "crucifying Jews" stand on the periphery of both discovery stories as shadowy and hostile narrative figures who try to impede the unstoppable triumph of Christianity at every turn. The vignette here ends with the claim that the emperor ordered all Jews to leave Italy. For an additional excerpt from the *Teaching of Addai*, see chapter 1.

> Protonike, the wife of Claudius Caesar, [...] when Simon, one of the disciples, was in the city of Rome, saw the signs and wonders and astonishing powers that he performed in the name of the messiah [and] recanted the paganism of her fathers in which she lived, even the pagan idols that she worshipped. She believed in our Lord the messiah, worshipped and glorified [him] along with those who were followers of Simon, and held him in great honor. Later she wished also to see Jerusalem and the places where the mighty deeds of our Lord had been performed. So she arose with zeal and went down from Rome to Jerusalem, she and her two sons with her and her one virgin daughter.
>
> When she entered Jerusalem, the city came out to meet her. They received her in great honor as due to the lady empress of the great region of the Romans. [As for] James, who was made leader and prefect over the church that was built for us there, when he heard why she had come there, he arose and went to her and entered in before her where she was dwelling in the great palace of the royal house of King Herod. When she saw him, she received him with great joy, even as [she had received] Simon Peter. He also showed her healings and miracles like Simon.

She said to him, "Show me Golgotha where the messiah was crucified, the wood of his cross on which he was hung by the Jews, and the grave where he was laid." James said to her, "These three things that your majesty wishes to see are under the authority of the Jews. They control them and do not permit us to go and pray there before Golgotha and the grave. They are not even willing to give us the wood of his cross. And not only this, but they persecute us that we not preach or proclaim in the name of the messiah. Often also they confine us in prison."

When she heard these things, the empress immediately ordered that they bring before her Onias, the son of Hanan the priest, Gedalia, the son of Caiaphas, and Judah, the son of Ebed Shalom, chiefs and officers of the Jews. She said to them, "Deliver Golgotha, the grave, and the wood of the cross to James and to those who follow him. Let no one hinder them from offering service there according to the custom of their worship."

When she had thus ordered the priests, she arose to go and see those places, and to hand over the area to James and to those who were with him. Later, when she entered the tomb, she found within the tomb three crosses, one belonging to our Lord, and two to the thieves who were crucified with him on his right and left sides. In the moment that she entered the tomb, she and her children with her, in that very instant, her virgin daughter fell down and died without pain, illness, or any cause of death. When the empress saw that her daughter had suddenly died, she kneeled and prayed within the tomb the following prayer: "The God who gave himself to death for all people, being crucified in this place and laid in this tomb, and who as God gives life to all, arose and brought many to life with him, whom the crucifying Jews will not hear as well as the erring pagans, whose idols, graven images, and pagan worship I have renounced. Now they will look on me with mockery." [. . .]

While she was saying these things in her prayer and was relating [them] in the suffering of her crying out in front of all who were there, her oldest son came near and said to her, "Listen to what I have to say, your majesty. In my mind and reasoning I think that this sudden death of my sister was not in vain; it was rather a marvelous visitation by which God could be glorified—it did not happen that his name be blasphemed—in order that those who hear might believe. Look, we entered the tomb and found three crosses in it. We do not know which one of them is the cross upon which the messiah was hung. By the death of my sister we are able to perceive and learn which cross is the messiah's because the messiah will not turn away from those who believe in and seek him." [. . .]

After she had waited a long time, she took the second cross from her daughter and, taking the third cross, placed it upon her daughter. When she attempted to raise her eyes to heaven and open her mouth in prayer, immediately, in that instant, in the twinkling of an eye, as the cross touched the corpse of her daughter, her daughter came back to life, suddenly arose, and glorified God who had restored her to life by his cross. [. . .] Then the crowd of Jews and pagans who had been happy at the beginning of this affair and cheerful became very sad at the end of it. [. . .]

When the empress went up from Jerusalem to the city of Rome, every city that she entered thronged together to catch a glimpse of her daughter. Upon entering Rome she related the things that had happened to Claudius Caesar. When Caesar heard it, he commanded all the Jews to leave the region of Italy, since in this whole region this event was spoken of by many. She also told Simon Peter what had happened.

ISAAC OF ANTIOCH, *HOMILIES AGAINST THE JEWS* 2

Late fifth century. West Syrian.

This series of homilies has been attributed to Isaac of Antioch, whom Jacob of Edessa (d. 708) notes spent time in Edessa and Antioch and flourished during the reign of the emperor Zeno in the late fifth century. Nevertheless, because Jacob refers to more than one person by this name, it is difficult to be certain of this text's context. This second homily in the series tries to discredit the notion that God loves the Jewish "people" more than the Christian "peoples" (or "nations"), and argues that the Jews' own scripture condemns them and their law. It includes a unique metaphor of circumcision as a temporary seal for protecting the riches of the lineage, with the Jews as a dragon protecting the treasure of the law. It argues, however, that through Christ the riches were removed and given to all the nations, leaving the Jews devoid of God's riches and removing the need for the fleshly seal.

I have a judgment with Jacob,
And a discourse with the Jews.
If we all have one Father,
Why should anyone feel superior to the [gentile] nations?

I belong to the nations,
And on behalf of my people I speak.
What do you think, O [Jewish] people,
Did the Lord not create us as well as you?

If God created us and you,
He loves us as well as you.
If your begetter did not beget us [too],
[Then] you have in mind another God.

But if your begetter is one,
He doesn't love you any more than me,
And you are no closer to [his] thoughts
Than I or my people. [. . .]

From this very law of yours
You may learn of its invalidation.
The weapon that you have seized [turns] against you,
And the arrow that you have shot is wounding you.

For since the law itself proclaims
That the righteous ones triumphed who did not observe it,
It [thereby] shows great contempt for those who observed it
But did not achieve the measure of the ancients.

By lengthily narrating the fame
Of those who were without the law,

It proclaims its own invalidation
Since the ancients lived without it. [. . .]

Is it not after you turned astray
From the Lord after the [golden] calf
[That] there came down for you from Mount Sinai
A chain for your bonds,

A heavy yoke that was cast
As if upon your rebellious neck.
And bonds and a shackle it was for you
That you would not leave your Lord. [. . .]

Moses revoked the judgment of Jacob,
And gave Reuben the inheritance.
The messiah revoked the curse of Moses,
And made the nations enter the inheritance. [. . .]

Circumcision, you fool, was [just] a seal.
It protected the treasury [that was] in your Father.
Now that [its] riches have come forth,
Of what use is the seal to you?

There is a sealed money bag that is empty.
Is [this] not you, O Jews?
The treasure is dug out from you.
Why do you use the seal? [. . .]

And when the riches within them went forth
Because of which they were sealed,
They remained open in a ruined state and were made
A latrine like you are.

So the Jews
Were stamped with circumcision
Because of the seed of everlasting life
That was preserved within them until the proper time.

And when that which [the seal] was [to protect] went forth,
Seal and stamp became ineffective.
Behold, they are ruined, destroyed, and despoiled,
And [yet] they are proud of the seal upon them.

The treasure is dug out and taken away.
[Its] riches have come forth, but the seal stands.
Now you might say, "Behold the treasure is with you.
Why do you not use the stamp?" [. . .]

O people, you were the guardians
Of the riches that were preserved for the nations.

You want to continue circumcising; you will not give peace.
Would that each of you would cut all the way. [. . .]

I am circumcised, not in [the] flesh,
But rather [with] circumcision that is not [done] with hands.
Not with the removal of flesh, but
In the spirit, by a removal that [removes] from evil.

I have removed the entire flesh
With the circumcision of baptism.
Not like you, who of the little
Flesh that you cut off are proud.

By nature I am your brother,
Though you have alienated us from you.
Come, inherit with me in the messiah.
I am not envious like you.

I do not bar you from entering
The house of holiness, as you have barred us.
For you put guards at the gates,
That the Ammonite would not enter.

I know that God will not
Reject you if you return.
And he loves you as [he loves] me,
If you follow the right course.

Come, inherit God with me,
And he will not recall your waywardness.
Seek vindication through the Son whom you have crucified,
And he will not remember your bitterness. [. . .]

Like a dragon upon a treasure
You sat on the law.
And like a heap of stones they cleared and cast you away,
That the riches beneath you might be used.

SIMEON OF BET ARSHAM, *LETTERS* 1

524. West Syrian.

This excerpt is a letter within a letter, the latter of which is attributed to Simeon of Bet Arsham and has been dated to 524. Simeon's letter states that during his recent travels to King Mundhir, the leader of the Christian Arab Lakhmids, the king had received a report recounting the death of a Christian king in the southern Arabian peninsula, the land's annexation by a Jewish king of Himyar, and the ensuing martyrdom of many of the region's Christians, including those of the city of Najran in the southwestern Arabian peninsula in 518 or 523. This excerpt is primarily from the letter to Mundhir included in Simeon's letter, with a few of Simeon's comments from his own letter at the end. These martyrdoms are unusual in Christian history for being attributed to a Jewish ruler.

"Let it be known, O my brother Mundhir the king, that the king whom the Kushites had established in our region died. The winter season came and the Kushites were not able to march out to our region to establish a Christian king as they were accustomed to do. Therefore I ruled over the entire territory of the Himyarites. At first, I captured all the Christians who confessed Christ unless they became Jews like us. And I killed 280 priests who were present, along with the Kushites who were guarding the church, and I turned their church into a synagogue of ours. Then with an army 120,000 strong I marched to Najran, their capital. After I besieged it for several days and could not subdue it, I swore oaths with them but I decided not to keep my promise to my enemies the Christians. So I detained them and required them to bring in their gold, silver, and properties, which they brought to me and I collected. I sought Paul their bishop and when they told me that he was dead, I did not believe them until they showed me his grave. So I exhumed his bones and burned them. I compelled their priests and all those whom I found taking refuge in their church, and the rest, to renounce Christ and the cross. But they did not want to. Rather, they confessed that he was God and the Son of the blessed one and chose to die for his sake.

Their chief said many things against me and insulted me, so I ordered that all their nobles be killed. We brought their wives and exhorted them to apostatize while they were witnessing the massacre of their husbands on account of Christ, and to have mercy on their sons and daughters, but they did not want to. But female monks insisted on being killed first, and the wives of the nobles reproached them, saying, 'We ought to die after our husbands!' And by our order all of them were killed except for Rehumi—wife of him who was to become king there—whom we did not let die. But we required her to renounce Christ in order to live and to become a Jew and have mercy upon her daughters and keep all that she had. So we ordered her to go and take counsel while accompanied by guards from our army. Nonetheless, she went out moving around in the streets and squares of the city bareheaded—a woman whose figure none has seen in the street since she came to maturity. [. . .]

When we heard the sound of wailing coming from the city, those who were dispatched came. And when they were asked, they told us as we wrote above, that Rehumi, while moving around in the city, spoke to the women who were her companions, encouraging them, and a wailing took place in the city. We were furious at the guards to the point of killing them—if we had not been persuaded not to—for allowing her to do these things. Finally, like a mad woman and with her head uncovered she came out from the city with her daughters; and she stood up before me without shame, holding her daughters by the hand, who were adorned as if for marriage. She untied the braids of her hair, wound them round her hands, stretched out her neck and bent her head, while shouting, 'I am a Christian and so are my daughters, and for Christ we die! Cut off our heads that we may go and reach our brothers and sisters and the father of my daughters!'

As for me, after all this madness, I exhorted her to renounce Christ and to say that he was only a man, but she did not want to. One of her daughters insulted us because we said this. As I realized that she would not renounce Christ in any way, in order to terrorize the rest of the Christians, I ordered her thrown on the ground; her daughters were slaughtered and their blood ran down to her mouth, and then her head was severed.

I swear by Adonai that I grieved very much because of her beauty and that of her daughters. My chief priests and I thought that according to the law it was not right that children should die because of the parents. Therefore, I assigned the boys and girls to the army to be raised. Once they come to maturity, if they become Jews they will live, and if they confess Christ they will die. I wrote these things and made them known to your majesty. And I am making a petition to you not to leave a Christian among your people unless he apostatizes and becomes one of yours. As for the Jews, my brothers and sisters who are under your authority, treat them kindly, my brother, and write and send word to me, and I will send what you wish in return for this."

All of these things were written to Mundhir by the impure Jewish king. [. . .] All the Christians of this place were distressed at these letters and at the news they heard. So, in order to inform the venerable bishops and believers about these events that happened in the land of the Himyarites, we wrote them down that they may keep the commemoration of the holy martyrs. We beg you, dearest, that the events be made known quickly to the abbots, bishops, and especially the patriarch of Alexandria so that he may write to the king of the Kushites to be prepared to help the Himyarites speedily. Let the chief priests of the Jews who are in Tiberias also be held and pressured to send a message to this Jewish king who has appeared, so that he may put an end to the strife and persecution in the land of the Himyarites.

BOOK OF THE HIMYARITES

Sixth to tenth century. West Syrian.

This anonymous book from a tenth-century manuscript includes stories of the early sixth-century Christian martyrs of the city of Najran on the Arabian peninsula. As noted in the excerpt above, the region of Himyar was at the time under the control of a Jewish king who sent forces to require the Christians in the nearby city of Najran to abandon their commitment to Christianity and become Jews. Sources describe a brutal massacre of Christians in Najran that eventually prompted the Christian Roman emperor Justin I to work with Ethiopian Christian leaders to overthrow the Himyarites. This excerpt about the women Habsa, Hayya, and Hayya is typical of Christian martyr narratives in some respects, but the emphasis on the fact that their persecutors are Jews sets this text apart. The text repeatedly refers to the Jews as "crucifiers," associating the martyrs' sixth-century opponents with those whom Christians blamed for killing the messiah. This epithet was commonplace in Christian literature, inspired in part by the Gospel of Matthew's implication that all future generations bore responsibility for the crucifixion. The text's insistence that survivors were hampered in their efforts to recover and honor the martyrs' bodies because of a "fear of the Jews" echoes language in the Gospel of John.

> There was in Najran among the other believing [Christian] freeborn women, those who were not yet seized by the Jews that they should deny [Christ], one freeborn woman also, the name of whom was Habsa, of the family of Hayyan, son of Hayyan, the teacher, him by the care of whom it is written above in the beginning of this book that Christianity was sown in the town of Najran and in the land of the Himyarites. When, then, this excellent woman heard about all the harm that was done to the freeborn women by the Jewish crucifiers on account of their belief in Christ, [who is] our hope, she grieved exceedingly that she was not among them, and so she wept and said, "Our Lord, Jesus Christ, regard not my sins and exclude me not from the rank of martyrdom for your sake, but deem me worthy, O my Lord, me also, to be added to the number of those who have loved you and have been put to death for the sake of your worshipped name." And on the day that followed that on which the [other] freeborn women [of Najran] had been crowned [i.e., martyred], which was Monday, this believing Habsa rose and took that little cross of brass she had, sewed it on to her headcloth over its edge, went out into the street, and cried, saying openly, "I am a Christian and I worship Christ." Then there went out to her two other women, freeborn friends of hers, the names of whom were as follows: the one Hayya, and she was an old woman, and the name of the other was Hayya too, and she was a girl. And many of the Najranites also, men and women, came together around them. And this Habsa looked and saw among them a man, her neighbor, who was a Jew. So she called him and said to him: "O you, Jew and crucifier, I renounce you and all who agree with you, since you deny Christ, saying that he is not God, and renounced be your king, that crucifier of his Lord. Go and tell him, "Look, Habsa, daughter of Hayyan, is crying out in the street that she is a Christian and renounces you and all who agree with you." [. . .] When, now, this shedder of innocent blood Masruq heard that from this magnate, he was violently disturbed and enraged against these freeborn women and commanded that they should speedily catch them and bring them before him. And it was quickly done as he had ordered. [. . .]
>
> The impious Masruq said to her, "Whose daughter are you?" Habsa said to him, "I am the daughter of Hayyan of the family of Hayyan, the teacher, him by whom our Lord sowed Christianity in our land. And Hayyan my father once burned your synagogues." The crucifier Masruq said to her, "So then you hold the same opinion as your father. And I think from your words that you too are ready to burn our synagogue just as your father burned it." Habsa said to him, "No, I will not set it on fire in my own person because I am ready speedily to go and join my brothers and sisters in Christ by this way of martyrdom. But we trust in the justice of Jesus Christ, our Lord and our God, that he will speedily remove and destroy your power from among humankind and break down your pride and your life, and extirpate your synagogues from our land, and build in it holy churches, and Christianity will increase or rule in it by the grace of our Lord, and by the prayers of our parents and brothers and sisters who died for the sake of Christ, our Lord. And you and the children of your people shall be an omen and a byword for ages to come, because of all that you as a man without God and without mercy have done to the holy churches and to the worshippers of Christ, God."

And the accursed serpent Masruq breathed out the rage of his heart, as it were, just as a serpent that seeks to suck the blood of a pigeon, and was troubled and oppressed because of all that he heard from Habsa, and planned how to find a manner of death that would suffice to torment this believing woman that had said to him words such as these. And he gave orders, and they threw before him a cross, and brought and placed near him a bowl in which was blood, just as he had done to those who had suffered martyrdom before her. Then he said to her, "Look, now you have spoken abundantly all that you want in your effrontery and you have let me hear things that not even the people before you have said to me. And I highly wonder how you treat me with contempt, as you think, and say this in your boldness. But since you are a woman, I must first ask you to turn back from your error; but afterward, if you do not hear me, I will let you perish bitterly as you deserve. But deny Christ immediately, and spit on this cross, and take with your finger from this blood, and say as we [say] that Christ was a mortal as everyone else, and be a Jew as we are and you shall live and I will give you to a freeborn man and forgive all that you have spoken."

Habsa said to him, "Your mouth that has blasphemed your maker will speedily be shut up from this temporal life, and no offspring will be left after you to revile its creator, O, you crucifier who has hung your Lord on the cross, you who have undertaken to destroy, as you think, all the people of the Christians that are in our land. But you will know that not only will I not say that Christ was a man, but I worship him and praise him because of all the benefits he has shown me. And I believe that he is God, maker of all creatures, and I take refuge in his cross. Now, since you know that I do not shrink from a single one of your tortures, invent all the sufferings you wish and bring them upon me."

The crucifier Masruq said to her, "Now I understand that what I had hoped, that you should be spared from a painful death, has not succeeded, and so your blood be on your head. Therefore I shall speedily deal with you thus, so that you will regret in your mind that you did not listen to my words." [. . .]

And it was done as he ordered and these crucifiers that executed the sentence on them said to them jestingly, "Will you now obey all that the king says to you or are you pleased with this death?" But because these believing ones were not able to speak, they made signs with their hands, meaning, "Yes, we wish to die." Then, in this immense suffering, the blessed Hayya the elder yielded up her spirit to the Lord and was crowned by a good confession for his sake. And when those crucifiers saw that she was dead, they cried aloud and laughed in their madness and said, "Excellently has Christ helped this woman who worshipped him? For he has not saved her from this suffering but, look, she has died like an animal. And they removed the body of the blessed Hayya and brought it out and threw it outside the encampment. But in the night, some of the Christians, those who were there in fear, not confessing themselves to be Christians, went and dug a grave and buried the good and blessed Hayya. But the servants of God, Habsa and the other Hayya, were thrown into great suffering, not being able to speak because of the blows with which they were struck unmercifully and because of their torments. And this crucifier Masruq commanded that they should bring wild camels and bind each of them to one and so send them out into the desert. His command was quickly carried out and so these servants of God, being dragged away by those wild camels, yielded up their spirits to their Lord and were crowned by this glorious confession that they confessed for his sake.

But Afʿu [. . .] and two other men with him went out on the tracks of those camels on the way where the blessed ones had been dragged. And when he had gone about twelve miles, they found the body of the excellent blessed Hayya, for the bonds that were fastened on the camel had broken and she was left there though the camel went on. And this Afʿu cut off and took in faith as a blessing the hair of the blessed Hayya and they dug a grave and buried her body on the spot. Then they went on and took the track of the other camel and continued and went on it about fifteen miles and found also the body of the woman fulfilled with victories, the servant of God, Habsa, and the camel lying down. When Afʿu saw her, he noiselessly ran on and with his sword cut off those ropes and the camel rose and went away, but the pure body of the servant of God remained. So he and those with him took the blessed Habsa and buried her beside the blessed Hayya. And Afʿu cut off and took in faith as a blessing the hair of the victorious Habsa also, and Afʿu and those with him buried together the two victorious ones, and erected a sign on their graves, and returned for fear of the Jews because they were still ruling the land.

This Afʿu gave us a blessing from the hair of them both, but when we asked him to give us also from their bones, he said to us, "We have not yet for fear of the Jews brought them to our town and we did not even take anything from their bones because the Jews immediately put to death everyone of the believers who was found wearing anything from the bones of the victorious martyrs."

LETTER OF THE JEWS TO THE EMPEROR MARCIAN

Sixth century. West Syrian.

Although brief, this text nevertheless contains a wealth of information about the rhetorical ways in which "Jews" were often used in intra-Christian arguments. The text claims to be a letter that Jews wrote to the emperor Marcian soon after the Council of Chalcedon in 451. In reality it seems to be a text produced by the West Syrian opponents of that council, most likely in the sixth century when similar rhetoric abounded in texts by authors like Severus of Antioch and Philoxenus of Mabbug. On the surface, it appears that in the letter the Jews are asking that they be pardoned and their synagogues returned since the council determined that their ancestors did not crucify God, as they had been accused of having done, but rather the human person Jesus. In context, this represents a common West Syrian accusation that Chalcedonian Christians, like Nestorius and the Jews before them, denied the full divinity of Christ through their doctrine of "two natures," one human and another divine. The text is rich in irony and implies, for a West Syrian audience, that the Chalcedonian doctrine is every bit as ridiculous as this request from "the Jews."

To the merciful emperor Marcian, [from] the people of the Hebrews. For such a long time we have been regarded as though our fathers had crucified God and not the man. Since, however, this holy Council of Chalcedon has assembled and has demonstrated that they crucified the man, and not God, we request for this reason that this fault should be pardoned to us and [that] our synagogues should be returned to us.

HISTORY OF THE "SLAVE OF CHRIST"

Mid-seventh to mid-ninth century. West Syrian.

This text tells the story of a young Jewish boy named Asher who comes to be called the "Slave of Christ" after he insists that his young Christian shepherd friends baptize him in a nearby spring so that he can eat and play with them while they tend their flocks. Heaven's blessing of the clergyless ritual is legible in the sweet aroma that follows and Asher's shining face that marks him as a saint. His new Christian identity is signaled by the enslaved person's mark of an earring, which eventually reveals his new identity to his father, Levi, a leader in the Jewish community. In this excerpt, the child becomes a martyr at the hands of his father at the very place where he had been baptized. The text is relevant both for its harshly anti-Jewish portrayal of the father Levi and for its fraught struggle to represent Jewish conversion to Christianity.

> That day was Friday, and when Saturday was approaching, the Jews had a great feast, during which his father prepared a great banquet. He invited and called his friends to supper, and he sent his servants after all his sons. He commanded that before Saturday came, they should gather apart from their flocks. When the holy one arrived there, he withdrew to the house of his mother. When he entered the door, the servants of his father seized him and brought him to the banquet. When his father, along with the Jews who were reclining with him, saw the earring in his ear, all of them were greatly agitated and troubled. His father then indignantly said to him, "Asher, who misled you and did this to you? Do you not know that this is the appearance of enslaved people who forsake freedom?" The holy one said, "Do not fear, old man, I know these things you say. But I have inscribed myself as enslaved for Christ forever, and I am a Christian." When his father heard, he became very angry, and he struck him in the face, threw him down among the guests, and was trampling him. The guests arose and said to him, "Leave him alone, for he is a boy, and he is out of his mind. Let us not take out our anger against him today, and let us not upset our banquet. For it is a feast. May there not be an uproar at it." All of them were silent, and they sat to eat. They were calling to him enticingly to eat with them. He was saying to them, "Do not err! For I am a Christian. It is not right for a Christian to eat with Jews." His father was afflicted with shame from what he said, and he arose to strike him once again in anger, but they did not let him. They said to the holy one three times, "Come, our beloved, eat with us, and the anger of your father will be pacified. We will be silent about the transgressing of the law that has been performed upon your ear because of your lack of education and because of the honor of the feast and banquet. Now, be convinced and come eat." The holy one said, "Had you known the things that have happened, perhaps you would not urge me to eat with you. For, until now, a veil has been set on the face of Moses, the establisher of the law."
>
> When they heard these things, they were in awe at the parables and also amazed by the courageousness of his words. They were saying to one another, "Maybe he did have some vision. For these words are not demonical, and this is not difficult with God. For many and great things came about among the prophets when they were but children, such as Moses, Joshua, Gideon, Samuel, David, Jeremiah, Daniel, the children who were with Hananiah,

as well as many others. Therefore, it would not be too much for one light of wonderment to appear among our people. For our tribe is not small in Israel, and God's laws are our pride." While they were saying these things, his father was silent. Then they said to the holy one, "Tell us, O beloved among brothers, who is that one whom we do not know? Show us, and let us learn. Demonstrate to us, and let us know." The holy one said to them, "That one whom your fathers killed in Jerusalem, I have seen that he is the lamb of God, whom John [the Baptist] proclaimed by the Jordan. I have been baptized in his name, and on account of his truth I will die. If you are not absolved by his baptism, you are responsible for the debt of your fathers. Thus, I proclaim to you the innocent blood that they shed by which the Gentiles have been saved, because they confessed him, whereas those who crucified him have perished. Take off the veil that is spread over your heart! Believe, be baptized, and be absolved!"

Then they were all filled with anger by these words, and his father sharpened a knife for his destruction. When the servants saw the uproar that had come about, they allowed the boy to flee. For they knew and understood that he intended to kill him. Then Levi, his father, got up angrily and with a hard heart, took a knife in his hand from the table that was before them, and ran after him in great anger. The child ʿAbda da-Mshiha [i.e., the slave of Christ] ran before him in the valley, until he came straight to that spring in which he had been baptized. Evening was near, and Saturday was approaching. While he was being chased from before him, and while the sun was setting in the West, he turned toward his father and said to him, "Observe your Sabbath, wretched one! If you are a Jew, stop your chase and sheathe your blade. If you are a disciple of Moses, do not make yourself liable for transgressing his law. But, if [you are a disciple] of Christ, as I am, do not defile your hand with the blood of his slave. For, I do not implore you so that I avoid being slaughtered on behalf of Christ, but so that you do not become an evil butcher and become even more lost." The more of these things that his father heard, the more embittered he became. He was gnashing his teeth like a lion at its prey and roaring like a ravenous wild beast thirsting for blood, as he spat out the bile of his blasphemy and shouted.

When the holy one arrived at the spring [where he had been baptized], he prostrated to pray, weeping. He said something like this, "O Christ, who pulled me out of the water, accept me among the number of the baptized. Upon this spring, again open the gate for me that I may enter among your martyrs and be included in the troop of your athletes. I offer you my blood as a pure offering. Accept me as a sweet smell and as the pleasure of your mercy, along with the company of my triumphant friends, whom you showed me were praising you with their hosannas. Make me also worthy, my Lord, to praise you and say, 'I have come to the altar of God and to the God who makes my youth happy. I will confess you with my lyre, God, my God.' Do not reckon this sin to the swift pursuer, my deceitful father. Make my mother, who gave birth to me and on whose knees I was raised, become to me a sister by the new mother, baptism—truly a mother—and also a partner in those rewards that are kept for those who fear you. Anyone who invokes my name on account of your name and whoever makes a remembrance of me in your name, be for them a helper in any appeal to you, my Lord, an answerer of requests, and a physician and a guardian of souls and bodies. May a blessing rest upon their homes. May they be delivered from the evil one and his power. May their souls be absolved. Thus, my blood is poured out for you as is the sacrifice of my thoughts on account of the fact that you made me a worker for you, you retrieved me from the deep pit, you revealed your truth in me, you made me your herald, you did not loath my impurity, and your greatness did not despise my smallness. Like a lamb to the slaughter, I hereby offer my neck for your sake. I have thus become a stranger to my brothers and a foreigner to my mother's children. Where are you, my beloved friends? Come, see my struggle that is due to your proclamation! Come, delight in the fruit of your teaching! By this deed I will finish the path that you have prepared for me. Come, be the best men at my wedding feast. Exult with me in the feast of blood that is prepared for me. Who hid from you the day of my marriage? It is the time in which friends are tested. It is the day on which beloved ones are invited. Would that someone show me the agony that is thrown at me and would that you join me in my great deeds. Good-bye, pray for me that I may be worthy to see you at the banquet of the heavenly bridegroom. Good-bye mother who gave birth to me and womb that carried me. Good-bye knees that raised me and breasts that nursed me. Good-bye my brothers, sons of my mother. If only you would become brothers to me through the womb of baptism as well!" While the holy one was praying these things and things like them and was crying with groans and wailing before God, his father overtook him like a lion that is thirsting for prey. He lowered his head onto the stone on which he was reclining, and he slew him like a lamb with the knife in his hand. He poured out his blood on that stone. [. . .]

When those children, the friends of the holy one, came as usual to water [their flocks] on Sunday after they had buried him, and when they saw that the stone had been rolled away from the tomb, that the body had been taken, that only the dirt that had been sprinkled with blood remained, and that a pleasing scent emitted from it, they were suddenly shocked and amazed, and, trembling, seized them. They lamented with groans in a loud voice and with bitter crying, hitting their faces, moaning bitterly. While one of them was saying that an animal ate him, another was saying that he was stolen by Christians, and still another was saying that his parents took him to bury him. Then, when they were amazed at the great calamity, every one of them went to the home of their parents and carefully told them the entire story of the holy one: how they had baptized him, the things that the athlete had told them, how they had found him killed, and how they had buried him. So, early in the morning, news went out everywhere that Levi the Jew had killed his son because he had become a Christian. From this news and from the story of the children, the faithful have been assured that as a martyr Asher had been killed by Levi his father and that now he truly was wealth and the one who makes wealthy. For, Asher is translated as "wealth."

DISPUTATION OF SERGIUS THE STYLITE AGAINST A JEW

Eighth century. West Syrian.

Disputations were a familiar narrative genre in late antiquity, and Syriac authors continued to produce them in later centuries under Islam. Disputation literature always offers a view sympathetic to the author's community and is polemical in varying degrees to the narrator's interlocutor. As with most examples of this genre, this text is unlikely to represent a conversation that actually took place, and it certainly represents an anti-Jewish Christian apology or defense speech. In this disputation, as is often the case in such texts, the Jewish speaker stands as a foil for the Christian narrator, as well as a literary device that prompts the author to explain Christian supersessionist teachings, sprinkled with anti-Jewish insults. The quotation marks around "The Jew" are a reminder that this character is a literary construction. This text adds to the topics of earlier Christian disputes with new questions about Christians' attraction to relics (i.e., pieces of saints' dead bodies) and Christians' alleged worship of the cross, as well as an explicit discussion of who should rightly be called "Jews" and "Israel."

Sergius: Since you have said, Jew, that no one pleases God and inherits the kingdom without the Sabbath and circumcision, what about Adam, Abel, Seth, Enosh, Kenan, Mehalalel, Jared, Enoch, Methuselah, Lamech, Noah, Shem, and Melchizedek? They were not circumcised, nor did they keep the Sabbath, and yet they pleased God more than you all who circumcise and keep the Sabbath. As of now each one of them has retired to life. And what about Abraham, Isaac, Jacob, Joseph, and the twelve heads of the tribes? None of them kept the Sabbath, and they pleased God more than you who keep the Sabbath. You circumcise a child on the Sabbath? Well, you've violated the Sabbath. But if you don't circumcise on the Sabbath, you've nullified the command about the eight-day-old child. Look how each one violates the other. When has the sun stopped running its course on the Sabbath, or springs stopped flowing, or trees stopped growing? God, too, is not idle on the Sabbath. [. . .]

Sergius: Let's talk a bit about what scripture and natural qualities show us. God said, "Let us make people in our image, and similar to us." While the word offers us many meanings about Christ, here it pursues one, showing that at their creation, people were created with the pattern of the cross. You hate the cross, but when you pray and stretch out your hands in prayer, even though you don't mean to, you display a cross. When you put on your clothes, you display a cross. Similarly, in the window of your house, in the brace and seed-holder of your plow. A bird, unless it spreads its wings and feet, won't mount the thin air. Jew, open your eyes and look at the bird, that splits and crosses the air with the power of the cross. It supplies the pattern: only with the power of the cross can someone fly through the clouds to meet our Lord in the air, as it is written about him. For he is the "son of man" who, Daniel says, approached the Ancient of Days, and he gave him authority so all peoples would serve him, for he will rule an imperishable reign, as Daniel has decreed. Then all his enemies will be put under his feet, and with "every knee bowing in the sky and on the earth and underground, every tongue will confess that Jesus Christ is Lord, to the glory of God, his father." For many things written in the prophets and in natural qualities demonstrate that everything subsists with the power of the cross of Christ. [. . .]

Sergius: [. . .] Anyone who strays from the commands is imprisoned under a curse, as in "Cursed is anyone who fails to do everything written in this book." Show me a single one of Abraham's descendants who hasn't strayed from the commands, except Christ, about whom Isaiah has testified and said, "He did no wrong, and no deceit was found in his mouth." Hence it is true that the verse, "all the peoples will bless themselves in your descendant," has been fulfilled in Christ: that is, they will bless themselves in the faith of Christ, and anything that is outside the faith of Christ—whether from the people or the peoples—is subject to the curse, and not close to the blessing of Abraham the faithful. Abraham put faith in God, and it was considered as righteousness for him. With this similarity to Abraham, anyone who puts faith in Christ, it will be considered as righteousness for them. Hence it is recognized and validated that those with faith in Christ are Abraham's children and God's Israel.

"The Jew": If things are like you say, why aren't you all called Jews and Israel? If you're the real Jews and Israel, you ought to be called Jews. So why do you shun the name?

Sergius: If you and we were referred to with the same name, each group and each unique essence would be indistinguishable, and there would be a huge confusion in the world. It's not right for grain to be thrown together with straw under the same name. This is why God has been happy to hang on to the old name for you all, as a disgrace, while we are referred to as Christian confessors. This name makes a distinction between confessors and rejectors, so that the genuine Jews are called Christians and, instead of synagogue, it is named the church. [. . .]

"The Jew": In the law it is written: Do not come close to the bones of a corpse, especially those who are priests. But you all, you carry the bones of corpses around in your clothes, and you defile yourselves with cadavers, rather than shunning them. But not only this, you also pray and bow down to decayed, dry bones, and you rub the dust that comes off them on your bodies, and act like it's something special. But if someone who comes close to a bone with the tip of their finger is unclean until the evening, how much more so the person that the pus of a corpse sticks to. You build them temples, paint them colorful images, assign them the name of martyrs, and you call these places prayer chapels. If you have testimonies about Christ from the books of the prophets, so what? Moses gave a command about the bones of a corpse, and Isaiah said: Those who defile their vessels with cadavers and those who eat pork, reptiles, and mice will come to an end together, says the Lord. But here you are defiling yourselves with cadavers and bones, eating pigs and other things God forbids in the Law. You all are guilty in this, and as far as I can see, you don't have a defense, but go ahead and answer.

TIMOTHY I, *LETTERS* 40

Late eighth century. East Syrian.

Timothy I was the celebrated katholikos of the East Syrian church centered in Baghdad, and during his long episcopacy (780–823) he remained close with four generations of 'Abbasid Muslim caliphs. Timothy seems to have composed this letter in his early years in office, and "Jews" appear in this text, as they did in past centuries, as a negative way of referring to the author's contemporary religious opponents, in this case Muslims, who in the author's view do not appropriately recognize Jesus as the Son of God. This letter begins with New Testament imagery that claims Jesus's victory over Satan, whom the text associates with "the Jews," and then refers to Muslims as "the new Jews" as a way of denigrating them. Timothy thus adapts a long tradition of Christian anti-Jewish rhetoric that linked Satan and the Jews with more recent Christian opponents (e.g., so-called Arians, Nestorians, or those who support the Council of Chalcedon) by making Muslims next in this nefarious genealogy. For additional excerpts from Timothy I, see chapters 9, 11, and 12.

To Mar Sergius, priest and teacher, from Timothy. Rejoice in the Lord.

There is nothing that is stronger than truth or weaker than falsehood. I will explain everything diligently. Just as the love of truth is an eternal victory, so also the love of the world is a false victory. A sign indicative of both is the defeat of Jesus on the cross and the victory of the Jews and Satan.

When it seemed that our Lord had been conquered by him, he conquered both the world and its prince, saying, "Take heart, I have conquered the world [John 16:33] and the prince of this world [John 17:31]." He was exalted above the heavens and seated at the right hand of God's throne [Hebrews 12:3]. When the prince of the world with his commanders, the Jews, thought that they had conquered him, they were conquered by him. When they thought that they were victorious, they were put to shame and confounded by him. That shame, being eternal, will never be forgotten.

In the days of Herod, Pilate, and the old Jews there was both defeat and victory, and truth and falsehood. So also, now, in the days of the present princes, in our time, and in the days of the new Jews among us, there is the same struggle and the same contest to distinguish falsehood and truth. The stumbling block of the cross has still not passed away, but there is nothing to fear from such a contest and struggle.

11

ISLAM

It is hard to overstate the importance of Syriac sources for the history of Christian-Muslim relations and for our understanding of earliest Islam. Syriac authors discussed Muslims in theological tractates, inscriptions, apocalypses, letters, jurisprudence, historical chronicles, scriptural commentaries, hagiographic texts, prayers, and scientific treatises. For the earliest centuries of Christian-Muslim interactions, Syriac texts constitute the largest surviving corpus of Christian writings on Islam and often contain eyewitness accounts to the events that they described. Coming from the perspective of seeing Islam from the outside, every Syriac text had its own bias and must, therefore, be read critically. Nevertheless, these works provide a treasure trove of information on the first Islamic centuries.

Even more important than the sheer number and antiquity of these sources, however, is the variety of experiences that they represent. Although Greek and Latin authors were far from uniform in their discussions of Islam, they frequently wrote from the context of military conflict or had little direct contact with Muslims. In contrast, just a few years after Muhammad's death, almost all Syriac Christians were under Muslim rule. By the 640s, Muslims were no longer military opponents, nor was Islam a distant phenomenon for Syriac Christians. Rather, Islam was an aspect of daily life. In the Islamic Empire, Syriac Christians held key government positions, attended the caliph's court in Baghdad, collaborated with Muslim scholars to translate Greek science and philosophy into Arabic, accompanied Muslim leaders on their military campaigns against Byzantine Christians, and helped fund monasteries through donations from Muslims—including money from the caliph himself. Syriac Christians ate with Muslims, married Muslims, bequeathed estates to Muslim heirs, taught Muslim children, and were soldiers in Muslim armies.

There are close to a hundred surviving premodern Syriac texts that address Muslims, Islam, and the Islamic Empire. They range in size from a short marginal note to a several hundred-page history book. Excerpts from the following ten texts help convey an array of Syriac reactions to the rise of Islam. These texts traverse more than five hundred years, all four early Syriac churches, and multiple genres.

Here you will find them in chronological order. The first four (the *Maronite Chronicle* through the *Disputation of Bet Ḥale*) were most likely written during the Umayyad dynasty (661–750), the next three (the *Chronicle of Zuqnin* through the *Syriac Baḥira Legend*) in the early ʿAbbasid era (750 to the ninth century), the final three authors (Michael the Syrian, Dionysius bar Ṣalibi, and Barhebraeus) wrote during the Crusades. If read sequentially, these texts illustrate how Syriac Christian understandings of Islam became increasingly detailed and developed. Nevertheless, this never resulted in a unified Syriac view of Islam. Instead, what makes these sources so valuable is the incredible diversity of their responses to Muslims. Ranging from overtly antagonistic to downright friendly, Syriac sources belie the notion of any monolithic Christian reaction to Islam and serve as an important corrective to the reductionist views that characterize many modern depictions of the history of Christian-Muslim relations.

Further Reading Volumes 1 through 4 of *Christian-Muslim Relations: A Bibliographic History* provide concise overviews for most of the early Christian sources on Islam, including many Syriac ones. See David Thomas et al., eds., *Christian-Muslim Relations: A Bibliographical History*, 5 vols. (Leiden: Brill, 2009–13). For English translations of almost all Syriac sources written before 750 that deal with Islam, see Michael Penn, *When Christians First Met Muslims: A Sourcebook of the Earliest Syriac Writings on Islam* (Oakland: University of California Press, 2015). More synthetic treatments of Syriac Christian reactions to Islam can be found in: Sidney Griffith. *The Church in the Shadow of the Mosque: Christians and Muslims in the World of Islam* (Princeton, NJ: Princeton University Press, 2008); Michael Penn, *Envisioning Islam: Syriac Christians and the Early Muslim World* (Philadelphia: University of Pennsylvania Press, 2015); and the second half of Jack Tannous, *The Making of the Medieval Middle East: Religion, Society, and Simple Believers* (Princeton, NJ: Princeton University Press, 2018).

MARONITE CHRONICLE

Ca. 670. Maronite.

The *Maronite Chronicle* is one of the earliest Christian works that speaks of Islam and it provides important data about mid-seventh century history and how Syriac Christians interpreted the events that occurred then. The surviving text begins with an allusion to the assassination of Caliph ʿAlī during the First Arab Civil War and follows with a particularly intriguing description of the Umayyad caliph Muʿāwiya (d. 680). Here Muʿāwiya oversees an intra-Christian debate (which the Maronites of course win) and visits holy sites in Jerusalem. But the caliph also accepts bribes from West Syrian Christians and issues coinage without the Christian sign of the cross. Although the factual accuracy of this account may be suspect, it remains an intriguing example of how early Syriac Christians depicted Islamic rulers.

> Then ʿAlī also threatened to rise up against Muʿāwiya again. They struck him while he was praying at Ḥira and killed him. Muʿāwiya went down to Ḥira, the entire Arab army there gave him allegiance, and he went back to Damascus.
>
> In the year 970 [of the Greeks = 659 CE], the seventeenth year of [Emperor] Constans, at the second hour on a Friday in the month of June, there was a devastating earthquake in the land of Palestine, in which many places collapsed.
>
> In the same month, the Jacobite bishops Theodore and Sabuk came to Damascus, and before Muʿāwiya they debated the faith with those of Mar Maron [i.e., the Maronites]. When the Jacobites were defeated, Muʿāwiya commanded them to give up twenty thousand denarii and be silent. And it became customary for the Jacobite bishops to give Muʿāwiya that [much] gold annually lest [his] protection of them slacken and they be punished by the [Maronite] clergy. He who was called patriarch by the Jacobites annually established what share of that gold the inhabitants of all the monasteries and convents would pay. Likewise, he established [the share] for the [other] followers of his faith. And he made Muʿāwiya heir [to his estate] so that out of fear of [Muʿāwiya] all the Jacobites would submit to him. On the ninth of the month during which the disputation with the Jacobites took place, at the eighth hour on a Sunday, [there was] an earthquake. [. . .]
>
> In the year 971 [of the Greeks = 660/661 CE], the eighteenth of Constans, many Arabs assembled in Jerusalem and made Muʿāwiya king. He ascended and sat at Golgotha. He prayed there, went to Gethsemane, descended to the tomb of the blessed Mary, and prayed there. In those days, while the Arabs were assembling there with Muʿāwiya, there was a tremor and a devastating earthquake. Most of Jericho collapsed, as did all its churches. Mar John's house by the Jordan, where our savior was baptized, was uprooted from its foundations. So, too, the monastery of Abba Euthymius, along with the dwellings of many monks and solitaries, as well as many [other] places, collapsed during [the earthquake].
>
> In the same year, in the month of July, the amirs and many [other] Arabs assembled and gave allegiance to Muʿāwiya. A command went out that he should be proclaimed king in all the villages and cities under his control and that they should make invocations and acclamations to him. He struck both gold and silver [coinage], but it was not accepted because it did not have a cross on it. Muʿāwiya also did not wear a crown like other kings in the world. He established his throne in Damascus but did not want to go to Muhammad's throne.

APOCALYPSE OF PSEUDO-METHODIUS

Ca. 690. West Syrian.

The *Apocalypse of Pseudo-Methodius* became the most widely read early Christian text on Islam. It was quickly translated into a multitude of languages, including Greek and Latin, and it spread throughout the late ancient world. Copies were even printed during the Turkish siege of Vienna in 1683. Falsely ascribed to the early fourth-century bishop Methodius (d. 312), this apocalyptic text was actually written toward the end of the seventh century. Heavily dependent on the biblical book of Daniel, the author envisions the world as having four kingdoms. According to *Pseudo-Methodius*, the children of Ishmael (i.e., Muslims) will defeat the last of these. They, in turn, will soon be defeated by the last Byzantine emperor, which will lead to the appearance of the anti-Christ and Jesus's second coming. Amid this apocalyptical mayhem appear some of the most negative depictions of Islam in Syriac literature.

When the kingdom of Persia has been destroyed, in its place the children of Ishmael, the children of Hagar—those whom Daniel calls the "arm of the South" [Daniel 11:5]—[will have] attacked the Romans. For they will attack them for ten weeks of years, because the time of the end has arrived and there is no intervening interval.

For this is the last millennium, the seventh, during which the kingdom of the Persians will be destroyed; the children of Ishmael will go out from the desert of Yathrib, and they will come and all assemble there at Gaba'ut Ramta. [. . .]

For the fatlings of the kingdom of the Greeks will be devastated in Gaba'ut, just as they had devastated the fatlings of the Hebrews and of the Persians. Thus, at Gaba'ut they too will be devastated by Ishmael, "the wild ass of the desert" [Genesis 16:12]. For in anger and wrath he will be sent against the entire world: against people, animals, livestock, trees, and plants. It is a merciless chastisement. These four evil princes will be sent before them against the entire earth: destruction, the destroyer, annihilation, and the annihilator.

For through Moses, [God] said to the children of Israel, "It is not because the Lord your God loves you that he brings you into the land of the Gentiles to inherit it, rather on account of the iniquity of its inhabitants" [Deuteronomy 9:5]. So, too, [concerning] these children of Ishmael, it was not because God loves them that he allowed them to enter and take control of the Christians' kingdom, rather on account of the iniquity and sin done by Christians, the like of which was not done by any previous generation. [. . .]

Until the time of wrath, [the children of Ishmael] will ride in boasting and be wrapped in arrogance. They will seize the entrances of the North, the roads of the East, and the ocean's crossings. People, livestock, animals, and birds will be yoked to the yoke of their enslavement. The oceans' waters will become enslaved to them.

Wasteland, widowed of its farmers, will be theirs. They will declare the mountains to be theirs. Theirs will be the fish in the ocean, the trees in the forest, the plants with their fruit, and the dust of the earth, along with its rocks and produce. The merchants' commerce, the farmers' work, the wealthy's inheritance, the holy ones' gifts of gold, silver, bronze, and iron, clothing, all their glorious vessels, adornment, food, confections, and everything desirable and luxurious—[all this] will be theirs. They will become so arrogant in their rage and boasting that they will demand tribute from the dead lying in the dust. They will take the poll tax from orphans, widows, and holy men. [. . .]

For these barbarian tyrants are not people. Rather, they are children of devastation set on devastation. They are annihilators and will be sent for annihilation. They are destruction and will come out for the destruction of everything. They are defiled and love defilement. And when they come out of the desert, they will split open pregnant women. They will snatch babies from their mothers' laps and dash them upon the rocks like defiled animals.

They will slaughter priests and deacons in the sanctuary as well as sleep with their wives and with female captives in the sanctuary. They will make holy vestments into clothes for themselves and their children. They will spread [them] over their horses and defile [the vestments] in their beds. They will tether their livestock to the sarcophagi of martyrs and to the holy ones' graves. They are rebels, murderers, blood shedders, and annihilators. They are a testing furnace for all Christians. [. . .]

Many who were children of the church will deny the Christians' true faith, the holy cross, and the glorious mysteries. Without compulsion, lashing, or blows, they will deny Christ and make themselves the equivalent of unbelievers. [. . .]

In that tenth week, during which the extent of their victory will be complete, affliction will grow strong, a double chastisement upon people, livestock, and animals. There will be a great famine, many will die, and their corpses will be thrown into the street like mud, without anyone to bury [them]. On one of those days, plagues of wrath will be sent upon people, two or three a day.

One will go to sleep in the evening, rise in the morning, and find outside their door two or three oppressors, demanders of tribute and money. All accounts of commerce and taxation will come to an end and vanish from the earth. At that time, people will sell their bronze and iron [goods] and their grave clothes.

In that tenth week, when everything will come to an end, they will give their sons and daughters to pagans for money.

JACOB OF EDESSA, *LETTERS*

Ca. 700. West Syrian.

Between his ordination as the West Syrian Bishop of Edessa in 684 and his death in 708, Jacob of Edessa wrote extensively on church regulations. Most of his legal opinions survive in letters composed in response to inquiries that other Christians had sent him. These include several key references to Islam. As a result, Jacob's letters provide some of the best surviving evidence for on-the-ground interactions between seventh- and early eighth-century Christians and Muslims. Jacob's letters are far from an objective lens of how things really were. Nevertheless, they almost certainly reflect—however imperfectly—a messy world where people frequently crossed confessional boundaries.

LETTER TO ADDAI

ADDAI: "Concerning a Christian woman who willingly marries a Hagarene [i.e., a Muslim], [I want to learn] if priests should give her the Eucharist and if one knows of a canon concerning this. [I want to learn]: if her husband were threatening to kill a priest, if he should not give her the Eucharist, should [the priest] temporarily consent because [otherwise the husband] would seek his death? Or would it be a sin for him to consent? Or, because her husband is compassionate toward Christians, is it better to give her the Eucharist and she not become a Hagarene?"

JACOB: "You have abolished all your doubts concerning this question because you said, 'If the Eucharist should be given to her and she not become a Hagarene.' So that she will not become a Hagarene, even if the priest would have sinned in giving it and even if her husband were not threatening [the priest], it would have been right for him to give her the Eucharist. But [in truth] he does not sin in giving [it] to her. Then, [as for] the other thing you said: 'If one knew of a canon concerning this.' If there is neither risk of apostasy nor her threatening husband, it is right for you to act in this way. Namely, because other women should fear lest they also stumble, for [this woman's] admonition she should fall under the canons[' sentence] for as long as it appears to those in authority that she is able to bear." [. . .]

ADDAI: "If they about to die, is a priest permitted to pardon someone who became a Hagarene or became a pagan?"

JACOB: "If they are about to die and a bishop is not near, [the priest] is permitted to pardon them, give them the Eucharist, and bury them if they die. But if they live, [the priest] should bring them to a bishop and [the bishop] impose on them a penance that he knows they are able to bear."

FIRST LETTER TO JOHN THE STYLITE

JOHN: "Is it right for a priest to give Hagarenes or pagans who are possessed by evil sprits some blessings from the holy ones or, likewise, [holy water mixed with the dust of relics, that is] *ḥnana*, [and] to spread it on them so that they might be healed?"

JACOB: "By all means. None should at all hinder anything like this. Rather, it should be given them for whatever sickness it might be. For I need not say that, while you should give them some blessings, it is God who gives them health. Clearly it is right for you to give [this] to them without hindrance."

DISPUTATION OF BET ḤALE

Ca. 725. East Syrian.

The *Disputation of Bet Ḥale* is one of the earliest surviving disputation texts concerning Islam. It claims to be an account of a sick Arab notable visiting the narrator's monastery and, during the ten days he was there, challenging the narrator's Christian beliefs. The sixteen pages of text present themselves as a transcript of this alleged exchange alternating between quotations attributed to "the Arab" and those attributed to "the monk." They discuss topics such as the Islamic conquests, circumcision, Christian theology, biblical interpretation, Muhammad, and the Qur'an. The text is almost certainly a literary construction of what was most likely an imaginary encounter. It remains, however, an invaluable record for what Syriac Christians thought were the most substantial theological differences between eighth-century Christianity and Islam. The following excerpts give a taste of the various topics discussed and how they were presented.

Next, by the help of God we will write down the disputation that took place between a certain Arab and a certain monk in the monastery of Bet Ḥale. [. . .]

Now, O master, that Arab man was one of the notables who [served] before the amir Maslama, and by reason of an illness he had [contracted,] he came to us, and he remained with us for ten days. And he assumed with us a freedom [of speech] and was well educated in our scriptures and their Qurʾan. And when he had observed our worship that is carried out, with its [appropriate] rites, seven times [a day]—just as the blessed David said, "Seven times a day I have praised you for your ordinances, O righteous one"—he called me to him. [. . .]

And [the Arab] says: "By night and day you are most diligent in prayer, and you do not cease, and you surpass us in prayer, and in fasting, and in your petitioning of God. But, according to my way of thinking, your religion will not allow your prayer to be received [by God]." [. . .]

The monk says: "Speak with me humbly so that I too may speak with you as is fitting! [. . .] But if you wish to learn the truth with precision, talk to me without a translator. [. . .] And even though we are of low estate, accept from us whatever statement you recognize to be the truth, for I know that the truth is loved by all who fear God." [. . .]

The Arab says: "We do [indeed] love the truth, but we do not accept all your scriptures."

The monk says: "Speak out about anything whose truth you doubt, and we, as far as we are able, will provide an answer, either from the scriptures, or from rational argument, and whatever you recognize to be the truth you should accept."

The Arab says: "I know that everyone's faith is dear to them, but tell me the truth: is our religion not better than all the [other] religions on earth?"

The monk says: "In what way?"

The Arab says: "If you want, [in that] we are vigilant concerning the commandments of Muhammad and the sacrifices of Abraham, or, if you would rather, [in that] we do not create a son for God, [one] who is visible and passible like us. And also [in] other ways; for we do not worship the cross, or the bones of martyrs, or images as you [do]; and you mislead people who are pagans and say to them: 'Everyone who is baptized and confesses the Son, their sins will be forgiven them.' And this is the sign that God loves us, and is pleased with our religion, that he has given us authority over all faiths and all peoples. And behold, they are our slaves and subjects! And so I want you to give me an honest answer about these things, without paying any regard to my status, and without protecting yourself with falsehood!" [. . .]

The monk says: "Speak each of your questions before me, and as soon as you have heard the response [given] concerning it, then add whatever you wish."

The Arab says: "Tell me first why you do not believe in Abraham and in his commandments, even though he is the father of the prophets and of the kings, and scripture bears witness to his righteousness?"

The monk says: "Which belief concerning Abraham do you ask of us, and which commandments of his do you wish us to perform?"

The Arab says: "Circumcision and sacrifice, because he received them from God."

The monk says: "It is true that Abraham is the father of the prophets and of the kings, and his righteousness is also clear to all who read the scriptures. But like a shadow in the place of a body, and speech in relation to a deed, so also is the guidance of our father Abraham in relation to the new things that Christ performed for the salvation of our lives." [. . .]

The Arab says: "I know that baptism among the Christians is like circumcision among the children of Abraham, but tell me, how is the sacrifice of Abraham a symbol of the sacrifice of Christ?"

The monk says: "Abraham was commanded to offer up his son as a sacrifice, so that he might be a type of our Lord who was going to suffer for us. And the fact that he took two boys along with him is a type of the two thieves who were crucified along with Christ. And the sticks upon the shoulder of Isaac are a type of the cross of our Lord, which was upon his shoulder. And the fact that Isaac was bound upon the altar is a symbol that [Christ's] divinity was accomplishing it. And that [passage]: 'Remove your hand from the boy, and do nothing to him,' . . . and 'behold a lamb hanging on the tree,' it is a symbol of the body that he received from us, which suffered on the cross, while his divinity was unharmed." [. . .]

The Arab says: "How is it possible, as you have said, that the divinity, which was with him on the cross and in the tomb, did not suffer and was not harmed?"

The monk says: "Truly it was with him, but not through mingling and mixture and confusion, as the heretics say, but through will. And [as for] how it was unharmed and did not suffer, hear two proofs that are most trustworthy for those who love God. Just as [when] the sun rests upon a wall, and you take a pickaxe and you demolish the wall, the sun is not stunned and neither does it suffer, so also the body [that Christ took] from us died, and was buried, and rose, while the divinity did not suffer. And just as iron, which they leave in the fire if they do not throw it into water for any [time], when they seek it, it increases its effectiveness, so also the eternal Son who inhabited the temple [of the body received] from us, on the cross and in the tomb and in its resurrection, he was with it, and he showed its effectiveness. [. . .] [Jesus] said: 'This is my body, which is broken for your sakes. Take and eat of it, all of you. And let it be for you for the remission of debts.' And, likewise, he also gave thanks over the cup, and said: 'This is my blood, which is shed for you for the forgiveness of sins. Take and drink of it, all of you. So, do in commemoration of me. Whenever, therefore, you eat of this bread, and drink of this cup, you shall recall my death until my [second] coming.' And so, from Christ until now, all Christians take delight in his sacrifice. The bread is of wheat, and the wine is of the vine, and by the mediation of priests and through the Holy Spirit if becomes the body and blood of Christ, just as he entrusted to us. And we are freed from animal sacrifices and from bloodshed." [. . .]

The Arab says: "I consider that you have spoken these things well. Now, tell me again, given that God is high and exalted, and is incomprehensible and invisible and ineffable and inexplicable, and is in every place but is not limited by any place, why do you thrust him down into baseness and proclaim that he has a son? And given that he is one, [why] do you say 'Father, and Son, and Holy Spirit?'"

The monk says: "You said truly that he is one, but he is known in the three persons of Father, and Son, and Holy Spirit, for he is one nature, one power, one will, one authority, a hidden being without beginning or end, the mighty one, and creator, and lord, and maker of all created things." And we know him in threefold manner, both from that [passage]: 'Let us make human in our image according to our likeness;' and from that [one]: 'Let us go down and there divide [their] languages;' and from the fact that the prophet saw in the midst of the temple the seraphim crying, 'holy, holy, mighty Lord! Heaven and earth are filled with his praises!' It is this utterance that bears the symbol of the holy Trinity. [. . .] And, just as the sun is a single sphere, and from it proceed illumination and warmth, [and] a human also is one, but is composed of bones and flesh and hair, so also God is one, and is known in three persons, and they are distinguished by their particular properties. And just as someone might light a fire in wintertime, and warms themselves, and benefits from its heat, but if they should extend their hand into it, and investigate its nature, they will be burned by it, so also we confess the Trinity, as it was delineated above, to be one and indivisible, and it is proclaimed and confessed in threefold manner, and whoever [so] believes and confesses is further enlightened by it. But if someone should investigate and pry [into it] they will surely be burned and their life shall be brought to an end. For just as a potter's vessel is not able to judge that which pertains to its fashioner or the origin of its existence, so also the nature of the maker is not known by those who are made. And [as for] that which you said, 'Why do you produce a son for [God]?' tell me, you son of Ishmael, whose son do you make him, he who is called by you 'Īsā son of Mariam, and by us Jesus Christ?"

The Arab says: "According to Muhammad our [prophet],—we also bear witness to what he said,—[he is]: 'The Word of God and his Spirit.'"

The monk says: "And you speak well! But Muhammad received this saying from the Gospel of Luke, in accordance with what the angel Gabriel proclaimed [when] he declared it to the blessed Mary: 'Peace be with you, who are full of grace! And our Lord is with you, blessed among women! For the Holy Spirit shall come, and the power of the most high shall rest upon you. Because of this, he who shall be born of you is holy, and he shall be called the Son of the most high.' Now, consider your saying, and understand what you have heard from Muhammad, because you bear witness that he proclaimed him to be 'the Word of God and his Spirit.' Now, I require one of two things from you; either you alienate the Word of God and his Spirit from him, or you correctly proclaim him to be the Son of God."

The Arab says: "Here we must take refuge in silence! But tell me the truth. Muhammad our prophet, how is he reckoned in your eyes?"

The monk says: "A wise and God-fearing man, who freed you from the worship of demons, and caused you to know the one true God."

The Arab says: "And [so] for what reason, given that he was wise, did he not teach us from the beginning about the mystery of the Trinity as you term [it]?"

The monk says: "You should know, O man, that a child, when it is born, because it does not possess fully formed senses [capable] of receiving whole food, they feed it with milk for two years, and [only] then do they give it food [consisting] of bread. So, also, Muhammad, because he saw your childishness and your lack of knowledge, he first caused you to know the one true God—a teaching that he received from [the Christian monk] Sergius Baḥira. Because you were childlike in knowledge, he did not teach you about the mystery of the Trinity, so that you should not go astray after multiple gods. For you might perhaps have said, 'Since Muhammad proclaimed three, let us make seven others, since ten would be even more powerful!' and [so] you would have run after the worship of carved idols, as previously."

The Arab says: "Truly you possess the truth, and it is no error, as [some] people have supposed! And Muhammad our prophet also said: 'As for those who live in monasteries, and those who dwell on the monasteries, and those who dwell on the mountains, they will enjoy the kingdom.' And truly, everyone who holds to your belief with this way of thinking, as you have repeated [it] before me, and is cleansed from iniquity and sin, God will not reject them. However, although I accept the truth of everything that you have said, [and] even though I have greatly wearied you, yet I wish to learn the whole truth from you concerning all the particularities. [So] answer me one small question."

The monk says: "What is your question?"

The Arab says: "I acknowledge that your religion is good, and also that your way of thinking is better than ours, [so] for what reason did God deliver you into our hands? And [why] are you led away by us like sheep to the slaughter, and [why] are your bishops and priests being killed, and the rest [of you] are being subjugated and belabored night and day by the impositions of the king that are more bitter than death?"

The monk says: "Moses said to the children of Israel, 'It is not because of your righteousness that God will lead you into the promised land so that you might inherit it, but because of the wickedness of its inhabitants.' And you also, you reigned for a period of sixty years, and [then] you were driven away by Gideon the Hebrew, and he killed four of your kings, ʿOib, Zib, Zabaḥ, and Ṣalmana. And the children of Israel also, even though they were a mighty people, yet they were enslaved by the Egyptians for four hundred years. [And] when they were taken captive by Nebuchadnezzar, they served in bondage in Babylon for seventy years. And they were [also] delivered into the hand of the Assyrians. And you also, children of Ishmael, God did not give you power over us because of your [own] righteousness, but because of our sins, and because the Lord loves us and does not wish to deprive us of his [heavenly] kingdom. For it is said: 'He whom God loves he chastises,' and 'if you [remain] without chastisement you will be strangers, and not sons.' The good and merciful God desired to chastise us in this passing world of brief and fleeting life so that there [in his kingdom] he might cause us to inherit eternal life.

The Arab says: "I said to you from the start that whatever you know to be true, tell me, and do not have regard for my status. And now I make you swear by Christ—for I know that you love him better than your own life—tell me the truth inasmuch as you know [it]: Will the children of Hagar enter the kingdom, or not?"

The monk says: "By Christ, through whom you have made me swear, hear [the words] from his holy mouth as he speaks in the Gospel of the blessed John: 'Anyone who is not born again shall not see the kingdom of God.' Nicodemus says to him, 'How can an old man be born again? Is he able to enter his mother's womb again for a second time and be born?' Jesus says to him, 'Truly, truly I say to you, that anyone who is not born of water and the spirit shall not enter the kingdom of God.' But if there should be someone who has fine deeds [to their credit], they may live through grace in [those] mansions that are far removed from the torment, but they shall be considered as a hired hand, and not as a child and heir."

The Arab says: "I testify that if it were not for fear of the government, and public shame, many would become Christians. But as for you, may you be blessed by God, for you have given me great ease through your speech with me."

The monk says: "To him from whom is everything, and in whom is everything, and through whom is everything, to him be praise from spiritual beings and corporeal beings and from my feeble self, who has proclaimed him! Glory be to his name, and on us be his mercy and his grace, for ever and ever, amen."

CHRONICLE OF ZUQNIN

Ca. 770. West Syrian.

The 380-page *Chronicle of Zuqnin* traces history from the world's beginning to the 770s. The anonymous author details the evil deeds of caliphs such as Yazid II (who he claimed tried to destroy all religious images, white animals, and blue-eyed people) and other governmental officials (who roasted abbots alive). But the author's greatest nemeses were Caliph al-Mansur and his governor of Mosul. The *Chronicle* states, "all the world's parchment would not suffice to write on them the evils that in our time came upon humanity." Nevertheless, the author gave it his best try and dedicated more than 170 pages to afflictions under this caliph. Although one suspects some exaggeration, the *Chronicle of Zuqnin* remains important for refuting the claim that Syriac Christians universally welcomed Islamic rule. The excerpt below recounts the alleged fate of a Christian who converted to Islam. Although highly stylized, it remains one of the earliest surviving accounts of a Christian's conversion to Islam.

It happened, as we said to you, that numerous people converted to paganism [i.e., Islam] and renounced Christ, baptism, the Eucharist, and the cross through which every human being was granted salvation. They renounced all the things that are part of Christ's program of salvation, only confessing that Christ was the Word and the Spirit of God. Nor did they admit to this very profession or understand what Moses had previously said: "In the beginning God created . . ." which the Son of Thunder [i.e., John the Evangelist] interpreted, saying: "In the beginning was the Word, and the Word was with God, and the Word was God. This one was in the beginning with God; everything came to exist through his hand, and without him not even one thing that was made came into existence. They did not understand, nor did they comprehend these words, because they walked in darkness." As soon as someone asked them, "This 'Word and Spirit of God in 'Īsā,' what is it?" they blasphemed, saying, "He is like Moses, Elijah, and Muhammad"—the prophet who was the founder of their faith. "He is simply a prophet, like other prophets, a person like you and me." But then they professed that he was not born from a human seed, like anyone else, but they denied him any divine substance. They only called him Word and Spirit of God, and prophet, and one not born from the seed of man; instead, God ordered Mary and she conceived him, as the trees are pollinated to produce fruit without the intervention of a male, since they are pollinated by the wind. Jeremiah the prophet called a dubious faith like this one "a leaky cistern." This apostasy was practiced not only by the young but also by adults, including many elderly people, and worst of all, by old priests and numerous deacons who cannot be numbered. I shall talk very briefly about one or two events that happened to them and that they reported and admitted publicly, and with that conclude my account of these people.

I was in Edessa at that time for some event that took place there. When I was there, people came and said before us, as well as before everyone, that a man, a deacon from the region of Edessa, had slipped into this pit and chasm of perdition. When the idea of apostasy occurred to him, all the notables and priests of the village seized him and begged him at length not to apostatize, but he was not persuaded. After imploring him with sad tears as well as with gifts to get rid of the bad will in which he found himself—more so because of the rank of the holy priesthood that had been conferred on him—and since he did not yield to them, they left him. As for him, he went to seek refuge in a man, one of the Arabs in that region, and asked that he might become an Arab at his hands. This man did not pressure him; on the contrary, he asked him not to do so lest he should regret it one day and return to his faith, in which case great tortures would then be inflicted upon him. But he said, "If the idea of repenting will occur to me, I will not turn away from your faith, because God indicated that to me." The man said to him, "Do you renounce Christ?" He said, "Yes." Then he said to him, "Do you renounce baptism?" He said, "I renounce it." He then said to him, "Do you renounce the cross, the Eucharist, and everything that Christians profess?" He replied, "I renounce them." At this point, the son of the devil added to these words insults not requested by the Arabs. After he made him apostatize in this manner, he asked him, "Do you believe in Muhammad as the messenger of God, and in the book that descended upon him from heaven?" He said, "I believe." Then he said, "Do you believe that 'Īsā is the Word and Spirit of God, that he is a prophet, and that he is not God?" He replied, saying, "Yes." Thus, he made him renounce everything in his free will. For no one among the people was forcibly driven by anyone else, unless by the devil his father, to renounce his faith, while many of them apostatized without any reason whatsoever. Then he ordered him, "Untie your belt and pray toward the south."

Now God was not disgusted to wash the feet of the betrayer or to allow him to share in the mystical supper; moreover, he even gave him the dipped and softened morsel, unlike the other apostles, and with his finger he pointed him out as the betrayer. So did God do to this wretched one. The Holy Spirit despised him more than the renegade despised the spirit he received in baptism and turned him into an object of dread for others. In like manner, we too shall set him as an example for the generations to come after us, so that all the believers who will read in this book will realize what happened to this wretched one and take care of the grace that they have received, lest the same thing should happen to them too.

After he untied his belt and kneeled to pray, his body shivered, and at the time of prostration something like a white and beautiful dove came out of his mouth and went up to the sky. When the wretched one saw this dove, he grievously wailed, like a woman, and terrified all those who were there, saying, "Woe unto me! Woe unto me! Woe unto me, what has happened to me!" After they calmed him down from screaming, he spoke before everyone about what he had seen and what had happened to him—he was talking openly and with many tears before everyone. Some of those who heard him reported the matter to me, but because at that time I did not pay enough attention to it, I forgot the name of the man and that of his father, as well as the name of his village. About this wretched man and about those who acted like him, the scripture says: "Lament, wail, and make lamentation like the jackal," because the Holy Spirit, a mistress, went out and the impure spirit, a man, came in, as says the scripture. [. . .]

Look, O believer, when you are in great fear, believe firmly in what is written, have faith at least in the prophets, and understand that a servant cannot serve two masters, that is the Holy Spirit and the impure spirit. It is not possible that a king and a slave live in one house. Therefore, God does not live in the soul that renounces him and confesses Satan.

TIMOTHY I, *LETTERS* 59

Ca. 770. East Syrian.

The East Syrian katholikos Timothy I (d. 823) speaks of Islam in a number of his writings, but nowhere more extensively than in *Letters* 59. Often called Timothy's "Apology", this almost one-hundred-page epistle recounts two audiences the patriarch had with Caliph al-Mahdi (d. 785) and their ensuing conversations regarding Christianity. Timothy frequently attended the caliph's court and it is quite possible that this letter reflects, however imperfectly, an actual discussion between the patriarch and al-Mahdi. But, as with other Syriac disputation texts, its current form is a carefully constructed literary work that remains far from a direct transcript of words truly exchanged. The passage below is set at the start of the second day of conversation. Here Timothy presents one of Christianity's most positive depictions of Muhammad. But the katholikos very carefully stops short of calling Muhammad a prophet. For additional excerpts from Timothy I's *Letters*, see chapters 9, 10, and 12.

The next day we entered before [the caliph al-Mahdi]. For this constantly took place, sometimes for a matter of state, sometimes owing to the love of wisdom burning in his soul (for as a lover of wisdom, he loved it whenever [wisdom] came from another person), sometimes owing to his enthusiasm to argue opposite us. After I recited the customary greeting to the king of kings, he began to converse and speak with us. Not angrily or harshly, for harshness and pride were far from his soul. Rather, pleasantly and humbly.

Our king of kings said to me, "Katholikos, did you bring with you the gospel as I asked?" I answered his majesty, "Our victorious and God-loving king, I have brought it." Our victorious king said to me, "Who gave you this book?" I answered him, "Our God-loving king, the Word of God gave us the gospel." Our king said, "Didn't four of the disciples write it?" I said to him, "As our king said, four of the apostles wrote it. But not on their own, rather from what they heard and learned from the Word of God. And on the one hand, if it is the case that the apostles wrote the gospel and, on the other hand, it is the case that the apostles wrote whatever they heard and learned from the Word of God, then the gospel was given by the Word of God. For also, on the one hand, the Torah was written by Moses. And, on the other hand, Moses heard and learned it from an angel and the angel from God. But we do not say the Torah was given by Moses, rather by God. Just as Muslims say, 'We received the Qur'an from Muhammad and Muhammad received the knowledge and the book from an angel.' But they do not say that it is a book that was given by Muhammad, nor by an angel, rather by God the Lord of prophets and angels. Thus, also, we Christians. Even if it is the case that the gospel came to being by the hands of the disciples and apostles, it is not from the apostles, rather from God. We believe the gospel was given to us by the Word of God and his Spirit. For also your majesty's books and documents are written by scribes and secretaries. But they neither come from nor are called the scribes'. Rather they come from the king of kings and the commander of the faithful."

And our peaceable king, full of wisdom said to me, "What do you say about Muhammad?" I answered his majesty, "O king, Muhammad is worthy of all exaltation from every rational being. He walked in the way of the prophets and he traveled on the path of the lovers of God. For if all of the prophets taught about the one God and if Muhammed taught about the one God, then it is evident that Muhammad walked on the path of the prophets. And if it is the case that all the prophets separated people from evil and brought them to good and if Muhammad separated his people from evil and brought them to good, then it is evident that also Muhammad walked in the way of the prophets. And if it is the case that all the prophets separated people from demon worship and from the reverence of idols and brought them to God and to his worship, and Muhammad separated his people from the reverence of demons and from idol worship and brought them to the knowledge and worship of the one God (who alone exists and there are no others beside him), then it is clear that Muhammad walked on the path of the prophets. And if it is the case that Muhammad taught about God, his Word, and his Spirit and all the prophets prophesied about God, his Word, and his Spirit, then Muhammad also walked on the path of all the prophets. Who would not exalt, praise, and glorify him who fought for God not only with words but who also showed his zeal for God with the sword? For just as Moses did to the Israelites when he saw that they had made the golden calf and were worshipping it—that is, he put all the calf worshippers to the sword and killed them—so, also, Muhammad showed zeal for God. He loved and honored God more than himself, his people, and his race. He praised, exalted, and honored those who, along with him, revered God. And he promised them the kingdom, the glory, and the honor that is from God, both in this world and in the other [world] in paradise. But he fought and made war against those who were worshipping images and not God. And he showed them the torments in Gehenna and the unquenchable fire in which the wicked will burn without end. Just as did Abraham, that dear friend of God, who turned his face from idols and from his race and all alone toward God became a teacher to his people about the one God. So, also, Muhammad did. For he turned his face from idols and their worship whether they belonged to his people or to foreigners. And he honored and worshipped alone him who is God alone.

Therefore, God also increased [Muhammad's] honor. And he subdued under his feet two strong kingdoms that were roaring in the world like lionesses, sounded like thunder, and whose dominion was over all the earth under heaven. I mean the kingdom of the Persians and that of the Byzantines. The former, that is the kingdom of the Persians, was worshipping creatures instead of their creator. The latter, that is the kingdom of the Byzantines, was causing to suffer and die in the flesh one who in no way or fashion can suffer or die. And through the commander of the faithful and his descendants he stretches his kingdom's rule from the East to the West and from the North to the South. Victorious king, who would not praise him whom God has praised. And who would not plait a crown of praise and glorify him whom God has praised and glorified? Our king, these and similar things, then, I and all the lovers of God say concerning Muhammad."

SYRIAC BAḤIRA LEGEND

Ca. 810. East Syrian.

By the early eighth century, Muslims claimed that a Christian monk named Baḥira met the young Muhammad and proclaimed that the boy would grow up to be a great prophet. Baḥira's prominence in Islamic traditions motivated one early ninth-century Syriac Christian to retell this narrative from a particularly Christian point of view. The resulting *Syriac Baḥira Legend* states that the Christian monk Baḥira actually taught Muhammad about monotheism, helped Muhammad concoct the religion of Islam, and—along with the help of a malicious Jew—wrote the Qur'an. This account became extremely popular among Christian circles and versions of it can be found in more than thirty surviving West Syrian, East Syrian, Armenian, Arabic, and Latin manuscripts. But despite its extremely polemical perspective, the *Syriac Baḥira Legend* also shows a surprisingly detailed knowledge of Islam illustrating how, especially as they became increasingly fluent in Arabic, 'Abbasid-era Syriac Christians were gaining a much more developed understanding of Muslim traditions and practices. These excerpts come from the middle of the East Syrian version of the *Syriac Baḥira Legend*, where the monk Baḥira first instructs the young Muhammad on how to create a new religion.

And on a certain day when they were coming to the well, Baḥira was standing outside his cell. He looked and saw them coming from far away, Muhammad being with them. And, when he saw him, he knew that something great was to become of the boy, as he saw a vision above him and he knew that in him his prophecy would be fulfilled. When they arrived at the well, they went to him in the cell, according to their habit. The boy Muhammad was sitting outside at the well, saying to himself, "When my brothers come out and leave, I will enter too." Then Mar Sergius Baḥira said to them, "There is someone with you who is bound to become great." They said to him, "There is a simpleminded foolish boy with us." Father Sergius said to them, "Call him, so that I can see him." And when he came in, Sergius stood up and sat down again. He told them about the vision that was above his head. They, however, were not aware of the vision. [. . .]

He then blessed him and said to him, "The Lord will magnify you and your sons after you, and you will become very mighty and numerous on the earth. Twelve kings will come forth from your loins, and their seat will be in the land of Babel. Your kingdom will be mighty on the whole earth and it will conquer many areas and cities and it will defeat strong kings. And there will be peace in the whole world. There is not one kingdom that draws near to them that they will not defeat."

When Muhammad had heard from Sergius that he had prophesied to him about his family and about him and his tribe, he asked Sergius, "From where did you receive this revelation?"

Sergius said, "From Mount Sinai where Moses received divine revelations."

Muhammad said, "For what reason?"

Sergius Baḥira said, "You are destined to become a master and a king and a prophet and a leader and a head of your people. Twenty-four kings will come forth from your loins and you will convert the children of your people from the worship of demons to the knowledge and worship of the one true God."

Muhammad said, "And you, which God do you worship?"

Mar Sergius said, "The God who made heaven and earth, light and darkness, the seas and the rivers, the birds of the sky and the animals and the cattle and all that creeps on the earth, and all of humankind, together with the orders of fire and of spirit. Him they worship and praise and cry 'Holy, holy, holy, Lord God almighty, by whose praises heaven and earth are filled.'"

Muhammad said, "And where is the dwelling place of the God about whom you say these things?'

Sergius said, "In heaven."

Muhammad said, "From where do you know him?"

Sergius said, "From his creation and from the ancient prophets." [. . .]

Muhammad said, "Who are they, the prophets?"

Sergius said, "They are righteous people, who fear God and keep his commandments. The Lord revealed himself to them through the Holy Spirit."

Muhammad said, "Who is the Holy Spirit?"

Sergius said, "The Spirit of God, who is sent from him to whoever fears him and does his will."

Muhammad said, "You, whom do you worship?"

Sergius said, "The living God."

Muhammad said, "And people, whom did they worship of old?"

Sergius said, "Some of them worshipped fire, some of them stones, some of them stars, some of them trees, some of them demons, and some of them graven images. And when God saw all this erring in the world, he pitied the human race and sent prophets to them and they turned the peoples from the false worship of the demons to the knowledge of truth and to the worship of one God."

Muhammad said, "Which one of those do you worship and what is your belief?"

Sergius said, "I am a Christian and I worship the one God."

Muhammad said, "What is Christianity?"

Sergius said, "It is the faith that Christ taught us."

Muhammad said, "Who is Christ?"

Sergius said, "Christ is the Word of God and his Spirit.'"

Muhammad said, "Is he a prophet or a human being like you and me?"

Sergius said, "The human being in whom God dwelled. The Word of God was sent from heaven through Gabriel the archangel to Mary the virgin, who descended from Abraham and from the seed of David. And she conceived without intercourse through the power of the Holy Spirit, and she gave birth to a son without intercourse as the prophets had prophesied." [. . .]

Muhammad said, "How did the virgin give birth without intercourse?"

Sergius said, "The Spirit of God descended from heaven and the Word clothed himself with a body from the virgin, and she gave birth to a son without intercourse and God came to be in a human being."

Muhammad said, "And where is Christ now?"

Sergius said, "After he rose from the grave he went to heaven."

Muhammad said, "And how long was he in the grave?"

Sergius said, "Three days."

Muhammad said, "And what was the cause of his death?"

Sergius said, "Willingly he came to the passion and not by force, and he delivered himself up into the hands of the Jews, the oppressors, and they crucified him in Jerusalem. He died and he was put in the grave and on the third day he rose from the grave and showed himself to his disciples and he gave them certainty about his resurrection. He stayed on earth for forty days and after that he went up to heaven and took a seat at the right hand of God, in the heavenly holiest of holy, above the principalities and powers. And as he came to be, likewise will be done to the whole of his race."

Muhammad said, "Why do you worship a crucified man?"

Sergius said, "It is him I worship, in the man by whom he worked many miracles and wonders on earth and whom he raised with him to heaven and through whom he will bring about the resurrection of the righteous and the wicked, for he is the adorable God in his invisible nature." [. . .]

Muhammad said, "Ask me anything you desire and I will do it for you, if these things will happen to me like you have told me."

Sergius said, "I make a request to you on behalf of the Christians, the followers of Christ, that those who will come forth from your loins and your religion will not shed the blood of Christian people, who have put on Christ. There are people among them who are dressed like me, and they are called 'monks,' being priests and deacons. They abandoned their parents and siblings and houses and cities and everything in the world, and they went out to the desert and the wilderness, and they built monasteries and convents. And they are humble, neither haughty nor arrogant. They fear God and keep his commandments, and they do not care for anything in the world, nor do they have women or children. Nay, all their hope depends on God. And, therefore, they set themselves apart and they abandoned the world, and they pray and beseech God, for the kings and the judges, for the righteous and the wicked, that we may live a quiet and peaceful life. And when you treat them with this kindness, God will lengthen your life and also that of your children after you. He will make them great and your kingdom will increase during all the years of the life of the world. And no kingdom that rises against them will be able to defeat them. None will defeat you, except the kingdom of the Romans, which has sought recourse with the cross, which is the strong, invincible weapon, on which Christ, savior of the world, was crucified."

Then Muhammad said to Mar Sergius, "Everything you ask will be for you, but how will they believe in me, not knowing a book?"

Mar Sergius said to him, "I will teach you everything."

Muhammad said, "I fear that they will not recognize me and that they will kill you and do me harm, and that they will regard me as an impostor."

Sergius said, "I will teach you everything at night, and you teach them during the day."

Muhammad said, "And if they say to me, 'Where did you receive this vision or teaching?' What shall I say to them?"

Sergius said, "Say to them, 'The angel Gabriel has come to me at night and he has taught me all that will happen.'"

Muhammad said, "And if they say to me, 'What is there in the other world?' What shall I say to them?"

Sergius said, "Say to them that there is a paradise and trees and that the best of all things are there."

Muhammad said, "And if they say to me, 'What will we eat and drink there?' What shall I say to them?"

Sergius said, "Say to them, 'you will eat and drink and enjoy in paradise,' and 'there are four rivers there, one of honey, one of milk, one of wine, and one of water.'"

Muhammad said, "When I say to them, 'you will eat and drink in paradise,' they will say to me, 'there is food and drink there and nature's call?'"

Sergius said, "Say to them, 'it will disappear from the body like sweat.'"

Muhammad said, "And when I say to them, 'you will eat and drink in paradise and enjoy,' and they say to me, 'we cannot endure there without intercourse,' what shall I say to them?"

Sergius said, "You tell them also, 'there are beautiful young girls there with big eyes and beautiful appearances and with lovely looks, who are very plump. Seven will be given to each man.'"

Muhammad said, "And if I say, 'fast and pray,' and they say to me, 'we will not pray and fast all day,' what shall I say to them?"

Sergius said, "Command |them| to fast thirty days only and say to them, 'eat and drink all night until you can distinguish a white from a black thread.'"

Muhammad said, "And if they say to me, 'what is allowed to us to eat and drink and from [what] should we abstain?' What shall I say to them?"

Sergius said, "Warn them against wine, fornication, gluttony, pork, and anything strangled and carrion, against murder, false witnessing, hypocrisy, adultery, and drunkenness, and against theft, rapine, and oppression. Treat the orphans and widows justly, and honor your father and your mother, so that days of your life will be many on the earth. [Then] your sins will be forgiven."

Muhammad said, "And where should one pray to God every day?"

Sergius said, "Build a house for God and pray five times a day and twice at night, every day of your lives. And strike the sounding-board. And let Friday be distinguished for you and more honored than all other days. And make a great congregation on it and a fixed prayer, because on that day you will have received the law."

Muhammad said, "And if they say to me, 'give us a testimony that your promise to us is true,' what shall I say to them?'"

Sergius said, "I will write a book for you and teach it to you. And on Friday I will put it on the horn of a cow and you go and gather all the children of your people in one place. Sit down with them and say to them, 'know that today God sends to you from heaven a great book of commandments and laws according to which you shall live every day of your lives.' And when you see the cow coming, stand up from your place, go toward her, and take the book from her horn in the presence of all of them. And say to them, 'this book descended from heaven, from God. The earth was not worthy to receive it, so this cow received it on her horn.'" And until this day it is called the "Scripture of the Cow."

Because he was a humble, simple boy, Muhammad liked the daily teaching of Mar Sergius. And Sergius wrote for them this book that they call "Qur'an," at the hands of Muhammad. They studied it every day of their lives until the death of Baḥira, he who prophesied to them.

DIONYSIUS BAR ṢALIBI, *A RESPONSE TO THE ARABS*

Late twelfth-century. West Syrian.

A key text from the Syriac Renaissance, *A Response to the Arabs* is the longest surviving Syriac disputation of Islam. It consists of thirty chapters that together take up 135 pages in modern translation. Of all surviving premodern writers of Syriac, its author, the West Syrian bishop Dionysius bar Ṣalibi (d. 1171), demonstrates the most comprehensive and in-depth knowledge of Islam. Dionysius addresses topics ranging from Islamic history to six chapters worth of specific Qur'anic verses and his direct refutation of each of them. Of the three excerpts below, the first is very similar to a passage found in Michael the Great's *Chronicle* (which immediately follows these excerpts from Dionysius). It suggests either that one of these authors borrowed from the other or that the two shared a similar source. This makes a comparison between Dionysius's and Michael's versions particularly illustrative. The second excerpt addresses the same question Timothy I did four centuries earlier—how to refute claims that Muhammad was God's prophet. The final excerpt is from Dionysius's conclusion. It not only summarizes the entire work but also curses whoever might dare to falsely take credit for having written his text. For an additional excerpt from Dionysius, see chapter 3.

Muhammad son of ʿAbdallah is said to have gone up from Yathrib, his city, to Palestine on business, and thanks to his involvement with various Jews, he learned the religion of one God and one unique essence. It was 933 [according to the Greeks = 621/622 CE] when he came to power, in the time of Emperor Heraclius. When he saw his people worshipping the idol ʿAkbar and the planet ʿUzzay, that is, Venus, he taught them the religion of one God, and when a few people listened to him and started to be better off, he immediately started domineering and commanding them to obey him.

Sometimes he would use threats, sometimes he would enact vengeance, and at other times he would praise the land of Palestine, saying, "Because of the religion of the one God it was given to the Jews." He would say to his people, "If you listen to me, God will make you heir to the land flowing with milk and honey." Once he had convinced a number of them, he immediately became king over them and started going out for war with a large army: wherever he went, he would take captives and plunder, and he made his people wealthier. This is why they were so bound to his affection, and they became extremely wealthy. Once he had convinced all the Ṭayyaye [i.e., Arabs], and they had converted to the religion of the one God, he himself no longer went out with them to fight, but he would send generals, capturing and plundering, to many different places, while he sat in his city in honor like a king. When their power had grown and expanded, these places were in large part subjugated to them and became their fixed kingdom. Twenty-five kings came in succession in this dominion. The kingdom of the Persians fell under their subjugation, and after a while they convinced the Persians to come to the religion of the one God, and they were converted, since the Persians used to worship the sun and fire. They also brought the Turks, Kurds, and other language groups into the religion of the one God.

Muhammad set as law for his people things he would say had been given to him directly from Gabriel—that is, Gabriel the angel—for him to enact. He taught them to confess one God, maker of everything, although not naming the Father, the Son, and the Holy Spirit, but saying that God is a single, unique essence, neither born nor producing a child, and having no son, no companions, and no partners. He accepts the book of Moses, the prophets, and parts of the gospel. He thinks that Christ is the one the prophets prophesied about, but a regular human being like one of the prophets, and not God or the son of God. He also says he was born, not out of a man's semen, but was created by the word and command of God out of Mary, through the breathing of the Spirit, like God created Adam through breathing. Sometimes he calls Christ the Word and Spirit of God, but a creation, and something made by the word of God. He says the Virgin Mary is the sister of Aaron, and that when Christ got close to the cross, he cast his shadow on one of the disciples, and [that one] was crucified and went to heaven.

Paradise is envisioned as a place for bodily sensations: food, drink, having sex, milk, honey, and fruits. They bring in fate, fortune, and predicting the future as meaningful. They take four free women as wives, and as many concubines as they want. If one of them divorces his wife with oaths, he cannot remarry her until she has become another man's wife, and then he is absolved.

They pray five times a day, kneeling down four times. They believe in the resurrection of the dead and that everyone will get retribution for what they have done. They have a daily fast, but they eat the whole night until dawn. Before praying they wash off, including their genitals, and if they have had a wet dream, they bathe. If water is unavailable, they use dust instead. They practice circumcision, and they worship the Kaʿba.

They call themselves Muslims, and when anyone asks about the meaning of the name Islam, they say it comes from the word for peace, but others say Islam is when you have submitted yourself to God, saved yourself from sins, and achieved salvation from what you have said and done with your hands.

Against them we say that if everyone who has achieved salvation from what they have said and done with their hands and body is a Muslim, then anyone who is just is a Muslim, and with this interpretation a majority of different peoples fit the description. So you do not have the real meaning of your own name in this name of Islam and its interpretation, since it is also shared with a majority of other peoples that are not like you.

[. . .]

"But how, they say, do you not recognize Muhammad?" Against them we say, "We have found no testimony about him in the prophets or the apostles. Another thing is that your own book affirms that Christ is a prophet, and his book, the gospel, is true. He has warned us and said, 'Be sure that, if someone says to you, they are a prophet, you don't accept them, because there won't be any prophets after me. Moses and the prophets have written about me, and there is no more need for prophecy.' Daniel said that when Christ comes, he will remove vision-seeing and prophets."

"Next, we do not accept your prophet since he wrote down laws that the prophets before him did not write. What they allowed, he forbids. For Moses says, 'Whoever divorces his wife must give her a divorce document and cannot go back to her. If he does go back for her, he has committed an unclean act.' Muhammad stands against the Torah and the gospel in these things. Muhammad says in his book that if someone leaves their wife ten times in a year, and someone else has sex with her, he can marry her again, which is against Moses and every prophet there has ever been."

"Or maybe he is known by miracles, or others have testified about him? This guy of yours did nothing amazing; nor have the prophets testified about him. Furthermore, Muhammad brought in another book in addition to the Torah and the gospel, and you testify that they have come down from heaven."

[. . .]

With our discourse against the Arabs—that is, the Ṭayyaye—confirmed up to this point, we have refuted their questioning about the Trinity as well as about the incarnation of the Son, having clearly demonstrated the truth of our position using proofs from nature, scripture, and the wise; having defeated them with many places from their own book, after which we arranged some parts of the Qurʾan in a single list, translated from their language into Syriac, and made a brief refutation of them on the following page (since we had already done so in the previous chapters), we have now reached the time to bring an end to this work.

Whoever reads and understands it, gets something from it and shares that benefit, they should offer up a prayer for Mar Dionysius, the foreigner, Jacob bar Ṣalibi of Melitine, metropolitan of Amid, who wrote this for us to remember. May they get a blessing from the Lord. But whoever dares to treat what is here as theirs and erases mention of our name, may they fall from the promise and get a curse.

MICHAEL THE GREAT, *CHRONICLE*

Ca. 1190. West Syrian.

Michael the Great (also known as Michael the Syrian) is among the most preeminent historians of the West Syrian literary tradition. Monk, abbot, and patriarch in Syria during the Crusades, he had direct contacts with Western, Byzantine, and Muslim rulers in a time of conquest and war. He sought to reform the hierarchy of the West Syrian church and maintain its autonomy in diplomatic relations. His *Chronicle* covers creation to 1195, incorporating prior historical works now lost. The only extant manuscript, written in 1598, is preserved in Aleppo. The first part of the excerpt below comes from Michael's initial discussion of Islamic rule and it occurs a little over halfway through the overall work. Like much of the *Chronicle*, this passage is heavily indebted to a no longer extant, mid-ninth-century history from a West Syrian patriarch named Dionysius (d. 845). But it is clear that Michael often modified and expanded the work of his predecessor. In this section Michael combines a strong knowledge of Islamic beliefs and practices alongside a tendency to depict them in a particularly negative light. Of particular interest is the contrast between this passage from a twelfth-century West Syrian patriarch and the writings of the eighth-century East Syrian katholikos Timothy I found earlier in this chapter. The second set of excerpts concern the complicated events, alliances, and wars of the twelfth-century Near East. These comprise the battles of the First Crusade, including the Muslim observations on the rise and demise of the Knights Templar, the siege and capture of Edessa ("the city of Abgar") by the Seljuk Turks in 1144, and the conquest of Jerusalem in 1187 by Saladin (Ṣalaḥ-al-din), as well as the Muslim cleansing of the Dome of the Rock. Michael records important and unique observations on the Crusades from the point of view of Syriac Christians, who for the most part had little say in the events that affected them. For an additional excerpt from Michael the Syrian, see chapter 1.

> The kingdom of the Arabs began in the year 993 of the Greeks [= 622 CE], the twelfth year of the Byzantine emperor Heraclius, and the thirty-third year of the Persian king Khosrau, when a man by the name of Muhammad of the tribe of Quraysh went to the land of Yathrib and proclaimed himself a prophet. They are called Arabs, Ishmaelites, and Hagarenes (because they are from Hagar and Ishmael), and Saracens (because they are from Sarah), and Midianites (because they come from Keturah's children). But even if these terms and tribes vary, nevertheless the general name for all of them is Arabian. They name themselves this term that comes from the name of Arabia Felix, which is their dwelling place. It is situated from north to south, from the Euphrates river until the Southern Sea, and from west to east from the Red Sea until the gulf—that is, the Persians' Sea.
> So, this Muhammad, son of Abd Allah, went from his city of Yathrib up to Palestine on a trading expedition. And when he had contact with Jews, he learned monotheism from them. Seeing his kin worshipping stones, wood, and all created things, he followed the doctrine of the Jews because he liked it. Returning to his own country, he placed this doc-

trine before his compatriots. At first he persuaded a few of them. But after many attached themselves to him, with authority he commanded that they obey him. Sometimes he would threaten them, sometimes he would praise the land of Palestine, saying, "Because of monotheism this good land was given to these ones [i.e., the Jews]." And he also said to them, "If you obey me, forsake these vain idols, and confess the one God, God will give you this good land." He enticed many with such things and from them he began to make himself an army and to go up and plant spies in the land of Palestine so that, whenever news reached them from there, he would send them to confirm it and they would subject themselves to him. Many times, he went there and back without harm. He took captives and came back laden with spoils. This situation was strengthened for them through lust for possessions, which, becoming a fixed practice, made it a habit by their going up and plundering; and some, too, before they were subjugated, when they were seeing that those who had attached themselves to him were abundantly supplied with possessions, they too were attaching themselves to him. And when many had submitted to him, he no longer himself went as the leader of those going to plunder. Rather, he sent others as the leader of his forces while he remained in his city in honor. Anyone who did not accept the teaching of his doctrine he subdued, in that case not by persuasion but by the sword, killing whoever resisted. After a little while, his forces began to enter and seize many lands. As this domination grew and expanded, he took possession of lands so that their peoples would pay him tribute. They had an established kingdom and, from man to man of those who ruled it, it became more powerful. They subdued most of the lands of the Byzantines and the entire kingdom of the Persians was under their control.

And Muhammad established for them those laws that he said were from God and given him to establish. He taught them to confess the one God, the maker of all (even if he does not name him Father, or Son, or Holy Spirit). But Muhammad says that he is a single divinity, person, and hypostasis who was not begotten nor begets and who has no son, companion, or associate. Muhammad accepts the book of Moses and of the prophets and also some things from the gospel, while he rejects much of it and says that he agrees with only a little [of the gospel]. Concerning Christ, Muhammad thinks and says that he is the one who the prophets prophesied would come—a righteous man and a prophet like one of the prophets—but not God or God's son as we Christians confess. Rather, for him Christ was the greatest of the other prophets because he was not born from a man's semen or from intercourse. Rather, he was created by God's word and came to be through Mary by the breath of the Spirit, just as by his breath God commanded and Adam was created from dust. That is, the Holy Spirit breathed into Adam and he stood up and came into existence. Therefore, they sometimes name him God's Word and his Spirit like one who is a creature and a creation of God's word. Thus, when we call him God's Son (for without suffering or division he was born from him, like speech from the mind), regarding this carnally, they wickedly allege that we confess something along the lines of his having had a son together with a woman. So, they blame us and speak wickedly against us who confess [Christ]. And they say that the holy virgin Mary is the sister of Aaron and Moses. None of them confess that Christ was crucified by the Jews. Rather they claim that one of his disciples, when he gave him his form, was crucified and died. And Christ himself, while hiding, was carried off to the garden and was received by God. Concerning the garden—that is, paradise—they quite stupidly think and say that it has carnal food, drink, sex with women, reclining on beds of gold, mattresses of fine materials, rivers of milk and honey, as well as desirable trees bearing fruit. And they introduce fate, fortune, and predicting the future as being from God.

They take up to four free women as wives and as many concubines as they want. And if one divorces his wife by oaths, he cannot remarry her or break his oaths until he has given her to another man. Then his oaths will be absolved and he can remarry her. They pray five times a day and make four genuflections with each prayer. They confess the resurrection of the dead and that there will be judgment and reckoning for everyone in accord with their deeds. And they are addicted to the love of the world: bodily pleasure, food, drink, clothing, and lots of sex with free women and concubines. And it is not forbidden that one divorce his wife and take another. They have a daytime fast for thirty days—that is, one month a year. But the entire night they eat until dawn. And they wash in water before they pray and even wash the body's orifices. When they approach a woman or have a wet dream, they wash their entire body and then pray. They worship in the direction of the Ka'ba; from any direction where they find themselves, they worship toward it. They circumcise males and females, although they do not follow the rule of Moses, which designates circumcision to be on the eighth day. Rather, they circumcise at whatever age one happens to be.

[. . .]

When the Turks ruled Syria and Palestine, they caused the Christians who prayed in Jerusalem evils: blows, mockery, head tax collected at the city gate, and even at Golgotha and in the [Holy] Sepulchre [Church]. In addition, whenever they saw multitudes of Christian crowds, especially those coming from Rome and [other] lands of Italy, they schemed to destroy them in various ways. As countless people died in this manner, kings and commanders, moved by zeal, marched out, and armies gathered with them from all these regions, coming by sea up to Constantinople. Now Alexios, the Greek emperor [Alexios I Komnenos, r. 1081–1118], hindered their crossing over, and they took the decision to take the capital away from the Greeks. They fought against the citizens of Constantinople for seven years, from 1401 to 1408 [the year of the Greeks = 1090–97 CE].

At the time when the Franks besieged Constantinople, Antioch collapsed in an earthquake. In the middle of the foundation of one of the towers that collapsed a large house was exposed in the ground, in which there were huge statues of brass in the likeness of Franks mounting horses, fully dressed and carrying weapons, spears and swords and the rest. All of them were of brass, harnessed and bound with iron. The governor, Aghusin the Turk, ordered an inquiry about them, and because no one knew anything about them and no book that shed light on them, he thought that they were cultic idols for pagans. Therefore he ordered them destroyed. Thereafter, a blind old woman was found who said, "I heard the ancients saying that there are under such and such tower talismans concerning the nation of the Franks that they will not march out and will not cross the sea." When the governor heard these things from the mouth of the old woman, he regretted that he shattered them. He said to her, "Did you hear about how they were made? Is it possible to make them?" When she answered, "No!" they hit her and killed her.

When the Franks crossed the sea, all of them gathered and promised the Lord that if he allowed them to invade Jerusalem, they would have peace with all the confessions of the Christians and would give churches and monasteries to every nation that confessed Christ.

In the meantime, Suleiman was killed by the Turk Alp-Arslan [the second Seljuk sultan].

With the Franks who came to Antioch were two kings and seven commanders: Ma'mūn and Tangri the kings; Rogel, Baimond, Bagdwin, Joscelin, Galeran, Gondofer, and Salgis. When they besieged Antioch, Theodore son of Hetum, who ruled Edessa after the killing of Buzan, heard of it, he sent a message to the Franks promising to give it to Godfrey the duke. The Franks greatly rejoiced and said, "Just as Edessa believed in Christ before Jerusalem, thus Christ our Lord gave Edessa to us before Jerusalem." Thus, Godfrey sent his brother Baldwin to reign over Edessa.

While the Franks were battling Antioch for nine months, the Turkish leaders in it were Gasian and Aghusin, and being under pressure, Aghusin left to go to Aleppo, but on the way, some Armenians fell upon him, cut his head off, and brought it to the Franks. Then, two other Armenian brothers who were established to keep guard on one of the towers on the mountain, committed treachery during the night; they made an agreement with Bohemond—to whom they surrendered the city.

Upon hearing that the Franks attacked Antioch, the sultan of Khorasan sent one hundred thousand cavalrymen with Khorabagad. On the same day, the Franks went into Antioch, and the Turks arrived in Baghras, and when they saw that the citadel, I mean Qal'a, was still with the Turks, they besieged it. The Franks were so much under the pressure of hunger that they ate their own horses. They sought refuge in prayer, and at that point, it was revealed to King Tancred in a dream; opening a place in the Church of Cassianus, they found there the nails of the cross of our Lord.

He made from them a cross and the tip of a spear, and taking them, he marched against the Turks and God gave the Franks a victory. They filled the ground with killed ones while pursuing the Turks as far as a one-day march. And when the Franks reigned over Antioch, the Turks ran away from the whole of Bet Nahrin, but [they came] to Ma'arra and Sarug, which belonged to Bani 'Uṭayr.

Before the expedition of the Franks, the Egyptians marched up and took Jerusalem away from the Turks, and when the Franks came, they first captured Jaffa in war, and then marched up against Jerusalem, in which was Faḍil the Egyptian. They set up a wooden tower in the middle of the eastern gate, that [of Mar] Stephen, and conquered it in Tammuz [i.e., July], the second year after their expedition. Many people among the Arabs were killed in it, and it was filled with corpses, especially the Temple of [Solomon], which they called Ṣakhra-Rock [Qubbat al-Ṣakhra; i.e., the Dome of the Rock]. They set the killed ones on fire. The first king of the Franks, Godfrey, reigned in it for two years [i.e., 1099–1100], and then Baldwin reigned for seven years [i.e., 1100–1118].

Until the time of this Alexios the emperor, our nation [i.e., the West Syrian Church] had one church in Constantinople, and another one [there] belonged to the Armenians, and in each one of them there was one priest and a group of lay people, traders, and others. A Syrian priest from Antioch went into our church, and when the priest, who was there and who was of Synnada, did not accept him, Satan possessed him. He went to say to the Greeks,

"These Syrians and Armenians who are in your city have schemes with the Turks." The emperor was furious, and upon his order, the two churches were burned down. The priests and other people were expelled but most of them became heretics. [. . .]

At the beginning of the kingdom [of Jerusalem] of Baldwin II [r. 1118–31], a Frankish man came from Rome to pray in Jerusalem. He had made a vow not to return to his land unless after three years, during which he, with thirty cavalrymen with him, would help the king in his wars, and thereafter he would become a monk and end his life in Jerusalem. When the king and his nobility saw that they succeeded in wars, assisting effectively the city through their service in this three-year period, they advised him that instead of becoming a monk and winning only his soul, he with those who followed him could serve the army and protect the lands from bandits. This man, whose name was Hodfayn [i.e., Hugues de Payens], accepted this advice, and the thirty cavalrymen agreed with him and followed him [and became the Knights Templar]. The king gave them the house of Solomon to inhabit and villages for their sustenance; likewise, the patriarch gave them some villages belonging to the church.

They imposed upon themselves to be guided by monastic rules, not to have wives, not to go into public baths, not to own anything whatsoever, but rather all their possessions belonged to the community. With such manners of conduct, they began to be illustrious and their reputation flew to all regions, in such a way [that] princes, kings, nobility, and the humble people used to come and join them in such a spiritual fraternity.

Anyone who joined them as a brother had to give to the community all that he possessed, whether villages or cities or even a trivial thing. They multiplied, expanded, and possessed regions not only in the lands of Palestine but also and mainly in the vast land of Italy and Rome. Their rules and regulations are written down in order. They would probe anyone who came to become a brother with them for one year, repeating to him the laws seven times, and each time they would tell him, "See lest you regret; perhaps you are not able to bear these rules to the end; confess and go back home." At the end of the year, the one who accepted and promised to bear the burden, they would pray over him and put on him their costume. Thereafter, the one who would retract from his promise, he would suffer the sword mercilessly and without intercession whatsoever.

Their rule was as follows: No one had the right to own a house or gold or possessions whatsoever. He could not leave without the permission of the leader. He could not sleep in any place other than in their estate. He could not consume bread at the table of the people. He had no right to refuse to go wherever he was ordered to go, even to death; rather, as he promised, he had to work to death in this group in faith. Anyone who died, they would dedicate forty sanctifications for him; in his commemoration, they would feed the poor for forty days, forty people a day; and his commemoration in the offering of the Eucharist in their churches was perpetual. Those who died in wars, they were considered as martyrs. Anyone who was found to have hidden something from the community or, while dying, was found that he had something with him that he did not give to the community, they considered him not worthy even of burial.

Their clothing consisted of one simple white dress, and other than it, they had no right to put on anything else. When they slept, they had no right to take off their cloths or to untie their belts. Their food was as follows: on Sundays, Tuesdays, and Thursdays they consumed meat; on the other days they consumed milk, eggs, and cheese; as for wine, they drank it every day during meals only. The priests and deacons among them served in churches, and the soldiers, I mean the cavalrymen, were engaged in their military service, and thus too the infantry during warfare. As for the skilled people, each type worked in his skill, and this is also the case of the peasants. In every city or village where they had estates, they had a superior and a steward, and according to his command, all of them worked, each in his domain.

Their general superior resided in Jerusalem. He ordered all of them that it was in no way lawful to have anything personal whatsoever. Everything that came in from the harvest of wheat or wine, or the rest, a tenth of it was set for the poor, and one tenth of the bread that was baked in every house had to be allocated to the needy.

Every day, the table was served of food for the brothers and the leftover was given to the poor, and twice a week, they allocated bread and wine specifically to the poor.

Their beginning was meant to protect pilgrims on roads, but later on, they marched out in war with the king against the Turks. Their numbers grew up to one hundred thousand. They owned fortresses and built fortified places in all the regions of the Christian dominion. Their possession of gold, all kinds of things, all types of weapons, and herds of sheep, cows, pigs, camels, and horses increased more than that of all kings. Yet, all of them were destitute and unencumbered with things. They agreed with and loved all who paid homage to the cross. They founded in all their regions, but especially in Jerusalem, hospitals so that any foreigner who became sick could find a place there, with people who cared about them and served them. If he was healed, they would give him sustenance and bid him well; if he died, they took care of his burial. [. . .]

The beginning of the first capture of Edessa that the Turks had taken away from the Franks happened as follows. For a long time, its inhabitants were as though in a prison at the hands of the Turks, and the city grew weakened in every aspect. Suddenly, Joscelin, lord of Edessa [i.e., Joscelin II, d. 1159], quarreled with Zangi, lord of Mosul [i.e., Imad al-Din Zengi, r. ca. 1085–1146], for the following reason. When Zangi was pursuing the lord of Ḥiṣn-Ziyad who sought refuge with Joscelin, the latter gave him the fortress of Bet Bula to help him against Zangi, just as he had helped Sultan Mas'ud. Now Joscelin did not understand that he had no advantage to quarrel with Turks on account of the Turk, [and so] he sent an army to assist Kara-Arslan. This became a pretext for Zangi. When Joscelin went to Antioch and was far away, the people of Ḥarran made known to Zangi that the city was without an army. Zangi gathered an army in the year 1456 [year of the Greeks = 1144 CE], and on the third day [of the week], the twenty-third of Second Teshrin [i.e., November], laid siege against Edessa with thousands, even myriads [of soldiers].

They pitched camp at the Gate of the Hours, near the Church of the Confessors. He sent to the citizens a word, saying, "Surrender so that you do not be perish! For you have no savior!" There was in it a leader, the Frank Papios, and they replied, "We do not surrender!" The latter was counting on the messengers that he dispatched to Antioch and Jerusalem that they may hasten to save the desirable city.

At the beginning of First Konun [i.e., December], at Zangi's order, the war began with all means: seven mangonels hurling stones and soldiers shooting arrows like drops of rain. As for the citizens, old and young, men and women, and the monks of the mountain, they stood on the wall fighting. When Zangi realized that the poor people were mightily fighting, he ordered [his troops] that they dig in the ground below the wall, and they dug deep and reached the foundation. Now the citizens dug from the inside and went against the ones outside and began fighting. Not [being] helped with this device, they began to build up a wall inside, opposite the place that had been dug. The outsiders dug under two towers, placing beams below them and below the wall from one tower to another. Atabeg [Zangi] sent a word: "We will give two men to be inside and send two [of yours] and see the wall that is dug. Surrender the city before you be taken by the sword, for I do not want that you [should] perish." Counting on the wall that [Papios] had built for them and waiting for the arrival of the Franks, they did not agree; rather, they scorned him and insulted him.

Then the Turks set the beams on fire. By the morning time the battle intensified, the air darkened with smoke, and knees and hearts trembled from the trumpets' sound, the messengers, and the scream of people. When the Turks burned the beams, bringing down the wall and the two towers, and the new wall appeared from inside, stupefaction befell them. They looked closely and saw a breach remaining between the new and the old walls, and at that point the troops gathered to enter, and the citizens assembled from inside with Papios and the bishops, preventing them from entering. The breach was filled with piles of the dead from among the defenders and invaders. And while the people stood in the breach fighting, and the wall was deserted, the Turks positioned ladders and climbed up, and a Kurd went up first and cried out and began stoning people. When the citizens saw him, they gave up out of fear, set their faces to the fortress, and fled.

Thereafter, what tongue could relate, or which finger would not tremble to write about the calamity that that took place at the time of the third hour of Saturday the third in First Konun [i.e., December]? The Turks invaded [the city], while their swords and lances brandished, drinking the blood of old men and children, women and men, priests and deacons, monks and hermits, nuns and virgins, babies, and bridegrooms and brides. The Assyrian pig ruled and trampled on lovely grapes. Ah, the bitter story! The city of Abgar, the friend of Christ, was trampled on because of our iniquity. The priests were destroyed, the deacons slaughtered, the subdeacons trampled, the churches pillaged, and the altars overturned. Ah, the affliction! Fathers denied their children and mothers lost compassion for their children, while the sword [was] destroyed, and everyone [was] rushed to the summit of the mountain.

Some gathered their children like a chicken and her chicks [Matthew 23:37], waiting either to die by the sword together or to be taken to slavery collectively. Old priests who were carrying relics of the martyrs, when they saw the wrath, said the word of the prophet [Micah]: "I will bear the anger of the Lord because I have sinned and angered him!" [Micah 7:9] Therefore, they did not escape, nor did they cease from prayer, until the sword silenced them. Thereafter, they were found in the same place, their blood covering their priestly vestments and the reliquaries of the holy ones in their hands. These were not taken away because of a [divine] sign that they received.

The Franks did not open the gate of the fortress to those who fled that they may enter, because Papios ordered them not to open it until they saw the face of the person. But while he could not come with the first arrival [of people], thousands were suffocated and the dead ones amassed to above the gate. When Papios arrived and the gate was opened, he could not enter on account of the multitude of cadavers that piled up on the ground. As he was struggling to enter, he fell between the suffocated ones, and one of the Turks shot him and killed him. When Zangi realized the calamity, he ordered that there should be no more killing. Then it happened that the bishop Basil was naked and being dragged with a rope. When Zangi saw that he was an old man with a shaven head, he asked about him, and when he learned that he was the bishop, he began interrogating him because the people did not want to surrender the city. He responded courageously, "The thing that happened is very good!" The amir [Zangi] said, "How?" The bishop said, "Yours is the great victory for you took us by the sword. But we have confidence in you that just as we did not break our oaths with the Franks, we will also respect the faithful oaths with you, for following God's order we became your servants." When he saw him courageous and lo, talking intelligibly in the Arabic language, he ordered that he be clothed with his tunic and brought into the tent. He sought his council about the rebuilding of the city, and the herald went out, [announcing], "Let all those who were spared the sword return to their houses!" After two days, those who were in the fortress took a pact for their lives and surrendered it, and all who survived from our people and from the Armenians and the Greeks were allowed to live, but they killed the Franks wherever they were found. [. . .]

In the year 1498 [of the Greeks = 1187 CE], Sultan Saladin [d. 1193] gathered an army from Egypt, Arabia, Syria, and Assyria, setting to fight against the Franks. On Saturday, the fourth of Tammuz [i.e., July], the Franks suffered desertion [by God] because of our sins, and they were utterly defeated. The king of Jerusalem and all his noble men were seized and all the brothers were killed. This defeat took place in Tiberias. The comes of Tripoli rebelled and fled. It is said about this one, because he expected that he should be established king but was prevented, he committed a perfidy against the Franks and left. I would say that without being deserted [by God,] their defeat would not have happened, because "no sparrow falls to the trap" without the sign from above [Matthew 10:29]. Saladin killed with his own hands the old man Arngad and three hundred brothers and washed himself with their blood. Then, he destroyed Tiberias in war, killing all who were in it. He went quickly to Acre, and all noble men who were in it fled by sea to Tyre. Those who remained in it surrendered it to Saladin. Then the people of Caesarea, Jaffa, Samaria, and Nazareth were taken into captivity and the whole universe was filled with captives. No word can describe how many insults, spitting, and abuses the Muslims made the persecuted Christian people endure in Damascus, Aleppo, Ḥarran, Edessa, Amid, Mardin, Mosul, and in the rest of their dominions.

In First Tishri [i.e., October] of the year 1499 [of the Greeks = 1188 CE], Saladin gave the Franks of Eshqalon, I mean Ascalon, oaths and freed the king who was captured by him and these surrendered the city to him. Then he marched up against Jerusalem, the land of peace. After he waged a few days of war against it and destroyed part of its wall in the northeast side, because there was no savior, the inhabitants agreed that every person would pay ten dinars to get out. Then he who was able to pay was able to get out—thousands and myriads left in cry and lamentation that splintered [even] stones. Those who were unable to pay, were subjected to servitude: Twenty thousand men and women; Saladin freed among them four thousand old men and women; he allocated six thousand to his armies as slaves; he sent five thousand to Egypt to build walls; and he left five thousand in

Jerusalem also to build the walls. As for the temple of Solomon which they call Ṣakhra, I mean Rock [i.e., Qubbat al-Ṣakhra; the Dome of the Rock]—they purified, according to their law, a second building erected by the Arabs, banning Christians from setting foot in it. They shut the Church of the Resurrection [i.e., the Holy Sepulchre] and other churches. The Christians, slaves, and others who remained would always head there to pray at the doors, while crying.

BARHEBRAEUS, *ECCLESIASTICAL CHRONICLE*

Thirteenth century. West Syrian.

Barhebraeus was a polymath of the highest order: he wrote on theology, philosophy, medicine, grammar, and history. His two historical works are the *Syriac Chronicle*, which covers secular events pertaining to Syriac Christianity, and the *Ecclesiastical Chronicle*, which covers Syriac church history and institutions. The latter extends to his death in 1286. Borrowing much from Michael the Syrian and an eleventh-century East Syrian Arabic work called the *Book of the Tower*, he nevertheless adds significant details, especially as he gets closer to his own time. He is unique in that he intermixes the history of the West and East Syrian patriarchates, though his focus is ultimately on the history of the office of maphrian, the West Syrian subpatriarch responsible for territories in the East. In the following selection dealing with the crusader period, the Frankish king Joscelin II, count of Edessa (see Michael the Syrian above), ransacks Mar Barsawma Monastery in 1148 and uses the relic of the right arm of the saint in battle against the Turks. The vignette depicts violence done among Christians during the Crusades and points out the difficult position of Syriac Christians throughout the twelfth and thirteenth centuries. For additional excerpts from Barhebraeus, see chapters 4 and 5.

> In the same year Joscelin the Frank, the lord of Edessa [i.e., Joscelin II; d. 1159], gave way to a wicked impulse. He assembled his forces, and after announcing his intention of going up to plunder the lands of the Turks, came to Ḥarran. Then he went up into the White Mountain, where he remained for three days, until he was recognized by the people of that region and fled. Then he said to his captains, "Since our march has been troubled, let us go to the nearest monastery, offer a prayer there, and then turn back."
>
> He suddenly arrived here [at the monastery of Mar Barsawma] on the morning of Sunday, the eighteenth of June [1148], and the monks rejoiced, because they thought he had come to pray, and they went out with crosses and gospels to meet him at the southern gate. When he saw the cross, he deceitfully dismounted from his horse, and humbly went inside and sat down. Then he disclosed his deceitful plan to several of his soldiers, who were as perverse as himself, and sent them to search the citadel.
>
> The monks immediately recognized the deceit of this inspection but were unable to prevent him. So five Franks went up and ordered the monk Hadbshabba and two servants

to leave. Joscelin imprisoned all the other monks in the church and summoned the eldest monks to him. Then he began to abuse them: "You put to flight the inhabitants of Qlaudia," he said. "Give me everything that was entrusted to you from the Turkish territories. I know you have hidden it here somewhere." The monks replied that if they did that, they could no longer live there. He angrily drove them out of the church and imprisoned them in the prison known as Kana. Then he sent the Frankish priests into the temple, who took away whatever they found: golden chalices, platters, glasses, crosses, thuribles, candlesticks, fans, gospels, books, and parchments. They also plundered the cells and collected whatever gold, silver, bronze, iron, clothing, and carpets they found. After searching the monastery throughout the Sabbath day, they took away whatever they could carry and, during the night, on the eve of the Lord's Day, they ordered the monks and all the other inhabitants of the monastery to leave and go with them. They spent the night by the "elephant's vine," near the riverbank, and they left the monastery under the guard of a gang of rogues and bandits, both Franks and Armenians.

Early on Sunday morning Joscelin again entered the monastery and sent men to search the cells. He even went up to the roof and sent plunderers into the cells of the servants. They loaded the spoil onto camels and mules. He also smashed another golden cross inside the monastery and gave it to his accomplices. He also took twelve mules and led off fifty monks. On the next day they came to Ghaktai. On the same night, while they were staying there, the holy saint Mar Barsawma appeared in a dream to three of the soldiers, saying, "Go, and tell your king that I was angry with my monks, and delivered them into your hands so that you might afflict them, and that they might repent and be converted. Now let them return to the monastery." But when the three men reported their dream to the king, he hardened his heart like Pharaoh, and said, "Unless they buy their freedom, I will not let them go." Then some of the king's servants saw a vision of a fiery sword held out from a citadel, in which was the saint's right hand, and heard a voice saying, "I tell you, Joscelin, unless you release my monks, I will destroy you and your kingdom with this sword." When they told him this, he imposed a fine of five thousand dinars on the monks, and released the elders David and Ya'qob, who arrived at the monastery in September 1460 [of the year of the Greeks = 1149 CE].

Meanwhile Joscelin was besieged by a Turkish force in Tel Bashir. Then, on his order, they held the saint's right arm above the wall and brandished it in the direction of the Turkish camp, while all the people stood by and wept with bared heads. Joscelin vowed that if he captured the enemy camp, he would send the right arm back to the monastery and would return all the other things he had plundered. The Turkish camp was stormed and captured in that very same hour, so Joscelin sent to the monastery and begged for forgiveness. The oldest monks led the saint back to the monastery in solemn procession. They entered the monastery at the beginning of January, on the feast of the holy doctors.

12

RELIGIONS OF THE SILK ROAD

Syriac Christianity was born in a religiously diverse environment. Syria and Mesopotamia were home to many religions, including indigenous and imported forms of pagan polytheism, Zoroastrianism, Manichaeism, and Judaism, as well as competing forms of Christianity. This chapter introduces the diverse religious landscape of Syriac Christianity's base in Syria and Mesopotamia, as well as Syriac Christians' encounters with religious "others" as they spread out from that base, especially eastward along the network of trade and communication in Central Asia that is commonly referred to as the "Silk Road."

Zoroastrianism was the state religion of successive ancient Persian empires, especially the Sasanians (224–651), who for centuries vied with the Romans for control of Syria and Mesopotamia. Syriac Christians settled in Sasanian territory as early as the third century and thus were in constant contact, and at times conflict, with Zoroastrianism and its royal patrons. The longstanding view has been that as Christianity became the state religion of Rome, Sasanian leaders viewed Christians in their midst as religiously and politically suspicious, and so subjected them to periodic, brutal persecution. More recent scholarship has cast that narrative into doubt, suggesting instead that Christians were integrated into the political elites, and that the persecutions might have been exaggerated in Christian hagiography. Nonetheless, some Christians were critical of Zoroastrianism's dualist cosmology of good and evil. Furthermore, the Zoroastrian veneration of the elements (water, earth, fire, and air) and especially the prominent role fire plays in Zoroastrian worship led some Christians to think of Zoroastrians as idolaters—that is, worshippers of created things (e.g., fire) rather than of the single creator.

Manichaeism was a religion founded in third-century Mesopotamia by the self-styled "apostle of light," Mani. Although he was raised in a Christian baptist sect and understood himself as a Christian and his message as the truth of Christianity, he was evidently also deeply influenced by Zoroastrian dualistic cosmology. Manichaeism was a wildly successful missionary religion. It spread as far west as Roman North Africa (where it initially counted the famed Latin theologian Augustine of Hippo among its ranks) and as far east as China (where it survived until the fourteenth century). Manichaeism flourished for a brief time under Sasanian patronage, especially under Shapur I (d. 272). All the missionary religions—Buddhism, Christianity, Manichaeism, and, later, Islam—competed for converts along the Silk Road. Manichaeism tended to adopt and adapt the religious vocabulary of its competitors. While this may have been a successful missionary strategy, it also had the effect of drawing the ire of confessional competitors.

The story of Syriac Christianity's spread along the Silk Road is fragmentary, although modern archaeological work is bringing more and more to light. We do know that especially the East Syrian Church, centered in Baghdad, invested in an unprecedented expansion eastward, reaching Chinese Turkestan and even Tibet. The most famous eastward mission is the one to China in 635, where Christians—called *jingjiao* or the "luminous religion" in China—established a community in Chang'an, capital of the Tang dynasty (618–907). In addition to the monumental bilingual Chinese and Syriac inscription erected by that community in 781, Christian texts in different languages (e.g., Chinese, Sogdian) have been found in the Silk Road oases of Turfan and Dunhuang. One such Chinese text from Dunhuang titled the *Discourse on the One God* is excerpted below.

The unification of several nomadic tribes in Mongolia under the leadership of Genghis Khan (d. 1227) led to the emergence of the Mongol Empire in the thirteenth and fourteenth centuries. The empire expanded rapidly, toppling other empires in its path, and it soon stretched from China to Central Europe—the largest contiguous land empire in history. With the rise of the Mongols, Western Christians took a keen and urgent interest in the Far East and discovered, to their surprise, that Christians were already in the court of the khans—although to them, these East Syrian Christians were "Nestorian" heretics. The final two sources provide a perspective on these encounters between Christians in the religiously diverse world of Mongol-controlled China and Central Asia, one from the Far Eastern and one from the Far Western point of view.

Further Reading An excellent place to begin is Richard Foltz, *Religions of the Silk Road: Premodern Patterns of Globalization* (New York: St. Martin's Press, 1999), along with Valerie Hansen, *The Silk Road: A New History* (New York: Oxford University Press, 2012). For more on Syriac Christians' encounters with Zoroastrians, see Joel Thomas Walker, the *Legend of Mar Qardagh: Narrative and Christian Heroism in Late Antique Iraq* (Berkeley: University of California Press, 2006); Richard E. Payne, *A State of Mixture: Christians, Zoroastrians, and Iranian Political Culture in Late Antiquity* (Berkeley: University of California Press, 2015). Hans-Joachim Klimkeit, *Gnosis on the Silk Road* (San Francisco:

HarperSanFrancisco, 1993) includes a good introduction to Manichaeism, as well as translations of Manichaean parables, hymns, and prayers from Central Asia. For more on *jingjiao* Christians in Tang-era China, see R. Todd Godwin, *Persian Christians at the Chinese Court* (London: I. B. Tauris, 2018). For more on the Latin missions to the Mongols, and Rabban Sawma's journey to the Europe, see Morris Rossabi, *Voyager from Xanadu: Rabban Sauma and the First Journey from China to the West* (Berkeley: University of California Press, 2010).

LEGEND OF MAR QARDAGH

Early seventh century. East Syrian.

This Christian martyr legend tells the story of Mar Qardagh, a fourth-century prince born into a noble family in the Sasanian empire. Mar Qardagh renounces his Zoroastrian heritage and converts to Christianity after meeting a Christian holy man named 'Abdisho'. For this conversion, he is sentenced to death by stoning by the Sasanian king Shapur II. This selection includes a dialogue between Mar Qardagh and 'Abdisho', who is in Mar Qardagh's custody before his conversion and martyrdom. The two of them enter into a theological dispute about the relative merits of Christian belief and traditional Zoroastrian worship of the "luminaries" (e.g., the sun and the moon) and "elements" (i.e., fire, water, earth, and air). Although scholars doubt that this legend is historically accurate, the dialogue is an important witness to the ways in which Syriac Christians imagined Zoroastrianism, the official religion of the Sasanian empire.

> And as soon as [Qardagh] took his seat, he ordered that they bring the holy 'Abdisho' into his presence. And he questioned him sharply and said to him, "Where are you from, man? And what is your profession?"
>
> But the blessed 'Abdisho' answered and said to him, "As it was told to me by my parents, they were from Ḥazza, a village in the lands of the Assyrians. But because they were Christians, they were driven out by impious pagans, and went and settled in Tamanon, a village in the land of the Kurds. But I have no fixed place or special abode to live in, because I heard from my Lord Christ who came and redeemed us by his holy death that "there was no place for him [the Son of man] to lay down his head," although verily heaven and earth and the things above and below are his, and he possesses and guides and preserves them.
>
> "But my 'work' [as you call it] is to offer ceaseless praise and to pay thanksgiving to God our maker and provider, he who created us in his own image and called us in his own likeness and saved us through his only begotten, who clothed himself in our body. And he gave us knowledge and understanding, lest we should reckon creatures to be gods, and lest we give, as you impious pagans give, the adoration that is due to him alone to the creatures he fashioned."
>
> And when Qardagh heard [this] he burned with anger, and he ordered that they strike the holy one upon his mouth. But while the blessed 'Abdisho' was being savagely beaten,

his eyes were gazing up into the heaven, and secretly he prayed to God that he might bring to completion in deed that which he had told him by revelation.

And Qardagh said to him indignantly, "Why do you call us worshippers of creatures, stupid old man?"

But the blessed 'Abdisho' was silent and did not give him an answer. And Qardagh said to him, "Will you not answer me? Do you now know that I have power over your life and death?"

But the blessed 'Abdisho' said to him, "Sir, I believe that a person who is struck upon the mouth is being taught that it is not right for him to speak; and because of this I have not answered your excellence. But what you have said about having power over my life and death is not true. You have the power to kill the body, but we who are servants of Christ and worshippers of the cross do not consider this to be death, but true immortal life! And over my soul and my life in Christ you do not have any power. Our Lord exhorts and commands us in his gospel when he says, "Do not fear those who kill the body, but are unable to kill the soul. But fear me, who am able to destroy both the body and the soul in Gehenna" [Matthew 10:20]. If, however, you desire me to speak with you, calm your wrath and control yourself. Kindly give me your attention and order them not to strike me again."

Then Qardagh swore to him, saying, "Speak as you please. No one will strike you again."

Then the holy 'Abdisho' replied and said to him, "Do you agree that everything that is an eternal entity and has not been made is a true god?"

The *marzbān* [i.e., an office in Sasanian administration, in this case Qardagh] said to him, "I agree."

The blessed one said to him, "And do you acknowledge that everything that has been made and is not an eternal entity is a creature?"

The *marzbān* said to him, "I acknowledge that it is so."

And again the blessed one said to him, "And you know that it is not right to worship creatures and that everyone who worships creatures angers God their creator?"

The *marzbān* said to him, "Sir, you have spoken truly. It is thus. But show me, who worships creatures?"

The blessed one said to him, "You and all your heathen companions. You are worshipping creatures!"

The *marzbān* said to him, "If you [can] show me that I worship creatures and anger God, gladly will I agree with you and follow your teaching. And I will hold you in the highest favor. But if you [can]not show me, be aware that you are making a grievous insult against me."

The blessed one said to him, "Do you not worship the sun and the moon, fire and water, air and earth, and call them gods and goddesses?"

Qardagh said to him, "Yes, I worship them because these things are eternal entities and have not been made."

The blessed one said to him, "Now from what have you deduced that the luminaries are eternal entities and have not been made?"

Qardagh said to him, "From their constant course, and because of the immutability of their nature, and from the fact that they endure by the strength of their nature and are not changed like other things and are set on high above."

The blessed one said to him, "These things about which you have spoken they have received from their creator as part of their constitution. The credit does not belong to their essence. That they [the luminaries] are not eternal entities is evident from the fact that they are not even alive. And if you say that these things are alive, I beseech you to tell me, indeed what kind of life do they possess? That of animals? Then why are they not nourished like animals? Or are they rational and capable of perception? And if you say that they are rational and capable of perception, then why do they not store up their warmth at times and rest from their course? For if the sun were rational, in winter it would dissipate the intensity of the frost and in summer it would not increase its heat. And it would grow warm in the region that is colder than its neighbor, and where it is hot it would restrain its rays. And from its constant course it would grow weary and suffer.

For everything that lives and belongs to the perceptible world and is in motion of its own accord also grows weary. And everything that does not live and does not grow weary has been set into motion by something else. A stone or an arrow or a cart is set into motion by something else, and they do not grow weary, since they also are not alive. Birds and animals move of their own accord and grow weary. If then the luminaries together with the elements move of their own accord, they should also grow weary and suffer, because they belong to the world of the senses. But because they do not move of their own accord, just so it is also evident that they are mute and soulless. And because of this they do not grow weary. And they are moved by the power of other things in the manner of a stone or an arrow or a cart. The former are moved by God; the latter by us."

The *marzbān* said to him, "Why do [the luminaries] possess a constant motion greater than these things on earth, and light and power that are exempt from change, corruption, or hindrance?"

The blessed one said to him, "Because they are in rank like the principal organs of the body: the brain, the liver, and the heart. For example, if someone removes a fingernail or hair or tooth from a body, the damage is partial. But if someone removes the brains or heart or liver, together with such things the whole animal would be destroyed. Just so, if one of those parts that are small in the constitution of the world, such as animals or seeds, perishes, the damage is partial. But if the creator allowed the luminaries to perish, the whole world would be destroyed. For the luminaries are the bond of the whole body of creation, for they are the chief members and eyes and brain of the world. And from them comes all the warmth that is in bodies and plants and the order of times and the numbering of the years, months, weeks, and days.

But they do not possess these qualities chiefly of their own accord. Rather, they receive them from the power and wisdom of their creator, while [they themselves] are neither alive nor sentient. Just as if there are ten men in one house, and one of them is blinded, he alone suffers in darkness, while those others escape his affliction. But if you [extinguish] the lamp that is inside the house or shut the door, the experience of the chastisement overtakes all of them in the house. Just as in the case of the loss of these [men in the dark house], so also [it would be for us] in the case [of the loss] of the luminaries. And from this, it is evident that the luminaries are not eternal entities but have been made. They are neither alive nor sentient, and anyone who worships them angers God their creator.

The same applies also to the elements. Earth, I mean, and water and fire and air are created entities. They are neither alive nor sentient. How can they be called eternal entities when each one is dissolved or corrupted by its companion, and the victory of each of them is the rout of the other? For earth is dissolved and even carried away by water. And water is absorbed by earth and perishes, and also vanishes into the air. Fire is extinguished by water and perishes. And air is enclosed in a wineskin and heated by the luminaries, and staleness and stench are mingled together with it. In sum, each of them is the destroyer of everything, even of its fellow [element].

[The elements] are also dissolved or changed or in need of each other. And everything that has needs has an origin. And everything that does not have an origin has no needs. For just as the origin-less thing is completely without needs, so also everything that has an origin has needs. Reality itself testifies to the neediness of the elements. For none of them, without its companion, can support its own internal parts. For earth needs water for germination. And water needs air to make it ascend and pour down. And fire also, without the wood that grows from earth, water, and air, cannot perform its activity.

Therefore, it is evident that the elements have needs, and if they have needs, they also have an origin. For what has no origin has no needs, neither with respect to its essence nor another [entity]. Being without origin, it is alive and also rational. But the elements are neither alive nor rational. For everything that lives and belongs to the perceptible world moves of its own accord and suffers, whereas the elements are not only irrational, they are not even alive or sentient. Indeed plants, together with animals, have life. For these things, because they grow and send up sprouts, [there is] also for them movement and change together with sense perception. The elements have not one of these things. But they are silent like rocks. And whoever worships these things and reckons them to be eternal entities angers God their creator. Rightly, therefore, I have called you creature-worshippers and strangers to God."

Where the *marzbān* heard these things, he burned with anger, because [his] error did not allow him to be persuaded by the words of the blessed one. And he ordered that the holy 'Abdisho' be bound with heavy chains and imprisoned in a dark place, and that each evening he be given a little bread but no water at all. And the holy one was bound and imprisoned, while he was rejoicing, singing, and saying, "Lord, my helper, I do not fear what man does to me."

One the next day, the *marzbān* went out for the chase and hunt. And he stretched his bow to shoot an arrow, but it dropped before his feet. And this same thing also happened to the soldiers who were with him. And although they tried many times, the air refused to support the arrows they were shooting. And when this happened, they were all very afraid. And the marzbān replied and said to those who were with him, "I think that old man whom we bound is a man of God. And by his prayers this marvel has occurred, and our weapons have been taken captive because we have provoked him."

And immediately he returned and entered his house in a state of great depression. And having neither food nor drink, he went to bed. He decided that in the morning he would release the blessed 'Abdisho'.

Now in the middle of the night, the house in which the blessed 'Abdisho' was imprisoned was filled with a splendid light. and a great crowd of spiritual beings appeared before him, chanting in a high voice and saying, "The righteous have called out, and the Lord has heard them, and set them free. The Lord is near those who call him in truth, and he does the will of those who fear him. He hears their request and redeems them."

While the blessed 'Abdisho' was chanting together with them and rejoicing, great fear fell upon all those who were nearby, surrounding the house in which the blessed one was imprisoned. And suddenly all the doors were opened. And an angel of the Lord touched the chains of the blessed one, and the chains fell off his hands and his feet. The angel grasped him by his hand and pulled him and led him out from the prison. And having led him outside, he released him from his hand and said to him, "Come after me." And the angel went before him in resplendent garments until he led him to his cave. Then he released him and departed.

THEODORE ABŪ QURRAH, *ON THE EXISTENCE OF GOD AND THE TRUE RELIGION*

Early ninth century. Chalcedonian. Arabic.

Theodore Abū Qurrah was the Chalcedonian bishop of Ḥarran and he is the first Christian known to have written in Arabic (he also wrote in Syriac, but none of his Syriac works have survived). Among his Arabic writings are a series of treatises in which he endeavors to discern the true religion. He is principally concerned to establish Christianity's truth (and specifically Chalcedonian orthodoxy) over against Islam, a recent arrival on the scene. In this treatise, Theodore offers a detailed narrative of contemporary religions, including those of pagans, Mazdeans, Samaritans, Jews, Christians, Manichaeans, Marcionites, Bardaisanites, and Muslims. In what is almost certainly a literary device, Theodore presents his material as if he were on a tour, spending time with each of these groups. This selection includes abbreviated discussions of Manichaean cosmology and anthropology, as well as a critique of Manichaeans' alleged sexual libertinism and refusal of almsgiving (both charges are highly suspect). According to Theodore, the Manichaeans regard themselves as the true Christians, in possession of the true gospel, and the caretakers of the one and only true church.

> I left them and was met by some Manichaeans, who are also called Zindiqs. They said, "Beware! Don't follow the Christians or listen to the words of their gospel. We have the true gospel, the one that the twelve apostles wrote. The only true religion is ours, and we are the only Christians. Our master Mani alone understands how to interpret the gospel. He taught us as follows: 'Before the world was created, there were two gods. These differed in essence. One was light and good (that is, the good god). The other was wicked and darkness (that is, Satan). In the beginning, each was in his own domain. The darkness then noticed the luminous one, as well as his beauty and his loveliness. Out of desire for him, he attacked him and fought with him, wanting to capture him. The luminous one sought to fight against him, but soon the darkness was on the point of victory. When the luminous one came to fear for himself, he cut off a piece of himself and threw it to him. This the darkness swallowed. Heaven and earth, as well as what is between them, is made—by way of mingling—from the nature of the darkness and from the piece that the luminous one threw to him.'

The human being, for instance, is created from an internal soul and an external body, and they suggest that the soul is from the nature of the luminous one, while the body is from the nature of Satan, the dark one. The same holds with regard to the state of things. Everything in them that is good and pleasant is from the nature of the dark one. For instance, water drowns those who are submerged in it but gives life and pleasure to those who drink it. The part that gives life is from the luminous one, while what drowns and destroys is from the darkness. As for snakes, scorpions, lions, panthers, creeping things, and the like, all these are from the darkness." This is the essence of their religion and how they describe their gods. As for the permitted and the forbidden, they pander to the worldly desires of those who wish to live a life of pleasure. They are not commanded to get married. Rather, whoever desires a woman can have her, and the same holds for women with regard to men. In fact, this is how they interpret the gospel, suggesting that when Christ said, "Give to whoever asks," he did not mean that when the poor ask for alms, you should give to them. Because it was God who caused the poor to have misery in this world, no one is allowed to give them anything, not even alms. If we do, we disobey God, who, if he desires, makes them wretched, and who, if he desires, makes them prosperous. If God had wished to make them prosperous, he would have given them wealth in the same way that he gave it to the one from whom alms were being asked and would not have caused them to be needy. As concerns their interpretation of Christ's words, "Give to whoever asks," this has to do with men and women. He is saying to the woman, "If a man asks you for yourself, don't refuse him," and to the man, "If a woman asks you for yourself, give yourself to her." This and the like do they teach with regard to the permitted and the forbidden and with regard to matters of divinity.

TIMOTHY I, *LETTERS* 41 AND 47

790s. East Syrian.

Timothy I (d. 823) was one of the greatest katholikoi of the East Syrian Church. Many of his letters survive, including these two that provide fascinating insights into the history of Christianity in Central Asia (dated 792/793 and between 795 and 798, respectively). During Timothy's reign, the East Syrian Church continued its expansion eastward into Central Asia, for which Timothy had to consecrate metropolitans in various places to the east of his patriarchal see in Baghdad. The extent of the church's reach can be seen in his consecration of a metropolitan for Christians among the Turks and his intention to do the same for Christians among the Tibetans. These letters bear witness to the missionary efforts and successes (albeit somewhat ephemeral ones) of the East Syrian Church among the peoples of Central Asia. For additional excerpts from Timothy I, see chapters 9, 10, and 11.

LETTERS 41

For behold, in all of the lands of Babel [i.e., Baghdad], Pars [i.e., Persia], and Atur [i.e., Assyria], and in all of the eastern lands and among Bet Hinduwaye [India] and indeed among Bet Ṣinaye [China], among Bet Tuptaye [Tibet] and likewise among Bet Ṭurkaye [Turkestan], and in all the domains under this patriarchal throne—this [throne] of which God commanded that we be its servants and likewise its ministers (that one who is this hypostasis) who is from eternity, without increase, who was crucified on our behalf—is proclaimed, indeed in different and diverse lands and races and languages.

For behold, even in our days—prior to these ten years that I have been entrusted with the service of the administration of the church, for even now I have been thirteen years more or less in this service—the king of the Ṭurkaye, with more or less all of his territory, has left the godless error from antiquity, for he has become acquainted with Christianity by the operation of the great power of the messiah, that by which all are subject to him. And he has asked us in his writings [about] how he might appoint a metropolitan for the territory of his kingdom. This also we have done [with the help of] God. And, also, the letter that we wrote to him we will send to you if it is pleasing to our Lord.

LETTERS 47

The Spirit has anointed in these days a metropolitan for Bet Ṭurkaye and we are also preparing to anoint another one for Bet Tuptaye.

JINGJIAO STELE

781. East Syrian.

This black limestone monument was discovered between 1623 and 1625 in modern-day Xi'an, formerly Chang'an, the capital city of the Tang dynasty in China (618–907). Erected in 781, the stele commemorates the arrival of East Syrian missionaries in Chang'an in 635, and the history of the community in the ensuing hundred and fifty years. The inscription was authored by a certain Jingjing, whose Syriac name was Adam; it is in classical Chinese, ringed by short sentences in Syriac. The monument's title, "A Eulogy in Celebration of the Arrival and Spread of the Luminous Religion of *Daqin* in the Middle Kingdom," attests to the name Christians were given in China (or took themselves): *jingjiao* or "the luminous religion." Daqin is a vague geographical marker in classical Chinese, sometimes used to refer to the Roman Empire, greater Syria, or some mythic West. "The Middle Kingdom" is an ancient name that successive Chinese dynasties gave themselves. The inscription describes Christianity in terms significantly drawn from Buddhism and Taoism. (Note: headings in italics are not a part of the inscription itself but have been added to aid the reader.)

Part 1. The Title of the Monument
A eulogy in celebration of the arrival and spread of the Luminous Religion of Daqin in the Middle Kingdom—with a prologue.
Written by Presbyter Jingjing of the Daqin church.
Adam, presbyter and chorepiscopus, and bishop of Chinastan.

FIGURE 14.

The *Kadamattom Cross*. In addition to textual references in sources like Timothy I's *Letters*, material remains also attest to the geographic expanse of medieval Syriac Christianity. This stone relief of a Persian-style cross comes from the Kadamattom Church in southern India and is traditionally dated to the ninth century. An inscription in Pahlavi, or Middle Persian, runs along the side. Images of Persian-style crosses proliferated among south Indian Syriac Christian communities from the sixth through ninth centuries; other such crosses have been found in Mailapur, Tamil Nadu; Kottayam, Kerala; and Sri Lanka, among other locations. The Pahlavi text and wing imagery to the side of the cross suggest a Persian origin of the image, and therefore a close connection between the Syriac Christian community in south India and Persian ecclesiastical and mercantile organizations in the medieval period. Some scholars have also noticed connections between the text of some of these crosses and copper plates granting certain rights to Christian communities in south Indian kingdoms (see figure 15). Whatever the exact source of the south Indian cross imagery, these crosses are some of the earliest surviving artifacts from Syriac Christian communities in India and their inscriptions constitute some of the earliest Christian writing in the Indian subcontinent. Today, the Persian or Nasrani cross continues to be a symbol of religious, ecclesiastic, and ethnic identity among Christians in India and the Indian diaspora. "Kokkarani" / WikiCommons; licensed under the CreativeCommons Attribution-Share Alike 3.0 license.

FIGURE 15.
The *Kollam Plate*. Inscribed around 849 under the Cera dynasty in the Indian port city of Kollam, southern Kerala, these copper plates record a grant of land and legal privileges from a local noble to a group of Persian Christians. They are written primarily in Old Malayalam, with signatures representing four religious communities (Jews, Muslims, Christians, and Zoroastrians) in Middle Persian, Arabic, and Judeo-Persian. Although similar grants were given to Buddhist, Hindu, and Jain communities under the Cera dynasty, the exact transcription, translation, and provenance of the Kollam copper plates have long been debated. Regardless of the exact terms of and reasons for the grant, however, the Kollam Plate represents one of our earliest indigenous written sources on Syriac Christianity in India and is a valuable source for understanding relations between the Syriac Christian community, south Indian nobility, and other religious communities in the region. The frame and multiple repairs to the plates given to them by later generations of Syriac Christians bear witness to their ongoing importance for the Syriac Christian community in India. Photo credit: Kesavan Veluthat.

Part 2. A Description of the Teaching of the Luminous Religion
   a) A Description of God
   As it is said: the one who is everlasting and truly serene, the one who is before all and without beginning, the one who is profound reality and spiritual emptiness, the one who is after all and has mysterious existence, the one who gathered the central principles and created all things, the one who is more wonderful than all the holy ones, and most honorable, he is the only mysterious Trinitarian being, he is indeed the preexistent true Lord, Aluohe [Chinese for Syriac *Alaha*, God]!
   b) A Description of Creation
   He divided the cross in order to establish the four cardinal points. He moved the original spirit and produced the two realms. The dark void was changed, and heaven and earth were separated. The sun and moon began to spin, and day and night were made. After he made all material things, he established the original human beings. In addition, he granted them goodness and harmony, and commanded them to subdue and transform the world. According to their original nature, they were pure and uninflated.
   In accordance with their pure heart, their inner self did not have any inordinate desire.

c) The Fall and Perversion of Humanity

But then Satan acted deceitfully, and he deceived humanity's upright nature. He disrupted peace and serenity in the place of rectitude. Instead he brought darkness into the place of perversion. Because of this, 365 kinds of sects followed shoulder-to-shoulder making one track. They competed to weave many sectarian nets. Some pointed to material things in order to trust and worship them. Some destroyed the distinction between the invisible and visible realms. Some prayed and sacrificed in order to obtain blessings. Some made a show of goodness in order to suppress people. Their wisdom and plans became utterly confused. Their thoughts and desires became completely enslaved. Because of their confusion and inability, they were harassed and anxious, and turned and burned. After accumulating much darkness, they lost the way. And after a long time of confusion, they ceased to return again.

d) The Incarnation and Ministry of the Messiah

Upon this, therefore, our Triune God divided his person, and the illustrious and honorable messiah, masking and hiding his true power, appeared as a human being. Thereupon, the spirits of heaven proclaimed the glad tidings. The virgin gave birth to a holy one in Daqin. An illustrious star announced the good news. The Persians, seeing the glory, came to present gifts. He fulfilled the words of the Old Testament by the twenty-four saints. He governed families and countries by his heavenly way. He established, through the pure Spirit of the Trinity, the new religion of no words. He established virtuous means for upright faith. By setting up the standard of the eight moral virtues, he refined people of dust to become people of truth. By revealing the three everlasting gates, he opened life and extinguished death. He raised the light of the sun in order to destroy the realm of darkness. Thereupon, the devil and anarchy were completely broken. He launched the ship of mercy in order to ascend to the palace of light. Thereupon, imprisoned spirits were released. Having completed this work of power, at noon he ascended to his true home.

e) The History of the Early Church (Apostolic Era)

He left behind twenty-seven scriptures. They proclaimed the great conversion in order to open the spiritual barrier. Through baptism and the Spirit, he purified superficial extravagance and cleansed barren emptiness. By holding the cross as a sign, they harmonized and enlightened the whole world in order to unite all without restriction. By striking the wood, they excite the sound of mercy and grace. By worshipping toward the East, they advance the way of life and glory. The reason they keep the beard is to have outward works. The reason they shave the head is to have no inner desire. They do not collect slaves or maidens but treat the noble and the poor alike. They do not gather possessions or wealth. Instead, they manifest simplicity and bequeath an example to us. They eat moderately to control their thoughts and become mature. They are disciplined to be quiet and alert, becoming firm. Seven times a day they worship and praise. They greatly aid the living and dying. Once every seven days, they cleanse the heart and return to simplicity.

f) A Summary of the Way

The true and everlasting Way is wonderful, but very difficult to name. Its meritorious results are luminously displayed, and we are forced to call it the Luminous Religion. Without the holy ones, the Way would not have spread. Without the Way, the holy ones would not have been great. When the Way and the holy ones are in harmony, the whole world becomes cultured and enlightened.

Part 3. The History of the Luminous Religion in China
   a) The Arrival of Aluoben

Taizong was a cultured emperor, who enlightened China and started a new era. Enlightenment and piety came to the people. At that time, the country of Daqin had a great sage, who was called Aluoben. He observed the heavens and carried the true scriptures. By observing the laws of the wind, he quickly passed through difficulties and dangers. In the ninth year of the Zhen Guan period, he arrived in Chang'an. The emperor sent his chief minister, Duke Fang Xuanling, who was the overall protector of the Western Regions, to welcome and escort his guest into the interior.

   b) Imperial Sanction of the Luminous Religion

After the scriptures and books were translated in the imperial library, the emperor researched the Way in his private quarters. And he became deeply convinced of its respectability and truth. So he specially decreed that it should be propagated and taught. In the autumn of the twelfth year and seventh month of the Zheng Guan period, an imperial mandate was issued, stating, "The Way does not always have the same name. The sage does not always have the same ritual. Heaven according to every place, appointed a particular religion, to aid quietly numerous peoples. Bishop Aluoben of the country of Daqin brought from afar scriptures and images and presented them at the supreme capital. The emperor carefully examined the meaning and intention of this teaching and found it to be profoundly wonderful and of silent operation. The emperor also observed its good aims and found that it promotes success and establishes essential principles. Its language does not have complicated expressions. Its principles can be compared to 'forget the trap when you have caught the fish.' It is helpful for the affairs of the world and beneficial for humanity. Therefore, it should be propagated throughout the empire."

   c) The Expansion of the Luminous Religion

Consequently, those in charge in the Yi-ning ward of the capital immediately constructed one Daqin monastery with an administration of twenty-one presbyters. The virtue of the House of Zhou had already died away, and the green carriage already ascended to the west. But during the Great Tang the Way was recovered, when the Luminous wind came to fan the East. Thereupon, it was decreed that those in charge take the portrait of the emperor and transfer a copy to the walls of the monastery. The celestial image disseminated bright colors. Its clarity and brightness shone upon the Luminous disciples. Divine miracles conferred blessings and enlightened the world forever.

   d) The Country of Daqin

According to the illustrated records of the Western Regions and the historical books of the Han and Wei dynasties, the country of Daqin on the south is bounded by the Coral Sea; on the north reaches to the Mountain of All Precious Things; on the west extends toward the borders of the immortals and flowery forests; on the east it strides the long winds and weak waters. Its soil produces fireproof cloth, soul-restoring incense, bright moon pearls, and night-shining gems. Among the common people there are no thieves and robbers. They all have much happiness and peace. None but the Luminous Religion prevails. None but the virtuous are raised to power. The land and terrain are vast and broad. Its culture and affairs are glorious and enlightened. [. . .]

Part 4. Chronological Notes

This monument was established in the second year of the Jian Zhong period of the great Tang dynasty, in the year of Zuo'e, in the first month on the seventh day, on the Great Yaosenwen Day [Sunday]. At this time, the spiritual master, Presbyter Ning-shu, is overseeing the congregations of the Luminous congregations in the East.

In the day of our father of fathers, my Lord Henanisho', Katholikos, Patriarch.

Written by Lu Xiuyan, secretary to council, with the title Chao Yi Lang, who was formerly the superintendent for Taizhou.

[On Bottom of Monument from right to left]

The assistant examiner and supervisor, the high official for ceremonies, who has been conferred with the purple robe, was the Abbot of the Monastery, Presbyter Yeli.

Gabriel, presbyter and archdeacon, and head of the Church of Kumdan [Chang'an] and Sarag [Luoyang].

The examiner and supervisor at the erection of the monument was Presbyter Xingtong.

Presbyter Sabraniso

Mar Sergius, presbyter and chorepiscopus

Adam the deacon, son of Yazedbuzid who is the chorepiscopus

Presbyter Lingbao

In the year of the Greeks one thousand and ninety-two [= 781 CE], my Lord Yazedbuzid, presbyter and chorepiscopus of Kumdan [Chang'an], the royal city, son of the deceased Milis, presbyter of Balkh, a city of Tahouristan, set up this tablet, whereon is inscribed the dispensation of our savior, and the preaching of our fathers to the kings of China. [. . .]

DISCOURSE ON THE ONE GOD

Seventh century. East Syrian.

In addition to the *Jingjiao Stele*, seven Christian manuscripts in Chinese were discovered in the early twentieth century in the Silk Road oasis town of Dunhuang. They were part of a large cache of scrolls that had been sealed in a cave in the eleventh century—presumably in order to protect them. Two of these seven texts, including this one, are thought to be from the earliest period of Christianity in China, having perhaps been in the possession of the Christian missionary, Aluoben, and his entourage, which reached Chang'an in 635. An internal date suggests that the *Discourse on the One God* was composed (or translated) soon after Aluoben's arrival around 635. The Dunhuang manuscripts are either translations into Chinese of some Syriac or Sogdian Christian texts now lost to us or, more likely, original compositions in Chinese. The Dunhuang manuscripts present many textual challenges, and in the case of this and the other early text, the quality of the Chinese is quite poor. Like the *Jingjiao Stele*, all Dunhuang manuscripts borrow heavily from Chinese religious terminology (i.e., Buddhism, Taoism, and Confucianism) to explain Christian teachings.

FIGURE 16.
A rubbing from the *Jingjiao Stele*. Erected in Chang'an (the capital of Tang-dynasty China) in 781 and unearthed in the seventeenth century, the *Jingjiao Stele* is one of our most important sources regarding Christianity in premodern China. The monument's inscription, authored by the East Syriac monk Jingjing, is a summary of Christian theology, and a history of Christianity in China, which goes by the name *jingjiao* or "luminous religion"; the bottom and sides include signatures written in Syriac. On top is a depiction of a cross over clouds (traditionally a Daoist symbol) flanked by lotus flowers (a Buddhist symbol). This imagery aligns with the theological portion of the monument's text, which makes heavy use of Buddhist and Daoist terminology, evidently an attempt to make Christian theology legible to a Chinese audience. University of Minnesota East Asian Library.

All things manifest [only] one God. All things are the things made by the one God. If the things that are seen are the things that were made, then the seen and the made manifest the same one God. Therefore, one can know that all things were created by this one God. The visible and the invisible were all created by this one God. Until today, things made by God can be seen.

So those things can stay in heaven or stand on earth, unchangeable until today. The sky has no pillar to support it. Should it not be made by the one God, how can it stay up there for forever, and not fall down? This is because of the wonderful power of the one God. Should it not be the work of the one God, who can stand and not fall down forever? Therefore, [we] know that it is because of the power of the one God that the sky can stay high above there alone. With this analogy, [we] know the wonderful power of the one God. Since it is the power of God, then we know that even though there is no pillar to support it, the sky can stay high above alone. Since the sky stays high above alone without the support of a pillar, we know that it does not stand by itself, but rather by the power of the one God, which is the same as a pillar there to be seen; and that with the power of the one God, there is no need to have pillars or walls. One sees that in heaven and on earth, one has no position there either. So one says that they have no place of rest. The so-called position is positioned upon water. But then upon what is water positioned? Upon wind! Then for a long time it [heaven and earth] has neither collapsed nor fallen down. Thousands of things move and turn, but not one thing is seen. However, there is the power of God that makes all things acquire what they had wished. It is like archery. One sees only the landing of the arrow but not the archer. Though one does not see the archer, the arrow cannot come by itself. There must be an archer who has shot it. So it is known with heaven and earth for which the one God gives power; it does not collapse or break down. Because of the power of God, the universe [i.e., heaven and earth] can stand for ever. Though one sees no one supporting and grasping the heaven and earth, there must be a supporter with wonder there. For instance, the archer, when his strength is gone, the arrow falls down. If God's power is not given, heaven and earth will break down. It is because of God's power that heaven and earth do not decay. Therefore, both heaven and earth are the power of the one God. The heaven does not fall down, so we know that the wonderful power of the one God has no end. There is no other god, but the power of this God, the only one God. He is both invisible, and he is visible in two manifestations. It is like the left and the right hands and feet, moving forward or backward, upward or downward, very similar and not much different.

Another example: within the one God, the idea of the one God is generated. That is to say, we know there is no left or right; no front or back; no up or down; the one God grasps all together one thing, no other second or third. No one can make it, and there is no master or maker or operator. We see the one God staying and standing in heaven and earth, but we do not see him holding the heaven and the earth. And he can provide for all beings. This is what can be seen. Another example: a house has one master who has one soul. If the house has more masters, then the house will be in trouble. If one person has several souls, then this person is not able to do good. Therefore, a person has no second soul or third. It is like a house having one master, no second or third. Heaven and earth have only one God, no other second or third. This one God cannot be seen in heaven and on earth, just like the soul in a person, which human eyes cannot see. The soul in a person cannot be grasped or seen, just like [the one God] not being seen under heaven. Everyone wants to see or grasp the soul in the body. The most holy one of great wisdom is equal to emptiness. He cannot be grasped. Only this one God is everywhere. And the soul in the body has also its own will.

There is only one God in the world. In heaven there is no border. The one God is not always in one place; nor does he hold one place. There is no border linking one place to the second place or one time period to the second time period.

For example, from here to Bosi [Persia], like from Bosi [Persia] to Fulin, there is no land border or time border. Another example, the morals and teachings of the holy Lord appear today. Then from now on, there will be no border limit or beginning of making [action], nor can the first and the second be possible again. There is only one God. Therefore, there is neither border nor the beginning of making [action], nor dwelling places, nor time period. It cannot be questioned, nor can it be known by questioning. Where is this one God? Wherever he stays, there is no limit or the beginning of making [action]. One cannot ask the one God when to do the action and when to begin. Neither can it be answered by questioning; nor can it be answered by not questioning. The permanent will not diminish. The diminishing is not permanent. Where the one God is, is in the permanence of all things. The one God has no beginning. His existence has no end. The place where the one God dwells is the place of the honored, though the honored is not seen. The one God made laws that are not different. His self-holiness has no limit. The intangible in the world was made by the heavenly Lord. In the place of the heavenly Lord, the tangible in the world can be seen. Some cannot be seen. For instance, one cannot see the appearance of the soul, but one has the desire to see it. [The soul] is similar to the knowledge of God in a person. All human beings have these two elements [i.e., the soul and spirit] that have the same root. It is like a tree that has two branches. The same is with a person who has both soul and spirit that are in this one person. If a person has no body, he is not complete; nor is he complete without soul; nor is he complete without spirit. Those that can be seen in the world are themselves not complete; but those that cannot be seen can be themselves complete. All things under heaven are of two kinds but of one root. If one asks, how can the one God know all things? Where are the invisible things? The answer is as follows: all the invisible things exist in the world, like the things used by the one God. For example, some of the things are operated by some men.

HISTORY OF THE LIFE AND TRAVELS OF RABBAN SAUMA

Late thirteenth or early fourteenth century. East Syrian.

Rabban Sauma (d. 1294) was an East Syrian monk of Turkic ethnicity born in China, which was then under the control of the Mongols. He set out with one of his students, Markos, on a pilgrimage to Jerusalem, but they never reached their destination. Along the way, in 1281, Markos was elected katholikos in Baghdad and assumed the name

Yahballaha III (d. 1317). In 1287, Rabban Sauma continued on to Europe as an ambassador from the Mongols, since the Mongol khan Arghun sought to form an alliance with the king of France against the Mamluk sultanate in Cairo. His travels took him to Constantinople, Paris, Gascony, and Rome. During his sojourn, he met with the Byzantine emperor Andronicus II Palaeologus, King Philip the Fair of France, King Edward I of England, and Pope Nicholas IV (here, "Mar Papa"), among others. He returned to Baghdad in 1288, where he remained for the rest of his life. He kept a journal in Persian, which was translated into Syriac and incorporated into this travelogue by an anonymous author who appears to have been an eyewitness to some of the events. The travelogue serves as a mirror image of Marco Polo's later and more famous account. This selection is from Rabban Sauma's sojourn in Rome: First he offers his confession of faith to the group of cardinals; then he celebrates the Eucharist in front a large assembly of people; finally, on Palm Sunday, he attends the Pope's celebration of the Eucharist, and receives the mysteries from the pontiff's own hands.

[The Confession of Rabban Sauma to the Cardinals]

I believe in one God, hidden, everlasting, without beginning and without end, Father, and Son, and Holy Spirit: three persons, coequal and indivisible; among whom there is none who is first, or last, or young, or old: in nature they are one, in persons they are three: the Father is the Begetter; the Son is the Begotten; the Spirit proceeds.

In the last time one of the persons of the royal Trinity, namely the Son, put on the perfect man, Jesus Christ, from Mary the holy virgin; and was united to him personally, and in him saved the world. In his divinity he is eternally of the Father; in his humanity he was born in the time of Mary; the union is inseparable and indivisible forever; the union is without mingling, and without mixture, and without compaction. The Son of this union is perfect God and perfect human, two natures [*kyane*], and two persons [*qnome*]—one *prosōpon* [*parsopa*].

The cardinals said to him, "Does the Holy Spirit proceed from the Father or from the Son, or is it separate?" Rabban Sawma replied, "Are the Father, and the Son, and the Spirit associated in the things that appertain to the nature or separate?" The cardinals answered, "They are associated in the things that concern the nature but are separate in respect of individual qualities." Rabban Sawma said, "What are their individual qualities?" The cardinals replied, "Of the Father, the act of begetting; of the Son the being begotten; of the Spirit the going forth." Rabban Sawma said, "Which of them is the cause of the other?" And the Cardinals replied, "The Father is the cause of the Son, and the Son is the cause of the Spirit." Rabban Sawma said, "If they are coequal in nature, and in operation, and in power, and in authority, and the three persons are one, how is it possible for one of them to be the cause of the other? For of necessity the Spirit also must be the cause of some other thing; but the discussion is extraneous to the confession of faith of wise men. We cannot find a demonstration resembling this statement of yours.

For behold, the soul is the cause both of the reasoning power and the act of living, but the reasoning power is not the cause of the act of living. The sphere of the sun is the cause of light and heat, and heat is not the cause of light. Thus we think that which is correct, namely, that the Father is the cause of the Son and the Spirit, and that both the Son and the Spirit are causations of his. Adam begot Seth, and made Eve to proceed [from him], and they are three; because in respect there is absolutely no difference between begetting and making to go forth [or proceed]."

Then the cardinals said unto him, "We confess that the Spirit proceeds from the Father and the Son, but not as we said, for we were only putting your modesty to the test." And Rabban Sawma said, "It is not right that to something that is one, two, three, or four causes should be [assigned]; on the contrary I do not think that this resembles our confession of faith." Now, though the cardinals restrained his speech by means of very many demonstrations, they held him in high esteem because of his power of argument.

Then Rabban Sawma said to them, "I have come from remote countries neither to discuss, nor to instruct in matter of the faith, but I came that I might receive a blessing from Mar Papa, and from the shrines of the saints and to make known the words of King [Arghan] and the katholikos. If it be pleasing in your eyes, let us set aside discussion, and give attention and direct someone to show us the churches here and the shrines of the saints; [if you will do this] you will confer a very great favor on your servant and disciple."

Some days later Rabban Sawma said to Mar Papa, "I wish to celebrate the Eucharist so that you might see our use"; and the pope commanded him to do as he had asked. And on that day a very large number of people were gathered together in order to see how the ambassador of the Mongols celebrated the Eucharist. And when they had seen, they had rejoiced and said, "The language is different, but the use is the same." Now the day on which he celebrated was the Sunday [on which the prayer beginning] *ainaw asya* [i.e., "Who is the physician"] is recited. And having performed the mysteries, he went to Mar Papa and saluted him. And the pope said unto Rabban Sawma, "May God receive your offering, and bless you, and pardon your transgressions and sins." Then Rabban Sawma said, "Beside the pardon of my transgressions and sins that I have received from you, O our Father, I beseech your fatherhood, O our holy Father, to let me receive the offering from your hands, so that the remission [of my sins] may be complete." And the pope said, "Let it be so!"

And on the following first day of the week, which was the Festival of Hosannas [i.e., Palm Sunday], from the break of day onward, countless thousands and tens of thousands of people gathered together before the papal throne, and brought branches of olives, which the pope blessed and gave to the cardinals, and then to the metropolitans and then to the bishops, and then to the princes, and then to the nobles, and then he cast them among all the people. And he rose up from the throne, and they brought him into the church with great ceremony. And he went into the apse of the altar and changed his apparel, and he put on a red vestment with threads of gold [running through it], and ornamented with precious stones, and [the gemstones] jacinths, and pearls down to the soles of his feet, that is to say, sandals. And he went to the altar, and then went forth to the pulpit, and addressed the people and admonished them. And he consecrated the mysteries and gave the Eucharist mystery to Rabban Sawma first of all—he having confessed his sins—and the pope pardoned his transgressions and his sins and those of his fathers. And Rabban Sawma rejoiced greatly in receiving the Eucharistic mystery from the hand of Mar Papa. And he received it with tears and sobs, giving thanks to God and meditating upon the mercies that had been poured out upon him.

And when these things had taken place, Rabban Sawma asked Mar Papa for [his] command to return. And Mar Papa said unto him, "We wish you to remain with us, and to abide with us, and we will guard you like the pupil of our eye." But Rabban Sawma replied, "O our father, I came on an embassy for your service. If my coming had been the result of my personal wish, I would willingly bring to an end the days of this my useless life in your service at the outer door of your palace. [But I must return], and I believe that when I go back and show those who are there the benefits that you have conferred upon my poor person, that the Christians will gain great content thereby. Now I beseech our holiness to bestow upon me some of the relics [of the saints] that you have with you."

And Mar Papa said, "If we had been in the habit of giving away these relics to the people [who come] in myriads, even though the relics were as large as the mountains, they would have come to an end long ago. But since you have come from a far country, we will give you a few." And he gave to Rabban Sawma a small piece of the apparel of our Lord Christ, and a piece of the cape, that is to say, the kerchief of my lady Mary, and some small fragments of the bodies of the saints that were there. And he sent to Mar Yahballaha a crown for his head that was of fine gold and was inlaid with precious stones; and sacred vestments made of red cloth through which ran threads of gold; and socks and sandals on which real pearls were sewn; and the ring from his finger; and a *pethikha* or bull that authorized him to exercise patriarchal dominion over all the children of the East. And he gave to Rabban Sawma a *pethikha* that authorized him to act as visitor-general over all Christians. And Mar Papa blessed him and he caused to be assigned to him for expenses on the road one thousand, five hundred *mathkale* of red gold. And to King Arghan he sent certain gifts. And he embraced Rabban Sawma and kissed him and dismissed him. And Rabban Sawma thanked our Lord who had held him to be worthy of such blessings as these.

MISSION OF FRIAR WILLIAM OF RUBRUCK

Late fourteenth century. Latin.

William of Rubruck (d. 1293) was a Franciscan missionary. He accompanied Louis IX of France on the Seventh Crusade in 1248; later, in 1253, Louis ordered him to undertake a mission to convert the Mongols to Christianity and thereby to enlist them as an ally against his Muslim adversaries, the 'Abbasids. William's journey took him deep into Mongol territory, after which he returned to Europe and wrote an account of his travels. In the court of the Mongols, William encountered Muslims, Buddhists, and Christians from the East Syrian Church, the latter of whom he refers to as "Nestorians." In the excerpt below, the Mongol khan Mangu asks William—with the aid of his fellow Christians, the "Nestorians" (of whose piety and practice he was quite critical)—to enter into debate with the "Saracens" (Muslims) and "Tuins" (Buddhists) about whose religion was true.

The following day he sent to me his secretaries, who said, "Our master is sending us to you with this message: 'Here are you, Christians, Saracens and Tuins, and each one of you claims that his religion is superior and that his writings or books contain more truth.' So he would like you all to assemble together and hold a conference, and each one to put his claims in writing, to enable the khan to learn the truth." At this I declared, "Blessed be God, Who put this in the khan's heart. But our Scripture says, 'It is not seemly for the servant of God to wrangle, but to be mild toward all' [2 Timothy 2:29]; for this reason I am ready, without bickering or recrimination, to explain the faith and hope of Christians to anyone who asks." They wrote down this speech and reported it to him. Then the Nestorians were ordered to see that they were prepared and to write down what they intended to say, and so were the Saracens and the Tuins in the same way.

The eve of Pentecost [i.e., May 30] arrived. The Nestorians wrote out a chronicle from the creation of the world as far as Christ's passion; and they went beyond the passion, to touch on the ascension, the resurrection of the dead and [Christ's] returning in judgment, a section that contained some faults that I pointed out to them. We for our part wrote down simply the creed of the Mass, *Credo in unum Deum*.

I next asked them how they wished to proceed, and they said that they wanted to debate with the Saracens first. "This would not be a good method," I explained, "since the Saracens agree with us in saying that there is one God and therefore provide allies for us against the Tuins." They agreed; and I then asked them whether they were aware how idolatry had originated in the world, which they did not know. So I told them, and they said, "You tell them these things and then allow us to speak, as it is difficult to speak through an interpreter." "Let us rehearse," I suggested, "to see how you will handle yourselves against them. I shall take the part of the Tuins and you maintain the Christian view. Now I belong to their sect and let us assume that they deny the existence of God: prove that he does exist." (For there is a sect there that asserts that any soul or any power in anything is the god of that thing, and that God does not exist otherwise.) But at this point the Nestorians were incapable of proving anything but could only relate what Scripture tells. "They do not believe in the Scriptures," I said: "if you tell them one story, they will quote another." Then I advised them to let me be the first to meet them [the Tuins] since, should I be worsted. they would still have an opportunity to speak, whereas if they were worsted, I should not receive a hearing afterward; and they agreed.

We assembled in our oratory, then, on the eve of Pentecost, and Mangu khan sent three secretaries to be umpires—one a Christian, one a Saracen and one a Tuin. The following announcement was made: "This is Mangu's decree, and let nobody dare claim that the decree of God is otherwise. He orders that no man shall be so bold as to make provocative or insulting remarks to his opponent, and that no one is to cause any commotion that might obstruct these proceedings, on pain of death." At this everyone fell silent. And a great many people were present, as each party had summoned the wiser men of their nation, and many others too had gathered. [. . .]

The Christians then placed me in the middle and told the Tuins to address me; and the latter, who were there in considerable numbers, began to murmur against Mangu khan, since no khan had ever attempted to probe their secrets. They confronted me with someone who had come from Cataia: he had his own interpreter, while I had Master William's son. He began by saying to me, "Friend, if you are brought to a halt, you may look for a wiser man than yourself." I did not reply. Next, he asked what I wanted to debate first: either how the world had been made, or what becomes of souls after death. "Friend," I answered, "that ought not to be the starting point of our discussion. All things are from God, and he is the fountainhead of all. Therefore, we should begin by speaking about God, for you hold a different view of him from us and Mangu wishes to learn whose belief is superior." The umpires ruled that this was fair.

They wanted to begin with the issues I have mentioned because they regard them as more important. All of them belong to the Manichaean heresy, to the effect that one half of things is evil and the other half good, or at least that there are two principles; and as regards souls, they all believe that they pass from one body to another. Even one of the wiser of the Nestorian priests asked me whether it was possible for the souls of animals to escape after death to any place where they would not be compelled to suffer. In support of this fallacy, moreover, so Master William told me, a boy was brought from Cataia, who, to judge by his physical size, was not three years old, yet was fully capable of rational thought: he said of himself that he was in his third incarnation, and he knew how to read and write.

I said, then, to the Tuin, "We firmly believe in our hearts and acknowledge with our lips that God exists, that there is only one God, and that he is one in a perfect unity. What do you believe?"

"It is fools," he said, "who claim there is only one God. Wise men say that there are several. Are there not great rulers in your country, and is not Mangu khan the chief lord here? It is the same with gods, inasmuch as there are different gods in different regions."

"You choose a bad example," I told him, "in drawing a parallel between humans and God: that way any powerful figure could be called a god in his own dominions."

But as I was seeking to demolish the analogy, he distracted me by asking, "What is your God like, of whom you claim that there is no other?"

"Our God," I replied, "beside whom there is no other, is all-powerful and therefore needs assistance from no one; in fact, we all stand in need of his. With people it is not so; no one is capable of all things, and for this reason there have to be a number of rulers on earth, since no one has the power to undertake the whole. Again, he is all-knowing and therefore needs no one as counselor: in fact, all wisdom is from him. And again, he is the supreme good and has no need of our goods: rather, 'in him we live and move and are' [Acts 17:28]. This is the nature of our God, and it is unnecessary, therefore, to postulate any other."

"That is not so," he declared. "On the contrary, there is one supreme god in heaven, of whose origin we are still ignorant, with ten others under him and one of lowest rank beneath them; while on earth they are without number." [...]

As he was about to spin yet more yarns, I asked about this supreme god: did he believe he was all-powerful, or was some other god? He was afraid to answer, and asked: "If your God is as you say, why has he made half of things evil?"

"That is an error," I said. "It is not God who created evil. Everything that exists is good." All the Tuins were amazed at this statement and recorded it in writing as something erroneous and impossible.

Next, he broached the question: "Where, then, does evil come from?"

"Your question is at fault," I said, "you ought first to ask what evil is before asking where it comes from. But go back to the first question, whether you believe that any god is all-powerful; and afterward I shall give an answer to every question you care to ask."

He sat for a long while reluctant to answer, with the result that the secretaries who were listening on the khan's behalf had to order him to reply. Finally he gave the answer that no god was all-powerful, at which all the Saracens burst into loud laughter. When silence was restored, I said, "So, then, not one of your gods is capable of rescuing you in every danger, inasmuch as a predicament may be met with where he does not have the power. Further, 'no man can serve two masters' [Matthew 6:24]. so how is it that you can serve so many gods in heaven and on earth?" The audience told him to reply; yet he remained speechless. But when I was seeking to put forward arguments for the unity of the divine essence and for the Trinity while everyone was listening, the local Nestorians told me it was enough, as they wanted to speak themselves.

At this point I made way for them. But when they sought to argue with the Saracens, the latter replied, "We concede that your religion is true and that everything in the gospel is true; and therefore we have no wish to debate any issue with you." And they admitted that in all their prayers they beg God to grant that they may die a Christian death.

There was present an old priest of the Iugur [Uygur] sect, which holds that there is one God but nevertheless makes idols; and they had a long discussion with him, relating everything down to the coming of Christ in judgment, and also using analogies to explain the Trinity to him and to the Saracens. Everybody listened without challenging a single word. But for all that no one said, "I believe, and wish to become a Christian." When it was all over, the Nestorians and Saracens alike sang in loud voices, while the Tuins remained silent; and after that everyone drank heavily.

APPENDIX A

TRANSLATIONS AND EDITIONS

CSCO = Corpus Scriptorum Christianorum Orientalium

PO = Patrologia Orientalis

SC = Sources chrétiennes

Page numbers of published translations correspond with reprinted excerpts. Editions are included to provide access to the entire text, not just the excerpted portions. As a result, page numbers are listed with an edition only when a published edition contains multiple works (e.g., the edition for the *Chronicle of Edessa* is listed as CSCO 1, 1–11 because only the first eleven pages in CSCO 1 contain the *Chronicle of Edessa* but the rest of that volume consists of other Syriac chronicles. The edition of Dionysius bar Ṣalibi, *Response to the Arabs*, is listed as CSCO 614 without page numbers because all of CSCO 614 is dedicated to just that one text). For collected hymns, homilies, and letters (e.g., Ephrem's *Hymns on Faith*), edition information is given for the entire collection.

CHAPTER 1. ORIGIN STORIES

Acts of Thomas, 1.1–16. Translation: Based on *Acts of Thomas*, trans. Harry Attridge (Salem, OR: Polebridge Press, 2010), 17–28, used with permission. Edition: *Acta Apostolorum Apocrypha*, ed. R. A. Lipsius and M. Bonnet, vol. 2 (Leipzig: Mendelssohn, 1898), 99–291.

Ephrem, *Hymns on Heresies*, 22.1–7. Translation: Adam Bremer-McCollum, used with permission. Edition: *Des heiligen Ephraem des Syrers Hymnen contra Haereses*, ed. E. Beck, CSCO 169 (1957).

Eusebius, *Ecclesiastical History*, 1.13. Translation: Based on *The History of the Church: A New Translation*, trans. Jeremy Schott (Berkeley: University of California Press, 2019), 72–73, used with permission. Edition: *Eusebius Werke*, ed. Eduard Schwartz, Theodor Mommsen, and Friedhelm Winkelmann, vol. 2 (Leipzig: Hinrichs, 1903–9).

Egeria, *Pilgrimage Journal*, 19. Translation: Based on *The Pilgrimage of Egeria: A New Translation of the* Itinerarium Egeriae *with Introduction and Commentary*, trans. Anne McGowan and Paul Bradshaw (Collegeville, MN: Liturgical Press, 2018), 136–41, used with permission. Edition: *Égérie: Journal de voyage (Itinéraire) et Lettre sur la Béatissime Égérie*, ed. Pierre Maraval (Paris: Cerf, 1982).

Teaching of Addai. Translation: Based on *The Teaching of Addai*, trans. George Howard (Chico, CA: Scholars Press, 1981), 3–17, 63–67, 105, used with permission. Edition: *The Teaching of Addai*, ed. Howard.

Chronicle of Edessa, 1. Translation: Based on *Edessa, the Blessed City*, trans. J. B. Segal (Oxford: Clarendon Press, 1970), 24–25, used with permission. Edition: *Chronica minora*, ed. I. Guidi, CSCO 1, 1–11 (1903).

Acts of Mar Mari, 1, 6–8, 19, 22–23, 25, 32–33. Translation: Based on *The Acts of Mār Mārī*, trans. Amir Harrak (Atlanta: Society of Biblical Literature, 2005), 3, 11–17, 43, 49–51, 57, 75–77, used with permission. Edition: *The Acts of Mār Mārī*, ed. Harrak.

Alexander Romance in the *Chronicle of Zuqnin*. Translation: Based on *The Chronicle of Zuqnīn: Parts I and II. From the Creation to the Year 506/7 AD*, trans. Amir Harrak (Piscataway, NJ: Gorgias Press, 2017), 82–86, used with permission. Edition: *The Chronicle of Zuqnīn*, ed. Harrak.

Michael the Great, *Chronicle*, 2.3. Translation: Michael Penn, used with permission. Edition: *The Edessa–Aleppo Syriac Codex of the Chronicle of Michael the Great*, ed. Gregorios Yuhanna Ibrahim (Piscataway, NJ: Gorgias Press, 2009).

CHAPTER 2. POETRY

Odes of Solomon, 24, 19. Translation: Based on *The Odes of Solomon: A Commentary*, trans. Michael Lattke (Minneapolis: Fortress Press, 2009), 340, 368, used with permission. Edition: *The Odes of Solomon*, ed. J. H. Charlesworth (Missoula, MT: Scholars Press, 1977).

Hymn of the Pearl. Translation: Based on *The Acts of Thomas*, trans. A. F. J. Klijn, 2nd ed. (Leiden: Brill, 2003), 182–87, used with permission. Edition: *The Apocryphal Acts of the Apostles*, ed. William Wright, vol. 1 (London: Williams and Norgate, 1871), 204–9.

Ephrem, *Hymns on Faith*, 81. Translation: Based on *St. Ephrem the Syrian: Hymns on Faith*, trans. Jeffrey T. Wickes (Washington, DC: Catholic University of America Press, 2015), 377–80, used with permission. Edition: *Des heiligen Ephraem des Syrers Hymnen de Fide*, ed. E. Beck, CSCO 154 (1955).

Ephrem, *Hymns on the Resurrection*, 1. Translation: Based on *Ephrem the Syrian: Select Poems*, trans. Sebastian P. Brock and George Kiraz (Provo, UT: Brigham Young University Press, 2006), 81–95, used with permission. Edition: *Ephrem the Syrian*, ed. Brock and Kiraz, 80–94.

Cyrillona, *On the Huns*, 240–314. Translation: Based on *The Works of Cyrillona*, trans. Carl Griffin (Piscataway, NJ: Gorgias Press, 2016), 158–62, used with permission. Edition: *The Works of Cyrillona*, ed. Griffin.

Narsai, *On Epiphany*, 1–70. Translation: Based on *Narsai's Metrical Homilies: On the Nativity, Epiphany, Passion, Resurrection, and Ascension*, trans. F. G. McLeod (Turnhout: Brepols, 1979), 71–75, used with permission. Edition: *Narsai's Metrical Homilies*, ed. McLeod.

Jacob of Serug, *On the Sinful Woman*, 239–408. Translation: *Jacob of Sarug's Homily on the Sinful Woman*, trans. Scott Fitzgerald Johnson (Piscataway, NJ: Gorgias Press, 2013), 50–68, used with permission. Edition: *Jacob of Sarug's Homily on the Sinful Woman*, ed. Johnson, 49–67.

On Mary and the Gardener. Translation: Based on "Mary and the Gardener: An East Syrian Dialogue Sogitha," trans. Sebastian P. Brock, *Parole de l'Orient* 11 (1983): 229–30, used with permission. Edition: Unedited; see the notes on the manuscript in "Mary and the Gardener," 226–27.

On the Cherub and the Thief. Translation: Based on *Sogiatha: Syriac Dialogue Hymns*, trans. Sebastian P. Brock (Mannanam: St. Joseph's Press, 1987), 28–35, used with permission. Edition: *Sughyotho mgabyotho*, ed. Mor Julius Çiçek (Glane: Dayra d–Mar 'Eprem Suryaya, 1982).

Giwargis Warda, *On Sin*. Translation: Based on *The Wardā: An East Syriac Hymnological Collection, Study and Critical Edition*, trans. Anton Pritula (Wiesbaden: Harrassowitz, 2015), 343–49, used with permission. Edition: *The Wardā*, ed. Pritula.

Khamis bar Qardaḥe, *Wine Song*. Translation: Based on "'Your Sweet Saliva is the Living Wine': Drink, Desire, and Devotion in the Syriac Wine Songs of Kāmīs Bar Qardāḥē," trans. David Taylor, in *The Syriac Renaissance*, ed. Herman Teule and Carmen Tauwinkl, (Leuven: Peeters, 2010), 39–40, used with permission. Edition: "'Your Sweet Saliva is the Living Wine,'" ed. Taylor, 39–40.

'Abdisho' bar Brika, *Metrical Catalogue of Syriac Authors*, 52, 53, 69, 70, 122, 123, 124, 165, 156, 157, 158, 159, 160, 161, 162, 198. Translation: Scott Fitzgerald Johnson, used with permission. Edition: *Bibliotheca Orientalis Clementino–Vaticana*, ed. J. S. Assemani, vol. 3 (Rome: Sacra Congregatio de Propaganda Fide, 1719–30), 325–62.

CHAPTER 3. DOCTRINE AND DISPUTATION

Ephrem, *Hymns on Faith*, 53.1–3, 10–14. Translation: Based on *St. Ephrem the Syrian: Hymns on Faith*, trans. Jeffrey T. Wickes (Washington, DC: Catholic University of America Press, 2015), 273–76. Edition: *Des heiligen Ephraem des Syrers Hymnen de Fide*, ed. E. Beck, CSCO 154 (1955).

Theodore of Mopsuestia, *On the Incarnation*, books 2, 5, and 7. Translation: Based on *Theodore of Mopsuestia*, trans. Frederick McLeod (New York: Routledge, 2009), 127–32, used with permission. Editions: Books 2 and 5 come from *Theodori Episcopi Mopsuesteni in Epistolas B. Pauli Commentarii*, ed. H. B. Swete, vol. 2 (Cambridge: Cambridge University Press, 1882), 290–312; Book 7 comes from *Patrologia Graeca*, ed. J.-P. Migne, vol. 66 (Paris: Imprimérie Catholique, 1864), 971–94.

Severus of Antioch, *Ad Nephalium Or. II*. Translation: Based on *Severus of Antioch*, trans. Pauline Allen (New York: Routledge, 2004), 59–66, used with permission. Edition: *Severi Antiocheni orationes ad Nephalium. Eiusdem ac Sergii Grammatici epistulae mutuae, I*, ed. I. Lebon, CSCO 119, 10–21 (1949).

Babai the Great, *Book of Union* 17. Translation: Adam Bremer-McCollum, used with permission. Edition: *Babai Magni liber de unione*, ed. A. Vaschalde, CSCO 79 (1915), 1–289.

George of Resh'ayna, *Life of Maximus the Confessor*, 1–26. Translation: Based on "An Early Syriac Life of Maximus the Confessor," trans. Sebastian P. Brock, *Analecta Bollandiana* 10 (1973): 314–19, used with permission. Edition: "An Early Syriac Life," ed. Brock, 302–13.

A Syriac Fragment of the Sixth Council. Translation: Based on "A Syriac Fragment of the Sixth Council," trans. Sebastian P. Brock, *Oriens Christianus* 57 (1973): 65, used with permission. Edition: "A Syriac Fragment," ed. Brock, 64–65.

Dionysius bar Ṣalibi, *Against the Melkites*, 3. Translation: Based on *Woodbrooke Studies*, vol. 1, trans. Alphonse Mingana (Cambridge: W. Heffer & Sons, 1927), 27–30. Edition: *Woodbrooke Studies*, ed. Mingana, 64–92.

CHAPTER 4. LITURGY

Acts of Thomas, 13.155–58. Translation: Based on *Acts of Thomas*, trans. Harry Attridge (Salem, OR: Polebridge Press, 2010), 115–18, used with permission. Edition: *Acta Apostolorum Apocrypha*, ed. R. A. Lipsius and M. Bonnet, vol. 2 (Leipzig: Hermann Mendelsohn, 1898), 99–291.

Didascalia Apostolorum, 16. Translation: Adam Bremer-McCollum and Michael Penn, used with permission. Edition: *The Didascalia Apostolorum in Syriac*, ed. A. Vööbus, CSCO 401 and 407 (1979).

Melkite Order for Emergency Baptism. Translation: Based on "A Short Melkite Baptismal Service in Syriac," trans. Sebastian P. Brock, *Parole de l'Orient* 3 (1972): 123–25, used with permission. Edition: "A Short Melkite Baptismal Service," ed. Brock, 122–23.

Testament of Our Lord, 2.5–89. Translation: Based on *Worship in the Early Church*, vol. 3, trans. Lawrence J. Johnson (Collegeville, MN: Liturgical Press, 2009), 329–32, used with permission. Edition: *Testamentum Domini nostri Jesu Christi*, ed. E. Rahmani (Mainz: Sumptibus F. Kirchheim, 1899).

Life of Rabban Hormizd, 11–12. Translation: Adam Bremer-McCollum and Michael Penn, used with permission. Edition: *The Histories of Rabban Hōrmīzd the Persian and Rabban Bar-'Idtā*, vol. 1, ed. E. A. Wallis Budge (London: Luzai, 1902).

John of Mardin, *Canons*, 24–25. Translation: Adam Bremer-McCollum, used with permission. Edition: *The Synodicon in the West Syrian Tradition*, II, ed. A. Vööbus, CSCO 375, 233–56 (1976).

Anaphora of Addai and Mari. Translation: Based on *Worship in the Early Church: An Anthology of Historical Sources*, trans. Lawrence J. Johnson (Collegeville, MN: Liturgical Press, 2009), 295–96, used with permission. Edition: *The Eucharistic Prayer of Addai and Mari*, ed. A. Gelston (Oxford: Clarendon Press, 1992), 47–54.

Barhebraeus, *Short Anaphora of Saint James*. Translation: Based on *West Syrian Anaphoras*, trans. Baby Varghese (Kottayam: St. Ephrem Ecumenical Research Institute, 2017), 33–45, used with permission. Edition: *West Syrian Anaphoras*, ed. Varghese, 32–44.

Service Book from Turfan, "A Memre for all Ranks" and "A Memre for Bishops and for an Eminent Person." Translation: Based on *A Syriac Service-Book from Turfan*, trans. Erica Hunter and J. F. Coakley (Turnhout, Belgium: Brepols, 2017), 254–56, used with permission. Edition: *A Syriac Service-Book from Turfan*, ed. Hunter and Coakley.

CHAPTER 5. ASCETICISM

Acts of Thomas, 1.9–16. Translation: Based on *Acts of Thomas*, trans. Harry Attridge (Salem, OR: Polebridge Press, 2010), 23–28, used with permission. Edition: *Acta Apostolorum Apocrypha*, ed. R. A. Lipsius and M. Bonnet, vol. 2 (Leipzig: Mendelssohn, 1898), 99–291.

Aphrahat, *Demonstrations*, 6.4, 7–8. Translation: Based on *The Demonstrations of Aphrahat, the Persian Sage*, trans. Adam Lehto (Piscataway, NJ: Gorgias Press, 2010), 179, 183–85, used with permission. Edition: *Patrologia Syriaca*, vol. 1, part 1, *Aphraatis Sapientis Persae Demonstrationes*, ed. Ioannes Parisot (Paris: Firmin–Didot, 1894).

Book of Steps, 15.1–2, 3b, 4a, 19. Translation: Based on *The Book of Steps: The Syriac Liber Graduum*, trans. Robert Kitchen and Martien Permentier (Kalamazoo, MI: Cistercian Publications, 2004), 139–42, 156–57, used with permission. Edition: *Patrologia Syriaca*, vol. 3, part 1, *Liber graduum*, ed. Michael Kmosko (Paris: Firmin–Didot, 1926).

Rules of Rabbula. Translation: Based on *The Rabbula Corpus*, trans. Robert Phenix and Cornelia Horn (Atlanta: Society of Biblical Literature Press, 2017), 95–101, used with permission. Edition: *The Rabbula Corpus*, ed. Phenix and Horn, 94–100.

Rules for Nuns. Translation: Based on *Syriac and Arabic Documents Regarding Legislation Relative to Syrian Asceticism*, trans. Arthur Vööbus (Stockholm: Papers of the Estonian Theological Society in Exile, 1960), 64–68. Edition: *Syriac and Arabic Documents*, ed. Vööbus, 64–68.

Philoxenus, *First Letter to the Monks of Bet Gaugal*. Translation: Based on *Three Letters of Philoxenus, Bishop of Mabbogh (485–519)*, trans. Arthur Vaschalde (Rome: Tipografia Della R. Accademia Dei Linchi, 1902), 106–7. Unedited.

Philoxenus, *Letter Concerning Zeal*. Translation: Based on *Syriac and Arabic Documents Regarding Legislation Relative to Syrian Asceticism*, trans. Arthur Vööbus (Stockholm: Papers of the Estonian Theological Society in Exile 1960), 53–54. Edition: *Syriac and Arabic Documents*, ed. Vööbus, 53–54.

Jacob of Serug, *On the Solitaries*, 149–226. Translation: Based on *Jacob of Sarug's Homilies on the Solitaries*, trans. Colby Scott and Morgan Reed (Piscataway, NJ: Gorgias Press, 2016), used with permission. Edition: *Jacob of Sarug's Homilies on the Solitaries*, ed. Scott and Reed.

Statutes of the School of Nisibis. Translation: Based on *The Statutes of the School of Nisibis: Edited, Translated and Furnished with a Commentary*, trans. Arthur Vööbus (Stockholm: Papers of the Estonian Theological Society in Exile, 1961), 73–85. Edition: *The Statutes of the School of Nisibis*, ed. Vööbus.

Elias, *Life of John of Tella*. Translation: Based on "The Biography of John of Tella (d. AD 537) by Elias, Translated from the Syriac with a Historical Introduction and Linguistic Commentaries," trans. Joseph Renee Ghanem (PhD diss., University of Wisconsin-Madison, 1970), 49–53. Edition: *Vitae virorum apud monophysitas celeberrimorum*, vol. 1, ed. E. W. Brooks, CSCO 7, 29–95 (1907).

John of Ephesus, *Life of Susan*, in John of Ephesus, *Lives of the Eastern Saints*. Translation: Based on *Holy Women of the Syrian Orient*, trans. Sebastian P. Brock and Susan Ashbrook Harvey (Berkeley: University of California Press, 1987), 133–36, 139–41, used with permission. Edition: *John of Ephesus: Lives of the Eastern Saints (I)*, ed. E. W. Brooks, PO 17.1 (1923), and *John of Ephesus: Lives of the Eastern Saints (II)*, ed. Brooks, PO 18.4 (1924).

Isaac of Nineveh, *Treatises on the Behavior of Excellence* and *Whereby the Beauty of Solitary Life is to be Preserved*. Translation: Based on *Mystic Treatises by Isaac of Nineveh*, trans. A. J. Wensinck (Amsterdam: Koninklijke Akademie van Wetenschappen, 1923), 1–2, 80–81. Edition: *Mar Isaacus Ninivita De perfectione religiosa*, ed. Paul Bedjan (Leipzig: Otto Harrassowitz, 1909).

Barhebraeus, *Book of the Dove*, introduction, 1, 3, 4, 10. Translation: Based on *Bar Hebraeus's Book of the Dove, Together with Some Chapters from his Ethikon*, trans. A. J. Wensinck (Leiden: Brill, 1919), 3–4, 19–20, 22, 49–50, 58–59. Edition: *Gregorii Barhebraei Chronicon Syriacum*, ed. Paul Bedjan (Paris: Maisonneuve, 1890).

CHAPTER 6. MYSTICISM AND PRAYER

Timothy of Constantinople, *On Those Who Come to the Church from Heretics*, 1–19 (selections). Translation: Based on *"Working the Earth of the Heart": The Messalian Controversy in History, Texts, and Language to A.D. 431*, trans. Columba Stewart (Oxford: Clarendon, 1991), 244–79, used with permission. Edition: *Patrologia Graeca*, ed. J.-P. Migne, vol. 86 (Paris: Imprimerie Catholique, 1868), 42–52.

Evagrius, *Praktikos*, 68. Translation: Charles M. Stang, used with permission. Edition: *Évagre le Pontique:* Traité pratique *ou* le Moine, ed. Antoine Guillaumont and Claire Guillaumont, vol. II, SC 171 (1971).

Babai the Great, *Commentary on Evagrius's* Kephalaia Gnostika, 3.9, 3.28, 3.55, 3.85, 4.39, 6.60. Translation: John Zaleski, used with permission. Edition: *Euagrius Ponticus*, ed. W. Frankenberg (Berlin: Weidmannsche Buchhandlung, 1912), 8–471.

Evagrius, *Letter to Melania*, 22–30. Translation: Adam Bremer-McCollum and Charles M. Stang, used with permission. Edition: *British Library Additional* 17192, folia 56b–72a.

Evagrius, *Kephalaia Gnostika*, 3.9, 3:28, 3.55, 3.85, 4.39, 6.60. Translation: Charles M. Stang, used with permission. Edition: *Évagre le Pontique:* Le Gnostique *ou à celui qui est devenu digne de la science*, ed. Antoine Guillaumont and Claire Guillaumont, SC 356 (1989).

Babai the Great, *Commentary on Evagrius's* Kephalaia Gnostikia, 3.9, 3.28, 3.55, 3.85, 4.39, 6.60. Translation: John Zaleski, used with permission. Edition: *Euagrius Ponticus*, ed. W. Frankenberg (Berlin: Weidmannsche Buchhandlung, 1912), 8–471.

Stephen bar Ṣudayli, *Book of the Holy Hierotheus*, 4.18–19, 21; 5.2. Translation: Based on *The Book of the Holy Hierotheos*, trans. F. S. Marsh (London: Text and Translation Society, 1927), 118–26, 131–32, used with permission. Edition: *The Book of the Holy Hierotheos*, ed. Marsh, 1–180.

Philoxenus, *Letter to Abraham and Orestes*. Translation: Based on *Stephen Bar Sudaili, the Syriac Mystic (c. 500 A.D.), and the Book of Hierotheos, on Hidden Treasures of the Divinity; with the Original Syriac Documents*, trans. Arthur L. Frothingham (Leiden: Brill, 1886): 29–33, 43–48, used with permission. Edition, *Stephen Bar Sudaili*, ed. Frothingham, 29–48.

Isaac of Nineveh, *On Gehenna*, 39.3, 6, 18–22. Translation: Based on *Isaac of Nineveh (Isaac the Syrian). "The Second Part,"* trans. Sebastian P. Brock, CSCO 555 (1995): 163–64, 165, 170–72, used with permission. Edition: *Isaac of Nineveh (Isaac the Syrian). "The Second Part"*, ed. Brock, CSCO 554 and 555 (1995).

John of Apamea, *On Prayer*, 1–7. Translation: Based on Sebastian P. Brock, "John the Solitary, On Prayer," *Journal of Theological Studies*, n.s. 30.1 (1979): 97–100, used with permission. Edition: "John the Solitary, *On Prayer*," ed. Brock, 89–96.

Isaac of Nineveh, *On Pure and Undistracted Prayer*, 15.2–11. Translation: Based on *Isaac of Nineveh (Isaac the Syrian). The Second Part*, trans. Sebastian P. Brock, CSCO 555 (1995), 84–87, used with permission. Edition: *Isaac of Nineveh (Isaac the Syrian). "The Second Part"*, ed. Brock, CSCO 554 and 555 (1995).

Dadisho' Qaṭraya, *Discourse on Stillness*. Translation: *The Syriac Fathers on Prayer and the Spiritual Life*, trans. Sebastian P. Brock (Kalamazoo, MI: Cistercian Publications, 1987), 306–10, used with permission. Edition: *Early Christian Mystics*, ed. Alphonse Mingana (Cambridge: W. Heffer & Sons, 1934), 232–34.

John of Dalyata, *Letters*, 12.1–3, 7–8. Translation: Based on *The Syriac Fathers on Prayer and the Spiritual Life*, trans. Sebastian P. Brock (Kalamazoo, MI: Cistercian Publications, 1987),333–37, used with permission. Edition: *La collection des lettres de Jean de Dalyatha*, ed. Robert Beulay, PO 39.3 (1978).

Joseph Ḥazzaya, *On the Stirrings of the Mind during Prayer*. Translation: *The Syriac Fathers on Prayer and the Spiritual Life*, trans. Sebastian P. Brock (Kalamazoo, MI: Cistercian Publications, 1987), 319–23, used with permission. Edition: *Early Christian Mystics*, ed. Alphonse Mingana (Cambridge: W. Heffer & Sons, 1934), 272–74.

CHAPTER 7. BIBLICAL INTERPRETATION

Aphrahat, *Demonstrations*, 12.2, 3, 8. Translation: Based on *The Demonstrations of Aphrahat, the Persian Sage*, trans. Adam Lehto (Piscataway, NJ: Gorgias Press, 2010), 278–80, 283–85, used with permission. Edition: *Patrologia Syriaca*, vol. 1, part 1, *Aphraatis sapientis Persae, Demonstrationes*, ed. Ioannes Parisot (Paris: Firmin–Didot, 1894).

Ephrem, *Commentary on the Diatessaron*, 16.1–3, 5, 8, 10. Translation: Based on *Saint Ephrem's Commentary on Tatian's Diatessaron*, trans. Carmel McCarthy (New York: Oxford, 1993), 243–47, used with permission. Editions: *Saint Éphrem, Commentaire de l'Evangile concordant, texte syriaque*, ed. Louis Leloir (Dublin: Hodges Figgis, 1963); *Saint Ephrem, Commentaire de l'Evangile concordant, texte syriaque, Folios additionels*, ed. Louis Leloir (Louvain: Peeters, 1990).

Ephrem, *The Repentance of Nineveh*, 5.1–10, 15–20, 38–47, 77–107. Translation: Christine Shepardson. Edition: *Des heiligen Ephraem des Syrers Sermones, II*, ed. E. Beck, CSCO 311 (1970).

Book of Steps, 15.6–7a, 8a. Translation: Based on *The Book of Steps: The Syriac Liber Graduum*, trans. Robert Kitchen and Martien Permentier (Kalamazoo, MI: Cistercian Publications, 2004), 143–45, used with permission. Edition: *Patrologia Syriaca*, vol. 3, part 1, *Liber graduum*, ed. Kmosko (Paris: Firmin–Didot, 1926).

Narsai, *On the Sacrifice of Isaac*. Translation: Based on *A Brief Outline of Syriac Literature*, trans. Sebastian P. Brock (Kottayam: St. Ephrem Ecumenical Research Institute, 1997), 186–88, used with permission. Edition: J. Frishman, "The Ways and Means of the Divine Economy: An Edition, Translation, and Study of Six Biblical Homilies by Narsai" (PhD diss., University of Leiden, 1992).

Homily on Genesis 22. Translation: Based on *A Brief Outline of Syriac Literature*, trans. Sebastian P. Brock (Kottayam: St. Ephrem Ecumenical Research Institute, 1997), 179–81, used with permission. Edition: "Two Syriac Verse Homilies on the Binding of Isaac," ed. Sebastian P. Brock, *Le Muséon* 99.1–2 (1986): 117–22.

Jacob of Serug, *Memra on Tamar*, 68–112, 125–55, 412–20. Translation: Based on "Jacob of Serugh's Verse Homily on Tamar (Gen. 38)," trans. Sebastian P. Brock, *Le Muséon* 115.3–4 (2002): 295–96, 302, used with permission. Edition: "Jacob of Serugh's Verse Homily," ed. Brock, 280–92.

The Cave of Treasures, Western Recension, 1.12–18; 2.12–25; Eastern Recension, 18.1–7; 19.11–13; 24.10–11; 44.1–5, 45–49; 46.8–18; 49.1–10. Translation: Adam Bremer-McCollum, used with permission. Edition: *La caverne des trésors: Les deux recensions syriaques*, ed. R. Su-Min Ri, CSCO 486 (1987).

Daniel of Ṣalaḥ, *Commentary on the Psalms*, "Psalm 1." Translation: Based on *A Brief Outline of Syriac Literature*, trans. Sebastian P. Brock (Kottayam: St. Ephrem Ecumenical Research Institute, 1997), 204–7, used with permission. Unedited.

Syriac Apocalypse of Daniel, 14–15, 21–22, 40. Translation: Based on *The Syriac Apocalypse of Daniel: Introduction, Text, and Commentary*, trans. Matthias Henze (Tübingen: Mohr Siebeck, 2001), 78–81, 89–90, 117, used with permission. Edition: *The Syriac Apocalypse of Daniel*, ed. Henze.

Solomon of Baṣra, *The Book of the Bee*, 1–2, 9, 24, 30, 33, 47, 49. Translation: Based on *The Book of the Bee*, trans. E. A. Wallis Budge (Oxford: Clarendon, 1886). Edition: *The Book of the Bee*, ed. Budge.

CHAPTER 8. HAGIOGRAPHY

Jacob of Serug, *On the Sleepers of Ephesus*. Translation: Based on "Jacob of Serugh's Poem on the Sleepers of Ephesus," trans. Sebastian P. Brock, in *"I Sowed Fruits into Hearts" (Odes Sol. 17:13): Festschrift for Professor Michael Lattke*, ed. Pauline Allen, Majella Franzmann, and Rick Strelan (Strathfield: St. Paul's Publications, 2007), 23–30, used with permission. Edition: *Acta Martyrum et Sanctorum*, ed. Paulus Bedjan, vol. 6 (Leipzig: Otto Harrassowitz, 1896), 324–30.

John of Ephesus, *Ecclesiastical History* in *Chronicle of Zuqnin*, part 3. Translation: Based on *The Chronicle of Zuqnin, Parts III and IV*, trans. Amir Harrak (Toronto: Pontifical Institute of Mediaeval Studies, 1999), 60–62. Edition: *Incerti auctoris Chronicon pseudo-Dionysianum vulgo dictum, II*, ed. I.-B. Chabot, CSCO 104 (1933).

Martyrdom of Abbot Barshebya. Translation: Based on *Constantine and the Captive Christians of Persia: Martyrdom and Religious Identity in Late Antiquity*, trans. Kyle Smith (Oakland: University of California Press, 2016), 193–95, used with permission. Edition: *Acta Martyrum et Sanctorum*, ed. Paulus Bedjan, vol. 2 (Leipzig: Otto Harrassowitz, 1891), 281–84.

Martyrdom of Anahid. Translation: Based on *Holy Women of the Syrian Orient*, trans. Sebastian P. Brock and Susan Ashbrook Harvey (Berkeley: University of California Press, 1987), 89–99, used with permission. Edition: *Acta Martyrum et Sanctorum*, ed. Paulus Bedjan, vol. 2 (Leipzig: Otto Harrassowitz, 1891), 565–603.

Stephen Mansūr, *Passion of Romanos the Neomartyr*, introduction, 22–24, 26. Translation: Based on *Three Christian Martyrdoms from Early Islamic Palestine*, trans. Stephen J. Shoemaker (Provo, UT: Brigham Young University Press, 2016), 151, 185–95, used with permission. Edition: *Three Christian Martyrdoms*, ed. Shoemaker, 150–96.

Theodoret, *History of the Monks of Syria*, 1–5, 10–14, 19, 22, 25–28. Translation: Based on *Theodoret and Antonius: The Lives of Simeon Stylites*, trans. Robert Doran (Kalamazoo, MI: Cistercian Publications, 1992), 69–84, used with permission. Edition: Théodoret de Cyr, *Histoire des moines de Syrie, tome II*, ed. Pierre Canivet and Alice Leroy-Molinghen, SC 257 (1979).

Syriac Life of Mary. Translation: Adam Bremer-McCollum and Michael Penn, used with permission. Edition: *Studia Sinaitica No. IX: Select Narratives of Holy Women from the Syro–Antiochene or Sinai Palimpsest*, ed. Agnes Smith Lewis (London: C. J. Clay and Sons, 1900), 48–61.

Thomas of Marga, *Book of Governors*, 4.21–22. Translation: Anuj Amin, Adam Bremer-McCollum, and Sunil Persad, used with permission. Edition: *The Book of Governors: The Historia Monastica of Thomas Bishop of Marga A.D. 840*, ed. E. A. Wallis Budge, vol. 1 (London: K. Paul, Trench, Trübner, 1893).

Life of Rabban Hormizd, 10. Translation: Adam Bremer-McCollum and Michael Penn, used with permission. Edition: *The Histories of Rabban Hōrmīzd the Persian and Rabban Bar-ʿIdtā*, ed. E. A. Wallis Budge, vol. 1 (London: Luzai, 1902).

CHAPTER 9. BOOKS, KNOWLEDGE, AND TRANSLATION

Book of the Laws of the Countries. Translation: Based on *The Book of the Laws of Countries: Dialogue on Fate of Bardaisan of Edessa*, trans. H. J. W. Drijvers (Assen: Van Gorcum, 1965), 39–63, used with permission. Edition: *The Book of the Laws of Countries*, ed. Drijvers.

Colophon from *British Library Additional 12150*. Translation: Michael Penn, used with permission. Edition: *Catalogue of Syriac Manuscripts in the British Museum Acquired Since the Year 1838*, ed. William Wright, vol. 2 (London: British Museum, 1871), 633. Colophon from *British Library Additional 14445*. Translation: Based on "Without Mushe of Nisibis, Where Would We Be? Some Reflections on the Transmission of Syriac Literature," trans. Sebastian P. Brock, *Journal of Eastern Christianity Studies* 56 (2004): 16.

Syro–Roman Law Book, 22–42, 84–86. Translation: Based on *The Syro–Roman Law Book*, trans. Arthur Vööbus, vol. 2 (Stockholm: Estonian Theological Society in Exile, 1983), 11–16, 36–38. Edition: *The Syro–Roman Law Book*, ed. Vööbus, vol. 1 (Stockholm: Estonian Theological Society in Exile, 1983).

Zacharias Rhetor, *Life of Severus*, 46–48, 51–57. Translation: Based on *The Life of Severus by Zechariah of Mytilene*, trans. Lena Ambjörn (Piscataway, NJ: Gorgias Press, 2008), 46, 50–56, used with permission. Edition: *The Life of Severus by Zechariah of Mytilene*, ed. Ambjörn.

Philoxenus of Mabbug, *Commentary on the Prologue of John*, 23. Translation: Based on *A Brief Outline of Syriac Literature*, trans. Sebastian P. Brock (Kottayam: St. Ephrem Ecumenical Research Institute, 1997), 195–97, used with permission. Edition: *Philoxène de Mabbog. Commentaire du Prologue johannique (Ms. Br. Mus. Add. 14, 534)*, ed. A. de Halleux, CSCO 380 (1977).

Sergius of Reshʿayna, *On the Aim of All of Aristotle's Writings*. Translation: *A Brief Outline of Syriac Literature*, trans. Sebastian P. Brock, (Kottayam: St. Ephrem Ecumenical Research Institute, 1997), 201–4, used with permission. Edition: Unedited, but see the notes on manuscripts in H. Hugonnard-Roche, *La logique d'Aristote du grec au syriaque: Études sur la transmission des textes de l'"Organon" et leur interprétation philosophique* (Paris: J. Vrin, 2004), 16n4.

Severus Sebokt, *Letter to the Periodeutes Basil of Cyprus*. Translation: Based on *A Brief Outline of Syriac Literature*, trans. Sebastian P. Brock (Kottayam: St. Ephrem Ecumenical Research Institute, 1997), 222–23, used with permission. Edition: F. Nau, "La cosmographie au VIIe siècle chez les syriens," *Révue de l'Orient Chrétien* 15 (1910): 249.

Timothy I, *Letters*, 43, 48, and 47. Translations: Based on "Two Letters of the Patriarch Timothy from the Late Eighth Century on Translations from Greek," trans. Sebastian P. Brock, *Arabic Sciences and Philosophy* 9 (1999): 235–40, used with permission; and *A Brief Outline of Syriac Literature*, trans. Sebastian P. Brock (Kottayam: St. Ephrem Ecumenical Research Institute, 1997), 245–50, used with permission. Editions: *Timotheos I., ostsyrischer Patriarch: Disputation mit dem Kalifen Al-Mahdi* and *Die Briefe des Ostsyrischen Patriarchen Timotheos I*, ed. M. Heimgartner, CSCO 631, 644, 661, 673, 700, 702 (2011–21).

Thomas of Marga, *Book of Governors*, 2.11. Translation: Based on *The Book of Governors*, trans. E. A. Wallis Budge, vol. 2 (London: K. Paul, Trench, Trübner, 1893), 176–79. Edition: *The Book of Governors*, ed. Budge, vol. 1 (London: K. Paul, Trench, Trübner, 1893).

Moshe bar Kepha, *Introduction to the Psalter*. Translation: Based on *A Brief Outline of Syriac Literature*, trans. Sebastian P. Brock (Kottayam: St. Ephrem Ecumenical Research Institute, 1997), 254–55, used with permission. Edition: Unedited, but see the summary and notes on the text in J.–M. Vosté, "L'Introduction de Mose Bar Kepa aux Psaumes de David," *Revue Biblique* (1929) 38: 214–28.

Hunayn b. Ishaq, *Risala*, 1, 2, 39, 72, 79, 110, 111. Translation: Based on *Hunayn ibn Ishaq on his Galen Translations*, trans. John C. Lamoreaux (Provo, UT: Brigham Young University Press, 2005), 2–6, 52, 78, 84, 108, used with permission. Edition: *Hunayn ibn Ishaq*, ed. Lamoreaux.

CHAPTER 10. JUDAISM

Didascalia Apostolorum, 21, 26. Translation: Adam Bremer-McCollum and Michael Penn, used with permission. Edition: *The Didascalia Apostolorum in Syriac*, ed. A. Vööbus, CSCO 401, 407 (1979).

Aphrahat, *Demonstrations*, 11.1, 2, 3, 11. Translation: Based on *The Demonstrations of Aphrahat, the Persian Sage*, trans. Adam Lehto (Piscataway, NJ: Gorgias Press, 2010), 262–65, 273–74, used with permission. Edition: *Patrologia Syriaca*, vol. 1, part 1, *Aphraatis Sapientis Persae, Demonstrationes*, ed. Ioannes Parisot (Paris: Firmin–Didot, 1894).

Ephrem, *Hymns on Unleavened Bread*, 19. Translation: *Anti-Judaism and Christian Orthodoxy: Ephrem's Hymns in Fourth-Century Syria*, trans. Christine Shepardson (Washington, DC: Catholic University of America, 2008), 32–33, used with permission. Edition: *Des heiligen Ephraem des Syrers Paschahymnen (De azymis, de crucifixione, de resurrectione)*, ed. E. Beck, CSCO 248 (1964).

Ephrem, *Hymns on Faith*, 87.1–3, 5–6, 9–14. Translation: Based on *St. Ephrem the Syrian: Hymns on Faith*, trans. Jeffrey T. Wickes (Washington, DC: Catholic University of America Press, 2015), 398–403, used with permission. Edition: *Des heiligen Ephraem des Syrers Hymnen de Fide*, ed. E. Beck, CSCO 154 (1955).

Ephrem, *Hymns on Virginity*, 28.2–5, 11. Translation: Based on *Ephrem the Syrian: Hymns*, trans. Kathleen McVey (New York: Paulist Press, 1989), 386–88, used with permission.

Edition: *Des heiligen Ephraem des Syrers Hymnen de virginitate*, ed. E. Beck, CSCO 223–24 (1962).

Teaching of Addai. Translation: Based on *The Teaching of Addai*, trans. George Howard (Chico, CA: Scholars Press, 1981) 21–33, used with permission. Edition: *The Teaching of Addai*, ed. Howard.

Isaac of Antioch, *Against the Jews*, 2. Translation: Based on "Isaac of Antioch's Homily against the Jews," trans. Stanley Kazan, *Oriens Christianus* 5 (1961): 31, 33–35, 42–49, used with permission. Edition: "Isaac of Antioch's Homily against the Jews," ed. Kazan, 30–53.

Simeon of Bet Arsham, *Letter*, 1, in John of Ephesus, *Church History*, II, in *The Chronicle of Zuqnin*, part 3. Translation: Based on *The Chronicle of Zuqnīn Parts III and IV*, trans. Amir Harrak (Piscataway, NJ: Gorgias Press, 2017), 78–81, used with permission. Edition: *Incerti auctoris Chronicon pseudo-Dionysianum vulgo dictum, II*, ed. I.-B. Chabot, CSCO 104 (1933).

Book of the Himyarites, 21. Translation: Based on *The Book of the Himyarites: Fragments of a Hitherto Unknown Syriac Work*, trans. Axel Moberg (Lund: C.W.K. Gleerup, 1924; Piscataway, NJ: Gorgias Press, 2010), xxii–cxxvi, used with permission. Edition: *The Book of the Himyarites*, ed. Moberg.

Letter of the Jews to the Emperor Marcian. Translation: Based on "A Letter of the Jews to the Emperor Marcian concerning the Council of Chalcedon," trans. Lucas Van Rompay, *Orientalia Lovaniensia periodica* 12 (1981): 215, used with permission. Edition: *Chronicon anonymum pseudo-Dionysianum vulgo dictum, I*, ed. I.-B. Chabot, CSCO 91, 226 (1927).

History of the "Slave of Christ," 10–13, 20. Translation: Based on *The History of the "Slave of Christ": From Jewish Child to Christian Martyr*, trans. Aaron Michael Butts and Simcha Gross (Piscataway, NJ: Gorgias Press, 2016), 116, 118, 120, 122, 124, 126, 128, 130, 144, 146, used with permission. Edition: *The History of the "Slave of Christ,"* ed. Butts and Gross.

Disputation of Sergius the Stylite Against a Jew, 4.1, 6.1–5, 11.5–9, 13.1. Translation: Adam Bremer-McCollum, used with permission. Edition: *The Disputation of Sergius the Stylite Against a Jew*, ed. A.P. Hayman, CSCO 338 (1973).

Timothy I, *Letters*, 40.1. Translation: Based on "Letter 40 of the Nestorian Patriarch Timothy I (727–823): An Edition and Translation" (Masters' thesis, Catholic University of America, 1981), trans. Thomas Hurst, 48. Editions: *Timotheos I., ostsyrischer Patriarch: Disputation mit dem Kalifen Al-Mahdi* and *Die Briefe des Ostsyrischen Patriarchen Timotheos I*, ed. M. Heimgartner, CSCO 631, 644, 661, 673, 700, 702 (2011–21).

CHAPTER 11. ISLAM

Maronite Chronicle. Translation: *When Christians First Met Muslims: A Sourcebook of the Earliest Syriac Writings on Islam*, trans. Michael Penn (Berkeley: University of California Press, 2015), 57–61, used with permission. Edition: *Chronica minora*, ed. E.W. Brooks, CSCO 3, 43–74 (1904).

Apocalypse of Pseudo–Methodius, 10–12. Translation: *When Christians First Met Muslims: A Sourcebook of the Earliest Syriac Writings on Islam*, trans. Michael Penn (Berkeley: University of California Press, 2015), 118, 120–23, used with permission. Edition: *Die Syrische Apokalypse des Pseudo-Methodius*, ed. G.J. Reinink, CSCO 540 (1993).

Jacob of Edessa, *Letter to Addai Questions 74–98, Q #75, Letter to Addai Question 99–116, Q #116, First Letter to John the Stylite, Q #6*. Translation: *When Christians First Met Muslims: A Sourcebook of the Earliest Syriac Writings on Islam*, trans. Michael Penn (Berkeley: University of California Press, 2015), 164–65, 167, 167–68, used with permission. Edition: *Letter to Addai Q#116: The Synodicon in the West Syrian Tradition, I*, ed. A. Vööbus, CSCO 367, 261 (1975). The others are unedited.

Disputation of Bet Ḥale, 1–9, 12–16, 19–22, 27–34, 53–62. Translation: Based on "The Disputation between a Muslim and a Monk of Bēt Ḥālē: Syriac Text and Annotated English Translation," trans. David G. K. Taylor, in *Christsein in der islamischen Welt: Festschrift für Martin Tamcke zum 60. Geburtstag*, ed. Sidney H. Griffith and Sven Grebenstein (Wiesbaden: Harrassowitz Verlag, 2015), 204–9, 211–12, 214–16, 219–24, 237–42, used with permission. Edition: "The Disputation between a Muslim and a Monk of Bēt Ḥālē," ed. Taylor, 187–242.

Chronicle of Zuqnin, part 4. Translation: Based on *The Chronicle of Zuqnin, Parts III and IV*, trans. Amir Harrak (Toronto: Pontifical Institute of Mediaeval Studies, 1999), 326–30. Edition: ed. I.-B. Chabot, *Incerti auctoris Chronicon pseudo-Dionysianum vulgo dictum*, II, ed. I.-B. Chabot, CSCO 104 (1933).

Timothy I, *Letters*, 59.14–15. Translation: Adam Bremer-McCollum and Michael Penn, used with permission. Editions: *Timotheos I., ostsyrischer Patriarch: Disputation mit dem Kalifen Al-Mahdi* and *Die Briefe des Ostsyrischen Patriarchen Timotheos I*, ed. M. Heimgartner, CSCO 631, 644, 661, 673, 700, 702 (2011–21).

Syriac Baḥira Legend, Eastern Recension, 12–16. Translation: Based on *The Legend of Sergius Baḥīrā: Eastern Christian Apologetics and Apocalyptic in Response to Islam*, trans. Barbara Roggema (Leiden: Brill, 2009), 271–85, used with permission. Edition: *The Legend of Sergius Baḥīrā*, ed. Rogemma.

Dionysius bar Ṣalibi, *Response to the Arabs*, 1, 20, colophon. Translation: Adam Bremer-McCollum, used with permission. Edition: *Dionysius bar Ṣalibi. A Response to the Arabs*, ed. J. P. Amar, CSCO 614 (2005).

Michael the Great, *Chronicle*, 11.2. Translation: Adam Bremer-McCollum and Michael Penn, used with permission. Edition: *The Edessa–Aleppo Syriac Codex of the Chronicle of Michael the Great*, ed. Gregorios Yuhanna Ibrahim (Piscataway, NJ: Gorgias Press, 2009). Michael the Syrian, *Chronicle*, 15.7.1–2, 15.11.3, 17.2.1, 21.6.1. Translation: Based on *The Chronicle of Michael the Great (the Edessa–Aleppo Syriac Codex): Books XV–XXI from the Year 1050 to 1195*, trans. Amir Harrak (Piscataway, NJ: Gorgias, 2019), 60–64, 100–104, 218–22, 450–52, used with permission. Edition: *The Chronicle of Michael the Great*, ed. Harrak.

Barhebraeus, *Ecclesiastical History*, section 1. Translation: Based on *Bar Hebraeus, The Ecclesiastical Chronicle: An English Translation*, trans. David Wilmshurst (Piscataway, NJ: Gorgias Press, 2016), 174–78, used with permission. Edition: *Bar Hebraeus*, ed. Wilmshurst.

CHAPTER 12. SILK ROAD

Legend of Mar Qardagh, 12–25. Translation: Based on *The Legend of Mar Qardagh*, trans. Joel Walker (Berkeley: University of California Press, 2006), 26–33, used with permission. Edition: *Acta Mar Ḳardaghi Assyriae praefecti qui sub Sapore II martyr occubuit, syriace juxta manuscriptum Amidense una cum versione Latina*, ed. J.-B. Abbeloos (Brussels: Société belge de libraire, 1890).

Theodore Abū Qurrah, *On the Existence of God and the True Religion*. Translation: Based on *Theodore Abū Qurrah*, trans. John C. Lamoureaux (Provo, UT: Brigham Young University Press, 2005), 4–5, used with permission. Edition: *Théodore Abuqurra: Traité de l'existence du Créateur et de la vraie religion*, ed. Ignace Dick (Rome: Pontificio Istituto Orientale, 1982), 200–258.

Timothy I, *Letters*, 41.1–2, *Letters*, 47. Translation: Based on "Patriarch Timothy I and the Metropolitan of the Turks," trans. Mark Dickens, *Journal of the Royal Asiatic Society*, series 3, 20.2 (2010): 118–19, used with permission. Editions: *Timotheos I., ostsyrischer Patriarch: Disputation mit dem Kalifen Al-Mahdi* and *Die Briefe des Ostsyrischen Patriarchen Timotheos I*, ed. M. Heimgartner, CSCO 631, 644, 661, 673, 700, 702 (2011–21).

Jingjiao Stele. Translation: Based on *Early Chinese Christianity: The Tang Christian Monument and Other Documents*, trans. Johan Ferreira (Strathfield: St. Paul's Publisher, 2014), 359–63, 370–71, used with permission. Edition: *Early Chinese Christianity*, ed. Ferreira, 160–208.

Discourse on the One God. Translation: Obtained from Li Tang, *A Study of the History of Nestorian Christianity in China and Its Literature in Chinese: Together with a New English Translation of the Dunhuang Nestorian Documents* (Frankfurt am Main: P. Lang, 2002), 156–60. Edition: *Hanyu Jingjiao wendian quanshi*, ed. Weng Shaojun (Beijing: Sanlian shudian, 1996), 113–55.

History of the Life and Travels of Rabban Sauma, 7. Translation: Based on *The Monks of Kublai Khan*, trans. E. A. Wallis Budge (London: Religious Tract Society, 1928), 55–56, 59, 60. Edition: *Histoire de Mar-Jabalaha: de trois autres patriarches, d'un prêtre et de deux laïques, Nestoriens*, ed. Paul Bedjan (Piscataway, NJ: Gorgias Press, 2007).

Mission of Friar William of Rubruck, 24. Translation: Based on *The Mission of Friar William of Rubruck*, trans. Peter Jackson (Indianapolis: Hackett, 2009), 150–52, used with permission. Edition: Francisque Michel and Thomas Wright, "Voyage en Orient du Frère Guillaume de Rubruk," in *Recueil de Voyages et de Mémoires*, vol. 4, ed. M. A. P. d'Avezac-Macaya (Paris: Société de Geographie, 1839), 213–396.

APPENDIX B

BIOGRAPHIES OF NAMED AUTHORS

'ABDISHO' BAR BRIKA

'Abdisho' bar Brika was an East Syrian author and bishop active from the late thirteenth century until his death in 1318. He was bishop of Sinjar and Bet 'Arbaye and later became metropolitan of Nisibis and Armenia around 1291. The dates of 'Abdisho''s activity place him around the tail end of the Syriac Renaissance. 'Abdisho' wrote scriptural commentary, legal works including a *Nomocanon*, an exposition of East Syrian theology called the *Marganita*, and another collection of poetry called the *Paradise of Eden*. Of these, the scriptural commentaries are largely lost, while much of his legal and theological work survives, with 'Abdisho''s legal compilation still being regarded as authoritative in the East Syrian Church today. 'Abdisho''s *Metrical Catalogue of Syrian Authors*, which lists all of the theological works known to him from the books of the Hebrew Bible to his own day, is regarded as an invaluable resource among scholars of the Syriac tradition. The *Catalogue* names numerous otherwise unknown Syriac authors and gives scholars a sense of the Greek theological works that were known to the East Syrian Church in 'Abdisho''s time.

APHRAHAT

Aphrahat wrote twenty-three prose *Demonstrations* in Syriac in the first half of the fourth century, during Shapur II's reign in Persia. Manuscripts often call him the "Persian Sage" or Jacob. The first twenty-two *Demonstrations* each start with one of the letters of the Syriac alphabet, forming an alphabetic acrostic. In *Demonstrations* 6, he addresses the *bnay* and *bnat qyama* (Children of the Covenant) and *iḥidaye* (solitary ones), early Syriac ascetics. Thus, like other early Syriac writers, Aphrahat places a strong emphasis on celibacy. In other *Demonstrations*, Aphrahat attempts to separate Christianity from Judaism and argues that the new, Christian covenant has superseded the old, Jewish one. At the same time, Aphrahat's writings themselves suggest that at least some ordinary Christians engaged in Jewish practices, including the observance of Passover. Aphrahat is also a witness to some level of persecution of Christians under Shapur II. In general, Aphrahat's writings show little influence from Hellenistic thought, but it is unclear whether he was unaware of Hellenistic Jewish and Christian thought or consciously developed an indigenous Syriac and Persian expression of Christian ideas.

BABAI

Often called Babai the Great, Babai was an East Syrian monk and writer active from the late sixth century until his death in 628. He studied at the School of Nisibis and lived at the "Great Monastery" founded by Abraham of Kashkar on two occasions, the first time as a monk and the second as its abbot. He also coadministered the East Syrian Church after the death of Katholikos Grigor in 609. Babai's writings on theology and spirituality have remained influential throughout the history of East Syrian Christianity. His *Book of the Union* outlines what has become the main position of East Syrian Christology. In it, Babai defends the claim that Christ had two natures and two persons (hypostases) against miaphysitism and the Chalcedonian position. Among his spiritual writings are a commentary on Evagrius of Pontus's *Kephalaia Gnostika*, which sought to tame more extreme interpretations of Evagrius's thought. Babai also criticized Messalianism by arguing that true *apatheia* was attainable only in the afterlife.

BARḤADBSHABA

Two important theological and historiographical works, both produced in the sixth or seventh century, are attributed to a Barḥadbshaba. Scholars debate whether these Barḥadbshaba are in fact the same author, but both works reflect the concerns of the East Syrian Church and discuss the School of Nisibis. The first of these is an *Ecclesiastical History* that addresses the fourth- and fifth-century Christological controversies from an East Syrian perspective. The final two chapters of this work describe the history of the School of Edessa and the School of Nisibis. The other work attributed to Barḥadbshaba, the *Cause of the Foundation of the Schools*, defends East Syrian Christianity as the truly orthodox form of Christianity. In so doing, it articulates Barḥadbshaba's epistemology and interprets history from creation to the author's own day as a series of schools, finishing with the School of Nisibis. Barḥadbshaba's works are early and influential examples of distinctively East Syrian models of theology and history, including the idea of pedagogical soteriology.

BARHEBRAEUS

Gregorios Bar 'Ebraya (Arabic: Gregory Abū al-Faraj) was a thirteenth-century West Syrian polymath and maphrian associated closely with the Syriac Renaissance. Educated in the Crusader states, Barhebraeus witnessed the Mongol conquest of Aleppo, where he was bishop, in

1260. In 1264, he became maphrian, now based in Mosul. Barhebraeus wrote in both Syriac and Arabic, interacted with Muslim and East Syrian scholars of his time, and modeled his works on Arabic and Persian styles. Many of his writings include compilations or abridgements of earlier writers, sometimes helping scholars reconstruct these works when they do not survive on their own. At the same time, there is increasing recognition that Barhebraeus was an innovative writer in his own right. His wide-ranging corpus includes the following: a *Nomocanon*; exegetical, theological, and mystical writings; an influential *Chronicle*; prose and verse writings on grammar and prosody; liturgical works; philosophical treatises; and medical and astronomical writing. Among his mystical works is a commentary on the *Book of the Holy Hierotheus* by Stephen bar Ṣudayli. Another work on spirituality, the *Book of the Dove*, places a strong emphasis on ascetic behavior and warns that even advanced ascetics may succumb to temptation.

CYRILLONA

Cyrillona was an early Syriac poet active in the late fourth century. Only six poems that may reliably be attributed to Cyrillona survive. Beyond these poems, Cyrillona's identity, and even the spelling and meaning of his name, are shrouded in mystery; there are no external references to an individual named Cyrillona in the time and place he wrote. One of Cyrillona's poems is notable for referring to the Huns' invasion of northern Mesopotamia, which allows this poem to be dated to roughly 396. His other poems discuss stories from the New Testament, including Jesus's washing of the disciples' feet, Holy Thursday, and the crucifixion. Unlike nearly all contemporary Christian theological literature (including the work of Ephrem the Syrian), Cyrillona's surviving corpus does not include a sustained treatment of any theological controversies of his day.

DADISHO' QAṬRAYA

A contemporary of Isaac of Nineveh from the same region (Bet Qaṭraye) and monastery (the monastery of Rabban Shapur), Dadisho' Qaṭraya was a late seventh-century East Syrian monk who wrote about spirituality, asceticism, and prayer. Alongside Isaac, John of Dalyata, and Joseph Ḥazzaya, Dadisho' belonged to a series of seventh- and eighth-century East Syrian authors who developed a sophisticated theology of prayer, including the idea of a spiritual state *beyond* prayer. In his *Discourse on Stillness*, Dadisho' draws on the ideas of Evagrius of Pontus to describe "pure prayer" and link it to four virtues. The only other works by Dadisho' that survive are commentaries on the work of Isaiah of Scetis and on the *Paradise of the Desert Fathers* and shorter works and letters dealing with stillness and spirituality.

DANIEL OF ṢALAḤ

Daniel of Ṣalaḥ was an influential West Syrian abbot and exegete most well-known in the later tradition for authoring an enormous commentary on the book of Psalms. Christological themes in his works, as well as his own mention of the year in his *Commentary*, indicate he was active in the mid-sixth century. The demonym "of Ṣalaḥ" was actually proposed by a modern scholar, and there is debate about whether Daniel was active in the present-day monastery of Ṣalaḥ; medieval and modern sources have also linked him to the monastery of Ṣaliḥe and that of Tella. Daniel's *Commentary on the Psalms*, the first extant commentary on the entire book of Psalms in Syriac, shows both polemical and spiritual concerns. Daniel does not interpret the Psalms systematically but proceeds according to what he finds relevant. In terms of format, the *Commentary* is arranged into a series of small sermons on each passage that Daniel discusses. The *Commentary* engages heavily with Christological controversies and opposed in particular Julianism, a subsect of miaphysite Christianity that taught that Christ's body was incorruptible even before his resurrection. At the same time, Daniel's work shows the influence of earlier Syriac exegetes, including Ephrem and Aphrahat. In addition to the *Commentary*, several medieval abridgements of the *Commentary* survive, and Daniel is also known to have composed letters and commentaries on other books and stories of the Old Testament. Only the *Commentary on the Psalms* is known to have survived.

DIONYSIUS BAR ṢALIBI

Dionysius bar Ṣalibi (d. 1171) was one of the most significant Syriac writer of the twelfth century. Born in Melitene in eastern Cappadocia, his baptismal name was Jacob. He took the episcopal name Dionysius when he was ordained bishop of Marʿash in 1148. Later Michael the Great appointed him West Syrian metropolitan of Amid. Dionysius wrote commentaries on the Old and New Testaments, thus being the first Syriac author to comment on the entire Bible whose work survives. He drew on Greek commentators in Syriac translation and, even though he was West Syrian, incorporated exegetical work from the East Syrian Church. He also wrote commentaries on the logical works of Aristotle and Porphyry, a commentary on the Greek mystical and ascetical writer Evagrius of Pontus, and polemical works against Muslims, Jews, and competing sects of Christians. An early polemical work, *On Providence*, which argues against John of Mardin that Edessa's fall was not due to divine providence, proved highly controversial and is now lost. We know of many other works that have been lost, including a historical chronicle, a book of letters, and poems dealing with current events. A *Life* of Dionysius by Michael the Great also does not survive.

EGERIA

A Western Christian pilgrim, Egeria left her home in Spain or France in 381 to go on a three-year pilgrimage to several biblical and Christian sites in the eastern Mediterranean. She addressed her travelogue to her "sisters" back home, possibly a monastic community, recounting her experiences in the Holy Land, Egypt, and Mesopotamia. Of particular interest for students of the Syriac world are Egeria's discussion of her visit to Edessa and her references to traditions of the Apostle Thomas's evangelization. Egeria describes several sites in fourth-century Edessa and makes extensive reference to the story that King Abgar exchanged letters with Jesus. According to Egeria, Jesus's reply to Abgar was used to protect Edessa from hostile armies. She mentions visiting a shrine to the apostle Thomas in Edessa and reports that he evangelized in Persia, but she seems unaware of the tradition, found in the *Acts of Thomas*, that Thomas reached India. Scholars are also interested in Egeria's writing as a source on fourth-century liturgical practices and as a witness to the linguistic development of Vulgar Latin.

ELIAS

Elias was a mid-sixth century follower of John of Tella who wrote an influential *Life* of him. All that is known of Elias's own life comes from this source. It appears likely that Elias was a monk, perhaps based in Kallinikos as John himself was. His reference to the Persian takeover of Kallinikos in 542 allows his *Life* to be dated to after that point. Interestingly, Elias also claims to have known John's mother and to have used her as a source.

EPHREM

Ephrem the Syrian (d. 373), sometimes called Ephrem of Nisibis or Ephrem of Edessa, was a prolific Syriac writer active in the fourth century. He served as a deacon in Nisibis until 363, when the city was transferred from the Romans to the Persians and he relocated to Edessa. Ephrem's surviving works encompass prose works, including his biblical commentaries; artistic prose; *madrashe* or hymns; and *memre* or verse sermons. Theologically, Ephrem defended Nicene orthodoxy and published polemics against Marcionism, Manichaeism, and Bardaisan's teachings. Ephrem was well regarded by Latin and Greek authors in late antiquity, and several of his works were translated into Greek and Armenian during this time. Additionally, numerous spurious works in Greek and Syriac were attributed to him, owing in part to his close association with the seven-syllable *memra* meter in the Syriac tradition. Largely fictional Greek and Syriac *Lives* of Ephrem closely associate him with the Greek Cappadocian Father, Basil the Great. In addition to being theologically interesting, his *Commentary on the Diatessaron* provides an invaluable witness to the Diatessaron, Tatian's largely lost harmonization of the gospels. Today, Ephrem is regarded as a virtuosic Syriac writer and theologians from various traditions are paying increased attention to his writings.

EUSEBIUS OF CEASAREA

Often considered the first Church historian, Eusebius of Caesarea was an influential Greek Christian writer, historian, and apologist most active in the early fourth century. His extant writings include the *Ecclesiastical History*, the *Preparation for the Gospel*, and the *Life of Constantine*. Eusebius wrote immediately after the legalization of Christianity in the Roman Empire under Constantine and is generally strongly in favor of Constantine's rule and the broader synthesis of Christianity with the Roman imperial apparatus. Eusebius was also deeply influenced by Origen and defended Origen's teachings in his writings. The writings of Eusebius play a significant role in Syriac history and scholarship on Syriac Christianity for several reasons. He presents the first datable report of the Abgar-Jesus correspondence, which he claims to have verified based on the archives of Edessa. He also represents an important Roman witness to Constantine's relations with the Sasanian king Shapur I. More generally, his writings were translated into Syriac at a relatively early date (by 400) and helped shape indigenous Syriac historical writing. For instance, many Syriac chroniclers, especially those in the West Syrian tradition, divide ecclesiastical and secular history into separate columns, following Eusebius's *Chronicle*.

EVAGRIUS OF PONTUS

Evagrius of Pontus (also Evagrius Ponticus, d. 399) was a Greek monk and a writer on spirituality very much influenced by Origen of Alexandria. Evagrius was born in Pontus and initially active in Constantinople, where he befriended the Cappadocian Fathers, before leaving for Palestine and staying under the care of Melania the Elder. At her suggestion, he went to become a monk in Egypt, where he practiced with some of the most prominent *abbas* of the Western desert. Evagrius's curriculum was divided between "practice" (*praktikē*) and "contemplation" (*theōria*), the latter culminating in a contemplation of the Holy Trinity. Evagrius taught a doctrine of universal salvation according to which minds would eventually reunite with God, and he insisted that *apatheia* could be attained in this life. Even during his lifetime, Evagrius's views were controversial, and his and Origen's views were anathematized at the Second Council of Constantinople of 553 under the Byzantine emperor Justinian. Because the East and West Syrian Churches did not recognize this council, Evagrius's works remained widely influential in the Syriac tradition, where a rich custom of commentary helped to tame some of his more extreme theological speculations. Some of Evagrius's more speculative writings survive only in Syriac; these include the *Letter to Melania* (sometimes called the *Great Letter*) and two versions of the *Kephalaia Gnostika* (*Gnostic Chapters*), one of which (S1) has toned down his more esoteric and heterodox teachings. Influential commentators on Evagrius in the Syriac tradition include Babai the Great and Dionysius bar Ṣalibi. Additionally, the *Book of the Holy Hierotheus*, likely written by Stephen bar Ṣudayli, is indebted to Evagrius's speculations.

GEORGE OF RESHʻAYNA

George of Reshʻayna was a monothelete Maronite writer who wrote a Syriac "antihagiography" of Maximus the Confessor sometime between 662 and 680. George mentions himself in the first person in this work, making it the only unambiguous source for his own life. Here George identifies himself as a bishop who attended a synod in Cyprus related to the monothelete controversy with Maximus. Although nothing else is known with certainty about George's life, scholars have proposed that George of Reshʻayna may have played a role in copying materials related to the Second Council of Constantinople and may have written a monothelete florilegium that survives in a single manuscript. Thematically, George's "antihagiography" is notable for portraying Maximus as a Nestorian and for suggesting that the Arab conquests of North Africa were God's punishment for the prevalence of dyotheletism.

GIWARGIS WARDA

To Giwargis (George) Warda is ascribed the *Ktaba Warda* ("Book of the Rose"), a thirteenth-century East Syrian collection of liturgical hymns in the *ʻonita* genre. Almost nothing can be reliably discerned regarding Giwargis Warda's life or which (if any) of the hymns in the *Ktaba Warda* were actually written by him. References to the Mongol invasions in the *Ktaba Warda* suggest it was composed in or after the first half of the thirteenth century, but additional details of its composition and compilation remain unclear. Giwargis's poems would have been read communally in the Eucharistic liturgies of the festivals to which they correspond. Structurally, they feature alphabetical acrostics. Poems attributed to Giwargis such as *On Sin* show a greater focus on self-reflection and communal contrition than earlier Syriac poems and make less use of imaginative retelling of biblical stories.

ḤUNAYN IBN ISḤAQ

Ḥunayn ibn Isḥaq (d. 873) was an East Syrian translator, scholar, physician, and scientist in 'Abbasid Baghdad. He was responsible for translating numerous works of medicine and philosophy from Greek into Syriac and Arabic. Trained as a medical doctor, he served as royal physician to Caliph al-Mutawakkil and founded a school of translators that translated almost all the writings of the ancient physician Galen, as well as works by Hippocrates and Dioscorides. The same school translated Greek philosophical works, including the writings of Plato, Aristotle, and Porphyry, into Syriac and Arabic. Depending on the needs of Ḥunayn's patron, Ḥunayn would variously translate Greek works into Syriac, Arabic (often by way of Syriac), or both. In addition to his activity as a doctor and translator, Ḥunayn wrote epitomes and original works on theology, linguistics, and medicine in both Syriac and Arabic. Several letters by Ḥunayn also survive, the most influential of which is his *Risala*, which explains his approach to translation. There, Ḥunayn discusses his travels in search of manuscripts of Greek works and his method of collating different copies of the same text. He also discusses earlier Syriac translations of Greek writings, including those of Sergius of Resh'ayna (sixth-century). Often, Ḥunayn either corrected or completely re-translated such works to accord with his own standards. Among the most visible examples of the place of Syriac in the 'Abbasid translation movement, Ḥunayn's writings illustrate how a Syriac-Greek-Arabic matrix defined the intellectual climate of Baghdad in the 'Abbasid period.

ISAAC OF ANTIOCH

A large collection of homilies and poetry is attributed to Isaac of Antioch. According to a letter by Jacob of Edessa (d. 708), Isaac was a priest active in Edessa and Antioch in the late fifth century, under Emperor Zeno. In fact, modern-day scholars suspect that works by several different writers were transmitted under the name "Isaac of Antioch." In some later East Syrian manuscripts, Isaac of Antioch is further conflated with the mystical writer Isaac of Nineveh. Identifying different perspectives and voices in the corpus attributed to Isaac of Antioch is not made easier by the relative lack of critical editions of his poems. All the same, some sets of poems and homilies share common themes, especially ascetical and eschatological topics. To Isaac of Antioch are also attributed a series of *Homilies Against the Jews*. These works show a supersessionist approach, arguing that the Jewish scriptures themselves have condemned the Jews, who have lost access to God's "riches" after the coming of Christ.

ISAAC OF NINEVEH

One of the most influential East Syrian mystical and ascetic writers, Isaac of Nineveh was a monk and, briefly, bishop of Nineveh active in the late seventh century. Isaac came from Bet Qaṭraye, a region of Arabia that included present-day Qatar. After his ordination, he was a hermit attached to the monastery of Rabban Shapur in the Shushtar region of Iran. Isaac's spiritual teachings were influenced by Evagrius of Pontus, whose more esoteric and advanced teachings were rejected by the Greek tradition after their official condemnation at the Second Council of Constantinople under Emperor Justinian in 553. In some of his writings, Isaac discusses states "beyond prayer" and shows universalist tendencies. At the same time, Isaac criticized those he characterized as Messalians, in part to distinguish his own views from theirs. Isaac's writings attracted a wide readership and were translated into Greek, Arabic, and, through Greek, Slavonic.

JACOB OF EDESSA

A West Syrian scholar originally from the province of Antioch, Jacob of Edessa served as bishop of Edessa from 684–89 and again in 708, the year of his death. In this capacity, Jacob was known for his devotion to canon law, initially resigning over what he perceived as laxities in the enforcement of that law. His writings, including his *Letters*, extensively discuss the interpretation and application of canon law. These letters also make reference to Islam in the regions in which Jacob was active, offering some of the best surviving evidence for on-the-ground interactions between Christians and Muslims in the seventh and eighth centuries. In addition to his career as a bishop, Jacob was an influential writer, translator, and scholar, who knew Greek and drew on Greek miaphysite theology and modes of writing. He was educated in Greek biblical exegesis at Qenneshre and Alexandria and taught, after his first tenure as a bishop, at the monasteries of Mar Jacob at Kaysum, Eusebona, and Tel 'Ada. His scholarly writings include a revised translation of the Old Testament into Syriac that drew on the Septuagint, translations of the miaphysite theologian Severus of Antioch, the first *Hexaemeron* originally composed in Syriac, biblical commentaries, and the aforementioned letters and works on canon law.

JACOB OF SERUG

Jacob of Serug (d. 521) was a widely regarded West Syrian bishop and poet-theologian. Jacob was a student at the School of Edessa, where he learned methods of biblical exegesis that go back to Theodore of Mopsuestia and the Antiochene tradition. In 519, he was consecrated bishop of Baṭnan. Jacob is most famous for hundreds of *memre* in the twelve-syllable meter; *madrashe*, *sogiyata*, anaphoras, prose homilies, and letters that have been attributed to him also survive, and at least some of these appear to be authentic. Most of his *memre* and homilies focus on poetic interpretation and imaginative retelling of biblical stories, such as his poem *On the Sinful Woman*; many other *memre*, including *On the Solitaries*, are hagiographic discussions of ascetics, solitaries, and saints. Although he is also venerated by the Maronite Church, Jacob sided with West Syrian miaphysites in the aftermath of the Council of Chalcedon and wrote a letter and *memra* lamenting the outcome of the council. Jacob is regarded as one of the most artful poet-theologians in Syriac, and by the Middle Ages his work had been translated into Arabic, Armenian, Ethiopic, and Georgian. Scholars have also noted numerous parallels between the content and themes of Jacob's writings and early Islamic literature, including the Qur'an; these are exemplified by the story of the *Seven Sleepers of Ephesus*.

JOHN OF APAMEA

Also known as John the Solitary (*iḥidaya*), John of Apamea was an early fifth-century spiritual writer who influenced both West and East Syrian traditions of spirituality and mysticism. His extant works consist primarily of essays on prayer and letters; some extant biblical commentaries survive under his name but appear to be spurious. John's spiritual writings outline two tripartite structures through which an individual could progress. The first of these moves from the "way of the body" to the "way of the soul" and ultimately to the "way of the spirit"; the second outlines levels of purity, serenity, and perfection that the believer could attain. In the treatise *On Prayer* included in this volume, John encourages silent prayer as the most spiritual way of addressing God and offers a fivefold typology of silence. Although John does not appear sympathetic to Messalianism, Katholikos Timothy I condemned him, John of Dalyata, and Joseph Ḥazzaya in the 780s for allegedly Messalian tendencies. However, in the 820s Katholikos Ishoʿ bar Nun reversed this condemnation. In the fifth century Philoxenus of Mabbug accused a John the Solitary of heresy, but scholars dispute whether this is the same as John of Apamea.

JOHN OF DALYATA

Also known as John the Elder, John of Dalyata was an eighth-century East Syrian monk, abbot, mystic, and writer. Initially John practiced as a monk in the monastery of Mar Yozadaq in the Qardu Mountains; after seven years there, he took up a solitary life in the mountains of Bet Dalyata. Later in life, he returned to the Qardu Mountains and was made an abbot. Like other East Syrian mystical authors in the seventh and eighth centuries, including Isaac of Nineveh and Joseph Ḥazzaya, John's spirituality drew on the thought of Evagrius of Pontus to theorize a state beyond prayer, which John called "wonder." At a synod in the late 780s, Katholikos Timothy I condemned John's writings, along with those of John of Apamea and Joseph Ḥazzaya, for allegedly Messalian tendencies. However, all three authors were rehabilitated forty years later under Katholikos Ishoʿ bar Nun (d. 828). The initial condemnation nevertheless stained John's reputation, so much so that many of his works in fact survive only in West Syrian manuscripts. Some of John's spiritual writings and sayings were transmitted anonymously into Arabic and Ethiopic; others among John's writings were translated into Greek.

JOHN OF EPHESUS

John of Ephesus (d. 589) was a West Syrian monk, historian, hagiographer, and titular bishop of Ephesus. John entered monastic life while still a child but was exiled in the 520s as the

Byzantine emperors Justin I and Justinian persecuted West Syrians. During his exile, he travelled the Eastern Roman Empire until settling in Constantinople around 540. Under Justinian, John led a missionary campaign to convert pagans in Asia Minor in 542. In 558, Jacob Baradeus consecrated John bishop of Ephesus, but he seems never to have resided in that city. John was imprisoned for his miaphysite views in the 570s under Justin II and died in prison. He wrote the *Lives of the Eastern Saints* in the 560s and an important *Ecclesiastical History* covering the years to 588. John's *Ecclesiastical History* does not survive in full but much of it is included as part of the eighth-century *Chronicle of Zuqnin* and is cited by Elias of Nisibis. Both of John's writings are notable for their defense of miaphysite doctrine and identity and their praise of monasticism and asceticism.

JOHN OF MARDIN

John of Mardin (d. 1165) was a West Syrian bishop and restorer of churches based in southeast Anatolia active in the twelfth century. He was appointed metropolitan of Mardin (sometimes called Mardre) in 1124 or 1125, and in this capacity he facilitated the restoration of several churches in the area and promoted monasticism. John's most influential writings include his legal canons, some of which were incorporated into the West Syrian *Synodicon*. Several of these discuss the proper performance of baptism and they provide important evidence for Syriac ritual practice during the crusader period. Perhaps most notable is a canon allowing for the special baptism of Muslim children without their converting to Christianity. This seems to have been an accommodation to Muslim parents who believed baptism provided spiritual protection for their children. In addition to his legal works, John wrote on liturgy and produced a work, since lost, claiming the fall of Edessa was separate from the will of God. Several biographical details are contained in his canons, and Michael the Great wrote a panegyric on John that remains unpublished.

JOSEPH ḤAZZAYA

Known by the epithet "the Seer" or "the Visionary" (*ḥazzaya*), Joseph was an eighth-century East Syrian monk and abbot credited with synthesizing the mystical thought of the East Syrian tradition up to his own day. Thanks to Ishoʿdnah of Baṣra's *Book of Chastity*, we know more about Joseph's life than we do about his contemporaries. Born to Zoroastrian parents around 710, he was captured and enslaved as a child. When he exhibited interest in the monks he saw in the region of Mount Qardu, he was baptized and eventually freed in order to pursue his own monastic vocation. He was both an abbot and a hermit at different times of his life, based in both Qardu and the mountains around Adiabene in Iraq. John's literary output was impressive and a number of his writings survive today, although some of his works, such as *On the Stirrings of the Mind During Prayer*, circulated under the name of his brother ʿAbdishoʿ, and others were attributed to Philoxenus of Mabbug. Katholikos Timothy I condemned Joseph's writings, along with those of John of Apamea and John Dalyata, at a synod in the late 780s for allegedly Messalian tendencies, but Joseph was later rehabilitated. Joseph also expressed universalist themes in some of his writings. As with many early medieval East Syrian mystics, Joseph's writings show Evagrian influences.

KHAMIS BAR QARDAḤE

A thirteenth-century East Syrian poet like Giwargis Warda, Khamis bar Qardaḥe wrote numerous poems in the *'onita* genre. He may have been a priest in the region of Arbela, although little else is known of his life. Like Giwargis Warda, Khamis wrote penitential hymns, hymns associated with feasts of the liturgical year, and martyrological or hagiographic hymns. However, Khamis also wrote on secular themes, including satire, invective, and epigrams. Such a combination of sacred and secular writing from one author is characteristic of both verse and prose from the medieval period. Khamis also wrote rhymed metrical commentaries on the gospels called *turgame*, which were read in liturgies. Khamis's writings were popular in the medieval and early modern period, and his poetic skill has earned praise from modern scholars. His poetry has been translated into Turkish and Neo-Aramaic.

MICHAEL THE GREAT

Michael the Great (also called Michael I or Michael the Syrian) served as patriarch of the West Syrian Church from 1166 until his death in 1199. Born in 1126 in Melitene, a city in the Cappadocia region of Anatolia, Michael became a monk at a young age. He was elected as part of a reform movement within the West Syrian Church. Michael was a skilled diplomat and recognized even by non-Syriac miaphysite Christians. He visited Latin-occupied Antioch and Jerusalem several times and, apart from a period in the 1180s, was recognized by the kingdoms of the Catholic crusaders. He was also in communication with the Seljuk sultan. As part of his reform project, Michael compiled and wrote liturgical, theological, and hagiographical works, but he is best remembered for his world *Chronicle*, which ranges from the creation of the world to his own day. Many of the historiographic materials that Michael discovered in monasteries were incorporated into *Chronicle*, preserving earlier Syriac historiography, including the ninth-century *Ecclesiastical History* by Dionysius of Tel Maḥre. Structurally, Michael's *Chronicle* parallels earlier West Syrian chronicles, dividing secular and ecclesiastical history into separate columns.

MUSHE BAR KEPHA

Mushe bar Kepha (d. 903) was the West Syrian bishop of Bet Ramman, north of Tikrit (Iraq). He produced a massive collection of biblical exegesis and theology and is recognized as one of the preeminent writers in the West Syrian tradition. His scholarship depended on compiling sections of previous works, showing him to have been well-versed in tradition and having had access to many books. This approach allowed Mushe to cover a wider range of theological and exegetical issues than earlier writers in his tradition had. Some scholars have suggested his compilations may have constituted an apologetic for Christianity amid the growing influence of Islam. His scholarship on the Old Testament is notable for its careful examination of different translations of the text, including the Greek Septuagint, the Peshiṭta Old Testament, and the Syro-Hexapla. This work draws on earlier sources, including Jacob of Edessa and Philoxenus of Mabbug. Mushe and Jacob also testify to a variation of the Abgar legend in which Abgar requests a Syriac translation of the Old Testament from the original Hebrew.

NARSAI

The head of the School of Edessa and possible founder of the School of Nisibis, Narsai (d. ca. 500) was one of the most prolific poets of the Syriac tradition and was the first major East Syrian hymnographer. He was born in the Persian Empire but studied in Roman Edessa, where he was influenced by the exegesis of Theodore of Mopsuestia and where he eventually became head of the School of Edessa. The writings of Barḥadbshaba and the statutes of the School of Nisibis attribute the founding of the latter school to Narsai. Through his eighty-one surviving *memre* on various subjects, including biblical interpretation and individual theological and ethical topics, he propounded the East Syrian Church's dyophysite theology, emphasizing the unmixed relationship of Christ's humanity and divinity in the incarnation. In his poetry, Narsai explicitly attacks Cyril of Alexandria and defends several Antiochene exegetes, including Nestorius; it is also alleged that he began writing *memre* in response to the miaphysite Christological views of Jacob of Serug. Most extant collections of Narsai's *memre* appear to have been organized for liturgical use in the East Syrian Church. *Sogiyata* and a cycle of *memra* on Joseph have also traditionally been attributed to Narsai but appear not to be authentic.

PHILOXENUS OF MABBUG

An influential polemicist and theologian for the West Syrian Church, Philoxenus (d. 523) served as Bishop of Mabbug (modern-day Manbij in Syria, also called Hierapolis) from 485 to 519. He spent the last four years of his life exiled on the orders of the Byzantine emperor Justin I. Philoxenus drew on both Greek and Syriac theology and sought to incorporate Greek Christological terminology into Syriac. To this end, he sponsored a new translation of the New Testament into Syriac, which in turn influenced the Harqlean translation of the New Testament, although neither overtook the Peshiṭta in popularity even in West Syrian circles. Other writings, including his famous *Discourses*, clearly operate within an ascetic context. Syriac asceticism also provides a valuable context within which to examine Philoxenus's letters to monks, in which he warns about what he perceives as heresy (including Chalcedonian Christology) and encourages the maintenance of a miaphysite identity. Other works by Philoxenus include commentaries and sermons, many of which only survive in the catena tradition.

SERGIUS OF RESH'AYNA

Sergius (d. 536) was a doctor, translator, and author, frequently designated the "Archiatros," or chief doctor, of Resh'ayna. Our main source for his life is a passage in the *Ecclesiastical History* of Pesudo-Zacharias, which mentions that Sergius received his medical education in Alexandria and died in Constantinople after delivering a letter to Pope Agapetus from Patriarch Ephrem of Antioch. Often associated with the first of two major Syriac translation movements, Sergius is best remembered for translating several Greek theological, philosophical, and medical works into Syriac. He is the most influential Syriac translator of Galen and the first Syriac translator of the pseudonymous *Corpus Dionysiacum*. He is also known to have translated some of Aristotle's writings, and Joseph Ḥazzaya seems to attribute to Sergius the translation of the unexpunged version of the *Kephalaia Gnostika* by Evagrius of Pontus. Sergius wrote original works on spirituality, philosophy, and translation theory; his treatise *On the Aim of Each of Aristotle's Writings* explains both Sergius's translation method and the place of Aristotle in Sergius's pedagogy and thought.

SEVERUS OF ANTIOCH

An architect of miaphysite orthodoxy and one of the foremost Greek theological writers of the sixth century, Severus served as patriarch of Antioch from 512 until his death in 538. However, he spent much of his life between Beirut, Gaza, Constantinople, and Egypt, where he died in exile. Born a pagan in Sozopolis in Pisidia, he studied in Alexandria and at the law school in Beirut, during which time he converted to Christianity. He became a monk in Gaza for a time before emerging as a major opponent of Chalcedonian Christology. His writings, originally written in Greek, were condemned by Emperor Justinian in 536, but early translations by Paul of Kallinikos guaranteed the survival of many of Severus's writings in Syriac. The Syriac translation of his writings was later revised by Jacob of Edessa. Severus's most famous writings were 125 *Cathedral Homilies*, which he gave during his time as patriarch. In addition to these homilies, anti-Chalcedonian and anti-Julianist writings by Severus survive in Syriac, as do letters and hymns. Syriac writers through the centuries have produced several biographies of Severus, indicating his continued importance in the West Syrian tradition.

SEVERUS SEBOKT

Severus Sebokt (d. 666 or 667) was the bishop of Qenneshre, a West Syrian monastery on the Euphrates south of Aleppo that became a major center of study for bilingual scholars of Greek and Syriac. Severus was an astronomer, philosopher, and mathematician, and he is said to have debated a Maronite bishop in front of the Muslim caliph Muʿāwiya at Damascus. His philosophical works, like most Syriac philosophy of the period, concerned Aristotle, especially the subject of logic. He may also have translated Middle Persian works of Paul the Persian on Aristotle into Syriac, indicating Severus's multilingual environment. His works also quote Plato. Few of Severus's astronomical works have been edited, but some of his surviving works on this topic include a *Treatise on the Astrolabe* and a *Treatise on Constellations*. Severus is an example of the cosmopolitan intellectual climate at Qenneshre and in the seventh-century Syriac world generally.

SIMEON OF BET ARSHAM

Simeon of Bet Arsham was a West Syrian polemicist and traveler active in the first half of the sixth century. Our main source of his life is a chapter in John of Ephesus's *Lives of the Eastern Saints*, but the value of John as a source has been questioned. According to John, Simeon was a bishop, but there was no known bishopric of Bet Arsham, suggesting Simeon may have been an itinerant bishop. Simeon was an influential polemicist against all forms of dyophysitism in Armenia, Persia, and the Byzantine empire. He was a vocal critic of the School of Edessa, identifying it as "Nestorian" in a heretical genealogy he traced back to Judaism. One letter, excerpted in this volume, discusses Simeon's travels among the Lakhmids, an Arab Christian kingdom, and reports the annexation of a Christian kingdom in South Arabia by the Jewish king of Himyar, leading to the martyrdom of many Christians in the region. Although Simeon's works are colored by anti-Judaism, this letter is notable for reporting an unusual case of Christian martyrdom under a Jewish ruler. More generally, Simeon's life and work are interesting for providing a witness to pre-Islamic Arab Christianity and Christological polemic in the sixth century.

SOLOMON OF BAṢRA

Solomon of Baṣra was a thirteenth-century East Syrian writer and the metropolitan of Baṣra. Little is known about Solomon other than that he attended a consecration in 1222. According to 'Abdisho' bar Brika, Solomon wrote several theological treatises and prayers; his most famous work today is the *Book of the Bee*. This work retells the history of the world from creation to Jesus's resurrection, and it includes several details, embellishments, and interpretations of biblical narratives. For instance, Solomon says that the order of creation in Genesis was intended to prevent later philosophers from claiming that the sun, rather than God, created the earth's plants. Like many Syriac texts, it also recognizes Syriac as the primordial human language, and makes an argument for the priority of its own (East Syrian) tradition over other forms of Christianity.

STEPHEN BAR ṢUDAYLI

Stephen bar Ṣudayli was a sixth-century Syriac monk and mystic who was accused of pantheist tendencies. Based on the testimony of the West Syrian patriarch Quryaqos in the late eighth century, scholars have concluded that Stephen is likely the author of the *Book of the Holy Hierotheus*. Closer to Stephen's own time, Jacob of Serug and Philoxenus of Mabbug wrote concerning him. Philoxenus also confirms the influence of Evagrius of Pontus on Stephen. In the *Book of the Holy Hierotheus*, Stephen presents a form of mysticism that draws on Evagrius, Origen of Alexandria, and the Pseudo-Dionysian corpus, but goes beyond all three. This text claims that minds may attain a state of extreme unification with God, by which they surpass both Christ and even God. Although several West Syrian authors criticized these ideas, the *Book of the Holy Hierotheus* was incorporated into orthodox West Syrian thought in part through a handful of medieval commentaries on the text, including one by Barhebraeus. The title and pseudonymous attribution of the book are allusions to the Pseudo-Dionysian corpus, which makes reference to a supposed teacher of Dionysius named Hierotheus.

STEPHEN MANSUR

Stephen Mansur (d. 780) was a Chalcedonian monk active at the monastery of Mar Saba. There he wrote the *Passion of Romanos the Neomartyr*, the story of a monk who was killed by Caliph al-Mahdi (here called Amir al-Mu'minin) after convincing some recent converts to Islam to revert to Christianity. The *Synaxarion* and the Georgian translation of the *Passion of Romanos the Neomartyr* indicate that Stephen was from Damascus and was, in fact, the nephew of John of Damascus. Stephen also wrote hymns, including one in praise of martyrs at Mar Saba. Stephen almost certainly wrote in Greek, but the *Passion of Romanos the Neomartyr* survives only in a Georgian translation. Stephen's martyrdom narrative notably takes a much more negative view of Caliph al-Mahdi than the East Syrian tradition does, and it is one of the few accounts (nearly all of which are Chalcedonian in origin) of Christian martyrdom under the early Islamic caliphate.

THEODORE ABŪ QURRAH

Theodore Abū Qurrah (d. after 829) was the Chalcedonian Bishop of Ḥarran and one of the first Christians known to have written in Arabic. Little is known of Theodore's life, although he was likely born in Edessa, and Michael the Great claims he was eventually deposed of his seat as bishop. He is also known to have traveled in Armenia in the early ninth century. Theodore's writings survive in Arabic and Greek, but he also wrote a number of Syriac works that are no longer extant. His extant writings show a concern for defending Christian truth-claims over Islam and a broader recognition of the religious diversity of the Near East in this period, also discussing pagans, Zoroastrians, Samaritans, Jews, Manichaeans, Marcionites, and Bardaisanites. While his work is polemical and at times exhibits stereotypes, he provides a valuable witness to Christian views of Islam and Manichaeans in the early ninth century.

THEODORE OF MOPSUESTIA

Theodore of Mopsuestia (d. 428) served as bishop of Mopsuestia and acquired fame for his exegetical and theological writings and homilies. He was educated in Antioch, studied with the pagan rhetor Libanius, and probably personally knew John Chrysostom and Diodore of Tarsus. Theodore is the foremost representative of the Antiochene school of exegesis and dyophysite Christology. Theodore was suspicious of allegorical interpretations of the Bible, a widespread practice associated mostly with the Jewish author Philo (d. ca. 50) and the Christian writer Origen (d. 253), both from Alexandria. Theodore interpreted the Bible principally in its historical integrity and was wary of reading the Old Testament as if it predicted or prefigured Christ. However, based partly on the apostle Paul's acceptance of allegorical interpretation, Theodore did not completely reject allegorical or typological interpretations of the Old Testament. His dyophiste Christology influenced Diodore, Nestorius, and the East Syrian tradition more broadly. Theodore's Christological views were formally condemned at the Second Council of Constantinople in 553, but the Council of Chalcedon had previously partly rehabilitated his views and he died in full communion with the Greek Church. Many of Theodore's writings were preserved in Syriac owing to their influence on the East Syrian tradition. His exegetical methods were taught in the Schools of Edessa and Nisibis, proving formative for generations of Syriac theologians.

THEODORET OF CYRRHUS

Theodoret of Cyrrhus (d. 466) was an Antiochene bishop, historian, hagiographer and theologian who left a sizeable influence on Syriac Christianity, especially East Syrian thought. He wrote in Greek but is known to have been fluent in spoken Syriac. A student of Theodore of Mopsuestia, Theodoret exemplified the Antiochene tradition of exegesis and was condemned at the Second Council of Ephesus (sometimes called the "Robber Synod") in 449. He wrote biblical commentaries and arguments against both paganism and miaphysitism. His historical writings include a continuation of Eusebius's writings to 428 and the *History of the Monks of Syria* (in Latin, *Historia religiosa*), which includes the earliest witness to Simeon the Stylite's life and to the Christian ascetic practice of stylitism. Theodoret met Simeon personally, and his hagiography of Simeon is interesting for its striving to present the unique piety of Syrian monastic practice to a wider, Western (here, Greek-speaking) audience.

THOMAS OF MARGA

Thomas of Marga was a ninth-century monk at the monastery of Bet 'Abe, the "Forest Monastery" northeast of Mosul (Iraq). In the 840s, he was appointed bishop of Marga under the East Syrian katholikos Abraham II (r. 837–850), who was himself a former monk and abbot at the monastery of Bet 'Abe. Thomas is most famous as the author of the *Book of Governors*, more properly called the *Book of the Abbots of Bet 'Abe* and also known by its Latin title, the *Historia Monastica*. The *Book of Governors* tells the history of Thomas's monastery and especially its relations to the many East Syrian monasteries founded between the sixth and the ninth centuries. It also features many vignettes about specific East Syrian monks and miracle stories. More generally, the *Book of Governors* provides a valuable witness to East Syrian monastic scholasticism, the missionary activities of the East Syrian Church, and Christian-Muslim relations in the ninth century. Thomas wrote other historiographical works that are either referenced by or incorporated into the *Book of Governors*, and he appears to have been an able poet, based on his inclusion of verse in the work.

TIMOTHY I

Considered one of the greatest katholikoi of the East Syrian Church, Timothy I (d. 823) served as katholikos from 780 until his death, through the reign of five caliphs. He undertook extensive efforts to consolidate the East Syrian Church and improve the status of Christians under Muslim rule. These included efforts to promote scholarship in the East Syrian Church. That scholarship includes the following: translating Greek works of scholarship, philosophy, and textual criticism; largely friendly dialogue with Muslim authorities, including the caliph al-Mahdi; and the consolidation of East Syrian law. Timothy is also famed for his missionary and administrative efforts in India, China, Tibet, Central Asia, and South Arabia. He consecrated several metropolitans for various locations in Central Asia and promoted indigenous leadership and theological writing in languages beside Syriac. Timothy's letters are a witness to his missionary efforts and scholarship and they provide a valuable source on numerous aspects of the East Syrian Church under Islam.

TIMOTHY OF CONSTANTINOPLE

Timothy was a Greek Chalcedonian priest in Constantinople active in the seventh or early eighth century. He wrote *On Those Who Come to the Church from the Heretics*, a heresiological work discussing what members of various "heretical" sects had to do to be admitted to the

Chalcedonian Church and classifying heresies more broadly. Timothy places each heresy into one of three categories: those whose members must be baptized to enter the Chalcedonian Church; those whose members must be anointed to join the Church; and those whose members must abjure a particular heresy without anointing or baptism. Timothy notably mentions Messalianism among the heresies he catalogued and ascribes a list of heretical doctrines to the Messalians, doctrines that may be derived from an earlier source. He is also an interesting witness to seventh-century Chalcedonian Christian understandings of Manichaeism and Chalcedonian views of the non-Chalcedonian Churches.

WILLIAM OF RUBRUCK

William of Rubruck (d.1293, fl. 1253–55) was a Flemish Franciscan missionary who wrote in Latin. He participated in the Seventh Crusade under King Louis IX of France in 1248. In 1253, Louis IX sent him to convert the Mongols to Christianity and secure a Franco-Mongol alliance against the 'Abbasids, the same alliance the Mongol khan Arghun would later send Rabban Sauma to promote. William's journey took him deep into Mongol territory, after which he returned to Europe and wrote an account of his travels. In the court of the Mongols, William encountered Muslims, Buddhists, and Christians from the East Syrian Church whom he refers to as "Nestorians." He participated in theological debates among these parties in the Mongol court, providing an outsider's witness to their theology and relationship to the state. Written approximately a generation before Marco Polo, William's travel account is praised for its attention to detail and accuracy and was cited by the English Franciscan philosopher-scientist Roger Bacon.

ZACHARIAS RHETOR

Zacharias Rhetor, sometimes called Zacharias Scholasticus, was a Christian lawyer, bishop, and writer active in the late fifth and early sixth centuries. He studied at Gaza and Alexandria, where he met Severus of Antioch, and he subsequently studied law with Severus in Beirut. Zacharias practiced law in Constantinople before becoming bishop of Mytilene in the 530s. Several writings by Zacharias have survived, many of which proved important for West Syrian thought and historiography after Chalcedon. Zacharias wrote an *Ecclesiastical History* covering the Council of Chalcedon (451) to the end of the reign of Emperor Zeno (491); while this text does not survive in full, it was incorporated into the Syriac *Chronicle of Pseudo-Zacharias* and Michael the Great's *Chronicle*, and Evagrius Scholasticus used the original Greek version when writing his own *Ecclesiastical History*. Zacharias also wrote an apologetic *Life of Severus* that covers the period prior to Severus's becoming the patriarch of Antioch. This *Life* was partly intended to refute a pamphlet alleging that Severus had engaged in pagan practices during his youth. Other writings by Zacharias that survive in Greek include a *Life* of a monk named Isaiah and fragments of a *Life* of the monk Peter the Iberian. In Greek, writings by Zacharias that criticize Aristotelian philosophy and Manichaeism survive.

APPENDIX C

GLOSSARY

AMIR Arabic title meaning "prince" or "commander." One of the titles of the caliph of the 'Umayyad and 'Abbasid dynasties was *Amir al-Mu'minin* or "commander of the believers." Syriac texts often apply the title of 'amir to the same individuals that Arabic texts do, including the caliph.

ANAPHORA From the Greek verb *anapherō*, "to bring or carry up," refers to Eucharistic prayers said in Eastern Christian liturgies, including those in the Syriac tradition. Dozens of anaphoras survive in Syriac, with variations that often express confessional differences.

ANTINOMIANISM Generally, any viewpoint that rejects the need to follow laws or moral norms, especially from a religious perspective. In Syriac Christianity, accusations of antinomianism were leveled against Messalianism; as a result of these accusations, later Syriac mystics and bishops sought to distance themselves from Messalian and antinomian tendencies.

APATHEIA A Greek philosophical and theological term referring to total freedom from passions. Some Greek and Syriac monks, including Evagrius of Pontus, believed *apatheia* was a state that could be attained in this life; later Syriac writers, including Babai the Great and Isaac of Nineveh, claimed *apatheia* could only be attained in the afterlife.

APOKATASTASIS A Greek term literally meaning "restoration," *apokatastasis* acquired theological meaning for Christians in part because of the use of the term in Acts 3:21. Among theologians influenced by Origen of Alexandria, the *apokatastasis* came to refer to an eschatological end of time in which all people are reconciled to God, a kind of universalism or universal salvation.

ARAMAIC A group of languages in the Semitic branch of the Afroasiatic language family. Aramaic has a lengthy history—from its adoption by the ancient Persians to its survival as a minority language in the Middle East and diaspora populations today. Syriac is a standardized dialect of Aramaic that was originally spoken in Edessa.

ARIUS Arius (d. 336) was an Alexandrian presbyter after whom later polemicists named the doctrine of Arianism. Arius ignited a controversy with his bishop, Alexander, by claiming that God's word (and thus the Son) is not coeternal with God. Despite Arius's close association with Arianism, recent scholarship has noted that these ideas likely predate Arius and may have been more theologically traditional than Alexander's position. Arius's teachings were rejected at the Council of Nicaea in 325, which the Chalcedonian, East Syrian, Maronite, and West Syrian Churches accepted.

COENOBITIC (sometimes spelled cenobitic) Forms of monasticism according to which monks live in a community, in contrast to eremitic monasticism, according to which a monk lives alone as a hermit. The term derives from Greek *koinos bios* ("common or shared life").

CHILDREN OF THE COVENANT (Syriac: *bnay qyama*) Early indigenous Syriac ascetic movement that practiced celibacy. Syriac writers, including Ephrem and Aphrahat, addressed the "covenanters" with moral guidance and exhortation. Later, the children of the covenant became more communal and were eventually superseded by coenobitic forms of asceticism based on Egyptian monasticism.

CHOREPISCOPUS See PERIODEUTES.

CHRISTOLOGY The branch of Christian theology that concerns the nature of Jesus Christ and especially the relationship between the incarnate Christ's human and divine natures. During late antiquity and the early Middle Ages, Eastern Christianity divided as a result of several Christological controversies.

CHURCH OF THE EAST Modern-day title for the Christian denomination that succeeded the dyophysite East Syrian Church in the Middle East. Its members often call themselves Assyrians, which is reflected in the church's title as the Assyrian Church of the East. The corresponding church in union with the Roman Catholic Church is called the Chaldean Catholic Church.

COLOPHON A note by a scribe added to the end of a manuscript that provides information about the context in which the manuscript was produced and, often, the scribe who wrote it. Colophons are valuable sources for understanding the transmission and organization of knowledge in premodern scribal cultures.

COUNCIL OF CHALCEDON A watershed church council, convened in 451, that focused on the Christological controversy between dyophysitism and miaphysitism. The council decided that Christ had two natures in one person, a result accepted by the Catholic and Eastern Orthodox Churches (including Maronite and Chalcedonian Syriac Christians) but rejected by the Oriental Orthodox Churches, including the West Syrian (later Syrian Orthodox), Coptic Orthodox, Armenian Apostolic, and Ethiopian Orthodox Churches.

COUNCIL OF EPHESUS, FIRST The third ecumenical council, held in 431. This council rejected certain forms of dyophysitism promoted by Nestorius and declared that Christ was one person. The East Syrian tradition, including the present-day Church of the East, did not accept this Council.

COUNCIL OF NICAEA The first ecumenical Christian council, convened in 325 under the Roman emperor Constantine. This council rejected the teachings of Arius, taught that the Son is coeternal with the Father, and produced the Nicene Creed, an expanded form of which is still recited in many Christian congregations today. The Chalcedonian, East Syrian, Maronite, and West Syrian Churches accepted the Council of Nicaea.

DYOPHYSITE Broadly, a Christological viewpoint that holds that Christ has two natures, one human and one divine. The East Syrian Church subscribed to a type of dyophysitism attributed to Nestorius and held in attenuated ways by both Greek and Syriac theologians. In the end, this association led the church to be labeled, erroneously, as Nestorian. This view held that Christ has both two natures and two persons. A moderated form of dyophysitism, according to which Christ has two natures and one person, was adopted by Chalcedonian Christians.

EAST SYRIAN Dyophysite Syriac Church that has historically been centered in Persia, with missionary activity in Greater Iran, Arabia, Central Asia, China, and India. The East Syrian Church developed into the modern Church of the East. Polemical writings and older scholarship sometimes called the East Syrian Church "Nestorian," but this is now recognized as pejorative.

KATHOLIKOS A title for high-ranking bishops or heads of churches in several branches of Eastern Christianity. The leader of the East Syrian Church (including the modern-day Church of the East) is formally called the katholikos or katholikos-patriarch; this office was originally based in Seleucia-Ctesiphon but moved to Baghdad in the eighth century.

MADRASHA (pl. MADRASHE) A genre of Syriac poetry often translated as "hymn." *Madrashe* were sung in liturgical settings. The defining feature of a *madrasha* is its meter (*qala*); in *madrashe*, each stanza follows a pattern, and lines are defined by the number of syllables.

MANICHAEISM Religion founded by the Persian prophet Mani in the third century that acquired a wide following both in the Roman Empire and along the Silk Road, including in China. Its followers are typically called Manichaeans. Along the Silk Road, Manichaeans competed with Syriac Christians for converts; in turn, Christian theologians published numerous works criticizing Manichaeism.

MAPHRIAN The second-highest rank of bishop in the West Syrian tradition, including the modern Syrian Orthodox Church. For much of the Middle Ages the maphrian operated the church hierarchy in lands east of the Roman Empire, in competition with East Syrian Christians. This position is sometimes called Maphrian of the East.

MAR Syriac word for "lord" or "my lord"; an honorific applied to saints and bishops in the Syriac tradition.

MARCIONITE A follower of the early Christian thinker Marcion (d. ca. 160), who was deemed heterodox by later Christian tradition. Marcion was most notorious for claiming that the God of the Old Testament was different from the true God revealed by Jesus Christ. Marcionites were present in Syria and Edessa by the late second century; early Syriac writers including Ephrem and Bardaisan polemicized against them.

MARONITE Syriac-speaking Chalcedonian Christians that originally broke from other Chalcedonian Christians because of their acceptance of monotheletism, which they later rejected. During the Crusades, the Maronites entered full communion with the Roman Catholic Church.

MELKITE A term that is frequently used pejoratively to refer to Chalcedonian Syriac Christians. It derives from the Syriac term for "king" or "emperor," as these Christians shared the Christological view endorsed by the Byzantine emperor.

MEMRA (pl. MEMRE) Genre of Syriac poetry often translated as "verse homilies." *Memre* consist of couplets (sets of two lines) each with the same number of syllables, often forming a consistent pattern named for a given author. *Memre* may discuss theological controversies, elaborate biblical narratives, or reflect on a recurring motif.

MESSALIANISM "Messalian," meaning "one who prays" (from the Syriac root for "to pray"), was a slur applied to early Syriac monks who believed *apatheia* and a direct sensory apprehension of the Trinity were possible in this life and who therefore rejected the need for the sacraments or following ecclesiastical norms. Ecclesiastical authorities in the Syriac world repeatedly condemned those they suspected of being Messalians.

MIAPHYSITE Refers to Christians who hold that Christ has one (*mia*) nature (*physis*), a view condemned by the Council of Chalcedon, but accepted by several Eastern Churches, including the West Syrian (later Syrian Orthodox) Church. Traditionally, the miaphysites were called monophysites, but that is seen today as derogatory.

MONOPHYSITE See MIAPHYSITE.

MONOTHELETISM Christological viewpoint that Christ had a single (*monos*) will (*thelēma*), two natures, and one person, promoted by the Byzantine emperor Heraclius (d. 641) and accepted for a time by Maronites. Monotheletism was formally condemned at the Third Council of Constantinople in 680/681.

NATURE English translation of the Greek term *physis* and the Syriac term *kyana*. In Trinitarian theology, "nature" refers to the Godhead shared by all three persons of the Trinity. In Christology, the term refers to the human and divine natures of the incarnate Christ. How these two natures interacted was the central question of the fifth-century councils.

PARTHIANS Persian dynasty lasting from 247 BCE to 224 CE, during which time it was the primary rival to the Roman Empire. The Parthians took control of Edessa, an early center of Syriac Christianity, from the Seleucids in the second century BCE.

PERSON English translation of two Greek terms, *prosopon* and *hypostasis*. In Trinitarian theology, either Greek term refers to the different "persons" of Father, Son, and Holy Spirit. In Nicene Trinitarian theology, these represent interchangeable Greek terms referring to the three "persons" of Father, Son, and Holy Spirit, who exist coeternally and consubstantially within one *ousia* or "being." In Christology, the human and divine natures are often said to coexist in the one "person" of the incarnate Christ.

PERIODEUTES A type of itinerant priest that historically served rural communities on behalf of urban bishops. The *periodeutes* largely replaced the chorepiscopus in the Christian East, which was a rank of bishop under the city bishop that was intended to serve rural areas. In some Syriac churches, the title "chorepiscopus" is still used to refer to auxiliary bishops.

PESHITTA Translation of the Bible into Syriac that has become a standard among all Syriac Churches. It consists of the Old Testament Peshitta, a translation from Hebrew completed in the third century, and the New Testament Peshitta, a translation of twenty-two books of the Greek New Testament, that was finished in the early fifth century.

RABBAN Syriac term literally meaning "our master" or "our teacher." Monks, abbots, and some priests are often called "rabban" in Syriac literature.

SASANIANS Persian dynasty lasting from 224 CE until its fall in the Islamic conquests of 651, during which time it was the primary rival of the Roman Empire. Syriac Christianity spread in Sasanian Persia, winning converts from Zoroastrianism but facing periodic persecution from the ruling elites.

SCHOOL OF NISIBIS Major center of Syriac learning that succeeded the School of the Persians or the School of Edessa. The school primarily trained East Syrian clerics in methods influenced by the Antiochene school of biblical exegesis, influencing East Syrian monastic and scholastic culture in subsequent centuries.

SELEUCIDS Greek dynasty that ruled parts of Persia and the East from 312 to 64 BCE as a result of Alexander the Great's conquest of the region. Edessa was established by the Seleucids in 303 BCE. Although the Seleucid Empire was defeated by the Parthians in the second century BCE and ceased to be an independent entity in 64 BCE, Seleucid culture deeply influenced Syriac Christianity, contributing the dating system of many Syriac chronicles and manuscripts, a system that is called the Year of the Greeks.

SEPTUAGINT The earliest translation of the Old Testament into Greek. According to legend, it was translated by seventy Jewish scholars in Alexandria in the third century BCE. While the Septuagint did not provide the basis for the Peshitta Old Testament translation, which was translated from Hebrew, it became increasingly prominent among later translators who emphasized fidelity to the Greek over the Hebrew.

SOGITA (pl. SOGIYATA) A genre of Syriac poetry and subgenre of the *madrasha* that encompasses dialogue poems between two parties. This is a continuation of the ancient Near Eastern genre of dispute literature.

SYRIAN ORTHODOX CHURCH (sometimes Syriac Orthodox Church) Modern-day church with a presence in India, the Middle East, and diaspora communities from both regions in Europe and the Americas. This church is the successor to the miaphysite West Syrian Church and retains many of its doctrines and rites.

WEST SYRIAN Miaphysite church that has historically been centered west of Persia and that developed into the modern Syrian Orthodox Church. Some older texts refer to this tradition as "Jacobite," after Jacob Baradeus. "Jacobite" was often used derogatively, but sometimes West Syrian texts apply it to themselves. In some contexts West Syrian refers to Chalcedonian Syriac Christianity as well.

YEAR OF THE GREEKS (Sometimes abbreviated AG for Latin *Anno Graecorum*.) Method of counting years that originated in the Seleucid Empire. The era begins in 312/311 BCE, commemorating Seleucus I Nicator's reconquest of Babylon. Syriac chroniclers adopted the Year of the Greeks with Babylonian month names, defining the new year as October 1 instead of January 1 as in the Gregorian Calendar commonly used today. As a result, unless a source specifies in which month an event takes place, conversion to BCE/CE (also known as BC/AD), results in a two-year range where "/" stands for "or" (e.g., 312/311 BCE).

ZOROASTRIANISM Ancient religion allegedly founded by the prophet Zoroaster that was the state religion of several pre-Islamic Iranian dynasties, including the Achaemenids and Sasanians. Persian Christians sometimes attempted to convert Sasanian Zoroastrians, occasionally leading to tension and conflict.

INDEX

Page numbers in italics indicate illustrations. Titled works are best found under the name of the author, unless they are anonymous. People with honorifics (Mar, Rabban, Saint) are alphabetized under their actual name (e.g., Rabban Sauma is listed under S), but place names starting with honorifics are placed by natural order (Bet Maron monastery is listed under B). Arabic names beginning with al- are indexed by first major element: Caliph al-Mutawakkil is in the Ms.

Mar 'Aba: canons of, 286; *Discourses on the Soul*, 285
'Abbasid caliphate, 17–18, 280, 355, 395, 407
'Abd al-Malik (caliph), 17
'Abdisho' (converter of Mar Qardagh), 354–58
'Abdisho' bar Brika, 23, 85–86, 389; *Marganita*, 23, 87, 389; *Metrical Catalogue of Syriac Authors*, 23, 51, 85–87, 389; *Nomocanon*, 23, 389; *Paradise of Eden*, 87, 389; self-composed list of texts written by, 87; on Solomon of Baṣra, 402
Abdu (Edessan noble), 41–42
Abgar V of Edessa (corresponding with Jesus), 4, 31, 32; Egeria on, 39–40, 392; in Eusebius, *Church History*, 37–38, 393; self-emasculation prohibited by, 266; Syriac translation of Old Testament and, 287, 399; in *Teaching of Addai*, 40–43, 305; translation of Old Testament into Syriac and, 287

Abgar VIII of Edessa, 4, 43–44
Abraham of Kashkar, 15, 19, 141, 172
Abraham Katina, 86
Abraham bar Kayli (Chalcedonian bishop of Amida), 235–37
Abraham of Natpar, 86
Abraham Saba, 86
Abu Nuḥ, 281
Achaemenids, 412. *See also* Persia and Persians
acrostics, 51, 62, 74, 81, 389, 395
Acts of Mar Mari, 32, 44–46
Acts of Thomas, 8–9, 32–33, 115; asceticism in, 33, 140, 142–45; first miracles of Thomas in India, 31, 33–35; *Hymn of the Pearl*, 9, 51, 54–59; India in, 9, 31, 33–35, 392; liturgy in, 113, 115–17
Addai (Thaddeus; apostle), 4, 31–32, 40–43, 44, 127, 287, 326. *See also Anaphora of Addai and Mari; Teaching of Addai*

413

Aetians/Anomeans/Eunomians (neo-Arians), 36, 175, 176, 299
Agapetus (bishop of Rome), 400
Alexander Romance, 22, 32, 46–48
Alexander the Great, 3, 32, 46–48, 87, 259, 411
Alexios I (emperor), 345–46
'Alī (caliph), assassination of, 323
allegorical exegesis, 403
Aluoben (East Syrian missionary), 18, 364, 365
Amazons, 264
Amida, monastery of, 142
Ammonian chapters, 277
'Amran bar Muhammad, 253–56
Anahid, *Martyrdom* of, 238–42
Ananias (courier of Abgar V), 37, 38, 39, 40. *See also* Hanan the archivist
Mar 'Anan'isho, 286–87
Anaphora of Addai and Mari, 127–30
Anastasius (emperor), 13
Anastasius of Edessa, 275
Anatolius the Alexandrian, 275
Andrew of Samosata, 96, 97
Andronicus II Palaiologus (emperor), 369
Anomeans/Eunomians/Aetians (neo-Arians), 36, 175, 176, 299
anti-Chalcedonian Christians, xxi, 90. *See also* West Syrian Christians
anti-Jewish polemic, 293–94, 299–300. *See also* Jews and Judaism
antinomianism, 171, 407
apatheia, 171, 173, 174, 175–76, 177, 390, 407
Aphrahat, *Demonstrations,* 10, 11, 21, 140, 203, 389–90; on asceticism/celibacy (*Demonstrations* 6), 140, 145–47; Daniel of Ṣalah influenced by, 392; distinguishing Christianity from Judaism, 146, 202, 203–5, 294, 298–99; on Passover (*Demonstrations* 12), 203–5; on supersessionism of new covenant (*Demonstrations* 11), 298–99; Syrian mystical theologies of prayer and, 172
Apocalypse of Pseudo-Methodius, 22, 324–25
apocalyptic literature, 17, 47, 221–24, 324–25
apocryphal literature, 8–9, 32–33, 115
apokatastasis (restoration), 171, 177, 178, 180, 407
apostolic succession in Edessa, 43
Apostolic Tradition, 119
Arabic language: Elias of Nisibis, Syriac-Arabic lexicon of, 20–21; Greek texts translated into, 18, 20, 260; Ḥunayn ibn Isḥaq, translations of, 278, 287–88; Latin West, Greek texts transmitted via Syriac and Arabic to, 260; rhyme from poetic verse of, 51; Syriac Christian use of, 18, 20, 24; Timothy I translating from Greek into, 280, 281, 283
Arabs: *Book of the Laws of the Countries (On Fate)* on, 263; First Arab Civil War, 323; Muhammad's conversion of, 339–40, 342–43; Mundhir (Arab Lakhmid leader), letter of Simeon of Bet Arsham to, 309–11; Najran, martyrdom of Christians of, 310, 311–14; wine poetry *(khamriyya)* of, 51, 84–85
Aramaic, 2, 3, 4, 49, 408
architectural framing of liturgy, 114, 129, 130
Arghun (Mongol khan), 369, 405
Aristotle: 'Abdisho' bar Brika's commentary on, 87; Mar 'Anan'isho writing philosophy in mode of, 286; *aulētrides,* use of, 283; Barhebraeus's encyclopedia of Aristotelian philosophy, 22; Dionysius bar Ṣalibi, commentaries of, 21, 107; Ḥunayn ibn Isḥaq, translations by, 288; Mar Mattai monastery, Timothy I seeking commentaries from, 280, 281–82; Paul the Persian on, Severus of Antioch's translation of, 401; *Poetics,* 281; *Refutation of the Sophists,* 281; *Rhetoric,* 281; Sergius of Resh'ayna, *On the Aim of All of Aristotle's Writings,* 277–79; Sergius of Resh'ayna, translations of, 400; Severus Sebokt and, 279; Syriac translation of, 260; *Topics,* translated into Arabic by Timothy I, 280, 281, 283; Zacharias Rhetor on, 405
Arius, Arians, and Arianism, 10, 36, 59, 88–89, 91, 294, 299, 408. *See also* neo-Arians
Arkadios (archbishop of Cyprus), 103–4
asceticism, 25, 140–42; in 1st to 4th centuries, 8, 9, 10; in 5th and 6th centuries, 11, 14, 15; in *Acts of Thomas,* 33, 140, 142–45; additional resources and further reading, 142; in Aphrahat, *Demonstrations,* 140, 145–47; Barhebraeus, *Book of the Dove,* 167–69; *bnay/bnat qyama* (children of the covenant), 10, 141, 146, 230, 389; in *Book of Steps,* 141, 147–49, 209–10; celibacy,

10, 15, 33, 140–49, 155, 160–61, 209–10, 390, 408; defined, 140; dendritism (living in a tree), 230; Elias, *Life of John of Tella*, 142, 160–62; encratism, 8, 9; in hagiographies, 229–30; *iḥidaye* (solitaries/single ones), 10, 140–41, 146, 154–57, 165, 166–67, 188, 193, 389; Isaac of Nineveh, *Treatises on the Behavior of Excellence*, 165–66; Isaac of Nineveh, *Whereby the Beauty of the Solitary Life is to be Preserved*, 165, 166–67; John of Ephesus, *Life of Susan*, 162–64; Messalianism and, 10, 170; *Statutes of the School of Nisibis*, 157–60; stylites and stylitism, 11, 15, 140, 229, 245, 248, 249, 404; Theodoret of Cyrrhus, *History of the Monks of Syria*, 244–47; "upright" (noncelibate) and "perfect" (celibate) Christian life, 10, 141, 147, 149, 209. See also monasticism

Assyrian Christians, xx

Atargatis (deity), 32

Athanasius of Alexandria, 96, 97, 274, 281

Athanasius of Balad, 282

Audians, 36

Augustine of Hippo, 353

Avicenna, 22

Awgen (monastic figure), 141

Babai the Great, 15, 99, 283, 390; *Book of the Union*, 90, 99–101, 390; Evagrius's *Gnostic Chapters*, commentary on, 16, 171, 175, 176–77, 179–80, 390, 394; Evagrius's *Skemmata*, commentary on, 175–76, 394; Stephen bar Ṣudayli, *Book of the Holy Hierotheus*, commentary on, 391

Babel, Tower of, 31, 49, 218

Bacon, Roger, 405

Bactrians, 263

Baghdad, capital of caliphate moved to, 17–18

Baḥira and *Syriac Baḥira Legend*, 322, 335–39

Baldwin I (king of Jerusalem), 345

Baldwin II (king of Jerusalem), 346

baptism: in *Acts of Thomas*, 116–17; Babai the Great on, 175, 176; *Chalcedonian order for emergency baptism of a child*, 118–19; for children of Muslims, 126, 127; of Constantine, 88; in *Didascalia*, 118; in *Disputation of Bet Ḥale*, 328; Ephrem's *Hymns on Faith* 81 on, 59; in *History of the "Slave of Christ,"* 315–17; of Jesus, 52; John of Mardin, *Canons*, on baptism, 126–27; in *Life of Rabban Hormizd*, 124–26; liturgical texts for, 114; Messalians on, 173, 176; *Testament of Our Lord*, on catechumens, 119–24

Bar-Bahlul, Syriac-Syriac lexicon, 20

Bardaisan, 4–8; *Book of the Laws of the Countries (On Fate)* and, 7–8, 261, 265; Ephrem on, 10, 86, 261, 299; heterodoxy of, 9, 36; works attributed to, 261

Bardaisanism/Bardaisanites, 261, 403

Barḥadbshaba, 15, 390

Barhebraeus, 20, 22, 167, 350, 390–91; on asceticism, 142, 167–69; *Book of the Dove*, 167–69, 390; *Candelabra of the Sanctuary*, 22; *Cream of Wisdom*, 22; Dionysius bar Ṣalibi and, 21; *Ecclesiastical Chronicle*, 22, 322, 350–51, 390; Michael the Great and, 350; *Nomocanon*, 390; *Short Anaphora of Saint James*, 131–36; Stephen bar Ṣudayli and, 402; *Syriac Chronicle*, 22, 350, 390

Abbot Barshebya, *Martyrdom* of, 237–38

Basil the Great, 11, 49, 273, 274, 393; *Hexaemeron*, 274

Beirut, law school of, 269, 273–75, 401, 405

Bel (deity), 32

Bet 'Abe, monastery of, 19, 253, 285, 286, 404

Bet Gaugal, Philoxenus's *First Letter to the Monks of*, 153–54

Bet Maron, monastery of, 17, 19

Bezkin, monastery of, 124, 125, 256–58

Bible. See Syriac Bible

biblical interpretation. See exegesis

bnay/bnat qyama (children of the covenant), 10, 141, 146, 230, 389, 408

Bod Peryadeuta, 86

Book of Jubilees, 22

Book of Steps, 10, 11, 141, 147–49, 202, 209–10

Book of the Causes of Causes, 20

Book of the Chaldeans, 264

Book of the Holy Hierotheus, 171, 180–83, 391, 394, 402

Book of the Himyarites, 311–14

Book of the Laws of the Countries (On Fate), 7–8, 21, 261–66

Book of the Tower, 350

books, knowledge, and translation, 25, 259–61; *Book of the Laws of the Countries (On Fate)*, 7–8, 21, 261–66; British Library Additional mss 14456 (scholarly gospel manuscript), 277; colophons from Syriac manuscripts, 260, 267, *268*, 269, 408; first translation movement (5th and 6th centuries), 14, 18, 278; Greek language/culture and Syriac Christianity, 11, 259; Ḥunayn ibn Isḥaq, *Risala*, 278, 287–90; Latin West, Greek texts transmitted via Syriac and Arabic to, 260; manuscript collection, 21–22, 260, 280–86; Mushe bar Kepha, *Introduction to the Psalter*, 287; Philoxenus of Mabbug, *Commentary on the Prologue of John*, 275–77; second translation movement (8th to 10th centuries), 18, 20, 260; Sergius of Reshʿayna, *On the Aim of All of Aristotle's Writings*, 277–79; Severus Sebokt, *Letter to the Periodeutes Basil of Cyprus*, 279–80; Syriac translation technique, 259; *Syro-Roman Lawbook*, 260, 269–72; Thomas of Marga, *Book of Governors* (on Mar ʿAnanʿisho), 286–87; Timothy I, *Letters* 43, 48, and 47, 280–86; additional sources and further reading, 260–61. *See also* Syriac Bible; *specific languages*

Borborians, 36

Brahmans, 262

breasts of the Father as inseminating agent for virgin conception of Jesus, 52, 53

British Library Additional mss: 7170 (Syriac Gospel Lectionary), 202, 226, *227*; 12150 (colophon), 267, *268*, 269; 14445 (colophon), 267; 14456 (scholarly gospel manuscript), 277

Britons, 263, 264

Buddhists/Buddhism: Dunhuang, China, library cave of, 19, 365; expansion of, along silk road, 25, 353; *Jingjiao Stele* and, 360; William of Rubruck's encounters with, 371–74, 405

Bulayiq, East Syrian textual fragments from, 19

Byzantine empire. *See* Roman/Byzantine empire

catechumens, *Testament of Our Lord* on, 119–24

Cave of Treasures, 22, 202, 215–19, 224

celibacy, 10, 15, 33, 140–49, 155, 160–61, 209–10, 390, 408

Chalcedon, Council of (451), 13, 90, 97–98, 107, 109, 154, 162, 219, 294, 314, 396, 404, 405, 408

Chalcedonian Christians: anti-Jewish polemic applied to, 294, 314; baptismal ritual, 118–19; *Chronicle of Edessa to 540*, 31, 43–44; defined, xx; Dionysius bar Ṣalibi, *Against the Melkites*, 90, 107–9; as formal church, 89–90; Jacob of Serug and, 69; Job the Chalcedonian, corresponding with Timothy I, 280, 281; in Mar Musa frescoes, *223*; monasticism of, 19; Philoxenus on monasticism and, 154, 400; Severus of Antioch versus, 401; Stephen Mansūr, *Passion of Romanos the Neomartyr*, 242–44, 402–3; Theodore Abū Qurrah, *On the Existence of God and the True Religion*, 358–59, 403; Timothy of Constantinople, *On Those Who Come to the Church from the Heretics*, 173–74, 404. *See also* Maronites

Chaldeans, 264, 265

Chao Yi Lang, 365

children of the covenant *(bnay/bnat qyama)*, 10, 141, 146, 230, 389, 408

China: *Book of the Laws of the Countries* on, 262, 264; Dunhuang, library cave of, 19, 353, 365; expansion of Syriac Christianity into, 18–19, 137–39; *jingjiao* (luminous religion), as name for Christianity in, 353, 360; *Jingjiao Stele*, 18, 19, 353, 360–65, *366*; Turfan, Syriac Christianity in, 18–19, 137–39, 353; Xi'an (ancient Chang'an), Christianity in, 18, 353, 360, 364, 365

Christ. *See* Jesus

Christological controversies: in 4th century, 10, 88–89; in 5th and 6th centuries, 9, 12–14, 89–90; in 7th through 9th centuries, 17, 19, 90, 101–2; anti-Jewish polemic used in, 314; definition of Christology, 408; exegesis as tool in, 202; Mar Musa frescoes reflecting, 223. *See also specific authors and writings*

Christotokos theology, 12, 89

Chronicle of 1234, 22

Chronicle of Edessa to 540, 31, 43–44

Chronicle of Zuqnin, 46–47, 235–36, 242, 322, 331–33, 398

Church of the East (modern East Syrian Church), xx, 11, 15, 88, 90, 99, 408
circumcision, 204, 208, 218–19, 265–66, 294, 298–99, 307–9, 318, 327, 328, 340, 344
Claudius (emperor), wife of, 305–6
coenobitic or communal ascetical life, development of, 141, 408. *See also* monasticism
colophons from Syriac manuscripts, 260, 267, 268, 269, 408
Confucianism, 365
Constans II (emperor), 101, 105–6, 323
Constantine I (emperor), 88, 231, 305, 393
Constantine IV (emperor), 106
Constantinople, First Council of (381), 10, 88, 91, 107
Constantinople, Second Council of (553), 13, 16, 89, 93, 165, 171, 396
Constantinople, Third Council of (680/681; Sixth Ecumenical Council), 90, 101, 106–7
consubstantial *(homoousios)*, 10, 12, 88, 91
contemplation *(theōria)* and practice *(praktikē)*, in monastic life, 171, 175, 195, 394
conversion: in *Acts of Thomas*, 34–35, 142–45; baptism for children of Muslims, 126, 127; *History of the "Slave of Christ"* (on Jewish boy converting to Christianity), 294, 315–17; to Islam, 18, 20, 331–33; of Seleucia to Syriac Christianity, by Addai, 45–46; from Zoroastrianism, 237, 354–58
Corpus Dionysiacum. *See* Pseudo-Dionysius the Areopagite and *Corpus Dionysiacum*
Councils: Chalcedon (451), 13, 90, 97–98, 107, 109, 154, 162, 219, 294, 314, 396, 404, 405, 408; Constantinople I (381), 10, 88, 91, 107; Constantinople II (553), 13, 16, 89, 93, 165, 171, 396; Constantinople III (680/681; Sixth Ecumenical Council), 90, 101, 106–7; Ephesus I (431), 12, 107, 109, 408–9; Ephesus II (robber council; 449), 12–13, 404; Nicaea (325), 10, 12, 88, 91, 96, 107, 109, 286, 299, 409
cross, worship of, 318–19
crucifixion of Jesus: anti-Jewish polemic regarding, 300–301, 305–6, 311, 314; *Cave of Treasures* on, 219; *On the Cherub and the Thief*, 51, 75–81. *See also* true cross
Crusades, 17, 20, 21, 49, 167, 322, 342, 344–51, 371, 405
Cureton, William, 269
Rabban Cyriacus, 253–56
Cyril of Alexandria, 12, 89, 96, 97, 98, 109, 274, 400
Cyrillona, *On the Huns*, 51, 65–67, 391
Cyrus (West Syrian martyr-priest), 236–37

Dadishoʿ Qaṭraya, *Discourse on Stillness*, 172, 191–93, 391
Damascus, capital of caliphate moved from, 17
Damniyas, 86
Daniel of Ṣalah, *Commentary of the Psalms*, 202, 219–21, 391–92
Darius (Persian ruler), 47, 48
daughters/sons of the covenant *(bnay/bnat qyama)*, 10, 141, 146, 230, 389, 408
deaconesses, 115, 118
"Dead Cities" region of Syria, 129
Dead Sea Scrolls, 281
demon in human soul, Messalians on, 173–74
Demonstrations (Aphrahat), 10
dendritism (living in a tree), 230
Diatessaron (Tatian): Ephrem, *Commentary on the Diatessaron*, 8, 10, 205–7, 393; as Gospel harmonization, 8, 201–2, 205
Didascalia Apostolorum, 117–18, 294, 295–97
Diodore of Tarsus, 13, 15, 92, 186, 403
Dionysius bar Ṣalibi, 21, 107, 392; Evagrius, commentaries on, 21, 107, 394; *Against the Melkites*, 90, 107–9; Michael the Great and, 21, 339, 392; *On Providence*, 392; *A Response to the Arabs*, 322, 339–41
Dionysius of Tel Maḥre, *Ecclesiastical History*, 22, 341, 342, 399
Dioscorus (bishop of Alexandria), 12–13
Discourse on the One God, 353, 365–68
disputation literature, 294; Dionysius bar Ṣalibi, *A Response to the Arabs*, 322, 339–41; *Disputation of Bet Ḥale*, 322, 326–31; *Disputation of Sergius the Stylite Against a Jew*, 294, 317–19; *Legend of Mar Qardagh*, 354–58; in *Maronite Chronicle*, 322–23; Timothy I, *Letters* 59 (on disputation with al-Mahdi), 333–35; William of Rubruck, *Mission of Friar William of Rubruck*, 371–74, 405

doctrine and disputation, 25, 88–91; Babai the Great, *Book of the Union*, 90, 99–101; Dionysius bar Ṣalibi, *Against the Melkites*, 90, 107–9; Ephrem the Syrian, *Hymns on Faith* 53, 91–92; George of Reshʿayna, antihagiographic *Life of Maximus the Confessor*, 90, 101–6; Severus of Antioch, *To Nephalius*, 96–98; *Syriac Fragment of the Sixth Council* (Maronite), 90, 106–7; Theodore of Mopsuestia, *On the Incarnation*, 92–96; additional resources and further reading, 91–92. *See also* Christological controversies; heterodoxy/heresy; *specific doctrinal issues*

Dome of the Rock, Jerusalem, 17, 342, 345, 350

dualism, 12, 352, 353

Dunhuang, China, library cave of, 19, 353, 365

Dura-Europos, Syriac parchments from, 4, 5

dyophysite theology, 67, 90, 99, 101, 294, 400, 403, 409

dyothelitism, 101, 102, 394

East Syrian Church: *Acts of Mar Mari*, 32, 44–46; anti-Jewish polemic applied to, 294; Arabic, use of, 18; Barhebraeus and, 350; canon law codes, 19; Dadishoʿ Qaṭraya, *Discourse on Stillness*, 172, 191–93, 391; defined, xx–xxi, 409; *Discourse on the One God*, 353, 365–68; *Disputation of Bet Ḥale*, 322, 326–31; dyophysite theology of, 67; Eucharistic liturgy of, 127, 131; formal separation from Roman imperial orthodoxy, 11, 12, 14, 88, 89–90; foundation texts of, 88, 90, 99; geographic expansion/missionary work of, 9, 18–19, 280, 353; *History of the Life and Travels of Rabban Sauma*, 368–71; Rabban Hormizd, *Life* of, 124–26, 256–58; Islamic world, interaction with, 17–18; *Jingjiao Stele*, 18, 19, 353, 360–65, *366*; Khamis bar Qardaḥe, *Wine Song*, 23, 51, 84–85, 399; *Legend of Mar Qardagh*, 354–58; liturgy of, 114; *Martyrdom of Abbot Barshebya*, 237–38; *Martyrdom of Anahid*, 238–42; monasticism in, 15, 19, 152, 256; under Mongol khanate, 22–23; mystical theologies of prayer in, 170, 172; origin stories, 32; Persian influence on, 12, 14, 15; School of Nisibis and, 11; Seleucia-Ctesiphon as seat of *katholikos* of, 12, 14, 17–18, 90; Solomon of Baṣra, *Book of the Bee*, 22, 202, 224–28, 402; *Statutes of the School of Nisibis*, 157–60; *Syriac Baḥira Legend*, 322, 335–39; Theodore of Mopsuestia, influence of, xx, 12, 15, 92, 186, 202, 294, 403; Turfan, China, service book from, 137–39; William of Rubruck's encounters with, 371–74, 405. *See also* ʿAbdishoʿ bar Brika; Babai the Great; Giwargis Warda; Isaac of Nineveh; John of Dalyata; Joseph Ḥazzaya; Narsai; Stephen bar Ṣudayli; Thomas of Marga; Timothy I

Edessa: apostolic succession in, 43; *Book of the Laws of the Countries (On Fate)* on, 263, 266; *Chronicle of Edessa to 540*, 31, 43–44; city archives of, 43, 44; Crusades and destruction of, 21; Egeria on visit to, 31, 38–40, 392; family portrait mosaic with Syriac inscriptions, 7; flood (201 CE), 31, 43–44; funerary couch mosaic with Syriac inscriptions, 6; as Latin Crusader state, 345, 347; paganism in, denunciations of, 32; Persian capture and control of, 3, 39; Pool of Abraham, 38, 39; Roman capture and control of, 3; School of the Persians in, 11, 14, 15, 67, 69, 89, 157, 210, 213, 396, 401, 404; Syriac Christianity in, 3–8, 31; Thomas, shrine to, 38, 392; Turkish capture and control of, 342, 347–49. *See also* Abgar V of Edessa

Edict of Milan (313), 88

education: law school of Beirut, 269, 273–75, 401, 405; School of Nisibis, 11, 14, 15, 67, 89, 99, 157–60, 210, 390, 400, 403, 411; School of Qenneshre, 19, 279; School of the Persians, Edessa, 11, 14, 15, 67, 69, 89, 157, 210, 213, 396, 401, 403; transmission of ancient culture and, 260; in Zacharias Rhetor's *Life of Severus of Antioch*, 260, 273–75

Edward I (king of England), 369

Egeria, *Pilgrimage Journal*, 31, 38–40, 392–93

Elias, *Life of John of Tella*, 142, 160–62, 393

Elias of Nisibis, 20–21; *Chronography*, 20; John of Ephesus cited by, 398; Syriac-Arabic lexicon, 20–21

Elisa of Lycia, 274–75

Emmanuel bar Shahhare, commentary on the *Hexaemeron*, 20

encratism, 8, 9
Ephesus, First Council of (431), 12, 107, 109, 409
Ephesus, Second Council of (robber council; 449), 12–13, 404
Ephesus, *Sleepers* of, 231–35, 397
Ephrem of Antioch, 400
Ephrem the Syrian, 10–11, 35, 205, 393; in 'Abdisho' bar Brika's *Metrical Catalogue*, 86; asceticism favored by, 140, 141; *Commentary on the Diatessaron*, 8, 10, 205–7, 393; Daniel of Ṣalah influenced by, 392; as "Harp of the Spirit," 299; *Hymns on Faith* 53, 91–92; *Hymns on Faith* 81, 51, 59–61; *Hymns on Faith* 87, 301–4; *Hymns on Heresies* 22, 32, 35–37, 261; *Hymns on the Resurrection* 1, 51, 62–65; *Hymns on Unleavened Bread* 19, 300–301; *Hymns on Virginity* 28, 304–5; *madrashe* (hymns/poems), 11, 21, 51, 205, 393; *memre* (verse sermons), 11, 51, 86, 205, 207, 393; Nicene orthodoxy, as defender of, 88, 91–92; on origins of Syriac language, 49; polemical works of, 32; pseudonymous attributions to, 74; reading Old Testament through Christian lens, 202, 205; *The Repentance of Nineveh*, 207–9; Sinful Woman, poem on, 69; on superiority of Christianity over Judaism, 202, 205, 207, 294, 299–305; Syriac *Life of Ephrem*, 11; Syrian mystical theologies of prayer and, 172; women's choirs, poetry liturgically performed by, 299
Epideictics, 282
Essenes, 4
Estrangela script, 123
Eucharist/Eucharistic liturgy, 114; in *Acts of Thomas*, 117; *Anaphora of Addai and Mari*, 127–30; Barhebraeus, *Short Anaphora of Saint James*, 131–36; in *Disputation of Bet Ḥale*, 328; Giwargis Warda, *On Sin*, 81; Messalians on, 173, 174; *'onita* genre associated with, 81
Eunomians/Anomeans/Aetians (neo-Arians), 36, 175, 176, 299
Eusebian canons, 277
Eusebius of Caesarea, 393–94; *Apology for Origen*, 285; *Ecclesiastical (Church) History*, 31, 37–38, 393; *Life of Constantine*, 393; *Preparation for the Gospel*, 393; in Syriac manuscript with colophons, 269; *Theophania*, 21
Eutyches, 13
Evagrius of Pontus, 15–16, 171, 175, 394; on *apokatastasis* (restoration), 171, 177, 178; commentary of Babai the Great on *Gnostic Chapters*, 16, 171, 175, 176–77, 179–80, 390, 394; commentary of Babai the Great on *Skemmata*, 175–76, 394; condemnation at Second Council of Constantinople (553), 171; Dadisho' Qaṭraya influenced by, 192, 391; Dionysius bar Ṣalibi, commentaries of, 21, 107, 394; *Gnostic Chapters (Kephalia Gnostika)*, 175, 176, 177, 179–80, 394, 400; Isaac of Nineveh influenced by, 165, 185–88, 396; John of Dalyata influenced by, 194; Joseph Ḥazzaya influenced by, 195, 398; *Letter to Melania (Great Letter)*, 177–78, 180, 394; monastic life, on practice (*praktikē*) and contemplation (*theōria*) in, 171, 175, 195, 394; mysticism and prayer in Syriac churches, influence on, 170, 171–72, 175–88, 192, 194, 195; *Praktikos*, 175; *Skemmata*, 175; Stephen bar Ṣudayli influenced by, 394, 402; on Trinity, 175, 178, 180
Evagrius of Samosata, 274–75
Evagrius Scholasticus, *Ecclesiastical History*, 405
exegesis, 25, 201–3; in 5th and 6th centuries, 11; allegorical, 404; Aphrahat, *Demonstrations* 12, 202, 203–5; *Book of Steps*, 202, 209–10; *Cave of Treasures*, 202, 215–19, 224; Christological controversies and, 202; Daniel of Ṣalah, *Commentary of the Psalms*, 202, 219–21; *Diatessaron*, Ephrem's commentary on, 8, 10, 205–7; Ephrem the Syrian, *The Repentance of Nineveh*, 207–9; in illustrated manuscripts and frescoes, 202, *216*, *223*, 226, *227*; Jacob of Serug, *Memra on Tamar*, 213–15; *Memra on Genesis* 22, 202, 211–13; Narsai, *On the Sacrifice of Isaac*, 210–11; Philoxenus of Mabbug, *Commentary on the Prologue of John*, 275–77; reading Old Testament through Christian lens, 202, 205, 210, 213; Solomon of Baṣra, *Book of the Bee*, 202, 224–28; *Syriac Apocalypse of Daniel*, 221–24; Syriac translations of Bible and, 201–2; *turgame* (metrical gospel commentaries), 399; additional resources and further reading, 203

family portrait mosaic with Syriac inscriptions, Edessa, 7
Fang Xuanling, 364
First Arab Civil War, 323
Flavian of Constantinople, 13
foundations of Syriac Christianity, 25. *See also* doctrine and disputation; origin stories; poetry
Franciscans, 371–74, 405
funerary couch mosaic with Syriac inscriptions, Edessa, 6
funerary liturgy, Turfan, China, 137–39

Galen, 288–90, 395, 400
Gauls, 263, 264
Gehenna, 185–88
Geli, 263, 266
gender. *See* women and gender
George of Resh'ayna, antihagiographic *Life of Maximus the Confessor*, 90, 101–6, 394
Germans, 263, 264
al-Ghazali, 167
Giwargis (George) Warda, 394–95; *Book of the Rose (Kitaba Warda)*, 23, 81, 394–95; Khamis bar Qardaḥe compared, 399; *On Sin*, 51, 81–84, 395
Gnosticism/gnosticizing texts, 7, 52, 54
gnostikoi, Evagrius on, 175
Godfrey of Boulogne, 345
Gog and Magog, 22, 47–48
Golgotha: as center of the world, 215–17; Mu'āwiya (caliph) at, 323; pilgrimage to site of, 306
"Great Monastery" of Abraham of Kashkar, 15, 99, 141
Greek language and culture: first translation movement, 14, 18, 278; hagiographic narratives, 229; Ḥunayn ibn Isḥaq, translations of, 278, 287–88; influence on Syriac Christianity, 11, 259; Latin West, Greek texts transmitted via Syriac and Arabic to, 260; Monastery of the Syrians, Egypt, manuscript collection of Syriac translations at, 21; second translation movement, 18, 20, 260; Septuagint, 201; Timothy I and translations from Greek, 280–86

Habsa, Hayya, and Hayya, martyrdom of, 294, 311–14
hagiography, 25, 229–30; asceticism in, 229–30; Elias, *Life of John of Tella*, 142, 160–62; extra-Christian and intra-Christian tensions in, 229, 230, 235, 237, 238, 253, 256; George of Resh'ayna, antihagiographic *Life of Maximus the Confessor*, 90, 101–6; Himyarite Jews, Christian martyrdoms attributed to, 294, 309–14, 402; Rabban Hormizd, *Life* of, 124–26, 256–58; Jacob of Serug, *On the Sleepers of Ephesus*, 231–35; John of Ephesus, *Ecclesiastical History*, 235–36; John of Ephesus, *Lives of the Eastern Saints*, 15, 141, 162–64, 398, 401; *Legend of Mar Qardagh*, 354–58; *Martyrdom of Abbot Barshebya*, 237–38; *Martyrdom of Anahid*, 238–42; Stephen Mansūr, *Passion of Romanos the Neomartyr*, 242–44; Syriac *Life of Mary*, 250–53; Syriac *Life of Simeon*, 249; Thecla (disciple of Paul), *Life* of, 161; Theodoret of Cyrrhus, *History of the Monks of Syria* (on Simeon the Stylite), 244–47; Thomas of Marga, *Book of Governors*, 253–56, 286–87; additional sources and further reading, 230
Hanan the archivist, 40, 41. *See also* Ananias
Harqlean Version of New Testament, 202, 277, 400
Hatra, 263, 266
Hayya, Hayya, and Habsa, martyrdom of, 294, 311–14
Hebrew Bible. *See* Old Testament/Hebrew Bible
Hebrew language, 34–35, 49
Hebrew manuscripts, discovered in cave near Jericho, 281, 284–85
Helena (mother of Constantine I), 305
Henanisho' (katholikos), 365
Henotikon (Zeno), 13
Heraclius (emperor), 16, 17, 47, 90, 101, 104–5, 287, 339, 342, 410
heterodoxy/heresy: anti-Jewish polemic applied to, 294, 299–300; early Christian heterodoxy, 9–10; Ephrem, *Hymns on Heresies* 22, 32, 35–37; in hagiographies, 229; Syriac Christianity sometimes viewed in West as heretical, 2; Timothy of Constantinople, *On Those Who Come to the Church from the*

Heretics, 173–74, 404. *See also* orthodoxy; *specific groups regarded as heretical*
Hiba (bishop of Edessa), 13
Hierotheus, 180
Himyar and Himyarites: *The Book of the Himyarites*, 311–14; letter of Simeon of Bet Arsham to Mundhir on, 309–11, 402
Hindus, 262, 264
Hippo Diarrhytus, monastery of, 105–6
Hippocratic works, translated by Ḥunayn ibn Isḥaq, 290
History of the Life and Travels of Rabban Sauma, 368–71
History of the "Slave of Christ," 294, 315–17
homoousios (consubstantial), 10, 12, 88, 91
homosexuality, in *Book of the Laws of the Countries*, 263, 264
Honorius (bishop of Rome), 103
Rabban Hormizd, *Life* of, 124–26, 256–58
Hugues de Payens, 346
Ḥunayn ibn Isḥaq, *Risala*, 278, 287–90, 395
Huns, 51, 65–67, 391
Hymn of the Pearl, 9, 51, 54–59
hypostasis/hypostatic union, 13, 89, 96–101, 343, 360, 390, 410

Ignatius of Melitene, 108
iḥidaye (solitaries/single ones), 10, 140–41, 146, 154–57, 165, 166–67, 188, 193, 389
incantation bowls, 123
incarnation of Jesus, 51, 62–65, 93–96, 98
India: in *Acts of Thomas*, 9, 31, 33–35, 392; astronomy in, 279, 280; Bod Peryadeuta's translations from Sanskrit (?), 86; *Book of the Laws of the Countries (On Fate)* on, 262; Brahmans in, 262; Hindus in, 262, 264; *Kadamattom Cross*, 361; *Kollam Plate*, 362; Syriac Christianity in, 1, 2, 4, 9, 131, 361, 362
interreligious encounters, 25. *See also* Islam/Muslims; Jews and Judaism; silk road; *specific additional religious traditions*
Isaac of Antioch, *Homilies Against the Jews*, 294, 307–9, 395
Isaac of Nineveh, 86, 165, 185–86, 396; Dadisho' Qatraya and, 391; Evagrius of Pontus, influence of, 165, 185–88, 396; Isaac of Antioch conflated with, 395; John of Dalyata compared, 397; *On Pure and Undisturbed Prayer*, 190–91; *On Gehenna*, 185–88; on Syrian mystical theologies of prayer, 172, 190–91; *Treatises on the Behavior of Excellence*, 165–66; *Whereby the Beauty of the Solitary Life is to be Preserved*, 165, 166–67
Isaiah of Scetis, 391
Rabban Isho', 107
Isho' bar Nun (East Syrian katholikos), 172, 397
Isho'dnah of Baṣra, 172
Isho'yahb III (East Syrian katholikos), 18, 19, 127
Isho'dnah of Baṣra, *Book of Chastity*, 398
Islamic conquests, 16–17; apocalyptic literature and, 17, 47, 221, 324; in *Disputation of Bet Ḥale*, 330; maps of Near East before and after, xxii–xxv; Maximus the Confessor, attributed to heresy of, 102, 104–6, 394
Islam/Muslims, 25, 321–22; 'Abbasid caliphate, 17–18, 280, 322, 404, 407; anti-Jewish rhetoric employed against, 294, 319–20; *Apocalypse of Pseudo-Methodius*, 324–25; baptism of children of Muslims, 126, 127; Barhebraeus, *Ecclesiastical Chronicle*, 322, 350–51; *Book of the Causes of Causes* attempting to explain Christianity to, 20; *Chronicle of Zuqnin*, 322, 331–33; conversion to Islam, 18, 20, 331–33; Dionysius bar Ṣalibi, *A Response to the Arabs*, 322, 339–41; discrimination against non-Muslims under, 18; *Disputation of Bet Ḥale*, 322, 326–31; historical significance of Syriac Christianity for Islam, 1, 2; interactions of Syriac Christians with early Muslims, 17–18, 321–22, 335; Jacob of Edessa, *Letters*, 325–26; Jews and Muhammad, 335, 342; jurisprudence, influence of, 19; *Kollam Plate*, India, 362; legal protections for Christianity under, 242; in Mar Musa frescoes, 223; *Maronite Chronicle*, 322–23; marriage between Muslims and Christians, 326; Michael the Great, *Chronicle*, 322, 342–50; Muhammad (prophet), 16, 321, 329, 330, 333–43; Qur'an, 231, 327, 335, 339; relics/holy items given to, 326; Seljuk Turks, 49, 342, 344–51; silk road, missionary work along, 353; Stephen Mansūr, *Passion of Romanos the Neomartyr*, 242–44; *Syriac Baḥira Legend*, 322, 335–39; Theodore Abū Qurrah on, 358, 403; Timothy I, *Letters* 59, 333–35; Umayyad

Islam/Muslims *(continued)*
　caliphate, 17, 322, 323; William of Rubruck's encounters with, 371–74, 405; additional resources and further reading, 322. *See also* Arabic language; Arabs

Jacob (scribe), 267, 269
Jacob bar Ṣalibi of Melitine, 341
Jacob Baradeus, 14, 398, 411
Jacob of Edessa, 396; 'Abdisho' bar Brika on, 86; edition of Old Testament/Hebrew Bible by, 201, 287, 396; on Isaac of Antioch, 307, 395; *Letters*, 325–26, 396; Michael the Great on, 49; Mushe bar Kepha and, 399; Severus of Antioch and, 401
Jacob of Serug, 15, 213, 396–97; asceticism of, 140, 141, 142, 153–57; John of Tella and, 160; *Memra on Tamar*, 213–15; *memre* by, 69, 213–15, 396, 397; Narsai and, 400; *On the Sinful Woman*, 51, 69–74, 397; *On the Sleepers of Ephesus*, 231–35, 397; *On the Solitaries*, 153–57, 396; pseudonymous attributions to, 74; reading Old Testament through Christian lens, 202, 213; on Stephen bar Ṣudayli, 402
Jacobites, xi, 411. *See also* West Syrian Christians
James, brother of Jesus, 131
Jerusalem: Crusader control of, 345; Dome of the Rock, 17, 342, 345, 350; Mar Saba, monastery of, 19; Muslim capture and control of, 342, 344, 345, 349–50; Persian capture of, 16; Temple, Roman destruction of (70 CE), 293
Jesus: baptism of, 52; incarnation of, 51, 62–65, 93–96, 98; Muslim view of, 343; nativity of, 218–19; as second Adam, 67–69; virgin conception of, 52, 53–54, 62–63. *See also* Abgar V of Edessa; Christological controversies; crucifixion of Jesus; resurrection of Jesus
Jews and Judaism, 25, 293–95; Abgar of Edessa on, 32; in *Acts of Thomas*, 34–35; anti-Jewish polemic, 293–94, 299–300; Aphrahat distinguishing Christianity from, 146, 202, 203–5, 298–99; apocalyptic literature of, 221; *Book of the Causes of Causes* attempting to explain Christianity to, 20; *The Book of the Himyarites*, 311–14; *Book of the Laws of the Countries* on, 261, 265–66; crucifixion of Jesus, blaming Jews for, 300–301, 305–6, 311, 314; *Didascalia Apostolorum* on, 294, 295–97; Dionysius bar Ṣalibi, on Jewish dietary laws, 108–9; *Disputation of Sergius the Stylite Against a Jew*, 294, 317–19; Ephrem on superiority of Christianity over, 202, 205, 207, 294, 299–305; Essenes, 4; historical interactions of Syriac Christians with, 2, 293–94; *History of the "Slave of Christ,"* 294, 315–17; intra-Christian use of anti-Jewish polemic, 294, 299–300, 314; Isaac of Antioch, *Homilies Against the Jews*, 294, 307–9, 395; *Kollam Plate*, India, 362; *Letter of the Jews to the Emperor Marcian*, 314; martyrdom stories and, 294, 309–14; Muhammad and, 335, 342; Muslims, anti-Jewish rhetoric employed against, 294, 319–20; "new Jews," use of, 154, 294, 299, 319; Simeon of Bet Arsham, *Letters* 1, 294, 309–11; supersessionist rhetoric on, 294, 298–99, 300, 395; *Teaching of Addai* on, 294, 305–6; Theodore Abū Qurrah on, 358, 403; Timothy I, *Letters* 40, 294, 319–20; additional resources and further reading, 294–95. *See also* Himyar and Himyarites; Old Testament/Hebrew Bible; Passover

jingjiao (luminous religion), as name for Christianity in China, 353, 360
Jingjiao Stele, 18, 19, 353, 360–65, *366*
Jingjing (Adam), 360, *366*
Job the Chalcedonian, corresponding with Timothy I, 280, 281
John of Apamea (John the Solitary), 188, 397; condemnation of writings of, 172, 194, 195, 397, 398; Evagrian influence on, 16; *On Prayer*, 172, 188–89, 397
John Chrysostom, 403
John of Dalyata (John the Elder), 86, 193–94, 397; condemnation/rehabilitation of writings of, 172, 194, 195, 397, 398; Dadisho' Qaṭraya and, 391; Evagrius influencing, 194; Isaac of Nineveh compared, 194; *Letters* 12, 172, 193–96
John of Damascus, 19
John of Ephesus, 14, 142, 162, 397–98; *Ecclesiastical (Church) History*, 162,

235–36, 398; *Life of Susan*, 162–64; *Lives of the Eastern Saints*, 15, 141, 162–64, 398, 401
John (bishop of Litharb), 49
John of Mardin, *Canons*, 126–27, 392, 398
John Rufus, 13
John the Stylite, 326
John of Tella, 14, 142, 160–62, 393
Joscelin II (lord of Edessa), 347, 350–51
Joseph Ḥazzaya ("the Visionary"), 195, 398; condemnation/rehabilitation of writings of, 172, 194, 195, 397, 398; Dadishoʿ Qaṭraya and, 391; John of Dalyata compared, 397; on Sergius of Reshʿayna's translation of Evagrius's *Kephalaia Gnostika*, 400; *On the Stirrings of the Mind During Prayer*, 172, 195–97, 398
Jubilees. book of, 22
Judaism. *See* Jews and Judaism
"Judaizing" practices, 293, 295, 299
Judas Thomas (apostle). *See Acts of Thomas*; Thomas
Julian of Halicarnassus, 219
Julian Saba, 141
Julianism, 86, 392, 401
Julius Africanus, 4–7
Justin I (emperor), 13, 14, 89, 160, 275, 311, 398, 400
Justin II (emperor), 398
Justin Martyr, 8
Justinian (emperor), 13, 14, 16, 89, 219, 396, 398, 401

Kadamattom Cross, India, 361
Katharaites, 36
Kerala, India, East Syrian Christians in, 9, 31, 362
Khamis bar Qardaḥe, *Wine Song*, 23, 51, 84–85, 399
khamriyya (Arabic wine poetry), 51, 84–85
Kharg Island, monastery of, 142
Khosrow/Khosrau (Persian ruler), 16, 342
Knights Templar, 342, 346–47
knowledge transmission. *See* books, knowledge, and translation
Kollam Plate, India, 362
Kushanians, 263, 266
Kyros of Alexandria, 103, 104

Latin authors: Egeria, *Pilgrimage Journal*, 31, 38–40, 392–93; William of Rubruck, *Mission* of, 371–74, 405
Latin Crusader States, 21, 49, 167, 345–51, 390, 399
Latin West, Greek texts transmitted via Syriac and Arabic to, 260
law and legal practices: ʿAbdishoʿ bar Brika's *Nomocanon*, 23; Beirut, law school of, 269, 273–75, 401, 405; canon law codes, 19; Islamic jurisprudence, influence of, 19; John of Mardin, *Canons*, on baptism, 126–27; *Statutes of the School of Nisibis*, 157–60; *Syro-Roman Lawbook*, 260, 269–72; transmission of ancient culture via, 260; Zacharias Rhetor, *Life of Severus of Antioch*, 260, 273–75
Legend of Mar Qardagh, 354–58
Leo I (bishop of Rome), 13
Letter of the Jews to the Emperor Marcian, 314
Libanius, 403
liturgy, 25, 113–14; 7th through 9th centuries, 19; additional resources and further reading, 114; in *Acts of Thomas*, 113, 115–17; architectural framing of, 114, 129, 130; British Library Additional 7170 (Syriac Gospel Lectionary), 202, 226, 227; *On the Cherub and the Thief* in, 76; connections with other churches and, 113–14; *Didascalia*, 117–18; Ephrem's poetry liturgically performed by women's choirs, 299; Giwargis Warda, *Book of the Rose*, liturgical use of, 23, 81, 394–95; Turfan, China, service book from, 114, 137–39. *See also* baptism; Eucharist/Eucharistic liturgy
Lives. See hagiography
Louis IX (king of France), 371, 405
Lu Xiuyan, 365

madrashe (lyric or stanzaic hymns), 11, 21, 51, 74, 205, 261, 393, 396, 409
al-Mahdi (caliph), 242, 402, 403
Mangi Chan (Mongol leader), 371
Mani, Manichaeans, and Manichaeism, 9, 10, 353, 409; on androgyny, 240; Bod Peryadeuta on, 86; *Book of the Laws of the Countries* and, 261; contact between Syriac Christianity and, 25, 352, 353; Ephrem on,

Mani, Manichaeans, and Manichaeism *(continued)* 35, 36, 393; geographic spread of, 353; meat, abstention from, 275; Philoxenus of Mabbug on, 299; "proto-Manichaean" script, 123; Pseudo-Clementine, *Recognitions*, 268; Theodore Abū Qurrah on, 358–59, 403; Timothy of Constantinople on, 405; Titus of Bostra, *Against the Manichaeans*, 21; William of Rubruck on, 373; Zacharias Rhetor on, 405; Zoroastrianism influencing, 353; additional resources and further reading, 354
al-Mansur (caliph), 331
manuscript collection, 21–22, 260, 280–86
maphrianate, 22, 167, 390–91, 409
maps: East Asia, *xxvi–xxvii*; Near East after Islamic conquest, *xxiv–xxv*; Near East before Islamic conquest, *xxii–xxiii*
Mar Barsawma, monastery of, 21, 350–51
Mar Mattai, monastery of, 280, 281
Mar Musa, frescoes at monastery of, 202, *223*
Mar Saba, monastery of, 19, 403
Marcian (emperor), 13, 109, 314
Marcion/Marcionites, 9, 10, 36, 86, 261, 299, 402, 409
Marco Polo, 23, 369, 405
Mari (apostle of Addai), 31, 32, 44–46, 127, 141. *See also Acts of Mar Mari; Anaphora of Addai and Mari*
Mark the Hermit, *Kephalaia*, 192–93
Mark the Monk, *memra* on baptism, 176
Markos (Yahbalaha III, katholikos of Baghdad), 22, 368–69
Maronite Chronicle, 256, 322–23
Maronites: Arabic language, use of, xx, 18; defined, 409; George of Resh'ayna, antihagiographic *Life of Maximus the Confessor*, 90, 101–6, 394; Jacob of Serug and, 396; monasticism in, 19; monothelitism and formation of, 17, 20, 88, 89–90, 409; Roman Catholicism and, 17, 21, 114; Severus Sebokt and, 401; *Syriac Fragment of the Sixth Council*, 90, 106–7
marriage: in *Acts of Thomas*, 33, 143–44; *Book of Steps* on, 147–49, 209–10; in *Book of the Laws of the Countries*, 264, 265, 266; celibacy in/instead of, 146, 148–49, 209–10; Jacob of Serug, *Memra on Tamar*, 213; John of Tella, *Life* of, 160–62; in *Martyrdom of Anahid*, 239; of monks/clerics, 15; Muslim practice of, 344; between Muslims and Christians, 326; in *Syro-Roman Lawbook*, 272
Martinos (bishop of Rome), 105, 106
Martyrdom of Abbot Barshebya, 237–38
Martyrdom of Anahid, 238–42
martyrs and martyrology. *See* hagiography; saints and sainthood; *specific martyrs*
Mary, mother of Jesus: *Cave of Treasures* on ancestry of, 218; Muslims and, 323, 340, 343; as *Theotokos* or *Christotokos*, 12, 89; virgin conception of Jesus by, 52, 53–54, 62–63
Mary Magdalene, in *On Mary and the Gardener*, 51, 74–75
Mary/Marinus, *Syriac Life* of, 250–53
Maryahb (Edessan noble), 41
Maximus the Confessor, 90, 101–6, 394
Mazdeans, 358
Media and Medes, 264, 266
medical texts, 288–90, 395, 400
Melkites, xx, 90, 107–9, 410. *See also* Chalcedonian Christians
memre (verse sermons), 51; by 'Abdisho' bar Brika, 87; in *Book of Steps*, 147; defined, 410; of Ephrem the Syrian, 11, 51, 86, 205, 207, 393; Jacob of Serug, *Memra on Tamar*, 213–15; of Jacob of Serug, 69, 213–15, 396, 397; Mark the Monk, *memra* on baptism, 176; *Memra on Genesis 22*, 202, 211–13; of Narsai, 86, 400; Turfan, service book from, 137–39
Messalianism, 10, 36, 170–71, 172, 173–77, 190, 390, 396, 397, 410
Methodius (4th-century bishop), 324
miaphysite theology, xi, 13, 14, 89, 90, 96, 99, 294, 396, 398, 400, 410
miaphysites. *See* West Syrian Christians
Michael the Great (Michael the Syrian), 20, 21–22, 49, 342, 399; Barhebraeus and, 350; *Chronicle*, 21–22, 31, 49, 322, 342–50, 399, 405; Dionysius bar Ṣalibi and, 21, 339, 392; Timothy I compared, 342
Milan, Edict of (313), 88
missionary work. *See* silk road
Monastery of the Syrians, Egypt, 21

monasticism, 141–42; 4th century, protomonastic origins in, 10; in 5th and 6th centuries, 10, 14, 15; in 7th through 9th centuries, 17, 19; in 10th through 14th centuries, 21; coenobitic or communitarian monasticism, development of, 141, 408; in East Syrian Church, 15, 19, 152, 256; female monastics, 141, 151–53, 162–64; John of Ephesus, *Life of Susan*, 162–64; Muhammad (prophet) on, 330; Philoxenus, *First Letter to the Monks of Bet Gaugal/Letter Concerning Zeal*, 153–54, 400; practice *(praktikē)* and contemplation *(theōria)*, Evagrius on, 171, 175, 195, 394; Rabbula of Edessa, *Rules* of, 149–51; *Rules for Nuns*, 151–53; *Statutes of the School of Nisibis*, 157–60; Syrian mystical theologies of prayer in, 172; in West Syrian Church, 19, 152, 162, 256

Mongols: conquests of, 20, 23, 81, 353, 390, 395; East Syrian Christians under, 22–23, 368–69; *History of the Life and Travels of Rabban Sauma*, 368–71; William of Rubruck's mission to, 371–74, 405

monophysite theology/monophysites. *See* miaphysite theology; West Syrian Church

monotheletism, 17, 88, 90, 101, 106, 410

Mount Izla, monastery of, 19

Muʿāwiya (caliph), 17, 105, 106, 323, 401

Muhammad (prophet), 16, 321, 329, 330, 333–43

Mundhir (Arab Lakhmid leader), 309–11

Mushe bar Kepha, *Introduction to the Psalter*, 287, 399

Mushe of Nisibis, 21

Muslims. *See* Islam/Muslims

al-Mutawakkil (caliph), 288, 395

mysticism and prayer, 25, 170–73; in 5th and 6th centuries, 11; 7th and 8th century efflorescence of Syrian mystical theologies of prayer, 170, 172, 188–97; *Acts of Thomas*, prayer in, 115–16; Dadishoʿ Qaṭraya, *Discourse on Stillness*, 172, 191–93; definition of mysticism, 170; John of Dalyata, *Letters* 12, 172, 193–96; Messalianism and, 10, 170–71, 172, 173–77; Philoxenus of Mabbug, *Letter to Abraham and Orestes*, 183–85; "pure prayer," 190–93, 194; silence/silent prayer, 172, 188–89, 397; Stephen bar Ṣudayli, *Book of the Holy Hierotheus*, 171, 180–83; Timothy of Constantinople, *On Those Who Come to the Church from the Heretics*, 173–74; "wonder," as state beyond prayer, 194–95; additional resources and further reading, 172–73. *See also* Babai the Great; Evagrius of Pontus; Isaac of Nineveh

Najran, martyrdom of Christians of, 310, 311–14

Narsai, 15, 67, 210, 400; in ʿAbdishoʿ bar Brika's *Metrical Catalogue*, 86; *On Epiphany*, 51, 67–69; as "Harp of the Spirit," 86; *Homilies*, 285–86; *memre* by, 86, 400; reading Old Testament through Christian lens, 202, 210; *On the Sacrifice of Isaac*, 210–11; Theodore of Mopsuestia influencing, 67, 210, 400

nativity of Jesus, 218–19

"nature," in Trinitarian and Christological thought, 12–13, 410

Nebo (deity), 32

Nemesius, 282

neo-Arians (Eunomians/Anomeans/Aetians), 36, 175, 176, 299

Nephalius (Chalcedonian), 96–98

Nestorians, xx–xxi, 102, 105. *See also* East Syrian Church

Nestorius (bishop of Constantinople), 12, 13, 15, 89, 92, 96, 97, 105, 109, 294, 314, 403

"new Jews," use of, 154, 294, 299, 319

New Testament, 201–2; British Library Additional mss 14456 (scholarly gospel manuscript), 277; Eusebian canons/Ammonian chapters, 277; Harqlean Version (7th century), 202, 277, 400; Jacob of Serug, *on the Sinful Woman* mixing accounts from all four Gospels, 69; New Testament Peshiṭta (5th century), 11, 14, 201, 202, 216, 400; Old Syriac Version, 8, 14, 201, 205; Philoxenus of Mabbug's version of, 11, 14, 202, 400; Rabbula of Edessa's version of, 11, 14, 201–2; Revelation, canonicity of book of, 221; Timothy I on composition of Gospels, 334. *See also Diatessaron*; exegesis

Nicaea, Council of (325), 10, 12, 88, 91, 96, 107, 109, 286, 299, 409

Nicholas IV (pope), 369

Ning-shu, 365

Nisibis: Mari in, 44–45; School of Nisibis, 11, 14, 15, 67, 89, 99, 157–60, 210, 390, 400, 404, 411

Odes of Solomon, 4, 51, 52–54, 113
Old Malayalam, 362
Old Syriac Version (of New Testament), 8, 14, 201, 205
Old Testament/Hebrew Bible, 201; Abgar of Edessa, version commissioned by, 287, 399; *Hexaemeron*, 396; Jacob of Edessa's version, 201, 287, 396; Mushe bar Kepha, *Introduction to the Psalter*, 287; Old Testament Peshitta, 8, 14, 201, 202, 287, 399; Paul of Tella, translations by, 201, 280, 287; Philoxenus of Mabbug on, 201, 287; Polycarp's 6th century version, 201; read through Christian lens, 202, 205, 210, 213; Septuagint, 201, 284, 285, 287, 396, 399, 411; Syro-Hexapla, 201, 280, 283–84, 287, 399; Timothy I on composition of Gospels, 334. *See also* exegesis
On Fate (Book of the Laws of the Countries), 7–8, 21, 261–66
On Mary and the Gardener, 51, 74–75
On the Cherub and the Thief, 51, 75–81
'onita genre, 23, 51, 81, 399
Ophites, 86
Oration to the Greeks (Tatian), 8
Origen of Alexandria/Origenism, 14–16, 103, 171, 177, 178, 180, 195, 201, 280, 285, 393, 394, 402, 407
origin stories, 25, 31–32; *Acts of Mar Mari*, 32, 44–46; *Acts of Thomas*, 31, 32–35; *Alexander Romance*, 32, 46–48; *Chronicle of Edessa to 540*, 31, 43–44; for East Syrian versus West Syrian Church, 32; Edessa, rise of Syriac Christianity in, 3–4, 31; Egeria, *Pilgrimage Journal*, 31, 38–40; Ephrem, *Hymns on Heresies* 22, 32, 35–37; Eusebius, *Church History*, 31, 37–38; imperial orthodoxy, rise of, and demand for, 9; Michael the Great, *Chronicle*, 31, 49; polemic against religious "others" in, 32; for Syriac language, 31, 49, 218; *Teaching of Addai*, 31, 40–43; additional resources and further reading, 32
orthodoxy: Ephrem the Syrian, as defender of Nicene orthodoxy, 88, 91–92; proto-orthodox Christianity, 9–10. *See also* heterodoxy/heresy; Roman imperial orthodoxy

paganism/polytheism, 32, 43, 49, 104, 108, 118, 183, 233, 247, 273, 274, 283, 305–6, 326, 327, 331, 344, 354. *See also* silk road; *specific religions or deities*
Paluṭ/Paluṭians, 36–37, 40, 43
pantheism, 183, 402
Papios (Frankish defender of Edessa), 347–49
Paradise of the Desert Fathers, 391
Paris Syriac 346, 279
Parthians, 3, 263, 264, 410, 411. *See also* Persia and Persians
Passover: in Aphrahat's *Demonstrations*, 203–5, 298; *Didascalia* on, 295–97
Paul of Kallinikos, 14, 401
Paul the Persian, 401
Paul of Tella, 201, 280, 287
Paula (translator of Athanasius), 281
Paulinians, 36
pearl motif, in Syriac poetry, 9, 51; 'Abdisho' bar Brika, *Marganita*, 23, 87; Ephrem the Syrian, *Hymns on Faith* 81, 51, 59–61; *Hymn of the Pearl*, 9, 51, 54–59
"perfect" (celibate) Christians, 10, 141, 147, 149, 209
Persia and Persians: Achaemenids, 412; *Book of the Laws of the Countries* on, 262–63, 264, 266; Byzantine-Persian Wars (7th century), 16, 17, 47; Christological controversies and, 12; East Syrian Church influenced by, 12, 14, 15; Edessa, capture and control of, 3, 39; Islamic conquests and end of, 16; Kadamattom Cross, India, 361; *Martyrdom of Abbot Barshebya*, 237–38; *Martyrdom of Anahid*, 238–42; Parthians, 3, 263, 264, 410, 411; Sasanians, 12, 15, 47, 230, 298, 352–55, 393, 411, 412; Seleucids, 3, 43, 410, 411. *See also* Zoroastrianism
"person," in Trinitarian and Christological thought, 12–13, 410
Peshitta, 411; New Testament Peshitta, 11, 14, 201, 202, 216, 400; Old Testament Peshitta, 8, 14, 201, 202, 287, 399
Peter the Iberian, 405
Petion Cycle, 239
Philip (disciple of Bardaisan), 7, 261, 265

Philip the Fair (king of France), 369
Philippus of Patara, 275
Philo of Alexandria, 404
Philoxenus of Mabbug, 90, 153–54, 183, 314, 400; asceticism of, 142, 153–54, 400; *Commentary on the Prologue of John*, 275–77; *Discourses*, 400; Evagrius and, 171; *First Letter to the Monks of Bet Gaugal*, 153–54, 400; on John of Apamea, 397; *Letter Concerning Zeal*, 153–54; *Letter to Abraham and Orestes*, 183–85; Mushe bar Kepha and, 399; New Testament, new Syriac translations of, 11, 14, 202, 400; Old Testament, new Syriac version of, 201, 287; on Stephen bar Ṣudayli, 402; West Syrian Church and, 13, 96; writings of Joseph Ḥazzaya attributed to, 398
Phokas of Edessa, 282
Photinians, 36
Plato: *Book of the Laws of the Countries*, Platonic-style dialogue of, 7, 261; Ḥunayn ibn Isḥaq, translations by, 288; Severus of Antioch quoting, 401; *Timaeus*, Severus Sebokt quoting, 279, 280; Timothy I looking for treatises on, 281–82
poetry, 25, 50–52; ʿAbdishoʿ bar Brika, *Metrical Catalogue of Syriac Authors*, 23, 51, 85–87; Arabic influences on, 51; Arabic wine poetry (*khamriyya*), 51; *On the Cherub and the Thief*, 51, 75–81; Cyrillona, *On the Huns*, 51, 65–67; *Hymn of the Pearl*, 9, 51, 54–59; Khamis bar Qardaḥe, *Wine Song*, 51, 84–85, 399; *madrashe* (lyric or stanzaic hymns), 11, 21, 51, 74, 205, 261, 393, 396, 409; Narsai, *On Epiphany*, 51, 67–69; *Odes of Solomon*, 4, 51, 52–54; *On Mary and the Gardener*, 51, 74–75; *On the Cherub and the Thief*, 51, 75–81; *ʿonita* genre, 23, 51, 81, 399; *qale* (syllabic meters), 51; *sogiyata* (dialogue poems), 51, 69, 74, 75, 396, 400, 411; *turgame* (metrical gospel commentaries), 399; *zmirata* (psalms or songs), 52; additional resources and further reading, 51–52. *See also* Ephrem the Syrian; Giwargis Warda; Jacob of Serug; *memre*; pearl motif, in Syriac poetry
polemic. *See* doctrine and disputation; *specific polemical subjects*
Polycarp, 201
polytheism. *See* paganism/polytheism

Pool of Abraham, Edessa, 38, 39
Porphyry, 21
practice (*praktikē*) and contemplation (*theōria*) in monastic life, 171, 175, 195, 394
practices, 25. *See also* asceticism; liturgy; mysticism and prayer
prayer. *See* mysticism and prayer
"proto-Manichaean" script, 123
protomonasticism, 10
proto-orthodox Christianity, 9–10
Pseudo-Clementine, *Recognitions*, 268
Pseudo-Dionysius the Areopagite and *Corpus Dionysiacum*, 180, 277, 282, 400, 402
Pseudo-Hierotheus, 180
Pseudo-Methodius, *Apocalypse* of, 22, 324–25
Pseudo-Zacharias, *Ecclesiastical History*, 400
Pulcheria (empress of Marcian and sister of Theodosius II), 13, 109
"pure prayer," 190–93, 194

Qalb Lawza basilica, 129
qale (syllabic meters), 51
Mar Qardagh, *Legend* of, 354–58
Qenneshre, monastery of, 19, 279
the Quqite, 36
Qurʾan, 231, 327, 335, 339

Rabban Shapur, monastery of, 19, 172, 185, 191, 391, 396
Rabbula Gospels, 202, 216
Rabbula of Edessa: New Testament, new Syriac translations of, 11, 14, 201–2; *Rules* of, 149–51
Rakamaeans, 263
relics: *Disputation of Sergius the Stylite Against a Jew* on, 318, 319; given to Muslims, 326; from Mar Barsawma monastery, 350–51; *Rules* of Rabbula of Edessa on, 151; Turkish capture of Edessa and, 348
resurrection of Jesus: Ephrem, *Hymns on the Resurrection* 1, 51, 62–65; *On Mary and the Gardener*, 51, 74–75
Revelation, canonicity of book of, 221
robber council (Second Council of Ephesus; 449), 12–13, 404
Roman Catholicism: Maronites and, 17, 21, 114; Syriac Christians sometimes viewed as heretics by, 2

Roman imperial orthodoxy: demand for Christian origin stories and rise of, 9; formal separation of some Syriac Christian communities from, 11, 88–90; Theodore of Mopsuestia, condemnation of, 13, 89, 93, 202, 210. *See also* Councils

Roman/Byzantine empire: *Book of the Laws of the Countries (On Fate)* on, 263, 264, 265; Byzantine-Persian Wars (7th century), 16, 17, 47; Edessa, capture and control of, 3; Islamic conquests, 15–17; Jerusalem Temple, destruction of (70 CE), 293

Romanos the Melode, 69

Romanos the Neomartyr, Stephen Mansūr's *Passion* of, 242–44

Sabellians, 36

sacraments. *See* baptism; Eucharist/Eucharistic liturgy; marriage

Saint Sergius, basilica of, Sergiopolis (modern Resafa), 130

saints and sainthood: asceticism, practice of, 140; Himyarite Jews, Christian martyrdoms attributed to, 294, 309–14, 402; transvestite saints and *Syriac Life of Mary*, 250–53. *See also* hagiography; relics; *specific saints*

Saladin, conquest of Jerusalem by, 342, 349–50

Samaritans, 358

Sasanians, 12, 15, 47, 230, 298, 352–55, 393, 411, 412. *See also* Persia and Persians

Rabban Sauma, 22–23, 368–71, 405

Sayfo, 2–3

School of Nisibis, 11, 14, 15, 67, 89, 99, 157–60, 210, 390, 400, 403, 411

School of Qenneshre, 19, 279

School of the Persians, Edessa, 11, 14, 15, 67, 69, 89, 157, 210, 213, 396, 401, 403

scripture/scriptural interpretation. *See* exegesis; Syriac Bible

Seleucia, conversion of, by Addai, 45–46

Seleucia-Ctesiphon, as seat of East Syrian Church, 12, 14, 17–18, 90

Seleucids, 3, 43, 410, 411. *See also* Persia and Persians

Seleucus I Nicator (Persian ruler), 411

Seljuk Turks, 49, 342, 344–51

Septuagint, 201, 284, 285, 287, 396, 399, 411

Serapion (bishop of Antioch), 43

Seres, 262, 264. *See also* China

Sergiopolis (modern Resafa), 130

Saint Sergius, cult of, 130

Sergius (patriarch of Constantinople), 103

Sergius of Reshʻayna, 14, 16, 400–401; *On the Aim of All of Aristotle's Writings*, 277–79, 401; Aristotle, translation of, 400; Evagrius, translation of, 16, 400; Ḥunayn ibn Isḥaq on, 288

Sergius the Stylite, *Disputation Against a Jew*, 294, 317–19

Severus of Antioch, 14, 90, 96, 260, 314, 401; *Cathedral Homilies*, 401; Jacob of Edessa influenced by, 396; *To Nephalius*, 96–98; *Treatise on Constellations*, 401; *Treatise on the Astrolabe*, 401; Zacharias Rhetor, *Life of Severus of Antioch*, 13, 260, 273–75, 405

Severus Sebokt, *Letter to the Periodeutes Basil of Cyprus*, 279–80, 401

Shapur I (Persian ruler), 353, 393

Shapur II (Persian ruler), 10, 203, 237, 354

Shmeshgram (Edessan noble), 41, 43

Shubhalishoʻ of Bet Daylamaye, 285

silence/silent prayer, 172, 188–89, 397

silk road, 25, 352–54; *Discourse on the One God*, 353, 365–68; expansion of East Syrian Christianity along, 9, 18–19, 280, 353; *History of the Life and Travels of Rabban Sauma*, 368–71; *Jingjiao Stele*, 18, 19, 353, 360–65, 366; *Kadamattom Cross*, India, 361; *Kollam Plate*, India, 362; *Legend of Mar Qardagh*, 354–58; Mongol conquests, 20, 23, 81, 353, 390, 395; Theodore Abū Qurrah, *On the Existence of God and the True Religion*, 358–59, 403; Timothy I, *Letters* 41 and 47 (on missionary work), 359–60; additional resources and further reading, 353–54. *See also* China; India; *specific Eastern religions*

Simeon of Bet Arsham, *Letters* 1, 294, 309–11, 401–2

Simeon of Kurdlah, 86

Simeon the Stylite (Simeon the Elder), 15, 141, 244–47, 248, 249, 404

single ones/solitaries *(iḥidaye)*, 10, 140–41, 146, 154–57, 165, 166–67, 188, 193, 389

Sixth Ecumenical Council (Third Council of Constantinople; 680/681), 90, 101, 106–7 slaves and slavery: in *Acts of Thomas*, 33, 56; in *Book of the Laws of the Countries*, 263, 266; *History of the "Slave of Christ,"* 294, 315–17; Jerusalem, Turkish conquest of, 349–50; Jews under Pharaoh, 204; Joseph Ḥazzaya, childhood slavery of, 195, 398; Maximus the Confessor, as son of slave girl, 102; metaphorical uses of, 100, 116, 155, 156, 162, 204, 246, 261; *Statutes of the School of Nisibis* on, 157; Syriac language, slave contract in, 4, 5, 6; in *Syro-Roman Lawbook*, 269–71; William of Rubruck, *Mission of Friar William of Rubruck*, 371–74, 405

Sogdians and Sogdian language, 19, 24, 365

sogiyata (dialogue poems), 51, 69, 74, 75, 396, 400, 411

solitary ascetical life: *bnay/bnat qyama* (children of the covenant), 10, 141, 146, 230, 389; *iḥidaye* (solitaries/single ones), 10, 140–41, 146, 154–57, 165, 166–67, 188, 193, 389

Solomon of Baṣra, *Book of the Bee*, 22, 202, 224–28, 402

sons/daughters of the covenant *(bnay/bnat qyama)*, 10, 141, 146, 230, 389, 408

Sophronios (bishop of Jerusalem), 103–4

Statutes of the School of Nisibis, 157–60

Stephen bar Ṣudayli, 180, 402; *Book of the Holy Hierotheus*, 171, 180–83, 391, 394, 402; Philoxenus warning against, 183–85

Stephen Mansūr, *Passion of Romanos the Neomartyr*, 242–44, 402–3

stillness, *Discourse* of Dadishoʿ Qaṭraya on, 191–93, 391

stylites and stylitism, 11, 15, 140, 229, 245, 248, 249, 404

supersessionist rhetoric, 294, 298–99, 300, 395

Susai of Shus, 86

Susan, John of Ephesus's *Life* of, 162–64

Synodicon, 119, 398

Syriac Apocalypse of Daniel, 221–24

Syriac Baḥira Legend, 322, 335–39

Syriac Bible, 201–2; 1st to 4th centuries, 8, 202; 5th and 6th centuries, 11, 14, 201–2; 7th century, 202; illustrated manuscripts, 202; Philoxenus of Mabbug, *Commentary on the Prologue of John*, on Syriac translations, 275–77; translation techniques and, 259; vocalized Syriac versions of, 20. See also exegesis; New Testament; Old Testament/Hebrew Bible

Syriac Christianity, 1–27; 1st through 4th centuries, 3–11; 5th and 6th centuries, 11–16; 7th through 9th centuries, 16–20; 10th through 14th centuries, 20–24; Aramaic/Syriac, use of, 2, 3, 4; conversion to Islam and waning numbers of, 18, 20; foundations, 25 (*See also* doctrine and disputation; origin stories; poetry); geographic spread of, 1, 18–19, 20, 22–23, 280; Greek influence on, 11; heretics, viewed as, 2; historical and theological significance of, 1–3; interreligious encounters, 25 (*See also* Islam/Muslims; Jews and Judaism; silk road; *specific additional religious traditions*); as living tradition, xx, 2–3; map of East Asia, *xxvi–xxvii*; map of Near East after Islamic conquest, *xxiv–xxv*; map of Near East before Islamic conquest, *xxii–xxiii*; nomenclature for branches of, xx–xxi (*See also* Chalcedonian Christians; East Syrian Church; Maronites; West Syrian Church); organization and framing of texts, 24–25; practices, 25 (*See also* asceticism; liturgy; mysticism and prayer); texts and textual transmission, 25 (*See also* books, knowledge, and translation; exegesis; hagiography); translation and transliteration of texts, xix–xx; additional resources and further reading, 26–27

Syriac language: 5th and 6th century translation of Greek texts into, 14; 7th through 9th century translation of Greek texts into, 20; 10th through 14th century efflorescence of, 20–21, 167; Aramaic, relationship to, 2, 3, 4, 49; Ḥunayn ibn Isḥaq, translations of, 278, 287–88; incantation bowl using Estrangela script, *123*; Latin West, Greek texts transmitted via Syriac and Arabic to, 260; Monastery of the Syrians, Egypt, manuscript collection of Syriac translations from Greek at, 21; non-Christian use of, 5–7, 6; origin story for, 31, 49, 218; prioritization of, in the volume, 24; slave contract written in, 4, 5, 6; vocalization of writing of, 20

Syriac *Life of Ephrem*, 11

Syriac *Life of Mary*, 250–53

Syriac *Life of Simeon*, 249
Syriac liturgy. *See* liturgy
Syrian Orthodox Church (modern West Syrian Church), xx, 11, 88, 89, 90, 96, 131, 411
Syro-Hexapla, 201, 280, 283–84, 287, 399
Syro-Roman Lawbook, 260, 269–72

Taizong (emperor), 364
Taoism, 360, 365
Tatian: Ephrem, *Commentary on the Diatessaron*, 8, 10, 205–7, 393; Gospel harmonization, *Diatessaron* as, 8, 201–2, 205; *Oration to the Greeks*, 8
Teaching of Addai, 31, 40–43, 44, 294, 305–6
Templars, 342, 346–47
Testament of Our Lord, 119–24
texts and textual transmission, 25. *See also* books, knowledge, and translation; exegesis; hagiography
Thaddeus (apostle). *See* Addai; *Anaphora of Addai and Mari*; *Teaching of Addai*
Thecla (disciple of Paul), *Life* of, 161
Theodora (empress of Justinian), 13
Theodore Abū Qurrah, *On the Existence of God and the True Religion*, 358–59, 403
Theodore of Mopsuestia, 92–93, 403–4; Christology of, 12, 89, 92–93; East Syrian Church and, xx, 12, 15, 92, 186, 202, 294, 404; *On the Incarnation*, 92–96; Isaac of Nineveh quoting, 186; Narsai influenced by, 67, 210, 400; orthodox condemnation of, 13, 89, 93, 202, 210; Theodoret of Cyrrhus as student of, 403
Theodore son of Hetum (ruler of Edessa), 345
Theodoret of Cyrrhus, 13, 96, 109, 403; *History of the Monks of Syria*, 15, 244–47, 404
Theodosius II (emperor), 12, 13, 109
theōria (contemplation) and *praktikē* (practice), in monastic life, 171, 175, 195, 394
Theotokos theology, 12, 89
Thomas (apostle): Addai and, 40, 41; Egeria on Edessa shrine of, 38, 392; Mari on, 44, 46. *See also Acts of Thomas*
Thomas Aquinas, 260
Thomas of Marga, 404; *Book of Governors*, 253–56, 286–87, 404; on Mar 'Anan'isho, 286–87; on Rabban Cyriacus, 253–56; Syriac mystical tradition and, 172

Timothy I (East Syrian katholikos), 280–81, 359, 405; anti-Jewish rhetoric employed against Muslims by, 294, 319–20; Aristotle's *Topics* translated into Arabic by, 280, 281, 283; Dionysius bar Ṣalibi compared, 339; Job the Chalcedonian, correspondence with, 280, 281; *Letters* 40 (to Mar Sergius of Elam), 294, 319–20; *Letters* 41 (on missionary work), 359–60; *Letters* 43 (to Rabban Mar Pethion), 280, 281–82; *Letters* 47 (to Mar Sergius of Elam), 280–81, 283–86, 380; *Letters* 48 (to Mar Sergius of Elam), 280, 282–83; *Letters* 59 (on disputation with al-Mahdi), 333–35; al-Mahdi and, 242, 280, 333–35; Messalianism, condemnations of, 172, 194, 195, 397, 398; Michael the Great compared, 342; missionary work of, 18, 280, 285, 359–60, 405
Timothy of Constantinople, *On Those Who Come to the Church from the Heretics*, 173–74, 405
Titus of Bostra, *Against the Manichaeans*, 21
Tobias son of Tobias the Jew, 41–42
Tower of Babel, 31, 49, 218
translation. *See* books, knowledge, and translation
transvestite saints, 250–53
tree, living in (dendritism), 230
Trinity: in *Disputation of Bet Ḥale*, 329; Evagrius on, 175, 178, 180; Messalianism and sensible perception of, 170, 171, 173, 174; Trinitarian controversy (Arius and Arians), 10, 36, 59, 88–89, 91
true cross: discovery of, 305–6; Persian capture/Byzantine recapture of, 16
Tur 'Abdin, monastery of, 142
Turfan, China, Syriac Christianity in, 18–19, 137–39, 353
turgame (metrical gospel commentaries), 399
Turks, 49, 342, 344–51
al-Ṭūsī, 22
twins and twinning, in early Christian tradition, 8–9

Umayyad caliphate, 17, 322, 323
universalism, 183, 185–88, 195, 398
"upright" (noncelibate) Christians, 10, 141, 147, 149, 209

Valentinus, 36
virgin conception of Jesus, 52, 53–54, 62–63
Virgin Mary. *See* Mary, mother of Jesus
"the Visionary." *See* Joseph Ḥazzaya
Vitae. *See* hagiography
vocalized written Syriac, 20

West Syrian Church: *Alexander Romance*, 22, 32, 46–48; anti-Jewish polemic, intra-Christian use of, 154, 294, 314; *Apocalypse of Pseudo-Methodius*, 22, 324–25; Arabic, use of, 18; *The Book of the Himyarites*, 311–14; *On the Cherub and the Thief*, 51, 75–81; colophons, 267, 268, 269; Daniel of Ṣalah, *Commentary of the Psalms*, 202, 219–21, 391–92; defined, xxi, 411; *Disputation of Sergius the Stylite Against a Jew*, 294, 317–19; Elias, *Life of John of Tella*, 142, 160–62; Eucharistic liturgy of, 131; formal separation from Roman imperial orthodoxy, 11, 14, 88, 89–90; foundational teachings of, 13–14, 96; geographic expansion of, 18; *History of the "Slave of Christ,"* 294, 315–17; Rabban Hormizd and East Syrians, conflict with, 124; Isaac of Antioch, *Homilies Against the Jews*, 294, 307–9; Jacob of Serug and, 69; John of Mardin, *Canons*, 126–27, 392, 398; *Letter of the Jews to the Emperor Marcian*, 314; liturgy of, 114; *On Mary and the Gardener*, 51, 74–75; monasticism in, 19, 152, 162, 256; Mushe bar Kepha, *Introduction to the Psalter*, 287, 399; origin stories, 32; *Rules for Nuns*, 151–53; Severus Sebokt, *Letter to the Periodeutes Basil of Cyprus*, 279–80, 401; Simeon of Bet Arsham, *Letters* I, 294, 309–11, 401–2; *Syriac Life of Mary*, 250–53; *Teaching of Addai*, 31, 40–43, 44, 294, 305–6. *See also* Barhebraeus; Dionysius bar Ṣalibi; Jacob of Edessa; Jacob of Serug; John of Ephesus; Michael the Great; Philoxenus of Mabbug; Rabbula of Edessa; Sergius of Resh'ayna; Severus of Antioch; Zacharias Rhetor
William of Rubruck, *Mission* of, 371–74, 405
wine poetry *(khamriyya)*, 51, 84–85

women and gender: androgyny, Manichaeans on, 240; daughters/sons of the covenant *(bnay/bnat qyama)*, 10, 141, 146, 230, 389, 408; Ephrem's poetry liturgically performed by women's choirs, 299; female monastics, 141, 151–53, 162–64; homosexuality, in *Book of the Laws of the Countries*, 263, 264; Jacob of Serug, *On the Sinful Woman*, 51, 69–74; transvestite saints and *Syriac Life of Mary*, 250–53. *See also* marriage
"wonder," as state beyond prayer, 194–95

Xi'an (ancient Chang'an), China, 18, 353, 360, 364, 365

Yahbalaha III (katholikos of Baghdad; formerly Markos), 22, 368–69
Yazdgard II (Persian ruler), 239
Yazedbuzid, 365
Yazid II (caliph), 331
Yazidad, *A Gleaning*, 86
Year of the Greeks, 411–12

Zacharias Rhetor (Zacharias Scholasticus), 13, 405; *Ecclesiastical History*, 406; *Life of Severus of Antioch*, 13, 260, 273–75, 406
Zangi (Imad al-Din Zengi), 347–49
Zeno (emperor): closure of School of Edessa by, 15, 157, 210; *Henotikon*, 13; Zacharias Rhetor on, 405
Zephyrinus (bishop of Rome), 43
Zoroastrianism, 352, 412; dualism of, 12, 352, 353; East Syrian Church influenced by, 12, 15; encounters of Syrian Christianity with, 25, 352; Joseph Ḥazzaya born to Zoroastrian parents, 195, 398; *Kollam Plate*, India, 362; Legend of Mar Qardagh and, 354–58; Manichaeism influenced by, 353; *Martyrdom of Abbot Barshebya*, 237–38; *Martyrdom of Anahid*, 238–42; persecution of Christians under, 203, 237, 239, 352; as state religion of successive Persian empires, 352; Theodore Abū Qurrah and, 403; additional resources and further reading, 353

Founded in 1893,
UNIVERSITY OF CALIFORNIA PRESS
publishes bold, progressive books and journals
on topics in the arts, humanities, social sciences,
and natural sciences—with a focus on social
justice issues—that inspire thought and action
among readers worldwide.

The UC PRESS FOUNDATION
raises funds to uphold the press's vital role
as an independent, nonprofit publisher, and
receives philanthropic support from a wide
range of individuals and institutions—and from
committed readers like you. To learn more, visit
ucpress.edu/supportus.

www.ingramcontent.com/pod-product-compliance
Lightning Source LLC
Chambersburg PA
CBHW081822230426
43668CB00017B/2349